FEDERAL INCOME TAX

OBJECTIVE

Third Edition

ROBERT G. POPOVICH
Pepperdine University School of Law
Southwestern Law School

Exam Pro ®

WEST
ACADEMIC
PUBLISHING

Exam Pro Series is a trademark registered in the U.S. Patent and Trademark Office.

© West, a Thomson business, 2002
© 2007 Thomson/West
© 2019 LEG, Inc. d/b/a West Academic
      444 Cedar Street, Suite 700
      St. Paul, MN 55101
      1-877-888-1330

West, West Academic Publishing, and West Academic are trademarks of West Publishing Corporation, used under license.

Printed in the United States of America

ISBN: 978-1-63460-910-4

To my two sons, Mark and Brian
The happiness and pride that you bring to my life is immeasurable;
as is my love for you.

FEDERAL INCOME TAX
PREFACE

TO THE STUDENT:

This book is the Federal Income Tax contribution to the West Academic's **Exam Pro** series. It is the **third** edition of this book, the first and second editions published in 2002 and 2007, respectively. The landscape of the "tax world" has changed many times since the first edition of this book. What has not changed, however, is my love of teaching Federal Income Tax. The course material is always fun as well as challenging. It is my sincere hope that you find the book helpful to your understanding of Federal Income Tax.

This book consists of eight examinations in Federal Income Tax, containing a total of 200 OBJECTIVE QUESTIONS. Virtually all of these questions are **actual, final exam questions** from my Federal Income Tax course (many originally in essay form), and all have been updated in this third edition (many being released for the first time). You will probably find most of the questions to be "challenging." Many of the questions contain multi-faceted fact patterns that are designed to raise multiple diverse and overlapping Federal Income Tax issues. The questions are designed to prepare you for whatever questions you see on your exams whether they be multiple-choice or essay.

Each exam consists of twenty-five objective problems, followed by four or five multiple-choice answers. As indicated, many of the questions are "challenging," and each exam may (read that as "will") take more than one hour to complete. Many of the questions can easily be split into simpler questions on an actual exam. It is my sincere hope that the questions and in-depth answers for questions applicable to the tax concepts covered in your course, will help provide you will the tools, and confidence, to answer any question that might come your way on an exam (or in class). In short, my sole reason for writing this book is assist you in your study of the various components that make up the exciting, and sometimes strange, world of federal income tax.

Each exam has an answer key with a thorough discussion of the relevant issues and a step-by-step, detailed explanation of the analysis for the problem. The answer key explains why the *best* answer is the best choice, and it explains why the other available answers are incorrect, or not the best possible choice. It also helps identify "red herring" answers that are intended to lure you into an appropriate-sounding, but incorrect, responses. Some of the question explanations are quite lengthy, but they are designed to assist you in a better understanding of the subject matter, and to illuminate other testable issues not specifically asked in the respective question. Federal Income Tax is a very "real-world" subject, and I have tried to reflect this in the questions, and the answer key discussions.

The study of Federal Income Tax does involve some math and many of the questions contain numbers (primarily for the purpose of more clearly defining the facts). However, the math utilized is <u>very basic</u> and should not be a source of concern for those of you who do not get excited at the sight of numbers. Actually, the only math skills necessary are those from the four basic "arithmetic" food groups: addition, subtraction, multiplication, and division. Appendix C contains a discussion of "Code" math and explains almost everything you need to know about how tax math.

In addition to the thorough answer key explanations, for each answer, the text provides relevant citations to Internal Revenue Code Sections, Treasury Regulations, Revenue Rulings, Internal Revenue Service Publications, Case law, and the like.

The breadth and depth of topics covered in Federal Income Tax courses can vary dramatically. In addition, courses in Federal Income Tax vary in credit hours from a single 2-credit course, to a multiple-part course in excess of 5 credits. I have attempted to cover most of the issues that are typically addressed in the basic Federal Income Tax course. As your study in Federal Income Tax progresses, however, you will quickly come to realize that 200 objective questions could be supplied for almost any <u>one</u> of the subjects covered in a typical Federal Income Tax course. Writing a study aid under such conditions is a challenge. To facilitate your use of this book, and to maximize your benefit from this book, following this PREFACE is an ORGANIZATION OF MATERIAL section which is designed to assist you: (1) in understanding the organization of the subject matter coverage in this book, and (2) in locating particular Federal Income Tax topics as they appear in the problems in the exams. No matter how many credit hours your Federal Income Tax course may be, which textbook book you use, or who your professor is, the problems in this book should provide you with a better understanding of Federal Income Tax, and help prepare you for your exams.

Federal Income Tax is also challenging from the standpoint that the tax laws are always in a state of flux. The *Tax Cuts and Jobs Act* (TCJA) signed into law in December 2017 (generally effective beginning in 2018) made significant changes to numerous tax issues relating to individuals. We shall explore many areas relating to individuals that have been impacted by the TCJA (some that are favorable and others that are decidedly unfavorable). The TCJA affected so many of the concepts covered in the previous two editions of this book, this third edition is, for all intents and purposes, almost an entirely new book. Of course, tax legislation is nothing new and while adjusting to changing tax landscapes is always challenging, it can also be the source of intellectual, and practical, interest.

This book could not have been written without the assistance of Ms. Melinda van Hemert, who spent long hours proofing countless drafts of the manuscript. I wish to offer my sincerest heartfelt thanks and gratitude for her painstaking attention to detail. I am forever indebted. Moreover, I would also like to thank the wonderful people at West Academic who have been so helpful with every aspect of this book. I had great fortune of meeting Ms. Staci Herr (currently the Executive Editor at Foundation Press, a part of West Academic) about twenty years ago, and she "got me onboard" to write the first edition of this book. First and foremost a lifelong friend, she helped me through the first, second and start of this third edition. Most of the work on this new third edition has been with the interminable encouragement and assistance of Dr. Jon Harkness (Senior Acquisitions Editor). Thank you, Jon. A big "shout out" to Mr. Gregory Olson (Manager, Editorial Productions) for all your help and support with the production side of things. Thank you, Greg.

No "thank you" would be complete if I did not mention my students, without whom I would not have the privilege of teaching Federal Income Tax.

Thank you, and I hope that you enjoy this book as much as I enjoy teaching Federal Income Tax.

ROBERT G. POPOVICH

PROFESSOR OF LAW

PEPPERDINE UNIVERSITY SCHOOL OF LAW

VISITING PROFESSOR OF LAW

SOUTHWESTERN LAW SCHOOL

JUNE 2019

ABOUT THE AUTHOR

Professor Robert Popovich is a respected scholar and award–winning classroom Professor of Law at Pepperdine University School of Law and as a frequent Visiting Professor of Law at Southwestern Law School. He has taught Federal Income Tax for over 25 years and has more than 35 years of experience in the tax field as both an attorney and CPA.

More importantly, Professor Popovich loves his work as a professor; in particular his passion for teaching. He comments, "My students know from the first day of class that they are my number one priority. Facilitating their learning of the law is, of course, a primary goal. Equally important is that every student knows that their well being is paramount to me." Professor Popovich was twice named a Luckman Distinguished Teaching Fellow, 1992-1997 and 1997-2002, was the recipient of the 2006 Howard A. White Award for Teaching Excellence, and named Teacher of the Year in 2005/06, 2008/09, and 2015/16.

In addition to Federal Income Tax, Professor Popovich teaches Federal Estate and Gift Taxation, Estate Planning, Wills & Trusts, Community Property, and first-year Contracts. He has also served, for most of his teaching career, as the faculty advisor to the Business and Tax Law Society.

FEDERAL INCOME TAX
ORGANIZATION OF MATERIAL

I.   Organization By Exams

Exams I through VI (and parts of Exam VII) focus primarily on the classic components that make up most Federal Income Tax courses: issues of income and exclusions, deductions, gains and losses, and the like. Exams VII and VIII contain questions in which all these elements are combined in the concepts of adjusted gross income and taxable income. Exam VIII also contains tax computations, credits, doctrines, procedures and constitutional matters.

EXAM I .... PRIMARILY ISSUES OF INCOME
GENERAL SCOPE OF INCOME
SPECIFIC INCLUSIONS IN INCOME
SPECIFIC EXCLUSIONS FROM INCOME

EXAM II .... PRIMARILY ISSUES OF DEDUCTIONS
BUSINESS DEDUCTIONS
NONBUSINESS DEDUCTIONS

EXAM III .... OVERLAPPING AND COMBINED ISSUES
INCOME & EXCLUSIONS
DEDUCTIONS
GAINS/LOSSES

EXAMS IV, V AND VI .... OVERLAPPING AND COMBINED ISSUES
INCOME & EXCLUSIONS
DEDUCTIONS
GAINS/LOSSES
CAPITAL GAINS/LOSSES
BARTER TRANSACTIONS

EXAM VII .... THE COMPLETE PICTURE (PLUS
OVERLAPPING & COMBINED ISSUES)
GAINS/LOSSES
ADJUSTED GROSS INCOME
TAXABLE INCOME
OVERLAPPING QUESTIONS

EXAM VIII .... TAX COMPUTATION (PLUS "THE
COMPLETE PICTURE")
TAXABLE INCOME
TAX CREDITS
MISCELLANEOUS TAX ITEMS
TAX DOCTRINES
TAX PROCEDURE
CONSTITUTIONAL ISSUES

II.   Table of Exam Topics

DEDUCTIONS

FEDERAL INCOME TAX
TABLE OF CONTENTS

FEDERAL INCOME TAX

OBJECTIVE

Third Edition

EXAM I

FEDERAL INCOME TAX
MULTIPLE-CHOICE OBJECTIVE QUESTIONS
EXAM I

1. Melinda is the sole shareholder of ABC, Incorporated ("ABC"). Melinda is also the sole employee of ABC. Two years ago, ABC obtained a loan from a bank upon the condition that some of Melinda's property be transferred to ABC as additional security for the loan. Pursuant to this condition, Melinda transferred ownership of her personal Porsche automobile to ABC two years ago. At all times subsequent to this transfer, Melinda has continued to use the Porsche for her personal use – totally unrelated to any matter or activity involving ABC. **For the current year, Melinda will most likely:**

    (a) Not be required to recognize any income because such use is an excludable fringe benefit pursuant to IRC § 132.

    (b) Not be required to recognize any income because as sole shareholder of ABC, Melinda is effectively using her own car and there is no net economic benefit or accession to wealth.

    (c) Be required to recognize income in the form of compensation from ABC because as an employee, she has experienced a net economic benefit (or net accession to wealth).

    (d) Not be required to recognize any income this year because income, if any, should have been recognized two years ago when she transferred the automobile to ABC.

2. Tricia purchased her home a few years ago. Late last year, something unexpected happened. While excavating a portion of her backyard to build a swimming pool, several unmarked cans containing close to 1,500 old gold coins were unearthed. The face value of the coins was $28,000 but because they were rare and in uncirculated "mint" condition, they had an aggregate fair market value of $10 million. The pool contractor, the previous owners of the house, and Tricia all claimed ownership. A week ago, a court with competent authority declared Tricia the unequivocal legal owner of the coins (still worth $10 million). **As a result of the foregoing, Tricia most likely:**

    (a) Has $28,000 of income in the current year.

    (b) Has $10 million of income in the current year.

    (c) Has no income in the current year, but will have income when, and if, she sells the coins.

    (d) Has no income because the coins were not the result of her labor, invested capital, or from both combined.

    (e) Has no income in the current year but should have reported income either years ago when she purchased the house, or last year when the coins were discovered.

3. Spencer, a U.S. citizen domiciled in Florida, receives interest from three sources: 1) a ten-year U.S. government note, 2) a savings account at First Bank of the Alps (A Swiss bank with all accounts and offices located in Switzerland), and 3) a thirty-year general obligation bond of the state of Maine (in registered form and not of a "private activity" or "arbitrage" nature). **For federal income tax purposes, Spencer's gross income most likely will include:**

    (a) The interest from all three sources.

    (b) The interest from the U.S. note, but not the interest from the Swiss bank account or the Maine government bond.

    (c) The Interest from the U.S. note and the Swiss bank account, but not the interest from the Maine government bond.

    (d) None of the interest from all three sources.

    (e) The interest from the Swiss bank account, but not the interest from the U.S. note or the Maine government bond.

4. Paul, while attending his brother's funeral, was shocked when he discovered that the funeral director had purposefully disfigured his brother's body. Paul suffered severe emotional trauma, so much so that he ultimately became physically ill and required hospitalization. He sued the funeral director based on the tort of "intentional infliction of emotional distress" and reached an out-of-court settlement, with Paul receiving a total of $100,000. Of this total, $50,000 was designated for Paul's physical pain and suffering, $10,000 for Paul's mental and emotional pain, $15,000 to cover Paul's hospital bills, and $25,000 to compensate Paul for wages lost as a result of missing work because of the incident. **With respect to the foregoing, Paul will, most likely, have to recognize:**

    (a) $25,000 of income.

    (b) $35,000 of income.

    (c) No income.

    (d) $100,000 of income.

    (e) None of the above answers is correct.

5. This fall, Staci will be starting law school at an ABA and AALS accredited university. Because of her outstanding LSAT score and undergraduate GPA, the law school is awarding her a $75,000 scholarship for her first year of study. The scholarship benefits are specifically identified as follows:

- $54,000 applied to fully offset her law school tuition.
- $1,000 applied to offset some of the costs of books required for her first-year classes.
- $15,000 applied to offset some of her on-campus housing costs.
- $5,000 in cash for her to use as she chooses with precatory language that the monies be used for food and other living costs.

How much of this scholarship, if any, will be taxable to Staci?

(a) $20,000, representing the $15,000 to be applied towards housing plus the $5,000 cash to be received. The balance will qualify as excludable scholarship benefits pursuant to IRC § 117.

(b) $5,000, representing the amount of cash to be received. The balance will qualify as excludable scholarship benefits pursuant to IRC § 117.

(c) None of the benefit received will be taxable. The entire $75,000 is designated as a scholarship that, pursuant to IRC § 117, is fully excludable from gross income.

(d) $21,000 representing the $1,000 and $15,000 to be applied towards books and housing, respectively, plus the $5,000 cash to be received. The $54,000 being used for tuition will qualify as an excludable scholarship pursuant to IRC § 117.

(e) A currently indeterminable amount. The total amount that she can exclude from gross income will depend on how much of the $5,000 cash she uses for food and living costs.

6. Staci, from problem 5, discovered that most of her professors for her first-year courses utilize casebooks and supplemental student resources from the legal publisher West Academic. During her free online registration for West Academic, she entered their "welcome to law school" giveaway. To her delight, she was selected (at random from all entrants) as the winner of the grand prize: a top-of-the-line laptop computer worth $3,000. **Which of the following statements best describes the income tax ramifications to Staci as a result of the foregoing?**

    (a) She will have gross income of $3,000 (the value of the computer) unless, before actually receiving the computer, she designates that it be transferred directly to a qualified charitable organization.

    (b) She will have gross income equal to West's cost of the computer. This will be included in her gross income regardless of any recipient designation.

    (c) She will have gross income of $3,000 (the value of the computer). This will be included in her gross income regardless of any recipient designation.

    (d) She will have no gross income because such prizes are excluded pursuant to IRC § 74.

    (e) While normally such a prize would constitute gross income, Staci will be able to exclude it therefrom because she can properly classify the benefit as part of a "scholarship."

7. Wendy was the owner/insured of a $100,000 (face amount) life insurance policy and husband Hank was the beneficiary. Wendy died unexpectedly in December of last year, and Hank decided not to receive the full $100,000 presently. Rather, he selected a payment option that allows him to leave all of the insurance proceeds with the insurer (insurance company) for as long as he wants, and they will pay him interest until he withdraws the proceeds (similar, in concept, to leaving money in the bank and collecting interest). At the time of Wendy's death, Hank had a 50-year life expectancy and he planned to leave all of the insurance proceeds with the insurer for 20 years. In the current year, Hank does not plan to withdraw any of the original $100,000 proceeds, but will receive $6,000 in interest from the insurer. **In the current year, as a result of the foregoing, Hank must recognize:**

    (a) The full $6,000 as income.

    (b) $4,000 of income; the difference between the $6,000 received and $2,000 ($100,000 divided by 50 years).

    (c) $1,000 of income; the difference between the $6,000 received and $5,000 ($100,000 divided by 20 years).

    (d) No income.

8. Brian, a recent college graduate, was hired as a design engineer for a company that makes very sophisticated, and expensive, metal die-cast scale models of automobiles, airplanes and boats. The company has only one place of business, a large multi-building facility located on many acres of land. The company prides itself on uncompromising quality in its products and workforce. To this end, the company operates, on the business premises, an impressive dining facility featuring one of the finest chefs in the state. All employees are entitled, but not required, to eat lunch at this dining facility. Employees eating at the facility are required to pay something for their lunches, but it is **much less** than what they would have to pay for such a quality meal in an "outside" restaurant. Brian eats lunch almost every day at this company dining facility. **Which of the following statements is the most accurate?**

  (a) Brian has no income resulting from this benefit because the dining facility is available to all of the company employees.

  (b) Brian has income equal to the difference between the value of the meals received (measured by what they would cost in a normal restaurant) and the price that he pays for the meals.

  (c) The difference between the value of the meals Brian receives (measured by what they would cost in a normal restaurant) and the price that he pays for them will not be income to him, but only if the employer deems it necessary that employees remain on the business premises during lunch.

  (d) Brian has no income resulting from this benefit assuming that the price employees pay for the lunches covers the employer's cost for the food and other direct operating costs of the facility.

9. Malcolm's regular job is that of a financial consultant. He also has a penchant for gambling and has won a substantial amount from this activity. In addition, he occasionally earns extra cash working as a "full-service" male escort (where he accepts money in exchange for sex). **Which answer best describes what should be included in Malcolm's gross income?**

  (a) Amounts earned from his regular job. The amounts earned from his gambling and escort services are included in gross income only if, and to the extent, that such activities are lawful.

  (b) Amounts earned from all of these sources.

  (c) Amounts earned from his regular job only. His other sources of earnings are excluded from income.

  (d) Amounts earned from his regular job and his services as an escort (regardless of its legality). Amounts earned from gambling, however, are excluded from income.

10. Marcee is sixty-six (66) years old, retired and receiving regular Social Security retirement benefits. **With respect to the Social Security benefits received, Marcee:**

    (a) May be taxed on them at rates up to 50% depending on the extent of her other income.

    (b) May be taxed on them at rates up to 85% depending on the extent of her other income.

    (c) Will not be taxed on any of these benefits regardless of her level of income. Historically, they were fully includible in gross income, but changes in tax laws over the past few decades have eliminated their inclusion.

    (d) Must include all of them in gross income regardless of her level of other income. Historically, they were fully excluded from gross income, but changes in tax laws over the past few decades have eliminated their exclusion.

    (e) None of the above responses is correct.

11. Laura purchased some United States Savings Bonds (Series EE) that mature many years in the future. Series EE U.S. Savings Bonds are purchased at a discount from their stated face amount and pay the stated face amount upon maturity. **Which of the following statements is the most accurate?**

    (a) The difference between the price for which Laura purchased the bonds and their stated face amount represents interest, all of which is excluded because it is interest from an obligation of the United States.

    (b) The difference between the price for which Laura purchased the bonds and their stated face amount represents taxable interest income, all of which is recognized in the year the bonds mature, unless Laura elects to recognize the interest in each year as it effectively accrues.

    (c) The difference between the price for which Laura purchased the bonds and their stated face amount represents taxable interest income. It is recognized in each year as it effectively accrues, unless Laura elects to defer it, in which case it will all be recognized in the year the bonds mature.

    (d) The difference between the price for which Laura purchased the bonds and their stated face amount represents taxable interest income that must be recognized in each year as it effectively accrues.

12. Deidre died and in her will she bequeathed/devised/left $10,000 to her nephew Nathan. While this testamentary gift to Nathan was not qualified in any way in Deidre's will, she owed Nathan $10,000 at the time of her death. Prior to Deidre's death, the two orally agreed that the debt would be paid to Nathan at Deidre's death by way of this bequest/devise/gift (this debt involved no interest). **With respect to the $10,000 Nathan received, he:**

(a) Can exclude it from income as a "gift, bequest or devise" pursuant to IRC § 102.

(b) Must include it in his gross income because it does not qualify as a gift/bequest/devise for purposes of IRC § 102.

(c) Can exclude it from income because Nathan did not derive an economic benefit or a "net accession to wealth."

(d) Must include it in his gross income because it is a "net accession to wealth."

13. Sandra and David are the sole shareholders of SewaClean, Inc. ("The Corporation"). The Corporation owns and operates a private sewage treatment facility that serves the sewage treatment needs of a moderately sized city. Sandra and David are the respective president and general manager of The Corporation. The sewage treatment plant occupies a fair amount of land, which The Corporation leases from the city. A small two-bedroom bungalow is located at one end of the property (as far away from the open sewage pits as possible) and Sandra and David reside there, paying no rent to The Corporation. Sandra wrote her and David's employment contracts on behalf of The Corporation, and as a condition of their employment, their contracts state that they must live in the bungalow located on the plant premises. The Corporation employs many individuals, but Sandra and David are the only employees who live on the premises and are there during "off-hours." **Relating to the couple's residency in the bungalow, they will:**

(a) Be required to include in their income, the fair rental value of their lodging. Even if it is necessary for the couple to be on the premises during off-hours, the fact that Sandra essentially "required" herself and David to live on the premises as a condition of their employment precludes any exclusion.

(b) Not be required to include anything in income with respect to the lodging because The Corporation is effectively the same person as Sandra and David by virtue of their 100% ownership of The Corporation. Income, for tax purposes, is not imputed to "themselves."

(c) Not be required to include the value of the lodging in their income if, by objective standards, it is important that the couple be on the premises during off-hours.

(d) Be required to include in their income the fair rental value of the lodging because even if it is necessary that the couple be on the premises during off-hours, The Corporation does not own the land on which the bungalow is situated.

14. Hannah is a highly acclaimed physician and is employed by a well-known medical school as a teaching physician. Hannah's employment contract, which she negotiated, is unusual in that it requires that her employer pay one-third of her monthly salary directly to her daughter, Denise. In a totally unrelated matter, the medical school operates an active "outreach" program where Hannah spends a fair amount of time each month caring for the medical needs of indigent patients. Sometimes, she receives fees, in accordance with applicable state statute, for these services. Pursuant to the standard employment contract with the university, she (as well as all other employees) is required to immediately remit any such fees received to the university. **With respect to the foregoing, which of the following statements is most accurate?**

   (a) Hannah must include, in her gross income, all of her salary (including the one-third paid to her daughter) as well as the fees that she receives from her work with indigent patients. She cannot assign this income to others.

   (b) Hannah must include, in her gross income, all of her salary (including the one-third paid to her daughter) as she cannot assign any of this income to others. She will not, however, be required to include in her income the fees that she receives relating to her work with indigent patients.

   (c) Hannah's assignment of one-third of her salary to Denise is valid as an "anticipatory" assignment, and Hannah need not include that portion of her salary in her gross income. She will also not be required to include in her income the fees that she receives relating to her work with indigent patients.

   (d) Hannah's assignment of one-third of her salary to Denise is valid as an "anticipatory" assignment, and Hannah need not include that portion of her salary in her gross income. She must include, in her gross income, the fees that she receives from her work with indigent patients but will be entitled to a corresponding charitable contribution deduction.

15. Tad hired contractor Carl to repair earthquake damage to his house. Tad claims that Carl originally told him that the total cost of the job would be $10,000. Carl completed the work and billed Tad $15,000 ($10,000 for labor and $5,000 for materials). Carl claims that he originally told Tad that the $10,000 was the total cost for his labor, and that materials costs would be added thereto. After much arguing, Carl reluctantly agreed to compromise his bill and accept $12,000 as payment, in full, for the job. Tad then paid Carl $12,000. **As a result of the foregoing, Tad will most likely:**

    (a) Realize and recognize the entire $3,000 debt reduction as income from discharge of indebtedness, unless Tad was insolvent at the time the debt was forgiven.

    (b) Not realize or recognize any income from discharge of indebtedness.

    (c) Realize and recognize the entire $3,000 debt reduction as income, but Tad will be able to add this amount to the adjusted basis of his home.

    (d) Not realize or recognize any income from discharge of indebtedness but will realize and recognize $12,000 in income as compensation for services.

16. A car hit Todd while he was crossing the street. Todd sued the driver of the car alleging that the driver was negligent. The parties reached an out-of-court settlement and Todd received $100,000. Of this total, $50,000 was designated for pain and suffering, $10,000 for negligent infliction of emotional distress, $15,000 for medical expenses (of which $5,000 were for medical expenses arising out of the emotional distress), and $25,000 to compensate Todd for wages lost because of the accident. **Of the amount received, Todd will, most likely, have to recognize:**

    (a) $25,000 of income.

    (b) $35,000 of income.

    (c) No income.

    (d) $50,000 of income.

    (e) None of the above responses is correct.

17. Taxpayer entered into an annuity contract with a well-known life insurance company. In exchange for a substantial one-time payment to the insurance company, Taxpayer was guaranteed to receive a specified dollar amount every month until their death. **Which of the following answers best describe the income tax treatment to Taxpayer with respect to the monthly payments to her?**

   (a) The payments received will be fully tax-free until the cumulative benefits received reach the amount Taxpayer originally paid to the insurance company. Payments received thereafter will be fully taxable.

   (b) A portion of each payment received will be tax-free until the cumulative tax-free amount equals the amount Taxpayer originally paid to the insurance company. Payments received thereafter will be fully taxable.

   (c) A portion of each payment received will be tax-free regardless of how long Taxpayer lives or the amount of benefits Taxpayer receives pursuant to the contract.

   (d) All payments received by Taxpayer will be totally tax-free because the benefits are paid pursuant to a contract with a life insurance company.

18. Sheryl's principal residence is in Austin, Texas and is located within easy driving distance of the "Circuit of the Americas" (COTA) motor racing track complex. Not a big racing fan, she prefers not to be in town during the two racing events that attract the largest crowds: the U.S. Formula One Grand Prix and the "Grand Prix of the Americas MotoGP" (motorcycle). She takes her absences as opportunities to rent her home to race fans and others. Last year, she rented her home for two six-day extended racing weekends (twelve days total) and received aggregate rents of $42,000 (the MotoGP event was especially lucrative renting her home to the Ducati Motorcycle Racing team's support staff). Other than these racing weekends (never exceeding twelve days in the aggregate), Sheryl does not rent out her home. **Which of the following statements is most accurate with respect to the foregoing?**

   (a) Sheryl must include the $42,000 in her gross income. She can, however, offset this income to the extent of her actual "out-of-pocket" home-related expenses associated with the rental periods.

   (b) Sheryl must include the $42,000 in her gross income. She can, however, deduct (offsetting this income) a fraction of her total "out-of-pocket" home-related expenses for the entire year. The numerator of this fraction is the number of days she rented her house and the denominator is the total number of days in the year, or $^{12}/_{365}$ in this case.

   (c) Sheryl must include the $42,000 in her gross income. She can, however, deduct (offsetting this income) her actual "out-of-pocket" home-related expenses and properly determined "depreciation" expenses for the rental periods.

   (d) Sheryl can exclude the entire $42,000 from her gross income. She is not entitled to extra deductions associated with renting her house.

   (e) Because of the amount of rent Sheryl received, she can exclude only a portion of it from her gross income. She may be entitled to some extra deductions associated with renting her house.

Questions 19 through 22 are based on the following facts:

Tillie, a successful businesswoman, owns and operates a chain of small, very expensive boutique hotels located in major cities throughout the United States. She provides certain benefits to her employees.

19. Tillie employs, at each hotel, a manager who is required to live at that hotel and be "on call" 24 hours a day (to handle problems that might arise). Each hotel manager is provided, free of charge, a simple one-bedroom unit in the hotel. Tillie's son, Sid, is the manager of her hotel in Chicago and she provides him with a luxurious three-bedroom penthouse suite in the hotel (at no cost to Sid). When asked by her accountant about this arrangement regarding her son, Tillie said only that, "she loves him dearly and would do almost anything for him." **Regarding the accommodations furnished to Sid, he most likely will have to include in his gross income:**

    (a) Nothing. The value of the lodging is excludable because his lodging is furnished on the hotel premises, it is a requirement of his employment, and it is for the convenience of his employer.

    (b) The full value of his lodging because the benefit discriminates in his favor when compared with the benefit given to the managers of Tillie's other hotels.

    (c) A portion of the value of the lodging received. This amount is the difference between the value of his luxurious accommodations and the value of the standard lodging provided to the managers of Tillie's other hotels.

    (d) Nothing. An amount equal to the value of standard lodging furnished to the managers of Tillie's other hotels is excludable because his lodging is furnished on the hotel premises, it is a requirement of his employment, and it is for the convenience of his employer. The additional value of his luxury accommodations is excludable as a gift.

20. One of the benefits that Tillie provides to all of her full-time employees is free lodging at any of her hotels if there are vacancies. Tillie extends this benefit to the families (company-defined as spouses, domestic partners, and dependent children) of all full-time employees regardless of whether they are accompanied by such employee. Gil is a full-time employee and his husband, Hunter (his legal spouse) recently stayed two nights, free of charge, in an otherwise vacant room at Tillie's Seattle hotel. Gil did not accompany Hunter on this trip. **Which of the following answers best describes the income tax ramification to Gil because of the foregoing?**

    (a) Gil recognizes no income because the value of the lodging provided to his spouse qualifies as an excludable IRC § 132 "no-additional-cost service" fringe benefit.

    (b) Gil must include, in his gross income, the entire value of the lodging because his spouse staying at the hotel was not "for the convenience of" Gil's employer.

    (c) Gil must include the value of the lodging in his gross income because Gil was not present.

    (d) Gil must include the value of the lodging in his gross income because same-sex spouses are not considered "spouses" for federal income tax purposes.

    (e) Gil will have to include the value of the lodging in his gross income assuming that he is considered a "highly compensated employee" for purposes of IRC § 132.

21. Alice, one of Tillie's employees, is a California domestic partner with Dalia (by law, a CA domestic partner is the equivalent to a spouse for property rights, inheritance, etc. purposes). Like question 20, above, Dalia recently stayed three nights, free of charge in an otherwise vacant room, at Tillie's Beverly Hills Hotel. Alice did not accompany Dalia on this trip. **Which of the following answers best describes the income tax ramification to Alice as a result of the foregoing?**

    (a) Alice recognizes no income because the value of the lodging provided to Dalia qualifies as an excludable IRC § 132 "no-additional-cost service" fringe benefit.

    (b) Alice must include, in her gross income, the entire value of the lodging because her domestic partner staying at the hotel was not "for the convenience of" Alice's employer.

    (c) Alice must include the value of the lodging in her gross income because Dalia is not a "spouse" for federal tax purposes even though she is legally treated as one under state law.

    (d) Alice will have to include the value of the lodging in her gross income assuming that she is considered a "highly compensated employee" for purposes of IRC § 132.

22. In addition to the benefit addressed in questions 20 and 21, above, Tillie also allows all of her full-time employees to stay, free of charge, four nights per year in any of her hotels even if they take the place of a paying customer (i.e., they can "bump" a paying customer). Recently, one of her Boston hotel employees, Elise, spent her four free nights at Tillie's fully-booked New York hotel (i.e., Elise took the place of a paying customer). **Elise most likely:**

   (a) Will have to include the full value of the four nights lodging in her gross income.

   (b) Will be able to exclude the value of the four nights lodging because this fringe benefit does not discriminate in favor of "highly compensated employees."

   (c) Will have to include 80% of the value of the four nights lodging in her gross income. The remaining 20% is excludable as a qualified employee discount.

   (d) Will be able to exclude a portion of the value of the four nights lodging equal to the "gross profit percentage" of Tillie's hotel business.

Questions 23 through 25 are based on the following facts:

Brandon operates a construction business as an unincorporated sole proprietor and has experienced severe financial difficulties. Hoping to keep Brandon in business and to assure his future patronage, one of Brandon's major sub-contractors agreed to "write off" $25,000 of an uncontested $50,000 debt that Brandon owed for services received. This happened on April 1 of this year. Just prior to this partial cancellation of the debt, Brandon's total liabilities were $350,000 and the aggregate adjusted bases of his assets were $340,000. At such time, the aggregate fair market values of such assets were $320,000.

23. **As a result of the foregoing, how much income, if any, must Brandon recognize this year?**

   (a) No income pursuant to IRC § 108(e)(5) since the sub-contractor (the provider of services) was also the creditor.

   (b) $15,000, representing the difference between the $25,000 cancellation and the $10,000 amount by which Brandon was insolvent immediately before the debt cancellation.

   (c) No income since at the time of the cancellation, Brandon was insolvent by more than the amount of the debt canceled.

   (d) Currently an indeterminable amount of income since we do not yet know the degree to which Brandon will be insolvent at the end of this tax year.

   (e) None of the above responses is correct

24. Brandon has a $5,000 net operating loss carryover (NOL) from a prior year, but has no business or minimum tax credits, capital losses or carryovers, passive activity loss or credit carryover, or foreign tax credit carryovers. **Assuming no special elections are made, what are the tax ramifications (other than inclusion or exclusion from income) of the partial cancellation of the debt?**

   (a) The adjusted basis of his assets will be reduced by $25,000.

   (b) The net operating loss carryover (NOL) will be eliminated, and the basis of his assets will be reduced by $20,000.

   (c) The net operating loss carryover (NOL) will be eliminated, but the basis of his assets will not be reduced.

   (d) The net operating loss carryover (NOL) will be eliminated, and the basis of his assets will be reduced by $10,000.

   (e) None of the above responses is correct.

25. For this question only, assume that later in the current year, Brandon satisfies the $25,000 remaining debt with the major sub-contractor not by paying $25,000 in cash but, rather, by performing services for the sub-contractor that were worth $25,000. **As a result, Brandon:**

   (a) Does not have realization of income, since he is merely repaying a debt.

   (b) Will realize $25,000 of income.

   (c) Will realize income only to the extent Brandon is solvent at the time of the satisfaction of the debt.

   (d) Does not have realization of income, because this is a nontaxable "barter" type exchange of equal value.

   (e) None of the above responses is correct.

END OF EXAMINATION QUESTIONS

EXAM II

FEDERAL INCOME TAX
MULTIPLE-CHOICE OBJECTIVE QUESTIONS
EXAM II

1. Alfred suffers from severe arthritis. At the insistence of his physician, he installed an elevator in his three-story house in an effort to help alleviate the discomforts caused by his condition. The elevator was installed last year at a cost of $20,000 and it increased the value of his home by $15,000. With respect to the elevator, Alfred paid $1,000 for maintenance of the elevator last year. In addition, last year Alfred paid $200 in over-the-counter (non-prescription) medicines that were recommended by his doctor. **Assuming Alfred was not reimbursed through insurance for any of the above costs, what amount will qualify as expenses paid for medical care for purposes of IRC § 213(a) <u>before</u> applying the "10% of adjusted gross income (AGI) floor?"**

    (a) $5,250.

    (b) $6,000.

    (c) $20,000.

    (d) $21,000.

    (e) None of the above is correct.

2. Tom is a partner in the prestigious Philadelphia law firm of Hungadunga, Hungadunga, Hungadunga, Hungadunga, and McCormack. During the year, Tom had various expenditures as discussed below. The firm is prestigious, but is also "thrifty" (i.e., cheap) and did not reimburse him for any of his expenditures (this policy applies to all partners and employees of the firm). Tom has friends in Providence, Rhode Island, and after earning a few days off, he decided to fly up for a visit. Prior to leaving, Tom's colleague asked him to handle a business matter with one of the firm's Providence clients while he was up there. He arrived in Providence early on Tuesday and returned to Philadelphia early on Sunday. He ended up meeting with the client for twelve hours on Friday. He spent the rest of the trip visiting with friends. He originally had planned on leaving early Saturday but decided to stay an extra day because the price for flights on Sunday were much less expensive. By staying the extra day, he saved more in airfare than it cost him for the extra lodging, meals and incidentals. **Assuming that all of Tom's expenditures for travel, lodging, meals and incidentals were reasonable in amount, how much will probably qualify as "IRC § 162" business expenses?**

(a) All of his transportation costs to/from Providence and his meals (at 50%), lodging and incidentals for Friday, and as many extra days to equal the amount of airfare saved by staying over Saturday.

(b) All of his transportation costs to/from Providence, and his meals (at 50%), lodging, and incidentals for Friday only.

(c) None of his transportation costs to/from Providence, but his meals (at 50%), lodging, and incidentals for Friday will qualify.

(d) None of his transportation costs to/from Providence, but his meals (at 50%), lodging, and incidentals for Friday and Saturday will qualify.

(e) None of his costs because the trip was primarily for pleasure and not for business.

3. **Can an individual, who is not engaged in the business of gambling, deduct gambling losses?**

   (a) No, losses from gambling are not deductible.

   (b) Yes, an individual can use gambling losses to offset gambling winnings, and report as income, only the net amount of any winnings. If the net amount is a loss, it is not deductible.

   (c) Yes, an individual can deduct, as "other" itemized deductions, gambling losses, but only to the extent that he or she has gambling winnings.

   (d) Yes, an individual can deduct gambling losses as "other" itemized deductions.

Questions 4 and 5 are based on the following facts:

Some years ago (pre-2010), Tim purchased his principal residence for $400,000, paying $200,000 down and borrowing $200,000 (evidenced by a mortgage secured by the house). The value of his home has risen substantially, and in the current year (assume this is 2018 or later) he decided to "tap into the equity" in his home and borrow against it. He took out a second mortgage or "home equity loan" (also secured by the home) in the amount of $160,000. He used $90,000 of these funds to add a bedroom to his home. He used the remaining $70,000 to purchase some stocks for investments and pay for a cruise vacation. Assume that the principal owed on his first mortgage remains undiminished at $200,000. Also in the current year (2018 or later), he bought a vacation cabin (used exclusively for personal purposes and not rented out), borrowing $100,000 in a separate mortgage loan (secured by the cabin). Tim owns no other real property.

4. **For the current year (assume this to be 2018 or later), Tim should be entitled to a deduction for the interest paid with respect to:**

    (a) The full amount of all of the loans.

    (b) Both the original $200,000 loan and the $100,000 cabin loan as "acquisition indebtedness," and a maximum of $100,000 of the home equity loan as "home equity indebtedness."

    (c) Only the original $200,000 loan as "acquisition indebtedness," and an aggregate maximum of $100,000 from the home equity and the cabin loans as "home equity indebtedness."

    (d) Both the original $200,000 loan and $90,000 of the home equity loan as "acquisition indebtedness," and an aggregate maximum of $100,000 from the remaining home equity loan and the cabin loan as "home equity indebtedness."

    (e) The sum of the original $200,000 loan, $90,000 of the home equity loan, and the $100,000 cabin loan as "acquisition indebtedness." Interest on the $70,000 balance of the home equity loan is not deductible.

5. For this question only, assume that Tim had to pay the applicable lender one (1) "point" to obtain each of the two loans obtained in the current year (the second mortgage on his home and the cabin loan). **In the current year, Tim will be entitled to deduct:**

   (a) One percent of the full amount of both loans.

   (b) One percent of both the $100,000 cabin loan and $90,000 of the home equity loan. The points paid with respect to the balance of the home equity loan must be amortized (deducted pro-rata) over the life of that loan.

   (c) One percent of only the $100,000 cabin loan. The points paid with respect to the entire home equity loan must be amortized (deducted pro-rata) over the life of that loan.

   (d) One percent of only $90,000 of the home equity loan. The points paid with respect to the $70,000 balance of the home equity loan and the entire $100,000 cabin loan must be amortized (deducted pro-rata) over the respective lives of the loans.

   (e) None of the above responses is correct.

6. After graduating from law school a couple of years ago, Ben set up his own law firm, specializing in personal injury law representing plaintiffs in tort actions (he is self-employed). Not having taken "federal income tax" in law school, but realizing it was important to know something about the subject, Ben recently attended a two-day state bar sponsored "basic taxation for lawyers" seminar (six hours of classroom time for each day). The seminar was in Neighborville (some 30 miles from his residence and office in Centerville) and it cost him $900 in course fees. In addition, he spent $150 in lodging (he stayed the night between the two seminar days at the conference hotel because they offered a special seminar room rate), $100 in meals for both days, and $50 in transportation costs to and from the seminar. **To what extent do these costs qualify as trade or business expenses to Ben?**

   (a) The $900 course fee, the $150 for lodging, and the $50 in transportation costs.

   (b) The $900 course fee, and the $50 in transportation costs.

   (c) The $900 course fee, the $150 for lodging, the $50 in transportation costs, and one-half of the $100 spent for meals.

   (d) Only the $900 course fee.

   (e) None of these costs qualify as trade or business expenses to Ben.

7. Abigail operates a very substantial light manufacturing business as an unincorporated sole proprietorship. Early this year, she constructed a new warehouse on property that she already owned, and purchased a few very expensive machines (each costing well in excess of $100,000) used in her manufacturing business. **Assuming that Abigail makes no special elections available to her under current law, which of the following statements is most accurate with respect to the income tax ramifications with respect to these expenditures?**

   (a) She can deduct the full cost of the equipment purchases in the current year as business expenses. The cost of the warehouse represents a capital expenditure and is not deductible, in full, in the current year but, rather, is "expensed" over more than one year in the form of depreciation deductions.

   (b) Both the warehouse and equipment costs represent capital expenditures and she cannot deduct their full cost as an expense in the current year. Rather, their cost will be "expensed" over more than one year in the form of depreciation deductions.

   (c) Because Abigail operates her business as an unincorporated sole proprietorship, as opposed to a corporation, she is entitled to deduct the full cost of the warehouse and equipment in the current year as business expenses.

   (d) Both the warehouse and equipment costs are not deductible in full in the current year. Rather, they are capitalized expenditures and she can elect, pursuant to IRC § 195, to deduct them over a statutorily-defined number of years.

8. Abigail, in question 7, above, has a manufacturing building (different from the newly constructed warehouse) for which she originally paid $1 million (this included the cost of the underlying land) some years ago. She has not made any major improvements to this building since purchasing it. This manufacturing building is the type of asset for which depreciation deductions would be allowed (this was all prior to 2017/2018 tax law changes). Abigail's business has always been very successful and her taxable income, for all years that she has had the business, has been substantial in amount. **Which of the following statements is most accurate with respect to Abigail's basis (adjusted basis or AB) in this building at the beginning of the current year (or at the end of the previous year)?**

   (a) Her basis (AB) in the property is her "cost" basis of $1 million.

   (b) Assuming Abigail actually claimed depreciation deductions allowed with respect to this building, her basis (AB) in the property is $1 million less the depreciation deductions actually taken.

   (c) Her basis (AB) in the property is the $1 million cost less the amount of depreciation deductions allowable to her regardless of whether or not she actually claimed the deductions.

   (d) Her basis (AB) in the property is not the $1 million less the amount of depreciation deductions allowable to her, because part of the original $1 million purchase price represented the cost of the underlying land (and land is generally not a depreciable asset).

Questions 9 through 11 are based on the following facts:

Wendy is self-employed and operates a business as an unincorporated sole proprietorship. Wendy's husband, Hank, is an elementary school teacher at a local public school and is not involved in her business. They live together in their house on the beach in Santa Monica, California (which is located immediately west of Downtown Los Angeles, California). Wendy owns and operates two retail stores that sell men's suits exclusively (very "high-end" Italian and custom-made). One store is in Malibu, California (approximately ten miles up the coast from their Santa Monica home) and the other store is in Downtown Los Angeles (about fifteen miles inland from their Santa Monica home). Most days she goes to both stores and while her routine varies, her normal pattern is to drive, from home, to the Los Angeles store in the morning, then drive directly to the Malibu store, and then drive home in the early evening. On occasion, she also drives to the homes or offices of "special" customers. Wendy drives her own car and keeps meticulous records of her miles. Last year, her total miles driven break down as follows: 30% for driving to/from home to either store, 25% for driving between the Los Angeles and Malibu stores, 15% for driving to/from special customers (sometimes directly from home and sometimes from one of her stores), and the remaining 30% driving for purely personal purposes.

9. **What percent of Wendy's miles driven will qualify as "business miles" for purposes of determining her deduction for business transportation costs?**

    (a) 15 percent.

    (b) 25 percent.

    (c) Between 25 and 40 percent. The exact percentage will depend on what portion of the 15 percent of miles driven to special customers originated from or terminated with either store location.

    (d) 40 percent.

    (e) None of the above response is correct.

10. Wendy and Hank are planning to fly up to Seattle for a two-week trip. Wendy says that she will be "combining business with pleasure." They vacation often in the Seattle area and for their upcoming trip, they plan to spend most of their time enjoying the sights. Wendy has seriously been thinking of opening a small boutique in Seattle, and she states that one purpose of the upcoming trip is to search out store locations, make business contacts, and talk to suppliers in the area. This contemplated store will, however, be quite a departure for Wendy – no men's suits but, rather, "clothing" exclusively for pets (dogs, cats, etc.). **Which of the following statements best describes the income tax consequences, if any, to Wendy with respect to the planned two-week trip?**

(a) It is unlikely that any of Wendy's airfare will qualify as a trade or business expense pursuant to IRC § 162. However, some of her costs for lodging, meals and incidentals while in Seattle may qualify as § 162 trade/business deductions, if retail "pet clothing" sales is considered the same business as her current business (or a logical extension thereof).

(b) It is unlikely that any of Wendy's airfare will qualify as a trade or business expense pursuant to IRC § 162. Additionally, she will not be entitled to deduct any of her costs for lodging, meals and incidentals while in Seattle, even if retail selling of pet clothing is considered the same trade/business as her current business.

(c) If the business of retail sales of pet clothing is considered the same trade or business as is Wendy's current business (or a logical extension thereof), then a portion of her airfare and some of her costs for lodging, meals and incidentals will qualify as business deductions pursuant to IRC § 162.

(d) If the business of retail sales of pet clothing is considered the same trade or business as is Wendy's current business (or a logical extension thereof), then all of her airfare and some of her costs for lodging, meals and incidentals will qualify as business deductions pursuant to IRC § 162.

(e) If the business of retail sales of pet clothing is considered the same trade or business as is Wendy's current business (or a logical extension thereof), then all of the cost for her airfare, lodging, incidentals, and 50% of the cost of her meals will qualify as business deductions pursuant to IRC § 162.

11. Assume the same facts as in question 10, above, except that for this question, Wendy is not contemplating any type of future business in Seattle. For this question, however, please assume that Hank indicates a business purpose for the upcoming Seattle trip. He will visit sites, take pictures and gather data on Native American tribes indigenous to the area, thereby better educating himself on the subject. Hank plans to utilize the information that he learns in his classroom teaching. **Most likely, will Hank be entitled to deduct, as business expenses, any of his costs associated with this trip?**

    (a) No, but only because he is an employee and not self-employed.

    (b) No, regardless of whether he is an employee or self-employed.

    (c) Yes, but only the costs for his lodging, incidentals and meals (at 50%) for the days actually spent on the above-described activities.

    (d) Yes, most likely he will be able to deduct the cost of his airfare. In addition he should be entitled to a deduction for the cost of his lodging, incidentals and meals (at 50%) for the days actually spent on the above-described activities.

12. Chad is overweight and has been diagnosed by his physician as suffering from obesity. Donna suffers from hypertension and her physician has directed her to lose weight as a treatment for the disease. Both Chad and Donna join a commercial weight-loss program requiring them to pay an initial fee and additional fees to attend periodic meetings. The program meetings consist of developing diet plans, learning about nutritional information, and group discussions about the participants' challenges encountered in dieting. This weight-loss program also sells their own line of special program-specific foods that participants are encouraged to purchase. Chad and Donna both purchased the weight-loss program's food items. **Assuming neither Chad nor Donna are reimbursed through insurance for any of these costs, what will qualify as expenses paid for medical care for purposes of IRC § 213(a) (<u>before</u> applying the "10% of adjusted gross income (AGI) floor")?**

    (a) Only Donna's weight-loss program fees (initial fee plus fees for meetings) qualify as medical care expenses. Chad's program/meeting fees do not qualify as medical care expenses. The costs of the program's special foods do not qualify as medical care expenses for either Donna or Chad.

    (b) Both Chad's and Donna's weight-loss program fees (initial fee plus fees for meetings) qualify as medical care expenses. However, the costs for the program's special foods do not qualify as medical care expenses for either Donna or Chad.

    (c) Both Chad's and Donna's weight-loss program fees (initial fee plus fees for meetings) qualify as medical care expenses. The costs for the program's diet foods also qualify as medical care expenses for both Chad and Donna.

    (d) Donna's weight-loss program fees (initial fee plus fees for meetings) and the cost of her special program foods qualify as medical care expenses. Chad's program/meeting fees and the special program food costs do not qualify as medical care expenses.

    (e) None of the above responses is correct.

13. Shirin graduated from law school last spring and recently began work as a self-employed attorney (operating as an unincorporated sole proprietorship). This was Shirin's first full-time work and she had few "professional" clothes. After working for about a month and "getting by" with frequent rotation of the few business clothes that she owned, she realized that major additions to her wardrobe were in order. She purchased several items including business suits, blouses, scarves, dress shoes, and the like. Shirin's work is such that she must wear professional attire while working and for most work-related functions. Outside of work (or work related functions), she rarely wears business attire. **In all likelihood, will Shirin's recent clothes expenditures qualify as a deductible IRC § 162 business expense?**

    (a) No, because she has just started working, and has not worked long enough in her profession as an attorney to be considered engaged in that trade or business.

    (b) Yes, but only if she can show that she does not wear these business clothes outside of work or work-related matters.

    (c) No, because the business clothes are considered adaptable to normal street wear.

    (d) Yes, because for all intents and purposes, her type of work requires that she wear professional business attire.

    (e) No, because IRC § 162 deduction is allowed, but she can elect, pursuant to IRC § 195, some current deduction and/or amortization of their cost over a period of years.

14. Shirin, in question 13, above, takes good care of her business wardrobe. It did not take her long, however, to discover how costly regular maintenance (e.g., dry cleaning) of a business wardrobe could be. **Which of the following statements most likely describes the deductibility of these maintenance costs?**

(a) A percentage of these costs qualify as a legitimate business expense equal to the percentage of time that they are worn for business purposes. This deduction is allowed even though the cost of her clothes did not give rise to a deduction.

(b) All of these costs will qualify as a legitimate business expense because the cost of the clothes qualified as deductible under either IRC § 162 or IRC § 195.

(c) None of these costs will qualify as a legitimate business expense because the cost of the clothes did not qualify as deductible under either IRC § 162 or IRC § 195.

(d) Regardless of whether or not the cost of the clothes gave rise to any business related deduction, maintenance costs do not qualify as a legitimate business expense.

15. Greg, an accomplished, award winning craft beer brew master, operates his beer making business as an unincorporated sole proprietorship. Recently, after an equipment failure, he rented replacement equipment for two days, costing him $2,000 plus sales tax of $160 (his state charges sales tax on rentals). In a totally unrelated transaction, he also recently purchased an exotic Italian motorcycle (an MV Agusta F4 RC) used solely for personal purposes, totally unrelated to his business. He paid $46,000 for the motorcycle plus sales tax of $3,700 on the purchase. **Which of the following statements is most accurate?**

   (a) The $2,000 equipment rental cost gives rise to a deduction, but the sales tax on neither the equipment rental nor motorcycle purchase is a deductible tax pursuant to IRC § 164.

   (b) The $2,160 total paid for the equipment rental (rental plus sales tax thereon) is deductible as a business expense, but his sales tax on the motorcycle is not a deductible tax pursuant to IRC § 164.

   (c) The $2,000 paid for the equipment rental is deductible as a business expense and the sales tax on both the equipment rental and motorcycle purchase is deductible pursuant to IRC § 164 because they are imposed by a state (and/or subdivision thereof).

   (d) The $2,160 total paid for the equipment rental (rental plus sales tax thereon) is deductible as a business expense. Greg may benefit, tax-wise, from the sales tax paid on the motorcycle purchase because of a possible deduction pursuant to IRC § 164.

   (e) None of these expenditures qualify for a deduction.

16. Ira owns two homes; his principle residence in California and a vacation home in Luxembourg (the European country) and in the current year, he paid property taxes of $5,000 and $9,000, respectively. Ira also paid $7,000 in California income taxes and $3,000 in California sales taxes in the current year. **Assuming that these represent all of the "taxes" Ira paid in the current year, and that the "current year" is 2018 or later, what is the maximum amount of his deduction pursuant to IRC § 164?**

   (a) $24,000.

   (b) $21,000.

   (c) $15,000.

   (d) $12,000.

   (e) $10,000.

17. Claudia lives in Washington State and this year she paid no income taxes (Washington does not impose an income tax) but did pay state sales taxes of $4,000. She owns a home there and this year she paid $5,000 in property taxes. She also owns a parcel of raw land in Connecticut on which she hopes to someday build a house and retire (currently, the land is vacant). In the current year, she paid $3,000 in property taxes with respect to this property. **Assuming that these represent all of the "taxes" Claudia paid in the current year, and that the "current year" is 2018 or later, what is the amount of her deduction pursuant to IRC § 164?**

   (a) $8,000.

   (b) $9,000.

   (c) $10,000.

   (d) $12,000.

18. Takuma is a self-employed Denver attorney practicing as an unincorporated sole proprietor specializing in estate planning. Recently, Takuma invited a prospective client, Christina, to a Colorado Rockies baseball game. While, at times, it was a bit difficult to talk during the ballgame, Takuma was able to make an effective "pitch" for why he could best serve Christina's estate planning needs. Christina was impressed, and during the game's "seventh inning stretch," they shook hands with Christina agreeing to meet with Takuma the following week to begin discussing her estate plan. During the game's last couple of innings, they even discussed some of the pertinent issues relating to Christina's estate. Takuma paid for the tickets to the game. Notwithstanding their meeting next week, the two had no formal business meetings either before or after the game. **Which of the following statements best describes the tax implications to Takuma as a result of the foregoing?**

  (a) He will not be entitled to any deduction for the cost of the tickets because these are considered entertainment activities. While the cost of entertainment activities may be deductible if the taxpayer establishes that the activity was directly related to the active conduct of a trade or business, the regulations provide that a sporting event is an environment that precludes this.

  (b) He will not be entitled to any deduction for the cost of the tickets because these are considered entertainment activities. Had he and Christina met in his office for a bona fide business meeting either immediately preceding or following the ballgame, some deduction would have been allowed.

  (c) He will be entitled to some deduction for the cost of the tickets even though these were considered entertainment activities. Takuma most likely will be able to establish that the activity was directly related to the active conduct of a trade or business notwithstanding the regulation's presumptive conclusion to the contrary.

  (d) He will be entitled to some deduction for the cost of the tickets even though these are considered entertainment activities. Because he and Christina agreed to meet the following week, the ballgame is considered a legitimate entertainment activity that is "associated with" the active conduct of a trade or business.

  (e) None of the above responses is correct.

19. Moving on from question 18, a week later, Takuma and Christina have their initial meeting in which they go over some basic, preliminary information as part of the estate planning process. Since this was not addressing complex matters, the two held their meeting over lunch, in a secluded booth in a nice restaurant. Takuma paid for lunch and the two then arranged for a future in-depth meeting at his office. **Most likely, to what extent is Takuma entitled to a deduction for the cost of this lunch?**

    (a) 100% of the cost because it meets the requirements of a IRC §162 ordinary and necessary business expense.

    (b) 100% of the cost because this is a valid business expense and it meets the more stringent "meal deduction" requirements of IRC § 274(k).

    (c) 50% of the cost because while it is a valid business expense and meets the "meal deduction" requirements of IRC § 274(k), it is still subject to the overall limitation of IRC § 274(n); limiting deductions for meals to 50%.

    (d) Takuma will, most likely, not be entitled to any deduction for the cost of the meal. While this is a valid business expense, meals, including business meals, are within the more restrictive umbrella of "entertainment" expenses. IRC § 274(a) is the controlling section here and while under prior law certain business entertainment expenses gave rise to potential deductions, recent legislation generally denies any deduction for entertainment expenses. Thus, the lunch would be considered an entertainment expense for which no deduction will be allowed.

20. Monet, a very successful and well-known self-employed business consultant, is planning a trip to France. Her principal reason for the trip is to meet with one of her corporate clients in Paris to negotiate a complex merger involving the company. After concluding her business related work in Paris, she plans to take some time off, vacationing in the French countryside before returning home to New York. She expects the trip's duration to total six weeks with about one-third (33.33%) of this time spent on pleasure travel. **With respect to the cost of her round-trip transportation from New York to Paris, which of the following statements is most accurate?**

    (a) She will be entitled to deduct approximately two-thirds (66.67%) of the transportation costs.

    (b) Because the trip is primarily for business, she will be entitled to deduct 100% of the transportation costs.

    (c) She will not be entitled to deduct any portion of her transportation costs. Although the trip is primarily for business, because this is "foreign travel" and she plans to spend more than twenty-five percent (25%) of the time for pleasure travel, the statute precludes any deduction for the transportation costs.

    (d) She will not be entitled to deduct any portion of her transportation costs. Although the trip is primarily for business, the statute precludes any deduction for her transportation costs because: this is "foreign travel," the trip will last longer than one week, and she plans to spend more than twenty-five percent (25%) of the time for pleasure travel.

21. Jeremy, a single individual, is a full-time tenth grade science teacher at a financially strapped public high school. He has been a high school science teacher for many years. This year, he purchased $1,000 of much needed supplies and software for use in his classroom. Jeremy's employer does not reimburse teachers for such expenditures. **Assuming "this year" is 2018 or later, which of the following statements best describes the income tax ramifications to Jeremy as a result of the foregoing?**

    (a) Jeremy is entitled to deduct $250 (adjusted for inflation) in computing his adjusted gross income (AGI). The remaining $750 is considered a "miscellaneous itemized deduction" which is deductible only to the extent that the aggregate of such category of deductions exceeds 2% of his AGI.

    (b) Jeremy is entitled to deduct the entire $1,000 in computing his adjusted gross income (AGI).

    (c) Jeremy is not entitled to deduct any portion of the $1,000 because he is an employee. Had he been "self-employed," he would have been entitled to deduct the full $1,000 in computing his adjusted gross income (AGI).

    (d) Jeremy is entitled to deduct $250 (adjusted for inflation) in computing his adjusted gross income (AGI). The remaining $750, while a legitimate business expense, will not give rise to any deduction.

    (e) The entire $1,000 is considered a "miscellaneous itemized deduction" which is deductible only to the extent that the aggregate of such category of deductions exceeds 2% of his AGI.

22. Teresa graduated from law school in May of 2018. She financed most of her full-time legal education with student loans (traditional, school-arranged type). In 2019, she expects to pay interest of $2,800 on these loans. Teresa is employed as an attorney and in 2019, she expects to have gross income of $145,000. **Which of the following statements is most accurate in describing Teresa's deductibility of interest in 2019 pursuant to IRC § 221?**

    (a) She will not be entitled to any deduction.

    (b) She will be entitled to a deduction, but it will be limited to $2,500.

    (c) Teresa will be entitled to at least some deduction, but only if she is married (and files a joint return).

    (d) Teresa may be entitled to a deduction even if she is single, but this depends on the type and the scope of other deductions that she might have.

23. Waynoka and Hector, a married couple filing a joint return, are both educators and parents. Waynoka is a full-time chemistry professor at a local university. Hector was teacher at a local grade school but now he is a work-at-home dad homeschooling, on a full-time basis, their two primary grade level children. This year, Waynoka purchased various chemistry-related classroom supplies for use by her students. The university does not reimburse employees for such expenditures. Hector, who follows a state-approved education curriculum, also spent money this year on books, supplies, and the like, used exclusively for his homeschooling activities. **Assuming "this year" is 2018 or later, which of the following statements best describes the income tax ramifications to Waynoka and Hector as a result of the foregoing?**

(a) Neither Waynoka's nor Hector's expenditures will give rise to a deduction

(b) Waynoka's expenditures are legitimate IRC § 162 business expenses but because she is an employee, she is not entitled to any deduction. Hector, however, is entitled to deduct up to $250 (adjusted for inflation) of such costs in computing adjusted gross income (AGI) but any excess will not give rise to a deduction.

(c) Waynoka is entitled to deduct up to $250 (adjusted for inflation) of such costs in computing adjusted gross income (AGI) but any excess, while legitimate business expenses, will not give rise to a deduction.

(d) Both Waynoka and Hector are each be entitled to deduct up to $250 (adjusted for inflation) of such costs in computing adjusted gross income (AGI). Any excess, however, will not give rise to a deduction.

(e) Both Waynoka's and Hector's expenditures qualify a deduction in computing adjusted gross income (AGI). The deduction amount, however, is limited to $250 in combined expenditures (i.e., not $250 each). Any excess will not give rise to a deduction.

24. Oscar, a landscape architect, started investing in the stock market last year. He bought most of his stocks on "margin" (paying only a percentage of the stock's actual price and borrowing the balance of the purchase price from the brokerage firm). Last year, he paid $3,000 in interest on these "margin" loans. Other than his stock market activities, his other investments consist only of money deposited in interest bearing savings accounts at various banks. Last year, his stocks paid (to him), a total of $500 in "qualified" dividends (the type of dividends that receive favorable tax treatment), and he sold none of the stocks in his portfolio. Also last year, he received $300 in interest from his savings accounts. **Assuming that he made no special tax elections last year, which of the following statements is most accurate with respect to Oscar's deduction for the "margin" interest that he paid?**

   (a) He would not be entitled to deduct any of the $3,000 in interest because it represents "personal interest."

   (b) He could deduct, last year, all of the $3,000 interest because the interest related to investments and not to funds borrowed for the purchase of personal-use assets.

   (c) He could deduct, last year, only $500 of the $3,000 interest that he paid. The excess not deducted ($2,500), is carried forward to future years and deducted to the extent that he has "net investment income."

   (d) He could deduct, last year, only $800 of the $3,000 interest that he paid. The excess not deducted ($2,200) is not available for any future deductions.

   (e) He could deduct, last year, only $300 of the $3,000 interest that he paid. The excess not deducted ($2,700) is carried forward to future years and deducted to the extent that he has "net investment income."

25. Julie, a recent law school graduate, is employed full-time at a large law firm. Throughout her life, Julie has had a love for horses and horseback riding. A few years ago, she purchased a horse and boards it at a local stable. The recurring costs of caring for her horse are rather high and include such things as food, veterinary care, boarding/stable fees, equipment, and the like. Having taken federal income tax in law school, she recognizes that none of these costs are deductible because she uses her horse for purely recreational purposes (going on rides in the late afternoons and on weekends and holidays). She also remembers from her tax course that "business expenses" are deductible and has come up with an idea that she believes will convert her substantial amount of horse-related costs from nondeductible to deductible expenses. She is thinking of renting out her horse for others to ride about once every month or so, generating income to her. She would then claim that she is operating a business which she then believes would enable her to claim all of her horse-related costs as business deductions. This "business" would generate substantial operating losses (the costs far exceeding the revenue) which she would like to use for tax purposes to help offset some of her salary and other income. **Most likely, will Julie's plan succeed for income tax purposes?**

  (a) Yes. Assuming that she gets a business license (if necessary), advertises and keeps adequate financial records, this activity could qualify as a business, and she can deduct all of her horse-related expenses.

  (b) No. She will not be entitled to deduct all of her horse-related expenses, generating business losses therefrom. However, she will probably be entitled to deduct her horse-related expenses up to the amount of the income that she derives from the activity.

  (c) No. She will not be entitled to deduct any of her horse-related expenses. In addition, any income she would derive from renting out her horse would be required to be included in her gross income for tax purposes.

  (d) No. The statute contains objective criteria to conclusively establish whether or not an activity constitutes engaging in a business for profit. The statutory criteria for a taxpayer to be a business requires that the taxpayer generate a profit, in a certain number of years over a given period of time. Failure to meet these tests will preclude Julie from qualifying her activity as a valid business.

END OF EXAMINATION QUESTIONS

EXAM III

FEDERAL INCOME TAX
MULTIPLE-CHOICE OBJECTIVE QUESTIONS
EXAM III

Questions 1 through 6 are based on the following facts:

Ann and Bob have been married for thirty years. Until recently, Bob was incarcerated for many years in state prison for a serious felony for which he maintained his innocence. Ann managed the frozen foods section of a large warehouse type store until September of last year. In September of last year, Ann was involved in a horrible accident. As she was entering the store's large walk-in freezer, a store employee driving a forklift, hit the freezer door, crushing Ann. Ann suffered severe spinal injuries and is now confined to a wheelchair. In January of last year, Bob was released from prison; wrongfully incarcerated after new evidence conclusively determined his innocence.

1. As a result of the freezer incident, Ann filed a lawsuit against the market claiming negligence. The case went to trial and in November of last year, a jury found in Ann's favor and awarded her compensatory damages, specifically identifying amounts for pain and suffering, medical costs, lost wages, and emotional distress suffered as a result of the incident. **With respect to the foregoing, Ann:**

    (a) Can exclude from gross income only the amount of the award identified for pain and suffering, and medical costs. She cannot exclude from income the amount of the award compensating her for lost wages or emotional distress.

    (b) Can exclude from gross income the entire amount of this award.

    (c) Cannot exclude from gross income the amount of the award compensating her for lost wages. She can, however, exclude from gross income, the balance of the award.

    (d) Cannot exclude from gross income the amount of the award identified as compensating her for emotional distress. She can, however, exclude from gross income, the balance of the award.

    (e) Must include in gross income, the entire amount of the award since they represent "compensatory" damages.

2. In addition to the compensatory damages awarded to Ann in question 1, above, the jury found the market's actions to be particularly egregious and awarded her punitive damages. **Which of the following statements is most accurate?**

   (a) The punitive damages received can be excluded from gross income because they stem from a physical injury.

   (b) The punitive damages received can only be excluded from gross income if state law expressly permitted the awarding of such damages, and such law was in effect on September 13, 1995.

   (c) The punitive damages received must be included in gross income because a portion of the underlying compensatory award included amounts for lost wages or emotional distress.

   (d) The punitive damages received must be included in gross income regardless of the foundation or composition of Ann's underlying award or the application of any state law.

3. Bob, who was visiting Ann at work the day of the freezer incident, witnessed, in horror, his wife being injured. As a result, he suffered severe emotional trauma, manifesting into actual physical sickness requiring medical treatment. In a separate action, Bob sued the market claiming negligent infliction of emotional distress. The market settled this lawsuit for a substantial sum, specifically identifying amounts for emotional pain/suffering, physical pain/suffering, and payments for medical costs incurred. **Must Bob include all or any part of this settlement in gross income?**

   (a) Yes, he must include all but the amount representing payment for his medical costs.

   (b) No, he is entitled to exclude the entire amount received because the cause of action was "tort or tort-like."

   (c) Yes, he must include the entire amount received because the cause of action was based on emotional distress.

   (d) No, he is entitled to exclude the entire amount received because even though the cause of action was emotional distress, it manifested into an actual physical injury thereby allowing for full exclusion.

4. Following the freezer incident, Ann discovered that Mike, the market's manager, had been talking to employees and customers about the incident, and had repeatedly said: "the whole thing was probably Ann's own fault. That old lady was probably half asleep or drunk at the time." Ann filed a separate defamation lawsuit against Mike, claiming that both her personal and business reputation had been injured as a result of his statements. Ann was neither asleep nor drunk at the time of the incident and the lawsuit was settled before going to trial with Ann receiving a substantial sum of money. **Which of the following statements is most accurate?**

   (a) If Ann can show that the primary component of her defamation claim was the injury to her personal reputation, she may be entitled to exclude the settlement from gross income.

   (b) If Ann can show that the primary component of her defamation claim was the injury to her business reputation, she may be entitled to exclude the settlement from gross income.

   (c) Ann cannot exclude the settlement from gross income regardless of whether the primary component of her claim was injury to her personal or business reputation.

   (d) Ann can exclude the settlement from gross income regardless of whether the primary component of her claim was injury to her personal or business reputation.

5. Turning to Bob, he owes his freedom to the dedicated work of law students and faculty at a local law school's program working to free those wrongfully accused. In Bob's case, new witness testimony and DNA evidence lead to the total exoneration, and freedom, after serving twenty years of a life sentence for a crime that he did not commit. As a result, Bob received, earlier this year, $1 million in state-mandated "compensation" for his lost years spent behind bars. **For federal income tax purposes, is Bob required to include any portion of the $1 million in his gross income?**

    (a) No, because this is equivalent to a personal injury award and therefore is excluded from income via IRC § 104.

    (b) Yes. The entire $1 million is included in gross income. While not adequate compensation for the injustice he suffered, it is considered "compensation" for which there is no exclusion from gross income.

    (c) Yes. Some of the money received will be included in income as compensation (the equivalent of wages). However, a portion of the amount will be considered payment for an injury, excludable by IRC § 104.

    (d) No. Bob will be entitled to exclude, from gross income, the full $1 million received.

6. After Ann's accident, it became clear that extensive modifications to their house would be necessary for wheelchair accessibility. They spent a substantial amount of money widening doorways and installing ramps, grab bars and railings. In addition, Ann spent a considerable amount of money to purchase a new motorized wheelchair. **With respect to these house modifications and wheelchair expenditures, which statement best describes their qualification as "expenses for medical care" for purposes of IRC § 213?**

(a) All of the expenditures will qualify as medical care expenses notwithstanding that they appear to be nondeductible capital expenditures pursuant to IRC § 263.

(b) The cost of the wheelchair will qualify as a medical care expense. However, the cost of the home modifications will qualify as medical care expenses only to extent that the costs exceed the increase in the value to their home as a result of the modifications. In the present case, this will most likely result in a substantial amount of the home modification expenditures not qualifying as medical care expenses.

(c) Neither the expenditures for the wheelchair nor the home modifications will qualify as medical care expenses because they represent capital expenditures that, pursuant to IRC § 263, are nondeductible.

(d) None of these expenditures will qualify as medical care expenses unless specifically prescribed by her doctor.

Questions 7 through 11 are based on the following facts:

Larry, a single individual, age 28 and a recent law school graduate, started work in August of last year, as an associate (employee) in his Mother's law firm. To date, Larry's work at the firm has been exemplary. Unbeknownst to his mother, Larry, while in law school, borrowed $15,000 from his grandmother, Glenda, and used the money to pay tuition. Larry, wanting everything to be "above board," gave Glenda a promissory note for the amount borrowed. The note provided that Larry would pay her interest only (monthly at a fair market rate) until such time, after graduating law school, when he obtained a job – at which time he would repay the full $15,000 principal.

7. **Pursuant to the promissory note, Larry paid $1,100 in interest to his grandmother, Glenda. Most likely, the interest that he paid is:**

    (a) Nondeductible personal interest.

    (b) Deductible as investment interest.

    (c) Deductible pursuant to IRC § 221 assuming that the level of Larry's income is not sufficient to reduce or eliminate the deduction.

    (d) Nondeductible because no interest deductions are allowed on loans between "related" individuals.

    (e) Deductible as "regular" interest.

8 Please assume **for this question only** that instead of borrowing the $15,000 from his grandmother Glenda, Larry borrowed the money from his aunt, Ann. **Pursuant to the promissory note, Larry paid $1,100 in interest to Ann. Most likely, the interest that he paid is:**

    (a) Nondeductible personal interest.

    (b) Deductible as investment interest.

    (c) Deductible pursuant to IRC § 221 assuming that the level of Larry's income is not sufficient to reduce or eliminate the deduction.

    (d) Nondeductible because no interest deductions are allowed on loans between "related" individuals.

    (e) Deductible as "regular" interest.

9. **Back to our original facts (Larry borrowed money from Glenda), as to Glenda, which of the following statements most accurately describes the income tax consequences with respect to the interest received from her grandson Larry?**

    (a) It is excludable from gross income as a gift between family members.

    (b) Its inclusion or exclusion from gross income depends on the deductibility or non-deductibility of the interest, respectively, as to Larry.

    (c) It is included in gross income.

    (d) It is included in gross income unless Glenda's other income is not sufficient to generate an income tax liability.

10. In August of last year, shortly after Larry began working, he realized that he was not in adequate financial shape to repay the $15,000 loan to Glenda as promised. Reluctantly, he told his grandmother that he could not pay her the principal at that time, but would continue to pay her interest and hoped to be in the position to pay her the principal within a few months. Without hesitation, Glenda told Larry, her favorite grandchild, not only to take as long as he needed to pay her back, but that she was forgiving $5,000 of the loan principal because she was so proud of him. **As a result of this compromise of debt principal, is it likely that Larry has taxable income?**

    (a) No, the $5,000 debt discharged would be excluded from income.

    (b) Yes, the $5,000 debt discharged represents income.

    (c) No, but only if Larry, immediately before the $5,000 forgiveness, was insolvent by at least that amount. Otherwise, some or all of the $5,000 is taxable to Larry.

    (d) Yes, the $5,000 debt discharged is income assuming Larry considered the loan a bona fide debt.

11. In October of last year, Larry's mom found out about Glenda's loan to Larry. Larry's mom felt somewhat embarrassed that her son borrowed the money from Glenda, and a bit hurt that Larry did not ask her for the money. Also proud of her son, Larry's mom paid the remaining $10,000 Larry owed to Glenda, renouncing any claim to repayment by Larry. **Which of the following statements is most accurate with respect to the income tax ramifications to Larry as result of the foregoing?**

    (a) Larry has $10,000 of income from discharge of indebtedness.

    (b) Larry has $10,000 of income in the form of compensation (albeit indirectly) because his employer (his mother) paid this obligation.

    (c) Larry can exclude some or all of the $10,000 from income if, immediately before his mom paid off the loan, he was insolvent.

    (d) Larry can exclude the $10,000 from income if he can show that his mother was acting out of "detached and disinterested generosity" in paying off the debt of her son.

Questions 12 through 14 are based on the following facts:

Harold and Wanda were divorced on May 1, 2019 and have not lived together at any time subsequent to the divorce. They have one child, Charles, who is in Wanda's custody. Neither Harold nor Wanda has remarried. If necessary, you are to assume that applicable state law has no provision regarding cessation of support obligations upon the death of a spouse receiving support payments.

12. For this question only, assume that the divorce decree requires that Harold pay Wanda $20,000 "alimony" per year for life or until she remarries. While Harold and Wanda are no longer that fond of each other, they are both less fond of the I.R.S. Also assume for this question that in a plot to "cheat the tax man," their divorce decree provides that the yearly payments are not income to Wanda (and not deductible by Harold), this despite the fact that the payments are labeled as "alimony." **Assuming that all such "alimony" will be paid for the current year:**

    (a) Wanda does not have to recognize any of the $20,000 as income, and Harold is not entitled to a deduction.

    (b) Wanda has to recognize $20,000 as income, and Harold is entitled to a corresponding $20,000 "above the line" deduction – they can affirmatively decide what **is** alimony, but they cannot treat the payments as not being alimony if they otherwise qualify.

    (c) Wanda has to recognize $20,000 as income, but Harold is not entitled to a deduction – Wanda has a net accession to wealth and the agreement that the payments "are not alimony" is effective only as to Harold.

    (d) Wanda has to recognize $20,000 as income, and Harold is entitled to a corresponding $20,000 "below the line" deduction – they can affirmatively decide what **is** alimony, but they cannot treat the payments as not being alimony if they otherwise qualify.

13. For this question only, assume the same facts as in question 12 with the exception that the couple's divorce decree did not contain any provision regarding the tax treatment of alimony payments. **Assuming that all such "alimony" will be paid for the current year:**

   (a) Wanda has to recognize $20,000 as income, and Harold is entitled to a corresponding $20,000 "above the line" deduction.

   (b) Wanda does not have to recognize any of the $20,000 as income, and Harold is not entitled to a deduction.

   (c) Wanda has to recognize $20,000 as income, but Harold is not entitled to a corresponding deduction.

   (d) While the couple was officially divorced on May 1 2019 (i.e., their divorce was final on that date) Wanda's recognition of income and Harold's availability of a deduction will depend on whether the couple filed for their divorce prior to 2019, or on/after January 1, 2019.

14. The couple's May 1, 2019 divorce decree awarded certain shares of XYZ Co. stock to Harold (the couple had purchased the stock many years ago for $5,000). In March of 2020, Wanda heard a tip that XYZ Co. was going to be acquired by another company, and that the price of the stock was going to skyrocket as a result. Harold was unaware of this rumor but, coincidentally, was desperately in need of cash at about the same time. Wanda offered to buy the stock from Harold for $50,000 (its then current fair market value), and he accepted, selling the stock to her in March of 2020. Harold's sale to Wanda was not related to anything in their divorce decree. Shortly thereafter, the news about the acquisition came out and the stock price of XYZ increased dramatically. Wanda sold these same XYZ shares for $150,000 in April of 2020 to an unrelated individual. **As a result of selling these shares, Wanda should have to:**

   (a) Recognize a $100,000 short-term capital gain because Wanda's purchase of the shares from Harold did not relate to the cessation of their marriage.

   (b) Recognize a $145,000 short-term capital gain; Wanda's purchase of the shares from Harold was incident to their divorce.

   (c) Recognize a $145,000 long-term capital gain; Wanda's purchase of the shares from Harold was incident to their divorce.

   (d) Recognize no gain or loss; Wanda's purchase, and sale, of the shares were incident to their divorce.

   (e) None of the above responses is correct.

15. Marisol operates her dental practice as an unincorporated sole proprietorship. This year, her business had a net profit (i.e., business income exceeded business expenses). For computing an individual's taxable income, the *Tax Cuts and Jobs Act* (TCJA) added a new, special statutory business-related deduction by enacting IRC § 199A. **Assuming "this year" is 2018 or later, is Marisol entitled to any deduction pursuant to IRC § 199A?**

    (a) Yes. This special deduction was created for business owners (as well as those in a partnership, LLC, and others) and she will be entitled to an extra deduction of at least 20% of her business's net profit (before this special deduction).

    (b) Possibly. Depending on the amount of her business's net profit (before this special deduction), she may be entitled to an IRC § 199A deduction of up to 20% of such net profit (before this special deduction).

    (c) No. As a dentist, her business consists, primarily, of her performing services. As such, she is not entitled to this special deduction.

    (d) Possibly. Depending on the amount of her overall taxable income (before this special deduction), she may be entitled to an IRC § 199A deduction of up to 20% of her business's net profit (before this special deduction).

<u>Questions 16 through 19 are based on the following facts:</u>

Alex is a general contractor in the business of building and remodeling single-family homes. His business is very successful, and he has a strong conviction that philanthropy is an obligatory moral companion of success. To this end, he actively contributes his time and wealth to eleemosynary causes. For purposes of this series of questions, please treat each as a separate and independent question, and any reference to the "current year" is 2018 or later.

16. Alex made a substantial cash gift to the American Red Cross in the current year. Also, almost every day he gave various amounts of cash to homeless individuals that he encountered. **Assuming that the foregoing represents all gifts made by Alex in the current year, he:**

   (a) Will be entitled to a charitable contribution deduction pursuant to IRC § 170 for all of the above cash gifts. However, such deduction cannot exceed, in the current year, 60% of his "contribution base" as defined in IRC § 170(b)(1).

   (b) Will be entitled to a charitable contribution deduction pursuant to IRC § 170 for all of the above cash gifts. However, the deductions for the gifts to the American Red Cross and his cash gifts to the homeless individuals cannot exceed 60% and 30%, respectively, of his "contribution base" as defined in IRC § 170(b)(1).

   (c) Will be entitled to a charitable contribution deduction pursuant to IRC § 170 only for his cash gift to the American Red Cross. However, such deduction cannot exceed, in the current year, 60% of his "contribution base" as defined in IRC § 170(b)(1).

   (d) Will be entitled to a charitable contribution deduction pursuant to IRC § 170 only for his cash gift to the American Red Cross. However, such deduction cannot exceed, in the current year, 30% of his "contribution base" as defined in IRC § 170(b)(1).

17. Alex is very active in the Habitat for Humanity organization (a qualified public charity) helping to construct homes for qualifying individuals. During the year, he spent most of his weekends working on building projects for this organization. His contributed labor, had he charged for it in the context of his normal business operations, would have been worth $20,000. For the year, in the aggregate, he drove thousands of miles from his home to (and back from) the various Habitat for Humanity building projects. **Which of the following statements is most accurate in describing the extent of Alex's charitable deduction with respect to the foregoing?**

   (a) While he cannot deduct the value of his services, he can deduct his transportation costs from his home to (and back from) the building projects. The amount of the charitable deduction for these transportation costs is the greater of his actual costs of driving or the statutory per-mile rate specified in IRC § 170.

   (b) He can deduct $20,000 for his services because this amount, as in a barter transaction, represents the fair value of his services. He is also entitled to deduct his transportation costs from his home to (and back from) the building projects using the greater of his actual costs of driving or the statutory per-mile rate specified in IRC § 170.

   (c) He cannot deduct the value of his services or his transportation costs from his home to (and back from) the building projects. Both of these do not represent qualified charitable contributions as defined in IRC § 170.

   (d) He can deduct $20,000 for his services because he is in the construction business. However, he cannot deduct his transportation costs unless his "home" is considered his "office" for his normal business operations.

   (e) He cannot deduct the $20,000 value of his services. In addition, he cannot deduct his transportation costs unless his "home" is considered his "office" for his normal business operations.

18. In the current year, Alex gave to the American Red Cross (a qualified public charity), his car that he used solely for personal purposes, totally unrelated to his business. He originally paid $30,000 for the car a few years ago, but it was worth only $10,000 when he gave it to the American Red Cross (the American Red Cross facilitated the donation but immediately sold it to a used car broker for $8,000). In addition, he gave shares of General Motors Corporation common stock worth $20,000 to the American Red Cross (he originally purchased these shares two years earlier for $12,000). Lastly, Alex attended a special American Red Cross "Cirque du Soleil" gala event, a special fund-raising performance benefiting the American Red Cross. The ticket for this event cost $500 with all of the proceeds going to the American Red Cross. Tickets for regular performances of Cirque du Soleil cost $100. **Assuming that all required documentation was obtained, which statement best describes the extent of Alex's charitable deduction with respect to the foregoing?**

    (a) Subject to certain "percent of contribution base" limits, Alex can deduct the $10,000 value of the car, the $12,000 cost of the General Motors stock, and the $500 paid for the fundraising tickets.

    (b) Subject to certain "percent of contribution base" limits, Alex can deduct the $10,000 value of the car, the $12,000 cost of the General Motors stock, but only $400 for the fundraising event (the difference between the $500 paid and the $100 representing the value of the benefit received as evidenced by the regular ticket price).

    (c) Subject to certain "percent of contribution base" limits, Alex can deduct the $10,000 value of the car, the $20,000 value of the General Motors stock, but only $400 for the fundraising event (the difference between the $500 paid and the $100 representing the value of the benefit received as evidenced by the regular ticket price).

    (d) Subject to certain "percent of contribution base" limits, Alex can deduct $8,000 with respect to his car donation, the $20,000, the value of the General Motors stock, but only $400 for the fundraising event (the difference between the $500 paid and the $100 representing the value of the benefit received as evidenced by the regular ticket price).

    (e) None of the above responses is correct.

19. Rose, Alex's niece, was recently accepted as a new undergraduate student at a private university. The university's tuition is substantial, but Alex has "taken care" of it. Alex recently made a cash contribution to this university (a qualified public charity) equal to the amount of a student's tuition with explicit instructions that it be used as a "scholarship" awarded to Rose covering the full amount of her tuition. The university accepted the money under these terms, awarding a "full scholarship" to Rose. **Which of the following answers is most accurate?**

   (a) Alex will be entitled to a charitable deduction for the amount contributed. Rose will be able to exclude the scholarship from income under IRC § 117.

   (b) Alex will not be entitled to a charitable deduction for the amount contributed. Rose will have to include the "scholarship" in her gross income.

   (c) Alex will be entitled to a charitable deduction for the amount contributed. Rose will have to include the "scholarship" in her gross income unless it can be determined that this was a "gift" excludable from gross income under IRC § 102.

   (d) Alex will not be entitled to a charitable deduction for the amount contributed. Rose, most likely, will not have to include the "scholarship" in her gross income.

Questions 20 through 22 are based on the following facts:

Amy is an officer of XYZ Industries ("XYZ"), a conglomerate with operations in various businesses including passenger airline, hotel, consumer electronics, and life insurance. She has worked for XYZ for more than 25 years and is very well liked by all of the other officers (she is not related to anyone at XYZ). Amy performs a substantial amount of work in all areas of company operations and she is considered a "highly compensated employee" for purposes of IRC § 132.

20. Amy was involved in an automobile accident while on vacation. While she was not hurt in the accident, her child suffered some injuries and her car was "totaled." In a gesture of kindness and compassion, XYZ made a gift to Amy of $5,000 in cash and a new automobile worth $30,000. **As a result of the foregoing, Amy will most likely:**

    (a) Not be required to recognize any amount as income if she can show that XYZ was acting with "detached and disinterested generosity."

    (b) Be required to recognize $5,000 (cash received) as income, but not be required to recognize any income with respect to the automobile assuming that she can show that XYZ was acting with "detached and disinterested generosity."

    (c) Be required to recognize as income both $5,000 (cash received) and $30,000 (the value of the automobile) regardless of XYZ's motive for making the gift.

    (d) Be required to recognize as income $5,000 (cash received) plus 80% of the $30,000 value of the automobile regardless of XYZ's motive in making the gift.

21. Amy, as well as all full-time employees of XYZ, is entitled to obtain a personal life insurance policy at a substantial discount when compared to the cost at which XYZ offers such policies to the general public. The available discount is 40%, which equals XYZ's "gross profit percentage" in the life insurance portion of its business. Assume that in the current year, only Amy and one other officer took advantage of this insurance deal. Amy obtained a life insurance policy at a cost of $6,000 (a 40% savings off the regular $10,000 cost to the public). **With respect to the foregoing, Amy must include in gross income:**

    (a) None of the discount.

    (b) $2,000.

    (c) $4,000.

    (d) $6,000.

22. As a matter of company policy, XYZ pays professional association dues and subscription fees to professional periodicals (print and online) for all "highly compensated employees" of XYZ. XYZ does not pay for these items for other XYZ employees. During the year, XYZ paid Amy's $700 annual dues to the American Society of Corporate Officers and $400 in annual subscription fees to various professional periodicals that directly related to her job function at XYZ. **How much income must Amy recognize with respect to XYZ's payment of these items?**

    (a) No income need be recognized.

    (b) $1,100, because the benefit is discriminatory.

    (c) $880 (80% of $1,100), because even though it doesn't qualify as a "no additional cost fringe," at least 20% will be excluded as a "qualified employee discount."

    (d) $400, representing the cost of the periodical subscriptions.

Questions 23 through 25 are based on the following facts:

For years, Martha has owned an apartment building as an investment. A tenant in the building was the on-site manager, taking care of all maintenance and collection of rents. At the end of each month, the manager would remit to Martha, all of the money representing rents for the month then ended. On April 16th of this year (assume this is 2018 or later), Martha made a gift of the apartment building to Steve, her son (legally transferred ownership). On April 30th, the apartment manager remitted the rent money to Steve, the then legal owner. On May 1st of this year, the apartment building was sold to Paulo, an unrelated purchaser, resulting in a substantial gain.

23. **With respect to the April rent and the gain from the sale of the property, which of the following statements is most accurate?**

    (a) Steve will recognize the rental income as legal owner, but Martha will have to recognize the gain assuming the sale deal was in the works at the time the property was given to Steve.

    (b) Martha and Steve will each recognize one-half of the rental income, but Steve will recognize the gain from the sale assuming the sale was Steve's idea and he made the deal after receiving the property.

    (c) Martha and Steve will each recognize one-half of the rental income, but Martha will have to recognize the gain from the sale since she cannot effectively assign the gain to anyone other than herself.

    (d) Martha will recognize the rental income (she cannot assign this to Steve), but Steve will recognize the gain from the sale assuming that the sale was his idea and he made the deal after receiving the property.

24. For this question, assume that Paulo, the purchaser of the apartment building, is an attorney who also plans to hold the apartment building as investment property for many years to come. County real property taxes are assessed on a calendar year basis and are payable in advance, on January 1st, for each year. On January 1st of this year, Martha paid $12,000 in property taxes for the apartment building. **How much of this property tax, if any, will Paulo most likely be entitled to deduct this year?**

    (a) No deduction will be allowed because Paulo was not the legal owner on January 1st.

    (b) Approximately $8,000, but only if Steve and Paulo actually apportioned the tax, and Paulo reimbursed Steve (or Martha) for this amount.

    (c) Approximately $8,000 regardless of whether Steve and Paulo actually apportioned the tax or whether Paulo reimbursed any of it to Steve (or Martha).

    (d) It is possible that Paulo may be entitled to deduct an apportioned amount of the property taxes, but his actual deduction may be limited by the $10,000 cap for deduction of state and local taxes.

    (e) The lesser of: 1) an apportioned amount of the $12,000 tax for the total based upon the date that Paulo purchased the property, or 2) the actual amount of the tax that Paulo reimbursed to Steve (or Martha).

25. Assume on January 1st of next year, that Paulo pays the real property tax for the full year on the apartment building. Also assume that he continues to hold the property as an investment. **Which of the following statements best describes the income tax consequences to Paulo with respect to the payment of these property taxes?**

    (a) He will be entitled to a deduction for the amount of tax paid, and it will be allowed as an "above the line" deduction in computing his adjusted gross income (AGI).

    (b) He will be entitled to a deduction for the amount of tax paid, and it will be allowed as a "below the line" deduction (part of the *itemized deductions* group to which the $10,000 cap for deduction of state and local taxes will apply) in computing his taxable income.

    (c) The payment of property taxes will generate no income tax deduction but, rather, will be added to Paulo's basis in the property.

    (d) He will be entitled to an exclusion, against his rental income from the property, for the amount of tax paid.

END OF EXAMINATION QUESTIONS

EXAM IV

FEDERAL INCOME TAX
MULTIPLE-CHOICE OBJECTIVE QUESTIONS
EXAM IV

Questions 1 and 2 are based on the following facts:

Roger is a self-employed computer consultant and operates his very profitable consulting business as an "unincorporated sole proprietorship." This year, Cassandra (a CPA) rendered tax advice to Roger. This tax advice related solely to Roger's consulting business and Roger was billed $4,000. Both Roger and Cassandra collect baseball cards for a hobby and just as Roger was about to pay Cassandra's bill, Cassandra inquired about a particular rare baseball card in Roger's collection. The card had a value of $4,000 and Cassandra asked whether Roger would consider making an even trade (the card in exchange for discharging the bill). Roger agreed to the exchange, which then took place. Roger was happy with the deal because he had purchased the card some three months earlier for only $2,500. Both Roger and Cassandra operate their respective businesses on a "cash basis."

1. **Which answer best describes the income tax ramifications to Cassandra as a result of the facts presented?**

    (a) There are no income tax ramifications to her because this was a barter transaction in which no cash changed hands.

    (b) She has $4,000 of gross income from services rendered, but has an offsetting $4,000 business deduction.

    (c) She has no immediate income tax consequences because, in effect, she merely purchased the baseball card. She may have a gain or loss if she subsequently sells the card.

    (d) She has $4,000 of gross income from services rendered. In addition, her adjusted basis in the card, for purposes of determining gain or loss on any subsequent sale, is zero.

    (e) None of the above responses is correct.

2. **Which answer best describes the income tax ramifications to <u>Roger</u> as a result of the facts presented?**

   (a) He has gross income of $4,000 because this is a taxable barter type transaction.

   (b) He has no gross income because he was not the party providing services, but he is entitled to a $2,500 deduction.

   (c) He has a realized gain of $1,500 and a $2,500 deduction pursuant to IRC § 162.

   (d) He has a realized gain of $1,500 and a $4,000 deduction pursuant to IRC § 212.

   (e) He has a realized gain of $1,500 and a $4,000 deduction pursuant to IRC § 162.

<u>Questions 3 through 5 are based on the following facts:</u>

In March of this year, Tom's grandmother, Gloria, died and Tom received shares of XYZ Co. stock from her as a devise (bequest). Gloria had purchased these shares for $50,000 just one month prior to her death. While the value of these shares had declined to $35,000 at the time of her death, their price rebounded some, and Tom sold them for $40,000 in May of this year.

3. **When Tom received the XYZ Co. shares from Gloria, he:**

   (a) Realizes a net accession to wealth of $35,000, but can exclude it from his gross income pursuant to IRC § 102.

   (b) Realizes a net accession to wealth of $35,000, and, because this was not an inter vivos gift, he must recognize this amount in his gross income.

   (c) Has no gain or loss realized or recognized because transfers between family members are "tax free."

   (d) Has no gain or loss realized or recognized because of the value of the shares at the time of the devise, and the price for which Tom subsequently sold them.

4. **When Tom subsequently sells the XYZ Co. shares, he:**

    (a) Realizes a gain of $5,000.

    (b) Realizes a loss of $10,000.

    (c) Realizes neither a gain nor a loss because the fair market value of the shares at the time of the transfer to Tom was less than Gloria's basis, and Tom subsequently sold them for a price in between these two values.

    (d) Realizes neither a gain nor a loss because the value of these shares is excluded from his gross income pursuant to IRC § 102.

5. **What is the extent and character of gain or loss recognized by Tom when he sells the XYZ Co. shares?**

    (a) There is no recognition of gain or loss because Tom realizes no gain or loss when he sells the shares. Characterization of a recognized gain or loss, therefore, is moot.

    (b) Tom has $5,000 of recognized gain. This gain is a short-term capital gain because although, pursuant to IRC § 1223(2) he can tack onto his holding period that of Gloria, the combined holding period is less than one year.

    (c) Tom has ($10,000) of recognized loss. This loss is a long-term capital loss because, pursuant to IRC § 1223(2) he can tack onto his holding period that of Gloria.

    (d) Tom has ($10,000) of recognized loss. This loss is a short-term capital loss because although, pursuant to IRC § 1223(2) he can tack onto his holding period that of Gloria, the combined holding period is less than one year.

    (e) None of the above responses is correct.

6. Brad purchased his house four years ago for $200,000. On the same day Brad bought the house, Gail, his girlfriend, moved in with him. The two have been living there ever since. Brad and Gail, still unmarried, will be moving overseas together and Brad is now selling his house (Gail has no ownership interest in this or any other house). **Assuming Brad sells his house to an unrelated individual at a gain, he:**

    (a) Will be able to exclude up to $250,000 of such gain pursuant to IRC § 121 because he meets both the "use" and "ownership" requirements contained therein.

    (b) Will not have to recognize any such gain because he has used the house as his principal residence. Had he been renting out the house, instead of living in it, then some or all of the gain would have been recognized.

    (c) Will be able to exclude up to $500,000 of such gain pursuant to IRC § 121 because he meets the "ownership" requirement, and both he and Gail meet the "use" requirement contained therein.

    (d) Will not have to recognize any such gain, regardless of the amount, assuming that within a two-year period, he buys (and occupies) a new house.

    (e) Will not have to recognize any such gain, regardless of the amount, assuming that his overseas move is work related.

7. **Would your answer to question 6, above, be different if, at the time of the sale, Brad and Gail had been married for six months?**

    (a) Yes. The maximum excludable gain would be $500,000, assuming that Gail had some ownership interest in the house at the time of the sale.

    (b) No, because they had not been married for a long enough period at the time of the house sale.

    (c) No, because the maximum amount of gain excludable pursuant to IRC § 121 would be the same in this scenario.

    (d) Yes. The maximum excludable gain would be $500,000 assuming that they file a joint return for the year in which the sale occurred.

Questions 8 through 12 are based on the following facts:

Sonia was both the original owner and the insured of a $100,000 life insurance policy. Willa, her wife, was the named beneficiary of the policy. Sonia died in December 2018. The total of all premiums paid on the policy up to the time of Sonia's death was $15,000.

8. In January 2019, Willa, as policy beneficiary, received a check for $100,000 from the insurance company. **With respect to this insurance benefit, Willa must recognize:**

    (a) $85,000 of income pursuant to § 1001 – the difference between the "amount realized" and the "adjusted basis" in the policy.

    (b) No income pursuant to § 101(a).

    (c) $100,000 of income as an "accession to wealth."

    (d) $15,000 of income because this amount represents Willa's "tax cost" of the policy.

9. Same as Question 8, above, except that instead of receiving a lump sum, Willa selected a payout option in which the insurance company promises to pay her $10,000 a year for the rest of her life. The insurance company estimated that Willa had a 40-year life expectancy. During 2019, Willa received her first $10,000 payment. **As a result, the amount of income Willa can exclude from this is:**

    (a) $10,000.

    (b) $7,500.

    (c) $2,500.

    (d) Zero.

10. Same as Question 9, above, except that we have traveled to the future and it is now forty-one years later (and, unrealistically, tax laws have remained unchanged) and Willa is still alive, and she receives her forty-first annual $10,000 payment from the insurance company. **As a result, the amount of income Willa must recognize is:**

    (a) $10,000 because Willa has fully recovered the otherwise tax-free amount of life insurance benefits.

    (b) Zero because Willa has outlived her life expectancy.

    (c) $7,500.

    (d) $2,500.

11. Same facts as in Question 8, above, except that in January 2017, Sonia and Willa divorced. In May 2018, Sonia transferred the policy to Willa in exchange for $30,000 worth of her property. This transfer was not pursuant to any written or oral agreement relating to their divorce. Subsequent to this exchange, but prior to Sonia's death, Willa paid $3,000 in insurance premiums on the policy. The aggregate sum of all premium payments made by Willa and Sonia (by either or both of them) remained the same at $15,000. Willa remained as policy beneficiary. **With respect to the $100,000 insurance benefit received by Willa in January 2019, Willa will most likely be able to exclude:**

   (a) $30,000, representing the consideration paid, because the transfer to Willa was not incident to the divorce.

   (b) $33,000, representing the sum of the consideration paid plus premiums paid subsequent to the transfer. This is because the transfer to Willa was not related to the cessation of the marriage.

   (c) Nothing, because the amounts received by Sonia in 2018 were not by reason of the death of the insured.

   (d) $100,000, representing the entire insurance proceeds. This is because transfers within six years of divorce are considered related to the cessation of the marriage.

   (e) Nothing, because life insurance proceeds received by reason of the death of the insured are fully excluded from income pursuant to IRC § 101(a).

12. Assume the same facts as in question 11, above, except that Willa and Sonia divorced in January of 2018. **Which of the following answers is most accurate with respect to the $100,000 insurance benefit received by Willa in January 2019?**

(a) Willa can exclude, from gross income, $30,000 representing the consideration that she paid to Sonia. The $70,000 balance is included in her gross income. This is because the transfer of the policy to Willa was <u>not</u> pursuant to their divorce decree and, therefore, not incident to the divorce.

(b) Willa can exclude, from gross income, $33,000 representing the sum of the consideration paid plus premiums paid subsequent to the transfer. The $67,000 balance is included in Willa's gross income. This is because the transfer of the policy to Willa was <u>not</u> pursuant to their divorce decree and, therefore, not incident to divorce.

(c) Willa can exclude, from gross income, the entire $100,000 received because life insurance proceeds received by the death of the insured are always excludable pursuant to IRC § 101.

(d) Willa can exclude, from gross income, the entire $100,000 received. This is because transfers within six years of divorce are considered related to the cessation of the marriage.

(e) Willa can exclude, from gross income, the entire $100,000 received. This is because the transfer of the policy to Willa was incident to divorce.

Questions 13 through 15 are based on the following facts:

Earlier this year, Roxanne received a gift of jewelry from Martha, her aunt (no gift tax resulted from this transfer). Martha had originally purchased the jewelry years ago for $20,000. It was worth $60,000 at the time of the gift. Later in the year, Roxanne became desperate for cash and sold the jewelry for $42,000, its then current fair market value.

13. **How much gain or loss did Roxanne realize from the sale of the jewelry?**

    (a) Neither a gain nor a loss because Roxanne sold it for a price that was between Martha's basis and the fair market value at the time of the gift.

    (b) A <u>loss</u> of $18,000.

    (c) A <u>gain</u> of $22,000.

    (d) A <u>gain</u> of $42,000 because Roxanne paid nothing for the jewelry (and, therefore had a basis of $0).

14. For this question only, assume that Roxanne did not receive cash in exchange for her "sale" of the jewelry. Rather, she gave the jewelry to Carl, an individual to whom she owed $40,000. Upon receipt of the jewelry, Carl discharged this debt. However, since the jewelry was worth $42,000, Carl, a dentist, also agreed to render $2,000 worth of dental services to Roxanne (which he did). **Does Roxanne realize any income as a result of the foregoing?**

    (a) Yes, she realized $42,000 in income: $40,000 of which was income from discharge of indebtedness.

    (b) Yes, she realized $40,000 income from discharge of indebtedness. The $2,000 value of services received is not income because this was not part of the debt discharged.

    (c) Yes, she realized no income from discharge of indebtedness, but did realize a gain of $22,000 from the disposition of the jewelry.

    (d) She realized no income from discharge of indebtedness, but did realize a gain of $20,000 from the disposition of the jewelry. The $2,000 services received is not part of the gain calculation but, rather, is income to her under the concept of a "net accession to wealth."

15. Assume that the $40,000 Roxanne originally owed Carl in question 14, above, was not related to Carl's dental practice (i.e., it was a personal loan to Roxanne outside of the context of Carl's business). **Referring to question 14, above, what are the income tax consequences to Carl?**

    (a) Carl has $2,000 of gross income from the performance of services.

    (b) Carl has gross income in the amount of $42,000: $2,000 from the performance of services and $40,000 because of the discharge of the debt.

    (c) Carl has no income from the transaction, as he was simply being repaid amounts owed to him.

    (d) Carl has no income but, rather, was merely "purchasing" the jewelry for $42,000.

    (e) Carl has $2,000 of gross income from the performance of services and a "bad debt" deduction of the $40,000 debt discharged.

16. This past year (assume this to be 2018 or later) was a particularly bad year for Dirk, a single individual. His bad year started in January, when he was fired from his engineering job of five years. During the two months following his termination, he received a total of $3,000 in regular "unemployment" benefits from his state's governmental unemployment compensation insurance program. **For income tax purposes the $3,000 in unemployment benefits:**

    (a) Are excludable from Dirk's gross income because they represent government affiliated welfare benefits.

    (b) Are excludable from Dirk's gross income pursuant to IRC § 104.

    (c) Are fully included in Dirk's gross income because they represent taxable unemployment compensation.

    (d) Are fully included in Dirk's gross income because they represent taxable employer fringe benefits.

17. Dirk, in question 16 above, had more financial woes last year (again, assume this to be 2018 or later). Frustrated, out of work, and low on funds, he sold his personal residence. His timing, however, could not have been worse. He had purchased the house five years ago at the peak of a real estate boom for $400,000, hoping that it would be a good investment. His instincts and timing, however, proved to be poor as he sold the house in March of last year just after the real estate bubble in his area had burst. Receiving only $360,000 from the sale, he was disappointed that the house did not prove to be a better investment. He lived in the house at all times during his ownership thereof. This house was the first, and only, house he has owned and, while he is currently employed, he is undecided as to whether he will buy another home in the near future. **With respect to the sale of the house in March of last year, Dirk:**

    (a) Realized a loss of $40,000. Because the house is a capital asset, this loss is a recognized long-term capital loss.

    (b) Realized a loss of $40,000. While the house is a capital asset, the loss is not recognized for income tax purposes.

    (c) Realized a loss of $40,000. Because the house is not a capital asset, this loss is recognized as an "ordinary" loss for income tax purposes.

    (d) Realized a loss of $40,000. While this loss is not recognized, the cost basis of any principal residence that is purchased (and occupied) within two years will be increased by $40,000.

    (e) None of the above responses is correct.

18. The bad year for Dirk, in questions 16 and 17 above, continued to worsen. To add insult to injury, in July of last year, his prior years' Federal and State income tax returns were audited (by the I.R.S. and applicable State authorities, respectively). He paid a CPA $1,000 to handle the audits. Even this did not turn out well, because as a result of the audits, he had to pay additional Federal and State income taxes of $2,000 and $750, respectively (no penalties or interest were assessed). **With respect to the foregoing, which of the following statements is most accurate?**

   (a) None of these items give rise to possible deductions for income tax purposes.

   (b) He may be entitled to some deduction, as part of his "itemized deductions," the $750 in State income taxes. None of the other items give rise to possible deductions for income tax purposes.

   (c) He is entitled to deduct, as part of his "itemized deductions," the $1,000 paid to his CPA and the $750 in State income taxes. The $2,000 in Federal taxes does not give rise to a deduction for income tax purposes.

   (d) He may be entitled to some deduction, as part of his "itemized deductions," the $1,000 paid to his CPA as a "miscellaneous" itemized deductions." Also, he may be entitled to some deduction, as part of his itemized deductions, the $750 in State income taxes. The $2,000 in Federal taxes does not give rise to a deduction for income tax purposes.

   (e) All of the above items give rise to possible deductions for income tax purposes.

19. Mark is an officer in Little Cub, Inc., the offices of which are located in a high-rise building in downtown Los Angeles. He is considered a "highly compensated employee" for purposes of IRC § 132. Little Cub pays for Mark's parking in the building. **With respect to this parking for 2019, Mark must include in income:**

    (a) Nothing for 2019, even if parking was not furnished to other employees of Little Cub.

    (b) Nothing for the value of parking up to $265 per month for 2019. This is true even if parking was not furnished to other employees of Little Cub.

    (c) Nothing for the value of parking up to $175 per month for 2019 unless this benefit was discriminatory in favor of a "highly compensated class of employees" in which case the entire value of the parking would be included.

    (d) Nothing for the value of parking up to $265 per month for 2019 unless this benefit was discriminatory in favor of a "highly compensated class of employees" in which case the value of the parking received in excess of that received by all employees would be included.

    (e) None of the above responses is correct.

20. In April of this year, Tiffany sold a diamond Rolex watch for $23,000. She received it as a gift from her aunt in 1975 upon graduating college. Tiffany's aunt originally paid $18,000 for the watch in 1973, and it had appreciated in value to $21,000 at the time of her gift to Tiffany. Tiffany's aunt incurred, and paid, gift taxes of $7,000 with respect to this gift. Tiffany wore the watch daily (i.e. it was not an investment). **As a result of selling the watch, Tiffany realized:**

    (a) A loss of $2,000.

    (b) A gain of $4,000.

    (c) A gain of $2,000.

    (d) A gain of $5,000.

    (e) None of the above responses is correct.

Questions 21 and 22 are based on the following facts:

Grant, Tia's grandfather, had been quite ill for some time and, unfortunately, not in the best financial health either. In March of last year, Tia made a gift to Grant of shares of stock in XYZ Co. with the hope that he would sell the stock and use the proceeds for his medical/living needs. These shares were worth $40,000 at the time of the gift (Tia originally paid $15,000 for them two years ago) and no gift tax resulted from this gift. Unfortunately, Grant died in November of last year. In addition to the sadness Tia experienced from the loss of her grandfather, she was also quite sad to learn that he never did sell or use the stock that she had given him to help ease his situation. These shares were worth $50,000 at the time of Grant's death. Grant's estate was not of sufficient size to incur any estate tax liability.

21. For this question, assume that Grant died with a will containing the following language: "In recognition of my beloved granddaughter Tia's selfless caring for me and the profound help that she has given me, I hereby give to her the shares of XYZ Co. stock." These shares of XYZ Co. stock were the same shares that she had given to him in March of last year. **What is the most likely income tax consequence to Tia as a result of receiving these shares?**

   (a) She will not have to recognize any income.

   (b) She will have $50,000 of gross income.

   (c) She will have $10,000 of gross income.

   (d) She will have gross income equal to the lesser of: $50,000, or the value of the services that she rendered to Grant in caring for him.

22. For this question, assume that Grant died intestate (without a will) and, pursuant to the applicable state intestate succession statute, Tia was the sole beneficiary of Grant's estate. **Tia's basis in the XYZ Co. shares that she receives as intestate beneficiary of Grant's estate is:**

   (a) $50,000.

   (b) $40,000.

   (c) $15,000.

   (d) None of the above responses is correct.

23. Jackie, a California domiciliary, recently incorporated her plumbing business in another state (one that does not have any state corporate income taxes) after hearing advertisements extolling numerous benefits by doing so. The benefits that she believes she heard advertised include: no state corporate income taxes, the ability to establish large amounts of corporate credit, the ability to have the corporation buy, for her personal-use, items such as houses, cars, furniture, sporting equipment, etc. In addition, she believes that she heard that he can use the corporation to pay, and deduct, all or most of her purely personal expenses such as her home mortgage, property taxes on her house and personal automobile (state registration fees), vacations, and the like. Jackie is the sole shareholder and employee of her new out-of-state corporation. **If Jackie's corporation does buy, on her behalf, personal-use assets and pays for her personal expenses, Jackie, the individual:**

    (a) Will have income equal to the amount of her personal expenses paid by the corporation, but not for the personal-use assets bought by the corporation on her behalf.

    (b) Will have no income because these items are not in relation to the corporation's business and Jackie is the sole owner of the corporation.

    (c) Will have income equal to the value of the personal-use assets purchased on her behalf and the amount of her personal expenses paid by the corporation.

    (d) Will have income only because she is domiciled in a state other than the state in which his business is incorporated.

24. Marshall is an engineer and is employed by a large computer chip manu-facturing company. All full-time employees qualify to participate in the company's "401(k)" plan (a qualified retirement/pension plan). The company, concerned about the financial well-being of its employees, recently introduced a new service to all of its employees participating in the company's 401(k) plan. Each such employee is entitled to receive, free of charge, professional financial consulting services covering information about the company's 401(k) plan as well as advice and information on retirement income planning and how the company's 401(k) plan fits into the employee's retirement income plan. Company employees, expert in financial planning matters, will provide these services. Marshall took advantage of this new service and received valuable retirement planning advice. The ser-vices Marshall received were worth in excess of $800. **Is Marshall required to include in gross income the value of the services received?**

    (a) No, because most likely this would be considered a tax-free "de minimis" fringe benefit.

    (b) No, but only if this service qualifies as an educational assistance program pursuant to IRC § 127.

    (c) No, because most likely this would qualify as a tax-free "working condition" fringe benefit.

    (d) Yes, because most likely this would be considered additional compensation not qualifying for exclusion.

    (e) None of the above responses is correct.

25. A few years ago, when Abe was 26 years old, he purchased some United States Series EE Savings Bonds. While he originally planned on holding them until they matured, he recently cashed them in (redeemed them). Abe is going to attend a state funded vocational school to become a certified air conditioning repairman. **The interest earned from the U.S. Savings Bonds that he recently cashed-in is fully:**

   (a) Includible in his gross income because he cashed in the bonds prior to their maturity,

   (b) Excludable from gross income because the interest is from an obligation of the United States.

   (c) Excludable from gross income if, 1) he uses, for his tuition, the entire amount of the bond proceeds constituting interest, and 2) his adjusted gross income, as modified, is below certain statutory thresholds.

   (d) Excludable from gross income if, 1) he uses, for his tuition, the entire amount of the bond proceeds, and 2) his adjusted gross income, as modified, is below certain statutory thresholds.

   (e) Includible in his gross income in this case because he is not attending an undergraduate or graduate college or university.

END OF EXAMINATION QUESTIONS

EXAM V

FEDERAL INCOME TAX
MULTIPLE-CHOICE OBJECTIVE QUESTIONS
EXAM V

Questions 1 through 3 are based on the following facts:

Exactly four years ago, Tom and his wife Edna purchased a house for $400,000 (paying all cash), taking title as joint tenants. Shortly after buying it, they spent $110,000 on major additions/improvements to the house. They bought the house strictly for investment purposes but decided to use it as their residence while the additions/improvements were being made (fully intending to move out and either sell it or rent it thereafter). Unfortunately, the cost of these additions/improvements was much more than the value that they added to the house (it was worth only $450,000 after the work was completed). It was after this work was completed that their marriage began to falter and they continued living together, albeit unhappily, in the house. Tom and Edna's marriage ended in divorce exactly two years ago and, pursuant to their divorce decree, Tom received 100% of the house.

1. **Immediately after the improvement/addition work had been completed, the couple's "adjusted basis" in the house was:**

   (a) $400,000.

   (b) $450,000.

   (c) $510,000.

   (d) None of the above responses is correct.

2. For this question only, assume that the $110,000 used for improve-ments/additions came from a second mortgage loan secured by the house (and this 2nd mortgage loan was obtained in 2018 or later). **The income tax ramifications of this loan are:**

   (a) The $110,000 represents income. The interest that they pay on this loan will not qualify as deductible interest because the loan exceeds the $100,000 limit for qualified home equity indebtedness.

   (b) The $110,000 is not income. Assuming that they have no other loans outstanding, the interest that they pay on only $100,000 of the loan, the limit for home equity indebtedness, will qualify as deductible interest.

   (c) The $110,000 is not income. Assuming that they have no other loans outstanding, the interest that they pay on the entire loan will qualify as deductible interest.

   (d) The $110,000 represents income. Assuming that they have no other loans outstanding, the interest that they pay on the entire loan will qualify as deductible interest.

   (e) The $110,000 is not income. The amount of any outstanding loans is irrelevant because interest on home equity loans is no longer deductible after 2017.

3. Assume for this question only, that the value of the house had declined to $350,000 when it was transferred to Tom two years ago pursuant to their divorce decree. After the divorce, Tom, still hoping that the house would prove to be a good investment, continued living there until he sold it today for $380,000. **Which answer best describes the income tax consequences to Tom resulting from the house sale?**

   (a) Tom has a realized and recognized loss of $130,000. This loss qualifies as a long-term capital loss.

   (b) Tom has a realized and recognized gain of $30,000. This gain qualifies as a long-term capital gain.

   (c) Tom realizes neither a gain nor a loss from the sale of the house.

   (d) Tom has a realized and recognized loss of $70,000. This loss does not qualify as a capital loss.

   (e) None of the above responses is correct.

Questions 4 through 8 are based on the following facts:

Todd is an employee in his mother's music company. In January of this year, following a financially great year, Todd's mother gave each of her thirty employees, including her son Todd, a "mint condition" commemorative plate that had been made for the company many years earlier to celebrate their then twentieth year in business. The company had commissioned the then unknown artist Andy Warhol to design the plates which, including the design fee, cost the company $50 each. These plates, of course, became rare collector's items and were worth $20,000 each when given to the employees in January and were in addition to their regular salaries.

4. **Not considering Todd for this question, will the receipt of the commemorative plate by company employees result in the recognition of gross income?**

   (a) No, because transfers of property to employees must be in the form of cash to be considered compensation/income when received. The employee's receipt of the plate results in the realization of income, but no income is recognized until the employee sells the plate.

   (b) No, assuming that this was a "gift" made by the company acting with "detached and disinterested generosity." Gifts are specifically excluded from gross income.

   (c) No, because this represents an excludable "de minimis" fringe benefit. This is because the cost of the plate to the employer is so small and this was a one-time transfer to employees.

   (d) Yes, regardless of the company's motive for giving the plates to their employees. The $20,000 value of the plate is considered compensation to the employee.

   (e) Yes, regardless of the company's motive for giving the plate to their employees. The employee has compensation of $50, representing the employer's cost of the plate.

5. **Specifically, with respect to Todd, which statement most likely describes the income tax consequences of his receipt of the commemorative plate?**

    (a) Todd has $20,000 of gross income in the form of compensation.

    (b) Todd has $50 of gross income in the form of compensation

    (c) Todd has no gross income because for him, as opposed to the other employees, this will be considered a gift.

    (d) Todd has no gross income because for tax purposes here, he is treated like the other employees.

6. Notwithstanding Todd, all of the company employees took great care of the commemorative plates received and held onto them as an investment. In March of this year, however, one of the company's employees, Marcia, sold her commemorative plate to an art dealer for $23,000. **To what extent does Marcia have a realized gain as a result of this sale?**

    (a) She has a realized gain of $22,950, the difference between the $23,000 selling price and her basis in the plate of $50.

    (b) She has a realized gain of $3,000, the difference between the $23,000 selling price and her basis in the plate of $20,000.

    (c) She has a realized gain of $23,000, the difference between the $23,000 selling price and her basis in the plate of zero.

    (d) She has no realized gain because the receipt of the plate was properly classified as either a gift or de minimis fringe benefit.

7. **As to Marcia's sale of the commemorative plate in question 6, above, which answer best describes the recognition and character of such gain?**

    (a) Because there was no realized gain, there is no recognition of gain. The "character" of such gain, therefore, is moot.

    (b) The realized gain is recognized and will be a long-term capital gain.

    (c) The realized gain is recognized and will be a short-term capital gain.

    (d) The realized gain is not recognized and, therefore, its character is irrelevant.

8. Todd, unlike other employees, did not take good care of his commemorative plate nor treat it as an investment. Rather, Todd used his plate as everyday dinnerware and it soon became scratched and nicked from daily use. In November of this year, Todd sold his "used" plate on an Internet auction site, receiving $14,000 for it. **Most likely Todd:**

 (a) Will have a recognized gain.

 (b) Will have a recognized loss.

 (c) Will have a realized gain which, however, will not be recognized.

 (d) Will have a realized loss which, however, will not be recognized.

 (e) Will have neither a realized nor recognized gain or loss.

9. Recently, Mark made a "gift" of a parcel of real property to his brother Brian. There was a loan secured by the property, but Brian did not assume it. Rather, Brian took the property "subject to" the loan. At the time of the gift to Brian, the amount of the loan was less than the fair market value of the property. There was no gift tax on the transfer. **In order to determine whether Mark realized any gross income from this transfer, which of the following variables must we know?**

   I. Mark's adjusted basis in the property.
   II. The fair market value of the property at the time of the gift.
   III. The amount of the loan on the property.
   IV. Whether Mark was personally liable on the loan.

 (a) I, II, III and IV.

 (b) I, II, III but not IV.

 (c) I and II only.

 (d) I and III only.

 (e) None of the above responses is correct.

10. **With respect to Brian in question 9, above, which of the following statements is most accurate?**

  (a) Because of the broad definition given to gross income, Brian has gross income equal to the value of the real property at the time of the gift. Brian's basis in the real property is equal to the amount of gross income realized as a result of the gift.

  (b) Gross income is broadly defined, and Brian must include, in gross income, an amount equal to the value of the real property at the time of the gift less the amount of the loan to which he took the property "subject to." This amount of gross income also represents Brian's resulting basis in the real property.

  (c) While gross income is broadly defined, Brian has no gross income as a result of his receipt of the real property. Brian's basis in the real property is equal to his brother Mark's basis (or adjusted basis) in the property at the time of the gift.

  (d) While gross income is broadly defined, Brian has no gross income as a result of his receipt of the real property. Brian's basis in the real property is equal to the amount of the loan to which he took the property "subject to."

  (e) While gross income broadly defined, Brian has no gross income as a result of his receipt of the real property. Brian's basis in the real property is equal to the greater of his brother Mark's basis (or adjusted basis) in the property at the time of the gift, or the amount of the loan to which he took the property "subject to."

Questions 11 and 12 are based on the following facts:

Last year (assume that "last year" was 2018 or later) was rather unsettling for Dan. In January of last year, he purchased a diamond engagement ring intending to propose marriage to Carol later in the year. A few months later, on the day before proposing to Carol, Dan's apartment was burglarized and the ring was stolen. The ring was worth $30,000 at the time of the burglary (which is what he had paid for it in January). Unfortunately, there is no chance of its recovery and he was not insured against its loss. Undeterred by the theft he proposed, as planned, to Carol. Not only did she say "no," when he returned, dejected, to where his car had been parked, it was not there. An errant, uninsured motorist had plowed into his car pushing it over a railing and into the river below. To make matters worse, Dan's auto insurance had lapsed and he recovered nothing from its loss (there was no salvage value either). Dan had purchased the car, which he used for non-business purposes only, less than six months ago for $40,000 and its value at the time of the accident was $35,000.

11. **As a result of the foregoing, which of the following statements is most accurate?**

    (a) Both the theft of the ring and the loss of the car are considered "casualty losses." Unfortunately, neither loss will give rise to a recognized/deductible loss for Dan.

    (b) Both the theft of the ring and the loss of the car are considered "casualty losses." Dan will be entitled to a deduction equal to the aggregate amount of losses ($70,000) less $100.

    (c) Both the theft of the ring and the loss of the car are considered "casualty losses." Dan will be entitled to a deduction equal to the aggregate amount of losses ($65,000) less $200 ($100 per casualty event).

    (d) Both the theft of the ring and the loss of the car are considered "casualty losses." Dan will be entitled to a deduction to the extent that his aggregate casualty losses of $65,000 less $200 ($100 per casualty event), exceeds 10% of his adjusted gross income (AGI) for the year.

    (e) Neither the theft of the ring nor the loss of the car constitutes a "casualty loss."

12. For this question only, assume that Dan used the car exclusively for business purposes (in his unincorporated sole proprietorship), and that the uninsured loss arising from its plunge into the river occurred when parked while he was attending a business meeting. **Which of the following answers is most accurate in stating the change in income tax consequences, if any, resulting from these changed facts?**

    (a) The loss would now qualify as a casualty loss.

    (b) Although already qualified as a casualty loss, the amount of loss would equal the adjusted basis (AB) of the car at the time of the loss and Dan would be entitled to a deduction for this amount.

    (c) Although already qualified as a casualty loss, the amount of loss would equal the greater of the car's fair market value or its adjusted basis (AB) of the car, both measured at the time of the loss. Dan would be entitled to a deduction for this amount.

    (d) Although already qualified as a casualty loss, the determination of the deduction would not require that it exceed any percentage of Dan's adjusted gross income (AGI). However, the first $100 of this loss would still not be deductible.

    (e) There would be no change in income tax consequences to Dan as a result of these changed facts.

13. While Dan, in questions 11 and 12, above, was having his bad year, Talia's year was as bad as Dan's, if not worse. Talia's home, and all its contents, were destroyed by a flood. Sadly, she had no insurance coverage for this loss and nothing was left when the flood waters receded. **Is Talia at least eligible for a tax deduction from this loss?**

    (a) Yes. She suffered a "casualty loss" and she is entitled to deduct the correctly determined aggregate amount of the loss in full.

    (b) No. While her loss is a "casualty loss," the law no longer allows a deduction when such losses are of a "personal" nature such as hers.

    (c) Maybe. She suffered a "casualty loss" but will not be entitled to any deduction unless the flood is a "federally declared disaster." If so, then she will be entitled to a "casualty loss" deduction of an amount calculated pursuant to the statutory allowance for personal casualty losses.

    (d) Yes. This is a "casualty loss" and the correctly determined aggregate amount of the loss, less $100, will be deductible to the extent that it exceeds 10% of the her adjusted gross income (AGI) for the year.

14. In March of last year, Thelma received a "gift" of some shares of XYZ Co. stock from her father, Frank. At the time of the gift, the stock was worth $4,000. This was less than the $5,000 Frank paid for the stock some two years earlier. Frank incurred, and paid, $2,000 in gift taxes on this transfer. By November of last year, these shares had increased in value and Thelma sold them for $6,000. **As a result of Thelma's sale, she realized:**

    (a) A gain of $2,000.

    (b) A gain of $1,000.

    (c) A loss of ($1,000).

    (d) Neither a gain nor loss.

    (e) None of the above responses is correct.

15. A California domiciled husband and wife purchased a vacant parcel of California real estate (i.e., raw land) many years ago hoping that it would appreciate in value. Fortunately, the parcel has steadily increased in value over the years, and it is anticipated that it will continue to appreciate in the future. When the first spouse dies, they want the surviving spouse to own 100% of the land. **For income tax purposes, is it better for them to own the property as *community property* (with the first spouse to die devising his/her one-half share to the surviving spouse) or as *joint tenancy* (with right of survivorship)?**

    (a) *Community property* is better because of the "double step-up" in basis pursuant to IRC §§ 1014(b)(6) and 1014(a).

    (b) *Joint tenancy* is better because there will be a gain with respect to the property and the non-recognition of gain/loss rule of IRC § 1041(a) does not apply to joint tenancy.

    (c) *Joint tenancy* is better because the special rule of IRC § 1014(b)(6) does not apply.

    (d) Neither is better; *joint tenancy* and *community property* will produce the same income tax consequences in their situation.

16. The exact same facts as question 15, above, except instead of spouses, the two individuals are California registered domestic partners (by law, a CA domestic partner is the equivalent to a spouse for property rights, including the availability of community property, inheritance, etc.). Similar to question 15, above, when the first partner dies, they want the surviving partner to own 100% of the land. **For income tax purposes, is it better for them to own the property as *community property* (with the first partner to die devising his/her one-half share to the surviving partner) or as *joint tenancy* (with right of survivorship)?**

    (a) *Community property* is better because of the "double step-up" in basis pursuant to IRC §§ 1014(b)(6) and 1014(a).

    (b) *Joint tenancy* is better because there will be a gain with respect to the property and the non-recognition of gain/loss rule of IRC § 1041(a) does not apply to joint tenancy.

    (c) *Joint tenancy* is better because the special rule of IRC § 1014(b)(6) does not apply.

    (d) Neither is better; *joint tenancy* and *community property* will produce the same income tax consequences in their situation

17. A California domiciled husband and wife purchased a vacant parcel of California real estate (i.e., raw land) many years ago hoping that it would appreciate in value. Unfortunately, its value has steadily declined over the years and it is not expected to regain its original value. When the first spouse dies, they want the surviving spouse to own 100% of the land. **For income tax purposes, is it better for them to own the property as *community property* (with the first spouse to die devising his/her one-half share to the surviving spouse) or as *joint tenancy* (with right of survivorship)?**

    (a) *Community property* is better because of the "double step-up" in basis pursuant to IRC §§ 1014(b)(6) and 1014(a).

    (b) *Joint tenancy* is better because there will be a loss with respect to the property and the non-recognition of gain/loss rule of IRC § 1041(a) does not apply to joint tenancy.

    (c) *Joint tenancy* is better because the special rule of IRC § 1014(b)(6) does not apply.

    (d) Neither is better – *joint tenancy* and *community property* will produce the same income tax consequences in their situation.

18. A few years ago, Sean purchased a parcel of raw land for investment purposes. Unfortunately, it did not prove to be a good investment as it declined substantially in value. Sean's mother, Marta, felt sorry for her son and offered to buy the property. While somewhat reluctant, Sean, financially strapped, sold the land to his mother Marta at its then current fair market value (which was substantially less than he originally paid for it). **Which of the following statements best describes the income tax consequences to Sean as a result of this sale to Marta?**

   (a) Sean's loss will not be recognized because the transaction is automatically considered to be a gift.

   (b) Sean's loss will not be recognized because the sale was to his mother.

   (c) Sean's loss will be recognized because it was the sale of investment property.

   (d) Sean's loss will be recognized assuming that Marta did not purchase the property out of a sense of "detached and disinterested generosity."

19. Sean, in question 18, above, owned another undeveloped parcel of raw land that he purchased a few years ago (This was also purchased and held for investment purposes). This property also suffered a substantial decline in value since he purchased it. Sean's brother-in-law Bob (his wife's brother), an individual for whom Sean holds little respect, inquired about the property. While not making false or fraudulent statements about the future prospects for the property, Sean "enhanced" its attributes just a bit. Bob bought the property for its then current fair market value (which was substantially less than Sean originally paid for it). **Which of the following statements best describes the income tax consequences to Sean as a result of this sale to Bob.**

   (a) Sean's loss is a recognized capital loss because the property was held for investment purposes.

   (b) Sean's loss is not recognized because he sold the property to his brother-in-law.

   (c) Sean's loss is recognized, and is an ordinary loss because the property was held for investment purposes.

   (d) Sean's loss is not recognized because the property was held for investment purposes and was not the result of a "casualty."

20. In April of this year, Tom sold a diamond Rolex watch for $23,000. He received it as a gift from his aunt in 1990 upon graduating college. Tom's aunt originally paid $18,000 for the watch in 1985, and it had appreciated in value to $21,000 at the time of her gift to Tom. She incurred, and paid, gift taxes of $7,000 with respect to this gift. Tom wore the watch daily (i.e. it was not an investment). **Upon selling the watch, Tom realized:**

    (a) A loss of $2,000.

    (b) A gain of $4,000.

    (c) A gain of $2,000.

    (d) A gain of $5,000.

    (e) None of the above responses is correct.

Questions 21 and 22 are based on the following facts:

Alicia, a lawyer, makes occasional investments in stocks. In March of last year, she bought 500 shares of XYZ Co. for $10,000. Shortly after buying the stock, it started to decline in value. Thinking that her hopes of rebound would never materialize, she gave up and sold the shares on December 27th of last year for $4,000. Casually discussing XYZ Co. with an investment professional at a party on January 1 of this year, she learned that the company was introducing a new line of products that would turn the company around. While reluctant to get involved with the stock again (it had continued to decline in price since her December sale), on January 5 of this year, she purchased 500 shares of XYZ Co for $3,500. The company experienced a dramatic turnaround and now that her 500 shares are worth $15,000, she is contemplating selling them.

21. **The loss Alicia realized as a result of her December sale of the XYZ Co. shares will:**

   (a) Not be recognized in December when sold but, rather, when, and if, she sells the shares purchased in January of this year.

   (b) Be recognized and because it was a sale of a capital asset, it was a capital loss. However, this capital loss (and any other capital losses recognized) can only be used to offset capital gains for that year, with any excess loss deductible up to $3,000.

   (c) Be recognized because these shares were sold in a year (last year) different from that in which she again purchased the XYZ Co. shares (this year).

   (d) Be recognized because even though she repurchased XYZ Co. shares, she did not have the requisite intent for this to be considered a "wash sale."

   (e) Not be recognized because of her purchase of XYZ Co. stock in January of this year.

22. Assume that Alicia decides to sell her 500 shares of XYZ Co. stock for their current fair market value of $15,000. **For purposes of computing her gain or loss realized from this sale, her adjusted basis (AB) in the stock is:**

   (a) $3,500.

   (b) $4,000.

   (c) $9,500.

   (d) $10,000.

   (e) None of the above answers is correct.

23. Derrick made a gift of highly appreciated shares of stock to his favorite granddaughter Gail, on the condition that she pay the gift tax resulting from the transfer. Gail gladly did so, as the tax was much less than the value of the shares. **Which of the following statements is most accurate?**

(a) Derrick's gift to Gail may result in the realization, and recognition, of a gain because he received consideration from Gail.

(b) Derrick has gross income equal to the amount of the gift tax Gail paid because the gift tax was Derrick's obligation.

(c) Gail will not be entitled to a deduction for the tax paid because she was not the obligor. Most likely, however, Derrick will be entitled to the deduction.

(d) Gail is not entitled to exclude any portion of the gift pursuant to IRC § 102 because she is deemed to have paid consideration.

24. Two years ago, Brenda invested a substantial amount of money in the stock market purchasing shares in a large, publicly-traded biopharmaceutical company, paying well over $100 per share for the company's common stock. Recently, the company has been rocked by two major scandals: accounting improprieties that substantially misrepresented the company's financial situations, and the falsification of research and patient data in applications made to the FDA as part of the approval process for major new medications. As a result, the company is in shambles and its common stock is currently trading at around 7¢ per share. Financial pundits hold out little hope for the company's long-term viability, and are predicting that sometime next year, the company is likely to file for bankruptcy and will dissolve without paying creditors and leaving nothing for shareholders. **Which of the following statements is most accurate?**

(a) Brenda's shares in the company are considered "worthless securities" and this entitles her to an "ordinary" loss deduction.

(b) Brenda's shares in the company are considered "worthless securities" and this results in her recognition of a long-term capital loss.

(c) Losing money is a risk of investing and assuming that the financial pundits are correct in their predictions about the company, Brenda is not likely to ever be entitled to any tax benefit if she continues holding onto her shares.

(d) Losing money is a risk of investing and assuming that the financial pundits are correct in their predictions about the company, Brenda is likely to recognize a long-term capital loss if she continues holding onto her shares.

25. A couple of years ago, Michael, a dentist, purchased a parcel of raw (vacant) land to hold for investment purposes. He paid $50,000 in cash for it and he has made no improvements to it (and it has remained vacant). Michael's investment strategy proved fruitful, as earlier this year, he sold the land to an unrelated individual for an agreed sales price of $200,000. They agreed that the buyer would pay Michael 10% of the sales price ($20,000) at the time of the sale (which was done), and 10% (or one-tenth) of the sales price each year for the next nine years. The buyer agreed to pay Michael interest, at a fair current market rate, each year on the then unpaid balance. This land was the only investment real estate that Michael owned. **Which of the following statements best describes Michael's recognition of gain resulting from the sale of the land?**

    (a) $20,000 of gain will be recognized in the current year, and $20,000 of gain will be recognized in each of the next nine years.

    (b) No gain will be recognized in the current year. Michael will start to recognize gain only after he has received payments (exclusive of interest) totaling his $50,000 cost.

    (c) $15,000 of gain will be recognized in the current year, and $15,000 of gain will be recognized in each of the next nine years.

    (d) Michael will recognize all of the gain in the current year, unless he elects to recognize the gain on the installment method over the years in which he receives payments of the sales price.

END OF EXAMINATION QUESTIONS

EXAM VI

FEDERAL INCOME TAX
MULTIPLE-CHOICE OBJECTIVE QUESTIONS
EXAM VI

Questions 1 through 3 are based on the following facts:

In July, Skip, who owns an auto body shop (operating as an unincorporated sole proprietorship), sold shares of XYZ Co. stock for $5,000. He says that he did not pay anything for them but, rather, received them as part of a deal for repairing/repainting a door for his friend, Paula's, personal use car earlier in the year. Skip provided $4,000 worth of repairs and in exchange, Paula, a professional photographer, gave him 1) these shares of XYZ Co. stock worth $2,700 at the time (Paula originally paid $500 for them a few months earlier) and, 2) her expert photography assistance, worth $1,300, regarding Skip's website photos.

1. **Once the "deal" between Skip and Paula was complete, which answer best describes the income tax ramifications, vis-à-vis recognition of income, to both parties as a result of this deal?**

    (a) Neither Skip nor Paula has income from the deal, as it represents a tax-free barter transaction.

    (b) Skip and Paula each has $4,000 of gross income because this is a barter type transaction and both parties have derived $4,000 of financial benefit.

    (c) Skip and Paula each has $1,300 of gross income representing the value of "services" exchanged in this barter transaction.

    (d) Skip and Paula have $4,000 and $1,300 of income, respectively, as compensation from their services. In addition, Paula has a realized gain of $2,200 from the disposition of the stock.

    (e) Skip and Paula have $4,000 and $1,300 of income, respectively, as compensation from their services. Paula has no realized gain from the disposition of the stock because she is merely paying for the extra services.

2. **When Skip sold the shares XYZ Co. stock in July, his realized gain was:**

    (a) $5,000.

    (b) $4,500.

    (c) $2,300.

    (d) $1,000.

    (e) None of the above responses is correct.

3. **Does the "deal" between Skip and Paula give rise to any possible deductions for purposes of computing taxable income?**

  (a) No.

  (b) Yes. Skip has $1,300 of qualifying IRC § 162 business expenses.

  (c) Yes. Paula has $4,000 of qualifying IRC § 162 business expenses.

  (d) Yes. Both parties have some deduction for IRC § 162 business expenses.

  (e) Yes. Both parties have some deduction: Skip for IRC § 162 business expenses and Paula for qualifying IRC § 212 expenses for the production of income.

4. Paula, from questions 1 through 3, above, leases a small office for he photography business (she too is an unincorporated sole proprietorship) and her lessor, Larry, needed a photographer for a huge holiday party. Larry agreed to forgive two month's rent in exchange for her handling all of the photo work for his party (which she did). **Does Paula have to recognize any income from the foregoing?**

  (a) Yes. She has "income from discharge of indebtedness" equal to the amount of the two month's rent forgiven. The value of the forgiven rent would not be considered an excluded gift because it is clear that Larry was not acting out of "detached and disinterested generosity."

  (b) No. Assuming that this is an equal exchange, Paula, in effect, supplied consideration and, therefore, she has no income for the rent forgiven.

  (c) No. This represents a classic barter transaction and does not result in the generation of income to Paula. The cornerstone gross income requirement of a "net accession to wealth" is not present in this situation.

  (d) Yes. While Paula has no "income from discharge of indebtedness," she did, effectively, receive payment for her services. Assuming the services she performed were equal to the two month's rent, she has income in that amount as payment for her services.

Questions 5 & 6 are based on the following facts:

Beatrice was the owner/insured of a $100,000 life insurance policy that named her son, Sam, as beneficiary. Sometime before Beatrice's death this year, Sam performed $4,000 worth of legal services for Beatrice for which she agreed to pay him. Instead of paying him in cash, she transferred this life insurance policy (i.e., ownership of the policy) to him which, at the time, was worth $10,000 (her basis in the policy was $5,000). In response to Sam's protests that she gave him too much ($6,000 too much), she told him to consider the extra amount a gift. Subsequent to the transfer of the policy to Sam, he paid one premium payment of $1,000 and shortly thereafter, Beatrice died. Sam recently collected the $100,000 benefit from the insurance company.

5. **Which of the following statements best describes the income tax consequences to Sam when Beatrice transferred the life insurance policy (ownership of the policy) to him?**

    (a) Sam had gross income of $10,000, the value of the life insurance policy at the time of the transfer. This was not a tax-free gift because Sam furnished consideration in the form of his services.

    (b) Sam had no recognition of gross income. The transfer of the policy culminated a transaction that was, in part, a sale and, in part, a gift. Because the consideration Sam was deemed to have paid was less than Beatrice's basis in the policy, the entire value of the policy Sam received constituted a tax-free gift pursuant to IRC § 102.

    (c) Sam had gross income of $4,000, the value of the services that he rendered to Beatrice. The additional value of the policy Sam received was a tax-free gift pursuant to IRC § 102.

    (d) Sam had no recognition of gross income because the value of the services Sam rendered was equal to the amount of consideration that he was deemed to have paid for the policy. The additional value of the policy he received was a tax-free gift pursuant to IRC § 102.

    (e) Sam had gross income of $6,000 representing the difference between the value of the policy and the consideration Sam was deemed to have paid for it.

6. **Must Sam recognize any income with respect to the $100,000 that he received from the insurance company as the policy beneficiary?**

   (a) Yes, he must recognize $4,000 of income; the value of the services performed for Beatrice.

   (b) No, the entire $100,000 is properly excluded from income.

   (c) Yes, he must recognize $96,000 of income.

   (d) Yes, he must recognize $95,000 of income.

   (e) None of the above responses is correct.

Questions 7 through 10 are based on the following facts:

Maureen, a single parent, purchased a house in Atlanta ten years ago for $125,000 (paying all cash). Five years ago, when the house's value had increased to $300,000, Maureen took out a $150,000 recourse mortgage loan that was secured by the house. She used this money to purchase a new car and pay off debts unrelated to the house. Shortly thereafter, Maureen was transferred to her employer's Chicago office and moved there, allowing her single adult daughter, Denise, to continue living in the Atlanta home (Denise had been living with her mother since birth). Exactly one year ago, Maureen gave the house to Denise (transferring title to her name by deed). At the time, the house was worth $400,000 and the mortgage, to which Denise took the house subject to, was undiminished at $150,000.

7. **Which of the following statements best describes the income tax consequences to Maureen as a result of her gift to Denise?**

   (a) She is entitled to a deduction for the gift up to the amount indicated in IRC § 2503(b); $10,000 as indexed for inflation.

   (b) Has gross income of $150,000 representing the mortgage taken "subject to" by Denise.

   (c) Has a realized loss of $350,000 representing the difference between the house's fair market value of $400,000 and the $150,000 "consideration" received.

   (d) Has a realized gain of $25,000 representing the difference between the $150,000 "consideration" received and Maureen's $125,000 basis in the house.

   (e) She has no gain or loss realized from the transfer because it represents a tax-free gift to Denise.

8. Assume for this question only, that today (exactly one year after receiving the house from her mother) Denise sold the house to an unrelated buyer for $450,000 (paying Denise $300,000 in cash and taking it subject to the still undiminished mortgage of $150,000). Also assume, for this question only, that Denise sold the house because she wants to buy a new house located closer to her job (of many years) in downtown Atlanta. **Does Denise have any recognized gain from the sale of this house?**

   (a) Yes. The full amount of her realized gain will be recognized in this situation.

   (b) Yes. She will have to recognize a gain only if, and to the extent, that her realized gain exceeds $250,000.

   (c) Yes. She will have to recognize a gain only if, and to the extent, that her realized gain exceeds $125,000.

   (d) No. Any realized gain is not recognized in this situation.

   (e) No, assuming that her new house cost at least $450,000 and that she purchases (and occupies) it within two years from the sale of her old home.

9. **Would your answer to question 8, above, be different if Denise sold her house and moved to Phoenix because her doctor told her that to control her increasingly serious bouts with asthma, she had to move to a drier climate?**

   (a) Yes. In this revised scenario she would be entitled to exclude a greater amount of her realized gain.

   (b) Yes. In this revised scenario she would be entitled to exclude a smaller amount of her realized gain.

   (c) No. There would be no difference with respect to gain recognition in this revised scenario.

   (d) Possibly. There may be a difference with respect to gain recognition in this revised scenario depending, in the previous question, on the distances between her old/new homes and her job in Atlanta.

10. For this question only, assume that Maureen never mortgaged the Atlanta house (i.e., there were no loans on the property when she gave it to Denise). Also assume for this question only, that today (exactly one year after receiving the house from her mother) Denise sold the house to an unrelated buyer for $450,000 (paying Denise $450,000 in cash). Finally, for this question only, assume that she sold the house because she is moving to an apartment closer to her job in Atlanta. **Which of the following statements is correct?**

   (a) Denise's basis, for purposes of determining gain or loss, is a carryover from that of her mothers. As a result of this, Denise can "tack" (add) on her mother's period of ownership, thereby qualifying for the $250,000 exclusion of gain provided in IRC § 121.

   (b) Denise will have to recognize the full amount of her realized gain from the sale. She is not entitled to exclude any portion of the gain because she does not meet the ownership requirement of IRC § 121.

   (c) Denise will be entitled to exclude up to $125,000 of any realized gain, but only if, within two years, she purchases (and occupies) a new home costing at least $450,000.

   (d) Denise will be entitled to exclude up to $250,000 of any realized gain, but only if, within two years, she reinvests the profit from the sale of her old home in the purchase of a new home.

   (e) None of the above statements is correct.

Questions 11 and 12 are based on the following facts:

In July of last year, Tina purchased a piece of fine crystal from her Uncle Jim for $5,000. At the time, this crystal had a true fair market value of $30,000. Jim, who purchased the crystal four years ago for only $4,000 (its fair market value at the time), was originally just going to give it to her, his favorite niece, for nothing. Tina, however, insisted on paying him and he reluctantly agreed. No gift tax resulted from this transfer from Jim to Tina. Jim became furious with her, however, when he found out that to get her hands on some quick cash, she sold the crystal less than a month later and received $28,000 for it.

11. **As to the transfer of the crystal from Jim to Tina in July of last year, which answer best describes the most likely income tax consequences to Tina and Jim?**

    (a) Jim has a recognized loss of $25,000 because he is deemed to have sold the crystal to Tina. Because Tina cannot consider any portion of this transaction to be a gift, she has income of $25,000 (the difference between the value of the property and the amount that she paid for it).

    (b) Jim has a realized loss of $25,000, but because this sale was to a related party, it is not recognized. Although Tina furnished consideration, the $25,000 gift element of this transaction is excluded from her gross income.

    (c) Jim has no recognized gain or loss as a result of this transaction because the substance of the transfer was a gift to Tina. Similarly, Tina can exclude from her gross income the net benefit that she received.

    (d) Jim has a recognized gain of $1,000 because he is deemed to have sold the crystal to Tina. Although Tina furnished consideration, the $25,000 gift element of this transaction is excluded from her gross income.

    (e) Jim has a recognized gain of $1,000 because he is deemed to have sold the crystal to Tina. Because Tina cannot consider any portion of this transaction to be a gift, she has income of $25,000 (the difference between the value of the property and the amount that she paid for it).

12. **As a result of Tina's sale of the crystal, she:**

   (a) Has a realized gain of $23,000. This gain is recognized and qualifies as a long-term capital gain.

   (b) Has a realized gain of $24,000. This gain is recognized and qualifies as a long-term capital gain.

   (c) Has a realized gain of $23,000. This gain is recognized and qualifies as a short-term capital gain.

   (d) Has a realized gain of $24,000. This gain is recognized and qualifies as a short-term capital gain.

   (e) Has no realized nor recognized gain because the crystal was a gift from Jim.

Questions 13 and 14 are based on the following facts:

Bill, a single individual, earned **$60,000** in wages last year. Other than the four capital gains and losses indicated below, he realized no additional income, nor incurred any deductions for last year. His capital gains and losses for last year were as follows:

Capital **Gains**	Capital **(Losses)**
Short-Term of $5,000	Short-Term of ($8,000)
Long-Term of $16,000	Long-Term of ($18,000)

13. **With respect to the foregoing, which of the following is the most accurate statement?**

   (a) Bill's adjusted gross income (AGI) for last year was $55,000.

   (b) Bill's adjusted gross income (AGI) for last year was 57,000, and there is a net short-term capital loss carryover to this year of $2,000.

   (c) Bill's adjusted gross income (AGI) for last year was 57,000, and there is a net long-term capital loss carryover to this year of $2,000.

   (d) Bill's adjusted gross income (AGI) for last year was $57,000, and there is a net capital loss carryover to this year of $3,000.

14. Continuing on from question 13, above, this year Bill again expects wages of $60,000. During the current year, he sold two automobiles used exclusively for pleasure. Bill sold automobile number <u>one</u> for $7,500 on April 1st. He received automobile number <u>one</u> as an inheritance from his Uncle Fred on March of this year (the day Fred died). Uncle Fred's adjusted basis in the automobile was $8,000 but it was worth only $4,000 on the date of his death. Automobile number <u>two</u> was sold for $3,000 on April 15th. Bill purchased automobile number <u>two</u> five years ago for $6,000. **Assuming that there are no other tax-related items for the current year, Bill's adjusted gross income for this year should be:**

    (a) $57,000.

    (b) $58,000.

    (c) $60,500.

    (d) $63,500.

    (e) None of the above is correct.

15. Kathleen ("Kath") is an employee of an advertising firm. Her job demands require her to travel extensively, by airplane, and her employer pays for all of her travel costs. Kath is enrolled in a major airline's frequent flyer program, and she has accumulated a huge number of "frequent flyer miles" because of her business trips. Kath's employer claims no rights to these frequent flyer miles, and Kath, and all other employees, are free to use them as they wish (i.e., in whatever manner permitted by the frequent flyer program). **Which of the following statements is most accurate?**

    (a) Kath will have gross income when she redeems the frequent flyer miles for non-business-related trips. The amount of income will equal the value of the ticket(s) received from the redemption(s).

    (b) Kath will have gross income as the frequent flyer miles are earned because her employer imposes no restrictions on their use.

    (c) Kath will have no gross income resulting in the accrual of frequent flyer miles or in their redemption because taxing such benefits would be in violation of the "Commerce Clause" of the Constitution.

    (d) Kath will have no gross income as the miles are earned, or when she redeems her miles for travel, travel-related in-kind benefits, or other non-cash benefits or services available to her under the frequent flyer plan.

16. Roberta, an attorney, purchased a single-family residence about four years ago. She has always held this property as an investment, renting it to individuals unrelated to her. This property has produced a net profit every year even after deducting the allowed amount of depreciation expense. Roberta sold the property this year for a substantial gain. **Which of the following statements is most accurate?**

    (a) Roberta's entire recognized gain from this sale will be considered "ordinary income" because the house was investment residential real estate.

    (b) Roberta's entire recognized gain from this sale will be considered a "long-term capital gain" because this was investment residential real estate.

    (c) Assuming Roberta made no special elections regarding depreciation for this property, it is likely that a portion of her recognized gain will be treated as "ordinary income." The balance of the gain will qualify as a "long-term capital gain."

    (d) Because this property was a single-family residence, Roberta will likely be able to exclude (not recognize) some or all the gain resulting from its sale. Any recognized portion will qualify as a "long-term capital gain."

17. Roberta, in problem 16, above, practices law as an unincorporated sole proprietor (a.k.a., self-employed or an independent contractor). A few years ago, she purchased some office furniture, and has been taking depreciation deductions with respect to such property. Roberta recently sold this furniture and, much to her surprise, she sold it for more than she originally paid for it. **Which of the following statements is most accurate?**

    (a) If she utilized an allowed "accelerated" method of depreciation regarding the property, then a portion of the total amount of depreciation deductions taken will be "recaptured" as "ordinary" income.

    (b) She is not required to recapture any amount of her gain as "ordinary" income because she is operating her business as an unincorporated sole proprietorship.

    (c) Notwithstanding any "deprecation recapture" provisions, all of her gain is ordinary income because the furniture is business property.

    (d) The total amount of her depreciation deductions taken with respect to the furniture will be "recaptured" as "ordinary" income.

18. Earlier this year, Greg, a plumber, loaned $5,000 to his good friend Tony. This was not a gift, but was a true loan evidenced by a promissory note. Tony indicated that he needed the money to pay some medical bills. Unbeknownst to Greg, Tony had a severe substance abuse problem, and the borrowed funds were quickly depleted on things other than medical bills. Tragically, Tony died within weeks of obtaining the loan from Greg. After Tony's death, it became apparent that no funds were available to repay Greg (or any of Tony's many other creditors). **Given that there is no chance of Greg being repaid any portion of the $5,000 he loaned to Tony, which answer best describes the federal income tax consequences to Greg.**

  (a) Greg is entitled to a $5,000 deduction.

  (b) This loss (a bad debt) is characterized by statute as a short-term capital loss to Greg, and the amount of this loss is limited to $3,000.

  (c) Greg is not entitled to any tax benefit (i.e., a deduction) because this is considered a "nonbusiness bad debt."

  (d) The financial loss Greg suffered is treated as a $5,000 short-term capital loss.

  (e) Greg is not entitled to any tax benefit (i.e., a deduction) because Greg had no "basis" in the debt.

19. Adjusted Gross Income (AGI) is significant for many reasons. **For what reasons is AGI important?**

  I.   The determination of the amounts or availability of deductions allowed in computing AGI itself.
  II. The determination of amounts or availability of exclusions from gross income.
  III. The determination of amounts or availability of deductions allowed from AGI to derive taxable income.
  IV. The determination of self-employment taxes for an unincorporated self-employed individual.

  (a) Items I, II, and III only.

  (b) Items II and III only.

  (c) Items I, II, III, and IV.

  (d) Items I and III only.

  (e) None of the above responses is correct.

20. Jim and Kathy, a married couple filing a joint return, have *Adjusted Gross Income* (AGI) of $40,000 in 2019. Jim turned 65 years old in September 2019 (Kathy is 58) and they both have good eyesight. In 2019, they paid real property taxes of $6,000 on their home, $8,000 in State income taxes, and $5,300 in qualifying charitable donations. Also, they paid $13,100 in prescription drugs (there was no reimbursement by insurance or otherwise for the medicine). **Based on the foregoing, should they *itemize* deductions or take the *standard deduction* for 2019?**

    (a) They can do either because the amount of their *itemized deductions* is equal to their *standard deduction*.

    (b) They should take the *standard deduction* because it is greater than their *itemized deductions*.

    (c) They should choose to take their *itemized deductions* because this amount exceeds their *standard deduction*.

    (d) They may consider doing neither because utilizing either deduction would preclude them from taking their *personal exemption deductions*, and the latter may yield a greater benefit to them.

Questions 21 through 23 are based on the following facts:

The year is **2018** and Tammy's only child Chuck, age 12, lives with her (Tammy's husband died almost ten years ago and Tammy has not remarried). Chuck does some acting work in commercials and will earn $5,000 this year. Tammy provides literally all of Chuck's support. Tammy also provides the majority of the support for her unmarried nephew Ned, whose parents (Tammy's brother and sister-in-law) tragically died in an accident a few years ago. Ned turned age 20 this year, and he just completed his second year of college (he lives with Tammy's sister, Susie). Ned will earn $5,000 in the current year from a part-time job. Besides the rigors of full-time school, Ned has had a difficult year dealing with, and recovering from, a serious medical matter. All parties are U.S. citizens.

21. Tammy is trying to determine who she can claim as a dependent for **2018** for purposes of the "child tax credit" and "credit for other dependents" (these are discussed in exam VIII). **Which of the following statements is most accurate?**

   (a) She can claim both Chuck and Ned. Chuck qualifies as Tammy's dependent because Chuck is a *qualifying child* pursuant to IRC § 152. Ned also qualifies as Tammy's dependent even though his gross income is not less than the statutory limit. Ned qualifies because he is a full-time student under the age of 24 at the end of the year, thus coming within the expansive definition of a *qualifying child*.

   (b) She can claim neither of them. While Chuck and Ned qualify as Tammy's dependents for certain income tax purposes, she cannot claim them as dependents for this question's stated purpose (child tax credit and credit for other dependents) because they both earned too much money.

   (c) She can claim Chuck but not Ned. Even though Chuck's gross income is not less than the statutory limit, he is, nonetheless, Tammy's *qualifying child*. While Ned is Tammy's "child" for purposes of a *qualifying child* and is also a "relative" for purposes of a *qualifying relative* under IRC § 152, Tammy is not entitled to claim him as her dependent.

   (d) She can claim Chuck but not Ned. Even though Chuck's gross income is not less than the statutory limit, he is, nonetheless, Tammy's *qualifying child,* because of his age. If Ned was Tammy's child instead of her nephew, she would be entitled to also claim Ned as her dependent even though his gross income is not less than the statutory limit.

   (e) None of the above responses is correct.

22. **Which of the following statements most accurately describes Tammy's probable filing status for 2018?**

    (a) She qualifies as "head of household" because she is unmarried and has a qualifying dependent in either Chuck or Ned.

    (b) She qualifies as "head of household" because Chuck is Tammy's *qualifying child*.

    (c) She qualifies as a "surviving spouse" because she was married, and Chuck qualifies as her dependent.

    (d) She qualifies as an "unmarried individual" (single) because of the answer to question 21, above.

23. During the current year (2018), Tammy paid $2,000 in health insurance premiums ($1,000 each for her and Chuck, respectively). In addition, she paid $7,000 of Ned's doctor and hospital costs resulting from his aforementioned medical matter (he has no insurance and these amounts will not be reimbursed or paid by any other means). **What is the extent of Tammy's qualified medical care expenses for purposes of IRC § 213?**

    (a) $2,000 representing the cost of the health insurance premiums for her and Chuck. The $7,000 that she paid for Ned's medical costs is not a qualifying medical care cost for her because she is not entitled to claim Ned as her dependent.

    (b) $9,000 representing the total cost of the health insurance premiums plus Ned's medical costs. She is entitled to count as qualifying medical care costs the health insurance and medical costs for both Chuck and Ned because both individuals qualify as her dependents for purposes of IRC § 213 medical expense deductions.

    (c) $1,000 representing the health insurance cost for her alone.

    (d) Zero, because the health insurance is not a qualified medical expense and, while Ned's medical costs are qualifying medical care expenses, Tammy is not entitled count them as qualifying medical care costs.

    (e) None of the above responses is correct.

Questions 24 and 25 are based on the following facts:

Robert died in mid-January of last year, and is survived by his spouse, Allison. Prior to Robert's death, the couple had consistently filed "joint returns." They had no children and now, at age 86, Allison lives alone (unmarried). Last year, Allison had substantial taxable income and expects the same for the current year.

24. **Which of the following statements most accurately describes Allison's "filing status" for <u>last year</u> for purposes of determining the rate schedule used in computing her tax liability?**

    (a) She can use the rate schedule in IRC § 1(a) [IRC § 1(j)(2)(A) for years 2018 through 2025] for "Married individuals filing joint returns and surviving spouses" because she qualifies as a "surviving spouse" pursuant to IRC § 2(a).

    (b) She must use the rate schedule in IRC § 1(c) [IRC § 1(j)(2)(C) for years 2018 through 2025] for "Unmarried individuals (other than surviving spouses and heads of households)" because marital status is determined as of the last day of the taxable year and Allison was not married at that time.

    (c) She can use the rate schedule in IRC § 1(a) [IRC § 1(j)(2)(A) for years 2018 through 2025] for "Married individuals filing joint returns and surviving spouses" because her husband died in the then current year and she had not remarried.

    (d) She must use the rate schedule in IRC § 1(d) [IRC § 1(j)(2)(D) for years 2018 through 2025] for "Married individuals filing separate returns" because income in the year of a spouse's death must be reported separately by the respective spouse.

25. Assuming Allison does not remarry, which of the following statements most accurately describes Allison's "filing status" for the <u>current year</u> for purposes of determining the rate schedule used in computing her tax liability?

   (a) She can use the rate schedule in IRC § 1(a) [IRC § 1(j)(2)(A) for years 2018 through 2025] for "Married individuals filing joint returns and surviving spouses" because she qualifies as a "surviving spouse" pursuant to IRC § 2(a).

   (b) She must use the rate schedule in IRC § 1(c) [IRC § 1(j)(2)(C) for years 2018 through 2025] for "Unmarried individuals (other than surviving spouses and heads of households)."

   (c) She can use the rate schedule in IRC § 1(b) [IRC § 1(j)(2)(B) for years 2018 through 2025] for "Heads of households" because although she does not qualify as a "surviving spouse" pursuant to IRC § 2(a), she does meet the requirements of IRC § 2(b).

   (d) She can choose between the respective rate schedules in IRC § 1(a) [IRC § 1(j)(2)(A) for years 2018 through 2025] or 1(b) [IRC § 1(j)(2)(B) for years 2018 through 2025] for "Unmarried individuals (other than surviving spouses and heads of households)" or "Married individuals filing joint returns and surviving spouses," respectfully.

END OF EXAMINATION QUESTIONS

EXAM VII

FEDERAL INCOME TAX
MULTIPLE-CHOICE OBJECTIVE QUESTIONS
EXAM VII

Note: Questions 1 through 7 represent a series of questions, in this Exam VII, that concentrate on the potential nonrecognition of gain from the sale of one's principal residence. The questions in this series are in different blocks with different fact patterns and get progressively more difficult. There will be some redundancy in the answer analysis portion. These questions are, however, "doable" and will emphasize the importance of going through a fairly consistent step-by-step approach. Question 1 through 7 have all been, in some form, questions (multiple choice or essay) in this professor's actual basic income tax class. There are other questions earlier in this book that introduced us to this area of the law and beginning with this question, we begin to add real-life layers to this important area of tax law.

1. Winnie has owned and lived in her house for five years (she purchased it for $300,000). Exactly two years ago, she married Herb and he moved into her house. Unfortunately, the couple divorced exactly one year ago and Herb immediately moved out of the house at that time. Pursuant to their divorce decree, however, Herb was awarded a one-half interest in Winnie's house. Also pursuant to the divorce decree, Winnie continued to live in the house by herself. Today, they each sold their one-half interest in the house to an unrelated buyer for a combined total of $500,000 (Herb and Winnie splitting the proceeds equally). **Which answer best describes the tax consequences to Winnie and Herb?**

    (a) Each will realize a $100,000 gain. Winnie's gain is fully excluded pursuant to IRC § 121. Herb, however, can exclude only a pro-rata one-half amount of the gain ($50,000) assuming a divorce (moving out and then selling his interest) is considered an "unforeseen circumstance."

    (b) Each will realize a $100,000 gain, and both can exclude all of it pursuant to IRC § 121.

    (c) Each will realize a $100,000 gain, and both can exclude all of it pursuant to IRC § 1041 because the sale was within one year of the divorce.

    (d) Winnie will realize a $200,000 gain, all of which will be fully excluded pursuant to IRC § 121. Herb has no gain because the transfer was incident to divorce.

    (e) Each will realize a $100,000 gain. Winnie can fully exclude her gain pursuant to IRC § 121. Herb, however, must recognize all of his gain even if his divorce (moving out and then selling his interest) is considered an "unforeseen circumstance."

Questions 2 through 4 are based on the following facts:

On January 1, 2004, Jon, a single individual, purchased a lakefront cabin for $200,000 (paying all cash). He bought this with the intent of using it as a vacation "getaway." While he did use it for vacations over the years, there were some years that he used it as his principal residence (years when he took a leave of absence from his job in City and others when still working but making a longer commute from the cabin). Jon's primary residence for the years he used the cabin for vacations was a rented apartment in City. Questions 2 through 4, that follow, present alternate fact patterns vis-à-vis Jon's use of the cabin for vacation and principal residence purposes. These were the two exclusive uses of the cabin for his entire period of ownership (i.e., he did not rent it out, use it for business purposes, etc.). On January 1, 2019, exactly 15 years after purchasing the cabin, Jon sold it for $500,000, resulting in a realized gain of $300,000 ($500,000 sales price less his $200,000 basis).

2. For this question only, assume that Jon used the cabin for vacation purposes for a total of 12 years as follows: 2004-2012 (9 years), 2014-2016 (3 years). Also assume, for this question only, that he used the cabin as his principal residence for 3 years as follows: 2013, 2017 & 2018. Each of these were full calendar years. **Which of the following statements best describes the recognition aspect of his gain (i.e., how much is included in his gross income and how much he can exclude/not recognize)?**

    (a) Jon will be able to use IRC § 121 to exclude/not recognize $250,000 of his $300,000 realized gain. He must recognize the remaining $50,000.

    (b) Jon is eligible to exclude/not recognize some of his gain pursuant to IRC § 121. Because not all his years are "qualified," he can exclude/not recognize only $160,000 of his $300,000 gain. He must recognize the $140,000 balance.

    (c) Jon is eligible to exclude/not recognize some of his gain pursuant to IRC § 121. Because not all his years are "qualified," he can exclude/not recognize only $60,000 of his $300,000 gain. He must recognize the $240,000 balance.

    (d) All $300,000 of Jon's realized gain will be recognized. He is not entitled to exclude/not recognize any gain pursuant to IRC § 121.

    (e) Jon is eligible to exclude/not recognize some of his gain pursuant to IRC § 121. Because not all his years are "qualified." he can exclude/not recognize only $120,000 of his $300,000 gain. He must recognize the $180,000 balance.

3. For this question only, assume that Jon used the cabin for vacation purposes the following years: 2004-2012 (9 years), 2015, 2016 & 2018 (3 years). Also assume, for this question only, that he used the cabin as his principal residence for 3 years as follows: 2013, 2014 & 2017. Each of these were full calendar years. **Which of the following statements best describes the recognition aspect of his gain (i.e., how much is included in his gross income and how much he can exclude/not recognize)?**

    (a) Jon will be able to use IRC § 121 to exclude/not recognize $250,000 of his $300,000 realized gain. He must recognize the remaining $50,000.

    (b) Jon is eligible to exclude/not recognize some of his gain pursuant to IRC § 121. Because not all his years are "qualified," he can exclude/not recognize only $220,000 of his $300,000 gain. He must recognize the $80,000 balance.

    (c) Jon is eligible to exclude/not recognize some of his gain pursuant to IRC § 121. Because not all his years are "qualified," he can exclude/not recognize only $160,000 of his $300,000 gain. He must recognize the $140,000 balance.

    (d) Jon is eligible to exclude/not recognize some of his gain pursuant to IRC § 121. Because not all his years are "qualified." he can exclude/not recognize only $180,000 of his $300,000 gain. He must recognize the $120,000 balance.

    (e) None of the above responses is correct.

4. For this question only, assume that Jon used the cabin for vacation purposes the following years: 2004-2012 (9 years), 2015-2018 (4 years). Also assume, for this question only, that he used the cabin as his principal residence for the following years: 2013 & 2014. Each of these were full calendar years. **Which of the following statements best describes the recognition aspect of his gain (i.e., how much is included in his gross income and how much he can exclude/not recognize)?**

    (a) Jon will be able to use IRC § 121 to exclude/not recognize $250,000 of his $300,000 realized gain. He must recognize the remaining $50,000.

    (b) Jon is eligible to exclude/not recognize some of his gain pursuant to IRC § 121. Because not all his years are "qualified," he can exclude/not recognize only $120,000 of his $300,000 gain. He must recognize the $180,000 balance.

    (c) Jon is eligible to exclude/not recognize some of his gain pursuant to IRC § 121. Because not all his years are "qualified," he can exclude/not recognize only $220,000 of his $300,000 gain. He must recognize the $80,000 balance.

    (d) All $300,000 of Jon's realized gain will be recognized. He is not entitled to exclude/not recognize any gain pursuant to IRC § 121.

    (e) None of the above responses is correct.

Questions 5 through 7 are based on the following facts:

On January 1, 2009, Jamie, then single, purchased a condominium (condo) in New Town for $100,000 (paying all cash). At the time, she was living in a rented apartment in nearby Old Town and bought the condo with the intent to occasionally use it for weekend getaways and perhaps live their full time. For all of 2009 and 2010 (two exact calendar years) she used the condo for an occasional weekend but kept living in her apartment. On 1/1/11, she and her then boyfriend, Manuel, moved into the condo and used it as their principal residence for all of 2011, 2012, and 2013. The couple married on 1/1/14 and moved out of the condo, living with Manuel's parents for 2014 and 2015. Jamie's condo remained vacant for these two years. Unfortunately, the couple divorced on 1/1/16 and pursuant to their divorce decree, Manuel was awarded a one-half interest in Jamie's condo (at the time, it was worth $300,000). Their divorce decree also gave Jamie exclusive rights to possession of the condo. The couple remained on good terms and neither envisioned selling the condo. Nevertheless, at some point they mutually agreed to sell it. On 1/1/19, they each sold their one-half interest in the condo to an unrelated buyer for a combined total of $500,000 (Jamie and Manuel splitting the sale proceeds equally). Each of the years presented in this set of questions represent a full calendar year.

5. For this question only, assume that Jamie used the condo as her principal residence for 2016 and 2017, but moved out on 1/1/18 leaving the condo vacant for all of 2018. Manuel was living with his parents for these three years. **Which of the following answers best describes the recognition aspect of Jamie's and Manuel's respective gain from the 1/1/19 condo sale (i.e., for each, how much is included in his/her gross income and how much can he/she exclude/not recognize)?**

   (a) Each will realize a $200,000 gain. Jamie's gain is fully excluded pursuant to IRC § 121. Manuel, however, is not eligible to use IRC § 121 and must recognize all his gain.

   (b) Each will realize a $200,000 gain, and both can exclude all of it pursuant to IRC § 121.

   (c) Each will realize a $200,000 gain and both will be eligible for some exclusion pursuant to IRC § 121. Because not all the 10 years of ownership are "qualified," Jamie can exclude only $120,000 of her $200,000 gain (she must recognize the $80,000 balance). The tax results for Manuel will be the same as Jamie's.

   (d) Each will realize a $200,000 gain and both will be eligible for some exclusion pursuant to IRC § 121. Because not all the 10 years of ownership are "qualified," Jamie can exclude only $120,000 of her $200,000 gain (she must recognize the $80,000 balance). Manuel's excluded portion of his $200,000 realized gain will be less than that of Jamie (i.e., Manuel must recognize a larger percentage of his gain compared to Jamie).

   (e) For tax purposes, the transfer of a half interest to Manuel at their divorce will be ignored and Jamie will realize the entire $400,000 gain. While eligible for some exclusion pursuant to IRC § 121, not all of her years of ownership are "qualified." As a result, she will be able to exclude (not recognize) only $125,000 (50% of the $250,000 maximum §121 exclusion). She must recognize the balance of her gain.

6. For this question only, assume that Jamie used the condo as her principal residence for 2016, but moved out on 1/1/17 leaving the condo vacant for all of 2017 and 2018. Manuel was living with his parents for these three years. **Which of the following answers best describes the most likely recognition aspect of Jamie's and Manuel's respective gain from the 1/1/19 condo sale (i.e., for each, how much is included in his/her gross income and how much cam he/she exclude/not recognize)?**

    (a) Each will realize a $200,000 gain. Jamie's gain is fully excluded pursuant to IRC § 121. Manuel, however, is not eligible to use IRC § 121 and must recognize all his gain.

    (b) Each will realize a $200,000 gain, and both can exclude all of it pursuant to IRC § 121.

    (c) Each will realize a $200,000 gain and both will be eligible for some exclusion pursuant to IRC § 121. Because not all the 10 years of ownership are "qualified," Jamie can exclude only $120,000 of her $200,000 gain (she must recognize the $80,000 balance). The tax results for Manuel will be the same as Jamie's.

    (d) Each will realize a $200,000 gain and neither are eligible for any exclusion pursuant to IRC § 121. Both Jamie and Manuel must recognize all of their respective $200,000 gain.

    (e) None of the above responses is correct.

7. For this question only, assume that Jamie did not use the condo after the couple's divorce (she moved to her old rented apartment in Old Town). Remaining on good terms with Manuel, and he being in need of a place to live, she permitted him to use it as his principal residence for 2016, 2017, and 2018. She thought this to be preferable to having it remain vacant. She did this even though their divorce decree granted her exclusive use of the condo. **Which of the following answers best describes the recognition aspect of Jamie's and Manuel's respective gain from the 1/1/19 condo sale (i.e., for each, how much is included in his/her gross income and how much can he/she exclude/not recognize)?**

    (a) Each will realize a $200,000 gain. Jamie's gain is fully excluded pursuant to IRC § 121. Manuel, however, is not eligible to use IRC § 121 and must recognize all his gain.

    (b) Each will realize a $200,000 gain, and both can exclude all of it pursuant to IRC § 121.

    (c) Each will realize a $200,000 gain and Manuel will be eligible for some exclusion pursuant to IRC § 121. Because not all the 10 years of ownership are "qualified," Manuel can exclude only $120,000 of her $200,000 gain (he must recognize the $80,000 balance). Jamie, however, will not be eligible to any portion of her $200,000 gain (i.e., she must recognize her entire gain).

    (d) Each will realize a $200,000 gain and both will be eligible for some exclusion pursuant to IRC § 121. Because not all the 10 years of ownership are "qualified," Jamie can exclude only $120,000 of her $200,000 gain (she must recognize the $80,000 balance). The tax results for Manuel will be the same as Jamie's.

    (e) Each will realize a $200,000 gain and neither are eligible for any exclusion pursuant to IRC § 121. Both Jamie and Manuel must recognize all of their respective $200,000 gain.

Questions 8 through 13 are based on the following facts:

Note: This series of questions are year-specific (2019) and are intended to both highlight specific income tax issues and illustrate how the pieces fit together in computing taxable income. In a form uncharacteristic to this professor's objective exams, the correct analysis of some of the following questions requires substantially correct analyses of other questions. [Appendix B contains relevant, year-specific information applicable to 2019.] This series of questions is easily adaptable to years different than 2019.

Daniel is 22 years old, single, with good eyesight, and a child of Mom. He is also a full-time college student and has gross income of $13,000 in 2019. For 2019, Daniel has no "above the line" deductions for purposes of computing adjusted gross income (AGI), nor does he have any qualifying "itemized" deductions. For 2019, Mom unequivocally provides more than one-half of Daniel's support and Daniel lives with her.

8. Daniel and his Mom are trying to determine if Daniel is Mom's "dependent" for tax purposes. While being a dependent is no longer relevant for claiming personal exemption deductions, they know that his dependency status is important for other tax matters. **For 2019, is Daniel considered Mom's dependent?**

    (a) Yes. Daniel qualifies as Mom's dependent because he is a *qualifying child* pursuant to IRC § 152. Even though Daniel's gross income is not less than the statutory limit, he is a full-time student under the age of 24 at the end of the year and, therefore, comes within the definition of a *qualifying child*.

    (b) No. Daniel is not Mom's dependent in 2019. While he meets most of the requirements of a *qualifying child*, his gross income is too high. This latter fact will preclude him from being Mom's dependent.

    (c) Yes. All that is necessary for Daniel to be considered Mom's dependent is whether or not Mom provided more than one-half of his support for the year and that he is her child.

    (d) No, Daniel is too old to be considered Mom's *qualifying child* and his income is too high to be considered Mom's *qualifying relative*. because of his age.

9. Assume for this question only, that all of Daniel's $13,000 of gross income in 2019 is from investment sources (e.g., taxable interest and dividends received). Also assume that Mom will properly claim Daniel as her dependent for 2019. **For purposes of computing Daniel's taxable income for 2019, Daniel's "standard deduction" will be:**

    (a) $12,200.

    (b) $3,000.

    (c) $850.

    (d) Zero.

    (e) None of the above responses is correct.

10. Assume for this question only, that $2,000 of Daniel's $13,000 of gross income comes from wages ("earned" income), and $11,000 is derived from investment sources (e.g., taxable interest and dividends received). Also assume that Mom will properly claim Daniel as her dependent for 2019. **For purposes of computing Daniel's taxable income for 2019, Daniel's "standard deduction" will be:**

    (a) Zero.

    (b) $1,100.

    (c) $2,000.

    (d) $12,200.

    (e) None of the above responses is correct.

11. Assume for this question only, that all of Daniel's $13,000 of gross income in 2019, is from wages ("earned" income). Also assume that Mom will properly claim Daniel as her dependent for 2019. **For purposes of computing Daniel's taxable income for 2019, Daniel's "standard deduction" will be:**

    (a) $13,350.

    (b) $13,000.

    (c) $12,200.

    (d) $12,000.

    (e) None of the above responses is correct.

12. Assume the same facts as in question 9, above (i.e., Daniel's $13,000 of gross income is derived solely from investment sources). **Daniel's "taxable income" for 2019 will be:**

    (a) Zero.

    (b) $800.

    (c) $11,900.

    (d) $13,000.

13. Assume, for this question only, that Daniel provides all of his own support for 2019 (and, therefore, Daniel is not Mom's dependent). Also assume, for this question only, that all of Daniel's $13,000 of gross income is from wages. **Daniel's "taxable income" for 2019 will be:**

    (a) Zero.

    (b) $800.

    (c) $11,900.

    (d) Something less than $800 because Daniel will be entitled to an IRC § 199A "pass-through" business-related deduction.

    (e) None of the above responses is correct.

Questions 14 through 25 are based on the following facts:

Note: This is a <u>comprehensive</u> and <u>sometimes "challenging"</u> series of questions that contain numerous income tax components, all pertinent to the computation of "taxable income." These questions are year specific (2019) and are intended to both highlight specific income tax issues and illustrate how the pieces fit together in computing taxable income. In a form <u>uncharacteristic</u> to this professor's objective exams, the correct analysis of some of the following questions requires substantially correct analyses of other questions. [Appendix B contains relevant, year-specific information applicable to 2019.] This series of questions is easily adaptable to years other than 2019.

Thian, a single individual with no children, is 27, and is visually impaired to such a degree that he has virtually no eyesight. He struggled with an addition problem soon after obtaining his bachelor's degree, culminating with a felony drug possession conviction. Fortunately, he turned his life around and for the past few years, he had been employed by a law firm, working as a paralegal. In August 2019, Thian left his job to attend an accredited Law School on a full-time basis. He earned $27,000 in wages, in 2019, prior to leaving the law firm. In 2019, he received a $30,000 scholarship covering a portion of his law school tuition for the 2019/2020 academic year (Fall and Spring semesters of his first year). The balance of his tuition for each semester of his first year is $5,000, and he paid for both semesters (i.e., the full $10,000) when he began school in the Fall. Thian paid $8,000, in 2019, for room and board while attending law school during his first fall semester.

Thian's other expenditures for 2019 are as follows:
- $3,000 in cash contributions to the American Heart Association.
- $ 600 in legitimate, unreimbursed business expenses for Thian's job while he was still employed earlier in the year.
- $1,000 in state income taxes.
- $1,000 in interest on federally sponsored student loans used for his undergraduate tuition.
- $800 in state "intangibles" taxes (an annual ad-valorem tax on stocks owned).
- $4,000 in veterinary fees for his Seeing Eye dog.
- $400 in "over the counter" allergy medicines recommended by Thian's doctor.
- $ 300 in federal and state gasoline taxes (Thian's mom, Marlo, often drives him and Thian pays for the gas; these taxes are paid at the pump and are included as part of the price of each gallon of gas).

Even though Thian had been working, his mother, Marlo, has continually been providing most of Thian's support (he had been living with her until he started law school in the Fall of 2019). Notwithstanding the scholarship awarded to Thian, Marlo provided more than one-half of his support for 2019. Marlo doesn't know if Thian qualifies as her dependent for 2019 but she has told him that she will not claim him as such even if he qualifies.

In each of the following questions, please assume that the foregoing represents all of the tax-related items pertaining to Thian for 2019.

14. **Which of the following statements is most accurate in describing Thian's "gross income" for 2019?**

    (a) The $27,000 of wages is fully included in gross income. The $30,000 scholarship is also fully included in Thian's gross income because law school is not considered education that is "below the graduate level" and, therefore, not excludable as qualified tuition reduction pursuant to IRC § 117(d)

    (b) The $27,000 of wages is fully included in gross income. The $30,000 scholarship is also fully included in Thian's gross income because law school is considered "graduate" level education and, therefore, not excludable pursuant to IRC § 127.

    (c) The $27,000 of wages is fully included in gross income. All but $5,250 of the $30,000 scholarship is also included in gross income. While law school is considered "graduate" level education, the 2001 Tax Act extended this IRC § 127 exclusion (maximum of $5,250) to include graduate level courses.

    (d) The $27,000 of wages is fully included in gross income. One-half of the $30,000 scholarship is also included in Thian's gross income because one-half of the benefit does not relate to the 2019 tax year but, rather, relates to 2020.

    (e) The $27,000 of wages is fully included in gross income. The $30,000 scholarship is fully excludable from Thian's gross income because "qualified scholarships" for purposes of exclusion under IRC § 117(a) make no distinction between graduate and non-graduate levels of education.

15. **Does either the $10,000 Thian paid in tuition (in the Fall of 2019) or the $8,000 he paid in room and board give rise to an income tax deduction for him in 2019?**

   (a) No. It used to be that a portion of the $10,000 Thian paid for tuition would have been deductible pursuant to IRC § 222. This deduction, however, terminated in 2018. His costs for room and board were not considered "qualified tuition and related expenses" under IRC § 222 and would not have been deductible even if this section's deduction was still in effect after 2017.

   (b) Yes. Thian is entitled to deduct $4,000 of the $10,000 paid for tuition assuming that his "adjusted gross income" (as defined in IRC § 222(b)(2)(C)) does not exceed a certain level. The $8,000 he paid in room and board will not qualify for a deduction pursuant to IRC § 222 because they are not "qualified tuition and related expenses."

   (c) Yes. Thian is entitled to deduct $5,000 paid for tuition for the Fall 2019 semester assuming that his "adjusted gross income" (as defined in IRC § 222(b)(2)(C)) does not exceed a certain level. No portion of the $5,000 paid that relates to the Spring 2020 semester's tuition is deductible in 2019 because it was paid too far in advance. He is not, however, entitled to any deduction for his room and board expenses because they do not qualify as excludable "qualified scholarship" amounts pursuant to IRC § 117(b).

   (d) Yes. The total amount of his $10,000 tuition paid will qualify as an exclusion pursuant to IRC § 117. There are no statutory deductions available to Thian for the $8,000 room and board costs.

   (e) No. Thian not entitled to deduct either of these because they are incurred at the "graduate" level. He would have been entitled to some deduction had these costs been incurred in his undergraduate studies.

16. **Does the tuition and room/board that Thian paid result in a potential income tax credit for him in 2019?**

    (a) Yes, the $10,000 and $8,000 that Thian paid for law school tuition and room/board, respectively, represent qualifying expenses for purposes of determining the "American Opportunity Credit."

    (b) Yes, the $10,000 that Thian paid in law school tuition is a qualifying expense for purposes of determining the "American Opportunity Credit."

    (c) Yes. $5,000 of the $10,000 law school tuition that Thian paid may qualify for the "Lifetime Learning Credit."

    (d) Yes, the $10,000 that Thian paid in law school tuition in 2019 may qualify in determining the "Lifetime Learning Credit."

    (e) None of the above responses is correct.

17. **Which of the following statements best describes the income tax consequences to Thian with respect to the $1,000 in interest that he paid on his undergraduate student loans in 2019?**

   (a) Thian is entitled to deduct the interest in full because, pursuant to IRC § 163(a), all interest paid on indebtedness is deductible. Since this interest is "personal" in nature, it is deductible "below the line" (from adjusted gross income) as an itemized deduction in computing taxable income.

   (b) Thian is not entitled to deduct any of this interest, as it is considered "personal interest."

   (c) Thian may be entitled to deduct some or all the $1,000 interest pursuant to IRC § 221 depending on whether, and to what extent, his "modified adjusted gross income" (as defined in IRC § 221(b)(2)(C)) exceeds certain statutory amounts. This deduction, to the extent that it qualifies under IRC § 221, is deductible "above the line" in computing adjusted gross income.

   (d) Assuming that Thian has not been paying interest on the student loans for more than 60 months, he may be entitled to deduct some or all the $1,000 interest pursuant to IRC § 221. The amount of his deduction, if any, depends on whether, and to what extent, his "modified adjusted gross income" (as defined in IRC § 221(b)(2)(C)) exceeds certain statutory amounts. This deduction, to the extent that it qualifies under IRC § 221, is deductible "above the line" in computing adjusted gross income.

   (e) Thian may be entitled to deduct some or all the $1,000 interest pursuant to IRC § 221 depending on whether, and to what extent, his "modified adjusted gross income" (as defined in IRC § 221(b)(2)(C)) exceeds certain statutory amounts. This deduction, to the extent that it qualifies under IRC § 221, is deductible "below the line" (from adjusted gross income) as an itemized deduction in computing taxable income.

18. **For 2019, which answer best describes what qualifies as deductible taxes for the amounts Thian paid for state income taxes, state "intangibles" taxes, and federal & state gasoline taxes?**

    (a) The $1,000 in state income taxes qualifies as a deductible tax. Thian is not entitled to a deduction for either the $800 intangibles taxes or the $300 federal and state gasoline taxes that he paid.

    (b) All of the taxes indicated in this question qualify as deductible taxes.

    (c) Thian is not entitled to deduct any portion or any of these taxes paid.

    (d) The $1,000 in state income taxes and $800 in state intangibles taxes both qualify as a deductible tax. The $300 that he paid in federal & state gasoline taxes are not eligible for deductions.

    (e) The $1,000 in state income taxes and the $300 is federal/state gasoline taxes qualify as deductible taxes. The $800 that he paid in state intangibles taxes does not, however, qualify as a deductible tax.

19. **Which of the following statements is most accurate in describing the deductibility in 2019 for the amounts that Thian paid for veterinary fees (for his Seeing Eye dog) and for his over-the-counter medicines?**

   (a) The veterinary fees that Thian paid will be considered qualifying medical care expenses, but only if Thian was originally required to pay to acquire the Seeing Eye dog, and such expenditure was deductible as a medical care expense. The over-the-counter allergy medicines are not considered qualified medical care and, therefore, are not deductible.

   (b) The veterinary fees that Thian paid are considered qualifying medical care expenses and are deductible to the extent that they, combined with any other qualifying medical care expenses, exceed 10% of his adjusted gross income (AGI). The over-the-counter allergy medicines are not considered qualified medical care and, therefore, are not deductible.

   (c) The veterinary fees that Thian paid are not deductible as medical care expenses because they represent medical care expenses for his dog. Deductions are allowed only for expenses for medical care for the taxpayer, the taxpayer's spouse, or the taxpayer's dependent. The Seeing Eye dog does not qualify as Thian's dependent. Additionally, the over-the-counter allergy medicines are not considered qualified medical care and, therefore, are not deductible.

   (d) The veterinary fees that Thian paid are not deductible as medical care expenses because they represent medical care expenses for his dog. Deductions are allowed only for expenses for medical care for the taxpayer, the taxpayer's spouse, or the taxpayer's dependent. The Seeing Eye dog does not qualify as Thian's dependent. Because the over-the-counter allergy medicines were recommended by Thian's doctor, they do qualify as medical care expenses and are deductible to the extent that they, combined with any other qualifying medical care expenses, exceed 10% of Thian's adjusted gross income (AGI).

   (e) The veterinary fees Thian paid are considered qualifying medical care expenses. So, too, are the costs of his over-the-counter allergy medicines because his doctor recommended them. Together, these expenses, combined with any other qualifying medical care expenses, are deductible to the extent that the total exceeds 10% of his adjusted gross income (AGI).

20. **Which of the following answers best describes the deductibility of Thian's $3,000 cash contributions that he made to the American Heart Association in 2019?**

   (a) Thian is entitled to a $3,000 charitable deduction which is an *above the line* deduction (a deduction from gross income to arrive at adjusted gross income (AGI).

   (b) Thian is not entitled to a charitable deduction because he is Marlo's dependent.

   (c) Thian is entitled to a $3,000 charitable deduction which is a *below the line* deduction, a component of his itemized deductions.

   (d) Thian is not entitled to a charitable deduction because the amount of the charitable contribution most likely exceeds the statutory limitation regarding such contributions.

21. **Does the $600 in expenses that Thian paid in connection with his paralegal job give rise to an income tax deduction for him in 2019?**

   (a) Yes. Thian is entitled to an *above the line* deduction (a deduction from gross income to arrive at adjusted gross income (AGI)) as an IRC § 162 trade/business expense.

   (b) No. Because Thian is attending a program of education (law school) that will qualify him to enter a new trade or business (the practice of law is a different trade or business from that of a paralegal), the $600 does not qualify as a deductible business expense.

   (c) Yes. Thian is entitled to a *below the line* deduction (a deduction from adjusted gross income (AGI) to arrive at taxable income) as an IRC § 162 trade/business expense. However, its actual deductibility, along with other "miscellaneous itemized deductions," is, in the aggregate, subject to a two percent (2%) of adjusted gross income (AGI) nondeductible floor.

   (d) No. Thian's expenditures qualify as IRC § 162 business expenses. Had he been self-employed, this would give rise to an *above the line* deduction. Because he incurred these expenses as an employee, they will not give rise to any deduction notwithstanding that they are legitimate IRC § 162 business expenses.

   (e) No. This expenditure does qualify as a business expense deduction and would be considered part of Thian's "itemized deductions." However, Thian is not entitled to benefit from itemized deductions because he is Marlo's dependent.

22. **For purposes of computing Thian's taxable income for 2019, his "standard deduction" will be:**

    (a) The greater of: 1) $1,000, or 2) the amount of Thian's "earned income" plus $350. This is a special standard deduction limitation applicable to persons who are *dependents* of another.

    (b) $12,200 but only because applying the special standard deduction limitation applicable in this case (because Thian is Marlo's dependent), results in an amount greater than the regular standard deduction for a single person.

    (c) $12,200.

    (d) $13,500.

    (e) $13,850.

23. **Based upon the above information, and assuming that deductions are taken whenever possible (even if it means forgoing a possible tax credit), Thian's "adjusted gross income" (AGI) for 2019 is:**

    (a) $23,000.

    (b) $24,000.

    (c) $26,000.

    (d) $27,000.

    (e) None of the above responses is correct.

24. **Based upon the above information, and assuming that deductions are taken whenever possible (even if it means forgoing a possible tax credit), Thian's "taxable income" for 2019 is:**

    (a) $12,150.

    (b) $13,800.

    (c) $17,200.

    (d) $19,800.

    (e) None of the above responses is correct.

25. For this question only, assume that in 2019, Thian incurred costs for doctor visits. Further assume for this question that Thian's mother, Marlo, paid for these costs and that they were not reimbursed by insurance or otherwise. **Is Marlo entitled to a deduction with respect to these medical costs that she paid on Thian's behalf?**

    (a) Yes, because Thian is her dependent for purposes of IRC § 213 medical expense deductions.

    (b) No, because Thian is not Marlo's *qualifying child* or *qualifying relative*.

    (c) Yes, regardless of whether or not Thian is Marlo's dependent, because she paid for the medical costs.

    (d) No, because Marlo is not entitled to claim Thian as a dependent on her tax return.

END OF EXAMINATION QUESTIONS

EXAM VIII

FEDERAL INCOME TAX
MULTIPLE-CHOICE OBJECTIVE QUESTIONS
EXAM VIII

Questions 1 through 5 are based on the following facts:

Note: This series of questions are year-specific (2019) and are intended to both highlight specific income tax issues and illustrate how the pieces fit together in computing taxable income. In a form uncharacteristic to this professor's objective exams, the correct analysis of some of the following questions requires substantially correct analyses of other questions. [Appendix B contains relevant, year-specific information applicable to 2019.] This series of questions is easily adaptable to years other than 2019.

Susan and Wally, both age 70, are married, have good eyesight, and will file a joint return for 2019. Neither Susan nor Wally receives Social Security benefits. Wally had $10,000 in wages for 2019 from working part-time. Susan, an attorney, has a small law practice (no employees) that she operates as an unincorporated sole proprietorship and had a net profit (income less IRC § 162 business expenses) of $70,000 in 2019. In 2019, the couple earned $20,000 in regular interest from their bank savings account. For 2019, other than Susan's business expenses reflected in her net profit, the couple had no other "above the line" deductions for purposes of computing adjusted gross income (AGI). The couple's cash contributions to qualified charities in 2019 were, in the aggregate, $11,000.

1. **For purposes of computing the joint "taxable income" for Susan and Wally for 2019, their "standard deduction" will be:**

    (a) $6,000.

    (b) $24,000

    (c) $24,400.

    (d) $27,000.

    (e) None of the above responses is correct.

2. IRC § 199A was enacted as part of the *Tax Cuts and Jobs Act* (TCJA) signed into law in December 2017 (generally effective beginning in 2018). This is the so-called "pass-through" deduction used to compute *taxable income* and it is available to some individuals who operate a business. **What is Susan's IRC § 199A deduction for 2019?**

    (a) $14,000.

    (b) Zero because as an attorney, she is considered performing a "specific services trade or business" (SSTB) and the deduction is disallowed for SSTB's.

    (c) Zero because Susan operates her law practice as an unincorporated sole proprietorship and this is not considered a "pass-through" entity (e.g., a partnership, LLC, S Corp and the like) for which the deduction is allowed.

    (d) $14,600.

    (e) None of the above responses is correct.

3. For this question only, assume that the couple's personal interest earned for 2019 was $15,000 instead of $20,000 as indicated in the general facts. **How, if at all, will this change of facts affect Susan's IRC § 199A deduction for 2019?**

    (a) It will have no impact because this deduction is based on her net business income and their interest earned is irrelevant in computing the deduction.

    (b) It will have no impact because she was never entitled to any such deduction to start. Her IRC § 199A deduction remains at zero.

    (c) It will decrease her IRC § 199A deduction by $400.

    (d) It will decrease her IRC § 199A deduction by $1,000.

    (e) It will decrease her IRC § 199A deduction by some amount but not by those indicated in answers (c) or (d).

4. **Reverting to our original facts (i.e., ignoring the one-off change of interest income in question 3, above) and assuming that the introductory facts to this series of questions represent all possible tax related items for Susan and Wally, their 2019 taxable income will be:**

    (a) $59,000.

    (b) $61,600.

    (c) $73,000.

    (d) $75,600.

    (e) None of the above responses is correct.

5. Using our original facts (i.e., ignoring the one-off change of interest income in question 3, above) and assuming that those facts represent all possible tax related items for Susan and Wally, what is their "regular" federal income tax for 2019 (ignoring any potential additional taxes and possible tax credits):

   (a) $13,717.

   (b) $8,372.

   (c) $7,080.

   (d) $6,699.

   (e) $6,692.

6. Robert succumbed to cancer five years ago (at age 36) and was survived by his spouse, Carol (now age 40). Carol has not remarried and lives alone (she and Robert had no children). In the current year (2019) Carol expects to have "taxable income" of $100,000. **Assuming Carol does not remarry during 2019, her "regular" federal income tax liability for 2019 (ignoring any potential additional taxes and before any tax credits) will be approximately:**

   (a) $13,717.

   (b) $16,754.

   (c) $18,174.

   (d) $24,000.

   (e) None of the above responses is correct.

7. Assume the same facts as in Question 6, above, except that for this question, Robert and Carol had one child, Samantha. Samantha turned 10 in 2019 and lives with Carol. Carol provides 100% of Samantha's support and qualifies as her "dependent." As in Question 6, Carol has not remarried and in the current year (2019), she expects to have "taxable income" of $100,000. **Assuming Carol does not remarry during 2019, her "regular" federal income tax liability for 2019 (ignoring any potential additional taxes and before any tax credits) will be approximately:**

   (a) $13,717.

   (b) $16,754.

   (c) $18,174.

   (d) $24,000.

   (e) None of the above responses is correct.

8. Marilee and Bill have, for many years, owned shares of stock of a publicly traded Vermont granite mining company. This year (assume the year is 2019), as always, the company paid dividends to its shareholders. In addition to these dividends, Marilee and Bill earned substantial sums from their respective medical practices (they are both doctors). **With respect to the dividends that Marilee and Bill received in the current year, which of the following statements is most accurate?**

   (a) They are "qualified dividends" and, as such, are excluded from their income and not subject to federal income tax.

   (b) They are fully included in their gross income.

   (c) They are "qualified dividends" and, as such, are excluded from their gross income but still subject to federal income tax (albeit at tax rates lower than regular income tax rates at their level of income).

   (d) Dividends, unlike interest, do not constitute income. Rather, they are considered a "return of capital" and, therefore, there is no net "accession to wealth."

   (e) They are "qualified dividends" and, as such, only a portion of the amount received is included in their gross income.

9. The *Tax Cuts and Jobs Act* (TCJA) was signed into law in December 2017 and was generally effective beginning in 2018. The TCJA made numerous tax law changes affecting both corporations and individuals. Concentrating on individuals, most of the TCJA provisions are effective for 2018 through 2025. In effect, the TCJA contains a "sunset provision" (through its application only through 2025). **Which of the following responses best describes the effect of this *sunset provision* for affected provisions in the TCJA?**

(a) Unless affirmatively changed by Congress and enacted into law, all the changes enacted by the TCJA that are effective through 2025 will disappear after December 31, 2025, and affected tax laws will revert to their status immediately prior to the enactment of the TCJA.

(b) All changes made, and provisions enacted by the TCJA that are effective through 2025 will disappear after December 31, 2025, and tax laws will revert to their status immediately prior to the enactment of the TCJA. This, however, will only occur if certain budget deficit thresholds are reached. Otherwise, the TCJA provisions set to expire after 2025 will automatically become permanent.

(c) The TCJA has an overriding provision that will automatically extend, for an additional ten years, the otherwise expiring provisions unless Congress affirmatively enacts legislation (that is signed into law) to "deactivate" this automatic extension provision. If the latter occurs, then the affected tax laws will revert to their status immediately prior to the enactment of the TCJA

(d) It is an example of Congress's bipartisan poetic expression that is rarely incorporated into law. It describes the beauty and soft tranquil glow of a late summer's day when the sun gently slips below the horizon, and all is right with the world.

10. **Notwithstanding any potential limitations, if a taxpayer has a choice of a tax deduction or a tax credit, of equal amounts, which is usually more beneficial to the taxpayer for income tax purposes?**

    (a) Neither is more beneficial as a tax deduction and a tax credit are both equally beneficial to a taxpayer.

    (b) A tax credit is more beneficial than a tax deduction because the former represents a dollar-for-dollar reduction of tax liability.

    (c) A tax deduction is more beneficial than a tax credit because the former reduces taxable income.

    (d) A tax credit is more beneficial than a tax deduction because the former represents taxes that the taxpayer has already paid which, if the total exceeds the tax liability, will be refunded.

11. There are numerous "tax credits" available to qualifying individuals. Two such credits are the "earned income credit" and the "lifetime learning credit." **Which of the following statements is most accurate regarding these two credits?**

    (a) The *earned income credit* and the *lifetime learning credit* are "refundable" and "nonrefundable" credits, respectively.

    (b) The *earned income credit* and the *lifetime learning credit* are "nonrefundable" and "refundable" credits, respectively.

    (c) Both the *earned income credit* and the *lifetime learning credit* are "refundable" credits.

    (d) Both the *earned income credit* and the *lifetime learning credit* are "nonrefundable" credits.

12. Baxter is a single parent with one child, Celia age 5. Celia lives with Baxter. He works full-time and in order to work, he needs someone to look after Celia. On many days, Baxter's mother, Monica, takes care of Celia (at no charge). Other days, Baxter pays an unrelated individual to come to his home to look after Celia. Celia is Baxter's dependent for tax purposes. **Most likely, is Baxter entitled to some tax benefit for the payments he makes for Celia's childcare?**

    (a) Assuming that Baxter's adjusted gross income (AGI) exceeds a certain amount, the answer is no.

    (b) Yes, but only if Celia's health is such that "taking care of" or "looking after" her requires some degree of medical care.

    (c) Yes. He will be entitled to a "childcare" credit regardless of the amount of his adjusted gross income (AGI).

    (d) No. Childcare is a nondeductible personal expense pursuant IRC § 262.

13. Pamela, a single parent, has three young children living with her. Their respective ages are 10 months, 2 years, and 4 years. In order for Pamela to be able to work full-time, during working hours her children are cared for in a full-service state licensed day care facility (on a daily basis, between twenty to thirty children are at this day care facility). For the current year, Pamela estimates that her costs for the day care will be $4,000 per child. She estimates that her adjusted gross income (AGI) for the current year will be $45,000. All three of Pamela's children are her dependents. Please assume that "the current year" is 2018 or later. **Most likely, Pamela's "child and dependent care" tax credit pursuant to IRC § 21 will be:**

    (a) $2,400.

    (b) $2,100.

    (c) $1,800.

    (d) $1,200.

    (e) None of the above responses is correct.

14. This year (assume the year is 2019) Sonia adopted a healthy two-year-old baby boy, Adam. She incurred, and paid, significant costs associated with his adoption including adoption fees, court costs and attorney fees. **Is Sonia entitled to an income tax credit in 2019 with regard to this adoption?**

   (a) Yes, assuming that Sonia's income does not exceed a certain amount, she may be entitled to a tax credit for her adoption-related costs up to $14,080.

   (b) No, because the adoption tax credit expired at the end of 2001, except for adoptions of "special needs" individuals.

   (c) Yes, assuming that Sonia's income does not exceed a certain amount, she may be entitled to a tax credit for her adoption-related costs to $10,000.

   (d) No, because adoption costs do not give rise to a tax credit. However, if Sonia's employer paid or reimbursed her for her adoption related costs, she may be entitled to exclude some or all of these amounts from her gross income.

15. Justin, a single individual age 38, wants to set up a "traditional" Individual Retirement Account (IRA) because he read an online article that they can produce some nice income tax benefits. He is currently working in the production department of a major entertainment company and he is covered by the company's pension/retirement plan (the company makes contributions to this plan on his behalf and he can make voluntary contributions to the plan). Justin makes a fair amount of money from his job, but he also makes substantial alimony payments to his ex-wife Ellen (they divorced in 2015 and his alimony payments qualify as deductions for Justin). **If Justin makes contributions to a "traditional" IRA, which of the following statements best describes Justin's current income tax benefits?**

    (a) Because he is a participant in his company's pension/retirement plan, he is not entitled to any deduction for contributions made to a "traditional" IRA.

    (b) He may be entitled to some deduction for contributions to a "traditional" IRA depending on his amount of adjusted gross income (AGI). In this regard, his alimony payments will be beneficial to him.

    (c) He may be entitled to some deduction for contributions to a "traditional" IRA depending on his amount of adjusted gross income (AGI). His alimony payments are irrelevant for purposes of this question.

    (d) He will be entitled to a deduction (within certain limits) for his contributions to a "traditional" IRA. The fact that he is a participant in another pension/retirement plan is no longer a relevant factor in determining the deductibility of such contributions.

16. Ellen, Justin's ex-wife in question 15, above, is also considering establishing an Individual Retirement Account (IRA) for her. She receives approximately $15,000 per year in alimony (they divorced in 2015 and the alimony she receives is includible in her gross income) and has minimal earnings of $1,500 from a part-time job. She does have other sources of income such as rental income, interest and dividends. She is 42 years old and has no interest in any company retirement or pension plan. Assume for this question that the year is 2019, and that Ellen wants to make a contribution to a "traditional" IRA up to the maximum amount allowed. **Most likely, how much of a deduction will she be entitled to as a result of this contribution?**

    (a) $6,000.

    (b) $1,500.

    (c) $6,000 or less depending on the amount of her adjusted gross income (AGI).

    (d) Zero because Ellen is not a full-time employee.

17. In general, is the "alternative minimum tax" (AMT) a good thing for individual taxpayers?

    (a) Yes, it is a special provision that, for some taxpayers, generates a smaller amount of income tax liability when compared with a regularly computed income tax liability.

    (b) No, it is a special provision that, for some taxpayers, generates a greater amount of income tax liability when compared with a regularly computed income tax liability.

    (c) Yes, but only if a "qualified" individual makes an affirmative election to this alternative method of tax computation.

    (d) No, but in rare situations, a "qualified" individual will elect this alternative method of computing tax because it can have a beneficial impact to certain "non-tax" matters.

18. Last year (2019), Victor paid substantial hospital costs following a serious illness. These costs were not covered by insurance. Last year tax-wise, Victor had substantial "taxable income" resulting in an income tax liability. After discovering errors in their accounting software and reviewing all patient accounts, the hospital discovered that they had overcharged Victor. This year (2020), Victor received a refund from the hospital in the amount overcharged. **Does this refund represent gross income to Victor this year?**

    (a) Yes, but only if, and to the extent by which, Victor benefited from a medical deduction last year. This would be the amount by which his qualifying medical care expenses exceeded 10% of his adjusted gross income (AGI).

    (b) Yes, but only if, and to the extent by which, Victor benefited from "itemizing" deductions last year. This would be the amount, if any, that his total allowed itemized deductions exceeded his standard deduction.

    (c) Yes, but only if, and to the extent by which, Victor benefited from a medical deduction last year. This would be the amount by which his qualifying medical care expenses exceeded 10% of his adjusted gross income (AGI), and then only if, and to the extent by which, his total allowed itemized deductions exceeded his standard deduction.

    (d) No, none of the refund represents income to Victor in the current year. Rather, he must go back and amend his income tax return for the prior year to reflect the corrected amount of qualifying medical expense.

    (e) It may represent income to Victor in the current year. He has a choice of either 1) reporting it as income in the current year to the extent that he benefited from the deduction in the prior year, or 2) amending his income tax return for the prior year to reflect the corrected amount of qualifying medical care expense.

19. Kim has, for the past eight years, filed individual income tax returns in a timely manner (at least one month before the April 15th due date), and paid what she believed was the correct amount of tax in each of these years. Now a second-year law student enrolled in a federal income tax course, Kim learned, for the first time, about the education-related "American Opportunity" and "Lifetime Learning" credits. She now realizes that she could have taken advantage of these credits in prior years to reduce her tax liabilities. **Can Kim do anything to take advantage of these missed opportunities?**

    (a) No. Any tax benefits are available only for the appropriate years and she cannot receive the benefit of them in the current year.

    (b) Yes. Kim can file amended income tax returns for prior years to claim the benefits and receive refunds resulting therefrom.

    (c) Yes. Kim can claim these credits in her current year's income tax return as long as they were not claimed in income tax returns for prior years.

    (d) Yes. Kim can file amended income tax returns (and claim any appropriate tax benefit) for any of her returns that were filed within the past three years.

    (e) Yes. Kim can file amended income tax returns (and claim any appropriate tax benefit) for any years' returns where the due date for filing such returns was within the last three years.

20. Terrance's income tax return for last year was audited and the I.R.S. has assessed a deficiency (i.e., additional tax owed). Terrence does not agree with the I.R.S.'s position but has been unable to resolve this controversy with the I.R.S. **Assuming that he has exhausted all possible means of appealing the assessment with the I.R.S., internally, which of the following courts are available to him for purposes of resolving the issue?**

      I.   The U.S. Tax Court.
      II. The U.S. District Court for the jurisdiction in which Terrance resides.
      III. A U.S. District Court in a jurisdiction other than that in which Terrance resides.
      IV. The U.S. Court of Federal Claims.
      V. The U.S. Court of Appeals for the jurisdiction in which Terrance resides.

(a) I, II, & IV only.

(b) I only.

(c) I and IV only.

(d) I and V only.

(e) None of the above responses is correct.

21. If Terrance, in question 20, above, wants to have his issue resolved in court, must he first pay the proposed I.R.S. assessment before bringing the action?

(a) Yes.

(b) No.

(c) Yes, but only if he wishes to, and can, bring the action in the U.S. Tax Court.

(d) No, but only if he wishes to, and can, bring the action in the U.S. Tax Court.

22. In our nation's early history, federal taxes were derived primarily from tariffs, duties, and other excise-type taxes. Federal income taxes first appeared during the Civil War in 1861 and were later abolished in 1872. Federal income taxes appeared again in 1894 and, shortly thereafter, were held to be unconstitutional. **"Modern-day" federal income taxes were first actually imposed upon individuals via the:**

   (a) 16th Amendment.

   (b) Article 1, § 8 of the Constitution.

   (c) Article 1, § 9 of the Constitution.

   (d) Revenue Act of 1913.

23. Assume that Congress has just passed a law whereby income taxes for the current year will be assessed according to income earned in prior years. Betty, a taxpayer, is upset by this new law and would like to challenge the retrospective manner through which taxes will be imposed. **Her best argument and the likely result would be:**

   (a) Betty can argue that this law violates her 5th Amendment Due Process rights, and she will most likely lose.

   (b) Betty can argue that this law violates her 5th Amendment Due Process rights, and she will most likely prevail.

   (c) Betty can argue that this law violates the 16th Amendment because taxes are limited to income earned in the current tax year, and she will most likely prevail.

   (d) Betty can argue that this law violates the 16th Amendment because Congress cannot modify the current tax structure, and she will most likely prevail.

24. Dave has earned income through various illicit sources and does not report it on his tax return. **Once caught, his best argument, and the likely outcome in any pending litigation would be:**

   (a) Dave could argue that such disclosure would violate his 5th Amendment right against self-incrimination, and he will most likely prevail.

   (b) Dave could argue that such disclosure would violate his 5th Amendment right against self-incrimination, and he will most likely lose.

   (c) Dave could argue that such disclosure violates the 16th Amendment since income derived through such means is not included in tax calculation, and he will most likely prevail.

   (d) Dave could argue that such disclosure is not specifically required by state law and is therefore unnecessary. Dave will most likely prevail.

25. **Critics of a consumption-based tax, in place of or augmenting the current income tax, argue that it:**

   (a) Lacks administrative simplicity.

   (b) Does not promote fairness since it is regressive.

   (c) Will cause unnecessary litigation.

   (d) Will encourage tax evasion.

END OF EXAMINATION QUESTIONS

ANSWER KEY
EXAM I

1. **The best answer is (c).** Melinda will be required to recognize income because of her personal use of the company owned Porsche. She has derived a net economic benefit that is not excludable from her gross income.

IRC § 61 defines gross income as "all income from whatever source derived." From your initial study of gross income's scope, you probably found it to be broadly defined, including the taxpayer's receipt of some net economic benefit or net accession to wealth. In class, you also discover that gross income is also not limited to the receipt of cash. [Reg. § 1.61-1(d) (compensation received in forms other than in cash).] Is Melinda receiving a net economic benefit from ABC vis-à-vis the use of the Porsche? The answer is yes. She has been given the free use of the automobile, the value of which can easily be determined based on a fair rental or lease rate for the car. Barring any specific income exclusion provisions, Melinda has gross income.

But wait, isn't Melinda merely using her own automobile? Gross income does not go so far as to impute income to one's own use of assets. For example, when you live in your own house, you are <u>not</u> required to assign a fair rental value to such use and include it in your gross income for income tax purposes. In effect, isn't this the situation with Melinda? Technically the corporation (ABC) owns the vehicle, but Melinda *is* the corporation, owning 100% of it. Unfortunately for Melinda, the "technical" fact that the corporation is the owner of the automobile <u>cannot</u> be ignored. Melinda's wholly owned corporation *is* a person or entity that is separate and distinct from Melinda for income tax purposes. [*Dean v. Comm'r*, 187 F.2d 1019 (3rd Cir.1951).] For purposes of this question, ABC could just as well be any other corporation, one in which Melinda has no ownership interests. When an employer provides an employee with "in-kind" economic benefits, their value nonetheless represents income. While certain employer-provided "fringe benefits" are excludable from income, these excludable benefits do not include the full-time personal use of an automobile.

While not one of the answers to this question, Melinda's gross income could alternatively be viewed as income in the form of a dividend as she is the sole shareholder of ABC.

Answer (a) is incorrect because this does not represent an excludable fringe benefit to Melinda. Please see other questions in this book dealing with excludable fringe benefits. **Answer (b) is incorrect** because, as discussed above, Melinda's corporation is treated as a separate person or entity for income tax purposes. **Answer (d) is incorrect** because it is Melinda's current personal "use" of the car that is a net economic benefit to her and, therefore, represents gross income.

2. **The best answer is (b).** IRC § 61 defines gross income as "all income from whatever source derived." From your initial study of gross income's scope, you probably found it to be broadly defined, including the taxpayer's receipt of some net economic benefit or net accession to wealth. In class, you also discover that gross income is also not limited to the receipt of cash. Tricia, the undisputed owner of the "treasure trove," has derived an economic benefit and the value of the property $10 million, represents income to her.

Directly on point, the Regulations specifically identify as income: "Treasure trove, to the extent of its value in United States currency, constitutes gross income for the taxable year in which it is reduced to undisputed possession." [Reg. § 1.61-14(a).]

The general public is usually shocked by the tax consequences in such circumstances, believing that either Tricia has no income from such a find or that income is only realized if, and when, Tricia sells the coins. Surely, just finding them is not the triggering event causing income. As stated, however, once Tricia is deemed to be the legal owner, she has income (and "don't call me Shirley"). The facts in this problem closely resemble the real-life 2013 find by John and Mary while walking on their property in California's "gold rush" region. Their treasure trove of gold coins, known as the "Saddle Ridge Hoard" made nation-wide news, as did the public disbelief that its $10 million value would be income to the couple. Media coverage of the tax consequences often cites the seminal case, found in many income tax casebooks, of *Cesarini v. United States* [296 F. Supp. 3, affirmed per curiam 428 F. 2d 812 (6th Cir. 1970)]. An interesting account of this can be found in numerous online sites including this in the 2014 San Francisco Chronicle article: [Kevin Fagan, *Gold Country couple discover $10 million in buried coins*, San Francisco Chronicle, February 25, 2014, https://www.sfchronicle.com/news/article/Gold-Country-couple-discover-10-million-in-5266314.php?psid=ThkC (last visited Apr 24, 2019)].

It should be noted that had this problem featured a discovery of sunken treasure at sea, the tax consequences could be different due to various, and often complex, international and maritime laws.

Answer (a) is incorrect because while Tricia has income for the current year, it is measured by the coins' *value* and not by their face amount. **Answer**

(c) is incorrect because as stated above in the explanation, she has income now, when she is determined to have legal possession. This answer, while incorrect, represents the most commonly viewed tax outcome in such situations. It should be noted that should Tricia ultimately sell the coins, she may realize additional income to the extent she sells them for more than the value when they were "reduced to undisputed possession." There are multiple "gain and loss" questions in other parts of this book. **Answer (d) in incorrect** because gross income is more broadly defined than the definition given in this answer. **Answer (e) is incorrect** because, as indicated above, it was not until the current year that the coins were "reduced to undisputed possession."

3.   **The most likely correct answer is (c).** Interest received is included in income unless there is a specific provision granting an exclusion from income. Of the three sources of Spencer's interest, only the interest from the Maine bond is excludable from gross income. IRC § 103(a) excludes, from income, interest from state and local bonds. Commonly, this is referred to as tax-free state or municipal (or "muni") bond interest. Interest from such bonds is not excluded from gross income, however, if the state or local bond is either not issued in registered form, is a "private activity" or "arbitrage" type of bond (Spencer's Maine bond is none of these types).

Interest from obligations of the United States is generally fully includible in gross income. This is sometimes the source of confusion among students. While not the subject of this book, interest from U.S. obligations is generally excluded from income for <u>state and local income tax purposes</u> (for those states, counties or cities imposing an income tax). Also not at issue in this problem is IRC § 135 that provides for a very limited and narrow exclusion of certain interest received by certain individuals from Series EE U.S. Savings Bonds, the proceeds of which are used for certain education purposes.

The interest that Spencer receives from his Swiss bank account is, most likely, also included in his gross income for U.S. income tax purposes. U.S. citizens and U.S. residents are taxed (for U.S. income tax purposes) on a "world-wide" basis. Simply put, this means that such individuals must include in gross income, unless otherwise excludable, all income regardless of its geographic source. Gross income includes "all income from whatever source derived." [IRC § 61(a).] There are a limited number of special situations for certain taxpayers, earning certain types of income in certain foreign countries. It is extremely unlikely that any such exception would apply to Spencer given our facts. There is a common public misconception that individuals are not taxed on income (interest) from "offshore" bank accounts and this is often conflated with attempts to make it more difficult for creditors to reach an individual's offshore funds. It should be noted that corporations may be subject to different rules vis-à-vis inclusion of income earned abroad.

Answers (a), (b), (d), and (e) are all incorrect because none reflects the correct combination of taxable interest.

4. **Answer (e) is the most accurate.** Paul will have to recognize all but $15,000 of the award amount (i.e., he must recognize $85,000 in gross income). Because this was not a "physical" tort, Paul can only exclude the $15,000 representing the amount of the award allocated to cover his actual medical costs.

Students universally dislike "none of the above" answers and are justified in doing so. They do provide, however, a powerful testing tool for professors and, in this case, none of the answers provided in (a) through (d) are correct. The "bottom line" correct numeric answer for this question is that Paul would have to recognize $85,000 of income or, to put it another way, he would be entitled to exclude from income $15,000 of the $100,000 received. This question involves the exclusion of "compensation for injuries or sickness" provided in IRC § 104. This section has a long, complex and capricious past vis-à-vis what is within its umbrella of exclusion. In its most basic form, an individual receiving damages, by award or settlement, for physical injuries or physical sickness can exclude such amounts from income. [IRC § 104(a)(2).] In its current form (reflecting changes made by the "Small Business Job Protection Act of 1996"), this section generally excludes amounts received (other than punitive damages) for awards and settlements arising from <u>physical injury or sickness</u>. In the body of IRC § 104(a), the law indicates that "emotional distress shall not be treated as a physical injury or physical sickness." At this point, it would appear that Paul would have to include the entire $100,000 received because his cause of action was that of emotional distress. However, the section goes on to effectively say that the recipient can exclude the amount of damage award/settlement that is payment for his/her costs of actual medical care attributable to the emotional distress. In our question, $15,000 of Paul's settlement was to cover his hospital costs and, therefore, representing the only portion of the settlement that is excludable from income.

Do not fall into the trap of trying to "bootstrap" this section's exclusion application to awards/settlements emanating from an emotional distress cause of action because the plaintiff's emotional distress manifests itself into an actual physical injury.

The difficulty of questions involving IRC § 104 can vary dramatically depending on how thoroughly one's professor covers the exclusion as to its history, policy foundations, and the like. This is a good area of tax law for in-depth class analysis, so take this into consideration when addressing questions involving the subject. Much of this Code section's history centered on the breadth of this exclusion with, at varying times, exclusions allowed for damages received from nonphysical tort or "tort type" causes of action, and punitive damages.

This material also provides a good example to illustrate that the Regulations may not always be up-to-date with actual current law. As indicated above, the current law, at IRC § 104(a)(2), limits the exclusion to amounts received for _physical_ injury or _physical_ sickness (generally, _physical tort_ awards or settlements), with the all-important word "physical" added by legislation in 1996. The corresponding regulations where not changed until 2012 and reading them prior to 2012, the critical word "physical" was missing from the exclusion for personal injuries or sickness. [Reg. § 1.104-1(a) prior to 2012 amendments.] This older version of Regulation § 1.104(c), defining what constituted excludable amounts received on account of personal injuries or sickness, referred to legal actions "based upon tort or tort type rights." Reading this older version of the regulations alone, and not coming back to what is actually stated in the law, could easily lead a student to incorrectly conclude that a taxpayer can exclude an award or settlement from, for example, a defamation claim; clearly a "tort." Similarly, a defamation claim is clearly based on a tort, but it is not a _physical_ one opening up the "exclusion from income doors." It took over fifteen years to update this regulation to properly reflect that the statutory exclusion is limited to awards or settlements arising from _physical_ injuries or sickness.

Answers (a), (b) and (c) are incorrect because each of these answers, in varying degrees, incorrectly brings within the scope of the IRC § 104(a)(2) exclusion, amounts received that arose from a "non-physical" injury/sickness. **Answer (d) is incorrect** because it fails to recognize the limited exclusion for the portion of Paul's emotional distress-based settlement identified to repay him for his actual medical expenses.

5.   **The correct answer is (a).** The receipt of a scholarship is clearly a financial benefit that, but for some specific exclusion, would be included in a taxpayer's gross income under the broad definition thereof. IRC § 117 excludes, from income, "qualified scholarships." In general, amounts received as a scholarship, scholarship grant or fellowship grant are excluded from income to the extent that they are used for tuition and fees required for enrollment, or for fees, books, supplies, and equipment required for courses. [IRC §§ 117(a) and (b).] In this question, the $54,000 and $1,000 going towards tuition and books, respectively, fit squarely within this scholarship exclusion. However, the $15,000 designated for Staci's housing costs and the $5,000 in cash, even if used for meals and living costs, do not

fit within the scope of excludable scholarship amounts under IRC § 117. [Prop.Reg. § 1.117-6(c).] Therefore, the $20,000 sum of these latter two amounts is included in Staci's gross income (i.e., they are "taxable").

It should be noted that this general scholarship exclusion rule applies only to students who are "candidates for a degree." In addition, this exclusion is available only for students attending a qualified educational institution, which means a school that normally maintains a regular faculty, curriculum and regularly enrolled student body in attendance. [IRC §§ 117(b)(2)(A) and 170(b)(1)(A)(ii).] Staci's enrollment at an accredited law school satisfies these requirements. While not pertinent to our facts, the growing trend of "distance learning" raises interesting questions as to what constitutes a "school" for scholarship exclusion purposes.

Students are often surprised that scholarship amounts for room and board, as well as cash as an "allowance" generally are not excludable from gross income. Not a semester goes by that this professor does not have a student who asks about a "friend's" scholarship experience in their undergraduate education in which this "friend" received room, board, and an allowance without any of it being taxable. Upon further discussion, the "friend's" determination of non-taxability usually came by way of this person not receiving any official statement or form (such as a W-2 or 1099) from the school indicating that anything was taxable. Students are also often then surprised to learn that they are not relieved of their requirement to report (e.g., taxable scholarships) merely because the payor (e.g., the university or college) failed in their obligation to send any required forms to the taxpayer or the I.R.S. In other words, the duty to report taxable income is incumbent on the taxpayer.

Is it possible that any of this "scholarship" can be excluded pursuant to some other Code provision? In class, you may have discussed the statutory exclusion for gifts, bequests and devises of IRC § 102. If so, can we attempt to use this section to exclude some or all of Staci's scholarship benefits in this question? The answer, unfortunately for Staci, is no. The regulations at Reg. § 1.117-1(a) state that "[t]he exclusion from gross income of an amount which is a scholarship or fellowship grant is controlled solely by section 117." While not the subject of this question, it should be noted that there are other education-related benefits that may qualify for exclusion such as tuition reduction/remission and education assistance programs. [See IRC §§ 117(d) and 127, respectively.]

Answers (b) and (c) are incorrect because both answers incorrectly expand the scope of amounts excludable as a qualified scholarship under IRC § 117. Answers (b) and (c) fail to include, in income, the $15,000 of the scholarship designated for housing costs and answer (c) additionally fails to include the $5,000 cash allowance component of the scholarship in income. **Answer (d) is incorrect** because it improperly includes in income the $1,000 component of the scholarship used for required books, which is within the scope of the IRC § 117 exclusion. **Answer (e) is incorrect** because, as discussed above, the $5,000 cash allowance component of the scholarship is not excludable in this situation.

6. **The most accurate statement is (c).** Westlaw Academic's law-school related products include numerous fantastic resources for law students (no self-aggrandizement intended but they publish, among many items, this Exam Pro book). Staci is very fortunate to have received such a nice prize. IRC § 61 defines gross income as "all income from whatever source derived . . ." From your initial study of gross income's scope, you probably found it to be broadly defined, including a taxpayer's net accession to wealth or receipt of an economic benefit. In class, you also discover that gross income is not limited to the receipt of cash. Staci received a net accession to wealth, or a financial benefit, of $3,000 (the value of the laptop) and this amount is included in her gross income. IRC § 74 specifically addresses "prizes and awards" and its general rule, at § 74(a), states: "Except as otherwise provided in this section or in section 117 (relating to qualified scholarships), gross income includes amounts received as prizes and awards."

    Answer (a) is incorrect but is an answer that is commonly selected. It appears to be a possible correct answer after a casual reading of IRC § 74(b). This provision does exclude from gross income certain prizes and awards that are directly assigned to a qualified charitable organization. However, this "exclusion by assignment" provision is applicable only to prizes and awards "made primarily in recognition of religious, charitable, scientific, educational, artistic, literary, or civic achievement." [IRC § 74(b) (emphasis added).] Additionally, this provision requires that the "recipient was selected *without* any action on his part to enter the contest or proceeding." [IRC § 74(b)(1) (emphasis added).] Think of the "Nobel" prize as an example to which this provision could apply. Staci's prize resulted from a typical contest, not from a prize situation meeting the requirements of IRC § 74(b). Knowing something about charitable deductions (discussed elsewhere in this book) one might logically wonder about the actual significance of this exclusion by assignment provision. What if Staci does assign her computer over to a charitable organization; so she has gross income equal to $3,000 but is she not then entitled to a $3,000 deduction resulting in the same net effect of the IRC § 74(b) exclusion provision? Yes, Staci would most likely be entitled to a $3,000 charitable deduction, but no, the end result is probably not the same, nor as favorable, as the IRC § 74(b) provision. This is because, as discussed in other problems in this book, Staci's charitable deduction is a "below the line" itemized deduction (a deduction from adjusted gross income (AGI) to compute taxable income). Depending on the extent of her other itemized deductions compared with her "standard deduction" she may not, when all is said and done, realize the full benefit of the deduction. Other unfavorable consequences may include disqualification for numerous deductions and exclusions or reduction of various deductions, based on her higher AGI that reflects the inclusion of the prize. [See Appendix A for more information about how income and deductions fit together in computing taxable income and AGI.]

Congratulations if you win the lottery, a sweepstakes, money or prizes on a game show, and the like, but be aware that the money and prizes are taxable.

Answer (b) is incorrect because the measure of income for property received is the fair market value of the property, not the transferor's basis in the property. **Answer (d) is also incorrect** but does introduce another commonly misunderstood provision of IRC § 74. IRC § 74(c) provides for another possible exclusion to the recipient of certain awards. There is a separate exclusion from gross income but it is limited to certain "low value" property awards for employee achievement such as for length of employment, safety record, retirement, and the like. Staci's laptop from Westlaw does not fit within this category. **Answer (e) is also incorrect** because Staci's prize does not meet the requirements for an excludable qualified scholarship pursuant to IRC § 117. Please see other questions in the book addressing qualified scholarships for more information.

7. **Answer (a) is correct.** With Wendy's death, Hank has suffered a terrible loss. He will, however, financially benefit as the beneficiary of the life insurance policy on Wendy's life. The $6,000 that Hank receives from the insurance company is income to him, as it does not represent receipt of the actual insurance proceeds. Rather, the money received represents interest on the proceeds left on deposit with the insurance company.

    While accessions to wealth arise when one receives life insurance benefits, the statute confers favorable tax treatment for much of the benefits associated with life insurance. IRC § 101(a) declares the general rule that life insurance proceeds received by reason of the insured's death are excluded from gross income of the beneficiary. Had Hank simply received the $100,000 from the insurance company, it would have been fully excluded from income. In this question, however, Hank leaves the funds on deposit with the insurance company, earning interest thereon. The exclusion of life insurance proceeds pursuant to IRC § 101 extends only to the life insurance proceeds and <u>not</u> to any earnings therefrom. The $6,000 Hank expects to receive will be fully included in his gross income.

IRC § 101(c) specifically addresses our situation and confirms the interest to be taxable. This provision does make sense. This is not different, in principle, to Hank depositing $100,000 in a bank account and earning interest thereon. Clearly, the interest in such a situation is includible in gross income. Similarly, when a donee receives a true gift of money and subsequently invests it, the gift itself may be excluded from income (IRC § 102; see questions elsewhere in this book) the monies earned from its subsequent investment is not excluded.

Answers (b) and (c) are incorrect because the inclusion of interest earned on life insurance proceeds has no correlation to one's life expectancy or the planned duration of the investment. See other questions in this book that involve an "annuity type payout" of life insurance benefits. **Answer (d) is incorrect** for the reasons discussed above. There is no exclusion "magic" merely because this interest comes from a life insurance company.

8. **The best answer is (d).** IRC § 61 defines gross income as "all income from whatever source derived." From your initial study of gross income's scope, you probably found it to be broadly defined, including the taxpayer's receipt of some net economic benefit or net accession to wealth. In class, you also discover that gross income is also not limited to the receipt of cash. [Reg. § 1.61-1(d) (compensation received in forms other than in cash).] Brian receives an economic benefit each day when he eats lunch at the company dining facility. He is receiving "something" (a fine meal) for less than its true value and he is receiving this benefit by reason of his employment. Barring a specific exclusion provision, the benefit he is receiving (the fair value of the meals on the "outside" less what he is paying for them) represents income to him.

Fortunately for Brian, he might be entitled to relief. A host of employee fringe benefits are excluded pursuant to IRC § 132, and the benefit Brian is receiving in this problem invokes the "de minimis" fringe benefit. [IRC §§ 132(a)(4) and 132(e).] More specifically, there is a special provision within the *de minimis* fringe material in the statute that addresses "certain eating facilities." [IRC § 132(e)(2).] The statute addresses situations exactly like the one presented in our facts. Where an employer operates an eating facility on (or near) the employer's business premises and the employees pay less than the true fair value of the meals provided, if certain requirements are met, the employees can exclude, as a *de minimis* fringe benefit, the extra value of the meals received.

The primary requirement for this special category of excludable *de minimis fringe* benefits is that the amount the employees do pay for the meals at least covers the employer's "direct operating costs of such facility." [IRC § 132(e)(2)(B).] The regulations define these costs to be the employer's cost of food (which is likely at wholesale prices) and other direct costs of operating the facility such as the cost of labor (cooks, waiters, etc.). [Reg. § 1.132-7(b).] The statute also requires that the employer not discriminate in favor of "highly compensated employees" as to the availability among employees to such eating facility. [IRC § 132(e)(2).]

Brian's employer makes this dining facility available to all employees and assuming that the price the employees pay for their meals at least equals the employer's "direct operating costs" for the facility, the benefit Brian receives is excludable from gross income.

Law students might be familiar with this type of eating facility when working for some of the larger law firms. Some such firms have an "attorneys' dining room" where otherwise expensive meals are available at a very reasonable cost to the employee. Most likely, the benefit received by employees (from the discounted meals) is excludable from gross income under these same provisions. It should be noted that an employer can discriminate and provide access to only certain employees (such as "attorneys") as long as it does not result in "per se" discrimination in favor of "highly compensated employees" (e.g., a "partners only" dining room, more than just a physical separation from other attorneys, would probably not qualify). [See Reg. § 1.132-8(d)(2).]

While not the subject of this question, one may ask to what extent is an employer entitled to deduct the costs of meals provided to employees who are within this excludable fringe benefit? With the enactment of the *Tax Cuts and Jobs Act* (TCJA) in December 2017 (generally effective beginning in 2018), the law for employer deductibility changed. Prior to 2018, an employer could deduct, as a business expense, 100% of the cost of such meals irrespective of any exclusion in employees' gross income. Beginning in 2018, pursuant to the TCJA, employers, generally, can only deduct 50% of such costs. [IRC § 274(n)(1)]. Also pursuant to the TCJA, no deduction is allowed for any such meals beginning in 2025. [IRC § 274(o)] While the TCJA does not impact the excludability of this benefit for employees (i.e., the above analysis of this question's answer), the TCJA's deduction limitations for employers may have a dampening effect vis-à-vis an employer's willingness to continue offering this employee fringe benefit.

Answer (a) is incorrect because it fails to reflect the statutory requirement that the employees cover at least the direct operating costs of the eating facility. **Answer (b) is not the best answer** because the benefit that Brian receives might be excluded as a *de minimis* fringe benefit as discussed above. **Answer (c) is also not correct.** This special category of the *de minimis* fringe benefit contains no requirement that the employer deems it necessary to have the employees remain on the business premises. If such is the case, then another employee related exclusion provision, IRC § 119, might be applicable. However, this answer is not correct because this latter provision in IRC § 119 is not the only reason why Brian might be able to exclude the benefit he is receiving.

9. **The correct answer is (b).** IRC § 61 defines gross income as "all income from whatever source derived." From your initial study of gross income's scope, you probably found it to be broadly defined, including a taxpayer's net accession to wealth or receipt of an economic benefit. Modernly, no distinction is made, for gross income purposes, whether the wealth is derived from legal or illegal activities. Malcolm must include, in gross income, amounts he earns from all three of the sources indicated.

    Answers (a), (c) and (d) are incorrect because each answer fails to include in Malcolm's gross income amounts earned from all of the sources indicated.

10. **Answer (e) is correct.** Social Security benefits historically were fully excluded from gross income under the auspices of that all legislatively provided social benefit programs for the promotion of the general welfare were not taxable. This changed in 1983 with the enactment of IRC § 86. This section, as modified over the years, makes Social Security benefits includible in gross income depending on the taxpayer's level of other types of income. If certain threshold limits are reached, then up to 85% of the Social Security benefits received will be included in the taxpayer's gross income.

    It should be noted that the depth of coverage given to IRC § 86 in the basic federal income tax course might vary considerably. This question covers only the basic concept of the taxability of Social Security benefits.

    Answers (a) and (b) are incorrect because Social Security benefits are <u>not</u> taxed at <u>rates</u> up to 50% or 80% but, rather, these represent the portion of one's Social Security benefits that may be included in gross income depending on the level of the taxpayer's other income. **Answer (c) is incorrect** because the stated answer is opposite to that what has transpired over the years with respect to the income tax laws relating to the inclusion of Social Security benefits in gross income. **Answer (d) is also incorrect.** While the historical perspective is generally correct, benefits are <u>not fully includible</u> in gross income. At most, 85% of Social Security benefits will be includible in a taxpayer's gross income.

11. **The best answer is (b).** United States Savings Bonds (Series EE) are issued in various "face amount" denominations (e.g. a $50 U.S. Savings Bond), but are purchased at a fraction of this face amount (usually at one-half of the

face amount). These bonds *do* pay interest, but not in the normal form of a stated interest rate on money invested (as with a savings account at a bank). Rather, the interest accrues on the original discounted purchase price. Traditionally, and much to the disappointment of many a young person who received a U.S. Savings Bond from his or her grandmother, the bond could not be "cashed in" right away, receiving the full face amount. One must wait many years until the bond "matures" to receive its face value. These years until the bond's maturity is the period when the interest accrues on the bond, bringing its value up from the original discounted purchase price to the face amount. This difference, therefore, represents interest, and it is taxable interest for U.S. income tax purposes.

Unless an individual affirmatively elects to report, as interest, the annual increases in such a bond's value, the recognition of interest is deferred until the bond matures (or is redeemed or otherwise disposed of sooner). [IRC § 454(a).] This deferred interest is all of the interest earned on the bond, which is measured by the difference between its face amount and its original discounted purchase price.

The use of the word "traditionally" earlier in this answer reflects a real-life change to how, and in what form, U.S. Savings Bonds are issued/sold. Beginning in 1935, pursuant to legislation signed into law by then President Franklin D Roosevelt, U.S. Savings Bonds (then only in $25 face/matured denominations) were issued/sold in paper form. Up through 2011, U.S. Savings Bonds could generally be purchased in paper form at most financial institutions (in varying denominations). The United States Treasury discontinued issuing the paper form of such bonds in 2012. Currently, U.S. Savings Bonds can still be purchased but must be done so online and in electronic form.

Answer (a) is incorrect. Interest from obligations of the United States is generally fully includible in gross income. This is sometimes the source of confusion among students. While not the subject of this book, interest from U.S. obligations is generally excluded from income for state and local income tax purposes (for those states, counties or cities imposing an income tax). Also not at issue in this problem is IRC § 135 that provides for a very limited and narrow exclusion of certain interest received by certain individuals from Series EE United States Savings Bonds, the proceeds of which are used for certain education purposes. **Answer (c) is also incorrect.** Taxpayers can affirmatively elect to recognize interest annually from U.S. Savings Bonds (Series EE), but the default recognition is at the bond's maturity. This answer switches the default and elective recognition of such interest. **Answer (d) is incorrect** because the annual recognition of such interest is an election, not a requirement. In addition, this answer does not reflect the default recognition of such interest at the bond's maturity.

12. **Answer (c) is correct.** When "bequest/devise, etc." appear in the facts, the inclination is to look at IRC § 102, the section that excludes from income amounts received by gift, bequest, devise, and inheritance. However, the fact that property or money comes from a decedent by way of a will (or intestate succession or through some other death-related means) does not assure the application of IRC § 102 or exclusion status. If, as it appears to be the case here, the devise is in satisfaction of some contractual agreement between the decedent and the beneficiary, then we do not view the transfer as an excludable devise pursuant to IRC § 102 but, rather, a fulfillment of the contract between the parties.

In this case, Nathan is not, for tax purposes, receiving a bequest/devise but, rather, is being repaid the money previously loaned to Deidre. While this is not an excludable devise, the repayment of a loan does <u>not</u> give rise to income to Nathan. Income, while broadly defined, does not include the repayment of monies loaned (we are ignoring any interest in this problem). Just as the debtor has no income when money is borrowed (there is no net accession to wealth to the debtor), there is no income to the creditor when the money is repaid (there is no net accession to wealth to the creditor). It is for this reason that Nathan has no income in this question.

Contrast the situation in our problem with one that would result in the recognition of income from a "bequest/devise." As an example, say that rather than Nathan loaning money to Deidre, he performed services for her that were worth $10,000 and that she promised to pay him for them and did prior to her death. This would, of course, result in compensation income to Nathan. An alternative situation that the promised $10,000 payment for Nathan's services came through Deidre's will as a devise would not change the character of the income to Nathan. In other words, there is no magical exclusion merely because property or cash is received from a decedent.

Answer (a) is incorrect. While Nathan has no gross income in this question, it is <u>not</u> because the $10,000 is an excludable devise pursuant to IRC § 102. **Answer (b) is also incorrect.** Although it does recognize that Nathan's receipt of the $10,000 is not excludable as a devise, this answer fails to correctly characterize the receipt of the money as a non-taxable event, the repayment of a loan. **Answer (d) is incorrect** because, as indicated above, Nathan has no net accession to wealth as a result of being repaid the money loaned to Deidre.

13. **The best answer is (c).** The possible exclusion of the value of the lodging provided to Sandra and David is under the auspices of IRC § 119, exclusion

of meals and lodging provided for the convenience of the employer. If there is a valid reason as to why it is important or necessary for the couple to be "on call" at the facility during off-hours, the value of their free lodging should be excluded from their income.

From your initial study of gross income's scope, you probably found it to be broadly defined, including the taxpayer's receipt of some net economic benefit or net accession to wealth. In class, you also discover that gross income is also not limited to the receipt of cash. [Reg. § 1.61-1(d) (compensation received in forms other than in cash).] Sandra and David are receiving an economic benefit as a result of the lodging provided, free of charge, by their employer, and the value of this benefit should be includible in their gross income. The fact that the couple owns 100% of their employer corporation does not, in and of itself, change this, as the corporation's separate identity must be respected for income tax purposes. [See *Dean v. Comm'r*, 187 F.2d 1019 (3rd Cir.1951).]

IRC § 119 provides that meals and lodging provided to an employee are excludable from the employee's income *if* they are provided for the *convenience of the employer*. In addition to being for the convenience of the employer, qualified lodging must be on the business premises of the employer <u>and</u> be a condition of the taxpayer's employment. [IRC § 119(a)(2).]

The determination of whether providing such a lodging benefit is for the convenience of the employer, one must look for substantial non-compensation factors or reasons. The most common situations in which IRC § 119 exclusions arise are those where it is necessary to have an employee on duty or on-call to handle business matters that might arise at any time, day or night. A typical example is that of an on-site manager of an apartment complex who may be required to handle tenant matters during off-hours (typically during overnight periods). Assuming it is important or commonplace for a sewage treatment plant to have an on-site manager at all times to handle situations that might arise, the couple's residency at the plant would appear to be for the convenience of the employer.

The bungalow is located on the business premises of The Corporation's sewage treatment facility (albeit as far away as possible from the open sewage pits as possible). The fact that The Corporation leases the underlying property does not undermine the application of IRC § 119 because this is still considered the employer's premises (The Corporation's leasehold interest is sufficient for this purpose).

With respect to the requirement that the couple lives on the premises as a condition of their employment, the fact that Sandra (as The Corporation's president) basically made this requirement of herself (and David) has a certain, excuse the pun, strange "odor" to it. When this "requirement" is made in situations where the employee is also the sole or majority shareholder, or in intra-family situations, the validity of the "requirement" is naturally suspect. A "requirement" solely for the purpose of meeting the "form" of the statutory requirement would clearly be a sham and would be ignored for these purposes. However, the relationship between the employer and employee does not preclude meeting a valid "requirement for employment" from existing. If the true nature of the required on-site lodging is legitimate, than the fact that a related party (or the same person) acting on behalf of the employer made this a requirement of employment, is legitimate. As long as there is a legitimate important business reason that Sandra (and/or David) resides at the facility, then their lodging should be excludable from their gross income.

Answer (a) is incorrect because, as indicated above, the fact that Sandra, acting as President of The Corporation, required herself and David to live at the facility will not, in and of itself, preclude the exclusion of lodging under IRC § 119. **Answer (b) is incorrect** because The Corporation is a separate and distinct person from Sandra and David, the individuals, notwithstanding their 100% ownership of The Corporation. The employees Sandra and David *did* receive a financial benefit from their employer and its value is includible in their gross income barring any exclusion. **Answer (d) is incorrect** because the fact that The Corporation has a leasehold interest in the land is sufficient to deem it to be The Corporation's business premises.

14. **The best answer is (b).** This question raises one of the classic doctrines in income tax law; "assignment of income." The "assignment of income" doctrine is, arguably, best known from the case *Lucas v. Earl.* [281 U.S. 111, 50 S.Ct. 241 (1930).] Income is income (for tax purposes) to the taxpayer who earns it. One cannot transfer the tax obligation to another person merely by "assigning" the income to such person. One cannot say, "I earned the income, but do not give it to me, give it to my son instead" (who happens to be in a much lower income tax bracket) and have it work that way for income tax purposes. As far as the contract regarding Hannah's salary, she cannot merely assign this income to her daughter, Denise. Hannah earned the income and she must include all of it in her gross income.

The fees received from her work with the school's outreach program present more of a problem. On the surface, there is little distinction from the situation regarding her salary payable to her daughter. Hannah earned this income and ostensibly, she cannot just assign it to another person. This is not to be confused with a concept of "disclaiming" (waiving, rejecting, etc.) income before it is earned. Such disclaimers may prevent recognition of income as long as they are made before the income is earned and there is no assignment of the disclaimed income (i.e., directing that it go to someone else). Relief for Hannah is found in I.R.S revenue rulings. In a factually similar situation, the I.R.S., while applying assignment of income rules and finding no escape, has held that, "the Internal Revenue Service has recognized that amounts that would otherwise be deemed income are not, in certain unique factual situations, subject to the broad rule of inclusion provided by section 61(a) of the Code." [Rev.Rul. 74-581, 1974-2 C.B. 25.] This revenue ruling held that a law professor receiving statutory fees for representing clients in the school's clinical program was not required to include them in gross income when their employment contract required that these amounts be remitted to the school. Similarly, Revenue Ruling 69-274 (1969-1 C.B. 36) held, in facts almost identical to ours, that the fees remitted to the employer as required by the employment contract were excludable from income. Therefore, it is very likely that Hannah will not have to include, in gross income, the fees that she receives and remits to the university pursuant to her employment contract.

Answer (a) is incorrect because, as discussed above, Hannah will most likely be able to exclude from income the outside fees received and remitted to her employer. **Answer (c) is incorrect** because even if the assignment is "anticipatory" (made before Hannah earned the income) such assignments are still ineffective for income tax purposes. Her assignment is not an unconditional waiver or disclaimer of her future earnings. **Answer (d) is also incorrect.** But for the Revenue Rulings discussed above, this would be a good answer.

15. **Answer (b) is correct.** We will conclude below that none of Tad's debt was discharged or forgiven and, therefore, Tad realizes no income.

Forgiving a debt, in whole or in part, generally results in the realization of gross income to the debtor. It makes sense that being relieved of a liability (a financial obligation) results in a net accession to wealth (i.e., income) to the debtor. This type of income is referred to as "income from discharge of indebtedness" and is specifically identified by the Code as constituting gross income. [IRC § 61(a)(12).] However, to realize income from discharge of indebtedness, one must first have a cognizable or liquidated "debt" that has been discharged or forgiven. In our question, what was the amount of debt Tad owed to Carl? Carl would assert that it was $15,000, yet Tad would assert that it was only $10,000. In our question the actual amount owed is in dispute. When there is a legitimate (good faith) disagreement as to what the actual amount of debt is, an agreement or settlement as to the debt amount is <u>not</u> considered a discharge or forgiveness of debt. It bears repeating that to have a discharge or forgiveness of debt (giving rise to income) one must first have a "debt" which is subsequently discharged/forgiven in whole or in part. This is what is sometimes referred to as the "contested or disputed liability doctrine." [See *Zarin v. Comm'r,* 916 F.2d 110 (3rd Cir.1990).]

In this problem, the liability was in dispute and the settled amount of $12,000 represents the cognizable or liquidated debt. Carl's compromise from $15,000 down to $12,000 does <u>not</u> represent income from discharge of indebtedness. Rather, pursuant to the contested/disputed liability doctrine, it is the process to determine the actual uncontested amount of the debt owed. Tad then fully pays the liquidated debt of $12,000. There is, therefore, no income to Tad from discharge of any debt. Although not the case in our question, if after the parties had settled on $12,000 as the amount owed and subsequently some or all of this amount was forgiven, then income from discharge of indebtedness would have resulted.

A word of caution about language used on exams. There are many instances where the common use of a term does not necessarily correspond to its official "tax" counterpart. Labels can be deceiving and do not be fooled by their use in lay terms on an exam. Problems involving what may appear to be income from discharge of indebtedness are fertile ground for tricky questions vis-à-vis terminology. The next to the last sentence in this question could have read, "Tad then paid Carl $12,000, *fully discharging the debt.*" Our answer to this question would have remained unchanged. The lay use of the word "discharge" (to fully pay off a debt) would not correspond to the official "tax" counterpart where "discharge" of debt represents a forgiveness of debt.

Answers (a) and (c) are incorrect because as indicated above, there is no income from discharge of indebtedness resulting from a settlement of a contested liability. While not relevant for this question, answer (a) does bring up an important concept. Had there been, in this case, income realized from discharge of indebtedness, it is always important to ask if such realized income is recognized? There are provisions that may exclude this from gross income. For example, income from forgiven debt may be excluded from income pursuant to IRC § 102, if it can be shown that the forgiveness was gratuitous. Another example of a possible exclusion lies in IRC § 108, applying to insolvent or bankrupt debtors. **Answer (d) is incorrect** because while Tad does not have income from discharge of indebtedness in our question, he does not have income from any services performed. <u>Carl</u> has income from services performed, but this is not germane to the question.

16. **Answer (c) is correct.** This question involves the exclusion of "compensation for injuries or sickness" provided in IRC § 104. This section has

a long, complex and capricious past vis-à-vis what is within its umbrella of this exclusion. In its most basic form, an individual receiving damages, by award or settlement, for physical injuries or physical sickness can exclude such amounts from income. [IRC § 104(a)(2).] In its current form (reflecting changes made by the "Small Business Job Protection Act of 1996"), this section generally excludes amounts received (other than punitive damages) for <u>physical tort</u> awards and settlements. The entire amount of Todd's award, in this question, originates from his physical injury arising from the negligence cause of action and, therefore, is excluded from gross income.

The difficulty of questions involving IRC § 104 can vary dramatically depending on how thoroughly one's professor covers the exclusion as to its history, policy foundations, and the like. This is a good area of tax law for in-depth class analysis, so take this into consideration when addressing questions involving the subject. Much of this Code section's history centered on the breadth of this exclusion with, at varying times, exclusions allowed for damages received from nonphysical tort or "tort type" causes of action, and punitive damages.

The problem students usually have with this question is the reluctance to exclude the portions of Todd's award identified as replacement for "lost wages" and "emotional distress." As for the replacement of lost wages, one might logically argue (as did the I.R.S. for many years) that they should not be within the scope of IRC § 104's exclusion because wages, had he not been injured, would have been taxable. Historically, this was the subject of much tax litigation. However, the answer is now clear that these amounts do not represent taxable wages even if the award amount is measured by the amount of wages that could have been earned but for the injuries. [Rev.Rul. 85-97, 1985-2 C.B. 50.]

Regarding the "emotional distress" component of the award, there is often confusion because of the language in the body of IRC § 104(a) that states, "emotional distress shall not be treated as a physical injury or physical sickness." Remembering that "physical" injury/sickness is required for exclusion, it might appear that the portion of Todd's award identified for emotional distress is not excludable. However, because Todd's cause of action was the physical injury, and the emotional distress emanated therefrom, the amount is within the scope of the exclusion.

Answers (a), (b), and (d) are incorrect because they all, to some degree, do not represent the full scope of the IRC § 104(a)(2) exclusion as it applies to this question. Please see the discussion for the correct answer (c), immediately above, for more information. **Answer (e) is incorrect** because there is a correct answer in response (c).

It should be noted that this question, and others in this book that specifically identify component parts of a personal injury award, are a bit removed from "real world" circumstances. Lawyers specializing in the practice of personal injury law will acknowledge that many, if not most, personal injury awards and settlements do not separate damage awards/settlements with such specificity. Correct application of income tax rules is further frustrated by the additional "real world" fact that the underlying cause of action, or basis on which a tort related lawsuit damages are awarded, is not always clear or separable from other causes of action.

17. **The correct answer is (b).** Annuities contracts come in many different varieties and the tax ramifications associated with payments thereunder can be complex. This question, however, is designed to address the basic or standard type of annuity contract (and the corresponding tax rules). The income tax ramifications of payments received pursuant to an annuity contract are contained in IRC § 72. One look at this section, that is well over a dozen pages long, gives some hint to the possible complexity of the subject. Be aware that your professor may cover the material in much greater depth than is addressed in this basic question.

The most basic example of an annuity contract is that you give money to someone (typically a life insurance company) and they promise to pay you a specific amount of money at set intervals for as long as you live. Without knowing anything more about the tax rules of annuity payments, logic tells us that you *should not* be taxed on the amount that you get back from them that is equal to the amount you gave them (i.e., you are merely getting your money back). Any "extra" amount you receive must be coming from earnings on your money (similar to interest on money deposited in a bank) and that *should* be taxable (represents gross income). Basically, this is how the most basic annuity taxation rules of IRC § 72 work.

The only real question is one of "timing." When does the *taxable portion* start? Do you get to first recoup the amount contributed, and only have gross income once you have received all of your contributed money back? The answer is no. IRC § 72 requires that an "exclusion ratio" be established based on certain criteria. In essence, a *portion* of each payment received from the annuity contract is excluded (recouping your original contribution) and a portion of each such payment is included in gross income (representing earnings on your money deposited). After applying this ratio to each payment received, once the taxpayer (the "annuitant") receives, in the aggregate, the amount of their original contribution, this prorated exclusion ends, and the full amount of each subsequent payment is included in income.

Again, this is the most basic of income tax rules of what, in reality, are a very complex set of rules associated with annuities.

It should be noted that the rules applicable to annuities are different from "annuity like payments of life insurance benefits" under a life insurance contract (paid by reason of the death of the insured). That issue is addressed in another question in this book.

Answer (a) is incorrect but would be the preferred way for a taxpayer to treat annuity payments. Unfortunately, the statute does not allow this method of nonrecognition. **Answer (c) is incorrect** because annuity payments do not garner such favorable tax treatment under the statute. However, please see at least one other question in this book addressing annuity type payment of life insurance benefits that do receive this favorable tax treatment. **Answer (d) is incorrect** because the statute does not provide for such degree of nonrecognition. The fact that life insurance companies are often involved in annuity contracts should not be confused with exclusions provided to life insurance benefits received by reason of the death of the insured. [See IRC § 101.]

18. **Answer (d) is correct.** There is no doubt that Sheryl received a financial benefit from her short-term rental activities and, barring any specific exclusion provision, the $42,000 would be included in her gross income. Fortunately for Sheryl, there is such an exclusion provision and it proves very beneficial to Sheryl in this case. IRC § 280A(g) provides that a taxpayer renting out his or her home for less than fifteen (15) days during the year, excludes, from gross income, any rent received for such period. The dollar amount of this exclusion is unlimited. To be fair, this section also precludes any rental expense deductions for this period. Basically, if the rental period of one's house is short enough, we pretend, for tax purposes, that is was not rented out at all. A very nice result for Sheryl in our problem.

While not the subject of this question, the tax law is very different for other popular short-term rentals of one's home where, in the aggregate, the rental period exceeds fourteen (14) days in one year (e.g. "Airbnb" situations). Such situations invoke a variety of very complex tax law and your professor's coverage of this may vary dramatically (from only a brief mention of such law to a comprehensive study of the rules).

Answers (a), (b), and (c) are incorrect because none of these answers properly reflects this short-term house rental exclusion from income. **Answer (e) is incorrect** because as long as Sheryl's home is rented for less than fifteen days, there is no statutory limit on the amount of rental income excludable.

19. **The most likely answer is probably, maybe (d), but answer (a) might also be acceptable.** This is a very close call and subject to some debate. In any event, as discussed below, Sid should be able to fully exclude the value of his use of the luxury penthouse suite from his gross income.

IRC § 61 defines gross income as "all income from whatever source derived." From your initial study of gross income's scope, you probably found it to be broadly defined, including the taxpayer's receipt of some net economic benefit or net accession to wealth. In class, you also discover that gross income is also not limited to the receipt of cash. [Reg. § 1.61-1(d) (compensation received in forms other than in cash).] Sid is clearly receiving a substantial economic benefit by being provided with the luxurious free lodging and, absent a specific exclusion provision, the value of this benefit represents income to Sid.

The primary exclusion of the value of Sid's lodging comes by way of IRC § 119. IRC § 119 provides that meals and lodging provided to an employee are excludable from the employee's income *if* they are provided for the *convenience of the employer*. In addition to being for the convenience of the employer, qualified lodging must be on the business premises of the employer <u>and</u> be a condition of the taxpayer's employment. [IRC § 119(a)(2).]

The determination of whether providing such a lodging benefit is for the convenience of the employer, one must look for substantial non-compensation factors or reasons. The most common situations in which IRC § 119 exclusions arise are those where it is necessary to have an employee on duty or on-call to handle business matters that might arise at any time, day or night. A typical example is that of an on-site manager of a hotel or an apartment complex who may be required to handle guest/tenant matters during off-hours (typically during overnight periods). It is quite logical to come to the conclusion that Sid's "on-site" living is for the convenience of his employer. In addition, this "living on the premises" (the hotel) is a requirement for all of Tillie's hotel manager employees.

The problem in our facts is with the type of free lodging being provided to Sid, especially when compared to that provided to all of her other hotel managers. A careful review of the Code and Regulations for IRC § 119 does not reveal any sort of "reasonableness" test. It is for that reason why **answer (a)** might be an acceptable response. However, the totality of the facts (the type of accommodations provided to Sid and that his employer is his mother who would do anything for her son) raises some suspicion. Specifically, the nexus between the "lodging provided for the <u>convenience of the employer</u>" and the degree of the benefit that is provided to Sid, appears to be a bit tenuous. The author would argue that a "reasonableness" standard is inherent in exclusion for lodging provided in IRC § 119. If this is the case, then the value of Tillie's typical hotel manager's lodging would be excluded by IRC § 119, but any excess would not be covered by this exclusion.

Continuing with the theme that not all of the value of Sid's lodging is excluded via IRC § 119, we must venture further to find tax relief for Sid. If you have studied the IRC § 102 exclusion for gifts, bequests and devises, that might be a logical place to look for a potential exclusion for this "extra" benefit that Sid receives. Under the general rule of § 102(a), gifts are excluded from the gross income of the donee/recipient. While no statutory definition of a gift exists, it is generally defined as a transfer without consideration that is made out of emotions of detached and disinterested generosity. [See *Comm'r v. Duberstein*, 363 U.S. 278, 80 S.Ct. 1190 (1960).] This sounds perfect for Sid as the facts clearly imply such that Tillie has such motives with respect to her son, Sid. However, we must address a major hurdle located at IRC § 102(c). This subsection provides, in general, that the possible exclusion from gross income of property acquired by gift, bequest or devise, does <u>not</u> apply to transfers between employers and employees. In other words, "gifts" to employees are not excludable from gross income under IRC § 102. As applied to most employees, this subsection is not merely a presumption. Rather, "gifts" to most employees are not excludable gifts at all.

The author, in the preceding paragraph, states that the IRC § 102(c) denial of excludable gifts applies with respect to "most employees." For discussion purposes and totally divorced from the facts of our question, suppose a parent employs a child. Let's further suppose that the employer (parent) makes no gifts to any employees but on the child's 25th birthday, the parent gives the child a new automobile. In the familial context, we have a parent making a gift to a child most likely out of emotions of detached and disinterested generosity, qualifying it for exclusion from income to the child pursuant to IRC § 102(a). However, we also factually have an employer making a gift to an employee that, pursuant to the language in IRC § 102(c), cannot be considered an excludable gift to the employee. Does this preclude any gifts, in the traditional and excludable sense, when the donor and donee happen to have an employment relationship such as this? Proposed regulations answer this question as follows: "For purposes of section 102(c), *extraordinary* transfers to the natural objects of an employer's bounty will *not be considered transfers to, or for the benefit of, an employee if the employee can show that the transfer was not made in recognition of the employee's employment. Accordingly, section 102(c) shall not apply to amounts transferred between related parties (e.g., father and son) if the purpose of the transfer can be substantially attributed to the familial relationship of the parties and not to the circumstances of their employment.*" [Prop.Reg. § 1.102-

1(f)(2) (emphasis added).] In the hypothetical presented in this paragraph, the parent's gift of the car to the child is, in all likelihood, an example of an excludable gift notwithstanding the employment relationship between the two.

Now back to the facts of the question presented. Sid is the "natural object" of his mother's "bounty" (using the somewhat odd vernacular of the regulations), and it appears that the excess benefit (the luxury penthouse three-bedroom suite) Tillie is providing Sid is extraordinary in nature. We can also logically infer from the facts that Tillie does not provide Sid with these luxurious accommodations in recognition of Sid's employment, or in the context of their employment relationship, but rather, it is attributable to their familial relationship. Based upon this, Sid should be able to exclude as a gift, pursuant to IRC § 102, the "excess" benefit he receives vis-à-vis his luxury accommodations.

Answer (a) is probably not the best answer for reasons mentioned above. Arguably, it could be an acceptable answer but the author, as discussed above, believes that a "reasonable" element in inherent in this IRC § 119 exclusion. **Answer (b) is incorrect.** This answer is a diversion to the statutory fringe benefits excluded pursuant to IRC § 132. As discussed in other questions in this book, many of the fringe benefits excluded pursuant to that Code provision contain a "nondiscrimination" requirement (regarding highly compensated employees) and if breached, the entire value of the benefit received is included in income. Sid's lodging benefit is not one of the IRC § 132 fringe benefits. **Answer (c) is also incorrect.** Assuming the "extra" benefit Sid receives is not excluded pursuant to IRC § 119, it is excludable as a gift under IRC § 102.

20. **The best answer is (a).** IRC § 61 defines gross income as "all income from whatever source derived." From your initial study of gross income's scope, you probably found it to be broadly defined, including the taxpayer's receipt of some net economic benefit or net accession to wealth. In class, you also discover that gross income is also not limited to the receipt of cash. [Reg. § 1.61-1(d) (compensation received in forms other than in cash).] Gil (by way of his spouse) received an economic benefit when Gil's husband was entitled to stay, free of charge, for the two nights in Seattle. It is by reason of Gil's employment that his spouse received this benefit and, absent a specific exclusion provision, the value of this benefit represents income to Gil.

Fortunately for Gil, he is entitled to relief in this case. A host of employee fringe benefits are excluded pursuant to IRC § 132, and the benefit Gil (through his spouse) is receiving in this problem invokes the "no-additional-cost service" fringe benefit. [IRC §§ 132(a)(1) and 132(b).] Perhaps you have worked for an airline and company policy allowed you to fly for free (or at a reduced fair) when empty seats were available. Or, as in our example, you worked for a hotel chain and could stay in any of the chain's hotels for free (or for a reduced charge) when rooms would otherwise remain vacant. If so, did you include, in income, the value of the benefit received? Most likely the answer is <u>no</u>, and the most likely reason is that the benefit you received was an excludable *no-additional-cost service* fringe. Although restrictions and limits may apply, the *no-additional-cost service* fringe enables employers to allow employees to receive free (or discounted) services that the employer provides to the public, without the value of such services being included in the employee's gross income.

There are two major requirements or limitations applicable to this fringe benefit. First, the service that the employee is receiving must be the type of service offered for sale to customers in the line of business in which the employee is working. [IRC § 132(b)(1).] This is the so-called "line of business" test. Ostensibly, this requirement exists to prevent conglomerates from providing across the board free or discounted services to all employees in all lines of the employer's business that are perceived to be unfair when compared to non-conglomerates. Gil's husband (because of Gil's employment) is receiving the free hotel nights (considered a service), and Gil is provided this benefit by working in the same line of business (the lodging industry). The "line of business" requirement is somewhat of a "non-issue" for most "single line" business such as Tillie's

The second major limitation is that the employer cannot incur substantial additional cost in providing such service to the employee. [IRC § 132(b)(2).] If an employer loses or foregoes revenue because of the service provided, this requirement is not met. The benefit provided in this question is free lodging "as long as there are vacancies." This condition placed on the fringe benefit in question assures that it will not be a substantial additional cost to Gil's employer. This situation is sometimes referred to as "excess capacity services." [See Reg. § 1.132-2(a)(2).] The fact that the employer incurs incidental costs, such as room housekeeping service, during an employee's stay, does not render the fringe benefit taxable, as these costs are not "substantial." [See Reg. § 1.132-2(a)(5)(ii).]

Does the fact that Gil's husband is receiving this benefit without Gil's presence impact what appears to be a tax-free *no-additional-cost service* fringe benefit? Fortunately for Gil, his spouse (and, while not in our question, dependent children) are part of an expanded definition of an employee for purposes of the *no-additional-cost service* fringe benefit (as well as the "qualified employee discount," another IRC § 132 fringe benefit). [IRC § 132(h)(2).]

Gil's spouse can be the beneficiaries of this fringe benefit (even without Gil's presence) and it does not jeopardize its otherwise tax-free status.

One last issue is the question of who is a "spouse?" While there was some confusion during transitional periods where same-sex marriages were not legally recognized in all states, the answer is now clear and uniform. A spouse is a spouse is a spouse; for federal income tax purposes, including for this fringe benefit section and all other federal tax provisions referencing or relating to "spouses," the gender of the spouses is irrelevant. Individuals who are legally *married* are "spouses." In real-life, an employer is generally free to extend fringe benefits to whomever they wish and here, Tillie extends the fringe benefit in question to include employees' spouses and Hunter is Gil's spouse.

While not an issue in this problem, it should be mentioned that the statute provides that an employer cannot provide some, but not all, of the fringe benefits enumerated in IRC § 132 to employees on a discriminatory basis (in favor of only highly compensated employees as defined by the statute). The *no-additional-cost service* is one such benefit that cannot be provided to employees in a discriminatory manner. [IRC § 132(j)(1).] This is not an issue in our question as the fringe benefit at issue is offered to all full-time employees and therefore, does not offend these discrimination rules. Limiting this benefit to just "full-time" employees is most likely not discriminatory for purpose of IRC § 132. [Reg. § 1.132-8(d)(2).] It should also be noted that if this fringe benefit were to discriminate in favor of highly compensated employees, the <u>entire</u> value of the free service received would be included in income (and not just any extra benefit that may be provided to such employees). [Reg. § 1.132-8(a)(2).]

It should also be noted that this is a fairly basic question regarding the *no-additional-cost service* fringe benefit. Your professor may cover the material in much greater depth and there are many ancillary issues regarding this and other IRC § 132 fringe benefits.

Answer (b) is incorrect because the *no-additional-cost service* fringe benefit, as well as all fringe benefits enumerated in IRC § 132, do not have as a requirement that the benefit be provided for the convenience of the employer. **Answer (c) is incorrect** because, as discussed above, this fringe benefit can be provided, without tax consequence, to the employee's spouse and there is no requirement that employee Gil accompany this covered individual. While not at issue in this question, this fringe benefit (as well as the "qualified employee discount") can also be provided to an employee's dependent (think, generally, of one's minor children), retired or disabled employees as well as a deceased employee's surviving spouse. [See IRC § 132(h) (and for an employee's "parents" in the case of airline travel as a *no-*

additional-cost service fringe benefit).] **Answer (d) is incorrect** because, as discussed above, a spouse is a spouse is a spouse and the gender of one's spouse is irrelevant. **Answer (e) is incorrect** because, as discussed above, the benefit is provided across the board to all full-time employees on a nondiscriminatory basis.

21. **The best answer is (c).** IRC § 61 defines gross income as "all income from whatever source derived." From your initial study of gross income's scope, you probably found it to be broadly defined, including the taxpayer's receipt of some net economic benefit or net accession to wealth. In class, you also discover that gross income is also not limited to the receipt of cash. [Reg. § 1.61-1(d) (compensation received in forms other than in cash).] Alice (by way of her domestic partner, Dalia) received an economic benefit when Dalia was entitled to stay, free of charge, for the three nights in Beverly Hills. It is by reason of Alice's employment that her domestic partner received this benefit and, absent a specific exclusion provision, the value of this benefit represents income to Alice.

Unfortunately for Alice, she is not entitled to any relief from including this value in her income. To reach this conclusion, however, takes us down a somewhat long path (very similar to that in the discussion of the answer to the immediately preceding question, 20). A host of employee fringe benefits are excluded pursuant to IRC § 132, and the benefit Alice (by way of her domestic partner) is receiving in this problem invokes the "no-additional-cost service" fringe benefit. [IRC §§ 132(a)(1) and 132(b).] Perhaps you have worked for an airline and were able to fly for free (or at a reduced fair) when empty seats were available. Or, as in our example, you worked for a hotel chain and could stay in any of the chain's hotels for free (or for a reduced charge) when rooms were available. If so, did you include, in income, the value of the benefit received? Most likely the answer is <u>no</u>, and the most likely reason is that the benefit you received was an excludable *no-additional-cost service* fringe. Although restrictions and limits may apply, the *no-additional-cost service* fringe enables employers to allow employees receive free (or discounted) services that the employer provides to the public, without the value of such services being included in the employee's gross income.

There are two major requirements or limitations applicable to this fringe benefit. First, the service that the employee is receiving must be the type of service offered for sale to customers in the line of business in which the employee is working. [IRC § 132(b)(1).] This is the so-called "line of business" test. Ostensibly, this requirement exists to prevent conglomerates from providing across the board free or discounted services to all employees in all lines of the employer's business that are perceived to be unfair when compared to non-conglomerates. Alice (by way of her domestic partner) is receiving the free hotel nights (considered a service), and she is provided this benefit by working in the same line of business (the lodging industry). The "line of business" requirement is somewhat of a "non-issue" for most "single line" business such as Tillie's.

The second major limitation is the employer cannot incur substantial additional cost in providing such service to the employee. [IRC § 132(b)(2).] If an employer loses or foregoes revenue because of the service provided, this requirement is not met. The benefit provided in this question is free lodging "as long as there are vacancies." This condition placed on the fringe benefit in question assures that it will not be a substantial additional cost to Alice's employer. This situation is sometimes referred to as "excess capacity services." [See Reg. § 1.132-2(a)(2).] The fact that the employer incurs incidental costs, such as room housekeeping service, during an employee's stay, does not render the fringe benefit taxable, as these costs are not "substantial." [See Reg. § 1.132-2(a)(5)(ii).]

In the answer to question 20, above, we saw that a "spouse" is part of an expanded definition of an employee to whom this, and other fringe benefits, can apply. [IRC § 132(h)(2).] While this expanded definition of an employee is expansive, and we know that it includes spouses, there is no language referring to domestic partners, civil unions, and the like. The determinative question, therefore, is whether a domestic partner (or a partner is a civil union) is considered a "spouse" for federal income tax purposes? As stated in the question, California domestic partners are, for all intents and purposes, equivalent to spouses for California purposes (California statutes effectively incorporate by reference domestic partners to other statutes referring to spouses). Unfortunately for Alice, while her domestic partner Dalia may have the same rights, benefits, duties, obligations, etc. as a spouse for California law, federal income tax law does conform, and they are not considered "spouses" for federal income tax purposes. This not only has application to this fringe benefit section, but throughout the Internal Revenue Code, any reference to a spouse does not include individuals in a valid domestic partnership or civil union, notwithstanding the degree to which state law may deem them to be equivalent to a spouse.

Here, because Dalia is not Alice's spouse, there is no applicable provision excluding the value of Alice's benefit (derived through her domestic partner, Dalia). It is great that Alice's employer in inclusive of domestic partners in offering this fringe benefit but, unfortunately, Alice is not entitled to the accompanying tax benefits which would be available for herself, a spouse and others (dependent children, retired employees, etc.).

It should also be noted that this is a fairly basic question regarding the *no-additional-cost service* fringe benefit. Your professor may cover the material in much greater depth and there are many ancillary issues regarding this and other IRC § 132 fringe benefits.

Answer (a) is incorrect because, as discussed above, Dalia is not Alice's spouse, and this precludes any exclusion as a *no-additional-cost service* fringe benefit. **Answer (b) is not the best answer.** While inclusion of the value of this benefit in Alice's income is correct, the "convenience of the employer" is not relevant. **Answer (d) is not be best answer** because inclusion of the value of this benefit is Alice's income is not related to the availability of the fringe benefit on a nondiscriminatory basis.

22. **The best answer is (c).** IRC § 61 defines gross income as "all income from whatever source derived." From your initial study of gross income's scope, you probably found it to be broadly defined, including the taxpayer's receipt of some net economic benefit or net accession to wealth. In class, you also discover that gross income is also not limited to the receipt of cash. [Reg. § 1.61-1(d) (compensation received in forms other than in cash).] Elise, the employee in question, derived an economic benefit with her four-night free stay at Tillie's fully booked New York hotel.

    Once again, we turn to the fringe benefits of IRC § 132 in search of relief for this employee. At first glance, one might go to the *no-additional-cost service* fringe benefit discussed in questions 20 and 21, above. In this case, however, the employer <u>did</u> incur substantial additional cost, in the form of lost revenue, by allowing the employee to "bump" a paying customer. [See Reg. § 1.132-2(a)(1)(ii) (foregone revenue is a substantial additional cost).]

    Next, we might consider the "de minimis" fringe benefit in IRC §§ 132(a)(4) and 132(e). A *de minimis* fringe "means any property or service the value of which is (after taking into account the frequency with which similar fringes are provided by the employer to the employer's employees) so small as to make accounting for it unreasonable or administratively impracticable." [IRC § 132(e)(1).] Looking at examples of *de minimis* fringe benefits in the regulations, a four-night free stay at a luxury hotel hardly seems to qualify (this is not the proverbial doughnuts and coffee at the office). The regulations, in examples of what sort of benefits do <u>not</u> constitute *de minimis* fringes include "use of employer-owned facilities (such as an apartment, hunting lodge, boat, etc.) for a weekend." [Reg. § 1.132-6(e)(2).]

    Elise still has hope for some relief and looking back to the regulations addressing the *no-additional-cost service* fringe, we are given some guidance. In discussing excess capacity as a potential indication of no cost incurred by an employer, the regulations state: "Employees who receive non-excess capacity services may, however, be eligible for a qualified employee discount

of up to 20 percent of the value of the service provided. See § 1.132-3."
[Reg. § 132-2(a)(2).] So off we go to the *qualified employee discount* fringe
benefit.

It is here that we find at least *some* relief for Elise. The *qualified employee discount*
fringe benefit can be found in IRC §§ 132(a)(2) and 132(c). While students
usually encounter this fringe benefit at some former job working in retail
and being entitled to a 15%, 20%, etc. employee discount on merchandise
purchased from the store. Although restrictions and limits may apply, the
qualified employee discount allows employers to allow employees to buy their
products or services at a discount, without that discount being included in
the employee's gross income. Elise's situation is a bit unusual as we are
examining the *qualified employee discount* in relation to the 100% discount that
she received. Nonetheless, it is a discount, and we can apply the *qualified
employee discount* rules to it.

There are two major requirements or limitations applicable to this *qualified
employee discount* fringe benefit. First, the discount the employee is receiving
must be with respect to products or services that are in the line of business
in which the employee is working. [IRC § 132(c)(4).] This is the so-called
"line of business" test. Ostensibly, this requirement exists to prevent
conglomerates from providing across the board discounts to all employees
in all lines of the employer's business that are perceived to be unfair when
compared to non-conglomerates. We have, in questions 20 and 21, above,
already addressed this requirement with respect to Tillie's employees, and
Elise passes this test.

The second major limitation is the amount of the discount available.
Basically, the *qualified employee discount* will be viewed as a tax-free fringe
benefit as long as "it doesn't cost the employer too much money" in
providing the benefit. The statutory maximum tax-free discount applicable
to employer provided "services" is 20%. [IRC 132(c)(1)(B).] In the case of
discounts for products (tangible personal property), the statute does not set
a specific discount percentage amount but, rather, states that the discount
cannot exceed the employer's "gross profit percentage." [IRC §
132(c)(1)(A).] The computation of a company's "gross profit percentage" is
defined in IRC § 132(c)(2) and can be a bit cumbersome to compute.
Fortunately, it should be fairly clear that Elise's free hotel stay is classified
as the receipt of a service, and, therefore, the statutory 20% maximum
discount applies. The repercussion to Elise is that she has received a
discount well in excess of the statutory allowed maximum (recall, she
received a 100% discount). The result is that Elise can exclude the statutory
maximum 20% discount applicable to services. In other words, Elise can
exclude, from income, 20% of the value of her four-night New York hotel

stay. She must include in income, however, 80% (the excess discount) of the value of her lodging.

Note that the fact that one fails to qualify for a particular tax-free fringe benefit (such as the *no-additional-cost service* fringe in Elise's case), does not preclude the application of another fringe benefit exclusion provision.

While not an issue in this problem, it should be mentioned that the statute provides that an employer cannot provide some, but not all, of the fringe benefits enumerated in IRC § 132 to employees on a discriminatory basis (in favor of only highly compensated employees as defined by the statute). The *qualified employee discount* is one such benefit that cannot be provided to employees in a discriminatory manner. [IRC § 132(j)(1).] This is not an issue in our question as the fringe benefit at issue is offered to all full-time employees and therefore, does not offend these discrimination rules. Limiting this benefit to just "full-time" employees is most likely not discriminatory for purpose of IRC § 132. [Reg. § 1.132-8(d)(2).] It should also be noted that if this fringe benefit were to discriminate in favor of highly compensated employees, the <u>entire</u> value of the free service received would be included in income (and not just any extra benefit that may be provided to such employees). [Reg. § 1.132-8(a)(2).]

23. **The best answer is (c).** Brandon will not have to recognize as income, any of the debt that was forgiven because of the degree of his insolvency.

This is a fairly difficult question and involves multiple steps to arrive at the correct answer. The two major questions that need to be answered are: 1) does Brandon, on a prima facie basis, have "income from discharge of indebtedness?" and 2) if so, is this income recognized or is there a statutory non-recognition (or exclusion) provision that is applicable?

Forgiving a debt, in whole or in part, generally results in the realization of gross income to the debtor. It makes sense that being relieved of a liability (a financial obligation) results in an economic benefit or net accession to wealth (i.e., income) to the debtor. This type of income is referred to as "income from discharge of indebtedness" and is specifically identified by the Code as constituting gross income. [IRC § 61(a)(12).] Brandon owed $50,000 to a sub-contractor, $25,000 of which was forgiven. So far, Brandon appears to have $25,000 in income from discharge of indebtedness. This $25,000 will be recognized in Brandon's gross income unless there is some specific Code provision allowing for its exclusion. In general, on any question (multiple choice or essay) where it appears that there is income to be recognized, do not just stop at that point. Go on to make sure that no exclusion or non-recognition provisions apply to the situation presented in the question.

In the area of "income from discharge of indebtedness," there are two major exclusion/non-recognition provisions to think about. The exclusion from gross income to the recipients of gifts (resulting from detached and disinterested generosity) under IRC § 102, and the potential exclusion of income from discharge of indebtedness for taxpayers in dire financial straits pursuant to IRC § 108. The former occurs where the facts give some indication that the debt was gratuitously forgiven, typically where there is a familial or close relationship between the debtor and creditor. There is no indication from our facts that the sub-contractor gratuitously forgave the $25,000. Exclusion as a gift, therefore, is not relevant. The latter exclusion, under IRC § 108, applying to certain debtors in poor financial straits, looks promising for Brandon.

IRC § 108(a)(1) provides, in part, that some or all of otherwise includible income from discharge of indebtedness is <u>excludable</u> from income for "insolvent debtors" or where the debt is discharged in a bankruptcy proceeding. For debts discharged or forgiven in a bankruptcy proceeding, there is full exclusion from gross income for the amount discharged. When the debt is not discharged in formal bankruptcy proceedings, the otherwise includible income from the forgiven debt may, nonetheless, be excluded from income (in whole or in part) if the debtor was "insolvent" at the time of the forgiveness. Insolvency is defined, in IRC § 108(d)(3), as an individual who, immediately before the debt in question is discharged, has total liabilities in excess of the total value of his or her assets. Unfortunately, many people fit this definition of insolvency including law students with huge student loan debt and little in the way of assets. Brandon's $25,000 of forgiven debt was not discharged in bankruptcy. However, his $350,000 of liabilities before the discharge exceeds his total assets valued at $320,000 and, therefore, Brandon was insolvent. For insolvent debtors, the exclusion from gross income may be limited, as the excluded amount cannot exceed the amount by which the debtor was insolvent immediately before the discharge. Any amount forgiven that exceeds the debtor's degree of insolvency is included in gross income. Brandon was insolvent to the tune of $30,000 ($350,000 of debt less the $320,000 <u>value</u> of his assets) and the debt forgiven was less, at $25,000. Therefore, Brandon has no income recognition as a result of the debt discharged.

Answer (a) is incorrect because the cited provision is not applicable to our facts. IRC § 108 is a very complex section and contains many special provisions. Depending on the depth in which your professor covers these provisions, you may or may not encounter the cited provision at § 108(e)(5). Basically, that section provides exclusion relief for "solvent" debtors in certain "purchase-money" debt situations. **Answer (b) is incorrect** because it reflects an improper determination of Brandon's insolvency. To determine insolvency, the total <u>value</u> of assets is used, not their adjusted basis. This answer incorrectly used Brandon's adjusted basis in his assets to determine insolvency. **Answer (d) is incorrect** because measurement of income and possible exclusion thereof from discharge of debts is determined at the time the debt is discharged, not at the end of the tax year.

24. **The answer to this <u>very</u> complex question is (e).** Students universally dislike "none of the above" answers and are justified in doing so. They do provide, however, a powerful testing tool for professors and, in this case, none of the answers provided in (a) through (d) are correct. The "bottom line" correct numeric answer for this question is that the net operating loss (NOL) carryover will be eliminated, and the basis of his assets will be reduced by <u>$15,000</u>. This question is a somewhat unfair extension of the immediately preceding question 23. It requires delving deeper into the quagmire of the IRC § 108 provisions excluding otherwise includible income resulting from discharge of indebtedness. This professor, over the past few years, has not covered IRC § 108 in sufficient depth to answer this question. Your professor, however, may cover this section more thoroughly and, if such is the case, this question is pertinent. This question is also a bit unfair in that it requires, in part, a correct analysis of the previous question. This professor would not ask such a series of interrelated multiple-choice questions on an exam. Rather, this series of questions was derived from an exam essay question.

With the introduction out of the way, we know, from the previous question, that Brandon's $25,000 discharge of indebtedness is properly excludable form gross income because he was "insolvent" by more than the amount of the debt forgiven. The issue, and the one addressed in this question, is whether Brandon has to pay some later "price" for the exclusion. No, Brandon does not have to recognize the previously excluded income should, for example, he become solvent down the road. However, Brandon may, indeed, have to pay some price for this exclusion that can be extracted by other indirect means. IRC § 108(b) is the potential payback provision titled "reduction of tax attributes." The basic concept here is that if a taxpayer qualified for the benefit of excluding otherwise taxable income from discharge of indebtedness, he or she may have to reduce other "good tax things" to which they may be entitled; we have to open up the taxpayer's tax treasure chest and possibly take out some beneficial items. This provision requires Brandon to take the $25,000 that he is entitled to exclude (because of his insolvency) and reduce, by up to that amount, certain "tax attributes" or benefits. This provision is difficult enough without the added difficulty that some, if not most, of these "tax attributes" may not readily be understood. These "tax attributes," in the order of their reduction, are as follows:

- Net operating losses (NOL).
- General business credits pursuant to IRC § 38.
- Minimum tax credits available pursuant to IRC § 53(b).
- Capital losses for the current year and carryovers to the current year under IRC § 1212.
- Reduction of adjusted basis in the taxpayer's property.
- Passive activity loss or credit carryover under IRC § 469(b).
- Foreign tax credit carryovers pursuant to IRC § 27.

Without presenting a treatise on the issue, we take Brandon's $25,000 and start eliminating or reducing, as the case may be, the above "tax attributes" in the order presented. Brandon's $5,000 net operating loss (NOL) is the first to go. The NOL is completely eliminated, using up $5,000 of his $25,000 excluded amount. We take the remaining $20,000 of benefit and go down the list. The facts indicate that he has no general business credits, or minimum tax credits or capital losses/carryovers. That takes us down to the reduction of the basis of his property. We can see that reducing Brandon's adjusted basis in his property by $20,000 will not be a beneficial thing for him. The mechanics of this adjusted basis reduction is not, however, that simple. The Code, in IRC § 108(b)(2)(D) directs us to IRC § 1017 for the mechanics of making this basis reduction. Unfortunately, IRC § 1017 is another daunting section. With some variations, the basic mechanism for basis reduction is to reduce the basis of the taxpayer's property with a maximum or limit on such reduction equal to the amount by which the taxpayer's total adjusted basis in property exceeds his or her total liabilities, both measured immediately after the discharge of debt. Huh? Let's use the facts in our problem to try to explain this. At this point, Brandon has $20,000 of excluded benefit for which he has not paid any price (recall he started with $25,000 of exclusion benefit, but $5,000 was used to eliminate his NOL). The total adjusted basis in Brandon's property is given as $340,000. Brandon's liabilities, immediately after the discharge, are $325,000 ($350,000 total liabilities less the $25,000 forgiven). Therefore, the maximum or limit for basis reduction for Brandon is $15,000 (the amount by which his $340,000 total adjusted basis in assets exceeds his $325,000 of debt).

We continue down our list of tax attributes because at this point, Brandon has not fully "paid" for his original $25,000 exclusion. We used up $5,000 by eliminating the net operating loss (NOL), and just reduced the basis of his assets by $15,000, for a total of $20,000; leaving $5,000 of exclusion left to offset other tax attributes on the list. Fortunately for Brandon (and for us), the facts indicate that he has no passive activity losses/credits nor foreign tax credits. Here is where we stop. Phew!

This finally brings us to our correct answer. Brandon was able to exclude the entire $25,000 of forgiven debt because of the degree of his insolvency. His "payback" was the elimination of his $5,000 net operating loss (NOL) and a reduction in the total adjusted basis of his assets to the tune of $15,000. Note that in this question, Brandon did not have to fully "pay" for his exclusion through the reduction of tax attributes.

Answers (b), (c) and (d) are incorrect because, to varying degrees, they do not reflect the proper method of reducing Brandon's tax attributes for the exclusion benefit that he received. **Answer (a) is incorrect** because, unless a special election is made (and the facts indicate that this is not the case) the tax attributes listed must be reduced in the order that they are presented above.

25. **Answer (b) is correct.** Normally, an individual does not have income when he or she repays a debt. Had Brandon paid his sub-contractor/creditor $25,000 in cash, Brandon would have no income realization; he has no net accession to wealth as gross income is commonly defined. However, Brandon paid off his debt with his services and that <u>does</u> create income for him. This is a concept upon which students sometimes stumble because it somehow does not seem fair to Brandon. In class, this professor utilizes a couple of methods or illustrations to help clarify the point. One such method is to recast, or view in a different light, the transaction in an equivalent manner (this professor often uses the phrase: "convert it to a cash transaction with money going back and forth so we can see all sides of what is happening"). We could break down the transaction into something like this. Brandon performs $25,000 worth of services for the sub-contractor and the sub-contractor <u>pays</u> Brandon $25,000 <u>in cash</u>. At this point, it is clear Brandon would have income. Next, Brandon turns around and gives $25,000 to the sub-contractor to pay off his debt. The payment of the debt is not the taxable component but, rather, it is the performance of services that generates the income to Brandon. In substance, we have the same result as given in the facts: Brandon performed services and the debt he owed was paid.

Another example used by this professor in class is as follows: I arranged with my University employer to give me loans or advances each month in an amount that equals my next month's salary. We agree that I will pay back these debts by performing teaching services. Should I not have any income with this plan? Does it seem unfair that I have income? I got paid, albeit in advance, for work performed. In effect, this is Brandon's situation in our question.

Answer (a) is not correct because while Brandon is paying a debt, he is also deriving a benefit from the services he performed. **Answer (c) is incorrect** because Brandon's repayment has nothing to do with discharge of indebtedness and the resulting potential exclusion based on insolvency. **Answer (d) is incorrect** because barter exchanges, involving services, is income to the party or parties rendering services. Brandon, in this question, rendered services for a benefit (the payment of his debt). **Answer (e) is incorrect** because we do have a correct response in (b).

ANSWER KEY
EXAM II

1. **Answer (b) is correct.** Alfred's qualifying medical care "expenses" consist of $5,000 of the elevator's costs and $1,000 for the cost of its maintenance.

   IRC § 213 allows for a deduction of certain qualified medical expenses. Once one makes the determination of what constitutes "qualified" medical care expenses, the subject of this question, the deduction is allowed as an "itemized deduction" only to the extent that the total qualifying expenses exceeds 10% of adjusted gross income (AGI). [See Appendix A for more information about how income and deductions fit together in computing taxable income.] Qualified medical care expenses include typical costs for doctors, dentists, hospital, health insurance, and the like. [See IRC § 213(d).]

   Addressing first the easier issue of Alfred's over-the-counter medicines that were recommended by his doctor. While logically it would appear that such costs would qualify, the Code specifically allows deductions only for prescription drugs (and insulin in those areas where its sale is allowed without a prescription). [IRC § 213(b).] Therefore, <u>none</u> of the $200 Alfred paid for the medicine will qualify as medical care expenses, even though his physician recommended the medicine.

   The cost of the elevator, and its maintenance, present other issues. The cost of a major and permanent improvement, such as an elevator, is not really an "expense" at all but, rather, is considered a "capital expenditure." Major improvement capital expenditures, are generally not deductible expenses but serve to increase the adjusted basis in the property being improved. [IRC §§ 263 and 1016.] However, if the capital expenditure is primarily health-related, as is the case for Alfred's elevator installation, a medical care expense is allowed but only to the extent that the cost of the improvement exceeds the increase in value to the underlying property resulting from the improvement. [See Reg. § 1.213-1(e)(iii).] For Alfred, the $20,000 cost of the elevator less the $15,000 resulting increase in the value of his home, or <u>$5,000</u> is the amount of qualifying medical care expense. The regulations go on to provide that 100% of the operating and maintenance costs associated with such an improvement are deductible regardless of the amount, if any, of the original expenditure for the medically related improvement that qualified as a medical care expense. This assumes, of course, that the medical condition, for which the expenditure was made, still exists. For Alfred, even though only a portion of the elevator installation costs qualified as a medical care expense, the entire $1,000 of maintenance costs qualifies.

While not really affecting the answer to this question, the *Tax Cuts and Jobs Act* (TCJA) signed into law in December 2017, did change one component of deductions for qualified medical expenditures. The TCJA did not materially affect what constitutes qualified medical expenses under IRC § 213, but it did change the extent to which taxpayers can claim medical expense deductions. Embedded in our question is a reference to the deduction being available only to the extent that total qualified medical expenses exceed 10% of Adjusted Gross Income. This is commonly referred to as a "floor" in computing an individual's actual deduction and does not work in the taxpayer's favor as it eliminates some, or all, of the actual deduction depending on the individuals Adjusted Gross Income (itself a somewhat complex calculation). Over the years, this percentage floor has varied from a low of 3% to what had been a stable 7.5% since 1986. The TCJA raised this floor to 10% for all taxpayers beginning in 2019. The lower this floor percentage, the better it is for individuals. Therefore, this most recent change, along with other changes to deductions discussed elsewhere in this book, is not beneficial to individuals.

Answer (a) is incorrect. This answer does accurately reflect the $5,000 qualifying medical care expense associated with the elevator's $20,000 installation cost (representing one-fourth of the total cost). However, it incorrectly prorates the maintenance costs, allowing only one-fourth of the total $1,000, or $250. **Answers (c) and (d) are incorrect** because both of these answers incorrectly include the entire $20,000 elevator installation costs as a qualifying medical care expense. **Answer (e) is incorrect because** a correct answer (b) is presented.

2. **The best answer is (c).** The principal Code section permitting business deductions is IRC § 162. None of Tom's cost for airfare to/from Providence is deductible because the trip was not primarily for business. However, the costs associated with his stay in Providence for the one day that he did conduct substantial business, Friday, qualify as deductible business expenses (meals qualifying at 50% of their costs). A more comprehensive analysis follows.

The first sentence of IRC § 162 (which appears in subsection (a)) enumerates, for all intents and purposes, four basic requirements for a business deduction. A business deduction is allowed for all (read as one continuous phrase with four distinct requirements):
  ➢ Ordinary and necessary
  ➢ Expenses
  ➢ Paid or incurred during the taxable year
  ➢ In carrying on any trade or business.

These four requirements often represent, in federal income tax classes and in real life, separate and significant points of contention. Business deductions come in a million different flavors, but all qualifying deductions must meet those four criteria. The study, in tax classes, of business deductions can be long and comprehensive. At times, it may seem like many business deductions have their own set of rules, as if permitted by a separate Code section. There are many business deductions that almost take on a life of their own primarily because of explanations and interpretations from the Code subsections, regulations, court decisions, I.R.S. pronouncements, and the like.

IRC § 162(a)(2) specifically identifies that expenditures associated with "traveling away from home" constitute qualifying business expenses. While this subsection appears to add additional requirements to the four listed above for such traveling expenditures, a careful examination of the statutory language reveals no more than a reiteration of the four basic requirements, albeit in a different form. It is clear that Tom, in this question, did spend some of his time on business matters on his trip to Providence. The regulations promulgated for IRC § 162 are extensive and help clarify the issues relating to Tom as well as many other business expense issues that are not the subject of this question. For discussion purposes, Tom's potential qualifying business expenses are bifurcated into two parts: his transportation costs to/from Providence, and his costs incurred during his stay in Providence. At the outset, however, before discussing these two components, it should be noted that this question addresses potential business travel "away from home" as distinguished from "local" business travel. Business travel "away from home" generally means traveling far enough and long enough away from one's home to require an overnight stay (i.e., it would not be reasonable to expect someone to travel long distances after a long business day's work). This is often referred to as the "sleep and rest" rule or test. [See *United States v. Correll*, 389 US 299, 88 S.Ct. 445 (1967).] Business travel "away from home" opens the door to potential deductions for lodging, non-entertainment meals, incidentals, etc. Other questions in this book address the issue of where a taxpayer's "home" is located, and the issue of "local" travel for business (usually concerned only with deductions for transportation related expenses).

Tom's transportation costs to/from Providence (his airfare) qualifies as a business expense if the "trip is related primarily to [his] . . . trade or business." [Reg. § 1.162-2(b)(1).] In Tom's case, we need not delve any further into the regulations to determine, based on a common sense analysis of the facts, that his trip to Providence was primarily for pleasure and not for business purposes. Just in case we want to verify this result, the regulations, at § 1.162-2(b)(2), provide that this determination be made based on the facts and circumstances in each case. These regulations indicate that an important factor for making this determination is the number of days spent on business compared to the number of days spent for pleasure. Again, hopefully it is fairly apparent from the facts that Tom's trip to Providence was <u>not</u> made primarily for business purposes. Tom's transportation costs to/from Providence (his airfare) do <u>not qualify</u> as deductible business expenses. Note that for domestic travel, as is the case in this problem, deduction of transportation costs for traveling away from home is generally an "all or nothing" proposition. If the trip is primarily for business, 100% of the taxpayer's transportation related costs generally qualify as business expenses pursuant to IRC § 162. Alternatively, as is the case with Tom, <u>none</u> of the transportation costs qualify as business expenses if the trip is primarily for pleasure. It should be noted that the rules for "foreign" travel may differ and proration of transportation costs between deductible business and nondeductible personal expenses may be appropriate.

The Regulations do provide, however, that "expenses while at the destination which are properly allocable to the taxpayer's trade or business are deductible even though the traveling expenses to and from the destination are not deductible." [Reg. §1.162-2(b).] The twelve hours that Tom spent on Friday meeting with the firm's client was clearly spent conducting business. For this one day, Friday, Tom was traveling away from home in connection with the conduct of a trade or business. Therefore, his expenses relating to that one day qualify as § 162 business expenses. These include the cost of his lodging and incidentals for Friday, as well as 50% of his meals for that day. The 50% deduction limitation for business meals comes not from IRC § 162 but, rather, is supplied by IRC § 274(n)(1). While not the subject of this question, the scope of this 50% limit covers more than unreimbursed employee business meals (as in this question). It is also applicable to most business meals and some entertainment-related business expenses that are otherwise allowed as deductions. Please see other questions in this book that relate to these other expenses.

It should be noted that an individual can incur qualifying § 162 expenses in the context of working as an employee or in an individual's own business (someone who alternatively is referred to as being self-employed, an independent contractor, or operating his or her business as an "unincorporated sole proprietorship"). Tom, in our question as a partner in a law firm, falls in the latter category (a partner is considered an owner/self-employed individual as opposed to an associate who would be an employee). The requirements for deductibility pursuant to § 162 are the same for an employee or a self-employed individual. However, the effective availability of an actual business deduction, and where it is deducted, varies dramatically depending on one's "work status." The *Tax Cuts and Jobs Act* (TCJA) signed into law in December 2017 (generally effective beginning in 2018) made significant changes, and not in a good way, for deductions of business expenses by employees. Under the TCJA (in its current state as of this writing), deductions for unreimbursed business expenses incurred by employees, have, for the most part, been "suspended" for 2018 through 2025. [IRC § 67(g)]. Earlier editions of this book had Tom, in our question, was an employee and the answer would be the same as this edition's revised question (i.e., the IRC § 162 qualifications for what constitutes a valid business expense remains the same). However, the TCJA has generally eliminated the actual deductibility of such business expenses if incurred as an employee. This topic, as well as one small exception, is addressed in other questions in this book.

Answer (a) is incorrect. First, his transportation costs to/from Providence are not deductible because his trip was primarily for pleasure and not primarily for business. The second part of this answer, deducting costs for pleasure days to the extent of the airfare savings derived by staying longer, is a legitimately allowed technique, but requires that the transportation costs qualify as business expenses. **Answer (b) is incorrect** because, as stated, his transportation costs are not deductible. **Answer (d) is incorrect** because Friday, and Tom's expenses associated with that day, qualifies as a business day for Tom. **Answer (e) is incorrect** because the fact that his trip was primarily for pleasure does not preclude the deduction for expense incurred while conducting business during the trip.

3.   **Answer (c) is correct.** IRC § 165(d) allows an individual to deduct gambling (or wagering) losses to the extent that such individual has wagering gains in the same year. However, an individual who is not engaged in the business of gambling cannot just offset gambling winnings with gambling losses. Such individuals, as all individuals, must include in gross income, total gross gambling winnings. They are entitled to claim gambling losses to the extent of these gross gambling winnings (but not more) as a separate deduction. This deduction is allowed *below the line* (a deduction from adjusted gross income to arrive at taxable income) as part of the group of deductions known collectively as *itemized deductions*. [Reg. § 1.165-10.] More specifically, this gambling loss deduction is part of a sub-group known as "other deductions." Other questions in this book discuss the logistics of where *itemized deductions* fit into the grand scheme of things (and when it is more beneficial for an individual to "take" *itemized deductions* in place of a later-discussed *standard deduction*).

Answer (a) is incorrect because in certain circumstances, as discussed above, gambling losses do give rise to a deduction. **Answer (b) is incorrect** because, as discussed above, when applicable gambling losses generate a separate deduction that does not serve to offset gambling winnings (the deduction is taken as part of *itemized deductions*). **Answer (d) is incorrect** because it does not reflect the conditional nature of the deduction (that it is allowed only to the extent of gambling winnings).

4. **Answer (e) is the best response.** This is a complex question involving the deductibility of interest. It is not really that complex, but the applicable statutes create a cumbersome labyrinth (with varying laws for different years), and we need to go through it step by step. We will conclude that Tim should be entitled to deduct the interest paid with respect to his original $200,000 home mortgage loan, $90,000 of the new $160,000 second mortgage loan on his house, and the new $100,000 mortgage loan used in purchasing his vacation cabin. The explanation is long (read that as: *LONG*), but don't give up; it takes some time to *digest* it all, but we shall cover this methodically.

Our primary statutory focus for this question is IRC § 163, dealing with the deductibility of interest paid. Summarizing the answer, "qualified residence interest" is deductible. To be classified as such, one must be paying interest on "acquisition" indebtedness that is secured by a "qualified residence" (two residences may qualify). Both Tim's principal residence and his vacation cabin are considered "qualified residences." Tim's "acquisition indebtedness" is comprised of the original $200,000 loan on his principal residence, $90,000 of the $160,000 second mortgage on his principal residence that was used for the bedroom addition, and the $100,000 mortgage loan to purchase the vacation cabin. The other $70,000 of the $160,000 second mortgage on his principal residence that was used to purchase stocks and pay for the cruise qualifies as "home equity indebtedness," but beginning in 2018 (pursuant to the *Tax Cuts and Jobs Act*, or TCJA), such home equity interest is no longer deductible. The total of his "acquisition" indebtedness does not exceed the statutory maximum for which interest thereon is allowed as a deduction. Therefore, all of the interest Tim pays with respect to all but $70,000 of his new second mortgage is deductible as "qualified residence interest." A more thorough analysis follows.

IRC § 163(a) provides a simple and broad sounding deduction for interest stating, in part: "There shall be allowed as a deduction all interest paid . . . within the taxable year on indebtedness." This sounds **great** and by just reading this, students rejoice at the thought of deductions for future interest paid on, among other things, their student loans. Alas, the Tax Reform Act of 1986 introduced subsection (h), located quite some written distance from the general allowance for interest deductions of subsection (a). IRC § 163(h) starts out deceptively, and unfavorably, simple by stating, in part: "In the case of a taxpayer other than a corporation, no deduction shall be allowed .

. . for personal interest paid . . . during the taxable year." The definition of "personal" interest, which is not deductible, is found in IRC § 163(h)(2) and takes the form of a negative definition; personal interest is interest "other than" those listed in subparagraphs (A) through (F). The key, therefore, to finding interest that is deductible, is to fit it within one of these specified categories of what does not constitute nondeductible personal interest. One such category of interest that is not considered personal interest is "qualified residence interest." [IRC § 163(h)(2)(D).]

Qualified residence interest is addressed in IRC §§ 163(h)(3) and (h)(4). To obtain deductible qualified residence interest status, a taxpayer must have two things:
  ➢ A "qualified residence."
  ➢ The property type of indebtedness associated with such qualified residence.

A qualified residence includes the taxpayer's principal residence and one other residence (e.g., a vacation home) that meets certain requirements. [IRC § 163(h)(4)(A).] A principal residence can include the typical house (as our couple's in this question), a condominium, townhouse, co-op, etc. A principal residence can consist of a boat, trailer, motor home, or similar vehicle if, generally, they contain sleeping, eating, and bathroom facilities. While the determination of one's principal residence is usually not at issue for most people (as it is not an issue here regarding Tim's *principal residence*), there are (i.e., your professor can discuss) situations that present more of a challenge. The "one other residence" as a qualified residence for purposes of deductible qualified residence can present its own host of issues, some involving rather complex statutory rules involving very convoluted definitions. For our facts, however, the classification of Tim's vacation cabin is fairly simple. Because he uses the cabin solely for personal purposes and it is not rented out during the year, it qualifies as a *qualified residence*. [IRC § 163(h)(4)(A)(iii).] While not at issue here, if the "one other residence" is rented out, the statute directs you to the somewhat bizarre definition rules in IRC § 280A(d)(1).

Ostensibly, there are two proper types of indebtedness recognized by the statute in this area: "acquisition indebtedness" and "home equity indebtedness." But be forewarned as things are not as they might first appear (the surprise has to do with the *home equity indebtedness* category, and it is not good news). We shall explain, below. It is important to recognize that the statute requires that either of these two types of loans must be **secured** by the applicable qualified residence in order to qualify. [IRC § 163(h)(3)(A).] All of Tim's loans in this question are secured by the appropriate *qualified residence* (the original and second mortgage loans secured by his principal residence and the vacation mortgage loan secured by his vacation cabin).

Acquisition indebtedness is defined in IRC § 163(h)(3)(B), and is fairly straightforward for most taxpayers. Acquisition loans are money borrowed to **acquire, construct, or substantially improve** a qualified residence. Tim's first mortgage loan, still at $200,000, was used to purchase his qualified principal residence and, therefore, is properly classified as *acquisition indebtedness*. His second mortgage of $160,000 presents a bit of a challenge as $90,000 of it was used for a room addition to his house, and the remaining $70,000 was used for things unrelated to the house (to purchase stocks and pay for a cruise). For debt classification purposes, we split this loan into component parts with the $90,000 of this loan used to "substantially improve" his qualified residence also qualifying as *acquisition indebtedness*. The remaining $70,000 portion of this loan is not acquisition indebtedness but, rather, is discussed below under *home equity indebtedness*. Tim's $100,000 loan to purchase the *qualified residence* vacation cabin is also *acquisition indebtedness*. So far, the interest Tim pays with respect to his $200,000 original house loan, $90,000 of his second mortgage on his house, and the $100,000 loan appears to be deductible under IRC § 163 as qualified residence interest. In the aggregate, Tim has $390,000 of *acquisition indebtedness* ($200,000 + $90,000 + $100,000).

One last issue to consider regarding the deduction of interest on *acquisition indebtedness* is that there is a cap or limit on the amount of loans qualifying as *acquisition indebtedness*. An initial read of the statute, at IRC § 163(h)(3)(B)(ii) appears to place a $1 million cap on such loans, meaning that for acquisition loans, only the interest on the first $1 million of such loans is deductible. Again, we are just looking at what the law *appears* to be. This $1 million cap is on the amount of loans and not a much larger $1 million cap on deductible interest. Also, pursuant to the statute, it should also be noted that this $1 million acquisition indebtedness cap is in the aggregate (i.e., $1 million total for all acquisition loans for the principal and one other qualifying residence and not a $1 million cap for each acquisition loan, or a separate $1million acquisition loan cap for each of two possible qualifying residences). So why does this author keep qualifying what is being discussed (and what is in the statute)? One must look deeper into the section to IRC § 163(h)(3)(F) that was "tacked on" by the *Tax Cuts and Jobs Act*, or TCJA, signed into law in December 2017 and effective, here, for years 2018 through 2025. A new, lower, aggregate cap of $750,000 replaces the $1 million cap for most acquisition debt loans obtained after 2017. While acquisition debt loans originated before 2017 generally retain the $1 million cap, later acquisition loans have this lower limit (again, it is the amount of the loan for which interest is paid and not the amount of interest paid). In our question, Tim has some "old" loans and the $90,000 portion of this new loan qualifying as *acquisition indebtedness*. This two-tiered cap can create a very messy situation for some individuals (with old and new loans) but fortunately for us, Tim's total *acquisition indebtedness* is $390,000 ($200,000 + $90,000 + $100,000), is well below even the newer $750,000 cap so we need not delve into the mathematical intricacies of how this is applied in determining the maximum amount of qualifying *acquisition indebtedness*.

While not at issue in this question, it should be noted that loans used to replace existing "acquisition indebtedness" (e.g., a straight refinancing), takes on the character of the loan being replaced and itself becomes acquisition indebtedness.

<u>Home equity indebtedness</u> is also an issue in this question. For now, let's just go with the code and see where it takes us (again, be forewarned that things are not as they may seem and, to some degree, we are going through an exercise in futility). Home equity indebtedness is defined in IRC § 163(h)(3)(C) and, typically, is money borrowed against an existing qualified residence (secured by the qualified residence) that is used for purposes *other than* substantial improvements to the qualified residence. Advertisements for "tapping the equity" in one's house to buy a new car or boat, go on a vacation, pay off credit card debts, student loans or consolidate all those existing bills, strike at the center of what "home equity indebtedness" is all about. From the statute, it appears that borrowing money, using your house, for such things as buying a car can generate deductible interest, while interest paid on a regular car loan from a bank, credit union or automotive financing companies will generally be nondeductible "personal" interest. This is, in part, what Tim has done with respect to the $160,000 second mortgage loan he took out on his principal residence. We have already determined that $90,000 of this loan qualifies as *acquisition indebtedness*, but what about the deductibility of interest Tim pays with respect to the remaining $70,000 of this loan that was used to purchase stocks and pay for a cruise? A statutory requirement of "home equity indebtedness" (in addition that it must be secured by the qualifying residence) is that such loan cannot exceed the "equity" in the qualified residence. "Equity" is the one figure of which most homeowners are constantly aware. Equity is the difference between the value of the home and the amount of outstanding loans with respect to the home. Say, for example, that you own a home worth $350,000, and that you have an outstanding first mortgage (acquisition debt) of $150,000. Your "equity" in the home is $200,000. This is the amount or value of your home that you really own; how much you would expect to "pocket in cash" upon selling (after the debt is paid off). In our problem, Tim has no problem with this equity limitation for *home equity indebtedness*.

Hold on, we are almost there and shall ultimately determine that Tim is **not** entitled to deduct the interest on this $70,000 portion of his home equity loan. But first, we continue with the statute and pursuant thereto [see IRC

§163(h)(3)(C)], it places a cap on the total amount of home equity indebtedness for which, ostensibly, interest paid thereon, is deductible. This statutory limit is $100,000 of home equity debt and, similar to acquisition debt discussed above, this is a cap for the aggregate of all home equity debt. The portion of Tim's second mortgage representing *home equity indebtedness* of $70,000 is less than the statutory cap. If we stopped at this point, it would appear that Tim would be entitled to deduct the interest on this $70,000 portion of his second mortgage. This would have been correct had it not been for the *Tax Cuts and Jobs Act* (TCJA) signed into law in December 2017. Here comes the letdown for Tim. The TCJA tacked on a new section, IRC § 163(h)(3)(F), that **totally eliminates** any deduction of interest on *home equity indebtedness* for years 2018 through 2025. [See, specifically, IRC §163(h)(3)(F)(i)(I)].

While not at issue in our question, it should be noted that the TCJA's elimination of interest deductions on qualified home equity debt applies irrespective of when such debt originated. It came as a "rude awakening" for taxpayers with pre-2018 home equity who, beginning in 2018, were no longer entitled to deduct interest on such loans even though they were entitled to do so in prior years.

In summary, A total of $390,000 of Tim's borrowing (the original home loan of $200,000, plus the $100,000 purchase loan for the cabin, plus $90,000 of the $160,000 second mortgage used for home improvements) constitutes *acquisition indebtedness* (and, more broadly, *qualified residence interest*) and he is entitled to deduct the interest paid on this amount of debt. The interest paid on the remaining $70,000 of his second mortgage, while technically qualifying as *home equity indebtedness*, is no longer deductible (for years 2018 through 2025) pursuant to changes made by the TCJA.

A word of **caution** about language used on exams. There are many instances where the common use of a term does not necessarily correspond to its official "tax" counterpart. Labels can be deceiving, and do not be fooled by their use in lay terms on an exam. The "home equity loan" label is a classic case in point. A home equity loan, a second mortgage, the cash portion of a cash-out refinance, a home equity-based line of credit, etc. are all typically referred to, in the real world, as home equity loans. Be careful here because, as we saw above in Tim's case, the fact that money is borrowed using the equity in a qualified residence as security does not necessarily render the loan as *home equity indebtedness*. If the borrowed funds are used to substantially improve the qualified residence, the loan, or applicable part thereof, is characterized as the more favorable *acquisition indebtedness*. Do not be fooled by language used to describe the facts of a loan. Tim's loan was, for loan description purposes, a home equity loan (he "tapped into the equity" of his house). However, an incorrect classification of the entire loan as *home equity indebtedness* for tax purposes would have resulted in an incorrect answer. As mentioned, the $90,000 of this loan used for the room addition is considered *acquisition indebtedness* which, as we saw, gave rise to an interest deduction (which would have vanished had it been classified as *home equity indebtedness*).

It should be noted that there are special rules applicable to older home-related loans incurred before October 14, 1987. [IRC § 163(h)(3)(D).]

Answer (a) is incorrect. This <u>was</u> the correct answer prior to the *Tax Cuts and Jobs Act* (TCJA) signed into law in December 2017 (generally effective beginning in 2018), but it is now incorrect because it effectively includes deductibility of interest paid on *home equity indebtedness* (such interest was, prior to 2018, deductible). **Answer (b) is incorrect** as it has one fall into the trap of characterizing all of Tim's $160,000 "home equity loan" (the commonly used label) as *home equity indebtedness* for tax purpose (and then subjects it to the $100,000 cap for such indebtedness and applies "old" law, pre 2018, regarding the deduction interest paid thereon). As discussed above, $90,000 of this "home equity loan" is classified, for tax purposes, as *acquisition indebtedness* because it was used to substantially improve Tim's *qualified* principal residence. **Answer (c) is incorrect** because it incorrectly classifies, for tax purpose, the entire $160,000 second mortgage loan and the $100,000 borrowed to purchase the vacation cabin as *home equity indebtedness* (and then subjects it to the $100,000 cap for such indebtedness and applies "old" law, pre 2018, regarding the deduction interest paid thereon). **Answer (d) is also incorrect** because it incorrectly classifies the vacation cabin purchase loan as *home equity indebtedness* (along with a portion of the home equity loan) and, then subjects it to the now irrelevant $100,000 cap for such indebtedness. Plus, it reflects "old" pre-2018 law regarding the deduction interest paid thereon.

5. **Answer (e) is correct.** Students universally dislike "none of the above" answers and are justified in doing so. They do provide, however, a powerful testing tool for professors and, in this case, none of the answers provided in (a) through (d) are correct. We will conclude, below, that Tim will be entitled to deduct, in the current year, only a portion of the "points" that he paid. Specifically, he can deduct, in full, one percent of $90,000 of his $160,000 home equity loan in the current year. The points paid with respect to the $100,000 loan for the cabin purchase will be deducted on a pro-rata basis over the respective lives of the loans. The points paid with respect to the $70,000 remaining balance of his $160,000 home equity loan will not give rise to any deduction (now or over the life of the loan). Recall that this question is asking about only the two new loans obtained in "the current" year (Tim's original loan to buy his principal residence is not at issue). The

answer to this problem has changed with this new 3rd edition of this book, reflecting changes in the tax laws.

This question is a logical extension of question 4, above, and while it is a bit unfair, as it requires a substantially correct analysis of the previous question, it does provide a more in-depth analysis of interest deductions. The "real-world" issue of deductibility of "points" paid with respect to obtaining home financing is a big issue and often misunderstood. One cannot hear a commercial, read an advertisement regarding home loans, or use an online home loan site and not be exposed to the issue of "points." It is not uncommon to see a lender's loan rates listed at various levels with corresponding variations in the number of *points* charged.

"Points" appear in the form of a number such as 1 point, 1.5 points, 2 points, etc., with the number corresponding to a "percentage" (e.g., 1 point = 1%). Although for first time borrowers the concept seems strange, this percentage number represents an amount of money that the <u>borrower</u> must pay to the lender in order to borrow the money; the applicable point percentage of the amount borrowed! For illustration purposes (facts unrelated to our problem), let us assume that you are purchasing your first home for $250,000, paying $50,000 in cash and obtaining a typical 30-year mortgage loan for the balance of the purchase price ($200,000). Let us further assume that the lender's interest rate is 3.15% plus "1.5 points." Of course, you will be making monthly payments on the money borrowed, but to just borrow the money, you would have to pay the lender 1.5% of $200,000, or $3,000. This is in addition to other fees that might be associated with the loan (e.g., title fees, appraisal fees, document charges, escrow fees, etc.).

What are points? They represent "interest" that is being "prepaid" to the lender when the loan is obtained. One only need venture to various Web sites to see a variety of lender's "loan packages," with differing loan rates related, inversely, to different "point" charges. The deductibility of points associated with a variety of personal-use home loans, involves two issues:

1) **Are** the points associated with loans for which the regular interest will be deductible as *qualified residence interest*, and if so,
2) **When** is the taxpayer entitled to deduct them.

Because points represent interest, albeit prepaid, it is necessary to first determine if they are deductible <u>at all</u>. For discussion purposes, we will not duplicate the exhaustive requirements for IRC § 163(h)(3) *qualified residence interest* (e.g., qualified residence(s), loans secured by the residence, loan limits for acquisition and home equity indebtedness, etc.). [See the answer for question 4, above.] But, making this determination, about the underlying loan upon which points are being paid, is critical. If points are paid with respect to any loan, or any portion of a loan, that will not give rise to deductible *qualified residence interest*, they (the points) will <u>not</u> be deductible. Rather, these points (or portion thereof) will be considered nondeductible *personal interest*.

As far as Tim is concerned, we determined, in problem 4, above, that all but $70,000 of his $160,000 home equity loan generates *qualified residence interest*. The $160,000 second mortgage loan that he obtained on his principal residence was split into two components: $90,000 of *acquisition indebtedness* (for the home improvement) and $70,000 of *home equity indebtedness* (for the investments and cruise vacation). The $100,000 loan used to purchase the vacation cabin qualified as *acquisition indebtedness*. The aggregate amount of Tim's loans in either category of qualified indebtedness did not exceed the statutory limits. We traveled a very long, tortuous road to ultimately determine that due to changes made by the *Tax Cuts and Jobs Act* (TCJA), interest paid on *home equity indebtedness* is no longer deductible (beginning in 2018).

At this juncture, we know that the "one point" that Tim paid with respect to some of the "current year's new loans" will be deductible (and some will not). Specifically, the one point that he paid on the $100,000 loan used to purchase his cabin and the one point that he paid with respect to $90,000 of his $160,000 home equity loan (the portion that was classified as *acquisition indebtedness*) <u>will be</u> deductible. The one point paid for the $70,000 balance of his home equity loan will not be deductible at all because as we saw in question 4, above, the interest on this portion is now (under the TCJA) classified as nondeductible interest on *home equity indebtedness*. While the question does not require us to actually compute the amount of money he was required to pay in points, the amount is easily determined. $1,000 for the cabin loan (1% of $100,000) and $900 in points for the $90,000 portion of his second mortgage (1% of $90,000). The **major issue** now, is <u>**when are these amounts deductible?**</u>

A simple reading of IRC §163 might infer that the above-mentioned amounts for deductible points ($1,000 plus $900), would be deductible in the current year; deductible in the year paid. Tim, as well as most borrowers, would like for this to be the result (for Tim it means a possible $1,900 interest deduction in addition to whatever regular monthly interest he will pay on these amounts of these new loans). However, deductions for prepayments of otherwise deductible expenses are usually not allowed for expenses that are properly attributable to future tax years. Points, by their nature, represent prepayment of a small amount of interest that would otherwise be payable over the entire life of the loan (typically 30 years).

Indeed, IRC §461(g)(1) generally disallows the deduction of prepaid interest, and requires the taxpayer to deduct the prepaid amount in a ratable fashion over the life of the loan.

In true law school form, there is an "exception" to this rule forbidding deductions of prepaid interest. IRC § 461(g)(2) allows for the current deduction, in the year paid, for points paid with respect to loans (otherwise qualifying as discussed above) that are used to "acquire" or "improve" one's "principal residence." Points paid for monies borrowed for those two purposes <u>are deductible now</u>, when paid. Points paid for other monies borrowed, for which deductions for interest are otherwise allowed, <u>are deductible ratably over the life of the loan</u>.

Applying these rules to Tim's loans obtained in the current year, we have some problems. The $100,000 loan obtained to acquire the cabin (while considered *acquisition indebtedness*) was <u>not</u> used to acquire Tim's <u>principal residence</u>. Therefore, the one point associated with that loan ($1,000) is <u>not</u> deductible in full in the current year but must be deducted ratably over the life of the loan (e.g., 1/30th each year for a thirty year loan). As for the $160,000 second mortgage obtained on his principal residence, we know that points paid with respect to only $90,000 of the loan is the only amount actually "in-play." Fortunately for Tim, this portion of the home equity loan <u>was</u> used to improve his principal residence (the other $70,000 was used for unrelated matters). As we did with determining the ongoing interest deductions for this loan (see question 4, above) this requires us to bifurcate the loan for point deductibility purposes. One point associated with the $90,000 used to improve his home (or $900) is deductible in full in the current year pursuant to IRC § 461(g)(2). We already know that the one point paid for the remaining $70,000 of this second mortgage ($700) is not deductible at all; not in the current year or ratably over the life of the loan. In the prior edition of this book, the answer to this question was different, reflecting that the points paid with this remaining portion of the home equity loan was deductible ratably over the life of the loan (this was prior to the TCJA where interest on *home equity indebtedness* was deductible, as were points attributable thereto; albeit not up front).

While this issue of point deductibility may appear confusing at first (and it is to many borrowers as well as misinformed lenders), the rules are fairly straightforward. Students sometimes run into problems when attempts are made to coordinate the current deductibility of points with the deductibility of different classifications of *qualified residence interest*.

While not at issue in this problem, points paid with respect to "refinancing" an existing loan (e.g. declining interest rates prompt a homeowner, to replace an existing home loan with a new, lower rate loan) are <u>not</u> deductible in the year paid. They do not meet the requirements of IRC §461(g)(2). [See Rev.Rul. 87-22, 1987-1 C.B. 146, (refinanced loans are not actually used to purchase or improve a principal residence but, rather, are at best, replacing such loans).]

Answer (a) is incorrect because under current law (reflecting the TCJA), the interest paid (including points) for all of his loans is not even deductible nor used to purchase or improve his principal residence. **Answer (b) is also incorrect.** While it is correct with respect to the $90,000 portion of the $160,000 second mortgage that Tim used for improving his principal residence, it incorrectly includes within the IRC §461(g)(2) provision, the points paid on his vacation cabin. The cabin is not his principal residence. This answer is also incorrect because all interest (including points) paid with respect to the $70,000 of his home equity loan not used to purchase or improve any qualified residence is no longer deductible at all (again, this is pursuant to the TCJA). **Answer (c) is incorrect** because it too does not properly identify the loans for which points can be deducted currently (and also misrepresents the deductibility, pursuant to the TCJA) of the $70,000 portion of his home equity loan. **Answer (d) is incorrect** but was the correct answer in the last edition of this book because it reflected that all of the interest (and therefore, all of the points paid) were at least deductible at some point with only the portion of the home equity loan used to improve his house being deductible up-front.

6. **The best answer is (b).** The primary focus for this question is IRC § 162, deductions for business expenses. Ben's $900 seminar course fee and the $50 in transportation costs to/from the seminar qualify as deductible business expenses pursuant to IRC § 162. His costs for lodging and meals do not qualify as deductible business expenses because he is not considered to be *traveling away from home*. A more comprehensive (and sorry, but lengthy) analysis follows.

The first sentence of IRC § 162 (which appears in subsection (a)) enumerates, for all intents and purposes, four basic requirements for a business deduction. A business deduction is allowed for all (read as one continuous phrase with four distinct requirements):
  ➢ Ordinary and necessary
  ➢ Expenses
  ➢ Paid or incurred during the taxable year
  ➢ In carrying on any trade or business.

These four requirements often represent, in federal income tax classes and in real life, separate and significant points of contention. Business deductions come in a million different flavors, but all qualifying deductions must meet those four criteria. The study, in tax classes, of business deductions can be long and comprehensive. At times, it may seem like many business deductions have their own set of rules, as if permitted by a separate Code section. There are many business deductions that almost take on a life of their own primarily because of explanations and interpretations from the Code subsections, regulations, court decisions, I.R.S. pronouncements, and the like.

In Ben's case, we are dealing with two or three sub-sets or specific types of IRC § 162 business expenses: business related education expenses and transportation expenses (with discussion of traveling away from home expenses for lodging and meals).

The "basic taxation for lawyers" seminar

The first issue, and partial foundation for our answer, is that of business related education: Ben's "basic taxation for lawyers" seminar. Of the four IRC § 162 requirements above, we have potential issues with whether the seminar was *ordinary and necessary*, and if it is with respect to Ben's *carrying on a trade or business*. While specific regulations under IRC § 162 provide guidance in the area of business-related education expenses, let us first try to analyze the facts in Ben's case using the basic IRC § 162 requirements. We then will turn to the regulations. The object here is not to create additional work nor extend the length of this analysis but, rather, it provides us with a good opportunity to work through the IRC § 162 requirements and then see how the regulations address the issue.

The seminar is necessary for Ben. "Necessary," for the purpose of IRC § 162, is not necessary in the sense that it is absolutely critical that Ben takes this course. Rather, "necessary" has been interpreted to be a taxpayer-*subjective* test of whether the taxpayer thought the expense was "appropriate or helpful." There is very little second-guessing here. Ben thought that this course would be appropriate or helpful and, therefore, it is necessary. The "ordinary" aspect of an IRC § 162 is an *objective* test; generally whether such an expenditure is common, accepted, customary, or usual in the taxpayer's line of business. Arguably, a lawyer taking a state bar sponsored course sounds fairly ordinary without much more information. Heck, if the state bar approves the course for attendance by lawyers, it almost has the "ordinary" seal of approval. Looking a bit deeper, it seems logical that a lawyer practicing in most areas of law, especially personal injury law (see IRC § 104 for example) would want to know something about tax law. Most likely, this is enough analysis to determine the seminar expenditure was *ordinary and necessary*. Whether attending the seminar relates to *carrying on* Ben's business, is effectively tied, in our facts, to whether the expense is *ordinary*. Ben is already a practicing lawyer (i.e., he is in a trade or business) and the seminar, learning something about income taxes, is in relation to that business. Most situations involving this issue involve questions of whether the expenditure is associated with the taxpayer entering a new or different business. A taxpayer can be engaged in business in various ways including as an employee or, as is the case for Ben in this question, as self-employed (a.k.a., independent contractor, or unincorporated sole proprietor), Ben appears to easily meet the in *carrying on a trade or business* requirement of IRC § 162. As of this point, Ben's $900 course fees appear to qualify as an IRC § 162 business expense. Now for further analysis of this issue referencing the regulations.

The regulations provide substantial guidance on business education issues. [Reg. § 1.162-5.] This is an example of where one type of business expense seems to take on a life of its own, and have its own set of rules and requirements. However, the regulation is merely providing interpretations or explanations of the basic IRC § 162 requirements as they pertain to business-related education expenses. In an interpretation of the general IRC § 162 requirements, the regulations provide that generally, education will qualify as a business expense, "if the education –

1) Maintains or improves skills required by the individual in his employment or other trade or business, or

2) Meets the express requirements of the individual's employer, or the requirement of applicable law or regulations, imposed as a condition to the retention by the individual of an established employment relationship, status, or rate of compensation."
[See Reg. § 1.162-5(a).]

A lawyer must maintain (and hopefully improve) one's skills in the practice of law. For Ben, the basic tax seminar appears to easily meet this requirement. The seminar may even meet the second test listed above, depending on his state's bar requirements for continuing legal education. If they impose continuing legal education requirements to maintain one's license to practice law (e.g., x number of hours of continuing legal education per year), Ben's state bar sponsored tax seminar would certainly qualify. The regulations go on to state instances where education will not qualify as an IRC § 162 business expense, and they include:

➢ "[E]ducation which is required of him in order to meet the minimum educational requirements for qualification in his employment or other trade or business" [Reg. § 1.162-5(b)(2).], and

> ➤ "[E]ducation which is part of a program of study being pursued by him which will lead to qualifying him in a new trade or business." [Reg. § 1.162-5(b)(3).]

Examples of the former might be education related to obtaining a teaching credential, so that one can become an elementary school teacher, law school education required to become a lawyer, etc. Examples of the latter tend to overlap the former and can include an engineer wanting to change jobs and embark on a field of study to become a veterinarian. Ben's tax seminar clearly does not fit within these examples of nondeductible education expenses.

We conclude that Ben's $900 seminar fee qualifies as an IRC § 162 business expense. Now on to his other expenditures related to the seminar experience.

Transportation costs related to business

Looking at transportation costs, we are faced with the same basic IRC § 162 requirements listed above. As with business education, particular rules have evolved regarding deductible business transportation. Distilled to its most basic form for this question, if the tax seminar Ben attended qualifies as a business expense, the cost of getting to and from it also qualify. This is no different than, for example, Ben driving to a client's office. At one point, the I.R.S. made distinctions whether business transportation initiated from home versus the office, but this is no longer relevant for transportation to what is considered a non-regular place of business. [Please see other problems in this book that address such issues in conjunction with nondeductible "commuting" transportation.] The facts indicate that Ben incurred $50 in transportation costs to/from the seminar. This $50, therefore qualifies as a § 162 expense. All that is left to discuss is Ben's costs for the lodging and meals, which brings up the issue of *traveling away from home*.

Is Ben "traveling away from home" on business?

IRC § 162(a)(2) specifically identifies that expenditures associated with "traveling away from home" constitute qualifying business expenses. While this subsection appears to add additional requirements to the four listed above for such traveling expenditures, a careful examination of the statutory language reveals no more than a reiteration of the four basic requirements, albeit in a different form. At the outset, an important issue needs to be addressed. *Traveling away from home* on business is a bit special and should be distinguished with what is commonly referred to as *local transportation*.

Traveling away from home is where you leave your office in Seattle to see a client in Chicago for a two-day business meeting. Local transportation is where you leave your office in Beverly Hills to see a client ten miles away in Santa Monica. Distinguishing between the two can make a huge difference for tax purposes (business deductions). Business travel *away from home* generally means traveling far enough and long enough away from one's home to require an overnight stay (i.e., it would not be reasonable to expect someone to travel long distances after a long business day's work). This is often referred to as the "sleep and rest" rule or test. [See *United States v. Correll*, 389 US 299, 88 S.Ct. 445 (1967).] Business travel *away from home* opens the tax doors to potential deductions (in addition to transportation costs) for lodging, non-entertainment meals, incidentals, etc. while traveling away from home on business. Whereas, local transportation for business purposes gives rise to deductions generally limited to transportation costs and parking charges at the business destination. For local transportation situations, meals are not deductible at all, and neither is lodging (client meals is a different issue and may give rise to some deductions).

Therefore, the key to deductions for his lodging and meals rests with the determination of whether Ben, traveling 30 miles each way to the seminar lasting six hours a day, is considered *traveling away from home*. Is it unreasonable for Ben to return 30 miles after spending six hours on business matters (the seminar)? The likely answer is no. Both the distance to the seminar and the time spent on business at that location, is too short to conclude that he is *traveling away from home*. Therefore, he is not entitled to a business deduction for the cost of his meals nor his lodging. A similar example is an everyday commute to work. Once you get there, you cannot deduct your meals (unless they relate to business) nor can you deduct lodging near work merely because you do not feel like driving home on a particular evening.

A potential twist that is not given as a possible answer to this question

There is a possible argument that Ben should be entitled to a little greater deductible amount than indicated in the correct answer to this problem (but rest assured, it is also not contained in any other answer provided). An I.R.S. Private Letter Ruling addressed the situation of a taxpayer traveling away from home primarily on business but spent some pleasure (non-business) days while on the trip. These pleasure days happened to coincide with the taxpayer's "Saturday night stay-over" which substantially reduced his or her airfare. This private letter ruling said, basically, that some of the otherwise nondeductible costs for the non-business days, *could* qualify for a business deduction to the extent such costs did not exceed the airfare saved by the Saturday night stay-over. The theory being that had the taxpayer left immediately after the business concluded, the airfare would have been much higher (and also deductible); so to the extent that the airfare would have been deductible (and the savings resulting from the Saturday night stay-over) represent business deductions for costs that are really not business related. [See Priv.Ltr.Rul. 9237014 (06/10/1992).] It is sort of a "fairness" principle. So why is this possibly relevant to Ben in our case? Had he gone back home after the first seminar day and returned for the next day, his transportation costs (most likely double the $50) would have been deductible as *local business transportation*. Utilizing the logic of the aforementioned I.R.S. Private Letter Ruling, one could make a case that at least $50, of his nondeductible lodging or meals (at 50% pursuant to IRC § 274(n)), should be deductible.

Lastly, it should be noted that an individual can incur qualifying § 162 expenses in the context of working as an employee or in an individual's own business (someone who alternatively referred to as being self-employed, an independent contractor, or operating his or her business as an "unincorporated sole proprietorship"). Ben, in our question, with his own law firm, falls in the latter category. The requirements for deductibility pursuant to § 162 are the same for an employee or a self-employed individual. However, the effective availability of an actual business deduction, and where it is deducted, varies dramatically depending on one's "work status." The *Tax Cuts and Jobs Act* (TCJA) signed into law in December 2017 (generally effective beginning in 2018) made significant changes, and not in a good way, for deductions of business expenses by employees. Under the TCJA, deductions for unreimbursed business expenses incurred by employees, have, for the most part, been "suspended" for 2018 through 2025. [IRC § 67(g)]. Earlier editions of this book had Ben, in our question, as an employee and the answer would be the same as this edition's revised question (i.e., the IRC § 162 qualifications for what constitutes a valid business expense remains the same). However, the TCJA as generally eliminates the actual deductibility of such business expenses if incurred as an employee. This topic, as well as one small exception, is addressed in other questions in this book.

Answer (a) is incorrect because the $150 in lodging is not a deductible business expense, as Ben was, most likely, not *traveling away from home*. **Similarly, Answer (c) is incorrect** because neither the lodging nor meals (at 50%) are deductible business expenses because Ben is, most likely, not *traveling away from home*. **Answer (d) is incorrect** because it fails to recognize that the $50 in transportation costs is a deductible business expense. **Answer (e) is incorrect** because it incorrectly presumes that the tax seminar (and all related costs) was not unrelated to Ben's current trade or business.

7. **The best answer is (b).** This question raises the issue of "depreciation" deductions. The *concept* of depreciation is not too difficult. Its real-world

application, however, with all of the analytical twists and turns, can be daunting. The study of depreciation varies considerably among law school tax courses: from a casual mention of the topic to a full-blown, in-depth analysis of the various depreciation methods (past and present), class lives, conventions, elective provisions, etc. For this book, the author has chosen to cover the issue of depreciation in its most basic form, and forego analysis of the many in-depth, analytical rules. This choice was made primarily to leave room for the host of other tax issues that require discussion. The author does acknowledge that this level of coverage may be disappointing for those students whose professor more fully covers the issue of depreciation in class.

Generally, the costs of major permanent improvements to existing business property or the purchase of business property having a useful life of more than one year are not fully deductible in that year. [IRC § 263.] These types of expenditures are commonly referred to as "capital expenditures." This result is also consistent with the requirements of the general business deduction section, IRC § 162. For expenditures to be fully deductible now (when incurred) IRC § 162 requires that the expenditure be (read as one continuous phrase with four distinct requirements):
- ➤ Ordinary and necessary
- ➤ Expense
- ➤ Paid or incurred during the taxable year
- ➤ In carrying on any trade or business.

Capital expenditures, as are Abigail's costs for the warehouse and manufacturing equipment, do not represent *expenses* and, therefore, do not qualify as business deductions pursuant to IRC § 162. *Capital expenditures* and *expenses* are mutually exclusive.

IRC § 167 provides, however, that the cost of most business (or investment) *capital expenditures* can be deducted over time (or expensed) through the concept of depreciation deductions. Do not be confused with the word "depreciation." For income tax purposes, property need not decline in value in order to claim deductions for depreciation. Rather, for income tax purposes, depreciation is the methodical deduction, over time, of a capitalized cost. Since Abigail's business expenditures for the warehouse and equipment are *capital expenditures*, their costs will be expensed over time in the form of depreciation deductions.

Well beyond the scope of the author's coverage of depreciation in this book, are the numerous methods of depreciation, depreciation elections, various periods of depreciation for different types of business assets, and elections for favorable "extra" depreciation deductions in the year in which certain assets are acquired. Be aware that while these extensive and complex rules are not discussed in this book, your professor may cover this issue in much greater detail.

Answer (a) is incorrect because the manufacturing equipment Abigail purchased for her business most assuredly represents capital expenditures. **Answer (c) is incorrect** because the fact that Abigail's business is operated as an unincorporated sole proprietorship does not allow her to "expense" these expenditures. The concepts of capitalization and depreciation apply to businesses regardless of their form. **Answer (d) is incorrect** because while Abigail's expenditures are not deductible in full in the current year, they do not represent "start-up" costs pursuant to IRC § 195.

8. **The most accurate answer is (c).** The general starting place for determining one's basis (adjusted basis hereinafter, AB) is one's cost. [IRC §§ 1011 and 1012.] Abigail paid $1million for the manufacturing building and that is our starting point for her AB. IRC § 1016 requires that certain adjustments be made to the basis of property. While not relevant in our facts, the AB of property is *increased* for such things as major improvements to the property. This section also provides that in general, a property's AB shall be *decreased* by (among other things) the amount of depreciation deductions *allowable* under the law. [IRC § 1016(a)(2).] This means that one's AB in property must be decreased by depreciation deductions that were allowed to the taxpayer regardless of whether the taxpayer actually claimed the deductions.

In our case, therefore, Abigail's AB in the manufacturing building will be the $1 million cost less depreciation *allowable* (even if she chose not to deduct any).

It should be noted that if a taxpayer does not claim the allowed depreciation deductions, the *allowable* depreciation that serves to reduce AB is computed using a particular method of depreciation (among many that might be available if the taxpayer actually claims depreciation deductions). While not at issue in our case, it also should be noted that the reduction of one's AB by depreciation allowed may be limited in certain circumstances when the depreciation allowed would not have resulted in a reduction of taxable income (e.g., the taxpayer had no taxable income before considering any allowed depreciation deductions).

Answer (a) is incorrect. While this is her initial cost basis in the property, as discussed above, it must be reduced by the depreciation that she could claim as deductions. **Answer (b) is not the most accurate answer** although it could be considered correct. As indicated above, one's AB in property is reduced by the amount of depreciation deductions *allowable*. AB reduction does not require, as implied by this answer, that the taxpayer actually claims the allowed depreciation deductions. **Answer (d) is incorrect** because while it is true that the land portion of property is generally not a depreciable asset, the cost of the building component is a depreciable asset. The AB of the land and building combined (the property) will be the total aggregate cost less the depreciation allowable (which is the amount related to the building component of the property).

9. **Answer (d) is correct.** The principal Code section permitting business deductions is IRC § 162. The first sentence of that section (contained in subsection (a)) enumerates, for all intents and purposes, the basic requirements for a business deduction. A deduction is allowed for all "ordinary and necessary" "expenses" "paid or incurred during the taxable year" "in carrying on any trade or business." The compartmentalized quotation marks signify what are commonly considered the four basic requirements for a business deduction. These four requirements often represent, in federal income tax classes and in real life, separate and significant points of contention. Business deductions come in a million different flavors, but all qualifying deductions must meet those four criteria. The study, in tax classes, of business deductions can be long and comprehensive. At times, it may seem like many business deductions have their own set of rules, as if permitted by a separate Code section. There are many business deductions that almost take on a life of their own primarily because of explanations and interpretations from the Code subsections, regulations, court decisions, I.R.S. pronouncements, and the like.

Deductions for transportation costs, the subject of this question, is one such business deduction that appears to have its own set of rules. Wendy, in our problem, drives her car to and from work, between work locations, etc. Some, but not all, of this driving is considered for business purposes (giving rise to deductions for the costs associated therewith). Currently, the general rules for what constitute business and nonbusiness transportation can be distilled into a few basic components.

- Driving to and from one's home and a "regular" (not temporary) place of work are <u>nondeductible</u> commuting miles.
- Driving between two or more "regular" places of work (including different jobs) <u>are</u> deductible business miles.
- Driving to and from a "regular" place of work and a "temporary" or "non-regular" place of work (e.g., a client's office) <u>are</u> deductible business miles.
- Driving to and from one's home and a "temporary" or "non-regular" place of work (e.g., a client's office) <u>are</u> deductible business miles.

A visual depiction of the deductible/nondeductible driving map, as applied to the facts in our question, is as follows:

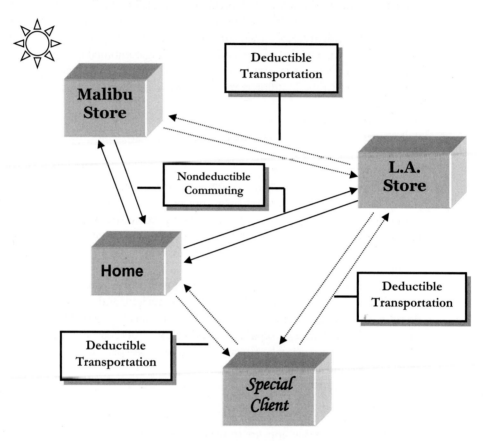

Wendy's driving percentages that qualify for business miles is 40%, the sum of the 25% store-to-store component and the 15% customer-to-home or office component.

This mileage rubric can easily be adapted to various occupations. A physician may have multiple "regular places of work" such as his or her office, and hospitals at which he or she regularly sees patients. An attorney may have an office and regularly make appearances at particular courthouse venues. Historically, the business mileage rules discussed above were different and not always as clear. Additionally, these are merely the "general" rules that apply to the most common business mileage situations. Your professor may cover material far beyond the current and most basic rules.

Answer (a) is incorrect because while the 15% portion of Wendy's miles do constitute business miles, this answer fails to include the additional 25%

qualifying portion. **Answer (b) is similarly incorrect**, failing to include the total qualifying business portions of Wendy's miles driven. **Answer (c) is incorrect** because this answer reflects what was a historical distinction made by the I.R.S. for travel between a temporary place of work, and one's regular place of work versus one's home. **Answer (e) is incorrect** because a correct response (d) is presented.

10. **Answer (a) is the best response.** Okay, so maybe a pet clothing boutique sounds like a bit of a stretch (no offense to pet owners), but it is sometimes difficult to come up with a fact pattern that encourages thoughtful discussion (this question was originally part of an exam essay question).

The principal Code section permitting business deductions is IRC § 162. Most likely, none of Wendy's cost for airfare to/from Seattle is deductible because based on the facts, the trip was not primarily for business. However, if the "pet clothing" sales business is considered the same business as her current business (or a logical expansion or extension thereof), then some of her costs while in Seattle will qualify as deductible business expenses. A more comprehensive analysis follows.

The first sentence of IRC § 162 (which appears in subsection (a)) enumerates, for all intents and purposes, four basic requirements for a business deduction. A business deduction is allowed for all (read as one continuous phrase with four distinct requirements):

> ➢ Ordinary and necessary
> ➢ Expenses
> ➢ Paid or incurred during the taxable year
> ➢ In carrying on any trade or business.

These four requirements often represent, in federal income tax classes and in real life, separate and significant points of contention. Business deductions come in a million different flavors, but all qualifying deductions must meet those four criteria. The study, in tax classes, of business deductions can be long and comprehensive. At times, it may seem like many business deductions have their own set of rules, as if permitted by a separate Code section. There are many business deductions that almost take on a life of their own primarily because of explanations and interpretations from the Code subsections, regulations, court decisions, I.R.S. pronouncements, and the like. In *Wendy's* case, the point of contention is the last of the four IRC § 162 requirements listed above.

Is Wendy Carrying on with Her Existing Business While in Seattle?

The issue distilled is whether or not the retail sale of pet clothing could be considered the same business, an expansion of, or a logical extension of, as that in which she is currently involved. In other words, for there to be *any possible* business deductions arising from her Seattle trip, she must be carrying on her existing trade or business. IRC § 162 deductions do not encompass expenses associated with starting up (or investigating) a new and different trade or business. As indicated, this question was originally part of an exam essay question and was designed to elicit insightful discussions. There is probably no *correct* answer to this particular element as extrapolation from examples in the regulations and from court decisions could point in either direction. If the two businesses are the same trade or business, then we can continue, but if they are considered two different trades or businesses, the discussion ends (with respect to IRC § 162 at least). Because some of the answers to this question contain "assuming that the two are the same" type of language, we will continue with our analysis of her Seattle trip vis-à-vis IRC § 162 business deductions.

<u>Wendy's Trip to Seattle and IRC § 162 Business Expense Deductions</u>

IRC § 162(a)(2) specifically identifies that expenditures associated with "traveling away from home" constitute qualifying business expenses. While this subsection appears to add additional requirements to the four listed above for such traveling expenditures, a careful examination of the statutory language reveals no more than a reiteration of the four basic requirements, albeit in a different form. If we are to assume that the "carrying on a trade or business" requirement of IRC § 162 is met, Wendy did spend some of her time in Seattle on business matters (searching out possible store locations, making business contacts, and talking with suppliers). The regulations promulgated for IRC § 162 are extensive and help to clarify the issues relating to Wendy as well as many other business expense issues that are not the subject of this question. For discussion purposes, Wendy's potential qualifying business expenses are bifurcated into <u>two parts</u>: her <u>transportation costs</u> to and from Los Angeles to Seattle, and her <u>costs incurred during her stay</u> in Seattle. At the outset, however, before discussing these two components, it should be noted that this question deals with potential business travel "away from home" as distinguished from "local" business travel. Business travel "away from home" generally means traveling far enough and long enough away from one's home to require an overnight stay. This is often referred to as the "sleep and rest" rule or test. [See *United States v. Correll*, 389 US 299, 88 S.Ct. 445 (1967).] Business travel "away from home" opens the door to potential deductions for lodging, non-entertainment meals, incidentals, etc. Other questions in this book address the issue of where a taxpayer's "home" is located and the issue of "local" travel for business (usually concerned only about deductions for transportation related expenses).

Wendy's transportation costs to/from Seattle (her airfare) qualifies as a business expense _if_ the "trip is related primarily to [her] . . . trade or business." [Reg. § 1.162-2(b)(1).] The regulations, at Reg. § 1.162-2(b)(2), provide some guidance in making this determination. The regulation indicates that this determination is to be made based on the facts and circumstances in each case. The regulation also indicates that an important factor for making this determination is the number of days spent on business compared to the number of days spent for pleasure. Basing a decision on the totality of our facts, we would most likely conclude that Wendy's Seattle trip was <u>not</u> made primarily for business purposes. Wendy's round-trip airfare from Los Angeles to Seattle does <u>not qualify</u> as a deductible business expense. Note that for domestic travel, as is the case in this problem, deduction of transportation costs for traveling away from home is an "all or nothing" proposition. If the trip is primarily for business, 100% of the taxpayer's transportation related costs generally qualify as business expenses pursuant to IRC § 162. Alternatively, as is the case with Wendy, <u>none</u> of the transportation costs qualify as business expenses if the trip is primarily for pleasure. It should be noted that the rules for "foreign" travel may differ and proration of transportation costs between deductible business and nondeductible personal expenses may be appropriate.

The Regulations do provide, however, that "expenses while at the destination which are properly allocable to the taxpayer's trade or business are deductible even though the traveling expenses to and from the destination are not deductible." The days that Wendy spent on business activities while in Seattle, should be considered as traveling away from home in connection with the conduct of a trade or business. Her expenses related to those days would qualify as IRC § 162 business expenses. While not necessary to answer this question, these expenses could include the cost of lodging and incidentals for full business-related days as well as 50% of her meals for days that she spent conducting business. The 50% deduction limitation for business meals comes not from IRC § 162 but, rather, is supplied by IRC § 274(n)(1). This 50% limitation is applicable to most business or entertainment meals that are otherwise allowed as deductions. Please see other questions in this book relating to meal and entertainment expenses.

It should be noted that an individual can incur qualifying IRC § 162 expenses in the context of working as an employee, or, like in Wendy's case, in an individual's own business (someone who is alternatively referred to as being self-employed, an independent contractor, or operating his or her business as an "unincorporated sole proprietorship"). The requirements for deductibility pursuant to § 162 are the same for an employee or a self-employed individual. However, the effective availability of an actual business deduction, and where it is deducted, varies dramatically depending on one's "work status." The *Tax Cuts and Jobs Act* (TCJA) signed into law in December 2017 (generally effective beginning in 2018) made significant changes, and not in a good way, for deductions of business expenses by employees. Under the TCJA, deductions for unreimbursed business expenses incurred by employees, have, for the most part, been "suspended" for 2018 through 2025. [IRC § 67(g)]. This distinction is not relevant for Wendy, but it is important to note that for employees, the TCJA now generally eliminates the actual deductibility of such business expenses if incurred as an employee. This topic, as well as one small exception, is addressed in other questions in this book.

While not specifically addressed in this question, our facts do raise another important tax issue (i.e., an issue that would be discussed if these facts were presented in essay question form). IRC § 195 addresses "start-up expenditures." Basically, these are expenditures that would qualify as IRC § 162 business expenses *but for the fact* that the taxpayer is not carrying on an existing trade or business. In essay form, our facts would elicit this issue because Wendy's contemplated pet clothing business is, arguably, a new and different business for her. In such a case, as discussed above, her business-related expenses (site investigation, supplier meetings, etc.) would not qualify as IRC § 162 expenses. If Wendy decided to enter this new business, these expenditures would, however, qualify as IRC § 195 start-up expenditures. While not a blanket allowance for an immediate deduction, IRC § 195 provides the taxpayer with an election to deduct up to $5,000 of such expenses when the taxpayer starts the business (but this immediate deduction is reduced or "phased-out" when aggregate start-up costs exceed specified amounts), with any excess of such expenses "amortized" (or deducted ratably) over a period of time (a minimum period of 180 months (15 years) starting with the month in which the business begins). [IRC § 195(b).]

Answer (b) is not correct because it incorrectly states that none of Wendy's costs while in Seattle qualify as IRC § 162 business expenses even if she is considered to be involved in the same trade or business. **Answer (c) is incorrect** because the transportation costs for domestic business travel is not prorated. Rather, it is fully deductible if the trip was primarily for business purposes or, not deductible at all if the trip was primarily for pleasure. **Answer (d) is incorrect** because her airfare is most likely not a deductible business expense. **Answer (e) is incorrect** because her transportation costs are most likely nondeductible, and at most, only some of her costs while in Seattle qualify as deductible business expenses.

11. **The correct answer is (b).** As with question 10, above, our analysis begins with deductions for business expenses under IRC § 162. An individual can incur qualifying § 162 expenses in the context of working as an employee, or, as a self-employed individual (a.k.a., independent contractor or unincorporated sole proprietor). The four basic requirements for qualified business expense deductions are the same for an employee or a self-employed individual (although, as discussed in other questions in this book, the *Tax Cuts and Jobs Act*, or TCJA, signed into law in December 2017 (generally effective beginning in 2018), effectively eliminates actual deductions by employees of otherwise qualifying IRC § 162 business expenses). In general, IRC § 162 allows for business deductions that are (read as one continuous phrase with four distinct requirements):

> ➤ Ordinary and necessary
> ➤ Expenses
> ➤ Paid or incurred during the taxable year
> ➤ In carrying on any trade or business.

Arguably, some of Hank's expenses while in Seattle would satisfy these requirements. However, to spare the reader from what would be a long, and in the end, an irrelevant discussion, another Code section is controlling here. While short and somewhat obscure, IRC § 274(m)(2) provides us with the ultimate answer that Hank's expenditures do <u>not</u> give rise to deductible expenses by stating: "No deduction shall be allowed under this chapter for expenses for travel as a form of education."

Answer (a) is incorrect because this deduction preclusion provision applies to both employees and self-employed individuals. **Answers (c) and (d) are both incorrect** because, as discussed above, none of Hank's costs associated with this trip are deductible.

12. **Answer (b) is correct.** The weight-loss program fees paid by Chad and Donna will qualify as medical care expenses pursuant to IRC § 213.

IRC § 213 allows for a deduction of certain qualified medical expenses. Once one makes the determination of what constitutes "qualified" medical care expenses, the subject of this question, the deduction is allowed as an "itemized deduction" only to the extent that the total qualifying expenses exceeds 10% of adjusted gross income (AGI). [See Appendix A for more information about how income and deductions fit together in computing taxable income.] Qualified medical care expenses include typical costs for doctors, dentists, hospital, health insurance, and the like. [See IRC § 213(d).] The I.R.S. had not, until 2002, been particularly lenient when it came to weight-loss programs qualifying as deductible medical care expenses.

Revenue Ruling 2002-19 presents facts that are essentially identical to those in our question, and the I.R.S. concludes that our answer (b) is correct. [Rev.Rul. 2002-19, 2002-16 I.R.B. 778.]

Historically, Donna's weight-loss program fees were more likely to qualify as medical care expenses than those for Chad. Losing weight to improve a taxpayer's general health is not considered a disease, giving rise to deductible medical health care expenses, and historically, it was not apparent that the I.R.S. considered obesity as a disease. However, in the above-cited Revenue Ruling, the I.R.S. does recognize obesity to be a "disease in its own right." Costs for losing weight to treat a disease, for Chad's obesity and directed by Donna's physician for her hypertension, are qualified medical care expenses.

However, the costs of the program's diet food items do not qualify as medical care expenses as they are substitutes for the food that Chad and Donna would "normally consume to satisfy their nutritional requirements." [Rev.Rul. 2002-19, 2002-16 I.R.B 778.]

While not really affecting the answer to this question, the *Tax Cuts and Jobs Act* (TCJA) signed into law in December 2017, did change one component of deductions for qualified medical expenditures. The TCJA did not materially affect what constitutes qualified medical expenses under IRC § 213, but it did change the extent to which taxpayers can claim medical expense deductions. Embedded in our question is a reference to the deduction being available only to the extent that total qualified medical expenses exceed 10% of Adjusted Gross Income. This is commonly referred to as a "floor" in computing an individual's actual deduction and does not work in the taxpayer's favor as it eliminates some, or all, of the actual deduction depending on the individual's Adjusted Gross Income (itself a somewhat complex calculation). Over the years, this percentage floor has varied from a low of 3% to what had been a stable 7.5% since 1986. The TCJA raised this floor to 10% for all taxpayers beginning in 2019. The lower this floor percentage, the better it is for individuals. Therefore, this most recent change, along with other changes to deductions discussed elsewhere in this book, is not beneficial to individuals.

Answer (a) is incorrect but, until the above-referenced 2002 Revenue Ruling, would have most likely been the correct answer. **Answer (c) is incorrect** because it incorrectly includes the diet foods as qualifying medical care expenses. **Answer (d) is incorrect** because it fails to recognize that Chad's weight-loss program/meeting fees qualify as medical care expenses. In addition, it incorrectly includes Donna's food costs as qualifying medical care expenses. **Answer (e) is incorrect** because a correct answer (b) is presented.

13. **The best answer is (c).** Shirin is facing the problem that many new (and not so new) professionals face: a huge outlay of funds for new clothes. Unfortunately, these costs are rarely deductible as business expenses. While those having to wear such attire may subjectively view this type of clothing as a *uniform*, objectively it is not the type of *uniform* for which business deductions are allowed.

In general, IRC § 162 allows for business deductions that are (read as one continuous phrase with four distinct requirements):
- ➢ Ordinary and necessary
- ➢ Expenses
- ➢ Paid or incurred during the taxable year
- ➢ In carrying on any trade or business.

Shirin may argue that her expenditures for her newly acquired business wardrobe meets these requirements, but the I.R.S. sees it otherwise. Their position is that *uniforms* qualify as deductible business expenses only if "(1) the uniforms are specifically required as a condition of employment and (2) are not of a type adaptable to general or continued usage to the extent that they take the place of ordinary clothing." [Rev.Rul. 70-474, 1970-2 C.B. 34.] The first requirement, as applicable to a self-employed individual, is effectively if the type of work one performs "requires" a particular type of *uniform*.] Work required safety clothes, helmets, work gloves, special boots, and the like, are examples of deductible items, as are uniforms worn by police, athletes, airline pilots, and the like (assuming the individual must pay for them and is not reimbursed for their cost).

Unfortunately, Shirin's business attire does not fit the I.R.S.'s interpretation of deductible work clothes. While most likely not applicable to Shirin, there have been rare instances, and under somewhat extraordinary circumstances, where certain clothing has been allowed as a business deduction notwithstanding that it could have been worn in public. [See *Betsy Lusk Yeomans*, 30 T.C 757 (1958), (fashion coordinator for high-end shoe manufacturer allowed to deduct costs of latest fashions that she was required to wear on the job that were not suitable for her private and personal use).] Another interesting case involved "America's favorite family, the "Nelsons." *The Adventures of Ozzie and Harriet*, a television series that aired long before most of today's students were born, had a little known "income tax" issue associated with the program. Ozzie deducted the costs of his and his family's everyday clothing used on the television series claiming that the test for deductibility should be applied on the basis of whether the clothing was actually worn in public. In this rare instance, the Tax Court agreed (as to the parent's clothes only, as they could not show that their two sons, David and the "irrepressible little Ricky," did not wear their "TV" clothes while off the set). [*Oswald Nelson v. Comm'r*, ¶ 66224 P-H T.C. (1966).]

Answer (a) is incorrect because even if this were a factor, her clothes would most likely not qualify for business deductions as discussed above. **Answer (b) is also incorrect**. While not likely in Shirin's case, there have been a few extraordinary instances where deductions have been allowed in such situations. **Answer (d) is incorrect** because the fact that Shirin's type of work requires that she wear such attire does not render it deductible as discussed above. **Answer (e) is incorrect** because these could not be considered qualifying "start-up" costs pursuant to IRC § 195, as they would not otherwise qualify, as discussed above, as deductible business expenses.

14. **Response (c) is the best answer.** This question is a bit unfair because the correct answer requires a substantially correct analysis of the previous question, 13. This professor would not ask both of these questions in an objective exam. Rather, these two questions were derived from an exam essay question. Unfortunately for Shirin, and most other individuals facing high costs of clothes maintenance (i.e., the costs of dry-cleaning), these costs do not qualify as deductible business expenses.

Maintenance costs for clothes, the purchase of which gave rise to a business deduction, are also deductible. For Shirin to deduct her clothes maintenance costs, this would mean that the cost of her business clothes would have had to qualify as deductible business expenses. As discussed above, unfortunately, her clothes are most likely not considered deductible *uniforms* because of the I.R.S.'s position on the issue. Recall that *uniforms* qualify as deductible business expenses only if "(1) the uniforms are specifically required as a condition of employment [or the nature of the business for a self-employed individual] and (2) are not of a type adaptable to general or continued usage to the extent that they take the place of ordinary clothing." [Rev.Rul. 70-474, 1970-2 C.B. 34.]

Answer (a) is incorrect because even the time she is wearing her clothes on business, the maintenance of them is not considered a deductible business expense. **Answer (b) is incorrect** because her clothes did not qualify as a deductible business expense as discussed in the analysis to question 13, above. **Answer (d) is incorrect** because in cases where the cost of clothing does give rise to legitimate business deductions, the cost of their maintenance also generally qualifies as a business expense.

15. Statement (d) is the most accurate. While we raise a glass of Greg's fine craft beer to toast this question, please note that a portion of this question makes for a somewhat clumsy analysis because it involves IRC § 164 and relevant facts, such as Greg's state of residence and other tax-related items, that are unknown to us (see below).

We first discuss the portion of the question that is <u>not</u> dependent on facts that are unknown: the business component of Greg's deductions here. The principal Code section permitting business deductions is IRC § 162. The first sentence of that section (contained in subsection (a)) enumerates, for all intents and purposes, the basic requirements for a business deduction. A deduction is allowed for all "ordinary and necessary" "expenses" "paid or incurred during the taxable year" "in carrying on any trade or business." The compartmentalized quotation marks signify what are commonly considered as the four basic requirements for a business deduction. These four requirements often represent, in federal income tax classes and in real life, separate and significant points of contention. Business deductions come in a million different flavors, but all qualifying deductions must meet those four criteria. The study, in tax classes, of business deductions can be long and comprehensive. At times, it may seem like many business deductions have their own set of rules, as if permitted by a separate Code section. There are many business deductions that almost take on a life of their own primarily because of explanations and interpretations from the Code subsections, regulations, court decisions, I.R.S. pronouncements, and the like.

The $2,000 Greg paid in rental costs for the construction equipment fits squarely within the requirements for business deductions under IRC § 162. The $160 in sales tax that was charged on the rental is also deductible as part of the rental cost pursuant to IRC § 162. Thus, Greg is entitled to deduct the full $2,160 associated with this equipment rental as a business expense.

For the deductibility of the $3,700 Greg paid in sales tax on his personal-use MV Agusta motorcycle (which, by the way, is an awesome bike), we need to turn to IRC § 164. This is where the explanation to this question becomes somewhat clumsy and fact-specific. IRC § 164(a) lists various taxes that are deductible including: state, local and foreign *income taxes* and real property taxes, and state and local personal property taxes. State and local sales taxes are not listed as deductible taxes in this part of the Code section and, if we just stopped there, the statute would preclude Greg from deducting the $3,700 in sales taxes paid on the purchase of the motorcycle. Beginning in 2004, IRC § 164 was amended to allow taxpayers the option to deduct state and local sales taxes paid *in lieu of* the otherwise allowed deduction for state and local income taxes. [The then new law added IRC § 164(b)(5))]. For taxpayers living in states which impose no state income tax, this choice is an easy, and, potentially, beneficial, one. At this point we have enough to answer this question; Greg *may benefit* from the possible deduction of sales taxes paid on the purchase of his motorcycle (in real-life, Greg would decide to deduct total state/local sales taxes he paid during the year only if the aggregate amount exceeded his total state/local income taxes paid during the year).

Remaining on the issue of Greg's potential deduction for sales taxes (in lieu of state/local income taxes) pursuant to IRC § 164, the author would be remiss if this answer did not include changes made by the *Tax Cuts and Tax Jobs Act* (TCJA) signed into law in December 2017 (generally effective beginning in 2018). As indicated above, IRC § 164 provides for deductions for various state and local taxes. These are of a personal nature and not taxes that are deductible as part, for example as in Greg's case, of business expenses (referring to the sales taxes paid on his business equipment rental). The §164 deductible taxes include, as mentioned in the discussion above, state, local and foreign *income taxes* (or, as we've seen, state and local sales taxes in lieu thereof) and real property taxes, and state and local personal property taxes. Examples of this basket of potential deduction for taxes paid include such items as one's state income taxes paid (e.g., through withholding, estimated tax payments, amounts owed when filing state income tax returns, etc.), property taxes on one's house and other property, a portion, in some states, of, for example, an annual motor vehicle registration fee, just to mention a few). Historically (including in earlier editions of this book), there was no real limit on the aggregate amount of deductible taxes pursuant to IRC § 164. The only real question was whether an individual had enough of these deductible taxes, combined with other *itemized deductions* (such as *charitable* deductions, *qualifying medical* expenses, *home mortgage interest*; please see other questions in this book addressing such deductions), to benefit from them (versus taking a *standard deduction*, also addressed in other questions in this book). With the TCJA now law, the rules have become much more complex and, sadly, less beneficial to individuals with respect to the IRC § 164 deduction for taxes. In a nutshell, the TCJA, beginning in 2018, puts an artificial $10,000 deduction cap for the aggregate of such state and local taxes. [IRC § 164(b)(6)] Known as the SALT (state and local taxes) tax deduction limit or just SALT, some taxpayers have, almost overnight, taken a huge tax "hit" because of this limit. Other questions in this book address the mechanics of SALT limit, but it is easy to see its large negative impact for a solidly middle-class homeowner, say for example, living in the state of this author (California) where pre TCJA deductions for such taxes could easily exceed $30,000. As of this writing, with the first full tax filing season under the TCJA now complete, the news is filled with stories of the deleterious impact of this one change, including calls by some members of Congress to abandon this $10,000 cap on SALT deductions.

Separately, in light of the SALT limit imposed by the TCJA, a number of states with income taxes on the higher end of the scale, have explored creative ways to "reclassify" their state's income tax as some form of *charitable* contribution, to effectuate a deduction that is outside those covered by SALT (as of this writing, the general consensus of their viability (and legality) among "tax folk" is not overly optimistic. Politics aside (the author apologizes for what may have sounded like an opinion-laden diversion), it should be noted that the $10,000 SALT limit is not a "per-person" limit for married individuals filing together (a *joint return* is the norm and is addressed in other questions in this book). Rather, it is just $10,000 per return and if a married couple elects to file separately (this is a complex issue addressed elsewhere in this book), each faces a $5,000 cap. [IRC § 164(b)(6)(B)]

Before leaving this question, we should go back and revisit a more overarching issue. The possible deductibility of sales taxes pursuant to multiple Code sections is often bothersome, or at least confusing, to students especially in situations such as those presented in this question. IRC § 164 appears to control deductions for taxes paid. Indeed, IRC § 164 lists *sales taxes,* albeit is an ungainly fashion through an "add-on" provision. Yet we found that sales taxes paid with respect to Greg's equipment rental (no different in substance or application) was a valid deduction pursuant to a different (and more beneficial) Code provision as a business expense via IRC § 162. Tax law is rife with such multi-sectional application to items and here, just because we would naturally turn first to IRC §164 state/local income and sales tax deductions does not mean that some other Code provision might apply (and yield a more beneficial deduction for a taxpayer). In Greg's case, the *sales tax* paid on the equipment rental, while a valid IRC §164 deduction, is also a qualified business deduction pursuant to IRC § 162 (and in his case, deductions via the latter section are more beneficial to him). The sales tax he paid on his motorcycle, however, is not deductible under some other Code provision. In other words, IRC § 164 does not limit or preclude a deduction via other Code provisions. While not relevant for this question, the possible multi-section availability for deductions that we see with respect to the sales tax paid on Greg's business equipment rental (IRC §§ 162 and 164; it is Greg's choice but it can't be deducted twice) can be distinguished from that of IRC § 163 dealing with deductions for interest paid. If a taxpayer pays interest, it must pass through the limitations and requirements imposed by IRC § 163 to be deductible at all; IRC § 163 acts as a clearinghouse for deductibility for all interest paid (as opposed to an alternative section for the deduction of interest paid).

While not part of this question, it should be noted that Greg's qualifying business expenses of $2,160 is deductible, along with other IRC § 162 business expenses, "above the line" to determine his "adjusted gross income" (AGI) which, in turn, is part of the computation of his taxable income. [Please see Appendix A for more information about how income and deductions fit together in the computation of taxable income and AGI]. Also, in our question, Greg is conducting business as a self-employed individual. [Please see other questions in this book that address IRC §162 business expenses and their actual deductibility, or lack thereof, for such business expenses incurred as an employee.]

Answer (a) is incorrect because it fails to recognize that the sales tax Greg paid with respect to the equipment rental does not require IRC § 164 to be deductible but, rather, is deductible as a business expense under IRC § 162. **Answer (b) is not the best answer** because of the special provision in IRC § 164(b)(5) which gives the taxpayer the option to deduct state/local sales taxes in lieu of state/local income taxes. **Answer (c) is not the best answer**. It is true that sales taxes <u>may</u> be deductible pursuant to IRC § 164 and Greg did incur $160 in sales taxes on his business equipment rental. As discussed above, however, this portion of sales taxes relating to the equipment rental is more appropriately (and to Greg's advantage) deductible as an IRC § 162 business expense. **Answer (e) is incorrect** because a correct answer (d) is available.

16. **Response (e) is the best answer.** This is a somewhat tedious question as it involves numerous aspects of what should be a simple tax provision. This section implicates IRC § 164, relating to deductions for various taxes paid by an individual. We will, in our discussion below, determine that Ira's deductible taxes presented in the question consist of the $5,000 property taxes on his home and the $7,000 he paid in state income taxes. Ultimately, however, we will determine that his total deduction will be limited to $10,000 pursuant to the *Tax Cuts and Jobs Act* signed into law in December 2017 (generally effective beginning in 2018). Unfortunately, a full discussion of this answer requires us to examine many other components of IRC § 164 and various changes made, thereto, by the TCJA (and earlier laws).

IRC § 164(a) is an example of a section that, with a cursory reading, is not overly complex. Not a political comment, but this section becomes more complex by new subsections that were added (tacked on contradictory provisions as opposed to being integrated into the section language) by the aforementioned TJCA as well as other tax laws). Our long analysis is not complex, but just cumbersome because of the structure of the statute as amended by tax laws over the years. So no worries, we will be methodical in our analysis. First, let's start with the basics of IRC § 164. The section (in subsection (a)) lists various taxes that are deductible including:
   ➤ State and local, and foreign, real property taxes
   ➤ State and local personal property taxes

> ➤ State and local, and foreign, income . . . taxes . . .

This subsection (a) of the statute has remained basically unchanged for years and if we stopped here, it would appear that more of Ira's taxes listed in this question would give rise to a deduction. Alas, we must read deeper into section 164.

Note that state and local sales taxes are not listed as deductible taxes in this first part of the section and here is where we come to our first "tacked on" revision. Beginning in 2004, IRC § 164 was amended to allow taxpayers the option to deduct state and local sales taxes paid *in lieu of* the otherwise allowed deduction for state and local income taxes. [The then new law added IRC § 164(b)(5))]. Ostensibly, this was done to assist taxpayers in states that impose no (or minimal) income taxes at the state level (e.g., Texas, Florida, Washington, to name a few). For taxpayers living in states which impose no state income tax, this choice is an easy, and, potentially, beneficial, one. At this point, there is enough information to analyze another piece of our question; Ira's $3,000 in California sales taxes are potentially deductible, but this deduction would be *in lieu* of his greater $7,000 paid in California Income taxes. At this juncture in the question analysis, while his California sales taxes are potentially deductible, he would not "take this" because it would preclude a larger state income tax deduction.

Looking back at our question, we see that Ira also paid $9,000 in property taxes on his vacation home in Luxembourg. It is easy to find that under the beginning part of section 164 [IRC § 164(a)], such foreign property taxes are listed among taxes that are deductible. Unfortunately for Ira, we must look further down the statute where we will find a "tacked-on" provision that will tell us something completely different. Again, not a model of statutory construction but, rather, the reflection of changes made to the law appear as "ad-on" parts as opposed to being reflected in revisions to earlier parts of the statute. The *Tax Jobs and Tax Jobs Act* (TCJA) signed into law in December 2017 (generally effective in 2018) added subsection (b)(6) to section 164 and its name alone is the harbinger of bad things, "Limitation on individual deductions for taxable years 2018 through 2025." Specifically, with respect to foreign property taxes listed as a deduction in subsection (a) of the section, subsection (b)(6)(A) overrides such deductions stating, "[F]oreign real property taxes shall not be taken into account under subsection (a)(1)." This TCJA provision effectively eliminates foreign property taxes as a deduction beginning in 2018. Turning back to Ira in our question, even though his foreign property taxes were deductible in years prior to 2018, they are no longer in his equation for deductible taxes under IRC § 164. While not at issue in our question, it should be noted that such deductions are still possible for businesses and business-like rental real estate operations. To reiterate where we are at this point for Ira in our question, he has deductible taxes consisting of his $5,000 domestic property taxes as well as his $7,000 in California income taxes.

We have a consistent theme that if we read no further in the statute, we would conclude that Ira's IRC §164 deduction for taxes paid would be a total of $12,000 ($5,000 domestic property taxes plus $7,000 state income taxes). Historically (including in the earlier edition of this book), this would have been the case (plus Ira would have been able to add the $9,000 foreign property taxes he paid to this total). But, of course, we must read more of the statute and we soon come across a second "bad" thing for taxpayers in the same subsection (b)(6) that eliminated the deduction for foreign property taxes beginning in 2018. Specifically, IRC §164 (b)(6)(B) places an artificial $10,000 deduction cap for the aggregate of otherwise deductible section 164 taxes paid. This provision, which was part of the TCJA, is now commonly known as the SALT (state and local taxes) tax deduction limit or just SALT. Turning to Ira in our question, his IRC § 164 deductions will be limited to $10,000 notwithstanding that under pre-TCJA law his tax deductions would have been much greater ($21,000 in his case; domestic and foreign property taxes and his state income taxes, the latter which were greater than his state sales taxes).

Not to be read as a political comment, but with the signing into law of the *Tax Cuts and Jobs Act* (TCJA) in December 2017, the rules have become much more complex and, sadly, less beneficial to individuals with respect to the IRC § 164 deduction for taxes paid. With the TCJA, some taxpayers have, almost overnight, taken a huge tax "hit" because of this limit. It is easy to imagine the large negative impact for a solidly middle-class homeowner, say for example, living in the state of this author (California) where pre TCJA IRC § 164 deductions for taxes could easily exceed $30,000. As of this writing, with the first full tax filing season under the TCJA now complete, the news is filled with stories of the deleterious impact of this one change, including calls by some members of Congress to abandon this $10,000 cap on SALT deductions. Separately, in light of the SALT limit imposed by the TCJA, a number of states with income taxes on the higher end of the scale, have explored creative ways to "reclassify" their state's income tax as some form of *charitable* contribution, to effectuate a deduction that is outside those covered by SALT (as of this writing, the general consensus of their viability (and legality) among "tax folk" is not overly optimistic. Politics aside (the author apologizes for the what may have sounded like an opinion-laden diversion), it should be noted that the $10,000 SALT limit is not a "per-person" limit for married individuals filing together (a *joint return* is the norm and is addressed in other questions in this book). Rather, it is just $10,000 per return and if a married couple elects to file separately (this is a complex

issue addressed elsewhere in this book), each faces a $5,000 cap. [IRC §
164(b)(6)(B)]

Other questions in this book address how these IRC § 164 deductions for
taxes fit into the larger picture of determining an individual's net or *taxable
income.*

Answer (a) is incorrect because it incorrectly includes all of the taxes Ira
paid as giving rise to a deduction. In addition, it does not apply the $10,000
SALT limit for total IRC §164 deductions enumerated in IRC §164(b)(6)(B).
Answer (b) is also incorrect. While it correctly reflects no deduction for
Ira's state sales taxes because it is not greater than state income taxes he
paid, it incorrectly includes the foreign property tax paid which, under the
TCJA, is not deductible pursuant to IRC 164(b)(6)(A). In addition, this
answer does not reflect the $10,000 SALT cap for total IRC § 164
deductions enumerated in IRC §164(b)(6)(B). **Answer (c) is incorrect.** It
appears to reflect an incorrect aggregation of both sales and income taxes
paid as being a legitimate deduction (it is the greater of the two) and adds
Ira's domestic property taxes paid. In addition, this answer does not reflect
the $10,000 SALT cap for total IRC § 164 deductions enumerated in IRC
§164(b)(6)(B). **Answer (d) is incorrect but is close to being correct.** It
properly reflects which of Ira's taxes are eligible for deductions (state
income tax plus domestic property tax) but fails to reflect the $10,000 SALT
cap for total IRC § 164 deductions enumerated in IRC §164(b)(6)(B).

17. **Response (c) is the best answer.** This question is somewhat similar to
the immediately preceding question 16. A full analysis will follow (and is a
bit repetitive of the response for question 16) but the shortened version is
as follows: This section implicates IRC § 164, relating to deductions for
various taxes paid by an individual. We will, in our discussion below,
determine that all of taxes Claudia paid in the current year ($4,000 sales
taxes, $5,000 and $3,000 property taxes on her Washington home and
Connecticut land, respectively) are "sort-of" deductible taxes. Ultimately,
however, we will determine that her total deduction will be limited to
$10,000 pursuant to the *Tax Cuts and Jobs Act* (TCJA) signed into law in
December 2017 (generally effective beginning in 2018). Unfortunately, a full
discussion of this answer requires us to examine many other components of
IRC § 164 and various changes made, thereto, by the TCJA (and earlier
laws).

IRC § 164(a) is an example of a section that, with a cursory reading, is not
overly complex. Not a political comment, but this section becomes more
complex by new subsections that were added (tacked on contradictory
provisions as opposed to being integrated into the section language) by the
aforementioned TJCA as well as other tax laws). Our long analysis is not

complex, but just cumbersome because of the structure of the statute as amended by tax laws over the years. So no worries, we will be methodical in our analysis.

First, let's start with the basics of IRC § 164. The section (in subsection (a)) lists various taxes that are deductible including:

> ➤ State and local, and foreign, real property taxes
> ➤ State and local personal property taxes
> ➤ State and local, and foreign, income . . . taxes . . .

This subsection (a) of the statute has remained basically unchanged for years and if we stopped here, it would appear that only Claudia's property taxes (for her Washington home and Connecticut property) would give rise to a deduction. We must, however, read deeper into section 164.

Note that state and local sales taxes are not listed as deductible taxes in this first part of the section and here is where we come to our first "tacked on" revision. Beginning in 2004, IRC § 164 was amended to allow taxpayers the option to deduct state and local sales taxes paid *in lieu of* the otherwise allowed deduction for state and local income taxes. [The then new law added IRC § 164(b)(5))]. Ostensibly, this was done to assist taxpayers in states that impose no (or minimal) income taxes at the state level (e.g., Texas, Florida, Washington, to name a few). For taxpayers living in states which impose no state income tax, this choice is an easy, and, potentially, beneficial, one. At this point we have enough information to analyze another piece of our question; the $4,000 that Claudia paid in Washington sales taxes is a potential IRC §164 deduction. This deduction would be *in lieu* of any state income tax that she paid and for Claudia, the choice is simple; she will "take," as a deduction, the sales taxes paid because it is larger than zero (what she paid in state income tax).

Next, we come to the property taxes that Claudia paid both on her Washington home and Connecticut land. Both of these taxes fit squarely within the basic list of "taxes" paid allowed as a deduction. It is irrelevant that these property taxes are levied in different states. Had she paid property taxes on property located in a foreign country, these would not be allowed (see discussion for question 16, above).

We have a consistent theme that if we read no further in the statute, we would conclude that Claudia's IRC §164 deduction for taxes paid would be a total of $12,000 ($4,000 sales taxes plus property taxes of $5,000 and $3,000). Historically (including in the earlier edition of this book), this have been the case. But, of course, we must read more of the statute and we soon come across something potentially very "bad" for taxpayers beginning in

2018. Specifically, IRC §164 (b)(6)(B) places an artificial $10,000 deduction cap for the aggregate of otherwise deductible section 164 taxes paid. This provision was part of the *Tax Cuts and Jobs Act* (TCJA) signed into law in 2017 (generally effective beginning in 2018). This new provision in IRC § 164, is now commonly known as the SALT (state and local taxes) tax deduction limit or just SALT. Turning to Claudia in our question, her IRC § 164 deductions will be limited to $10,000 notwithstanding that under pre-TCJA law her tax deductions would have been greater ($12,000 in her case; sales taxes plus both property tax amounts).

Not to be read as a political comment, but with the signing into law of the *Tax Cuts and Jobs Act* (TCJA) in December 2017, the rules have become much more complex and, sadly, less beneficial to individuals with respect to the IRC § 164 deduction for taxes paid. With the TCJA, some taxpayers have, almost overnight, taken a huge tax "hit" because of this limit. While Claudia, in our current problem, does not suffer too badly from the changes, it is easy to imagine the large negative impact for a solidly middle-class homeowner, say for example, living in the state of this author (California) where pre TCJA IRC § 164 deductions for taxes could easily exceed $30,000. As of this writing, with the first full tax filing season under the TCJA now complete, the news is filled with stories of the deleterious impact of this one change, including calls by some members of Congress to abandon this $10,000 cap on SALT deductions.

Separately, in light of the SALT limit imposed by the TCJA, a number of states with income taxes on the higher end of the scale, have explored creative ways to "reclassify" their state's income tax as some form of *charitable* contribution, to effectuate a deduction that is outside those covered by SALT (as of this writing, the general consensus of their viability (and legality) among "tax folk" is not overly optimistic. Politics aside (the author apologizes for the what may have sounded like an opinion-laden diversion), it should be noted that the $10,000 SALT limit is not a "per-person" limit for married individuals filing together (a *joint return* is the norm and is addressed in other questions in this book). Rather, it is just $10,000 per return and if a married couple elects to file separately (this is a complex issue addressed elsewhere in this book), each faces a $5,000 cap. [IRC § 164(b)(6)(B)]

Other questions in this book address how these IRC § 164 deductions for taxes fit into the larger picture of determining an individual's net or *taxable income*.

Answer (a) is incorrect because while it appears to include what Claudia paid in property taxes on both of her properties, it does not reflect the available deduction for sales taxes (in lieu of her income taxes which were zero). **Answer (b) is incorrect** because it appears to include only her Washington-based sales and property taxes but does not include an otherwise viable deduction for her Connecticut property taxes. **Answer (d) is incorrect** because while it includes all of the appropriate taxes deductible under IRC § 164, it does not reflect the $10,000 SALT cap for total IRC § 164 deductions enumerated in IRC §164(b)(6)(B).

18. **The most accurate statement is (e).** This problem, in a modified form, appeared in the last edition of this book. The answer then was quite different from now and began with this ominous statement: "The path to reach the conclusion in this question is somewhat long." In this edition of the book, we will see that the analysis is much shorter, and the end result is that Takuma will not be entitled to a deduction the cost of the tickets for the baseball game (as an entertainment or business expense). The answer, therefore, is the dreaded "none of the above" response. While bottom line is that he will not be entitled to any deduction here, the facts do merit analysis (albeit much less complex than for this question in the previous edition of the book).

Takuma's activities appear to be business related and would seem to be deductible if we were to apply the requirements for business deductions of IRC § 162 (that the expenditures be *ordinary and necessary expenses paid in connection with carrying on a trade or business*). [Please see other questions in this book addressing the general business deduction requirements of IRC § 162.] Because of the "entertainment" like nature of these business activities, the more restrictive provisions of IRC § 274 are applicable. IRC § 274 is a limiting section, enacted to curtail what were considered abuses to entertainment-related business deductions. In earlier editions of this book, we would go through a rather tedious journey through IRC § 274 and see that if certain requirements were met, one could deduct 50% of qualifying entertainment expenses. The *Tax Cuts and Jobs Act* (TCJA) signed into law in December 2017 (generally effective beginning in 2018) made dramatic changes to the deductibility of business expenses that fall within what is considered "entertainment" (think of when business activities have an entertainment, amusement, or fun sort of "flavor" to them). Beginning in 2018, and pursuant to the TCJA, entertainment-related business expenses are, generally, no longer deductible at all. [IRC § 274(a)(1)].

We could continue with an analysis of the pre-TCJA rules and requirements, but such requirements (e.g., such expenses had to be either be *directly related to*, or *associated with*, the active conduct of a trade or business in order to obtain a 50% deduction for such expenses), but such requirements have been rendered moot in light of current law.

Answers (a) through (d) are all incorrect because to some degree, each of these answers incorporate pre-TCJA concepts for deduction of entertainment type business expenses.

19. **Statement (b) is the most accurate.** This question is an extension of question 18, above, and the analysis is somewhat similar but, as we shall see, will have a different conclusion. Specifically, Takuma will be entitled to deduct 50% of the cost of his lunch with Christina. First, the cost of his lunch with her qualifies as an IRC § 162 business expense. Because we are dealing with a "meal," we must then turn to IRC § 274 where, we will conclude, his deduction will be limited to 50% of the cost of the lunch. A more thorough analysis follows, and it requires us to look at new, and somewhat conflicting, provisions enacted by the *Tax Cuts and Jobs Act* (TCJA) signed into law in December 2017 (generally effective beginning in 2018).

The first step in our analysis is determining whether Takuma's lunch with Christina is a deductible business expense. IRC §162 is the core section and the first sentence of the section (which appears in subsection (a) enumerates, for all intents and purposes, four basic requirements for a valid business deduction. A business deduction is allowed for all (read as one continuous phrase with four distinct requirements):
   ➢ Ordinary and necessary
   ➢ Expenses
   ➢ Paid or incurred during the taxable year
   ➢ In carrying on any trade or business.

These four requirements often represent, in federal income tax classes and in real life, separate and significant points of contention. Business deductions come in a million different flavors, but all qualifying deductions must meet those four criteria. The study, in tax classes, of business deductions can be long and comprehensive. At times, it may seem like many business deductions have their own set of rules, as if permitted by a separate Code section. There are many business deductions that almost take on a life of their own primarily because of explanations and interpretations from the Code subsections, regulations, court decisions, I.R.S. pronouncements, and the like.

For Takuma, there is little question that his lunch with Christina is clearly of a business nature, meeting all four of the core requirements for deductibility under IRC § 162. His lunch with Christina, however, implicates another code section; IRC § 274. This is the next step in our analysis,

IRC § 274 was enacted to curb what were considered abuses for business deductions when such expenses were of the nature that could be considered entertainment-related. While such expenses may be valid section 162 business deductions, IRC § 274 established a second hurdle to deductibility for expenses that were entertainment-related. Historically, such expenses had to satisfy various tests in order to be deductible (e.g., they had to be either be *directly related to*, or *associated with*, the active conduct of a trade or business), and even if they did, section 274 limited the deduction to 50% of the actual amount of such expense. In the analysis of the answer to the previous question 18, we saw that the *Tax Cuts and Jobs Act* (TCJA) signed into law in December 2017 (generally effective beginning in 2018) made dramatic changes to the deductibility of business expenses that fall within the "entertainment" category. As we discussed in our answer to question 19, beginning in 2018, and pursuant to the TCJA, entertainment-related business expenses are, generally, no longer deductible at all. [IRC § 274(a)(1)]. So how do, as in this question 19, "business meals" fit into the equation?

Historically, business meals fell within the parameters of IRC § 274 and were, for all intents and purposes, considered a form of "entertainment." While business meals, such as Takuma's in this question, were generally considered entertainment, historically he would have at least been entitled to a deduction equal to 50% of their costs. [IRC § 274(n)(1)]. When the TCJA became law, the tax community wrestled with how or if this new total disallowance of deductions for entertainment-related business expenses also applied to "business meals?" The TCJA-revised statute was unclear and, arguably, pointed in both directions of no deduction or retaining a 50% deduction. In October 2018, the I.R.S. issued Notice 2018-76 [2018-42 I.R.B. 599] appropriately titled: *EXPENSES FOR BUSINESS MEALS UNDER § 274 OF THE INTERNAL REVENUE CODE*. The pertinent part of this IRS Notice provides:

> *The Act did not change the definition of entertainment under § 274(a)(1); therefore, the regulations under § 274(a)(1) that define entertainment continue to apply. The Act did not address the circumstances in which the provision of food and beverages might constitute entertainment. However, the legislative history of the Act clarifies that taxpayers generally may continue to deduct 50 percent of the food and beverage expenses associated with operating their trade or business. [Citation omitted.]*

> *The Treasury Department and the IRS intend to publish proposed regulations under § 274 clarifying when business meal expenses are nondeductible entertainment expenses and when they are 50 percent deductible expenses. Until the proposed regulations are effective, taxpayers may rely on the guidance in this notice for the treatment under § 274 of expenses for certain business meals.*

> *Under this notice, taxpayers may deduct 50 percent of an otherwise allowable business meal expense if:*

1. The expense is an ordinary and necessary expense under § 162(a) paid or incurred during the taxable year in carrying on any trade or business;
2. The expense is not lavish or extravagant under the circumstances;
3. The taxpayer, or an employee of the taxpayer, is present at the furnishing of the food or beverages;
4. The food and beverages are provided to a current or potential business customer, client, consultant, or similar business contact; and
5. In the case of food and beverages provided during or at an entertainment activity, the food and beverages are purchased separately from the entertainment, or the cost of the food and beverages is stated separately from the cost of the entertainment on one or more bills, invoices, or receipts. The entertainment disallowance rule may not be circumvented through inflating the amount charged for food and beverages.

This I.R.S. Notice (issued almost a year after the TCJA was signed into law) answers the perplexing question about business meals and provides the answer to this question. Takuma's lunch with Christina complies with the Notice's guidelines and, therefore, he is entitled to deduct 50% of the cost of the lunch.

Answer (a) is not the best response because while it is true that his lunch meets the requirement of IRC § 162 (business deductions) it fails to recognize that because this is a business meal, IRC § 274 limits his deduction to 50% of the cost. **Answer (b) is not the best response.** It is correct that Takuma's business meal meets the requirements of IRC § 274(k) (this subsection contains some of the guideline requirements of the above-referenced I.R.S. Notice 2018-76). However, a deduction is still limited to 50% pursuant to IRC § 274(n). **Answer (d) is not the best response.** This answer highlights the TCJA-created conundrum vis-à-vis business meals and other business entertainment expenses that was clarified in the above-referenced I.R.S. Notice 2018-76.

20. **The most accurate answer is (a).** Ostensibly, our analysis of this question begins with IRC § 162; deductions for business-related expenses. We will see that Monet's trip to France is considered primarily for business purposes. However, because of statutory provisions applicable to certain foreign travel, her transportation costs will have to be allocated based upon the respective time spent on business and pleasure. A more thorough analysis follows.

As indicated, the starting point for our analysis is IRC § 162. The first sentence of IRC § 162 (which appears in subsection (a)) enumerates, for all intents and purposes, four basic requirements for a business deduction. A business deduction is allowed for all (read as one continuous phrase with four distinct requirements):

> ➢ Ordinary and necessary
> ➢ Expenses
> ➢ Paid or incurred during the taxable year
> ➢ In carrying on any trade or business.

These four requirements often represent, in federal income tax classes and in real life, separate and significant points of contention. Business deductions come in a million different flavors, but all qualifying deductions must meet those four criteria. The study, in tax classes, of business deductions can be long and comprehensive. At times, it may seem like many business deductions have their own set of rules, as if permitted by a separate Code section. There are many business deductions that almost take on a life of their own primarily because of explanations and interpretations from the Code subsections, regulations, court decisions, I.R.S. pronouncements, and the like.

IRC § 162(a)(2) specifically identifies that expenditures associated with "traveling away from home" constitute qualifying business expenses. While this subsection appears to add additional requirements to the four listed above for such traveling expenditures, a careful examination of the statutory language reveals no more than a reiteration of the four basic requirements, albeit in a different form. It is clear that Monet plans to spend the majority of her trip to France on business matters. Had this question involved domestic, as opposed to foreign travel, our answer would be relatively simple. The regulations promulgated for IRC § 162 are extensive and specifically address business transportation costs in general. For purposes of IRC § 162 qualification, transportation costs are deductible, in full, if the "trip is related primarily to [her] . . . trade or business." [Reg. 1.162-2(b)(1).] At this point, in Monet's case, we need probably not delve any further into the regulations to determine that her trip to France is primarily for business purposes. Just in case we want to verify this result, the regulations, at Reg. § 1.162-2(b)(2), provide that this determination be made based on the facts and circumstances in each case. These regulations indicate that an important factor for making this determination is the number of days spent on business compared to the number of days spent for pleasure. Hopefully, it is fairly apparent from the facts that Monet's trip to France is primarily for business purposes.

Thus far, we have only addressed the requirements of IRC § 162 which, if this were the extent of the law applicable to Monet's trip, would result in a deduction of 100% of her transportation costs. And that is how it works for <u>domestic travel</u> – deduction of transportation costs for traveling away from home is an "all or nothing" proposition. If the trip is primarily for business, then 100% of the taxpayer's transportation related costs generally qualify as business expenses pursuant to IRC § 162. Alternatively, none of the transportation costs qualify as business expenses if the trip is primarily for pleasure. Monet's is <u>not</u> a domestic trip but, rather, involves foreign travel, and foreign business travel triggers the application of additional statutory provisions.

IRC § 274(c) addresses *foreign business travel* and its rules for deductibility of transportation costs may diverge from those for domestic travel discussed above. The general rule for deductibility of foreign travel <u>is</u> the same as that for domestic travel <u>if</u>:
> ➢ The foreign travel does not exceed one week, **or**
> ➢ The pleasure portion of the foreign travel is less than 25% of the total foreign travel time. [IRC § 274(c)(2).]

If the foreign travel does *not* meet these criteria, then the statute requires that the foreign transportation costs be prorated based on business and non-business days, with only the business portion deductible. [IRC § 274(c)(1).] In Monet's case, her trip is expected to last more than one week, and her one-third pleasure travel portion of the trip exceeds 25%. Therefore, for deduction purposes she must prorate her transportation costs – two-thirds (her business portion of the trip) of such costs being deductible and the balance nondeductible.

Please note that this is a rather simplified question involving foreign business travel. The regulations contain many <u>very</u> specific rules regarding numerous aspects of foreign travel that your professor may choose to address.

Answer (b) is incorrect. This would be the correct answer if Monet's trip involved domestic travel only. As indicated above, and in other problems in this book, that if a domestic trip is made primarily for business purposes, then 100% of the round-trip transportation costs are qualified business deductions pursuant to IRC § 162 notwithstanding that the taxpayer enjoys some pleasure days while on the trip. **Answers (c) and (d) are also incorrect.** While both answers introduce the IRC § 274(c) restrictions for foreign travel, they both incorrectly conclude that none of Monet's transportation costs are deductible.

21. **The most accurate statement is (d).** Here we have another example of the ever-changing world of tax law. Pursuant to changes first made by the *"Job Creation and Worker Assistance Act of 2002"* (and later extensions of these changes by subsequent legislation, see below), Jeremy is entitled to deduct $250 in computing his adjusted gross income (AGI). The remaining $750, while we shall see is a legitimate business expense, no longer gives rise to

any deduction for him. This latter non-deductibility of any remaining business expense is a casualty of the *Tax Cuts and Jobs Act* (TCJA) signed into law in December (generally effective beginning in 2018). In the prior edition of this book, this remaining $750 was classified as a "miscellaneous itemized deduction" which he could have deducted but only to the extent that the aggregate of such category of deductions exceeded 2% of his adjusted gross income (AGI).

Jeremy's expenditures for supplies and computer software qualify as deductible IRC § 162 trade or business expenses. The first sentence of IRC § 162 (contained in subsection (a)) enumerates, for all intents and purposes, the basic requirements for a business deduction. A deduction is allowed for all "ordinary and necessary" "expenses" "paid or incurred during the taxable year" "in carrying on any trade or business." The compartmentalized quotation marks signify what are commonly considered the four basic requirements for a business deduction. These four requirements often represent, in tax classes and in real life, separate and significant points of contention. Business deductions come in a million different flavors, but all qualifying deductions meet those four criteria. The study, in tax classes, of business deductions can be long and comprehensive. Without too much strain, it appears that Jeremy's $1,000 in expenditures meet all of the IRC § 162 requirements.

The key issues in this question are where and how, in computing Jeremy's taxable income, this $1,000 is deductible. The requirements for deductibility pursuant to § 162 are the same for an employee or a self-employed individual. However, the effective availability of an actual business deduction, and where it is deducted, varies dramatically depending on one's "work status." The *Tax Cuts and Jobs Act* (TCJA) signed into law in December 2017 (generally effective beginning in 2018) made significant changes, and not in a good way, for deductions of business expenses by employees. Other questions in this book address the deductibility of IRC § 162 business expenses incurred by individuals who are self-employed (independent contractors, unincorporated sole proprietorship, etc.) and generally, those remain deductible under the TCJA. However, under the TCJA, deductions for unreimbursed business expenses incurred by employees, have, for the most part, been "suspended" for 2018 through 2025. [IRC § 67(g)].

At this point, it appears that we have selected the wrong "correct" answer. All of Jeremy's $1,000 in expenses, while qualifying as IRC § 162 business expenses, would appear to no longer be deductible pursuant to the TCJA. [See IRC § 67(g) added by the TCJA generally eliminating deductions for unreimbursed business expenses for employees.]

Jeremy, however, gets a bit of a tax break for his otherwise lost classroom business expenses. As indicated above, the *Job Creation and Worker Assistance Act of 2002* introduced a provision was enacted that specifically applies in Jeremy's situation. This provision (adding IRC § 62(a)(2)(D)) allows a full-time elementary or secondary school teacher (grades K-12) to deduct "above the line" (to compute AGI), up to $250 spent on books, supplies (with some restrictions for certain items for health and physical education courses), computer related items, etc., that are for use in the classroom as well as school-related seminars. Originally, this special deduction for K-12 teachers was to last for only two years (2002 and 2003). Subsequent legislation extended this deduction, on an almost year-by-year basis, and the TCJA has made this "permanent" (subject to, of course, any potential future changes). The TCJA also made the $250 per year (per person) limit subject to inflation adjustments. [IRC § 62(d)(3); adjusted in $50 increments when the cumulative cost of living index reaches the point of adjustment and as of this writing, and for 2019, the amount deduction limit remains at $250]. While not at issue in this question, it should be noted that this special teacher deduction is allowed on a per-person basis (e.g., a married couple where both are K-12 teachers are each allowed up to $250 in above the line deductions, adjusted for inflation).

Therefore, Jeremy's 2019 expenditures for classroom supplies and computer software qualify and $250 of the $1,000 he spent is deductible as an "above the line" in computing his AGI. The remaining $750 he spent, although a legitimate IRC § 162 business expense, is not, pursuant to the TCJA, deductible because he incurred this as an employee.

Note that this IRC § 62(a)(2)(D) is relatively small, albeit beneficial to K-12 teachers. Because of its limited benefit, your professor may, or may not, cover this provision.

Answer (a) is incorrect. This was the correct answer in the prior edition of this book. It is now incorrect because the $750 remainder of Jeremy's costs are no longer deductible at all pursuant to the TCJA. The TCJA eliminated the category of deductible "miscellaneous itemized deductions" subject to a 2% of AGI floor. **Answer (b) is incorrect** because qualifying unreimbursed IRC § 162 business expenses, for most employees, are not deductible "above the line" in computing AGI. The limited IRC § 62(a)(2)(D) provision for certain school teacher expenditures is an exception, but it is limited to $250 (see above discussion). **Answer (c) is incorrect.** This would be a correct answer but for the allowance of the limited $250 deduction allowed by IRC § 62(a)(2)(D). **Answer (e) is incorrect** because it fails to recognize the limited $250 deduction allowed by IRC § 62(a)(2)(D) and because pursuant to the TCJA, the former allowance of an employee's business expenses are no longer deductible (the *miscellaneous itemized deduction* category subject to a 2% of AGI floor no longer, for all intents and purposes, exists).

22. **The correct answer is (d).** First, this is a year-specific question (2019) but is easily adaptable to other tax years. Second, this is a difficult and a somewhat tricky question. Additionally, this material is not covered in all federal income tax classes sufficiently to answer this question. With that said, Teresa may be entitled to deduct some of the interest she expects to pay in 2019 on her law school loans, but this depends on the amount of her "modified" adjusted gross income for 2019.

IRC § 163 is the primary section at issue for deductions related to interest paid. For casual readers of the Code, IRC § 163(a) provides a simple and broad sounding deduction for interest stating, in part: "There shall be allowed as a deduction all interest paid . . . within the taxable year on indebtedness." Under this general definition, the interest Teresa pays on her law school loans would give rise to a deduction. However, the Tax Reform Act of 1986 added subsection (h) to IRC § 163 located quite some written distance from the general allowance for interest deductions of subsection (a). IRC § 163(h) starts out deceptively, and unfavorably, simple by stating, in part: "In the case of a taxpayer other than a corporation, no deduction shall be allowed . . . for personal interest paid . . . during the taxable year."

The definition of *personal interest*, which is not deductible, is found in IRC § 163(h)(2) and takes the form of a negative definition; *personal interest* is interest "other than" those listed in subparagraphs (A) through (F). The key, therefore, to finding interest that is deductible, is to fit within one of these specified categories of what does not constitute nondeductible personal interest. Among the categories of interest that are not personal interest is what might be the familiar category of "qualified residence interest" (typical interest paid on a home mortgage). [IRC § 163(h)(2)(D).] Somewhat less familiar, but logically not included as personal interest, is "interest properly allocable to a trade or business." [IRC § 163(h)(2)(A).]. Also listed among the categories of interest that is not considered personal interest is, "any interest allowable as a deduction under section 221 (relating to interest on educational loans)." [§ 163(h)(2)(F).] We will, below, conclude that the interest Teresa pays on her student loans in 2019 *may* qualify as deductible education loan interest pursuant to IRC § 221.

IRC § 221 (which came to life in 1998) allows for a limited deduction for certain interest paid on certain educational loans. This deduction, if allowed, is a valuable "above the line" deduction; a deduction from gross income in computing adjusted gross income (AGI). To qualify as an educational loan for this section, the loan proceeds generally must be used for tuition, fees, books, room/board or related expenses while attending a college, university or vocational school. This includes graduate, post graduate studies, professional degree programs, etc. So far, Teresa's loan qualifies. Qualified educational loans do <u>not</u> include money borrowed from certain "related parties." [IRC § 221(d)(1).] Teresa's loans were from traditional law school loan sources (not from "related" individuals) and her loans are considered *qualified education loans* used for *qualified higher education expenses.*

It should be noted that your professor may dive deeper into the complex waters of what constitutes *qualified educational loans* and *qualified higher education expenses.* Our question does not require us to do so

The interest Teresa pays on this qualified higher education loan is subject to two important limitations. First, the amount of interest deductible under IRC § 221 is limited, by statute, to $2,500 per year (in the aggregate for all such loans). While this question does not ask for a specific numeric answer, Teresa's expected $2,800 of interest exceeds this limit and, therefore, her deduction for interest would, at this point, be limited to $2,500. If allowed, as discussed below, this deduction is taken "above the line" in computing Teresa's adjusted gross income (AGI) (i.e., it is an amount that is subtracted from *gross income* to compute AGI). [Please see Appendix A for more information about how income and deductions fit together to compute AGI and taxable income.]

The second important limitation kicks in if the taxpayer's adjusted gross income (AGI), as modified by IRC § 221(b)(2)(C), exceeds certain levels. If it does, the otherwise allowed IRC § 221 interest deduction is reduced or "phased-out" utilizing a formula contained in the statute. Pursuant to IRC § 221(b)(2)(B), the level of "modified adjusted gross income" at which this deduction starts to "phase-out" (be reduced) is $50,000 for single individuals or $100,00 for married individuals filing a joint return. The deduction for student loan interest is completely eliminated for single individuals with "modified adjusted gross income" of $65,000 or more, and at $130,000 or more for married individuals filing a joint return. The statute uses the term "modified adjusted gross income" because true adjusted gross income will reflect any deduction allowed by this IRC § 221 (see above). Modified adjusted gross income is basically *adjusted gross income* computed before you compute any possible deduction under this IRC § 221 (and other sections not applicable to this problem). [IRC § 221(b)(2)(C).] It is **very important to note** that these "phase-out" thresholds appearing here and in the statute are "adjusted for inflation: (i.e., these threshold amounts are *indexed* for inflation) and are <u>not</u> the actual amounts for the current year but, rather, are the pre-inflation "phase-out" amounts.

For 2019, the year in question in our problem, the level of "modified adjusted gross income" at which this deduction starts to "phase-out" is $70,000 for single individuals or $140,000 for married individuals filing a joint return. For 2019, the deduction for student loan interest is completely eliminated for single individuals with "modified adjusted gross income" of $85,000 or more, and at $170,000 or more for married individuals filing a joint return. [Appendix B contains the "phase-out" threshold amounts for the year 2019 (the most current at the time of this printing)].

As for Teresa, we do not know her marital status or what her "modified adjusted gross income" will be for 2019. We do know that she expects to have "gross income" of $145,000 for 2019, but gross income is not the measuring rod for reductions of possible deductions under IRC § 221. We do not know the extent of Teresa's other possible *above the line* deductions for 2019 that will be subtracted from gross income to arrive at her *adjusted gross income* (and basically, her "modified adjusted gross income"). At this point, it might help to discuss, using illustrations or examples, why answers (a), (b) and (c) are not the best answers.

Answer (a) is not the best answer. It cannot be said for sure that Teresa will not be entitled to any deduction for her student loan interest. Let us assume for the moment that Teresa is married (filing a joint return with her spouse). Even if she has no other *above the line* deductions, her modified adjusted gross income would be $145,000, allowing at least some deduction of her student loan interest under IRC § 221. In the alternative, let us assume for the moment that she is single. It is possible that she could have enough other *above the line* deductions that when subtracted from her $145,000 of gross income, her "modified adjusted gross income" would be within the range of $70,000 to $85,000 (the phase-out range for 2019, thus allowing for some deduction.

Answer (b) is also not the best answer. It cannot be said for sure that Teresa will be entitled to a $2,500 deduction for her student loan interest. Let us assume for the moment that Teresa is single and further that she has no other *above the line* deductions for 2019. Her resulting "modified adjusted gross income" at $145,000 would be well in excess of the $85,000 2019 maximum limit and she would be entitled to <u>no</u> deduction for her student loan interest under IRC § 221. Similarly, let us assume for the moment that Teresa is married (and files a joint return with her spouse) and she has no other *above the line* deductions. Again, her "modified adjusted gross income" would be $145,000, which would be in excess of $140,000, the beginning of the range where the IRC § 221 deduction would be reduced for 2019.

Answer (c) is also not the best answer. It is true that if Teresa is married (and files a joint return with her spouse) she will be entitled to at least a partial deduction of her student loan interest in 2019. However, it is not true that "only if she is married" will she possibly be entitled to a deduction for her student loan interest. As indicated in the discussion of the incorrect answer (a) above, she could be *single* and have substantial *above the line* deductions to reduce her "modified adjusted gross income" to levels between $70,000 and $85,000 (2019 phase-out range) thereby allowing some deduction for her student loan interest.

23. **The most accurate statement is (a).** On the surface, this question may appear very similar to question 21, above. In that question, we had Jeremy, a full-time high school science teacher spending $1,000 on school supplies. **Spoiler alert**: we concluded that he was entitled to an "above the line" $250 deduction and the balance, while legitimate IRC § 162 business expenses, were ultimately nondeductible. The result, for our current question, will be quite different with neither Waynoka nor Hector being entitled to any tax deductions for their education-related expenses.

One might logically start with an exploration of whether our taxpayers' expenses are legitimate IRC § 162 business deductions. Other questions in this book address what is required for an expenditure to be considered a valid business expense. To save us from a long analysis that will end poorly for our taxpayers, we can summarize the IRC § 162 results as follows:

Waynoka's course-related expenses

These would give rise to legitimate IRC § 162 business expenses but, unfortunately for her, such expenses as an employee are no longer deductible pursuant to the *Tax Cuts and Jobs Act* (TCJA) signed into law in December 2017 (generally effective beginning in 2018). Other questions in this book deal with this issue in more detail.

Hector's homeschooling expenses

Hector's homeschooling activities do not constitute a business for federal income tax purposes and his costs incurred for this activity does not give rise to any IRC § 162 business expenses. Rather, such costs are considered personal-type expenses for which the I.R.C. provides no accompanying deductions.

As discussed in the analysis to question 21, we have an additional avenue of exploration for the deduction of education-related expenses. The *Job Creation and Worker Assistance Act of 2002* added IRC § 62(a)(2)(D)). This provision allows full-time elementary or secondary school teachers (grades K-12) to deduct "above the line" (to compute AGI), up to $250 spent on books, supplies (with some restrictions for certain items for health and physical education courses), computer related items, etc., that are for use in the classroom as well as school-related seminars. Originally, this special deduction for K-12 teachers was to last for only two years (2002 and 2003). Subsequent legislation extended this deduction, on an almost year-by-year basis, and the TCJA has made this "permanent" (subject to, of course, any potential future changes). The TCJA also made the $250 per year (per person) limit subject to inflation adjustments. [IRC § 62(d)(3); adjusted in $50 increments when the cumulative cost of living index reaches the point of adjustment. As of this writing, and for 2019, the amount deduction limit remains at $250]. This special teacher deduction is allowed on a per-person basis (e.g., a married couple where both are K-12 teachers are each allowed up to $250 in above the line deductions, adjusted for inflation). Let's examine how, or if, this special deduction applies to our taxpayers in this question:

Waynoka's course-related expenses

This special IRC § 62(a)(2)(D) deduction is available only to "eligible educators" and, unfortunately Waynoka does not meet the statutory definition. Therefore, she will not be entitled to this special deduction. IRC § 62(d)(1)(A) defines a *eligible educator* as "an individual who is a kindergarten through grade 12 teacher, instructor, counselor, principal, or aid in a school for at least 900 hours during the school year." Waynoka, a college professor, clearly does not meet the definition of an *eligible educator* as she is not teaching at the K-12 level.

Hector's homeschooling expenses

The special IRC § 62(a)(2)(D) deduction for educators' expenses is <u>not</u> applicable for homeschooling. [See I.R.S. Pub. 529, "Miscellaneous Deductions."] While it may appear that Hector is engaged in K-12 education, homeschooling, for a variety of reasons, does not fit within the form of education that would qualify him for this special deduction.

The end result is that neither Waynoka nor Hector are entitled to a tax deduction for their respective school-related expenses.

Note that this IRC § 62(a)(2)(D) is relatively small, albeit beneficial to K-12 teachers. Because of its limited benefit, your professor may, or may not, cover this provision.

Answer (b) is incorrect. The first part of this answer, referencing Waynoka, is correct. However, the portion referring to Hector is not correct because, as stated above, his homeschooling expenses do not qualify for the special $250 (maximum) educator's deduction. **Answer (c) is incorrect**

because, as discussed above, Waynoka is not eligible for the special $250 (maximum) educator's deduction because she is not a K-12 teacher. **Answer (d) is incorrect** because neither Waynoka nor Hector qualify for the special $250 (maximum) educator's deduction. Had both been K-12 teachers at a school, then this would be the correct answer; each would be entitled to a $250 (maximum) deduction. **Answer (e) is incorrect.** As indicated, neither of them qualifies for the special educator's deduction. In addition, had they both qualified for the deduction, the portion of this answer stating that the $250 is a combined limitation is incorrect (it is a per-person $250 limitation).

24. **The best answer is (e).** IRC § 163 is the primary section at issue for deductions related to interest paid. For casual readers of the Code, IRC § 163(a) provides a simple and broad sounding deduction for interest stating, in part: "There shall be allowed as a deduction all interest paid . . . within the taxable year on indebtedness." Under this general definition, the "margin" loan interest that Oscar paid would give rise to a deduction. However, the Tax Reform Act of 1986 added subsection (h) to IRC § 163, located quite some written distance from the general allowance for interest deductions of subsection (a). IRC § 163(h) starts out deceptively, and unfavorably, simply by stating, in part: "In the case of a taxpayer other than a corporation, no deduction shall be allowed . . . for personal interest paid . . . during the taxable year."

The definition of *personal interest*, which is not deductible, is found in IRC § 163(h)(2) and takes the form of a negative definition; *personal interest* is interest "other than" those listed in subparagraphs (A) through (F). The key, therefore, to finding interest that is deductible, is to fit within one of these specified categories of what does not constitute nondeductible personal interest. Among the categories of interest that are not personal interest is what might be the familiar category of "qualified residence interest" (typical interest paid on a home mortgage). [IRC § 163(h)(2)(D).] Somewhat less familiar, but logically not included as personal interest, is "interest properly allocable to a trade or business." [IRC § 163(h)(2)(A).] Also listed among the categories of interest that are not considered personal interest is, "any investment interest (within the meaning of subsection (d))." [§ 163 (h)(2)(B).] We will, below, conclude that Oscar's "margin" loan interest represents "investment interest" that, pursuant to IRC §163(d), is deductible only to the extent that he has "net investment income" in the year. Any excess nondeductible interest is carried over to future years and deductible to the extent of "net investment income."

Basically, *Investment interest*, is interest paid on monies used for investment purposes. Interest paid on "margin" loans to purchase stocks for investment purposes is a classic example of *investment interest*. IRC § 163(d) allows for an individual to deduct such interest, but only to the extent of the individual's "net investment income" for the year. [IRC § 163(d)(1).] While the definition of *net investment income* can, at times, be rather complex, it generally means the aggregate amount of net income that the individual earns from his or her investments (gross income from all investment activities less investment-related expenses other than *investment interest*). In effect, this provision limiting deductions for *investment interest*, prevents such interest from being used to reduce an individual's other, non-investment, income (e.g., wages or net business earnings).

Oscar's situation is somewhat simple in that his investment activities are comprised of his stock ownership and monies invested in savings accounts. It would appear, that his *net investment income* for last year was $800, consisting of $500 dividend income (from his stocks) and $300 in interest from his savings accounts. There is, however, one catch in our case. His dividends are indicated as "qualified dividends" and while it is well beyond the scope of this question to discuss the tax favorable nature of such dividends (please see other questions in this book), they <u>do</u> affect what is considered *net investment income* for purposes of our IRC § 163 interest deduction. Qualified dividends are <u>not</u> included in determining *net investment income*. This leaves Oscar with only the $300 interest constituting his *net investment income*. Therefore, of the $3,000 that Oscar paid last year in *investment interest*, he could only deduct (last year) $300, the amount of his *net investment income*. Notice that this brings his net profit from his investment activities (for tax purposes) to zero. It should be noted that recipients of "qualified dividends" can elect to forego their favorable tax treatment and, if such is the case, the dividends would be included in the calculation of an individual's *net investment income*. [This is the reason for the language in our question that indicates Oscar made no special tax elections last year.] While not applicable in this fact pattern, *net investment income* can include certain gains from sales of investment property. [See IRC § 163(d)(4)(B).]

What happens to Oscar's *investment interest* that he was not entitled to deduct last year because of this *net investment income* limitation? It is not lost but, rather, is carried forward to succeeding taxable years, and deducted to the extent of the applicable year's *net investment income*. [IRC § 163(d)(2).] For Oscar, the $2,700 of *investment interest* that he could not deduct last year ($3,000 less the $300 of deductible interest), is carried forward to this year and as many succeeding years as necessary to deduct the interest to the extent of *net investment income*.

Please note that the area of *investment interest* can be very complex, and your professor may cover this material in much greater depth than is presented in this problem.

Answer (a) is incorrect because Oscar's interest is not nondeductible "personal interest." Answer (b) is incorrect because, as discussed above, the deduction for investment interest is limited. Answer (c) is incorrect because it does not properly reflect Oscar's total "net investment income" for the year (it improperly includes his $500 in qualified dividends and does not include his $300 in interest). Answer (d) is incorrect because it does not properly reflect his net investment income (it improperly includes his $500 in qualified dividends) and it also fails to recognize the carryover aspect of nondeductible investment interest.

25. **The best answer is (c).** It is great that Julie remembers some of the material from her tax class and that she is thinking creatively about tax issues. Unfortunately, her plan most likely falls within what are known as the "hobby loss" rules of IRC § 183. This section addresses the deductibility of expenses for activities "not engaged in for profit." In the prior edition of this book, the correct answer was (c) allowing, as discussed below, a limited amount of deductions. Unfortunately, Julie will have to deal with changes, detrimental to her, introduced by the *Tax Cuts and Jobs Act* (TCJA) signed into law in December 2017 (generally effective beginning in 2018). Pursuant to changes made by the TCJA, she will not be entitled to any deductions (and will have to report any income from renting out her horse).

For now, let's assume that Julie's contemplated plan will be considered an activity not engaged in for profit. If such is the case, IRC § 183 appears to allow for some deductions. IRC § 183(a) generally limits the allowable deductions associated with this activity to the amount of income generated from this activity (with some exceptions not applicable here). In other words, it appears that the best Julie can do, tax wise, is to "break-even." But wait; we are not yet done and, as we shall see, our analysis of applicable law will result in an even worse outcome for Julie.

To be considered in an activity engaged in for profit, making a profit must be the **primary** motive for engaging in the activity. Profit as a secondary or incidental motive is not enough. Making a profit from an activity such as that contemplated by Julie is essentially not even on the map. Activities that are too centered around someone's hobby, where fun and personal pleasure are paramount, almost always run afoul with these rules. The statute does provide a "presumptive" test. It is presumed to be engaged in for profit (and thereby allowing deductions for all business expenses) if the activity shows a profit for any three or more out of five consecutive years (or two out of seven years for horse breeding, racing, or showing). [IRC § 183(d).] This is merely a presumptive test, and taxpayers legitimately engaged in a trade or business for profit can be considered a "for profit" business despite failing this test.

So with Julie clearly in the "an activity not engaged in for profit" arena, we come back to IRC § 183 and its limitation of deductions to the extent of her income derived from this activity. What we will not find in IRC § 183, however, is the logistics of how this deduction limitation works. Logically, one might think that Julie would report any income and then offset this with deductions to the point of "break-even" (i.e., showing no net income, nor a loss, from her "hobby"). Unfortunately for Julie, this is not how it works.

Julie would have to report, in gross income, all income derived from renting out her horse. The deductions that are allowed by IRC § 183 are/were deductible someplace else as part of a group of deductions known as "miscellaneous itemized deductions." The historical significance of this sub-group of deductions is that they were deductible, in the aggregate, to the extent that they exceeded 2% of an individual's AGI. This entire group of *miscellaneous itemized deductions* was a casualty of the *Tax Cuts and Jobs Act* (TCJA) signed into law in December 2017 (generally effective beginning in 2018). The TCJA "suspended" any deductions of *miscellaneous itemized deductions* for the years 2018 through 2025. [IRC § 67(g)]

Putting everything together, Julie's plan would result in her having to report in her gross income, all income she would derive from renting out her horse. To make matters worse, because she is not really conducting a business (an activity not engaged in for profit), she will not benefit from any deductions; pursuant to the TCJA, not even deductions to the extent she has income from the activity.

Answer (a) is incorrect because "looking" like a business will not, by itself, constitute a "for profit" business activity. **Answer (b) is also incorrect.** This was close to the correct answer in the previous edition of this book because under pre-TCJA law, IRC § 183 generally allowed deductions to the extent of income derived from an activity not engaged in for profit (i.e., she could "break even" but not report a net loss from such an activity). **Answer (d) is incorrect** even though the end result (no expense deductions) is correct. It is incorrect because the criteria for determining "for profit" business activity enumerated in the statute at IRC § 183(d) is only a presumptive test and not, as indicated in this answer, a conclusive criteria-based test.

ANSWER KEY
EXAM III

FEDERAL INCOME TAX
ANSWER KEY AND EXPLANATIONS
EXAM III

1. **Answer (b) is correct.** This question involves the exclusion of "compensation for injuries or sickness" provided in IRC § 104. This section has a long, complex and capricious past vis-à-vis what is within its umbrella of this exclusion. In its most basic form, an individual receiving damages, by award or settlement, for physical injuries or physical sickness can exclude such amounts from income. [IRC § 104(a)(2).] In its current form (reflecting changes made by the "Small Business Job Protection Act of 1996"), this section generally excludes amounts received (other than punitive damages) for <u>physical</u> injury or sickness awards and settlements. The entire amount of Ann's award, in this question, originates from her physical injury arising from the negligence cause of action and, therefore, is excluded from gross income.

The difficulty of questions involving IRC § 104 can vary dramatically depending on how thoroughly one's professor covers the exclusion as to its history, policy foundations, and the like. This is a good area of tax law for in-depth class analysis, so take this into consideration when addressing questions involving the subject. Much of this Code section's history centered on the breadth of this exclusion with, at varying times, exclusions allowed for damages received from nonphysical tort or "tort type" causes of action, and punitive damages.

The problem students usually have with this question is the reluctance to exclude the portions of Ann's award identified as replacement for "lost wages" and "emotional distress." As for the replacement of lost wages, one might logically argue (as did the I.R.S. for many years) that they should not be within the scope of IRC § 104's exclusion because wages, had she not been injured, would have been taxable. Historically, this was the subject of much tax litigation. However, the answer is now clear that these amounts do not represent taxable wages even if the award amount is measured by the amount of wages that could have been earned but for the injuries. [Rev.Rul. 85-97, 1985-2 C.B. 50.]

Regarding the "emotional distress" component of the award, there is often confusion because of the language in the body of IRC § 104(a) that states, "emotional distress shall not be treated as a physical injury or physical sickness." Remembering that "physical" injury/sickness is required for exclusion, it might appear that the portion of Ann's award identified for emotional distress is not excludable. However, because Ann's cause of action was the physical injury, and the emotional distress emanated therefrom, the amount is within the scope of the exclusion.

Answers (a), (c) and (d) are incorrect because they all, to some degree, do not represent the full scope of the IRC § 104(a)(2) exclusion as it applies to this question. Please see the discussion for the correct answer (b), immediately above, for more information. **Answer (e) is incorrect** because the exclusion provided in IRC § 104(a)(2), as has been discussed, is designed specifically for compensatory damages resulting from a physical injury or sickness.

It should be noted that this question, and others in this book that specifically identify component parts of a personal injury award, are a bit removed from "real world" circumstances. Lawyers specializing in the practice of personal injury law will acknowledge that many, if not most, personal injury awards and settlements do not separate damage awards/settlements with such specificity. Correct application of income tax rules is further frustrated by the additional "real world" fact that the underlying cause of action, or basis on which a tort related lawsuit damages are awarded, is not always clear or separable from other causes of action.

2. **Answer (d) is the most accurate.** With one narrow exception (see discussion of incorrect answer (b) below), punitive damages are not within the scope of excludable awards for physical injury/sickness as provided in IRC § 104(a)(2). While historically, exclusion of punitive damages has varied, current law is very clear on the matter. A plain reading of the statute (at IRC § 104(a)(2)) reveals, in a parenthetical phrase, that punitive damages are not within the scope of the exclusion. Therefore, in this question, the punitive damage award Ann receives is included, in full, in gross income.

    As indicated above, the difficulty of questions involving IRC § 104 can vary dramatically depending on how thoroughly one's professor covers the exclusion as to its history, policy foundations, and the like. This is a good area of tax law for in-depth class analysis, so take this into consideration when addressing questions involving the subject. Much of this Code section's history centered on the breadth of this exclusion with, at varying times, exclusions allowed for damages received from non-physical tort or "tort type" causes of action, and punitive damages.

    Answer (a) is incorrect but is a commonly selected answer because it corresponds to what could have been a correct answer had this question asked about the historical application of IRC § 104. One iteration of this Code section (at one time) arguably allowed for the exclusion of punitive damages arising from an underlying physical tort or tort type cause of action.

However, this is no longer the case and such a distinction is irrelevant for exclusion purposes. **Answer (b) is incorrect** because there is no such qualified exception to the rule of punitive damage inclusion applicable to our fact pattern. However, there is, in IRC § 104(c), a narrow exception where one can exclude punitive damages received. Specifically, punitive damages are excluded from gross income if they were awarded based on a "wrongful death" action <u>and</u> under applicable state law, which was in effect on September 13, 1995, punitive damages are the only type of damages that can be awarded in such an action. The facts in our question do not fit within this very limited exception. **Answer (c) is incorrect** because no such correlation for inclusion or exclusion exists.

3. **Answer (a) is correct.** As in questions 1 and 2, above, this question involves the exclusion of "compensation for injuries or sickness" provided in IRC § 104. Also, as previously indicated, this section has a long, complex and capricious past vis-à-vis what is within its umbrella of exclusion. As discussed above, in its current form (reflecting changes made by the "*Small Business Job Protection Act of 1996*"), this section generally excludes amounts received (other than punitive damages) for <u>physical</u> injury or sickness awards and settlements. In the body of IRC § 104(a), the law specifies that "emotional distress shall not be treated as a physical injury or physical sickness." This Code section goes on to effectively say that notwithstanding that emotional distress is not a physical injury or sickness, amounts received from an award/settlement arising therefrom are excludable to the extent that it represents payment for his/her costs of actual medical care attributable to the emotional distress. In our question, because Bob's claim is based on the tort of emotional distress, his settlement would not be excludable except for the amount designated as payment for his actual medical costs.

As indicated in another question in this book, do not fall into the trap of trying to "bootstrap" within this section's exclusion, awards/settlements emanating from an emotional distress cause of action because the plaintiff's emotional distress manifests itself into an actual physical injury. **Answer (d) is incorrect** for this reason.

It bears repeating that the difficulty of questions involving IRC § 104 can vary dramatically depending on how thoroughly one's professor covers the exclusion as to its history, policy foundations, and the like. This is a good area of tax law for in-depth class analysis, so take this into consideration when addressing questions involving the subject. Much of this Code section's history centered on the breadth of this exclusion with, at varying times, exclusions allowed for damages received from non-physical tort or "tort type" causes of action, and punitive damages.

Answer (b) is incorrect but is the source of some confusion because of the historical application of IRC § 104. Under old law, the basic starting point for exclusion under this section was whether the award/settlement arose from a "tort or tort type" cause of action. Using this as a benchmark for qualification under the current statute, however, is far too broad. **Answer (c) is incorrect** because it fails to recognize the limited exclusion for payments of medical costs for otherwise includible emotional distress based claims. **Answer (d)** is incorrect as explained above.

4. **Answer (c) is the most accurate.** As in questions 1, 2 and 3, above, this question involves the exclusion of "compensation for injuries or sickness" provided in IRC § 104. Without duplicating the entire analysis of those questions, the key item in this question 4, is that Ann's defamation action is not a physical injury/sickness and, therefore, not excludable from gross income. To be sure, defamation is a tort but damages therefrom do not meet the current law's narrower definition of the IRC § 104 exclusion.

This question, like in question 3, immediately above, also provides a good example of where the Regulations sometimes lag, by quite a long time, changes made to the underlying code section. While IRC § 104(a)(2) was changed some years ago to limit the exclusion to physical injuries or sickness, the corresponding Regulations were not amended to reflect this change until many years later. It took more than 15 years for the regulations to "catch up" to the changes in IRC § 104 requiring a physical injury or sickness. During this gap in time, the corresponding Regulation did not include the critical word "physical" from the exclusion for personal injuries or sickness. In this outdated Regulation [former § 1.104(c)] defining what constitutes excludable amounts received on account of personal injuries or sickness, refers to legal actions "based upon tort or tort type rights." Reading this outdated Regulation alone, and not looking at the actual statutory changes, it could have easily lead a student to incorrectly conclude that a taxpayer can exclude an award or settlement from, as is the case here, a defamation claim (defamation is clearly a "tort"). This would not be a correct analysis. A defamation claim is clearly based on a tort and under old law, as depicted in an outdated Regulation, one could incorrectly conclude that damages resulting therefrom would be excluded from income. While the Regulation in question has been changed to reflect current law, the Regulations are rife with examples of "out-of-date" law.

Answers (a), (b) and (d) are incorrect because Ann's defamation cause of action from which the settlement arose, was not a "physical" injury/sickness. As mentioned in the analysis of the answers to the previous questions in this series, the law in this area has changed dramatically over the years, generally narrowing the scope of the IRC § 104 exclusion. Your professor may discuss, in some depth, the historical progression of this section. There was a time when non-physical torts, such as defamation, gave rise to excludable damage awards. At one time there was, arguably, a distinction as to whether the harm was to one's personal reputation (excludable), or to their business/professional reputation (potentially non-excludable). However, with the narrowing of the statute to physical injury/sickness, most of these contentious issues have evaporated.

5. **The best answer is (d).** With the advances in more sophisticated means of obtaining evidence plus the hard work of dedicated people (law schools, organizations, and the like) the number of individuals who were wrongfully incarcerated has soared. While proper "justice" may ultimately have been served, how does society repay the injustice of wrongful imprisonment (sometimes lasting decades)? Time cannot be rewound but monetary compensation is awarded for federal wrongful incarceration and, as of this writing, in approximately 65% of states. Among the states authorizing compensation for wrongful imprisonment, the amount varies (dramatically).

Not ignoring the injustice for spending years in prison for a crime that Bob did not commit, our question addresses the taxability of the $1 Million that he received from his state for this wrongful incarceration. Prior to 2015, the analysis revolved around the exclusion in IRC § 104 for physical injury (see questions 1 through 4, above) and a determination of taxability pursuant to this statute was, at best, cumbersome and inconsistent. The *Wrongful Convictions Tax Relief Act of 2015* gave us a clear answer by adding IRC § 139F.

This relatively new section (as of this writing) is fairly straightforward and provides an exclusion for the $1 million Bob received for his wrongful incarceration. Therefore, Bob will be entitled to fully exclude, from income, his state-mandated "compensation."

This provision, while important, is a bit obscure and may not covered in all tax courses.

Answer (a) is incorrect but is close to the correct answer. Before the enactment of IRC § 139F, payments received for wrongful incarceration were analyzed using the IRC § 104 exclusion for physical injuries. As discussed above, this resulted in complex and inconsistent tax results. Now, IRC § 139F is the exclusive section for analysis for payments such as those received by Bob. **Answers (b) and (c) are incorrect** because, as discussed above, the entire amount received by Bob will be excluded from income via IRC § 139F.

6. **The best answer is (a).** IRC § 213 allows for a deduction of certain qualified medical expenses. Once one makes the determination of what

constitutes "qualified" medical care expenses, the subject of this question, the deduction is allowed as an "itemized deduction" only to the extent that the total qualifying expenses exceeds 10% of adjusted gross income (AGI). [See Appendix A for more information about how income and deductions fit together in computing taxable income.] Qualified medical care expenses include typical costs for doctors, dentists, hospital, health insurance, and the like. [See IRC § 213(d).]

Ann and Bob made substantial modifications to their home that were related to Ann's medical condition: installation of ramps, railings, widening doorways for wheelchair access, etc. In addition, they purchased an expensive motorized wheelchair for Ann. Do these expenditures qualify as medical care *expenses*? These costs are not really "expenses" at all but, rather, are considered "capital expenditures." Capital expenditures (permanent-like improvements and most asset purchases) are generally not deductible expenses but serve to either increase the adjusted basis in the property being improved or create a basis in the property acquired, as the case may be. [IRC §§ 263 and 1016.] However, if capital expenditures are primarily health-related, which would be the case for the house modifications and the wheel-chair in our facts, they are not precluded from qualifying as medical care expenses.

The regulations, at Reg. § 1.213-1(e)(1)(iii) indicate that costs for such medically related *capital expenditures* as Seeing Eye dogs, artificial teeth and limbs, wheelchairs, and the like represent *qualifying medical care expenses*. [Reg. § 1.213-1(e)(1)(iii).] The cost of Ann's wheelchair most likely fully qualifies as a medical care expense. For health-related capital improvements to the property, the normal rule is that a medical care expense is allowed but only to the extent that the cost of the improvement exceeds the increase in value to the underlying property resulting from the improvement. [See Reg. § 1.213-1(e)(1)(iii).] Certain improvements, by their nature, add minimal or no value to the underlying property and, therefore, qualify, in full, as a medical care expense. The home modifications made by the taxpayers in our problem most likely qualify, in full, as medical care expenses. [See Rev.Rul. 87-106, 1987-2 C.B. 67 (I.R.S. holding that accommodating expenditures such as those in our problem generally do not increase the fair market value of a personal residence, and, therefore, fully qualify as a medical care expense).]

In summary, all of the costs of the home modifications and Ann's wheelchair most likely qualify for medical care expenses notwithstanding that they are capital expenditures.

Answer (b) is most likely incorrect. This answer presents a correct analysis of the rules but gets off track in applying the facts of our case. The house modifications will most likely <u>not</u> increase the value of their house and, therefore, will not preclude their costs from qualifying as medical care expenses. **Answer (c) is incorrect** because it fails to recognize that in the medical area, capital expenditures and medical care expenses are <u>not</u> mutually exclusive. **Answer (d) is incorrect** because with medical related items such as those involved in our case, a physician need not specifically prescribe them.

7.   **Answer (a) is correct.** Larry is not entitled to any interest deduction here because the interest that he pays to his grandmother, Glenda, is considered nondeductible personal interest pursuant to IRC § 163(h).

IRC § 163 is the primary section at issue for deductions related to interest paid. For casual readers of the Code, IRC § 163(a) provides a simple and broad sounding deduction for interest stating, in part: "There shall be allowed as a deduction all interest paid . . . within the taxable year on indebtedness." Under this general definition, the interest Larry paid to Glenda would give rise to a deduction. However, the Tax Reform Act of 1986 added subsection (h) to § 163, located quite some written distance from the general allowance for interest deductions of subsection (a). IRC § 163(h) starts out deceptively, and unfavorably, simply by stating, in part: "In the case of a taxpayer other than a corporation, no deduction shall be allowed . . . for personal interest paid . . . during the taxable year."

The definition of *personal interest*, which is not deductible, is found in IRC § 163(h)(2) and takes the form of a negative definition; *personal interest* is interest "other than" those listed in subparagraphs (A) through (F). The key, therefore, to finding interest that <u>is</u> deductible, is to fit within one of these specified categories of what does <u>not</u> constitute nondeductible personal interest. Among the categories of interest that are <u>not</u> personal interest is what might be the familiar category of "qualified residence interest" (typical interest paid on a home mortgage). [IRC § 163(h)(2)(D).] Somewhat less familiar, but logically not included as personal interest, is "interest properly allocable to a trade or business." [IRC § 163(h)(2)(A).] As seen in other questions in this book, "business" interest, rather oddly, does not include business interest incurred by an employee. Unfortunately for Larry, there is no category listed that would remove the nondeductible *personal interest* taint from the interest he pays to his grandmother. Therefore, the interest is not deductible.

Answer (b) is incorrect because the interest Larry pays to his grandmother is not "investment interest." Investment interest is a special category of potentially deductible interest associated with the purchase, maintenance, etc. of investment property such as a rental house, stocks, etc. [IRC § 163(d).] At least one question in this book deals with the issue of investment interest. **Answer (c) is also incorrect.** While IRC § 221 does allow, in certain circumstances, deduction for interest on loans used for education, this section is not applicable here. Not to get into too much detail here, the loan between Glenda and Larry is not the type of loan that qualifies for the IRC § 221 deduction of interest because Larry borrowed the money from a "related party," his grandmother, who is an ancestor. [See IRC § 221(d)(1) and question 8, below.] **Answer (d) is incorrect** because there is no such broad restriction regarding deductible interest. **Answer (e) is incorrect** because, as discussed above, the interest Larry pays to his grandmother is nondeductible personal interest.

8. **The correct answer is (c).** This is a somewhat tricky question, and this professor would not present such a question on an exam immediately following the preceding, very similar question. This question is an example of how critical the facts can be for a correct analysis of a question; one slight change to the facts can make a dramatic change to the outcome, as it does here.

    As indicated in the analysis for question 7, above, IRC § 163 is the primary section dealing with the deductibility of interest. We saw that Larry's interest payments to grandmother, Glenda did not result in a deduction because the interest was classified as nondeductible personal interest pursuant to IRC § 163(h). We, once again, need to turn to IRC § 163(h) to see if the interest paid on the loan from his aunt Ann, in this question, yields a different result.

    The definition of *personal interest*, which is not deductible, is found in IRC § 163(h)(2) and takes the form of a negative definition – *personal interest* is interest "other than" those listed in subparagraphs (A) through (F). The key, therefore, to finding interest that is deductible, is to fit within one of these specified categories of what does <u>not</u> constitute nondeductible personal interest. Listed among the categories of interest that are <u>not</u> considered personal interest is, "any interest allowable as a deduction under section 221 (relating to interest on educational loans)." [IRC § 163(h)(2)(F).] We will conclude, below, that the interest Larry paid to his aunt Ann may qualify as deductible education loan interest pursuant to IRC § 221.

    IRC § 221 (which came to life in 1998) allows for a limited deduction for certain interest paid on certain educational loans. This deduction, if allowed, is a valuable "above the line" deduction; a deduction from gross income in computing adjusted gross income (AGI). To qualify as an educational loan for this section, the loan proceeds generally must be used for tuition, fees, books, room/board or related expenses while attending a college, university or vocational school. This includes graduate, post graduate studies, professional degree programs, etc. So far, Larry's loan qualifies. Qualified educational loans do <u>not</u>, however, include money borrowed from "related parties." [IRC § 221(d)(1).] In a familial situation, such as Larry's in this question, the definition of who is considered related, is very specific and includes only, "brothers and sisters (whether by the whole or half-blood), spouse, ancestors, and lineal descendants." [IRC § 267(c)(4) (definition as directed to by IRC § 221(d)(1).] Larry's aunt, Ann is <u>not</u> a related individual pursuant to this definition (an aunt is the lineal descendant [daughter] of an ancestor [grandparent], or the sibling [sister] of an ancestor [parent]). Therefore, Larry's loan from his aunt Ann is a qualified education loan used for qualified higher education expenses. Note that this is a very different result from that in question 7, above, where the loan was from Larry's grandmother. Unlike Larry's aunt Ann in this question, his grandmother is an ancestor (who is considered a *related party*).

The interest Larry pays on this qualified higher education loan is subject to two important limitations. First, the amount of interest deductible under IRC § 221 is limited, by statute, to $2,500 per year (in the aggregate for all such loans). Larry's $1,100 in interest is well under this maximum deduction. The second limitation kicks in if the taxpayer's adjusted gross income (AGI), as modified by IRC § 221(b)(2)(C), exceeds certain levels. If it does, the otherwise allowed IRC § 221 interest deduction is reduced or "phased-out" utilizing a formula contained in the statute. We now have our answer to this question that Larry is entitled to a deduction of this interest paid assuming that his income is not sufficient to invoke the phase-out provisions reducing or eliminating the deduction. It is beyond the scope of this question to discuss, in detail, the mechanics of this phase-out provision. At least one question in this book addresses IRC § 221 in more detail, utilizing numbers to analyze the phase-out provision.

Answer (a) is incorrect because, as discussed above, the interest Larry paid to his aunt, Ann is not "personal interest" but, rather, qualifies as deductible education loan interest under IRC § 221. **Answer (b) is incorrect** because the interest Larry pays to his aunt is not "investment interest." Investment interest is a special category of potentially deductible interest associated with the purchase, maintenance, etc. of investment property such as a rental house, stocks, etc. [IRC § 163(d).] At least one question in this book deals with the issue of investment interest. **Answer (d) is incorrect** because there is not such a broad restriction regarding deductible interest. **Answer (e) is incorrect** because, as discussed above, the interest Larry pays to his aunt is deductible, if at all, as IRC § 221 student loan interest, and is otherwise nondeductible personal interest.

9. **Answer (c) is correct.** This is a very straightforward question. Gross income is defined in IRC § 61 as income from whatever source derived. You know from your initial study of the subject that this definition is broadly defined. We do not have to go too broad to find that the interest received is included in the recipient's gross income. Interest is specifically identified as an example of gross income at IRC § 61(a)(4). Therefore, the interest Larry pays Glenda is included in her gross income.

   Answer (a) is incorrect because Larry's payment of interest, pursuant to a promissory note, cannot be considered a gift. There is no magical provision that strips away all income tax consequences with respect to familial transactions. While it is possible for a gift to arise in situations similar to ours, there is no information that, for this question, the loan was gratuitous in nature (that the loan to Larry was evidenced by a promissory note also points to this not being any form of a gift). **Answer (b) is incorrect** because the inclusion in income by one party is not determined by the availability of a deduction to the payor. For example, you pay to have someone wash your personal car. The payment is not deductible by you but does represent gross income to the payee. **Answer (d) is also incorrect.** The fact that a taxpayer does not have sufficient taxable income to generate a tax is irrelevant for purposes of determining what is or is not included in gross income.

10. **Answer (a) is most accurate.** While at first, this discharge of Larry's debt looks like a classic case of "income from discharge of indebtedness, the gratuitous nature of the debt forgiveness results in a gift, excluded from his gross income under IRC § 102. To properly analyze this question, there are two major questions that need to be answered: 1) Does Larry, on a prima facie basis, have "income from discharge of indebtedness?" and 2) if so, is this income recognized or is there a statutory non-recognition (or exclusion) provision that is applicable?

   Forgiving a debt, in whole or in part, generally results in the realization of gross income to the debtor. It makes sense that being relieved of a liability (a financial obligation) results in a net accession to wealth (i.e., income) to the debtor. This type of income is referred to as income from discharge of indebtedness and is specifically identified by the Code as constituting gross income. [IRC § 61(a)(12).] Larry owed $15,000 to his grandmother, Glenda, of which $5,000 was forgiven. So far, Larry appears to have $5,000 in income from discharge of indebtedness. This $5,000 will be recognized in Larry's gross income unless there is some specific Code provision allowing for its exclusion. In general, on any question (multiple choice or essay) where it appears that there is income to be recognized, do not just stop at that point. Go on to make sure that no exclusion or non-recognition provisions apply to the situation presented in the question.

In the area of "income from discharge of indebtedness," there are two major exclusion/non-recognition provisions to think about. The exclusion from gross income to the recipients of gifts (made out of detached and disinterested generosity) under IRC § 102, and the potential exclusion of income from discharge of indebtedness for taxpayers in dire financial straits pursuant to IRC § 108. The former occurs where the facts give some indication that the debt was gratuitously forgiven, typically where there is a familial or close relationship between the debtor and creditor. This, most likely, is applicable to Larry's situation in this question. This situation is replete with facts indicating that Glenda acted out of detached and disinterested generosity, the general definition of a gift for purposes of exclusion under IRC § 102. Larry was her "favorite grandchild," "without hesitation" she forgave $5,000 of the loan, she even told him to "take as long as he needed to pay her back." All of which point to a gratuitous motive for the discharge. Larry, therefore, can exclude, as a gift under § 102, the $5,000 debt forgiven.

Answer (b) is incorrect because this answer fails to recognize that the income from discharge of indebtedness is subject to exclusion, in Larry's case as a gift. **Answer (c) is also incorrect.** This answer could possibly be correct, but for the way in which the answer is worded. While it is possible that Larry could exclude, from income, the $5,000 discharged because of insolvency, it is not the *only* possibility for exclusion (i.e., the answer ignores the [more likely] possibility that the exclusion can result from the discharge of debt representing a gift). For more information about exclusion of income from discharge of indebtedness by reason of insolvency, please see other questions in this book. **Answer (d) is incorrect** because it too fails to recognize that income from indebtedness is subject to possible exclusion.

11. **This is a close call, but (d) is the most accurate statement.** To start, the payment of one's debt by one's employer is usually treated as compensation received, albeit indirectly. From your initial exploration of the scope of gross income, you probably learned that income need not be in the form of cash. Specifically regarding compensation, it can take the form of property, services received or, as here, an indirect financial benefit represented by the employer's payment of an employee's obligation. Initially, therefore, it appears that Larry has $10,000 in compensation income from his employer's payment of Larry's debt. In substance, it is as if Larry's employer gave Larry a $10,000 cash bonus that Larry then used to pay off the debt. The "compensation" element might be easier to see in this recast state.

The next logical question to ask is whether any provision in the Code would apply to exclude, from income, the $10,000 that Larry effectively received.

If you have studied the IRC § 102 exclusion for gifts, bequests and devises, that might be a logical place to look for a potential exclusion. Under the general rule of § 102(a), gifts are excluded from the gross income of the donee/recipient. While no statutory definition of a gift exists, it is generally defined as a transfer without consideration that is made out of emotions of detached and disinterested generosity. [See *Comm'r v. Duberstein*, 363 U.S. 278, 80 S.Ct. 1190 (1960).] Ultimately, our analysis will find that the $10,000 Larry indirectly received is excludable by this section as a gift. However, we first have to address a major hurdle located at IRC § 102(c). This subsection provides, in general, that the possible exclusion from gross income of property acquired by gift, bequest or devise, does <u>not</u> apply to transfers between employers and employees. In other words, "gifts" to employees are not excludable from gross income under IRC § 102. As applied to most employees, this subsection is not merely a presumption. Rather, "gifts" to most employees are not excludable gifts at all.

The author, in the preceding paragraph, states that the IRC § 102(c) denial of excludable gifts applies with respect to "most employees." For discussion purposes and totally divorced from the facts of our question, suppose a parent employs a child. Let us further suppose that the employer (parent) makes no gifts to any employees but on the child's 25th birthday, the parent gives the child a new automobile. In the familial context, we have a parent making a gift to a child most likely out of emotions of detached and disinterested generosity, qualifying it for exclusion from income to the child pursuant to IRC § 102(a). However, we also factually have an employer making a gift to an employee that, pursuant to the language in IRC § 102(c), cannot be considered an excludable gift to the employee. Does this preclude any gifts, in the traditional and excludable sense, when the donor and donee happen to have an employment relationship such as this? Proposed regulations answer this question as follows: "For purposes of section 102(c), *extraordinary* transfers to the natural objects of an employer's bounty will *not be considered transfers to, or for the benefit of, an employee if the employee can show that the transfer was not made in recognition of the employee's employment. Accordingly, section 102(c) shall not apply to amounts transferred between related parties (e.g., father and son) if the purpose of the transfer can be substantially attributed to the familial relationship of the parties and not to the circumstances of their employment.*" [Prop.Reg. § 1.102-1(f)(2) (emphasis added).] In the hypothetical presented in this paragraph, the parent's gift of the car to the child is, in all likelihood, an example of an excludable gift notwithstanding the employment relationship between the two.

Now back to the facts of the question presented. Larry is the "natural object" of his mother's "bounty" (using the somewhat odd vernacular of the regulations), and it appears that this transfer (although indirect) is extraordinary in nature. We can also logically infer from the facts that Larry's mom did not make this payment on Larry's behalf in recognition of Larry's employment or in the context of their employment relationship, but rather, it was attributable to their familial relationship. Based upon this, Larry can exclude the $10,000 benefit that he received as a gift pursuant to IRC § 102.

Answer (a) is incorrect because Larry's debt was not "discharged" in the tax sense (no debt was forgiven by the creditor but, rather, the debt was fully repaid, albeit not by Larry. **Answer (b) is also incorrect**. This answer would be correct but for the gift exclusion provision that the author believes is applicable to these facts. **Answer (c) is incorrect** because like incorrect answer (a), it incorrectly concludes that there is a discharge of indebtedness issue in these facts.

12. **Answer (a) is correct.** The "alimony" payments that Wanda receives will <u>not</u> be income to her nor give rise to a deduction for Harold. WOW, how the tax landscape has changed in the blink of an eye through legislative action. The *Tax Cuts and Jobs Act* (TCJA) signed into law in December 2017 (generally effective beginning in 2018 but a bit later for our discussion of this material) upended some 77 years of fairly consistent tax law regarding alimony. Historically, and in prior editions of this book, we would be looking at IRC §§ 71 and 215. Now, however, the TCJA has stricken these sections effective for divorces after 2018. While we will discuss a bit of history of the tax treatment of alimony, below, for the 2019 divorce in our question, the answer is clear; the recipient ex-spouse does not report alimony as income and the payor ex-spouse is not entitled to a deduction for alimony. The couple's agreement in this problem, while relevant under prior law, has, for all intents and purposes, no relevancy now; the answer is the same with or without such an agreement; Alimony is not income to the recipient ex-spouse nor is it a deduction for the payor ex-spouse (a complete reversal of what had been settled law for 77 years).

The changes that the TCJA brought to the tax treatment of alimony are massive and the ripple effects have put many a family lawyer (and courts) in unfamiliar territory vis-à-vis determining the amounts and duration of alimony. A bit of history is in order (and this still applies to alimony stemming from divorces before 2019). For over seven decades, "Alimony" was income to the payee ex-spouse and a corresponding deduction to the payor ex-spouse via IRC §§ 71(a) and 215(a), respectively. The law contained detailed elements of what constituted alimony and many a tax question, as well as real-life family law alimony-related planning, dealt with these elements. It is unnecessary for us to go through these requirements of what constituted alimony as such requirements were, effectively, tossed out the window by the TCJA's elimination of these sections.

In prior editions of this book, this question would have invoked one of the IRC § 71 elements to determine whether or not the payments made constituted alimony (and, of course, had relevance to their tax treatment). Under old law, even if the "alimony" payments met all of the IRC § 71 requirements, parties could agree to "opt out" of the default tax treatment of alimony where payments would not be income to the recipient ex-spouse nor a deduction to the payor ex-spouse. Again, this is of no relevance now as current law provides for exactly this result (regardless of any agreement or whether all of the prior law requirements for alimony were met).

Historically, we would also be careful to distinguish payment for "child support" from those for alimony (spousal support). Historically, unlike alimony, child support was neither income to the recipient ex-spouse nor a deduction to the payor ex-spouse. Again, with the TCJA, this distinction has become meaningless for tax purposes.

While not relevant to our question, nor the post TCJA law for alimony, one might wonder about the reasoning behind the prior law of alimony being income to the recipient and a corresponding deduction to the payor. Prior to the 1940's the tax ramifications of alimony were a bit of a mess but generally, alimony was not income to the payee/recipient spouse and no deduction was allowed for the payor spouse (basically what we now have pursuant to the TCJA). Top marginal tax rates (discussed elsewhere in this book) were on the rise (in part to help fund the Nation's efforts in WWII) and remained well above 50% (up to above 90% in a few years) for decades thereafter (with the highest average tax rates near 50%). The law was changed in 1942 to reverse this; alimony became income to the payee spouse and the payor spouse received a corresponding tax deduction (the basic framework until the TCJA changes). The impetus for the 1942 tax change for alimony was a mathematical conundrum from the alimony payor's side. If, for example, a payor spouse was required to pay alimony of upwards of 50% of his or her income, without a tax deduction, and he or she was being taxed at rates near 50% on their total income, the combination of alimony payments and tax obligations could account for almost 100% of the payor individual's total income (leaving little behind for him or her). Once you make alimony payments deductible for the payor spouse, then such individual is being taxed on a somewhat "net" basis (leaving the payor spouse with something). The compliment a deduction to the payor of alimony was that it be included in the gross income of the recipient. While tax rates have changed over the years (generally decreasing), the built-in tax ramifications of alimony and child support (the first giving rise to income/deduction and the latter having no tax impact to recipient or payor) lead to tax/alimony/child support planning playing an integral, and often substantial, role for family lawyers (and supportive software companies).

So, you might ask, why did the TCJA change the rules for alimony? Money! More specifically, to help pay for some of the tax-favorable provisions of the TCJA (primarily business-related). Reversing the law for alimony was calculated to raise approximately $7 billion (over ten years) in additional revenue (the tax cost to the Treasury of deductions for alimony by the payor spouse substantially outweigh the tax revenue derived from including alimony in the income of the recipient spouse).

Answers (b), (c) and (d) are incorrect because these answers, to varying degrees, represent pre TCJA law that alimony is potentially income to the recipient spouse and potentially a deduction to the payor spouse.

13. **Answer (b) is correct.** Wanda does not have any income from the receipt of alimony and Harold is not entitled to a deduction for any of his payments. This question is very similar to question 12, above. Please excuse the degree of repetition in this answer (this author did not want you to have to refer back to any prior answer explanation; hence much of what you will see is the same analysis for question 12).

WOW, how the tax landscape has changed in the blink of an eye through legislative action. The *Tax Cuts and Jobs Act* (TCJA) signed into law in December 2017 (generally effective beginning in 2018 but a bit later for our discussion of this material) upended some 77 years of fairly consistent tax law regarding alimony. Historically, and in prior editions of this book, we would be looking at IRC §§ 71 and 215. Now, however, the TCJA has stricken these sections effective for divorces after 2018. While we will discuss a bit of history of the tax treatment of alimony, below, for the 2019 divorce in our question, the answer is clear; the recipient ex-spouse does not report alimony as income and the payor ex-spouse is not entitled to a deduction for alimony. While the couple may have filed for divorce prior to the effective date of the TCJA changes on January 1, 2019, it is the date of the couple's actual divorce (May 1, 2019 when it became "final") that is controlling. Because this actual divorce date was on or after December 1, 2019, they are subject to the new alimony provisions of the TCJA; Alimony is not income to the recipient ex-spouse nor is it a deduction for the payor ex-spouse. This new law was a complete reversal of what had been settled law for 77 years.

The changes that the TCJA brought to the tax treatment of alimony are massive and the ripple effects have put many a family lawyer (and courts) in unfamiliar territory vis-à-vis determining the amounts and duration of alimony. A bit of history is in order (and this still applies to alimony stemming from divorces before 2019). For over seven decades, "Alimony" was income to the payee ex-spouse and a corresponding deduction to the payor ex-spouse via IRC §§ 71(a) and 215(a), respectively. The law contained detailed elements of what constituted alimony and many a tax question, as well as real-life family law alimony-related planning, dealt with these elements. It is unnecessary for us to go through these requirements of what constituted alimony as such requirements were, effectively, tossed out the window by the TCJA's elimination of these sections.

Historically, we would also be careful to distinguish payment for "child support" from those for alimony (spousal support). This was, in the prior editions of this book (in a revised question) the primary issue. Historically, unlike alimony, child support was neither income to the recipient ex-spouse nor a deduction to the payor ex-spouse. Again, with the TCJA, this distinction has become meaningless for tax purposes.

While not relevant to our question, nor the post TCJA law for alimony, one might wonder about the reasoning behind the prior law of alimony being income to the recipient and a corresponding deduction to the payor. Prior to the 1940's the tax ramifications of alimony were a bit of a mess but generally, alimony was not income to the payee/recipient spouse and no deduction was allowed for the payor spouse (basically what we now have pursuant to the TCJA). Top marginal tax rates (discussed elsewhere in this book) were on the rise (in part to help fund the Nation's efforts in WWII) and remained well above 50% (up to above 90% in a few years) for decades thereafter (with the highest average tax rates near 50%). The law was changed in 1942 to reverse this; alimony became income to the payee spouse and the payor spouse received a corresponding tax deduction (the basic framework until the TCJA changes). The impetus for the 1942 tax change for alimony was a mathematical conundrum from the alimony payor's side. If, for example, a payor spouse was required to pay alimony of upwards of 50% of his or her income, without a tax deduction, and he or she was being taxed at rates near 50% on their total income, the combination of alimony payments and tax obligations could account for almost 100% of the payor individual's total income (leaving little behind for him or her). Once you make alimony payments deductible for the payor spouse, then such individual is being taxes on a somewhat "net" basis (leaving the payor spouse with something). The compliment a deduction to the payor of alimony was that it be included in the gross income of the recipient. While tax rates have changed over the years (generally decreasing), the built-in tax ramifications of alimony and child support (the first giving rise to income/deduction and the latter having no tax impact to recipient or payor) lead to tax/alimony/child support planning playing an integral, and often substantial, role for family lawyers (and supportive software companies).

So, you might ask, why did the TCJA change the rules for alimony? Money! More specifically, to help pay for some of the tax-favorable provisions of the TCJA (primarily business-related). Reversing the law for alimony was calculated to raise approximately $7 billion (over ten years) in additional revenue (the tax cost to the Treasury of deductions for alimony by the payor spouse substantially outweigh the tax revenue derived from including alimony in the income of the recipient spouse).

Answers (a) and (b) are not correct because, to varying degrees, they implicate the old, pre TCJA, law regarding alimony. Pursuant to the changes made to the tax ramifications of alimony, Wanda will not recognize any income as the recipient. Additionally, the new provisions eliminate any issue regarding Harold's entitlement to a deduction for alimony paid. **Answer (d) is incorrect** because the new provisions of the TCJA are effective for divorces after December 31, 2018 (i.e., when the divorce is "final"). The fact that the couple may have filed for divorce prior to the effective date of the changes regarding alimony, is irrelevant. As a side note, this created a huge logistics problem for couples in the midst of a divorce with the impending law change. You can imagine the rush to finalize prior to 2019 if representing the payor spouse and the "let's take our time" mindset of the recipient spouse.

14. **The correct answer is (c).** This is a good example of a question that, to a student studying income tax, may appear to exist purely as an academic exercise. While it does contain aspects that present an academic challenge, this question reflects a surprisingly common "real world" tax situation. Wanda will have to recognize $145,000 of gain from the sale of the XYZ shares. This gain is characterized as "long-term capital gain."

In every fact pattern in which something is sold (or otherwise disposed of), the author likes to go through the following analysis:

1) Does the sale (or disposition) result in a <u>realized</u> gain or loss and if so, what is the <u>amount</u>?
2) If we have a <u>realized</u> gain or loss, is it <u>recognized</u> (i.e., reportable for income tax purposes)?
3) If the gain or loss is recognized, is it accorded "capital" gain or loss treatment?

Because this question involves a multi-step analysis and because the author recognizes the value of your time, both **abbreviated/short** and **comprehensive/long** analyses are provided below.

The <u>abbreviated/short</u> version of the analysis for this question is that Wanda's realized gain is the difference between the $150,000 sales price and her basis in the shares of $5,000, or $145,000. Her basis in the shares is a $5,000 carryover basis from Harold rather than the $50,000 that she paid for them because her purchase from Harold was from her former spouse and it was "incident to divorce (occurring within one year of their divorce). [See IRC § 1041.] This gain is recognized and is characterized as a long-term capital gain. This is because the shares represent capital assets and Wanda's holding period, with the tacking of Harold's and the couple's holding period, was more than one year. [See IRC §§ 1221, 1222 and 1223(2).]

The following comprehensive/long (very long) analysis presents a step-by-step discussion of the answer to this question that can be applied to other gain/loss questions.

The first step is determining whether Wanda has a realized gain or loss on the sale of the stock. For this, we need two basic components: her sales price ("amount realized" or, hereinafter, AR) and her basis in the shares ("adjusted basis or, hereinafter, AB). The difference between the two represents a realized gain or loss. [IRC § 1001(a).] Each of these two components, AR and AB, can present a variety of complex tax issues for exam and real-world tax purposes. The AR side is straightforward in our question and is her $150,000 sales price. Other questions in this book present more complex issues involving a taxpayer's AR. The AB component is a bit more difficult to derive in this question.

The general starting place for determining one's AB in property is one's cost. [IRC §§ 1011 and 1012.] "Adjustments" to one's basis, while not at issue in this question, can result from many reasons including capital improvements (increasing basis), and depreciation expenses (reducing basis). [IRC § 1016.] Applying the general cost basis rule in our question, Wanda's AB would appear to be $50,000, the amount that she paid Harold for the shares. There are, however, statutory exceptions where one's cost is not the general starting point in determining one's AB. Some of these exceptions, such as property received as a gift or devise, are the subject of other questions in this book. A major exception that is relevant to our question, is the special basis rule when we have transfers between spouses or transfers between former spouses that are considered "incident to divorce." IRC § 1041(b) provides, in a nutshell, that when spouses transfer property to each other, or when former spouses transfer property to each other and such transfer is "incident to their divorce," the transferee spouse (or former spouse) takes a carryover basis. This section does not distinguish as to the type of inter vivos transfer involved; it covers gifts, sales, exchanges, etc.

In our question, we have two transfers potentially subject to this special AB rule: 1) the awarding of the shares to Harold at the time of their divorce on

May 1, 2019, and 2) Harold's sale of the shares to Wanda in March of 2020. The focus in our question will be on the latter transaction (although the divorce transfer to Harold will be addressed). As to Wanda, the consequences of coming within the scope of IRC § 1041 will make a dramatic difference in her AB in the shares. If we find that Wanda's purchase of the shares from Harold is within the confines of IRC § 1041, she will have an AB in the shares of only $5,000 (carried over from Harold's original purchase price). Alternatively, if this purchase does not fit within the confines of IRC § 1041, Wanda's AB in the shares will be her $50,000 cost of the shares. The difference in AB will, of course, impact the amount of gain she realizes from her subsequent sale of the shares.

At this point, we are at the critical juncture of whether or not Harold's sale of the shares to Wanda in March of 2020 is within the parameters of IRC § 1041; was this a transfer between spouses or former spouses that is "incident to divorce?" Clearly, it was not a transfer between spouses as they were divorced at the time (they divorced on May 1, 2019; see the general facts presented for this series of problems 12 through 14). It was a transfer between former spouses, but was it considered "incident to divorce" as required by the statute? A transfer "incident to divorce" has a statutory definition as being either 1) <u>any</u> transfer within one year of the divorce, or 2) a transfer "relating to the cessation of the marriage." (See IRC § 1041(c)). Temporary regulations define transfers that are considered "relating to the cessation of the marriage" as a transfer provided for by a "divorce or separation instrument" (suffice it to say, that their divorce decree is the classic type of such an instrument) and is transferred, pursuant to this instrument, within six years of the divorce. [Temp.Reg. § 1.1041-1T(b) Q & A-7.]

The facts indicate that Harold's sale of the shares to Wanda occurred in March of 2020 and that they divorced on May 1, 2019. This March "sale" was within one year of their divorce and, therefore, is deemed to be a transfer that is "incident to divorce." With this sale being deemed a transfer incident to divorce, Wanda's AB in the shares is not her $50,000 purchase price but, rather, a $5,000 carryover basis from that of Harold. Until now, we have not addressed Harold's AB in the shares. However, it is not too difficult to see that his AB was also governed by IRC § 1041. The transfer of the shares to him was clearly "incident to divorce" (he received them not only within one year of the divorce, but also pursuant to the decree and within six years of the divorce). Harold's AB, therefore, is a carryover from the couple's original $5,000 purchase price. This hardly seems fair to Wanda, but it is the law and provides students with a great illustration of why it is important to know the tax ramifications of one's legal advice (i.e., a malpractice claim may await Wanda's attorney if he or she did not apprise Wanda of this result).

Note that the sale of these shares between Harold and Wanda is deemed "incident to divorce" notwithstanding the fact that it was not pursuant to any agreement relating to their divorce. This is often an elusive point with students. IRC § 1041(c) dictates a <u>non-rebuttable</u> presumption that any transfer within one year of divorce is deemed incident to divorce. To extend this classification to transfers made more than one year after divorce, the transfer must be pursuant to their divorce or separation instrument (e.g., divorce decree). [See Temp.Reg. 1.1041-1T(b) Q & A-7.]

A corollary provision of IRC § 1041 is that the <u>transferor</u> recognizes no gain or loss from a transfer "incident to divorce." While not at issue in our question, Harold's sale to Wanda resulted in a <u>realized</u> gain to him of $45,000 ($50,000 AR less $5,000 AB), this gain is <u>not recognized</u> (i.e., not reported for income tax purposes).

Now back to the income tax consequences to Wanda of her sale of the shares in April 2020 for $150,000. We can now answer the question in the first step of our gain/loss analysis: the amount of Wanda's <u>realized</u> gain. Wanda has a <u>realized</u> gain of $145,000 representing her AR (sales price) of $150,000 less her AB (as determined above) of only $5,000.

The next step in our analysis of gain/loss situations is to determine the extent to which any <u>realized</u> gain is <u>recognized</u>. Recognition of gain basically means that it is reported as income for income tax purposes. IRC § 1001(c) provides that unless otherwise provided for in the Code, all realized gains and losses are recognized. The above-discussed provision of IRC § 1041 is one such "otherwise provided for" non-recognition provisions (and is the reason why Harold's realized gain is a recognized gain). Another frequently addressed non-recognition provision is the IRC § 121 exclusion of gain from the sale of a principal residence (see other questions in this book addressing this issue). For realized losses, there are many "non-recognition" provisions that are discussed elsewhere in this book. Unfortunately for Wanda, there are no exclusion or non-recognition provisions applicable in these facts and her $145,000 realized gain will be <u>recognized</u>. Do not fall into the trap that some students do in this question, reasoning that because Wanda's subsequent sale of the shares in April 2020 was within one year of her divorce that the non-recognition provisions of IRC § 1041 apply to that sale. IRC § 1041 applies only to transfers between spouses and former spouses. Wanda's sale of the shares in April was to someone other than Harold, her former spouse. Had her sale in April been back to Harold, then, indeed, the non-recognition and carryover basis provisions of IRC § 1041 would again be applicable. Always be careful with questions involving transfers between spouses and former spouses.

The last part of the analysis is to determine whether Wanda's $145,000 of recognized gain is accorded special "capital gain" treatment. Historically, gains from the sale of certain types of assets have been accorded preferential tax treatment. While it is far beyond the scope of analysis for this question, modernly, "long-term" capital gains ("net capital gains" to be more specific), while included in a taxpayer's gross and taxable incomes, may be taxed at favorable (i.e., lower) tax rates. A capital gain analysis requires that we first determine that we are dealing with a "capital asset," after which the gain is characterized as having either long-term or short-term status.

IRC § 1221(a) defines a capital asset in a negative fashion, but for purposes of this analysis, it includes, by process of elimination, assets held for investment and personal-use purposes. There is little question that Wanda's XYZ Co. shares qualify as a capital asset. Long-term status is reserved for those assets held for <u>more than one year</u> (short-term status for assets held one year or less). [See IRC § 1222.] On the surface, Wanda purchased the shares from Harold in March 2020 and sold them one month later in April 2020. At first brush, Wanda's capital gain from the sale of the shares appears to be a short-term capital gain. Determining the holding period, for short- and long-term gain/loss classification, is controlled by IRC § 1223. At IRC § 1223(2), we have the so-called "tacking" rule, which essentially applies to situations where the taxpayer's AB is a carryover AB. Where this is the case, as it is in our question because Harold's sale to Wanda was a transfer incident to divorce, the transferee (Wanda) can add to her holding period, that of the transferor (Harold). Tacking on Harold's holding period from their divorce on May 1, 2019, Wanda, at the time of her sale, still has a holding period that is shy of one year. We apply IRC § 1223(2) again because Harold received the shares incident to divorce and, therefore, has the $5,000 carryover AB dating back to "many years ago" when the couple first purchased the stock. Adding all of this time together, it becomes clear that Wanda is deemed to have held the shares for more than one year, thus resulting in a <u>long-term capital gain</u>.

Other situations where this tacking rule often applies is with respect to inter vivos gifts where a transferee's AB is usually the same as the transferor's AB. The language of the statute more specifically makes this rule applicable where the transferee's AB is determined "in whole or in part" with reference to the transferor's AB. This language allows for tacking of the holding period to apply to gift situations where a gift tax results, and the transferee's AB is increased pursuant to IRC § 1015(d) because of the gift tax. Be careful with gifts, however, where the "special loss rule" (discussed elsewhere in this book) applies or where the transaction in which the taxpayer received the property was in part a sale and in part a gift (also discussed elsewhere in this book). In those gift related situations, the tacking rule may or may not apply depending on whether the transferee's AB was or was not essentially a carryover AB.

Answer (b) is incorrect. While it indicates the correct $145,000 or recognized gain, it fails to utilize the tacking rules for Wanda's holding period as discussed above. **Answer (a) is incorrect.** However, it is probably the incorrect answer that is selected most often. In our question, Wanda's purchase of the stock from Harold is deemed "incident to divorce" notwithstanding the fact that it was not pursuant to any agreement relating to their divorce. This is often an elusive point with students. IRC § 1041(c) dictates a non-rebuttable presumption that any transfer within one year of divorce is deemed incident to divorce. It is bothersome to many that a transaction such as this, which clearly had nothing to do with their divorce, is, nonetheless, a transaction that is deemed incident to their divorce. On essay questions similar to this fact pattern, it is not unusual for a student to logically, but <u>incorrectly</u> respond: "While Harold's sale to Wanda occurred within one year of their divorce, it did not relate to their divorce (i.e., it was not pursuant to their divorce decree) and, therefore, is not incident to the divorce." It is true, however, that extending this IRC § 1041 classification to transfers made more than one year after divorce, the transfer must be pursuant to their divorce or separation instrument (e.g., divorce decree). [See Temp.Reg. § 1.1041-1T(b) Q & A-7.]

Answer (d) is also incorrect. However, it too is a commonly selected incorrect answer. As warned above, do not fall into the trap that because Wanda's subsequent sale of the shares in April 2020 was within one year of her divorce, the non-recognition provisions of IRC § 1041 apply to that sale. IRC § 1041 applies only to transfers between spouses and former spouses. Wanda's sale of the shares in April 2020 was to someone other than Harold, her former spouse. Had her sale in April been back to Harold, then, indeed, the non-recognition and carryover basis provisions of IRC § 1041 would be applicable (and Harold would have a $5,000 carryover AB with a "tacked" long-term holding period).

15. **Answer (d) is the most accurate.** Now for something completely different. This question involves a tax provision that did not exist prior to the *Tax Cuts and Jobs Act* (TCJA) signed into law in December 2017 (generally effective beginning in 2018). One of the most touted provisions of the TCJA for individuals was "business tax cuts." To be sure, the TCJA had a huge impact on corporate taxes, but for the individual business owner (and those owing a business in partnership, LLC, "S Corp," etc. form), IRC § 199A was the section that implemented a new and special deduction for some businesses. This new provision was commonly referred to as the "pass-through deduction" for businesses. This new provision is not to be

confused with regular IRC § 162 deductions for business expenses that are covered in some detail in many questions in this book. Rather, it is an additional deduction for qualifying businesses and unlike regular business deductions, this new IRC § 199A *pass-through* deduction is reflected not in computing one's net business income but, rather, is tacked on as a deduction in computing an individual's taxable income. [Please see Appendix A and other questions in this book addressing the logistics of how this deduction fits in computing taxable income.] Before getting to the answer to this question, be aware that IRC § 199A is <u>very</u> complex (it took the Treasury Department/IRS more than a year after the section was enacted to issue guidance and regulations) and your professor may cover this section in varying degrees of detail (if at all). This section is more likely to be covered in greater detail in an advanced "corporate/business entities/etc." tax course than it is in the basic federal income tax course. For this book, the author presents only a light summary of some of the more salient provisions of this provision.

Turning to Marisol, she may be entitled to this special *pass-through* deduction" via IRC § 199A depending on her overall *taxable income* for the year. Depending on her level of *taxable income*, this special extra deduction may be up to 20% of her dentistry's business net income.

The previous paragraph contains many complex items that are well beyond the scope of this question, but we shall cover some of the basics. As indicated, IRC § 199A is very complex with multiple "layers" of tests for determining the proper deduction (if any). It is fair to say that this section may allow for a deduction of up to 20% of an individual's "Qualified Business Income." Computing an individual's *qualified business income* can be a laborious task but, basically, in a simple case such as ours, it is equivalent to the net profit (income less regular business expenses). The statute separates businesses, which in turn affects the calculation for this special deduction, into two camps: those that are deemed a "specified service trade or business" (SSTB) and those that are not. An SSTB is a trade or business that performs services in health, law, accounting, actuarial science, performing arts, consulting, athletics, financial services, brokerage services, investing and investment management, trading, dealing in securities, or a trade or business where the principal asset is the reputation or skill of one or more of its employees or owners." [See Reg. § 1.199A-5] Great; we now know that Marisol's dentistry is an SSTB; so what in the world is the significance of this? The IRC § 199A special deduction can be more restrictive for SSTB's than for non-SSTB's. What? Confused? Yes, everyone was confused when IRC § 199A was enacted. In a nutshell, if an individual's *taxable income* (this is their total taxable income before this special deduction is considered, and not just one's net business income) exceeds certain threshold amounts (varying by filing status and by tax year), then the section's 20% deduction is reduced. If an individual's *taxable income* is greater than an "upper-limit" threshold, then for SSTB's, like Marisol's dental practice, this special deduction is completely phased out (i.e., no special, extra IRC § 199A deduction). However, for businesses other than SSTB's there still may be some IRC § 199A deduction available even when an individual's *taxable income* exceeds this "upper-limit" threshold. Yikes, this is messy and the actual application of the rules (with numbers) and computation of this deduction is extraordinarily complex. But for us, in this question, this is as far as we need to go down this torturous path that is IRC § 199A. [Please see other questions later in this book that delve deeper into the IRC § 199A *pass-through* deduction.]

To summarize, answer (d) is correct because depending on Marisol's taxable income for the year (without regard to this special deduction) – i.e., if it is not too much, she will be entitled to an IRC § 199A deduction up to 20% of her net dentistry business income. If her *taxable income* is too high (exceeding the upper-limit threshold in the statute), then she would not be entitled to any such deduction. This latter non-allowance of a deduction could be different if her business was other than the service-type businesses mentioned above. It bears repeating that this material is covered in varying degrees of depth depending on your tax professor.

Answer (a) is incorrect because it fails to reflect the various statutory limitations for this deduction. It is also incorrect stating that the deduction is "at least" 20% of her business's net profit. If Marisol qualifies, the deduction is "up to" 20% of such business profit. **Answer (b) is almost correct.** It goes awry with the phasing out of this deduction being dependent on the amount of her business's net profit instead of her *taxable income*. **Answer (c) is incorrect** because while it reflects the statutory distinction of certain service-type businesses, it is not true, as discussed above, that such service businesses are not eligible for the IRC § 199A deduction. Rather, the "phase out" of the deduction is less favorable for such service-type businesses.

16. **The correct answer is (c).** Each year, Americans give billions of dollars to charities. Fostering charitable giving has long been an important component of government tax policy. A deduction, for income tax purposes, for contributions made to charitable organizations has had a long-time presence in our country's tax structure. IRC § 170(a) facilitates deductions for contributions of cash and property to qualified charities. One need not be a student in income tax to surmise that the American Red Cross qualifies as charitable organization. Indeed, the American Red Cross is a qualified charitable organization as generally defined in IRC § 170(c) and Alex's cash gifts thereto will be tax deductible (subject to limits discussed

below). Contrary to what is a common public belief, contributions made to an individual (unless to an individual acting as an agent for a qualified organization) do not give rise to charitable deductions. Therefore, Alex's cash gifts to the homeless individuals are not tax deductible.

The total amount of an individual's charitable deductions in any one year is limited or capped at a ceiling that varies depending on the nature of contribution (cash or property) and the charitable recipients. This deduction ceiling or limit for <u>cash gifts</u> made to most charitable organizations (commonly referred to as "public charities") is a percentage of the taxpayer's "contribution base." The Code, in IRC § 170(b)(1)(A) sets this percentage as 50% but the *Tax Cuts and Jobs Act* (TCJA) signed into law in December 2017 (generally effective beginning in 2018) increases this ceiling to 60% [IRC § 170(b)(1)(G)]. Alex's cash contributions to the American Red Cross (representing all of his qualified charitable contributions in the year for this question) are deductible up to 60% of his contribution base. While not necessary to answer this question, an individual's "contribution base" is basically the individual's adjusted gross income (AGI) calculated before deducting any "net operating loss" (NOL) carryback (most individuals do not have a NOL carryback, so their AGI is their "contribution base"). [See IRC § 170(b)(1)(H).]

While also not a part of this question, it should be noted that charitable contributions made in any year that, in the aggregate, exceed the deduction ceiling, are carried forward for up to the next five tax years (and deductible subject to the applicable year's limits).

It also should be noted that while not part of this question, tax deductible charitable contributions are, in calculating an individual's taxable income, part of a group of deductions known as "itemized deductions." As discussed in other questions in this book, not everyone obtains an actual benefit from *itemized deductions* because in calculating taxable income, one selects the greater of total *itemized deductions* or something called the "standard deduction." Other questions address the *standard deduction* as well as how all of this fits together in computing one's taxable income (also see Appendix A for more information). The TCJA dramatically increased the *standard deduction* for most individuals (beginning in 2018) and a "knock-off" effect is that fewer individuals benefit, tax-wise, from charitable deductions because these are part of *itemized deductions* which, in turn, may be less than the increased *standard deduction* (i.e., a larger *standard deduction* means fewer individuals taking *itemized deductions*, a component of which are charitable deductions).

Answers (a) and (b) are incorrect because those answers incorrectly include as deductible charitable contributions, Alex's cash gifts made to homeless individuals. **Answer (d) is incorrect** because it applies the wrong deduction limit or ceiling. Other questions in this book discuss the application of a lower 30% of "contribution base" ceiling for other charitable contribution situations.

17. **The correct answer is (a).** Unfortunately for Alex, and contrary to popular belief, no charitable deduction arises from the contribution of one's services. [Reg. § 1.170A-1(g).] Alex's contributed services, like that of a lawyer providing pro bono services, is commendable, meritorious, and a very rewarding public service. The rewards for such service do not, however, include tax deductions.

Alex <u>is</u> entitled to a charitable deduction, however, for costs that he incurs in connection with the charitable work he performs. [Reg. § 1.170A-1(g).] His driving costs related to the charitable services that he performs for Habitat for Humanity is a deductible expense. Generally, an individual can deduct (subject to charitable contribution ceilings) either the actual operating costs of his or her vehicle for the charitable related miles, or a statutory rate per charitable mile driven (14¢ per mile as of this writing).

It also should be noted that while not part of this question, tax deductible charitable contributions are, in calculating an individual's taxable income, part of a group of deductions known as "itemized deductions." As discussed in other questions in this book, not everyone obtains an actual benefit from *itemized deductions* because in calculating taxable income, one selects the greater of total *itemized deductions* or something called the "standard deduction." Other questions address the *standard deduction* as well as how all of this fits together in computing one's taxable income (also see Appendix A for more information). The TCJA dramatically increased the *standard deduction* for most individuals (beginning in 2018) and a "knock-off" effect is that fewer individuals benefit, tax-wise, from charitable deductions because these are part of *itemized deductions* which, in turn, may be less than the increased *standard deduction* (i.e., a larger *standard deduction*).

Answers (b) and (d) are incorrect because Alex is not entitled to a deduction for the value of his services rendered. Additionally, answer (d) is incorrect because a taxpayer is entitled to deduct charitable related transportation notwithstanding from where the trips originate. **Answer (c) is incorrect** because it does not reflect the deductible charitable miles. **Answer (e) in incorrect** because, as mentioned, a taxpayer is entitled to deduct charitable related transportation notwithstanding from where the trips originate.

18. Answer (d) is the best response. IRC § 170(a) facilitates deductions for contributions of cash and property to qualified charities. As indicated in the answer to question 16, above, the American Red Cross is a qualified charitable organization. This question is a good, albeit unfortunate, example of how changes to tax laws over the years have added layers of analysis to our answer.

The <u>value</u> of the property donated is usually the measurement for the charitable deduction. [Reg. § 1.170A-1(c).] There are, however, a few important caveats to this general rule. First, we have Alex's donation of his personal-use car to the American Red Cross and we are told that it was worth $10,000 at the time (probably determined by Alex looking up the value on one of many Internet websites). At one time, we would stop here and say that this would be the measurement of his charitable deduction. Students used to hear, some years ago, advertisements extolling the tax benefits of donating a car, boat or other property to charity: "*and you may be entitled to a tax deduction equal to the full fair market value of your car, often more than you would receive on a trade-in. Consult your tax advisor for more information.*" You are the "tax advisor" here and prior to 2005, you might have advised Alex that he was entitle to deduct the full $10,000 value of the car. However, due to perceived abuses in this area of charitable donations, the "*American Job Creation Act of 2004*" put limits to such deductions starting in 2005. Generally, the deduction for charitable donations for cars (or boats and planes) is limited to the gross proceeds from the sale of the vehicle by the charity (and this is usually what is done by the recipient charity or a third party acting on their behalf in a used-car auction setting). There are some rare exceptions that may entitle the taxpayer to a larger deduction for donations of cars (or boats or planes); the most common, albeit still infrequent, where the charity actually uses the donated vehicle for their charitable purposes and does not sell it. [See IRC § 170(f)(12) for more information.] So in our problem, Alex's car donation would yield a charitable deduction of $8,000, the proceeds that the American Red Cross received from the sale of the car.

Alex's donation of the GM stock is treated a bit different. This does not fall within the aforementioned limitations for donations of vehicles (cars, boats or planes). Rather, we go back to the previously stated general rule that a taxpayer is entitled to a charitable deduction equal to the fair market value of property. The appreciated fair market value of the GM stock Alex donated qualifies as a charitable contribution. This too is advertised by charities as being beneficial because the taxpayer is usually entitled to deduct the appreciated fair market value of the property without any recognition of gain (which would be the case if the stock had been sold and the cash proceeds donated to the charity). While it may be beyond the scope of discussion in many tax classes, it should be noted that a deduction equal to the fair market value of appreciated property is generally limited to property that would have produced a long-term capital gain if it had been sold (as is the case with Alex's GM stock in this question).

As with cash contributions in question 16, above, the deduction for charitable donations of property is limited by a ceiling, based on a per-centage of the taxpayer's "contribution base" (usually the taxpayer's AGI). [IRC § 170(b)(1).] While this question does not specifically refer to this limit, generally the deduction for contributions of non-appreciated property (e.g. Alex's car) is limited (in the aggregate combined with all additional such contributions and contributions of cash) to 60% of the taxpayer's "contribution base." [See question 16 for discussion of recent law changes affecting this ceiling percentage number.] Deduction for contributions of most appreciated property (e.g., Alex's GM stock) is limited (in the aggregate combined with all additional such contributions and contributions of cash) to 30% of the taxpayer's "contribution base" (AGI for most individuals). [IRC § 170(b)(1)(C).] Be aware that your professor may cover this material in much greater depth, with more detailed attention to contribution limits and other issues including special elections that may be made with respect to donations of appreciated property.

Finally, we come to the $500 that Alex paid for the tickets to the special American Red Cross Cirque du Soleil event. One might logically think that he would be entitled to a charitable contribution deduction of $500, the amount paid. However, when the donor receives something in return, the charitable deduction is normally limited to the amount contributed less the value of what is received. [Reg. § 1.170A-1(h).] In this case, Alex received the Cirque du Soleil tickets, worth $100 in return for his $500 contribution. Therefore, his charitable deduction is the $400 difference. This is a logical conclusion. Otherwise, an individual could generate deductible charitable contributions for non-charitable expenditures.

Again, your professor may cover the charitable deduction area in much greater detail. Not mentioned in this, or other problems in this book, are different deduction ceilings for donations to "non-public" charities (e.g., many "private foundations"), charitable contributions of business-related property, requirements for receipts for deductions of certain amounts of cash or property contributions, etc.

It also should be noted that while not part of this question, tax deductible charitable contributions are, in calculating an individual's taxable income, part of a group of deductions known as "itemized deductions." As discussed in other questions in this book, not everyone obtains an actual benefit from *itemized deductions* because in calculating taxable income, one selects the greater of total *itemized deductions* or something called the "standard deduction." Other questions address the *standard deduction* as well as how all of this fits together in computing one's taxable income (also see Appendix A for more information). The TCJA dramatically increased the *standard deduction* for most individuals (beginning in 2018) and a "knock-off" effect is that fewer individuals benefit, tax-wise, from charitable deductions because these are part of *itemized deductions* which, in turn, may be less than the increased *standard deduction* (i.e., a larger *standard deduction*).

Answer (a) is incorrect because it indicates the wrong charitable deduction assessment for the GM shares donated and overstates the charitable deduction for the Cirque du Soleil event donation. **Answer (b) is incorrect** because it indicates the wrong charitable deduction assessment for the GM shares donated. **Answer (c) is incorrect** because it fails to incorporate the special limitations placed on deductions with respect to donations of automobiles. This answer (c) would have been the correct answer in years prior to 2005. **Answer (e) is incorrect** because a correct answer (d) is presented.

19. **The correct answer is (d).** IRC § 170(a) facilitates deductions for contributions of cash and property to qualified charities. The facts indicate that the "university" in this question is a qualified charitable organization. However, as discussed below, Alex's "contribution" to the university will not give rise to a charitable deduction because in substance, it is the payment of his niece's tuition. Rose will not have gross income resulting from this most likely because it constitutes a gift, albeit an indirect one, from her uncle.

As for Alex's "contribution" to the university, the analysis is similar to that in question 18, above. When a donor receives something in return for the contribution to charity, the deduction is normally limited to the amount contributed less the value of what is received. [Reg. § 1.170A-1(h).] In this case, Alex received the benefit of Rose's tuition being covered in exchange for his contribution of an equivalent amount. Therefore, he is not entitled to any net charitable deduction. This is a logical conclusion. Otherwise, an individual could generate deductible charitable contributions for non-charitable expenditures. Specifically on point, is Revenue Ruling 83-104. [Rev.Rul. 83-104, 1983-2 C.B. 46.] It states that, "the presence of one or more of the following factors creates a presumption that the payment is not a charitable contribution: the existence of a contract under which a taxpayer agrees to make a "contribution" and which contains provisions ensuring the admission of the taxpayer's child; a plan allowing taxpayers either to pay tuition or to make "contributions" in exchange for schooling; the earmarking of a contribution for the direct benefit of a particular individual; or the otherwise-unexplained denial of admission or readmission to a school of children of taxpayers who are financially able, but who do not contribute." Clearly, Alex's "contribution" fits squarely within the borders of this revenue ruling.

As for Rose, she received a financial or economic benefit that will be income unless an exclusion provision applies. While it is debatable whether the "scholarship" could be considered a qualified scholarship and excludable pursuant to IRC § 117, it is more likely an indirect gift to her from Alex. IRC § 102 excludes, from gross income, amounts received as a gift. While other questions in this book address the issue of gifts in more detail, suffice it to say that Alex's motives for benefiting his niece were almost assuredly of the requisite "detached and disinterested generosity" variety.

Answer (a) is incorrect because, as discussed above, Alex will not be entitled to a charitable deduction for his "contribution" to the university. Rose's exclusion of the scholarship pursuant to IRC § 117 is also debatable. **Answer (b) is incorrect** because Rose will be able to exclude the benefit that she received – most likely it will be considered a gift from her uncle. **Answer (c) is incorrect** because Alex will not be entitled to a charitable deduction for his "contribution" to the university.

20. **The best response is (c).** Both the cash and the value of the car that Amy received will be included in her gross income. They do not represent excludable gifts because of Amy's employment relationship with XYZ.

From your initial study of gross income's scope, you probably found it to be broadly defined, including the taxpayer's receipt of an economic benefit or a net accession to wealth. Gross income is also not limited to the receipt of cash. [See Reg. § 1.61-2(d) (compensation paid in forms other than in cash).] Amy clearly received a net financial benefit upon receiving both the cash and automobile. Barring any specific income exclusion provision that might be applicable in this situation, Amy would include, in her gross income the $5,000 cash received plus the $30,000 value of the property received. [Reg. § 1.61-2(d).] While this result reflects the correct answer to this question, we should further explore this issue to better understand the subject and to rule out other possible answers to this question. It will also aid in reviewing issues arising in other questions in this book.

One specific income exclusion provision that is potentially relevant here is IRC § 102. This section's general rule provides for a very beneficial exclusion from income of amounts received as gifts, bequests, devises, and inheritances. [IRC § 102(a).] While not defined in statutes, a gift, for purposes of this exclusion, is a transfer made for insufficient consideration with the donor acting from "detached and disinterested generosity." [See *Comm'r v. Duberstein*, 363 U.S. 278, 80 S.Ct. 1190 (1960).] It could be argued that XYZ, Amy's employer, had such motives in giving the cash and automobile to Amy and, therefore, Amy could exclude them from gross income. Unfortunately for Amy, the general exclusion rule of IRC § 102(a) is nullified by subsection IRC § 102(c). This subsection provides, in general, that the possible exclusion from gross income of property acquired by gift (or bequest, devise or inheritance) does <u>not</u> apply to transfers between employers and employees. In other words, "gifts" to employees are not excludable from gross income under IRC § 102. This subsection is not merely a presumption. Thus, "gifts" to employees are not excludable by this section notwithstanding that an employer can demonstrate that the gift was made out of "detached and disinterested generosity." Therefore, despite the likelihood that XYZ's motives for making the gift were genuinely gratuitous, the $5,000 cash and $30,000 value of the automobile both represent income to Amy in the form of compensation.

The proposed regulations provide for a limited exception to this IRC § 102(c) exclusion denial for gifts to employees. Proposed Regulation § 1.102-1(f)(2) states that "[f]or purposes of section 102(c), extraordinary transfers to the natural objects of an employer's bounty will not be considered transfers to, or for the benefit of, an employee if the employee can show that the transfer was not made in recognition of the employee's employment. Accordingly, section 102(c) shall not apply to amounts transferred between related parties (e.g., father and son) if the purpose of the transfer can be substantially attributed to the familial relationship of the parties and not to the circumstances of their employment." Other questions in this book address this particular issue and this regulation exception is not necessarily limited to "gifts" to family member/employee. Unfortunately for Amy, the "gifts" to her would not fit within this limited exception notwithstanding her employer's motives for making them.

Answer (a) is not the best response. As indicated above, IRC § 102(c) generally precludes excludable gifts from employers to employees notwithstanding the employer's motives for making the gift. **Answer (b) is incorrect** because there is no relevant distinction applicable in these facts, for gift or compensation purposes, between transfers of money and transfers of property. With some exceptions, not applicable here, both represent income to the recipient employee. **Answer (d) is incorrect.** This answer hints of statutory exclusions relevant to employee "fringe benefits." However, no such fringe benefit provisions are applicable to the facts in this question.

21. **Answer (b) is correct.** We have some math here but it's not bad so don't shy away even if the site of numbers does not warm your heart. Amy must include $2,000 of the $4,000 discount that she received with respect to the

life insurance policy. This is because the discount that she received exceeds the maximum amount allowed by statute.

IRC § 61 defines gross income as "all income from whatever source derived." From your initial study of gross income's scope, you probably found it to be broadly defined, including the taxpayer's receipt of some net economic benefit or net accession to wealth. In class, you also discover that gross income is also not limited to the receipt of cash. [Reg. § 1.61-1(d) (compensation received in forms other than in cash).] Amy received an economic benefit when she purchased the life insurance policy from her employer in the form of the discount that she received. It is by reason of her employment that she received the $4,000 discount and, barring a specific exclusion provision, this amount represents income to her.

Fortunately for Amy, she is entitled to *some* relief. A host of employee fringe benefits are excluded pursuant to IRC § 132, and the benefit Amy is receiving in this problem invokes the "qualified employee discount" fringe benefit. [IRC §§ 132(a)(2) and 132(c).] Anyone who has ever worked in retail is probably familiar with this fringe benefit. Did you include, in income, the 15% or 20% employee discount that you received on merchandise purchased while working at that store? Most likely the answer is <u>no</u>, and the most likely reason is that the benefit that you received was an excludable *qualified employee discount*. Although restrictions and limits may apply, the *qualified employee discount* allows employers to allow employees to buy their products or services at a discount, without that discount being included in the employee's gross income.

There are two major requirements or limitations applicable to this fringe benefit. First, the discount the employee is receiving must be with respect to products or services that are in the line of business in which the employee is working. [IRC § 132(c)(4).] This is the so-called "line of business" test. Ostensibly, this requirement exists to prevent conglomerates from providing across the board discounts to all employees in all lines of the employer's business that are perceived to be unfair when compared to non-conglomerates. Amy is receiving a discount in XYZ's insurance line of business. The facts indicate that Amy, as an officer of XYZ, performs a substantial amount of work in all areas of XYZ's operations. Amy *does* satisfy this line of business test. The fact that she works in more than one of the company's line of business does not preclude her from the *qualified employee discount* fringe benefit. [Reg. § 1.132-4(a)(1)(iii).] Examples of an employee not satisfying this requirement would start with a company with many different lines of business (say hotels, insurance and consumer electronics). The *line of business test* would not be satisfied when, for example, a desk clerk working in the company's hotel line of business receiving a discount on insurance purchased from the company, or that same employee receiving discounts in XYZ's consumer electronics products.

The second major limitation is the amount of the discount available. Basically, the *qualified employee discount* will be viewed as a tax-free fringe benefit as long as "it does not cost the employer too much money" in providing the benefit. The statutory maximum tax-free discount applicable to employer provided "services" is a flat 20%. [IRC 132(c)(1)(B).] In the case of discounts for products (tangible personal property), the statute does not set a specific discount percentage amount but, rather, states that the discount cannot exceed the employer's "gross profit percentage." [IRC § 132(c)(1)(A).] The computation of a company's "gross profit percentage" is defined in IRC § 132(c)(2) (basically, it is the company's overall gross profit in a particular line of business as a percentage of sales). The facts for this question indicate that XYZ's "gross profit percentage" in their insurance line of business is 40%. At first glance, it looks as if Amy's 40% discount she received on the purchase of the life insurance policy does not exceed the maximum discount allowed. Unfortunately, "life insurance" is considered a "service" and not a "product" (tangible personal property). The repercussion to Amy is that she has received a discount in excess of the statutory allowed maximum (recall, this is a flat 20% maximum tax-free discount for services). The result is that Amy can exclude the statutory maximum 20% discount applicable to services. The value of the discount that she received in excess of this will be includible in her gross income. Putting numbers to this, the policy normally sells for $10,000 and she received a 40% discount or $4,000. Her maximum exclusion is only 20% of the $10,000 cost of the policy or $2,000. Therefore, the amount includible in Amy's gross income is the $4,000 discount she received, less the $2,000 allowed maximum, or $2,000 ($4,000 - $2,000).

There is one last issue to consider in this question. The statute provides that an employer cannot provide some, but not all, of the fringe benefits enumerated in IRC § 132 to employees on a discriminatory basis (in favor of only highly compensated employees as defined by the statute). The *qualified employee discount* is one such benefit that cannot be provided to employees in a discriminatory manner. [IRC § 132(j)(1).] While Amy is a "highly compensated employee," this insurance discount is offered to all full-time employees and therefore, does not offend these discrimination rules. Limiting this benefit to just "full-time" employees is most likely not discriminatory for purpose of IRC § 132. [Reg. § 1.132-8(d)(2).] The fact that in the current year only Amy and one other officer took advantage of the insurance discount does not render it discriminatory, as it was available to all full-time employees. It should be noted that if the discount benefit did discriminate in favor of highly compensated employees, the entire discount received by a highly compensated employee would be included in income (and not just the extra benefit provided to such employees). [Reg. § 1.132-8(a)(2).]

It should also be noted that this is a fairly basic question regarding the *qualified employee discount* fringe benefit. Your professor may cover the material in much greater depth and there are many ancillary issues regarding this and other IRC § 132 fringe benefits. Other questions in this book address some of these issues.

Answer (a) is incorrect because the maximum excludable employee discount available is 20% (because life insurance is considered a service). **Answer (c) is incorrect** because Amy need not include the entire amount of the discount that she received. **Answer (d) is also incorrect.** $6,000 represents the amount Amy *paid* for the policy. With the *qualified employee discount,* we are focusing on the benefit that she receives vis-à-vis her discount.

22. **Answer (a) is correct.** XYZ's payment of Amy's dues and periodical costs represent tax-free "working condition" fringe benefits.

IRC § 61 defines gross income as "all income from whatever source derived." From your initial study of gross income's scope, you probably found it to be broadly defined, including the taxpayer's receipt of some net economic benefit or net accession to wealth. In class, you also discover that gross income is also not limited to the receipt of cash. [Reg. § 1.61-1(d) (compensation received in forms other than in cash).] It is clear that Amy is receiving some economic benefit from her XYZ's payment of her association dues and the cost of the periodicals. This will represent income to Amy unless it is specifically excluded by some provision.

A host of employee fringe benefits are excluded pursuant to IRC § 132, and the benefit Amy is receiving in this problem is excludable as a "working condition" fringe benefit. [IRC §§ 132(a)(3) and 132(d).] Basically, an excludable *working condition fringe* is any property or service provided to an employee which would, had the employee had to pay for such items, have given rise to a valid business expense for such employee. In other words, if an employee were to make an expenditure for something that would be considered a qualified business expense, then having the employer pay for it instead will <u>not</u> be considered income to the employee (i.e., a *working condition fringe* benefit). The exclusion of an employer provided benefit as a *working condition fringe,* rests on whether the item paid for by the employer would have given rise to a qualified business expenses for the employee under IRC § 162 (had the employee paid for the item).

In general, IRC § 162 allows for business deductions that are (read as one continuous phrase with four distinct requirements):
> ➤ Ordinary and necessary
> ➤ Expenses
> ➤ Paid or incurred during the taxable year
> ➤ In carrying on any trade or business.

Had Amy paid for her association dues and business related periodicals, there is little doubt that they would have been considered qualified business expenses. Therefore, XYZ's payment of these items result in an excludable *working condition fringe* benefit to Amy and she need not recognize any income because of this.

Unlike some of the other excludable fringe benefits of IRC § 132, an employer can provide a *working condition fringe* benefit to employees on a discriminatory basis (in favor of highly compensated employees). Therefore, the fact that XYZ's policy of providing these benefits only to "highly compensated employees" (such as Amy) does not preclude the exclusion.

While not necessary to answer this question, one may ask why the *working condition fringe* benefit is really necessary. If the employer paid benefit were to be included in an employee's income, would not the employee then be entitled to a corresponding IRC § 162 business deduction, thus resulting in no net difference than if the amount was excluded form income in the first place? Those students familiar with "how" and "where" an employee's business expenses are deductible, may see the benefit of the *working condition fringe* exclusion. In prior editions of this book then explained that for most employees, IRC § 162 business expenses were deductible in a less favored *below the line* location (deductions from adjusted gross income (AGI) to compute taxable income) and were in a special subgroup of "miscellaneous itemized deductions" (these yielding an actual deduction to the extent that, in the aggregate, they exceeded 2% of an individual's adjusted gross income). The *Tax Cuts and Jobs Act* (TCJA) signed into law in December 2017 (generally effective beginning in 2018) made significant changes, and not in a good way, for deductions of business expenses by employees. Under the TCJA, deductions for unreimbursed business expenses incurred by employees, have, for the most part, been "suspended" for 2018 through 2025. [IRC § 67(g)]. The requirements for a valid IRC § 162 business expense are identical for employees and self-employed individuals. However, the TCJA has generally eliminated the actual deductibility of such business expenses if incurred as an employee. This topic, as well as one small exception, is addressed in other questions in this book. Our *working condition fringe* that is the core of this question, now seems to provide an even better benefit under the TCJA; an exclusion from income because it was paid for by Amy's employer but if it were unreimbursed and she had paid for it, it would not give rise to an actual tax deduction for her. In the latter example she would have incurred a legitimate IRC § 162 business expense but as an employee, other sections would now effectively yield no actual tax deduction. The key to her exclusion under a *working condition fringe* benefit is only that had she paid for it, it would qualify as an IRC § 162 business expense (and not that it would actually yield a tax deduction for her).

Answer (b) is incorrect because an employer can discriminate in favor of certain classes of employees for purposes of the *working condition fringe* benefit. **Answer (c) is incorrect** because the benefit provided to Amy in this question is not a "qualified employee discount." **Answer (d) is incorrect** because Amy's professional business related periodicals qualify as legitimate business expenses for her.

23. **The best answer is (b).** This question raises some of the most classic doctrines in income tax law. We have two parts to this question and both involve issues of "to whom does the income/gain belong." Or more appropriately, who <u>must</u> recognize the income derived. The first part of the problem is the issue of the April rents, and the second part is the sale of the property in May. Both issues involve essentially the same tax concepts.

The analysis starts with the "assignment of income" doctrine that arguably is best known from the case *Lucas v. Earl.* [281 U.S. 111, 50 S.Ct 241 (1930).] Income is income (for tax purposes) to the taxpayer who earns it. One cannot transfer the tax obligation to another person merely by "assigning" the income to such person. One cannot say, "I earned the income, but do not give it to me, give it to my child instead" (who happens to be in a much lower income tax bracket), and have it work that way for income tax purposes.

Similarly, income from property is the income of the owner of the property and cannot be "detached" and given to someone else. For tax purposes, it will not work if one says, "the interest earned on my money deposited with your bank, I do not want it given to me. Rather, give the interest to my child" (who happens to be in a much lower income tax bracket). Of course, this can be done, but the owner of the account will have to recognize the interest earned on the money. This is the so-called "fruit and tree" doctrine. The fruit (income) that the tree (the underlying property) produces, belongs to the owner of the tree (the property). If one wishes another person to recognize income earned from the property, the underlying property must be transferred to such person. The fruit cannot just be "picked" or separated from the tree and given to another, without first giving the tree.

Corollary to this fruit and tree concept is that one cannot avoid recognition of income from property that is already earned but has not yet been received. One cannot transfer a tree to another with fruit already "ripened" and have the picked fruit be considered belonging to the new owner. This is sometimes referred to as the doctrine of "ripeness;" once the fruit is ripe, it belongs to the owner of the tree notwithstanding that the tree is transferred to another before the fruit is picked.

Back from the garden to address the April rental income from the apartment building. Martha, the owner at the beginning of the April rent period, transferred the apartment building to her son, Steve midway through the month. Back to our garden analogy, the rental income earned up through the middle of April represents "ripened" fruit for Martha. While the rental income was not actually received until after she transferred the property (the tree), she cannot effectively assign the rental income earned up to the time of transfer. In other words, half of the April rents belong to, and must be recognized by, Martha (it is her fruit!). From the period that Steve owned the property in mid-April, the rental income earned belongs to him. Therefore, the April rents should be recognized one-half by Martha and one-half by Steve.

As for the sale of the property, we have the same concept of "ripeness" to consider. Had Martha, before transferring the property to Steve, arranged the sale of the property to Paulo and, for all intents and purposes, contracted to sell the property to Paulo, the income (gain in this case) has "ripened." Transferring the property at this point would not result in the transfer (or assignment) of the gain to Steve. However, we have no facts in the problem indicating what, if anything, Martha did vis-à-vis the sale to Paulo, while she still owned the property. If Martha was not involved with the sale prior to her transfer of the property to Steve, then whatever income Steve derives from the property (including gain from its sale) correctly belongs to him (and will be recognized by him). The only answer that correctly reflects this (and the issue of the April rents) is (b).

Answer (a) is incorrect because the April rental income is not all recognizable by Steve as discussed above. The latter part of this answer may be true depending on the degree of Martha's involvement regarding the sale prior to her transferring the property to Steve. **Answer (c) is incorrect** because the gain from the sale is not necessarily Martha's to recognize. There is no assignment of income when the fruit has not yet ripened. **Answer (d) is incorrect** because Martha does not recognize all of the April rents. The rental income earned after the transfer of the property to Steve belongs to Steve, not Martha.

24. The best answer is (c). IRC § 164 is a key section for addressing deductions for taxes paid. This section allows a deduction for, among other taxes, "state and local real property taxes" that have been "paid." While the real property tax in our problem is clearly the type of tax deductible pursuant to IRC § 164, there is some question as to Paulo's "payment of it." On January 1st of this year, Martha paid the $12,000 in property taxes for the full year. What happens when this property is sold to Paulo during the year vis-à-vis property taxes? In most real-life instances, the buyer reimburses the seller (as part of the sales transaction) a proportionate amount of the property taxes that were paid by the seller. This apportioned amount represents the period for which the seller paid taxes for the property that is now owned by the buyer. In our simplified calendar year property tax scenario, Paulo's purchase of the property on May 1st is four months into the twelve-month assessment period, or 4/12ths (one-third). Paulo's share of the assessment year for which property taxes have already been paid is the other 8/12ths (two-thirds). Again, in real-world transactions of this sort, Paulo would reimburse the seller 8/12ths (two-thirds) of the taxes paid or $8,000 of the $12,000 taxes paid in our facts.

The above method of apportionment is generally *required* for purposes of determining *who* gets to deduct *what* amount of property tax in sale situations such as ours. [IRC § 164(d).] Pursuant to this provision, the purchaser Paulo, is entitled to an apportioned $8,000 deduction of the total $12,000 property taxes paid (and the seller is entitled to a deduction for the remaining $4,000 of property taxes). The Regulations indicate that this method of apportionment "shall apply whether or not the seller and the purchaser apportion such tax." [Reg. § 1.164-6(b)(1)(i).] Therefore, Paulo's property tax deduction is approximately $8,000 regardless of whether he made the reimbursement to Steve (or Martha).

Please note that the answer indicates "approximate" values as the method of apportionment that is required under the Code (and as is the case in real-world transactions) is based upon actual *days* of ownership as opposed to whole months as used in our problem.

Answer (a) is incorrect. While Paulo was not the owner of the property when the taxes were paid on January 1st, the statute requires apportionment of the deduction for property taxes nonetheless. **Answer (b) is incorrect** because as mentioned above, apportionment of the deduction of property taxes pursuant to IRC § 164(d) does not require that the buyer and seller actually apportion such taxes between themselves for purposes of reimbursement. **Answer (d) is incorrect** because property taxes *are* deductible taxes pursuant to IRC § 164 (and possibly under other sections as well). The $10,000 cap mentioned in this answer is addressed in other questions in this book (this is part of the *Tax Cuts and Jobs Act* (TCJA) signed into law in December 2017) but is not implicated given the facts of this question. **Answer (e) is incorrect** because the apportionment rule discussed above does not require actual apportionment and reimbursement of property taxes between buyer and seller.

25. **The most accurate statement is (a).** This is not so much a question of *what* is deductible by Paulo, but, rather, *where* Paulo is entitled to deductions relating to his rental property for purposes of computing "taxable income." The "*what is* deductible portion" of this problem is easy. IRC § 164 is one section that allows for the deduction of real property taxes. There is little doubt that next year, Paulo will be entitled to deduct the property taxes he will pay with respect to the apartment building. As discussed below, Paulo will be entitled to this deduction "above the line" in computing his adjusted gross income (AGI). Independently, we can look to IRC § 212 as a source for Paulo's deduction in our question. In a nutshell, this section entitles an individual to deductions for investment-related expenses. Other questions in this book cover IRC § 212 in greater detail, but the property taxes paid for his apartment building are, for all intents and purposes, the same for most of his apartment-related expenses (e.g., maintenance costs, utilities, advertising, etc.). One might naturally gravitate to the "property tax-specific" IRC § 164 for determining the source for Paulo's deduction. However, IRC § 212 is a perfectly good section as a source for deducting his property taxes given that the apartment building is an investment-type activity. So actually, we have two different sections that give us the answer for "*what is* deductible" regarding Paulo's property taxes. Of course, Paulo cannot "double-dip" and take two deductions for the same property tax paid just because it may be allowed as a deduction by more than one section.

As far as deductions are concerned, there are two major camps of deductions for purposes of computing taxable income. There are deductions that are subtracted from *gross income* to arrive at our intermediary AGI. These are commonly referred to as "above the line" deductions, with AGI representing "the line." The other camp of deductions is comprised of those that are subtracted from AGI to arrive at *taxable income*. These are commonly referred to as "below the line" deductions. The components making up this camp of *below the line* deductions can include something called the "standard deduction" or, in the alternative, a group of deductions called "itemized deductions." [For more information about how this all fits together, please see IRC § 62; Appendix A; other questions in this book.]

IRC § 62 is a "signpost" section identifying those deductions (allowed by other Code sections) that are deductible "above the line" in computing adjusted gross income AGI. We find, at IRC § 62(a)(4) the answer to our question. "Deductions attributable to rents and royalties," such as the property taxes that Paulo will pay with respect to his apartment building, are deductible "above the line" in computing AGI. While not necessary to answer this question, Paulo's other deductible expenses associated with his apartment building (e.g., maintenance, repairs, insurance, and the like as well as possible interest and depreciation deductions) are also deductible above the line pursuant to IRC § 62(a)(4). Although well beyond the scope of this question, it should be noted that various limitations and restrictions might be applicable to deductions related to certain types of rental activities.

Answer (b) is incorrect because these property taxes are related to Paulo's investment/rental activities. Had this been real property taxes paid with respect to Paulo's personal residence, then this could have been a correct answer (please see other questions in this book that address this issue). **Answer (c) is incorrect** because payment of property taxes in this situation *does* give rise to deductions. There is also no provision applicable here that would provide for the property taxes paid to be added to the basis of the property. **Answer (d) is incorrect** because an "exclusion" represents an item that is otherwise included in gross income but is not because of some "exclusion" or nonrecognition provision. Property taxes paid represent deductions, and not exclusions from income.

FEDERAL INCOME TAX
ANSWER KEY AND EXPLANATIONS
EXAM IV

1. **Answer (e) is the correct answer.** Situations involving the exchange, between two parties, of services and/or property, usually result in some confusion among students at first. The bottom-line answer with respect to Cassandra is that she rendered $4,000 worth of services and was compensated for them, albeit not in cash form, but by receiving other "stuff" (the baseball card) worth $4,000. Cassandra has $4,000 of income as a result. To eliminate other possible answers presented, she is also deemed to have "paid" $4,000 for the baseball card and, therefore has a basis in the card of $4,000. The correct answer, by process of elimination, is the awful "none of the above."

What is bothersome for students in such exchange transactions, is the lack of cash being received for services rendered or property transferred. Somehow the resulting income tax consequences seem to be incorrect or unfair. A more thorough discussion of the transaction from Cassandra's perspective follows. Please see question 2 (immediately following this question), for the analysis of the facts from <u>Roger's</u> perspective.

The transaction from Cassandra's perspective

Early on in classroom discussions of gross income, we discover that gross income need not be in the form of cash. A lawyer, for example, who performs legal work for a client and is paid in cash has gross income. A lawyer who performs legal work for a client and receives property as payment has gross income equal to the fair market value of the property received. A lawyer who performs legal work for a client and receives a combination of cash and property as payment has gross income equal to the cash plus the fair market value of the property received. A lawyer who performs legal work for a client and receives the client's services as payment (in exchange) has income equal to the value of the services. A lawyer who performs legal work for a client and receives cash, property and the client's services as payment has gross income equal to the cash, the fair market value of the property, and the fair market value of the services. [See Reg. § 1.61-1(d) (compensation received in forms other than in cash).] When an individual performs services and receives "something" in exchange, that "something" (or the value thereof) represents gross income. The form of that "something" is generally irrelevant. In our question, Cassandra rendered $4,000 worth of services and received $4,000 worth of stuff in return: $4,000 worth of property in the baseball card.

In class, this professor likes to recast, or view in a different light, exchange or barter transactions in an essentially equivalent manner involving the transfer of cash back and forth between the parties. We could break down the transaction between Cassandra and Roger into something like this. Cassandra performs $4,000 worth of services for Roger and Roger pays Cassandra $4,000 in cash. At this point, it is clear Cassandra would have income. Next, Cassandra buys a rare baseball card worth $4,000 from Roger, paying him $4,000 in cash. The economic substance of viewing the transaction in this manner (with cash going back and forth) is the same as that given in our facts, but it sometimes helps to identify the separate components involved.

Because Cassandra is deemed to have "paid" Roger $4,000 for the baseball, that represents her basis (or adjusted basis (AB)) pursuant to the general "cost" basis rules of IRC §§ 1011 and 1012.

[For more information about barter/exchange transactions, see Reg. § 1.61-1(d); Rev.Rul. 79-24, 1979-1 C.B. 60.]

Answer (a) is incorrect because, as discussed above, the "barter transactions" in our facts does result in income tax ramifications to Cassandra. **Answer (b) is also incorrect**. It correctly identifies Cassandra's gross income of $4,000, but provides for a bogus business deduction for purchasing the baseball card. **Answer (c) is incorrect** because Cassandra does have immediate income tax consequences in the recognition of $4,000 of income for her services rendered. **Answer (d) is also incorrect.** It, too, correctly identifies the $4,000 of gross income to Cassandra, but incorrectly states her basis in the baseball card received in exchange.

2. **The best answer is (e).** As mentioned in the analysis to the companion question 1, above, situations involving the exchange, between two parties, of services and/or property, usually result in some confusion among students at first. Roger did two things: Roger paid for $4,000 of tax advice, albeit not in the form of cash, but in the form of property (the baseball card) which gives rise to a deductible IRC § 162 business expense. Roger also disposed of his baseball card worth $4,000 and received consideration for it, albeit not in the form of cash, but by receiving other stuff (services from Cassandra) worth $4,000. Roger's receipt of $4,000 consideration for the baseball card less his cost basis ("adjusted basis" hereinafter AB) of $2,500, results in a realized gain of $1,500.

What is bothersome for students in such exchange transactions, is the lack of cash being received for services rendered or property transferred. Somehow the resulting income tax consequences seem to be incorrect or unfair. A more thorough discussion of the transaction from Roger's perspective follows. Please see question 1 (immediately preceding this question), for the analysis of the facts from <u>Cassandra's</u> perspective.

The transaction from Roger's perspective

Let us view these tax results to Roger utilizing our "recast" cash version of this barter transaction (from the analysis of question 1, above). We break down the transaction between Cassandra and Roger as follows: Cassandra performs $4,000 worth of services for Roger and Roger <u>pays</u> Cassandra $4,000 <u>in cash</u>. Next, Cassandra buys a rare baseball card worth $4,000 from Roger, <u>paying</u> him $4,000 <u>in cash</u>. The economic substance of viewing the transaction in this manner (with cash going back and forth) is the same as that given in our facts, but it sometimes helps identify the separate components involved.

Roger effectively paid $4,000 for tax advice related solely to his unincorporated sole proprietor computer consulting business. In general, IRC § 162 allows for business deductions that are (read as one continuous phrase with four distinct requirements):
  ➤ Ordinary and necessary
  ➤ Expenses
  ➤ Paid or incurred during the taxable year
  ➤ In carrying on any trade or business.

We need not dig too deep here to see that Roger's "expenditure" for tax advice qualifies as a business expense deduction. The fact that he "paid" for this business related expense in a form other than cash is irrelevant.

The other part of the transaction from Roger's perspective was the disposition of his baseball card. A sale or disposition of property results in the realization of a gain or loss to transferor measured by the difference between the "amount realized" (AR) and the transferor's AB. [IRC § 1001(a).] The AR side of this sale or disposition equation is obscured just a bit. One's AR from a sale or disposition of property is usually received in the form of cash. However, AR is broader than that, and basically includes the value of any "stuff" received in exchange for property whether it be other property or services (money's worth). Here Roger received $4,000 worth of "stuff" (Cassandra's services) as consideration. Roger's AB is straightforward in this question, and is his $2,500 original cost of the baseball card. [See IRC §§ 1011 and 1012.] In effect, Roger sold the baseball card and received $4,000 consideration (in the form of Cassandra's services), resulting in a realized gain of $1,500 ($4,000 AR less his AB of $2,500).

In the aggregate, therefore, Roger has a $4,000 IRC § 162 business expense deduction, and a $1,500 realized gain from the sale of his baseball card.

[For more information about barter/exchange transactions, see Reg. § 1.61-1(d); Rev.Rul. 79-24, 1979-1 C.B. 60.]

Answer (a) is incorrect but is sometimes chosen as the answer under the misconception that anytime there is a barter transaction, both parties have equal amounts of income. While this may be true if the barter transaction is a straight "services for services" exchange, our facts present a different situation that requires a careful analysis of each component part. **Answer (b) is also incorrect**. While Roger has no income from the performance of services, he does have income in the form of gain from the disposition of the baseball card. In addition, the indicated amount of his deduction is incorrect. **Answer (c) is incorrect** because while it does indicate the correct amount of gain realized, the amount for his business deduction is wrong. **Answer (d) is incorrect** but it is commonly selected as the correct answer. The problem with this answer lies in the classification of Roger's $4,000 deduction. There is some overlap in IRC §§ 162 and 212. IRC § 212 does allow a deduction for tax advice type fees. [IRC § 212(3).] However, IRC § 212 expenses, by their definition, are not expenses associated with one's trade or business. Rather, IRC § 212 provides deductions for investment-related activities and nonbusiness tax related fees (advice, tax return preparation, tax audit assistance, etc.). In Roger's case, this tax advice was related solely to his consulting business and, therefore, is properly classified as IRC § 162 trade or business related expense. [Please see other questions in this book that address IRC § 212 in greater detail.]

3. **Answer (a) is correct.** Tom, with the death of his grandmother, suffered a terrible personal loss. While one hates to think of financial or tax benefits at times like this, a big tax benefit <u>does</u> exist. IRC § 102 is a wonderful section for recipients of gifts, bequests and devises. While Tom did realize a net accession to wealth (he was better off financially by reason of the devise to him), the full $35,000 value of the shares received is excluded from gross income by IRC § 102. This exclusion section is usually fairly straightforward, as it is here, but one need be on the watch for potential problem areas, usually revolving around what exactly constitutes a "gift" or "bequest/devise." Specifically in the bequest/devise area, while not at issue in this question, are situations where the "bequest/devise" may not be such but, rather, some contractual benefit received pursuant to a will.

    Answer (b) is incorrect because the exclusion in IRC § 102 applies to testamentary bequests/devises as well as inter vivos gifts. **Answer (c) is incorrect** because there is no blanket "tax-free" provision for transfers between family members. **Answer (d) is incorrect** because the exclusion of IRC § 102 is not dependent on any subsequent transaction by the donee, beneficiary/devisee.

4. **Answer (a) is correct.** When Tom sells the shares of stock, he realizes a gain or a loss measured by the difference between the sales price (or in tax terms: the amount realized or AR) and his adjusted basis (AB) in the shares. [IRC § 1001(a).] The AR portion of the equation in this problem is simply the $40,000 sales price for the shares. The key component to this question is the determination of Tom's AB in the shares.

While a taxpayer's cost is normally the starting point for determination of one's AB in property (IRC §§ 1011 and 1012), when property is received as a bequest/devise, as is the case here, there really is no "cost" to the taxpayer. The seemingly logical result of a zero AB is neither desirable nor, thankfully, appropriate. IRC § 1014(a)(1) provides the general rule that the AB of property acquired from a decedent shall be the property's fair market value at the date of the decedent's death. The shares Tom received were worth $35,000 at his grandmother's death and, therefore, represents Tom's AB in the shares.

When Tom sells the property for $40,000, his realized gain is the difference between the $40,000 and his basis of $35,000 or $5,000.

Note, that the fair market value basis rule of IRC § 1014(a)(1) is commonly referred to as the "step-up" in basis for property received from a decedent. This is because we like to think, or at least hope, that property has appreciated in the hands of the decedent and the testamentary beneficiary gets as his/her basis a new "higher" or "stepped-up" basis. For appreciated property, this Code provision is a great tax savings device that effectively makes, for income tax purposes, any gains from unrealized appreciation in the decedent's hands evaporate. Unfortunately, when property has depreciated in the decedent's hands, the testamentary beneficiary effectively gets a "stepped-down" basis.

Answer (b) is incorrect because to have a ($10,000) realized loss as result of Tom's sale, his basis would have had to be $50,000. Students sometimes select this answer because they mistakenly use the general inter vivos gift "carryover" basis rule of IRC § 1015(a). **Answer (c) is similarly incorrect**. This answer, again, has the student in the incorrect arena of determination of a transferee's basis in an inter vivos gift environment. Specifically, the potential application of the "special loss rule" of IRC § 1015(a) and the regulations addressing subsequent sales by the donee at a price between that of the donor's basis and the lower fair market value at the time of the inter vivos gift. [Reg. § 1.1015-1(a)(2).] **Answer (d) is incorrect** because it does not really address Tom's subsequent sale of the shares. It is true that he has no income pursuant to IRC § 102 from the receipt of these shares from his grandmother's devise to him, but that exclusion has no application to gains derived from a subsequent sale of such property.

5. **Answer (e) is correct.** This question, unfortunately, requires, in part, a correct analysis of the previous question. This professor would not ask such a series of interrelated multiple-choice questions on an exam. Rather, this series of questions was derived from an exam essay question. With that said, we know, from the previous question, that Tom's realized gain was $5,000. The only available answer with the correct amount of realized gain is (b) and, therefore, it must be eliminated if that answer is correct. Response (b) is almost correct in that the realized gain was $5,000. The gain is recognized pursuant to IRC § 1001(c), as all gains are recognized unless there is some specific non-recognition or exclusion section. No such non-recognition or exclusion section exists with respect to our facts. Further, the gain is a "capital" gain as the shares of stock, as investments, represent capital assets. [IRC § 1221(a).] However, we will conclude that Tom's $5,000 capital gain is a long-term capital gain.

Because Tom's capital gain is long-term (and why it is long-term), it renders answer (b) incorrect (and by default, (e) is the correct answer). Determining the holding period, for short- and long-term gain/loss classification, is controlled by IRC § 1223. While long-term status is generally reserved for assets held for more than one year (IRC § 1222), property received from a decedent effectively gets automatic long-term status in most situations pursuant to IRC § 1223(9). This is not the so called "tacking" of holding period pursuant to IRC § 1223(2) which effectively applies to situations where there is a "carryover" basis such as with most inter vivos gifts. Even if tacking were to apply here, which it does not, adding Gloria's holding period to that of Tom's would still result in a "short-term" period of one year or less.

Note, that as the law now stands, receipt of appreciated property from a decedent can have very beneficial effects: a "stepped-up" basis to the beneficiary and automatic long-term holding period for capital gain purposes.

One might wonder why so much is made out of properly classifying capital gains and losses as short-term and long-term. Historically, gains from the sale of certain types of assets (capital assets) that has been accorded preferential tax treatment. While it is far beyond the scope of the analysis for this question, modernly, "long-term" capital gains ("net capital gains" to be more specific), while included in a taxpayer's gross and taxable incomes, may be taxed at favorable (i.e., lower) tax rates. Proper classification of losses and gains is critical in determining the extent of favorably taxed long-term capital gains.

Answer (b) is incorrect because Tom's capital gain is a long-term gain because of IRC § 1223(9), as discussed above. **Answers (a), (c) and (d) are incorrect** prima facially because the amount of recognized gain (or lack thereof) indicated is not the correct amount. Additionally, answers (c) and (d) again incorrectly apply the holding period rules of § 1223(2) to this fact pattern.

6. **The correct answer is (a).**   This question involves the application of the gain exclusion provisions of IRC § 121. Effective for sales of a taxpayer's principal residence after May 6, 1997, IRC § 121 provides for the exclusion of up to $250,000 of gain ($500,000 in the case of certain married individuals) if certain conditions are met. The provisions of this section took an ominous and complex turn with the "Housing Assistance Tax Act of 2008" (sounds like a good thing but it can, in reality, be quite a negative thing for many taxpayers). We shall explain.

It may be a bit of an overkill for what is necessary for this particular question, but a summary of the way to approach such a problem might be helpful.

The **first step** in any problem that involves a sale or disposition of an asset is to always ask these three questions:

1) Do we have a **Realized** Gain (or Loss) & how much? This is computing the amount of gain (or loss). It is the AR (amount realized) less one's AB (adjusted basis). See other problems in this book addressing this issue.

2) If yes, is the realized gain (or loss) **Recognized**? This simply means, is it reported in one's income for tax purposes. This is the issue that we are currently addressing. As a taxpayer, you would like the answer to be NO for gains; I do not want to recognize, report, the gain (said another way, I'd like to be able to exclude this gain from my income).

3) If gain is recognized, is it given any **special character** or treatment? This is primarily the issue of "capital gains (or losses)" that are treated differently for income tax purposes. This is not the issue in this question (see other problems in this book).

Brad, in our question, clearly has a ***realized gain***. We do not know the exact amount as no sales price (AR) is given in the facts. Brad's $200,000 cost for his house represents his AB or "adjusted basis" (please see other questions in this book that address the many nuances of determining an individual's adjusted basis (AB) in property). At this point, we can conclude that Brad does have a ***realized gain*** (we just don't know the exact amount).

On to the second question of whether or not his realized gain is ***recognized*** (reported in his income). As discussed in other problems in this book, all realized gains are recognized unless there is some specific "non-recognition" (or exclusion) provision in the Code. The law has, for a long time, given some relief (non-recognition) to homeowners with respect to the sale of one's principal residence. We find this in IRC § 121 and it is often referred to as an "exclusion of gain from sale of principal residence." More accurately, IRC § 121 is a non-recognition (of gain) provision. Effective for sales of a taxpayer's principal residence after May 6, 1997, IRC § 121 provides for the exclusion of up to $250,000 of gain ($500,000 in the case of certain married individuals), if certain conditions are met.

Again, it may be helpful to first present the landscape of this analysis. Immediately below is a slide that this professor uses in class to address the various components of IRC § 121. The application and analysis of these steps follows.

§121 NON-RECOGNITION

Step 1: Does non recognition (exclusion) even apply?
    a) Ownership test <u>and</u>
    b) Use Test
       (if necessary, look to prorating provision §121(c))

Step 2: Okay, we qualify for non-recognition. Now to the new (in 2009) "overlay" for "qualified/non-qualified" use in §121(b)(5): <u>If required to do so</u>, split the <u>total realized gain</u> into two parts:

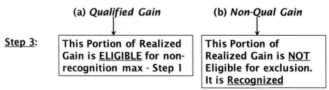

	(a) *Qualified Gain*	(b) *Non-Qual Gain*
Step 3:	This Portion of Realized Gain is <u>ELIGIBLE</u> for non-recognition max - Step 1	This Portion of Realized Gain is <u>NOT</u> Eligible for exclusion. It is <u>Recognized</u>

From 1997 through 2008 (and in prior editions of this book), IRC § 121 was much simpler. Our analysis consisted of only "Step 1," above (there were no steps 2 and 3). Fortunately for Brad, we shall see that we need not address Steps 2 & 3 in his case (please see other problems in this book that cover the entire scope of this section.)

Step 1 of our IRC § 121 analysis consists of the two basic requirements for this exclusion, commonly referred to as the "ownership" and "use" tests. The taxpayer must have owned the house for at least two years (looking back five years from the date of sale) **and** must have used it as his or her principal residence for two years (looking back five years from the date of sale). [IRC § 121(a).] Brad clearly meets both the ownership and use tests having owned and used the house as his principal residence for at least two years within the last five years (he has owned the house and has lived there for four years in this question). Therefore, he will be entitled to exclude the gain from the sale of his house up to a maximum of $250,000. Should he have gain in excess of $250,000, it will be recognized, as there are no other non-recognition or exclusion provisions applicable here.

The new (as of 2008) Steps 2 & 3 are not at issue for Brad. These additional steps are necessary for situations where an individual has at any time during the entire period he or she owned the house, used it for something other than his or her principal residence for the entire period that they owned it (e.g., used it as a vacation home, left it vacant, rented it out, etc.). If this were the case, it can be harmful (tax-wise) and we would have much longer trek to determine the proper outcome. Fortunately for Brad, the facts in this question have him using the house as his principal residence for the entire time of his ownership. Therefore, we need not proceed any further. This question, as well as the next question, 7, are meant to serve as a "soft" introduction to the IRC § 121 sale of a house non-recognition provision. Other questions in this book are more complex taking us down the entire tortuous road of IRC § 121.

While not at issue in this problem, it should be noted that generally, the exclusion provisions of IRC § 121 cannot be used more than once in a two-year period. [IRC § 121(b)(3).] It is a logical assumption from the facts presented that this limitation would not apply to Brad in this question.

It should also be noted that the statute does not require that the requisite two-year "use" and "ownership" period be co-extensive. While again, this is not an issue in this question, it is a common misunderstanding (read as "good testing area") that the two "two-year" qualifying periods must be at the same time. It is also a common misunderstanding (again, read as "good testing area") that the "five-year look back period" for purposes of determining two-year ownership and use somehow requires that the taxpayer either owned or used the house for at least five years. This is not correct, and again, while this is not at issue in this question, it might be helpful for your analysis of other IRC § 121 related questions.

Answers (b) and (e) are incorrect because there are simply no such provisions in the Code. **Answer (c) is incorrect** because while the exclusion limit of IRC § 121 increases to $500,000 in the case of certain married individuals, Brad and Gail are not, in this question, married. Gail is not entitled to any exclusion on her own because she is not an owner of the property.

Answer (d) is incorrect but is the source of much confusion among students and the general public. Prior to the $250,000/$500,000 exclusion of IRC § 121, the primary provision affecting gain recognition from the sale of a principal residence was IRC § 1034. This latter section, which was repealed and replaced by current IRC § 121 in 1997, also provided for gain exclusion, but its mechanism for doing so was very different. Basically, this old section provided that if you purchased (and occupied) a new principal residence within a two-year period of selling your old principal residence (either before or, as was more common, after the sale), then gain was recognized only to the extent, if any, that the purchase price of the new house was less than the sales price of the old house. In other words, if a taxpayer always "moved-up" to a more expensive house, gain was not recognized. However, this old IRC § 1034 provision was merely a "deferral" mechanism because any gain not recognized pursuant to this provision, served to reduce the adjusted basis of the new house (to be potentially recognized upon a subsequent sale). As indicated, this old § 1034 is no longer valid law (but if your professor covers this material in greater depth, be aware that prior deferrals of gain under that law may still be reflected in a taxpayer's adjusted basis for their home). Current IRC § 121 does not require that the taxpayer purchase a new house, and any gain excluded pursuant to the section is a real exclusion (not merely a deferral of recognition) with no effect on the adjusted basis of any subsequent house purchase.

Not to add additional superfluous information, there was an "old" IRC § 121 that was also repealed with enactment of current IRC § 121 in 1997. The old section was a "once in a lifetime" exclusion of a certain dollar amount of gain from the sale of a principal residence for taxpayers fifty-five years of age or older. This old IRC § 121 was in addition to old IRC § 1034, and their combination was a logistics mess (and a difficult area for instruction) when compared to the relatively straightforward rules of current IRC § 121. The current IRC § 121 has no age limit, can be used over and over again to exclude gain (generally just not more than once every two years), and has larger exclusion limitations. Again, while this old IRC § 121 is no longer valid law, it is the source of some confusion among taxpayers.

7. **The correct answer is (e).** This question is very similar to question 6, above. It would be appropriate to duplicate the very long analysis framework for questions such as this, but to save you from reading the same material

again, we can dispense with most of it. Please refer to the introduction analysis for question 6, above and note that for this question 7, we are dealing with the same issue as in question 6 (Brad has a realized gain from the sale of his house and we are determining how much can be excluded via IRC § 121; and again, we do not have the more complex situation where we need address steps 2 & 3 of the IRC § 121 analysis. So here we go.

The maximum gain from the sale of a principal residence doubles from $250,000 to $500,000 for certain married individuals. Spouses who file a joint return are entitled to this larger exclusion if both spouses meet the two-year "use" test, and either spouse meets the two-year "ownership" test. [IRC § 121(b)(2).] Note that only one spouse need meet the ownership test and in our question, Brad qualifies. Gail's lack of ownership interest in the property does not preclude them from this larger exclusion limitation. As indicated, both spouses must meet the "use" test for this larger exclusion and here, both Brad and Gail have used this house as their principal residence for at least two years (looking back five years). There is no statutory requirement that their two years of use must be while they were married (or co-extensive for that matter). Students sometimes suspect that because our couple was married for only six months prior to the sale, it negatively affects the application of this larger exclusion for married couples. However, the requirement is only that they be married at the time of the sale and that they file a joint return. [IRC § 121(b)(2).]

Answer (a) is incorrect because as mentioned above, for married individuals filing a joint return, there is no requirement that both spouses own the property for the requisite two-year period. **Answers (b) and (d) are incorrect** because they both reflect the mistaken belief that their qualifying two-year "use" period had to be when they were married. **Answer (c) is incorrect** because they do qualify for a larger exclusion than in the previous question.

8. **The correct answer is (b).** Willa has suffered a terrible loss with the death of her wife, Sonia. However, Willa has received an immediate net accession to wealth upon receipt of the $100,000 life insurance proceeds. Given the broad and inclusive nature of gross income, this $100,000 will be income unless there is a specific "exclusion" provision in the law. Fortunately, for Willa, there is in IRC § 101. This section's general rule is that life insurance proceeds received by reason of the insured's death are excluded from gross income of the beneficiary. This question is a straightforward life insurance question and the entire $100,000 Willa receives is excludable from income pursuant to the general rule of IRC § 101(a).

It should be noted that this general exclusion for life insurance proceeds has no dollar limitations. Ten million dollars of life insurance proceeds are as excludable as one thousand dollars of proceeds. Also, the beneficiary need not be related (through blood or marriage) for the exclusion to apply (e.g., a beneficiary can be a friend, acquaintance, or even a stranger).

Note that while this question contains specific dates, it is _not_ a year-specific question. Rather, specific dates were used only for the purpose of helping to navigate the question (and the other questions in this series 8 through 12).

Answer (a) is incorrect because the receipt of life insurance proceeds by reason of the insured's death is not treated as a sale or other disposition transaction with gain or loss realized. Rather, as discussed above, the proceeds are simply excluded in full under the general rule of IRC § 101(a). **Answer (c) is incorrect** because while there is an accession to wealth, IRC § 101(a) specifically provides for its exclusion under the facts in this question. **Answer (d) is incorrect** because it is simply not true and has no foundation in income tax laws.

9. **The correct answer is (c).** From the analysis to question 8, above, we know that life insurance proceeds receive favorable income tax treatment pursuant to IRC § 101. In general, the proceeds are excludable from gross income. Instead of receiving the $100,000 death benefit right now, that we know from the previous question would be tax-free, Willa has selected an annual lifetime payout option. Note that this is not a "tax thing" but, rather, a common option that life insurance companies present to beneficiaries as an alternative to receiving the insurance benefits in a lump sum. Assuming that Willa remains alive for exactly forty years, she will have received a total of $400,000 from the life insurance company ($10,000/year multiplied by 40 years). Where does all of this money come from, and how can the insurance company afford to pay so much more? The insurance company continues to invest the retained portion of the $100,000 it does not have to currently pay out and Willa benefits, in part, from these subsequent earnings. In effect, Willa is investing with the insurance company, the $100,000 owed to her. We need know very little about income tax rules to logically conclude that Willa will be able to exclude from income a total of $100,000 under IRC § 101(a) as this amount represents the actual death benefit proceeds. The excess she receives ($300,000 if she lives exactly forty years) is not excludable but, rather, represents taxable earnings on her invested money. The issue is in what manner do we reflect the exclusion when life insurance proceeds are paid out over time as they are here?

IRC § 104(d) and the regulations (at Reg. § 1.101-4), prescribe a "pro rata" method. Again, logic prevails, and even the most math sensitive student should have little difficulty reaching the correct conclusion here. We already have the numbers necessary and can compute the prorated exclusion in at least two different, and equally correct, ways. In our question, $100,000 is the total amount to be excluded. Dividing the $100,000 by 40 (the given life expectancy for Willa) equals $2,500, and this is the portion of each $10,000 annual payment that is excludable (the other $7,500 of each annual payment is income).

$$\frac{\text{Lump Sum Death Benefit}}{\text{Life Expectancy}} \quad = \quad \text{Amount Excluded}$$

The numbers in our problem:

$$\frac{\$100,000}{40 \text{ Years}} \quad = \quad \begin{array}{l}\$2,500 \text{ Excluded} \\ \text{per Year}\end{array}$$

An alternative approach is taking $100,000 (the total excludable benefit) and dividing it by $400,000 (the total we calculated Willa will receive over 40 years). This quotient is ¼ or 25%. One-fourth (or 25%) of each $10,000 payment ($2,500) is excludable and the balance is income.

$$\frac{\text{Excludable Death Benefit}}{\text{Total Expected Return}} \quad = \quad \% \text{ of Each Payment Excluded}$$

The numbers in our problem:

$$\frac{\$100,000}{\$400,000} \quad = \quad \begin{array}{l}25\% \text{ or } ¼ \text{ of} \\ \text{Each Payment Excluded}\end{array}$$

Answer (a), (b), and (d) are incorrect because they do not correspond to the method of prorating payments prescribed by the Code and regulations.

10. **The correct answer is (c).** In question 9, above, we calculated Willa's pro-rated excluded amount of each payment based on her given forty-year life expectancy. In that question we calculated that her $10,000 annual payment was split into non-taxable and taxable components of $2,500 and $7,500, respectively. That conclusion sounds fine for the payments to be received over the forty-year life expectancy. After forty years of payments, Willa will have excluded the full $100,000 of death benefits. Logic might dictate that when Willa receives her forty-first payment, it would be fully taxable having already excluded, over the past forty years, the full $100,000 original death benefit; everything from this point on would appear to be taxable "gravy." Fortunately, and somewhat surprisingly, this logic is wrong. Willa continues

to use the same excludable/includible portions as originally calculated regardless if she "outlives" her life expectancy. [See Reg. § 1.101-4(c).]

Please note that in this series of questions we are concerned with <u>life insurance</u>. Specifically in this question 10 and question 9 above, we have an "annuity type" payout of life insurance benefits. The rules for true annuity contracts (where typically a living individual, the annuitant, gives money to a life insurance company and the company pays the annuitant a specified periodic dollar amount for his/her life) are different. Please see other questions in this book that address the income tax consequences of annuities.

Answer (a) is incorrect, although it is a logical choice. As indicated above, the exclusion/inclusion portions of each payment, as originally calculated, continue regardless of how long the recipient lives. **Answer (b) is incorrect** and, if anything, is the opposite of what one might logically expect. **Answer (d) is incorrect** but is a commonly selected answer. Please be careful when reading the "call of a question." Unlike question 9 that asks for the <u>excluded</u> portion, this question 10 asks for the portion of the payment <u>included</u> in Willa's gross income. Unfortunately some students, who know how this bifurcated exclusion/inclusion rule works, answer this question incorrectly because of the call of the question. **Answer (e) is incorrect** because of the application of the partial exclusion "consideration" rule discussed above.

11. **The most accurate answer is (b).** This is a difficult question that requires us to explore many diverse income tax issues. We will conclude that Willa will only be able to exclude, from income, $33,000 of the $100,000 insurance proceeds received. The excludable portion represents the sum of the $30,000 consideration that she paid for the policy, plus the $3,000 in premiums paid subsequent to her receipt of the policy.

From the preceding questions in this series, we are well versed in the general rule of IRC § 101(a) excluding from income, the proceeds of life insurance paid by reason of the insured's death. This question introduces an important issue in the life insurance area. When there has been a transfer, for valuable consideration, of a life insurance policy during the insured's life, the aforementioned general rule of full exclusion may not be applicable to benefits received by reason of the insured's death. We are about to start a trek down a long and tortured road that requires careful attention to statutory road signs. Be aware, that this intricate material makes for very fertile testing grounds.

IRC § 101(a)(2) contains this exception the general exclusion rule of life insurance benefits. When a life insurance policy has been transferred for consideration, as it was in the facts of our question, the exclusion for benefits proceeds received at the insured's death is <u>limited</u> to the consideration paid by the transferee plus any additional premiums paid by the transferee subsequent to the transfer. In our problem, transferee Willa paid $30,000 in consideration for the policy plus $3,000 in policy premiums subsequent to the transfer. Applying this "consideration" limitation of IRC § 101(a)(2) to these facts, Willa's exclusion is limited to only <u>$33,000</u> ($30,000 plus $3,000) of the $100,000 received. The $67,000 of remaining proceeds would not be excluded pursuant to this rule. This ends up being the correct answer (b) in this question. We should, however, further explore this issue to better understand the subject and to rule out other possible answers to this question. It will also aid in reviewing issues that arise in questions unrelated to life insurance.

The "consideration" exception (IRC § 101(a)(2)) to the general full exclusion rule (IRC § 101(a)) has, in classic law school form, exceptions thereto. One such "exception to the exception" is at issue in this question, and it requires the application of Code sections seemingly unrelated to the insurance provisions at issue. Specifically, § 101(a)(2)(a) effectively provides that you can forget the aforementioned "consideration" limitation and qualify for full exclusion of life insurance proceeds even if the policy was transferred for consideration <u>if</u>, the basis of the policy in the hands of the transferee is "determined in whole or in part by reference" to the basis of the policy in the hands of the transferor. In other words, even though there has been a transfer of a policy for consideration, if the transferee's basis is essentially a carryover basis from the transferor, the "consideration" limitation evaporates, and proceeds from the policy are fully excluded.

The issues of basis (or adjusted basis) in property is more thoroughly discussed in other questions in this book, typically in those involving sales, gains, losses, etc. Generally, one's basis in property is determined by the taxpayer's cost of the property. [IRC §§ 1011 and 1012.] Applying this general rule in our fact pattern, Willa's basis in the life insurance policy purchased from Sonia is his $30,000 cost. There are a few instances, however, when the consideration paid does not necessarily represent one's resulting basis. These situations are critical to the analysis of this question. One such situation is when we have transfers between spouses or former spouses that are considered "incident to divorce." IRC § 1041(b) provides, in a nutshell, that when spouses transfer property to each other, or when former spouses transfer property to each other and it is "incident to their divorce," the transferee spouse (or former spouse) takes a carryover basis. This section does not distinguish as to the type of inter vivos transfer involved; it covers gifts, sales, exchanges, etc. Also, as discussed in other questions in this book, a spouse is a spouse is a spouse, and no legal distinction exists based on gender.

Let us step back for a second and see where we are at this point. If we find that Sonia's sale of the insurance policy to Willa is within the confines of IRC § 1041, Willa will have a carryover basis in the policy. This, in turn, will place her squarely within the exception of IRC § 101(a)(2)(A) which, in turn, overrides the "consideration" limitation, which ultimately would result in exclusion of the full $100,000 insurance proceeds received. Alternatively, if her purchase does not fit within the confines of IRC § 1041, Willa has a "cost" basis rather than a carryover basis. In turn, she would not qualify under the exception in IRC § 101(a)(2)(A), which ultimately would result in her exclusion of the life insurance proceeds being limited to $33,000.

After having read the preceding paragraph a few times to get our bearings, we are ready to continue with our analysis. We are at the critical juncture of whether or not Sonia's transfer of the insurance policy to Willa in May 2018 is within the parameters of IRC § 1041; was this a transfer between spouses or former spouses that is "incident to divorce?" Clearly, it was not a transfer between spouses as they were divorced at the time (they divorced in January 2017). It was a transfer between former spouses, but was it considered "incident to divorce" as required by the statute? A transfer "incident to divorce" has a statutory definition as being either 1) any transfer within one year of the divorce, or 2) a transfer "relating to the cessation of the marriage." [See IRC § 1041(c).] Temporary regulations define transfers that are considered "relating to the cessation of the marriage" as a transfer provided for by a "divorce or separation instrument" and is transferred, pursuant to this instrument, within six years of the divorce. [Temp.Reg. §1.1041-1T(b); Please see other questions in this book relating to divorce issues for more information.] We now see that Willa's purchase of the policy from Sonia was not a transfer "incident to divorce." Willa's purchase of the policy from Sonia was not within one year of their divorce. Alternatively, even though the transfer occurred within six years of their divorce, it was not called for by their divorce decree (this is indicated in the facts) and, therefore, is not related to the cessation of the marriage. This means that the transfer between Sonia and Willa does not fall within the parameters of IRC § 1041 which, in turn, means Willa does not have a carryover basis in the policy. As previously indicated, Willa, consequently, does not fit within the IRC § 101(a)(2)(A) exception to the limited exclusion "consideration" rule. Willa, therefore, can only exclude $33,000 of the $100,000 insurance proceeds received (the $30,000 consideration that she paid plus the $3,000 in premiums subsequent to his purchase).

Note that while this question contains specific dates, it is not a year-specific question. Rather, specific dates were used only for the purpose of helping to navigate the question (and the other questions in this series 8 through 12).

Answer (a) is incorrect but is close to being correct. It is true that Willa's purchase of the policy from Sonia was not incident to divorce and, therefore, she is stuck with the limited exclusion under the "consideration" rule. Willa paid consideration of $30,000, which is excludable, but she is also entitled to exclude the $3,000 that she paid in insurance premiums subsequent to her purchase. **Answer (d) is incorrect** because as indicated above, not just any transfer within six years of divorce is considered "relating to the cessation of the marriage." If the transfer occurs more than one year after the divorce, the divorce or separation instrument must have called for such a transfer. Here, the facts indicate that Willa's purchase of the policy was not pursuant to any oral or written agreement relating to the divorce. Since the transfer was not, by definition, incident to divorce, IRC § 1041(b) does not apply, so the exception in IRC § 101(a)(2)(A) does not apply and Willa cannot exclude the full amount of the proceeds. **Answer (c) is incorrect** because it has no relationship to the law and the facts of the question.

12. **Answer (e) is the most accurate.** This is very similar to question 11, above. On an actual class exam, the author would not include a question so similar and in such proximity to the question immediately preceding it. It is presented here, however, as a good review and to illustrate the marked difference in the answer resulting from a slight change in the facts.

So as not to torture the reader, the lengthy analysis for the preceding question, while relevant, will not be repeated here in full. We will pick up near the end of the analysis from the previous question dealing with the determination of Willa's basis in the insurance policy. Recall that Willa's goal of full exclusion rests on whether or not her basis in the policy was essentially a carryover basis from Sonia. As discussed above, this requires that her May 2018 purchase of the policy be considered a "transfer incident to divorce." Recall that in question 11 (a January 2017 divorce), we found this not to be the case because the transfer was neither within one year of the divorce, nor pursuant to their "divorce or separation instrument" and occurring within six years. In the revised facts of this question, however, the May 2018 transfer was within one year of their January 2018 divorce and, therefore, is deemed "incident to divorce." The significance of this makes a dramatic difference in the tax consequences to Willa. With the transfer incident to divorce, she has a carryover basis in the policy, she meets the exception in IRC § 101(a)(2)(A) to the limited exclusion "consideration" rule, and the general full exclusion rule of IRC § 101(a) applies.

Note that the sale of the life insurance policy between Sonia and Willa is deemed "incident to divorce" notwithstanding the fact that it was not pursuant to any agreement relating to their divorce. This is often an elusive point with students. IRC § 1041(c) dictates a non-rebuttable presumption that any transfer within one year of divorce is deemed incident to divorce. To extend this classification to transfers made more than one year after divorce, the transfer must be pursuant to their divorce or separation instrument (e.g., a divorce decree). [See Temp.Reg. § 1.1041-1T(b) Q & A-7.]

Answers (a) and (b) are not correct because as discussed above, Willa is not relegated to a limited exclusion based on the consideration that she paid. **Answers (c) and (d) are also incorrect.** They both have the correct numeric answer that the full proceeds are excludable from Willa's gross income, but they state an incorrect reason for this exclusion.

13. **The correct answer is (c).** This is a relatively straightforward problem. Determining Roxanne's realized gain or loss in this question requires us to identify two basic components: her sales price ("amount realized" or, hereinafter, AR) and her basis in the jewelry ("adjusted basis or, hereinafter, AB). The difference between the two represents a realized gain or loss. [IRC § 1001(a).] Each of these two components, AR and AB, can present a variety of complex tax issues for exam and real-world tax purposes. The AR side is straightforward in our question and is her $42,000 sales price. Other questions in this book present more complex issues involving a taxpayer's AR.

The AB component is the more challenging part of this question (but not as complex as AB issues presented in other questions in this book). While a taxpayer's cost is normally the starting point for determination of one's basis in property (IRC §§ 1011 and 1012), when property is received as a gift, as is the case here, there really is no "cost" to the taxpayer. The seemingly logical result of a zero basis is neither desirable nor, thankfully, appropriate. IRC § 1015 provides us with the rules for determining a donee's AB in property received as a gift. The general rule for most gifts is that the donee takes the donor's AB in the property, or what is commonly referred to as a "carryover" AB. In Roxanne's case, this would be her aunt Martha's original $20,000 cost of the jewelry. There are no other facts presented in this problem that require any further adjustments to Roxanne's carryover AB (e.g., gift tax paid adjustment, special loss rule, etc.).

The calculation of Roxanne's gain is now a simple matter. Her AR of $42,000 less her $20,000 AB results in a realized gain of $22,000. While not the subject of this question, issues of gain recognition and characterization (i.e., capital gain materials), are related testable material. For information purposes, Roxanne's $22,000 gain would be recognized and characterized as a "long-term capital gain." [Please see other questions presented in this book where recognition and characterization issues are addressed.]

Answer (a) is incorrect because it is a misrepresentation of a certain situation involving the "special loss rule" when determining the AB of property received as a gift. The special loss rule can apply when the fair market value of the gift (at the time of the gift) is less than the donor's AB in the property. Our facts do not implicate the *special loss rule*. **Answer (b) is incorrect** because this answer reflects the mistaken belief that Roxanne's AB is equal to the fair market value at the time of the gift. This answer would have been correct had Roxanne received the jewelry from Martha at Martha's death by devise, bequest or inheritance as the rules for determining the transferee's AB in such situations are quite different. Please see other problems in this book addressing the issue of the AB of property received from a decedent. **Answer (d) is incorrect** because it fails to reflect the AB rules for gifts as discussed above.

14. **Answer (c) is correct.** Situations involving the exchange, between two parties, of services and/or property, usually result in some initial confusion among students. Although it is a bit obscured in this problem, Roxanne really did two things in this transaction: sold the jewelry worth $42,000 to Carl in exchange for $42,000 of consideration, and she effectively paid Carl $2,000 for his dental services. With respect to the former, the consideration Roxanne received from the jewelry transfer was not in the form of cash but, rather, she received $42,000 worth of stuff (the payoff of her $40,000 loan to Carl, plus Carl's services worth $2,000). Roxanne's receipt of $42,000 consideration for the jewelry less his basis ("adjusted basis" hereinafter AB) in the jewelry of $20,000 (carryover gift AB from her aunt), results in a realized <u>gain</u> to Roxanne of <u>$22,000</u>.

What is bothersome for students in such exchange transactions, is the lack of cash being received for services rendered or property transferred. Somehow the resulting income tax consequences seem to be incorrect or unfair. A more thorough discussion of the transaction from <u>Roxanne's</u> perspective follows. [Please see question 15, immediately following this question, for the analysis of the facts and income tax consequences from Carl's perspective.]

The transaction from Roxanne's perspective

In class, this professor likes to recast, or view in a different light, exchange or barter transactions in an essentially equivalent manner involving the transfer of cash back and forth between the parties. We could break down the transaction between Roxanne and Carl into something like this. Roxanne *sells* the jewelry to Carl for $42,000 in cash. Roxanne then takes $40,000 of this cash and gives it back to *Carl,* fully paying off her $40,000 debt to him. Roxanne then takes the remaining $2,000 of cash that she has left after paying off the debt, and then pays Carl $2,000 for the dental work he performs for her. The economic substance of viewing the transaction in this manner (with cash going back and forth) is the same as given in our facts, but it sometimes helps identify the separate components involved. Either way we look at it, in the end Roxanne has no cash; no longer has the jewelry; her debt has been repaid, and she has received dental services.

Now let us look at Roxanne's disposition of the jewelry. A sale or disposition of property results in the realization of a gain or loss to transferor measured by the difference between the "amount realized" (AR) and the transferor's AB. [IRC § 1001(a).] The "AR" side of this sale or disposition equation is easy if viewed in light of our "recast" facts. Roxanne sold the jewelry for $42,000 and that is her AR. One's AR need not be comprised of cash as AR is much broader than that. AR basically includes the value of any "stuff" received in exchange for property whether it be other property or services (money's worth). Viewed through the tangled actual facts of the problem Roxanne received $42,000 worth of "stuff." She received the benefit of her $40,000 debt to Carl being fully paid off (she no longer has this obligation) plus she received $2,000 worth of Carl's dental services, for a total of $42,000. Turning to Roxanne's AB in the jewelry, her AB is $20,000. This is a carryover AB from her aunt Martha, from whom she received the gift (see question 13, above for a more thorough discussion of AB in property received as a gift).

At this point, Roxanne's gain calculation is simple: her AR of $42,000 less her $20,000 AB results in a realized gain of $22,000.

A word of caution about language used in this question and on exams in general. There are many instances where the common use of a term does not necessarily correspond to its official "tax" counterpart. Labels can be deceiving so do not be fooled by their use in lay terms on an exam. Problems involving what may appear to be income from discharge of indebtedness are fertile ground for tricky questions vis-à-vis terminology. For example, in this question, after receiving the jewelry from Roxanne, "Carl *discharged the debt.*" The lay use of the word *discharge* in our question (to fully pay off a debt) does not correspond to the official "tax" counterpart where "discharge" of debt represents a forgiveness of debt (and prima facie realization of income).

While not required to answer this question, there is one more tax-related item that is pertinent if we are to consider *all* of the income tax implications of the facts. We indicated that Roxanne effectively *paid* Carl for $2,000 worth of dental services. Discussed in more detail in other questions in this book, this $2,000 would be a qualifying medical care expense for Roxanne for deduction purposes under IRC § 213.

[For more information about barter/exchange transactions, see Reg. § 1.61-1(d); Rev.Rul. 79-24, 1979-1 C.B. 60.]

Answers (a) and (b) are incorrect because for both there was no *discharge of indebtedness,* from an income tax perspective, involved in this problem. Carl did not "forgive" any portion of the amount Roxanne owed to him. Please see the "caution about language" discussion above. **Answer (d) is also incorrect** but is the most commonly selected incorrect answer. While it correctly notes that Roxanne realizes no income from discharge of indebtedness, it incorrectly classifies the $2,000 services she received as some general form of income instead of being part of her AR from the disposition of the jewelry. She wasn't paid for services rendered. Rather, she paid, albeit indirectly with property, for services rendered to her. If it helps, when you go to a salon/barbershop/etc. for work on your hair, you are receiving the benefit of someone's services, but you are paying for them. It would be crazy tax law if you were required to recognize income for receiving services for which you paid (see question 15 immediately below).

15. **The correct answer is (a).** As mentioned in the analysis to the companion question 14, above, Situations involving the exchange, between two parties, of services and/or property, usually result in some confusion among students at first. Although it is a bit obscured in this problem, Carl really did just one thing, that results in the realization of income, for purposes of this question: he rendered services worth $2,000 to Roxanne in exchange for $2,000 of consideration. Separately, from a tax perspective, Roxanne repaid the debt that she owed to Carl.

What is bothersome for students in such exchange transactions, is the lack of cash being received for services rendered or property transferred. Somehow, the resulting income tax consequences seem to be incorrect or unfair. A more thorough discussion of the transaction from <u>Carl's</u> perspective follows. [Please see question 14, immediately preceding this question, for the analysis of the facts and income tax consequences from Roxanne's perspective.]

The transaction from Carl's perspective

Recall how we recast this barter transaction in the analysis of question 14, above, in an essentially equivalent manner involving the transfer of cash back and forth between the parties. We broke down the transaction between Roxanne and Carl into something like this. Carl *buys* the jewelry from Roxanne $42,000 in cash. Roxanne then takes $40,000 of this cash and gives it back to *Carl,* with Carl accepting this money as payment, in full, for the $40,000 Roxanne owed to him (on a personal loan unrelated to his business). Carl then performs $2,000 worth of dental work for Roxanne and she *pays* him $2,000 in cash for the work (this was all the money that she had left after paying off the debt). The economic substance of viewing the transaction in this manner (with cash going back and forth) is the same as given in our facts, but it sometimes helps identify the separate components involved. Either way we look at it, in the end Carl had the debt Roxanne owed to him fully repaid, and Carl received *payment* for his $2,000 worth of dental services.

With respect to Roxanne's repayment of the $40,000 she owed Carl, this does not give rise to any income to Carl. You probably learned early on in your discovery of *gross income* that borrowing money is not income to the debtor (as there is no net accession to wealth, or net economic benefit) and similarly, there is no income to the creditor when the amount is repaid. When we break down the transaction into its component pieces, this is what is happening when Carl accepts the jewelry, in part, as payment for Roxanne's debt.

As for Carl's dental services rendered to Roxanne, early on in classroom discussion of gross income, we discover that gross income need not be in the form of cash. A lawyer, for example, who performs legal work for a client and is paid in cash, has gross income. A lawyer who performs legal work for a client and receives property as payment has gross income equal to the fair market value of the property received. A lawyer who performs legal work for a client and receives a combination of cash and property as payment has gross income equal to the cash plus the fair market value of the property received. A lawyer who performs legal work for a client and receives the client's services as payment (in exchange) has income equal to the value of the services. A lawyer who performs legal work for a client and receives cash, property and the client's services as payment has gross income equal to the cash, the fair market value of the property, and the fair market value of the services. [See Reg. § 1.61-1(d) (compensation received in forms other than in cash).] When an individual performs services and receives **"something"** in exchange, that "something" (or the value thereof) represents gross income. The form of that "something" is generally irrelevant. In our question, Carl rendered $2,000 worth of services and received $2,000 worth of stuff in return: the value of the jewelry in excess of the amount going to pay off the debt.

In summary, Carl has $2,000 of gross income in the form of compensation for his services.

Answer (b) is incorrect because Carl does not have income merely when a debt owed to him is repaid. See the discussion above for more information. **Answers (c) and (d) are incorrect** because they both fail to reflect Carl's income from his services to Roxanne. **Answer (e) is incorrect** because the debt owed to him has been fully repaid.

16. **The best answer is (c).** We know that the "gross income" net is large, including just about every economic benefit a taxpayer might receive (with, of course, numerous holes for escape through specific statutory exclusions). Just in case there is any question about the inclusion of federal or state unemployment benefits, IRC § 85 specifically provides for their inclusion in gross income. Dirk's benefits are, therefore, included in his gross income.

Answer (a) is incorrect. Modernly, unemployment benefits are included in the recipient's gross income. However, this was not always the case as at one time, unemployment benefits were excluded under the belief that general governmental welfare benefits should not be taxed. **Answer (b) is incorrect** because unemployment compensation does not qualify for exclusion under IRC § 104 as compensation for injuries or sickness. This is distinguished from government *disability* benefits, which may be excludable from gross income. **Answer (d) is incorrect** because there is no such fringe benefit, or other employer/employee related exclusion, applicable to government paid unemployment benefits.

17. **Answer (b) is correct.** As with other questions presented in this book, every time a fact pattern presents a sale (or other disposition) of property, the author likes to go through the following analysis; always ask these three questions:

    1) Do we have a **Realized** Gain (or Loss) & how much? This is computing the amount of gain (or loss). It is the AR (amount realized) less one's AB (adjusted basis). See other problems in this book addressing this issue.

    2) If yes, is the realized gain (or loss) **Recognized**? This simply means, is it reported in one's income for tax purposes. This is the issue that we are currently addressing. As a taxpayer, you would like the answer to be NO for gains; I do not want to recognize, report, the

gain (said another way, I'd like to be able to exclude this gain from my income).

3) If gain is recognized, is it given any **special character** or treatment? This is primarily the issue of "capital gains (or losses)" that are treated differently for income tax purposes. This is not the issue in this question (see other problems in this book).

Dirk does realize a $40,000 loss on the sale of his house, the difference between the $360,000 sales price and his basis in the house of $400,000. His basis in the house is his original $400,000 purchase price. This $40,000 loss, however, is not recognized pursuant to IRC § 165(c) as Dirk used the house for personal purposes (living there as opposed to using it for business or investment purposes). Since Dirk's loss is not recognized, its characterization as a "capital loss" is neither relevant nor appropriate. A more comprehensive analysis of this answer follows.

The first step is determining whether Dirk has realized a gain or loss on the sale of the house. For this, we need two basic components: his sales price ("amount realized" or, hereinafter, AR) and his basis in the shares ("adjusted basis or, hereinafter, AB). The difference between the two represents a realized gain or loss. [IRC § 1001(a).] Each of these two components, AR and AB, can present a variety of complex tax issues for exam and real-world tax purposes. The AR side is straightforward in our question and is his $360,000 sales price. Other questions in this book present more complex issues involving a taxpayer's AR.

The AB component in this problem is also fairly straightforward. The general starting place for determining one's AB is one's cost. [IRC §§ 1011 and 1012.] Our starting, and ending, point is what Dirk paid for the house five years ago. The $400,000 Dirk originally paid for the property represents his AB. Computing Dirk's gain or loss realized from the sale of the house is not a simple matter. His AR (selling price) of $360,000 less his AB of $400,000 results in a realized loss of $40,000.

Now to the second step of our gain/loss analysis: whether Dirk's $40,000 loss is recognized. IRC § 1001(c) provides that, unless otherwise indicated in the Code, all realized gains and losses are recognized. This would cement the recognition of Dirk's loss, if it were not for an "otherwise indicated" Code section, namely IRC § 165. At first glance, the "general rule" in IRC § 165(a) looks to be in Dirk's favor allowing a deduction for "any loss sustained during the taxable year . . ." Reading further at IRC § 165(c) we come across an ominous sounding subsection: "Limitation on losses of individuals." In class, this professor refers to this as the "section 165(c) hoop," complete with graphic depictions on the board/slides. Figuratively, the goal is to jump from the "realized" loss side, through the hoop to the land of "recognized" losses. This hoop, however, is more akin to a **semi-permeable membrane** than an unobstructed open space. [Ha! Who would think we'd ever use the phrase *semipermeable membrane* in law school, let alone in a tax class?] We see, in IRC §§ 165(c)(1)-(c)(3), that business losses, investment losses and personal-use "casualty" losses, break on through to the recognized loss side. By default, however, losses from personal-use assets (other than casualty losses) do not make it through this "section 165(c) hoop" and go unrecognized. [To complete the *semipermeable membrane* analogy, their molecular size is too large to pass through to the land of *recognition*.] This explains why, for example, when you sell your personal-use car for a loss (which is almost always the case), the loss is realized but not recognized; i.e., you get no tax benefit from such a loss.

This, then, brings us to Dirk's realized loss. While the facts indicate that he had hoped his house would have been a better *investment*, the fact that he used the house as his residence negates, for tax purposes, any investment intentions. These facts represent a very common misconception about personal residences vis-à-vis their "investment" status for loss recognition. Dirk's use of the house as his personal residence relegates it to a personal-use asset, notwithstanding the magnitude or conviction of his accompanying investment intentions. Dirk is left, therefore, with a $40,000 realized loss that is <u>not</u> recognized. And, unfortunately for Dirk, this is where the answer ends.

Dirk's house is a capital asset as defined in IRC § 1221 (capital assets are generally, by definitional default, investment or personal-use assets). This has, however, no relevance to the answer, but it is a correct statement. There is often some confusion with respect to this as Dirk's house meets the definition of a capital asset. [IRC § 1221 (capital assets are generally, by definitional default, investment or personal-use assets).] If Dirk's house is a capital asset, which it is, then why isn't the loss on the sale thereof a capital loss? The answer to this can be found in the definition of capital losses in IRC §§ 1222(2) or 1222(4). Capital losses are losses from the sale or exchange of a capital asset "if and to the extent that such loss is taken into account in computing taxable income." We hit the IRC § 165(c) barrier with respect to personal-use assets and losses resulting from their sale or ex-change are <u>not</u> taken into account in computing taxable income. In class, this professor stresses to students the importance of going "step-by-step" through the above discussed three prong analysis whenever an asset is sold (or exchanged). Students often run into trouble when losses are at issue, and they leapfrog over the "recognition" step two.

Students are often bothered by the lack of symmetry in that gains from the sale of personal-use assets <u>are</u> recognized (must be included in income unless a specific exclusion provision is applicable), but losses from the sale of such assets are not recognized (no tax benefit for these losses). Unfortunately, income tax laws are not always fair.

Here is a copy of the slide (albeit without some cool animation and colors better depicting the semipermeable membrane) that this professor uses in class for a visual representation of IRC § 165(c).

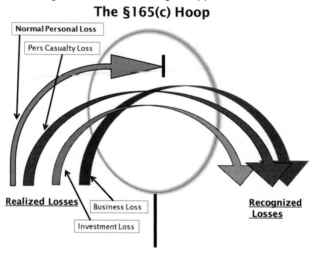

The §165(c) Hoop

Answer (a) is incorrect. As discussed above, this is a common misunderstanding dealing with losses from the sale of personal-use assets. As discussed above, Dirk's house is, indeed, a capital asset. However, because his realized loss is precluded form recognition by IRC § 165(c), no capital loss results. Capital losses can result only from losses that pass our second step of recognition. Characterization of the loss as either a long-term or short-term capital loss is neither relevant nor appropriate because the loss must first be recognized, which it is not in this case. **Answer (c) is incorrect** because it reflects an incorrect recognition of Dirk's loss from the sale of his house. While not particularly relevant, this answer is also incorrect for stating that the house is not a capital asset. **Answer (d) is also incorrect.** While the answer correctly states that Dirk's $40,000 loss is not recognized, there is no such provision allowing him to increase the basis in any new house by the amount of unrecognized loss from the sale of this house. Dirk's unrecognized loss is just "gone" with no tax benefits (present, past or future) resulting therefrom. **Answer (e) is incorrect** because a correct answer (b) is presented.

18. **Answer (b) is correct.** There are two major parts to this question: 1) *which* of Dirk's expenditures give rise to deductions, and 2) *where or how* any such deductions are allowed for purposes of computing his taxable income. As

to which of Dirk's expenditures give rise to deductions, IRC § 164 is the key section for addressing the taxes paid, and IRC § 212 is our primary focus for the CPA fees paid. Compared to this question's answer in prior editions of this book, Dirk has, unfortunately, been negatively impacted by the *Tax Cuts and Jobs Act* (TCJA) signed into law in December (generally effective beginning in 2018). Ultimately, we will conclude that Dirk may be entitled to some deduction of the $750 state income taxes paid as part of his "itemized deductions." Because of the TCJA, he will no longer be entitled to any actual deduction for the $1,000 paid to his CPA. Lastly, the $2,000 that he paid in Federal taxes will not give rise to a deduction for income tax purposes.

As indicated, IRC § 164 is the delimiting section for deducting taxes paid. State income taxes are among those listed as deductible (IRC § 164(a)(3)), so the $750 in state income taxes paid is deductible. However, <u>no</u> deduction is allowed for *federal income taxes* paid. Federal income tax is not among those listed as deductible in IRC § 164, and, just to be sure, IRC § 275 specifically denies any deduction of federal income taxes. The $2,000 Dirk paid in federal income taxes are, therefore, not deductible.

While not directly at issue in this question, it should be noted that the TCJA made significant changes with respect to IRC § 164 deductions for state and local taxes and not just for state income taxes as in our question but also for a host of other allowable "tax" deductions; most notably real property taxes. Prior to the TCJA, there was no cap or ceiling on the amount of IRC § 164 state and local taxes (now commonly known collectively as SALT). Specifically, IRC §164 (b)(6)(B) places an artificial $10,000 deduction cap for the aggregate of otherwise deductible section 164 taxes paid. This TCJA imposition of a $10,000 cap can have a huge impact on taxpayers. As we do not know the full extent of Dirk's other taxes paid (regular state income taxes, property taxes, etc.) we cannot say for sure that he will be entitled to a full deduction of the $750 state taxes paid because of his audit. This is the reason for the wording of the answer that he "may be entitled to some deductions." [Please see other questions in this book that address the TCJA's impact of IRC § 164 SALT deductions.]

The deductibility of the $1,000 in CPA fees Dirk paid for assistance with his federal and state income tax audits has also been impacted, negatively, by the TCJA. But first, a proper analysis of the deductibility of this expense and we begin at IRC § 212. IRC § 212 allows for deductions for ordinary and necessary expenses paid in connection with, "1) the production or collection of income; 2) the management, conservation, or maintenance of property held for the production of income; or 3) *the determination, collection or refund of any tax.*" [IRC § 212 (emphasis added).] The $1,000 Dirk paid qualifies under the last (the third) category listed in IRC § 212. Other common examples qualifying here include tax preparation fees (including annual personal tax preparation software) and amounts paid for personal tax advice.

Now that we have identified that the $750 and $1,000 Dirk paid in state income taxes and CPA fees, respectively, are deductible, the next issue is where and how they are deducted in computing taxable income. This is necessary to distinguish answers (c), (d) and possibly (e).

In very broad terms, there are two camps of deductions for purposes of computing taxable income. There are deductions that are subtracted from *gross income* to arrive at an intermediary point called *adjusted gross income* (AGI). These are commonly referred to as "above the line" deductions, with AGI representing "the line." The other camp of deductions is comprised of those that are subtracted from AGI to arrive at *taxable income*. These are commonly referred to as "below the line" deductions. The components making up this camp of *below the line* deductions can include something called the "standard deduction" or, in the alternative, a group of deductions called "itemized deductions." In addition, a new TCJA *pass-through* business-related deduction (IRC § 199A) may be included as a separate *below the line* deduction. [For more information about how this all fits together, please see IRC § 62, Appendix A, and other questions in this book.]

Dirk's deductible state income tax and CPA fees are part of the group of deductions known collectively as "itemized deductions." This *itemized deduction* grouping is comprised of various types of deductions including certain medical care expenses (IRC § 213), certain interest and tax expenses (IRC §§ 163 and 164), charitable contributions (IRC § 170), and others. Dirk's $750 in state income taxes, allowed by IRC § 164 as discussed above, fits clearly within this *itemized deduction* group. One sub-group of *itemized deductions* is a specific category referred to as "miscellaneous itemized deductions." This sub-group of *miscellaneous itemized deductions* contains IRC § 212 expenses (other than those related to rentals or royalties which is not the case here). While not at issue in this question, this sub-group of *miscellaneous itemized deductions* also contains unreimbursed employee IRC § 162 business expenses. The significance of this sub-group of deductions was always important but has taken on greater significance under the TCJA. Not to spend too much time on the historical significance but prior to the TCJA, IRC § 67 allowed for their deductibility only to the extent that they (in the aggregate) exceed 2% of the individual's AGI. Dirk's CPA fees, as IRC § 212 expenses, fit into this category of *miscellaneous itemized deductions* and in prior editions of this book, we would be done with this question. This entire group of *miscellaneous itemized deductions* was a casualty of the TCJA with the new law "suspending" any deductions of *miscellaneous itemized deductions* for the years 2018 through 2025. [IRC § 67(g)] Now we are done and, unfortunately for Dirk, while the $1,000 he spent in CPA fees are, ostensibly, a valid IRC § 212 expense, the TCJA has eliminated any actual deduction of these expenses for Dirk. It should be noted that nowhere in IRC § 212 will you see anything about the elimination of this deduction and this points to the importance of sometimes, such as here, it is a completely different section (IRC § 67(g) which is not even referenced in IRC § 212) that denies any deduction for such expenses.

Other questions in this book address, in greater detail, how all items of income and deductions fit together in determining an individual's taxable income.

Answer (a) is incorrect because, as discussed above, the state income taxes may give rise to a possible deduction. **Answer (c) is incorrect.** It properly identifies the state income tax as a deductible expense and that there is no deduction for federal income taxes paid. However, it incorrectly identifies the CPA fees giving rise to a deduction. **Answer (d) is incorrect** but would have been an acceptable answer prior to the TCJA (again, it is now incorrect because the CPA fees Dirk paid will no longer give rise to a possible deduction). **Answer (e) is incorrect** because, as explained above, neither the $2,000 federal income tax Dirk paid nor the CPA fees give rise to deductions for federal income tax purpose.

19. **The best answer is (b).** The Parking provided to Mark by his employer is excludable from his gross income up to $265 per month (for 2019) as a "qualified transportation" fringe benefit. Please note that this question is *year-specific* (for 2019), but can easily be adapted to other years, or be asked in a more generic non-year-specific form.

It is clear that Mark's free parking at work results in his receipt of a financial benefit or net accession to wealth that will be included in gross income unless it is specifically excluded by some provision. A host of employee fringe benefits are excluded pursuant to IRC § 132, and employer provided parking is among them. One such excludable fringe benefit is "Qualified parking" (a sub-part of the "qualified transportation" fringe benefits). [IRC § 132(f).] *Qualified Parking* includes employer provided parking provided to an employee on or near the employer's business premises, as is provided to Mark in our question. [IRC § 132(f)(5)(C).] There is, however, a statutory dollar limit to the amount of this qualified parking fringe benefit; which is listed in IRC § 132(f)(2)(B) as $175 per month (of parking benefit received). As with many dollar amounts listed in the statute, the monthly dollar limit of excludable parking value is "indexed" for inflation. [IRC § 132(f)(6).] The maximum value of parking provided by an employer that can be excluded under this provision (for 2019) is $265. The monthly value of parking provided in excess of this amount (or the appropriate amount for the year in question) represents income.

Unlike some of the other excludable fringe benefits of IRC § 132, an employer can provide the qualified parking fringe benefit (part of the qualified transportation fringe benefit) to employees on a discriminatory basis (in favor of highly compensated employees). Therefore, the parking provided to Mark by his employer is excludable up to $265 per month (for 2019) regardless of whether this benefit is offered to other employees.

Students familiar with other IRC § 132 fringe benefits may question whether employer provided parking (at the work location) may be considered an excludable "working condition fringe" – an expense, had the employee paid for it would have given rise to a IRC § 162 business deduction. This, however, is generally not the case as parking at one's place of work (as an employee or a self-employed individual) is considered part of nondeductible personal "commuting" expenses. It is interesting to note that at one time (prior to 1993) the "qualified transportation" category of excludable fringe benefits did not exist, but employer provided parking was included in a special category of excludable "working condition" fringes.

The *Tax Cut's and Jobs Act* (TCJA) signed into law in December 2017 (generally effective beginning in 2018) made some significant changes to many areas of fringe benefits including this question's *qualified transportation fringes*. The changes made do not directly impact the answer to our question but should be noted to more fully explain other aspects of these fringe benefits. Not to be read as a political statement, but none of the TCJA's changes to IRC § 132 are favorable to employees or employers. Prior to the TCJA, *qualified transportation fringes* included, in addition to qualified parking and other items, a *qualified bicycle commuting reimbursement* fringe benefit. This particular fringe benefit, which was insignificant in terms of lost revenue for the Treasury, was, oddly, singled out and eliminated (technically, "suspended" for 2018 through 2025).

Again, not a direct component of our question but fleshing it out in the contexts of changes made by the TCJA, a more significant change to the entire group of the IRC § 132 *qualified transportation fringes* affects employers providing such fringe benefits. While not the subject of this question, one may ask to what extent is an employer entitled to deduct the costs of employer provided *qualified transportation fringe* benefits (e.g., the qualified parking, the value of which up to a certain monthly value, employees can exclude from income)? Prior to the TCJA, an employer could deduct, as a business expense, 100% of the cost of such fringe benefits (e.g., the cost of the parking for the employee) irrespective of any exclusion in employees' gross income. Beginning in 2018, pursuant to the TCJA, employers, generally, can no longer deduct any costs associated with *qualified transportation fringe benefits*. While the TCJA does not impact the excludability of this benefit for employees (i.e., the above analysis of this question's answer), the TCJA's deduction limitations for employers may have a dampening effect vis-à-vis an employer's willingness to continue this employee fringe benefit. This is a major topic of discussion among businesses pitting an employer's desire to not increase their tax liabilities due to the loss of deductions, and providing such excludable fringe benefits as an incentive for employees (current and potential). It is way beyond the scope of this book but "tax exempt" organizations (e.g., hospitals, schools/colleges/law schools, religious institutions, etc.) providing otherwise excludable "qualified transportation" fringes (e.g., parking for doctors, staff, faculty, etc.) tan an even great hit under the provisions of the TCJA.

Answer (a) is incorrect because it fails to recognize the existence of the qualified parking/transportation fringe benefit under IRC § 132. **Answers (c) and (d) are incorrect** because the qualified parking/transportation fringe benefit can be offered on a discriminatory basis (in favor of highly compensated employees). Answer (c) is also incorrect because it states the excluded dollar amount as it appears in the statute before adjustments for inflation. **Answer (e) is incorrect** because a correct answer (b) is presented.

20. **Answer (c) is correct.** This question, except for one critical date in the facts, is identical to another question appearing elsewhere in this book. The answer, however, is quite different with Tiffany's realized gain equal to $2,000.

Determining Tiffany's realized gain or loss in this question requires us to identify two basic components: her sales price ("amount realized" or, hereinafter, AR) and her basis in the watch ("adjusted basis or, hereinafter, AB). The difference between the two represents a _realized_ gain or loss. [IRC § 1001(a).] Each of these two components, AR and AB, can present a variety of complex tax issues for exam and real-world tax purposes. The AR side is straightforward in our question and is her $23,000 sales price. Other questions in this book present more complex issues involving a taxpayer's AR. The AB component is the more challenging component of this question.

While a taxpayer's cost is normally the starting point for determination of one's basis in property (IRC §§ 1011 and 1012), when property is received as a gift, as is the case here, there really is no "cost" to the taxpayer. The seemingly logical result of a zero basis is neither desirable nor, thankfully, appropriate. IRC § 1015 provides us with the rules for determining a donee's AB in property received as a gift. The general rule for most gifts is that the donee takes the donor's AB in the property, or what is commonly referred to as a "carryover" AB. In Tiffany's case, this would be Tiffany's Aunt's original $18,000 cost. This is Tiffany's starting point in determining her AB.

We say "starting point" because there was a gift tax paid in connection with the 1975 gift to Tiffany. Discussion of gift taxes is beyond the scope of this book, and most basic federal income tax courses. Suffice it to say that a gift tax is based on the value of the property transferred and the tax is an obligation of the donor/transferor. It is a given, in our facts, that Tiffany's Aunt incurred and paid a $7,000 gift tax on the 1975 gift to Tiffany. While the study of gift taxes is beyond our scope, their effect on a donee/transferee's AB is not. IRC § 1015(d) provides for a "gift tax paid adjustment" to AB (an increase to AB). The method of calculating this positive, and favorable, adjustment varies depending on when the gift was made, with the critical date (of the gift) being December 31, 1976. The gift to Tiffany was in <u>1975</u> and the "gift tax paid adjustment" rules for pre-1977 gifts are contained in § 1015(d)(1). Basically, the donee/transferee is entitled to add to his or her AB, the gift tax paid on the transfer with a limit that the result cannot exceed the fair market value of the property at the time of the gift. Adding the $7,000 gift tax to Tiffany's carryover AB of $18,000 equals $25,000. However, this is more than the $21,000 value at the time of the gift in 1975, so <u>Tiffany's AB is limited to $21,000</u>. The gift tax paid adjustment to AB for gifts made after December 31, 1976, is the subject of at least one question presented elsewhere in this book.

The calculation of Tiffany's gain is now a simple matter. Her AR of $23,000 less her $21,000 AB results in <u>a realized gain of $2,000</u>. While not the subject of this question, issues of gain <u>recognition</u> and <u>characterization</u> (i.e., capital gain materials) are related testable material. For information purposes, Tiffany's $2,000 gain would be recognized and characterized as a "long-term capital gain." Please see other questions presented in this book addressing the recognition and characterization of gains and losses.

Answer (a) is incorrect. This answer utilizes the correct pre-1977 "gift tax paid adjustment" to the degree that the $7,000 gift tax is added to Tiffany's carryover AB. However it fails to limit the resulting AB to the $21,000 fair market value at the time of the gift. Incorrectly ignoring this AB limitation, Tiffany's AB would have been $25,000 ($18,000 carryover AB plus $7,000 gift tax paid adjustment). Incorrectly using this as Tiffany's basis results in a ($2,000) loss when subsequently sold for $23,000. **Answer (b) is incorrect** because it utilizes the "gift tax paid adjustment" rules for post-1976 gifts found in IRC § 1015(d)(6). An analysis of these rules is presented elsewhere in this book. **Answer (d) is incorrect** because it fails to reflect any "gift tax paid adjustment," rendering Tiffany's AB in the watch as a straight "carryover" of $18,000. **Answer (e) is incorrect** because a correct response (c) is presented.

21. **Answer (a) is the most likely result.** From all indications, Tia dearly loved her grandfather, Grant, and his death is a sad loss for Tia. One hates to think of income taxes at moments like these, but we must for purposes of this analysis. Tia, with the receipt of the XYZ shares has realized a financial benefit or net accession to wealth, the general measuring rod inclusion in the broadly defined definition of gross income. There is, however, a specific exclusion section in IRC § 102 that is most likely applicable here. This section's general rule provides for a very beneficial exclusion from income of amounts received as gifts, bequests, devises, and inheritances. [IRC § 102(a).] Grant's devise of the XYZ shares to Tia in his will seems to fit within this exclusion and, is the most likely result in this question.

An excludable devise/bequest is similar to excludable inter vivos gifts in that the primary motivation by the transferor is donative in nature. The language of Grant's devise raises the possibility (at least for exam discussion purposes) that perhaps the devise was made as payment for services that Tia had rendered to her grandfather. The fact that property or money comes from a decedent by way of a will does not assure exclusion status. For example, if the facts were such that Tia performed services with a determinable value for Grant, an unrelated individual, and Grant promised to pay her for them and did so prior to his death, this would result in compensation income to Tia (yes, we are using concepts from first-year contracts). The alternative situation, that the promised payment for her services came through Grant's will as a devise, does not change the character of the income to Tia. In other words, there is no magical exclusion merely because property or cash is received from a decedent. Having said that, statements of devises given as a "thank you" or "in appreciation of" or like sentiments, do not characterize the devise as a contract-based payment for services. Rather, as it most likely is the case in our question, such statements are more general statements of affection and appreciation, and absent more concrete evidence of a "bargained for" contractual situation, the devise is excludable pursuant to IRC § 102.

Answers (b), (c), and (d) are all incorrect because to some degree all of these answers incorrectly classify the excludable devise to Tia as income.

22. **The correct answer is (c).** While a taxpayer's cost is normally the starting point for determination of one's basis in property (IRC §§ 1011 and 1012), when property is received as a bequest/devise, as is the case here, there really is no "cost" to the taxpayer. The seemingly logical result of a zero basis is

neither desirable nor, thankfully, appropriate. IRC § 1014(a)(1) provides the *general* rule that the basis of property acquired from a decedent shall be the property's fair market value at the date of the decedent's death. Note that this *general* fair market value basis rule of IRC § 1014(a)(1) is commonly referred to as the "step-up" in basis for property received from a decedent. This is because we would like to think, or at least hope, that property has appreciated in the hands of the decedent and the testamentary beneficiary gets, as his or her basis, a new "higher" or "stepped-up" basis. For appreciated property, the general rule of this Code provision is a great tax savings device that effectively makes, for income tax purposes, the unrealized appreciation and gain in the decedent's hands evaporate. Utilizing this *general* rule of § 1014(a)(1) it would appear that Tia's basis in the XYZ shares received as a devise from her grandfather, Grant, would be their $50,000 fair market value at Grant's death.

Unfortunately, Tia innocently falls into a special provision designed to prevent a manipulation of basis among taxpayers in certain situations. For discussion purposes, let us assume that Tia did not transfer the stock to her grandfather with the hope that he would use it for his benefit. Rather, let us assume that she knew Grant would not live that long and that he would most likely devise, back to her, anything that she gave to him before his death. Looking at her meager $15,000 cost basis in the XYZ shares, she comes up with a rather morbid plan: give the shares to her dying grandfather and when she gets them back at his death (by devise or other similar means), voila, she has a "new and improved" "stepped-up" basis of $50,000. To prevent this sort of basis manipulation (yes, people actually do such things) IRC § 1014(e) was enacted. Basically, this provision says that if appreciated property was acquired by the decedent by gift within one year of his or her death, <u>and</u> the property (at the decedent's death) goes back to the donor who made the gift (or the donor's spouse), then the beneficiary is treated as receiving an inter vivos gift. The general basis rules for gifts result in a "carryover" basis. The result is that the original donor, trying to get a stepped-up basis, ends up having the same basis with which he or she started.

Now back to our situation. While Tia's gift to her grandfather hardly smells of such a devious plot to get a stepped-up basis in the shares, the gift to Grant was within one year of his death, and she did get the shares back at his death (by intestate succession). This special provision in IRC § 1014(e) is applied notwithstanding the motives behind Tia's transfer to Grant or the fact that Tia received the shares back through intestate succession. This provision does apply to Tia, and her basis in the XYZ shares received from Grant is $15,000 (her original cost).

Answer (a) is incorrect because, as discussed above, the general fair market value basis rule for property received from a decedent, does not apply to this set of facts. **Answer (b) is also incorrect.** When Tia made a gift of the shares to her grandfather, he took, as his basis, the carryover $15,000 basis from Tia (pursuant to the general gift rules of IRC § 1015). Grant's basis in the shares was not $40,000, the fair market value at the time of the gift. Since Tia takes Grant's basis on his death (because of the application of IRC § 1014(e) to these facts), her basis is $15,000. **Answer (d) is incorrect** because a correct response (c) is presented.

23. **The correct answer is (c).** IRC § 61 defines gross income as "all income from whatever source derived." From your initial study of gross income's scope, you probably found it to be broadly defined, including the taxpayer's receipt of some net economic benefit or net accession to wealth. In class, you also discover that gross income is also not limited to the receipt of cash. Is Jackie receiving net economic benefit from her corporation by its purchase of assets used by Jackie for personal purposes and its payment of her personal expenses? The answer is yes.

For assets purchased by the corporation that Jackie uses for personal purposes, she has <u>income</u> equal to the fair value of such use. For example, if her corporation purchases a house and she lives in it without paying rent to the corporation, she will have income equal to the fair rental value of the house. Similarly, if her corporation pays for her personal expenses, she will have <u>income</u> equal to the amount that her corporation paid on her behalf.

The confusion that surrounds this area is based on the belief that the corporation and the sole shareholder (and employee in this case) are really the same person. The concept of gross income for tax purposes does not go so far as to impute income to one's own use of assets. For example, when you live in your own house, you are <u>not</u> required to assign a fair rental value to such use and include it in your gross income for income tax purposes. In effect that is what many people believe to be the case in situations such as Jackie's. Sure, technically the corporation may own the assets and pay the bills, but since Jackie owns 100% of the corporation, isn't it merely Jackie paying for such things? Unfortunately for Jackie, the "technical" fact that the corporation and Jackie (the individual) are <u>two distinct entities</u>, is a distinction that is <u>not</u> ignored for income tax purposes. Jackie's wholly owned corporation *is* a person or entity that is separate and distinct from Jackie for income tax purposes. [See *Dean v. Comm'r*, 187 F.2d 1019 (3rd Cir.1951).] For purposes of this question, Jackie's corporation could just as well be any other corporation, one in which Jackie has no ownership interests. When an employer provides an employee with "in-kind" economic benefits, their value nonetheless represents income. [Reg. § 1.61-1(d).] While certain employer-provided "fringe benefits" are excludable from income, these excludable benefits do not include the non-work related personal items in this question.

Answer (a) is incorrect because Jackie will also have income associated with the personal-use of assets purchased (and owned) by the corporation. **Answer (b) is incorrect** for the reasons discussed above. **Answer (d) is incorrect** because the state of incorporation and domicile of its owner is irrelevant to the income tax consequences discussed here.

24. **The correct answer is (e).** The author apologizes for another of the dreaded "none of the above" answers. The Economic Growth and Tax Relief Reconciliation Act of 2001 (the "2001 Tax Act"), which was signed into law in 2001, made numerous changes in tax law. Added by the 2001 Tax Act are IRC §§ 132(a)(7) and 132(m), providing for a new excludable fringe benefit for employer provided retirement planning services. Absent some exclusion section, Marshall's receipt of this economic benefit would constitute gross income. [IRC § 61(a)(1).] IRC § 132 provides a host of excludable fringe benefits (many of which are explored elsewhere in this book). As indicated, the 2001 Tax Act added an excludable fringe benefit specifically covering the retirement related services that Marshall received in this question.

This excludable fringe benefit is defined in IRC § 132(m) and generally covers "any retirement planning advice or information provided to an employee and his spouse by an employer maintaining a qualified employer plan." [IRC § 132(m)(1).] Suffice it to say that the 401(k) plan in which Marshall is a participant, is a "qualified employer plan." The House Report explaining this new provision of the law states, in part, that; "[t]he exclusion is not limited to information regarding the qualified plan, and, thus, for example, applies to advice and information regarding retirement income planning for an individual and his or her spouse and how the employer's plan fits into the individual's overall retirement income plan. On the other hand, the exclusion does not apply to services that may be related to retirement planning, such as tax preparation, accounting, legal or brokerage services." [H.R. CONF. REP. 107-84.]

Similar to some, but not all, of the other fringe benefit exclusions listed in IRC § 132, this provision is subject to certain nondiscrimination rules (the availability cannot favor "highly compensated" employees). [IRC § 132(m)(2).] The retirement planning services provided by Marshall's employer is available on a nondiscriminatory basis and, therefore, the value of Marshall's retirement planning services that he received is excludable from gross income.

Answer (a) is not the best answer. Prior to enactment of this excludable fringe benefit, there was some thought that the employer provided retirement planning services might be excludable as a "de minimis" fringe benefit. Basically, excludable de minimis fringe benefits are property transfers and services provided to employees that are so small as to make accounting for them unreasonable or administratively impracticable." [IRC § 132(e).] The aforementioned House Report refers to this possibility. Indeed, services of relatively minor value could qualify as a de minimis fringe. However, services received that are of substantial value, as the $800 value of services that Marshall received in our question, would likely not qualify as a de minimis fringe benefit.

Answer (b) is close but, is also not the best answer. The retirement planning services that Marshall received might also be excludable under another Code provision: IRC § 127 educational assistance programs. Basically, if certain requirements are met, up to $5,250 of employer provided educational assistance can be excluded from an employee's gross income each year. The specific rules of this section are far beyond the scope of this problem and although the services provided to Marshall in this problem are not typical of those covered by this section, the exclusion under § 127 would, nonetheless, most likely be excludable. The aforementioned House Report also refers to the possible application of IRC § 127 to employer provided retirement planning advice. The reason why this answer (b) is not the best answer lies in the language of this answer: IRC § 127 is <u>not the only</u> statutory provision excluding the benefit Marshall received. In fact, the IRC § 132 fringe discussed above is more directly on point regarding the source of Marshall's exclusion.

Answer (c) is also not correct. The "working condition fringe" benefit is explained in IRC § 132(d). This excluded fringe benefit is basically any benefit paid for by the employer, that had the employee paid for it, would have given rise to an IRC § 162 business expense. A typical example of a working condition fringe is a law firm (employer) paying an associate lawyer's (employee) state bar association dues. This benefit would be excludable from the associate lawyer's gross income because such employee would have a qualifying IRC § 162 business expense had he or she paid such association dues. While deductions for business expenses are the source of other questions in this book, had Marshall paid for the retirement planning services himself, it probably would <u>not</u> have given rise to a valid business expense. Again, beyond the scope of this question, such a payment by Marshall probably would have given rise to an IRC § 212 investment related expense deduction. However, the working condition fringe exclusion does cover "would have been deductible expenses" pursuant to IRC § 212.

Answer (d) is not correct because, as discussed above, we have at least one exclusion section applicable to the retirement planning services that Marshall received.

25. **Answer (d) is correct.** Interest on debt obligations of the U.S. is, despite some common belief to the contrary, generally included in gross income for federal income tax purposes. U.S. Savings Bonds (Series EE) are U.S. obligations and the interest earned on them is also included in gross income, barring any specific exclusion thereof. There is a limited and rather narrow statutory exclusion provision regarding U.S. EE Savings Bond interest where the bond proceeds are used for certain education purposes. This is IRC § 135 and may apply to Abe depending on various factors discussed below.

The method and timing of reporting such interest for tax purposes is a bit different from typical interest-bearing instruments. United States Savings Bonds (Series EE) are issued in various "face amount" denominations (e.g. a $50 U.S. Savings Bond) but are purchased at a fraction of this face amount (usually at one-half the face amount). These bonds *do* pay interest, but not in the normal form of a stated interest rate on money invested (as with a savings account at a bank). Rather, the interest accrues on the original discounted purchase price. Traditionally, and much to the disappointment of many a young person who received a U.S. Savings Bond from his or her grandparent, the bond cannot be "cashed in" right away with the receipt of the face amount. One must wait many years until the bond "matures" to receive its face value. These years until the bond's maturity is the period when the interest accrues on the bond, bringing its value up from the original discounted purchase price to the face amount. This difference, therefore, represents interest, and it is taxable interest for U.S. income tax purposes.

Unless an individual affirmatively elects to report, as interest, the annual increases in such a bond's value, the recognition of interest is deferred until the bond matures (or is redeemed or otherwise disposed of sooner). [IRC § 454(a).] This deferred interest is all of the interest earned on the bond, which is measured by the difference between its face amount and its original discounted purchase price. One can "cash in" or redeem U.S. Savings Bonds prior to their maturity, as is the case with Abe in our problem. Of course, something less than the face value of the bond is received, but the difference between the amount received and the original discounted purchase price still represents taxable interest (at the time of redemption unless an election is made to report the annual accrued interest).

The use of the word "traditionally" earlier in this answer reflects a real-life change to how, and in what form, U.S. Savings Bonds are issued/sold. Beginning in 1935, pursuant to legislation signed into law by then President Franklin D Roosevelt, U.S. Savings Bonds (then only in $25 face/matured denominations) were issued/sold in paper form. Up through 2011, U.S. Savings Bonds could generally be purchased in paper form at most financial institutions (in varying denominations). The United States Treasury discontinued issuing the paper form of such bonds in 2012. Currently, U.S. Savings Bonds can still be purchased but must be done so online and in electronic form. An interesting interlude, but now back to our question.

IRC § 135 provides that if the proceeds from "qualified U.S. Savings Bonds" are used for "qualified higher education expenses" then the interest component of the proceeds will be excluded from the taxpayer's gross income as long as the taxpayer's income does not exceed certain levels. The term "qualified U.S. savings bonds means U.S. Series EE Savings Bonds issued after 1989, to an individual 24 years of age or older. [IRC § 135(c)(1).] The bonds that Abe redeemed meet this definition (and Abe purchased them when he was 26 years old).

IRC § 135 next requires that the proceeds of a qualifying bond be used for "qualified higher education expenses." Qualified higher education expenses means "tuition and fees for the enrollment or attendance of" the taxpayer, the taxpayer's spouse, or any dependent of the taxpayer (see IRC § 151 and other questions in this book) at an "eligible educational institution." *Eligible educational institutions* include most colleges, universities, community (junior) colleges, and vocational and nursing schools. [IRC § 135(c)(3).] Abe's vocational school tuition should qualify. It should be noted that the exclusion under IRC § 135 is based upon the full proceeds from the Bonds redeemed being used for qualifying expenses, and not merely the "interest" component of the bond proceeds. The statute allows for a potential pro-rata exclusion based upon the percentage of the bonds used for qualified purposes. [IRC § 135(b)(1).] While not applicable here, it should be noted that courses involving sports, games or hobbies do not qualify unless as part of a degree program. [IRC § 135(c)(2)(B).]

Unfortunately, the use of this IRC § 135 exclusion is limited for individuals whose adjusted gross income (AGI), as modified, exceeds a certain threshold amount. [IRC § 135(b)(2).] The level of AGI (as modified) at which this "phase-out" of the exclusion begins varies depending on one's filing status and changes every year (the thresholds are indexed for inflation). Our question does not involve dollar amounts, but for information purposes, the threshold level at which this phase-out begins is, for 2019, $81,100 for most single individuals, and $121,600 for most married individuals filing a joint return. The mechanism for the actual reduction of the exclusion is a bit complex, but the IRC § 135 exclusion is completely eliminated, in 2019, for taxpayer's with AGI (as modified) reaches $96,100 or $151,600 for single and joint filers, respectively.

Therefore, Abe may be entitled to exclude the otherwise taxable U.S. Savings Bond interest if he uses the entire proceeds from their redemption for his vocational school tuition, and his income is below the phase-out threshold applicable to him.

It should be noted that there are many other education-related benefits provided by the Code and there are numerous rules relating to their interaction that may affect anticipated benefits.

Answer (a) is incorrect because it fails to recognize the potential exclusion of this interest pursuant to IRC § 135. **Answer (b) is incorrect** because interest from obligations of the U.S. is generally taxable. **Answer (c) is incorrect** because full exclusion under IRC § 135 requires use of the full proceeds from the bond redemption for qualifying educational costs, not just the interest component of the bond proceeds. **Answer (e) is incorrect** because the IRC § 135 exclusion provision is not that restrictive.

ANSWER KEY
EXAM V

1. **The correct answer is (c).** Pursuant to IRC § 1011(a), the adjusted basis in property (hereinafter AB) is the "cost basis" of the property adjusted for certain items. The cost basis is, in most instances, simply the cost of the property. [IRC § 1012.] In the present case, the $400,000 Tom and Edna originally paid for the property four years ago represents their cost basis, the starting point for determining their AB, of the property. Adjustments increasing the basis of their property resulted from the major additions and improvements they made to the property. Similar to the purchase of their house, their AB in the house is increased by the $110,000 <u>cost</u> of such additions/improvements. [IRC § 1016(a); Reg. § 1.1016-2(a).] The resulting AB is, therefore, <u>$510,000</u> ($400,000 plus $110,000).

    The AB of property is important for many reasons including, as is ultimately the case in this series of questions, determining the amount of gain or (loss) resulting from a subsequent sale of the property. Because gain or (loss) is generally computed by subtracting the AB from the sales price (or amount realized, AR), the greater the AB, the lower the potential taxable gain (or greater the potential deductible loss) results. For "real-world" purposes, it is important, therefore, to keep track of improvements made to one's house and other property. This professor always suggests to students to keep a receipt box or drawer where one can toss receipts for home, or other property, related expenditures. The new patio cover, the landscaping project, the new kitchen fixtures, and the like are examples of expenditures that may increase one's AB in property. It is surprising how much of those weekend visits to the home improvement store can affect the AB in one's house or other property. While not pertinent to this question, issues can arise as to what constitutes an improvement versus expenditures for normal maintenance and repairs that do not increase the AB in property.

    Answer (a) is incorrect because it does not reflect the addition to the AB of the house resulting from the improvements. **Answer (b) is incorrect** because the increase to the house's AB is the cost of the improvements and not the increase in value because of the improvements (either more or less, as is the case here, than their cost). While not at issue in this question, there is one situation, where the cost of improvements is medically related, where the value added by the improvement is a factor. Please see other questions in this book dealing with that medical related issue. **Answer (d) is incorrect** because a correct answer (c) is presented.

2. **Answer (c) is the best response.** The couple's borrowing of the $110,000 does not, in and of itself, represent a taxable event. No income is realized

from borrowing money, as there is no net accession to wealth (a general prerequisite for income realization). [See *Comm'r v. Glenshaw Glass Co.*, 348 U.S. 426, 75 S.Ct. 473 (1955).] If borrowed funds are not repaid and the debt is discharged in whole or in part, then there is a net accession to wealth and, with some exceptions, income is recognized. This latter point, however, is not an issue in this question.

As for the deduction of interest paid on this $110,000 loan, we must turn to IRC § 163 dealing with deductions for interest paid. As discussed below, the interest the couple pays with respect to this loan is deductible "qualified residence" interest, with this entire loan deemed to be "acquisition indebtedness." A more thorough explanation follows.

IRC § 163(a) provides a simple and broad sounding deduction for interest stating, in part: "There shall be allowed as a deduction all interest paid . . . within the taxable year on indebtedness." This sounds **great** and by just reading this, students rejoice at the thought of deductions for future interest paid on, among other things, their student loans. Alas, the Tax Reform Act of 1986 introduced subsection (h), located quite some written distance from the general allowance for interest deductions of subsection (a). IRC § 163(h) starts out deceptively, and unfavorably, simple by stating, in part: "In the case of a taxpayer other than a corporation, no deduction shall be allowed . . . for personal interest paid . . . during the taxable year." The definition of "personal" interest, which is not deductible, is found in IRC § 163(h)(2) and takes the form of a negative definition; personal interest is interest "other than" those listed in subparagraphs (A) through (F). The key, therefore, to finding interest that is deductible, is to fit within one of these specified categories of what does not constitute nondeductible personal interest. One such category of interest that is not considered personal interest is "qualified residence interest." [IRC § 163(h)(2)(D).]

Qualified residence interest is addressed in IRC §§ 163(h)(3) and (h)(4). To obtain deductible qualified residence interest status, a taxpayer must have two things:
  ➤ A "qualified residence."
  ➤ The property type of indebtedness associated with such qualified residence.

A qualified residence includes the taxpayer's principal residence and one other residence (e.g., a vacation home) that meets certain requirements. [IRC § 163(h)(4)(A).] A principal residence can include the typical house (as our couple's in this question), a condominium, townhouse, co-op, etc. A principal residence can consist of a boat, trailer, motor home, or similar vehicle if, generally, they contain sleeping, eating and bathroom facilities.

While the determination of one's principal residence is usually not at issue for most people, there are (i.e., your professor can discuss) situations that present more of a challenge. The "one other residence" as a qualified residence for purposes of deductible qualified residence interest can present its own host of issues, some involving rather complex statutory rules. Some of these issues are presented in other questions in this book.

Ostensibly, there are two <u>proper types of indebtedness</u> recognized by the statute in this area: "acquisition indebtedness" and "home equity indebtedness." But be forewarned as things are not as they might first appear (the surprise has to do with the *home equity indebtedness* category, and it is not good news). We shall explain, below. It is important to recognize that the statute requires that <u>either of these two types of loans must be **secured** by the applicable qualified residence</u> in order to qualify. [IRC § 163(h)(3)(A).] The couple's loan, in our question, is secured by a qualified residence (their house).

<u>Acquisition indebtedness</u> is defined in IRC § 163(h)(3)(B), and is fairly straightforward for most taxpayers. Acquisition loans are money borrowed to **acquire, construct, or substantially improve** a qualified residence. Our couple's loan in this question was used to "substantially improve" their qualified residence (their house) and, therefore, constitutes <u>acquisition indebtedness</u>. While not at issue in this question, it should be noted that loans used to replace existing "acquisition indebtedness" (e.g., a straight refinancing), takes on the character of the loan being replaced and itself becomes acquisition indebtedness.

At this point, we are close to concluding the analysis of our facts. So far, the interest on Tom and Edna's $110,000 loan appears to be deductible under § 163 as qualified residence interest (their house as a qualified residence and the loan secured thereby qualifying as acquisition indebtedness). There is, however, one last issue to consider regarding the deduction of interest on *acquisition indebtedness*. An initial read of the statute, at IRC § 163(h)(3)(B)(ii) appears to place a $1 million cap on such loans, meaning that for acquisition loans, only the interest on the first $1 million of such loans is deductible. Again, we are just looking at what the law *appears* to be. This $1 million cap is on the amount of loans and <u>not</u> a much larger $1 million cap on deductible interest. Also, pursuant to the statute, it should also be noted that this $1 million acquisition indebtedness cap is in the aggregate (i.e., $1 million total for all acquisition loans for the principal and one other qualifying residence and not a $1 million cap for each acquisition loan, or a separate $1million acquisition loan cap for each of two possible qualifying residences). So why does this author keep qualifying what is being discussed (and what is in the statute)? One must look deeper into the section to IRC § 163(h)(3)(F) that was "tacked on" by the *Tax Cuts and Jobs Act*, or TCJA, signed into law in

December 2017 and effective, here, for years 2018 through 2025. A new, lower, aggregate cap of $750,000 replaces the $1 million cap for most acquisition debt loans obtained after 2017. While acquisition debt loans originated before 2017 generally retain the $1 million cap, later acquisition loans have this lower limit (again, it is the amount of the loan for which interest is paid and not the amount of interest paid). This two-tiered cap can create a very messy situation for some individuals (with old and new loans). This is not at issue in our questions. Tom and Edna have no problem with this acquisition debt limit in our facts as the $110,000, given as their only loan, is well below the $750,000 cap for such loans. It follows that all of the interest our couple pays on this loan is deductible qualified residence interest. [We are, of course, assuming that this property is the couple's only *qualified residence.*]

Home equity indebtedness is not at issue in this question, but is addressed here to better understand the subject, and to clear up any confusion that might exist regarding Tom and Edna's loan in this question. For now, let's just go with the code and see where it takes us (again, be forewarned that things are not as they may seem and, to some degree, we are going through an exercise in futility). Home equity indebtedness is defined in IRC § 163(h)(3)(C) and, typically, is money borrowed against an existing qualified residence (secured by the qualified residence) that is used for purposes other than substantial improvements to the qualified residence. Advertisements for "tapping the equity" in one's house to buy a new car or boat, go on a vacation, pay off credit card debts, student loans or consolidate all those existing bills, strike at the center of what "home equity indebtedness" is all about. From the statute, it appears that borrowing money, using your house, for such things as buying a car can generate deductible interest while interest paid on a regular car loan from a bank, credit union or automotive financing companies will generally be nondeductible "personal" interest.

Again, sticking with the statute, a *home equity indebtedness* requirement (in addition that it must be secured by the qualifying residence) is that such loan amount cannot exceed the "equity" in the qualified residence. "Equity" is the one figure of which most homeowners are constantly aware. Equity is the difference between the value of the home and the amount of outstanding loans with respect to the home. Say, for example, you own a home worth $350,000, and you have an outstanding first mortgage (acquisition debt) of $150,000. Your "equity" in the home is $200,000. This is the amount or value of your home that you really own – how much you would expect to "pocket in cash" upon selling (after the debt is paid off).

Hold on, we are almost done with our analysis of *home equity indebtedness.* For now, we shall continue with the statute and pursuant thereto [see IRC

§163(h)(3)(C)], it places a cap on the total amount of home equity indebtedness for which, ostensibly, interest paid thereon, is deductible. This statutory limit is $100,000 of home equity debt and, similar to acquisition debt discussed above, this is cap for the aggregate of all home equity debt. While Tom and Edna in our question have no *home equity indebtedness,* it is important to carry on with our discussion for future reference. There is danger in not reading the full statute because this area of the law, deductibility of interest on *home equity indebtedness* has been dramatically altered by the *Tax Cuts and Jobs Act* (TCJA) signed into law in December 2017. Here comes the letdown for affected taxpayers. The TCJA tacked on a new section, IRC § 163(h)(3)(F), that **totally eliminates** any deduction of interest on *home equity indebtedness* for years 2018 through 2025. [See, specifically, IRC §163(h)(3)(F)(i)(I)].

While not at issue in our question, it should be noted that the TCJA's elimination of interest deductions on qualified home equity debt applies irrespective of when such debt originated. It came as a "rude awakening" for taxpayers with pre-2018 home equity who, beginning in 2018, were no longer entitled to deduct interest on such loans even though they were entitled to do so in prior years.

A home equity loan, a second mortgage, the cash portion of a cash-out refinance, a home equity-based line of credit typically characterize home equity indebtedness. Be careful here because, as we saw above in our couple's case, the fact that money is borrowed using the equity in a qualified residence as security does not, thankfully, necessarily render the loan as home equity indebtedness. If the borrowed funds are used to substantially improve the qualified residence, the loan is characterized as more favorable *acquisition indebtedness.* Do not be fooled by language used to describe the facts of a loan. Tom and Edna's loan was, for loan description purposes, a home equity loan. However, such classification for tax purposes would have invoked the new TCJA total elimination of any deductions for interest paid on the loan. As mentioned, for tax purposes their loan is considered acquisition indebtedness (with interest deductible in full as their aggregate *acquisition indebtedness* loans do not exceed the new, lower, statutory $750,000 cap).

It should be noted that there are special rules applicable to loans incurred before October 14, 1987. [IRC § 163(h)(3)(D).]

Answers (a) and (d) are incorrect because the initial statement in these answers, that the $110,000 borrowed represents income, is incorrect. **Answer (b) is incorrect** because it incorrectly characterized the couple's loan as "home equity indebtedness" and also incorrectly, imposes the pre-TCJA $100,000 cap applicable on such loans. **Answer (e) is also incorrect.**

It correctly reflects the TCJA's impact for *home equity indebtedness* and the non-deductibility of interest, but our couple's loan is not *acquisition indebtedness* and is, as discussed above, treated differently (allowing the deduction of interest).

3. **Answer (e) is correct.** Students universally dislike "none of the above" answers and are justified in doing so. They do provide, however, a powerful testing tool for professors and, in this case, none of the answers provided in (a) through (d) are correct. This question is a bit unfair, as its analysis requires a correct answer to question 1, above. This professor would not ask such a series of interrelated multiple-choice questions on an exam. Rather, this series of questions was derived from an exam essay question. The "bottom line" correct numeric answer for this question is that Tom realizes a $130,000 loss from the sale of the house, but this loss is <u>not</u> recognized (i.e., the loss results in no income tax benefit to Tom).

    This is a good example of a question that, to a student studying income tax, may appear to exist purely as an academic exercise. While it does contain aspects that present an academic challenge, this question reflects a surprisingly common "real world" tax situation.

    In every fact pattern in which something is sold (or otherwise disposed of), the author likes to go through the following analysis; always ask these three questions:

    1) Does the sale (or disposition) result in a <u>realized</u> gain or loss and if so, what is the <u>amount</u>? This is computing the amount of gain (or loss). It is the AR (amount realized) less one's AB (adjusted basis).

    2) If we have a <u>realized</u> gain or loss, is it <u>recognized</u> (i.e. reportable for income tax purposes)? As a taxpayer, you would like the answer to be NO for gains; I do not want to recognize, report, the gain (said another way, I'd like to be able to exclude this gain from my income).

    3) If the gain or loss is recognized, is it accorded "capital" gain or loss treatment? This is primarily the issue of "capital gains (or losses)" that are treated differently for income tax purposes.

    Because this question involves a multi-step analysis and because the author recognizes the value of your time, both **abbreviated/short** and **comprehensive/long** analyses are provided below.

    The <u>abbreviated/short</u> version of the analysis for this question is that Tom's realized loss is the difference between the $380,000 sales price and his basis in the house of $510,000, or <u>$130,000</u>. His basis in the house is a $510,000 carryover basis from his and Edna's basis (the $400,000 purchase price increased by the $110,000 of additions/improvements) because he received the house (his and Edna's share) "incident to their divorce." [See IRC § 1041.] Tom's loss is <u>not</u> recognized pursuant to IRC § 165(c) as the house was used for personal purposes. Since Tom's loss is not recognized, its characterization as a "capital loss" is neither relevant nor appropriate.

The following <u>comprehensive/long</u> (very long) analysis presents a step-by-step discussion of the answer to this question that can be applied to other gain/loss questions.

The first step is determining whether Tom has a <u>realized</u> gain or loss on the sale of the house. For this, we need two basic components: his sales price ("amount realized" or, hereinafter, AR) and his basis in the shares ("adjusted basis or, hereinafter, AB). The difference between the two represents a <u>realized</u> gain or loss. [IRC § 1001(a).] Each of these two components, AR and AB, can present a variety of complex tax issues for exam and real-world tax purposes. The AR side is straightforward in our question and is his $380,000 sales price. Other questions in this book present more complex issues involving a taxpayer's AR.

The AB component is slightly more difficult to derive in this question. The general starting place for determining one's AB is one's cost. [IRC §§ 1011 and 1012.] Our starting point is what Tom and Edna paid for the house four years ago. The $400,000 Tom and Edna originally paid for the property represents their cost basis. As previously discussed, adjustments increasing the basis of their property resulted from the major additions and improvements they made to the property. Similar to the purchase of their house, their AB in the house is increased by the $110,000 <u>cost</u> of such additions/improvements. [IRC § 1016(a); Reg. § 1.1016-2(a).] The resulting AB is, therefore, <u>$510,000</u> ($400,000 plus $110,000). In this question, Tom ends up owning 100% of the house when Edna's interest is transferred to him two years ago pursuant to their divorce decree. While the question does not state the form of title in which Tom and Edna held the house nor the respective interests Tom and Edna had in the house while married, such information is not particularly relevant, as discussed below. We do know that Tom was awarded the entire house by the divorce decree, and it is relevant that Tom received Edna's interest in the manner in which he did (pursuant to the divorce decree).

IRC § 1041 provides, in part, special rules for determining the AB in property that is transferred between former spouses. If such transfer between former spouses is considered a transfer "incident to divorce," then the transferee ex-spouse takes a carryover AB from the transferor ex-spouse. [IRC § 1041(b).] This section does not distinguish as to the type of inter vivos transfer involved; it covers gifts, sales, exchanges, etc. In our question, we have only one transfer potentially subject to this special AB rule: the awarding of the house to Tom at the time of their divorce two years ago. Specifically, the issue is whether Tom's receipt of the house (whatever Edna's interest was in the house) is "incident to divorce" resulting in a carryover AB of $510,000. A transfer "incident to divorce" has a statutory definition as being either 1) <u>any</u> transfer within one year of the divorce, or 2) a transfer "relating to the cessation of the marriage." [See IRC § 1041(c).] Temporary regulations define transfers that are considered "relating to the cessation of the marriage" as a transfer provided for by a "divorce or separation instrument" and is transferred, pursuant to this instrument, within six years of the divorce. [Temp.Reg. § 1.1041-1T(b) Q & A-7.] It is fairly easy to see that Tom's AB in the house is governed by IRC § 1041. The transfer of the house to him was clearly "incident to divorce" (he received all of the house not only within one year of the divorce, but also pursuant to the decree and within six years of the divorce). Tom's AB in the house, therefore, is a carryover from the couple's AB of $510,000. [Please see other questions in this book addressing other aspects of IRC § 1041 and more complex issues relating thereto.]

Having determined Tom's AB to be $510,000, it is easy to compute his realized gain or loss: AR (selling price) of $380,000 less his AB of $510,000 resulting in a realized <u>loss</u> of $130,000.

Now to the second step of our gain/loss analysis: whether Tom's $130,000 loss is recognized. IRC § 1001(c) provides that, unless otherwise indicated in the Code, all realized gains and losses are recognized. This would cement the recognition of Tom's loss if it were not for an "otherwise indicated" Code section, namely IRC § 165. At first glance, the "general rule" in IRC § 165(a) looks to be in Tom's favor allowing a deduction for "any loss sustained during the taxable year . . . ." Reading further at IRC § 165(c) we come across an ominous sounding subsection: "Limitation on losses of individuals." In class, this professor refers to this as the "section 165(c) hoop," complete with graphic depictions on the board/slides. Figuratively, the goal is to jump from the "realized" loss side, through the hoop to the land of "recognized" losses. This hoop, however, is more akin to a **semi-permeable membrane** than an unobstructed open space. [Ha! Who would think we'd ever use the phrase *semipermeable membrane* in law school, let alone in a tax class?] We see, in IRC §§ 165(c)(1)-(c)(3), that business losses, investment losses and personal-use "casualty" losses, break on through to the recognized loss side. By default, however, losses from personal-use assets (other than casualty losses) do not make it through this "section 165(c) hoop" and go unrecognized. [To complete the *semipermeable membrane* analogy, their molecular size is too large to pass through to the land of *recognition.*] This explains why, for example, when you sell your personal-use car for a loss (which is almost always the case), the loss is realized but not recognized; i.e., you get no tax benefit from such a loss.

This, then, brings us to poor Tom. Oh, the facts sound good: "[t]hey bought the house strictly for investment purposes" fully intending to either sell it or rent it after they made their additions/improvements. And that Tom, after the divorce, was still hoping that the house would "prove to be a good investment." These facts represent a very common misconception about personal residences vis-à-vis their "investment" status for loss recognition. Tom's (and the couple's) use of the house as their personal residence relegates it to a personal-use asset, notwithstanding the magnitude or conviction of their investment intentions. We are left, therefore, with a realized loss from the sale of a personal-use asset that, by definition, is not a recognized loss. And, unfortunately for Tom, this is where the answer ends.

Students are often bothered by the lack of symmetry in that gains from the sale of personal-use assets <u>are</u> recognized (must be included in income unless a specific exclusion provision is applicable) but losses from the sale of such assets are not recognized (no tax benefit for these losses). Unfortunately, income tax laws are not always fair.

Here is a copy of the slide (albeit without some cool animation and colors better depicting the semipermeable membrane) that this professor uses in class for a visual representation of IRC § 165(c).

The §165(c) Hoop

Answer (a) is incorrect because Tom's $130,000 loss is <u>not</u> recognized. Characterization of the loss as either a long-term or short-term capital loss is neither relevant nor appropriate. There is often some confusion with respect to this as Tom's house meets the definition of a capital asset. [IRC § 1221 (capital assets are generally, by definitional default, investment or personal-use assets).] If Tom's house is a capital asset, which it is, then why isn't the loss on the sale thereof a capital loss? The answer to this can be found in the definition of capital losses in IRC §§ 1222(2) or 1222(4). Capital losses are losses from the sale or exchange of a capital asset "if and to the extent that such loss is taken into account in computing taxable income." We hit the IRC § 165(c) barrier with respect to personal-use assets and losses resulting from their sale or exchange which are <u>not</u> taken into account when computing taxable income. In class, this professor stresses to students the importance of going "step-by-step" through the above discussed three prong analysis whenever an asset is sold (or exchanged). Students often run into trouble when losses are at issue and they leapfrog over the "recognition" step two.

Answer (b) is incorrect because it utilizes an incorrect AB (the fair market value of the property at the time of their divorce) in determining Tom's gain or loss. **Answer (c) is incorrect** because Tom does realize a loss on the sale of the house. **Answer (d) is incorrect** because Tom's loss is <u>not</u> recognized.

4. **Answer (d) is correct.** Compensation need not be paid in cash to be considered income. When an employee receives property, it will be, barring any exclusion, included in the employee's gross income measured by the value of the property received. [Reg. § 1.61-1(d) (compensation received in forms other than in cash).] On the surface the employees in this question (other than Todd at this point) each have income of $20,000, the value of the commemorative plate received. This, we will see, ends up being the correct answer. For tax purposes, this is equivalent to each employee receiving a cash bonus of $20,000, and then having them turn around and buying this plate for $20,000 (this analogy will be useful for later questions). **This eliminates response (a) as a correct answer** as compensation need not be in the form of cash.

The next logical question to ask is whether any provision in the Code would apply to exclude, from income, the plate received. Foraging through the "fringe benefit" exclusions of IRC § 132, one might try to apply the exclusion for "de minimis" benefits. However, that exclusion requires that the value of the property (or service) received by the employee be "so small as to make accounting for it unreasonable or administratively impracticable." Commemorative plates worth $20,000 each hardly qualify. **This eliminates response (c) as a correct answer.**

If you have studied the IRC § 102 exclusion for gifts, bequests and devises, that might be the next logical place to look for a potential exclusion for the receipt of the commemorative plates. Unfortunately, The Tax Reform Act of 1986 essentially eliminated that possibility here by enacting IRC § 102(c). This subsection provides, in general, that the possible exclusion from gross income of property acquired by gift, bequest or devise, does <u>not</u> apply to transfers between employers and employees. In other words, "gifts" to employees are not excludable from gross income under IRC § 102. This subsection is not merely a presumption. Thus, "gifts" to employees are not excludable by this section even if the employer can show that the gift was made out of "detached and disinterested generosity," the general standard for defining a gift for this section. **This eliminates response (b) as a correct answer.**

As mentioned above, the <u>value</u> of property received by an employee represents compensation income. Each employee (not considering Todd at this point) therefore has income of $20,000. **Response (e) is incorrect** because while the reason for inclusion in income is correct, it is incorrect as to the amount of income includible in gross income.

5. **Answer (a) is correct.** Borrowing from the analysis of the answer to question 4, above, we came to the conclusion that each employee has compensation income of $20,000 resulting from the receipt of the commemorative plate. How then, you might ask, could the answer to this question possibly be any different? In our problem, the answer <u>is</u> the same, and Todd also has $20,000 of income in the form of compensation. But this question does bring up an important issue that requires discussion, if only to rule out other possible answers.

For discussion purposes and totally divorced from the facts of our question, suppose a parent employs a child. Let us further suppose that the employer (parent) makes no gifts to any employees but on the child's 25th birthday, the parent gives the child a new automobile. In the familial context, we have a parent making a gift to a child most likely out of emotions of detached and disinterested generosity, qualifying it for exclusion from income to the child pursuant to IRC § 102(a). However, we also factually have an employer making a gift to an employee that, pursuant to the language in IRC § 102(c), cannot be considered an excludable gift to the employee. Does this preclude any gifts, in the traditional and excludable sense, when the donor and donee happen to have an employment relationship such as this? The proposed regulations answer this question as follows: "For purposes of section 102(c), *extraordinary* transfers to the natural objects of an employer's bounty will *not be considered transfers to, or for the benefit of, an employee if the employee can show that the transfer was not made in recognition of the employee's employment. Accordingly, section 102(c) shall not apply to amounts transferred between related parties (e.g., father and son) if the purpose of the transfer can be substantially attributed to the familial relationship of the parties and not to the circumstances of their employment."* [Prop.Reg. § 1.102-1(f)(2) (emphasis added).] In the hypothetical presented in this paragraph, the parent's gift of the car to the child is, in all likelihood, an example of an excludable gift notwithstanding the employment relationship between the two.

Now back to the facts of the question presented. While Todd is the "natural object" of his mother's "bounty" (using the somewhat odd vernacular of the regulations), it would be an unreasonable application of this regulation exception to the facts given. The transfer was not "extraordinary" when compared to every other employee; the "gift" to Todd was identical to the "gift" made to every employee. Similarly, the fact that everyone received the same "gift" would make it extremely unlikely that Todd would be able to show that the gift was attributable to the familial relationship with his mother and not in the employment context. One must examine this familial gift in relation to the employment gifts. Because they are identical, then Todd's gift would fall within the "non-exclusion" provisions of IRC § 102(c).

Answer (b) is incorrect because income to Todd is measured by the $20,000 value of the property received, and not the employer's cost. **Answer (c) is incorrect** based on the above discussion. **Answer (d) is incorrect.** While he is treated like other employees, he, and the other employees, each have $20,000 of gross income from the "gift."

6. **The correct answer is (b).** This is a basic gain calculation with a slight twist. When Marcia sells the commemorative plate, she realizes a gain or loss measured by the difference between the sales price (or in tax terms: the amount realized or AR) and her adjusted basis (AB) in the property. [IRC § 1001(a).] The amount realized (AR) portion of the equation in this problem is simply the $23,000 sales price for the plate. The key component to this question is the determination of Marcia's adjusted basis in the property. We will conclude, below, that $20,000 will be her adjusted basis in the commemorative plate, thus resulting in a realized gain of $3,000.

A taxpayer's cost is normally the starting point for determining one's basis in property. [IRC §§ 1011 and 1012.] Here, while it is a bit obscured, Marcia paid $20,000 for the commemorative plate. From the analysis of the correct answer to question 4, above, we know that Marcia had $20,000 in income, in the form of compensation, upon receipt of the plate (income equal to the value of the property received). At this point, it might be helpful to recast, or view in a different light, the transaction of receiving the plate. In effect, we could view this as equivalent to Marcia receiving a cash bonus of $20,000, and then turning around and purchasing the commemorative plate for $20,000. The end result is the same, Marcia with the plate, but breaking the transaction down this way may make it easier to see the component parts. As we said, she had compensation of $20,000 and we can also see that she paid $20,000 for the commemorative plate (her resulting AB in the property). This concept in determining Marcia's basis in property received as compensation is sometimes referred to as her "tax cost" and is described, albeit in a somewhat cryptic fashion, in the regulations at Reg. § 1.61-2(d)(2)(i).

The gain calculation is now easy to accomplish. The $23,000 sales price (AR) less her $20,000 basis (AB) results in a realized gain of $3,000.

Answers (a) and (c) are incorrect because Marcia's adjusted basis (AB) as stated in both of these answers is incorrect, resulting in an incorrect gain calculation. **Answer (d) is incorrect** because Marcia's subsequent sale of the commemorative plate is a separate transaction from the receipt of the plate (which, is also incorrectly stated in this answer).

7.   **Answer (c) is correct.** Gains that are "realized," as was Marcia's gain from her sale of the plate, are also "recognized" (or reported as income for tax purposes) unless there is some specific non-recognition or exclusion Code provision. [IRC § 1001(c).] No such non-recognition or exclusion section exists with respect to our facts. Further, the gain is a "capital" gain as Marcia held the commemorative plate for investment purposes (rendering it a capital asset). [IRC § 1221(a).] Lastly, Marcia's capital gain from the sale of the plate is a "short-term" capital gain because she did not hold the property for more than one year. [See IRC § 1222.] She received it (in effect purchased it) in January of this year and sold it in March of the same year.

     Answer (a) is incorrect because, as discussed in question 6, above, her sale of the commemorative plate did result in a gain. **Answers (b) is not correct** because she did not hold the property for the requisite length of time. **Answer (d) is incorrect** because there is no "non-recognition" or gain exclusion Code provision applicable to the facts presented in this question.

8.   **The answer that is most likely correct is (d).** This is a difficult question and the author recognizes that there may be some disagreement as to the "most likely" answer. Todd's sale of his plate for $14,000, results in a "realized" loss to him of $6,000. As discussed in the analysis of question 6, above, this is derived from the difference between the selling price (AR) and his basis (AB). Unlike Marcia, however, Todd's sale resulted in a loss. It is

with the "recognition" of this loss (something that Todd would like to do as it would have the same effect as a deduction) where issues arise.

As previously mentioned, IRC § 1001(c) provides that, unless otherwise indicated in the Code, all realized gains and losses are recognized. This would cement the recognition of Todd's loss if it were not for an "otherwise indicated" Code section, namely IRC § 165. At first glance, the "general rule" in IRC § 165(a) looks to be in Todd's favor allowing a deduction for "any loss sustained during the taxable year . . ." Reading further at IRC § 165(c) we come across an ominous sounding subsection: "Limitation on losses of individuals." In class, this professor refers to this as the "section 165(c) hoop," complete with graphic depictions on the board/slides. Figuratively, the goal is to jump from the "realized" loss side, through the hoop to the land of "recognized" losses. This hoop, however, is more akin to a **semi-permeable membrane** than an unobstructed open space. [Ha! Who would think we'd ever use the phrase *semipermeable membrane* in law school, let alone in a tax class?] We see, in IRC §§ 165(c)(1)-(c)(3), that business losses, investment losses and personal-use "casualty" losses, break on through to the recognized loss side. By default, however, losses from personal-use assets (other than casualty losses) do not make it through this "section 165(c) hoop" and go unrecognized. [To complete the *semipermeable membrane* analogy, their molecular size is too large to pass through to the land of *recognition*.] This explains why, for example, when you sell your personal-use car for a loss (which is almost always the case), the loss is realized but not recognized – i.e., you get no tax benefit from such a loss.

This, then, brings us to poor Todd. The facts of this question indicated that once he received his commemorative plate, he rather foolishly used it for everyday dinnerware, not the sort of behavior one associates with holding property for investment purposes. In an attempt to solidify his use as personal, the facts also indicated that he did not treat the plate as an investment. We are left, therefore, with a realized loss from the sale of a personal-use asset which, by definition, is not a recognized loss.

Here is a copy of the slide (albeit without some cool animation and colors better depicting the semipermeable membrane) that this professor uses in class for a visual representation of IRC § 165(c).

The §165(c) Hoop

While the author believes (d) is the most likely result, a possible argument can be made that personal-use of an asset and holding an asset for investment purposes are not mutually exclusive. Perhaps Todd could consider the commemorative plate as an investment asset notwithstanding his use of it as every day dinnerware. This is, however, a weak argument. It is basically the same argument used when an individual sells a principal residence for a loss and attempts to recognize the loss claiming that the house was purchased primarily with investment intentions. Use of the house as a personal residence, however, trumps any investment intention, and the law is clear that a loss realized from the sale thereof is not recognized. Another example the author uses in class to illustrate this issue is where someone, usually a spouse, attempts to justify to someone else, usually the other spouse, the purchase of an expensive automobile (e.g., a Porsche) as a good "investment" even though it will be used for everyday personal driving. Later, if the car is sold for a loss, it too will not be recognized (no deduction for the loss) despite claims that it was purchased as an investment. **Answer (b) is not the most likely answer** but, as discussed above, is a close second.

Students are often bothered by the lack of symmetry in that gains from the sale of personal-use assets <u>are</u> recognized (must be included in income unless a specific exclusion provision applies) but losses from the sale of such assets are not recognized (no tax benefit for these losses). Unfortunately, income tax laws are not always fair.

Answers (a) and (c) are incorrect because Todd does not have a realized gain from the sale of the commemorative plate. **Answer (e) is incorrect** because Todd does have a realized loss from the sale of the property. This answer (e), however, is a fairly popular selection, perhaps being confused with the sale of property that had been received as a gift that, in certain fact patterns, result in no gain or loss realization.

9.   **Answer (d) is the best answer.** To properly determine whether Mark realizes a gain on the transfer of the property to Brian, we need to know two things: Mark's adjusted basis (AB) in the property, and the amount of the loan on the property.

A gift of property generally does not result in realization of gain or loss to a donor. However, under certain circumstances (i.e., if a donor receives "consideration"), a gift may in fact constitute a "part sale/part gift" with a resulting realization of gain. In a part sale/part gift situation, gain is realized to the extent the consideration received (amount realized" or hereinafter AR) by the donor exceeds the donor's basis ("adjusted basis" or hereinafter AB) in the property. [Reg. § 1.1001-1(e).] This is consistent with the general principals of IRC § 1001(a); the difference between the AR and AB represents <u>realized</u> gain or loss. When Mark makes the gift to Brian, Mark does not have an AR in the traditional sense such as in a sale of property. However, Mark is deemed to have received consideration (an AR) for income tax purposes. Pursuant to *Crane v. Commissioner* (331 U.S. 1, 67 S.Ct. 1047 (1947)), a liability associated with transferred property is considered an amount realized even when a transferee merely takes property "subject to" a mortgage. It is irrelevant, here, whether or not Mark was personally liable for the loan (i.e., for this fact pattern, it does not matter whether Mark's loan was "recourse" or "nonrecourse"). Additionally, when the transferee of property takes it "subject to" the loan (or "assumes" it for that matter) the AR includes the full amount of the loan regardless of the property's fair market value (even if the property is worth less than the amount of mortgage). [See *Comm'r v. Tufts* 461 U.S. 300, 103 S.Ct. 1826 (1983).] Therefore, while this appears to be just a gift, it is, in reality, a part sale/part gift situation with Mark deemed to have received consideration (AR) equal to the amount of the loan taken "subject to" by Brian.

To determine if Mark has a realized gain from this transfer to Brian, we do need to know his AB in the property transferred. As mentioned above, if the loan amount (the consideration received by Mark or his AR) exceeds his AB in the property, a realized gain will result. Therefore, the items that we need to make this determination are only items I and III: Mark's adjusted basis in the property and the amount of the loan, respectively.

Answers (a) and (b) are incorrect because both answers include, to different degrees, components that are not necessary for purposes of determining Mark's realized gain, if any. **Answer (c) is incorrect** because it does not contain one of the critical components (the amount of the loan being taken "subject to" by Brian) for purposes of determining Mark's realized gain, if any. **Answer (e) is incorrect** because the correct answer (d) presented.

10. **Answer (e) is correct.** This question, unfortunately, requires, in part, a correct analysis of the previous question. This professor would not ask such a combination of interrelated multiple-choice questions on an actual exam. This question is presented here, however, to reinforce understanding of the subject. Brian has no income as a result of receiving the property from his brother Mark. Brian's adjusted basis (AB) in the property is equal to the greater of Mark's AB in the property at the time of the gift, or the amount of the loan to which Brian took the property "subject to."

As discussed in the analysis of question 9, above, the "gift" to Brian was actually a part sale/part gift situation. The transfer was in part a sale because Brian was deemed to provide consideration, as discussed below, in the form of taking the property subject to the mortgage. The transfer was also, in part, a gift because the consideration paid (the amount of the loan) was given in the facts to be less than the value of the property. As for the true "gift" element of this transaction, Brian does <u>not</u> have to include it (or any amount) in his gross income. While it is true that "gross income" is broadly defined, gifts made out of detached and disinterested generosity are generally excludable from gross income under IRC § 102 (general exclusion for gifts, bequests, devises and inheritances). Mark's gift to Brian (of the portion considered to be a gift) would most likely be excluded from Brian's gross income.

As for Brian's resulting basis in the real property, because this was a "part sale/part gift" transaction, there are two basis (or adjusted basis hereinafter AB) rules that logically could apply: those for a gift and those for a sale (or purchase with respect to Brian). In such part sale/part gift situations, the resulting transferee's AB is the <u>greater</u> of: (1) the amount paid by the donee, or (2) the donor's AB at the time of the gift. [Reg. 1.1015-4(a) (the greater of these two is also increased for any gift tax paid adjustment – this is not present here).] While in this question, Brian did not pay any monies to Mark to acquire the house, the aforementioned *Crane* case also stands for the proposition that a mortgage loan taken "subject to" by a transferee is deemed consideration paid. [See *Crane v. Comm'r* (331 U.S. 1, 67 S.Ct. 1047 (1947).] The amount of the loan to which Brian took the property "subject to," therefore, represents the amount paid for purposes of determining AB. Therefore, Brian's AB is equal to the greater of his brother Mark's AB in the property at the time of the gift, or the amount of the loan to which he took the property "subject to."

Answers (a) and (b) are incorrect because the only part of this transaction which could be considered income to Brian, represents an excludable gift. Answers (c) and (d) are not the best answers. While both answers correctly reflect the exclusion from Brian's gross income of the gift, they do not adequately reflect the correct method for determining Brian's basis in the property received. Had this question provided numbers for Mark's AB in the property and the amount of the loan to which Brian took the property "subject to," one of these answers, depending on the numbers, would be correct.

11. **Answer (a) is correct.** We have some encouraging words for poor Dan. Your broken heart will eventually heal and forget about the ring and the car; there are more important things in life. Okay, the author will stick to income tax issues. Here, unfortunately, we do not have any good news for Dan. The answer to this question in prior editions of this book was very different and once again we see the common thread of some detrimental changes to tax law made pursuant to the *Tax Cuts and Jobs Act* (TCJA) signed into law in December 2017 (generally effective beginning in 2018). We will conclude, below, that while both of Dan's losses (the theft and the "unusual" automobile mishap) are designated as "casualty losses," the TCJA has severely limited any corresponding tax deduction to specific situations (none of which will apply to Dan). The result will be that Dan receives no tax benefit from either of these losses. In earlier editions of this book, and prior to the TCJA, Dan may have been entitled to tax deductions from the two unfortunate events.

Our analysis will be somewhat tedious as we do have to cover relevant law that, ultimately, will not give rise to any tax benefit for Dan. We begin with IRC § 165 as that is the primary section at issue in this question. Individuals suffering a "casualty loss" may be entitled to some deduction (much less so after passage of the TCJA) even if the property involved is of a personal-use nature (as is the case with Dan's property losses). [IRC § 165(h).] A *casualty loss* for personal-use property (property not used in a business or investment activity) is one that occurs from "fire, storm, shipwreck, or other casualty, or from theft." [IRC § 165(c)(3).] The loss must have resulted from some sudden, unexpected, or unusual cause. The theft of Dan's ring, as well as the loss of his car, represent classic examples of casualty losses (although not under conditions as unique as Dan's situation).

We continue with the law that will, until we get to the end of our analysis, sound encouraging, tax-wise, for Dan. Basically, the law that remains unchanged by the TCJA until we get to a huge "let-down" a bit later. The measurement of the loss for *casualty loss* purposes is prescribed by the regulations. For thefts of personal-use property, the loss is the lesser of: 1) the property's basis (adjusted basis or AB) of the property immediately before the theft, or 2) the fair market value of the property immediately before the theft. [Reg. §§ 1.165-7(b) and 1.165-8(c).] Either amount is reduced by any compensation from insurance or otherwise. For Dan, the ring was worth $30,000 at the time of the theft (which was the same as what he paid for it), so the amount of his *casualty loss* will be $30,000 (since his cost and its value at the time of the theft were the same, the "lower" of the two is also the same). He received no compensation from insurance or other sources. So far, this still sounds like Dan may be entitled to some tax benefit for his loss but, alas, we are far from done.

Similarly, for other casualties involving personal-use property, the loss is also the lesser of: 1) the property's AB immediately before the casualty, or 2) the property's fair market value immediately before the casualty. [Reg. § 1.165-7(b).] For property that is totally destroyed, such as in Dan's car, either amount must be reduced by any salvage value, insurance proceeds or other amounts received on account of the loss. Dan's car was a total loss having no salvage value and he received no compensation for this loss from insurance or other sources. Comparing his $40,000 AB in the car with its $35,000 fair market value at the time of the incident, the amount of his *casualty loss* will be the lower $35,000 (its fair market value). Again, so far, this still sounds like Dan may at least get some tax relief from this mishap.

At this point, we have correctly concluded that Dan has suffered "casualty losses" from the theft and the destruction of his car. We shall move on and continue our analysis of the statute to determine how, if at all, Dan may benefit, tax-wise, from these casualty losses. Be forewarned that our analysis will follow the statutory framework of IRC § 165 casualty losses as to how we compute any allowable deduction but in proceeding in this manner, it may be a bit misleading until we hit a huge roadblock at the end.

Per IRC § 165, once the amount of one's *casualty loss* is determined (see our above analysis) an individual's prima facie deduction is initially limited in two ways (we'll see that the TCJA added a third hurdle). First, for **each** casualty, $100 is not deductible. [IRC 165(h)(1).] This concept is similar to that of car insurance where you may have a $100 or $500 "deductible," the amount that you have to pay before the insurance kicks in. This Code provision is basically a $100 "deductible" plan with the government – no potential benefit (tax deduction) for the first $100 of loss per casualty.

The second, and more detrimental limit is that once you take off the first $100 per casualty, the remaining aggregate amount of *casualty loss* is deductible only to the extent that it exceeds 10% of the taxpayer's adjusted gross income (AGI). [IRC § 165(h)(2)(A).] AGI is discussed elsewhere in this book, but basically it is an intermediate point in the computation of taxable income. Gross income less certain deductions (listed in IRC § 62 and known as *above the line deductions*) take you to AGI. Other deductions (known as *below the line deductions*) are then subtracted to arrive at *taxable income*. While not required for this problem, the amount calculated as a deductible *casualty loss* is included as part of a group of *below the line* deductions known collectively as *itemized deductions*. This group of deductions is taken (if larger than the taxpayer's *standard deduction*) from adjusted gross income (AGI) in computing taxable income. [See Appendix A for more information about how various items of income and deductions fit together in the computation of taxable income and AGI.] This 10% of AGI floor was introduced into tax law in the early 1980's and is a substantial hurdle for the actual deduction of casualty losses (notwithstanding an additional hurdle that came with the TCJA; see below after the calculations).

While not required for this problem, let us use Dan's *casualty losses* to illustrate the operation of these limitations. Recall that Dan's *casualty losses* were $30,000 for the ring and $35,000 for the automobile. Let us assume, for illustration purposes, that Dan's AGI is a lofty $300,000. His actual *casualty loss* deduction (so far) would be $34,800 calculated as follows:

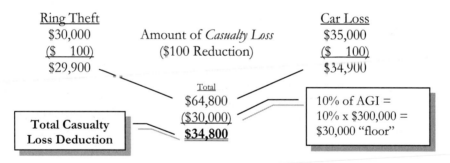

This is where our analysis stopped for this question in prior editions of this book. Unfortunately for Dan, we now finally come to a provision added to IRC § 165 by the TCJA that eliminates any prospect of a tax deduction for Dan's casualty losses. As discussed elsewhere in this book, the TCJA made changes that were dramatically beneficial mostly for corporate-related (and some business-related) taxes. This is not to be taken as a political statement, but to offset the lost revenue (to the government), other provisions of the TCJA made changes designed to raise revenue (i.e., provisions not favorable to taxpayers). IRC § 165 *casualty losses* is one such area where the post TCJA law is detrimental for many taxpayers, including Dan in our question.

The TCJA tacked on a new subpart of IRC § 165, specifically (h)(5) and the title "Limitations for taxable years 2018 through 2025" sets up what is now another hurdle for allowing actual deductions for *casualty losses.* The pertinent part of this new subsection states that a *casualty loss* deduction will be allowed (after the above-mentioned deductible and 10% AGI floor) "*only to the extent it [the casualty loss] is attributable to a Federally declared disaster . . .*" Federally declared disasters are then defined to be a "*disaster subsequently determined by the President of the United States to warrant assistance by the Federal Government under the Robert T. Stafford Disaster Relief and Emergency Assistance Act.*" And a disaster area "*means the area so determined to warrant such assistance.*" [See IRC § 165(i)(5)]

Prior to the TCJA, there was no requirement that a *casualty loss* be coupled with a federally declared disaster. As mentioned, in prior editions of this book which predates the TCJA, Dan would have qualified for a potential deduction for both of his *casualty losses.* Now, however, because Dan's losses are unrelated to a such a disaster area, he is not entitled to any deduction.

Answer (b) is incorrect because it fails to recognize the new TCJA restrictions of casualty losses to federally declared disaster areas. It also incorrectly reflects the amount of his casualty loss (using incorrect dollar amounts for the property, not applying the $100 "deductible" per casualty, and no application of the 10% of AGI floor). **Answer (c) is incorrect** because it also fails to recognize the new TCJA restrictions for casualty losses (no federally declared disaster area in this problem). This answer correctly calculates the amount of his *casualty losses* but fails to reflect the 10% of AGI floor. **Answer (d) is incorrect** but would have been correct but for the changes made by the TCJA. The answer fails to reflect the TCJA's limitation for deductions only to federally declared disaster areas. **Answer (e) is incorrect** because both the ring theft and the car loss represent legitimate *casualty losses.* It is just that these *casualty losses* will not give rise to any deduction for Dan.

12. **The correct answer is (b).** The loss of Dan's business-use car (as is the case in this question) is still characterized as a *casualty loss.* [IRC § 165.] However, the rules for the amount of the *casualty loss,* and its deductibility differ from those previously discussed regarding personal-use assets (as seen in question, 11).

The measurement of the loss for *casualty loss* purposes is generally the same as those used for personal-use casualties: the lesser of: 1) the AB of the property immediately before the casualty, or 2) the fair market value of the property immediately before the casualty. [Reg. § 1.165-7(b).] However, when a business-use asset is totally destroyed, the property's AB is the measurement of the *casualty loss* (notwithstanding its fair market value at the time). [Reg. § 1.165-7(b)(1).] Because Tom's business-use automobile (in this question) was a total loss, the amount of his *casualty loss* is the car's AB at the time of the loss, which is our answer (b).

Unlike the *casualty loss* deduction for individuals regarding personal-use property, *casualty losses* of business-use property is not subject to the $100 "per casualty" nondeductible amount. Nor are such business *casualty losses* subject to the 10% of AGI nondeductible floor that applies to personal-use casualty losses. We saw, in the previous question 11, that the *Tax Cuts & Jobs Act* (TCJA) signed into law in December 2017 (generally effective beginning in 2018) also precludes deductions for personal *casualty losses* unless they are attributable to a "federally declared disaster." Thankfully for Dan in this question 12, this restriction does not apply to business *casualty losses*.

Answer (a) is incorrect because the personal-use loss Dan suffered with respect to his car is also a *casualty loss*, as discussed in problem 11, above. There is no change in this regard because the loss in this problem stems from a business-use asset. **Answer (c) is also incorrect**. This answer states the general rule for determining the amount of *casualty loss* for business-use assets. However, as indicated above, the regulations provide that a "total loss" of a business-use asset results in the amount of *casualty loss* equal to the property's AB, regardless of its value. **Answer (d) is also incorrect.** While this answer properly reflects that business-use *casualty losses* are not subject to the 10% of AGI nondeductible floor, it is incorrect in applying the $100 per casualty nondeductible amount to business-use *casualty losses*. **Answer (e) is incorrect** because the amount of Dan's *casualty loss* changes from that in the previous problem 11, as does the amount of the actual deduction for the *casualty loss*.

13. **Answer (c) is correct.** Talia's total loss of her house and belongings to torrential flood waters was tragic. While one hates to think of "tax" at a time like this, Talia may be entitled to some tax relief from her uninsured losses. This question is very similar to question 11, above (Dan's stolen engagement ring and "disappearing" car) and much of the analysis of that question is repeated here. The ending, tax-wise, for Talia will be different, however, from that for Dan (he received no tax benefit for his losses). As in our analysis of Dan's unfortunate circumstances in question 11, above, we will need to explore the application of changes made by the *Tax Cuts and Jobs Act* (TCJA) signed into law in December 2017 (generally effective beginning in 2018) but for Talia, we will determine that the TCJA does not negatively affect the final outcome like it did for Dan in question 11.

Our analysis will be somewhat tedious as we do have to cover relevant law that, ultimately, will may give rise to a tax benefit for Talia. We begin with IRC § 165 as that is the primary section at issue in this question. Individuals suffering a "casualty loss" may be entitled to some deduction (much less so after passage of the TCJA) even if the property involved is of a personal-use nature (as is the case with Talia's house and belongings). [IRC § 165(h).] A *casualty loss* for personal-use property (property not used in a business or investment activity) is one that occurs from "fire, storm, shipwreck, or other casualty, or from theft." [IRC § 165(c)(3).] The loss must have resulted from some sudden, unexpected, or unusual cause. The flood that destroyed Talia's house and belongings represent classic examples of casualty losses.

We continue with the law. Basically, the law that remains unchanged by the TCJA until we get to a huge change (a "let-down" for many taxpayers) a bit later. The measurement of the loss for *casualty loss* purposes is prescribed by the regulations. These can be rather complex but generally, the tax loss is the lesser of: 1) the property's basis (adjusted basis or AB) of the property immediately before the loss, or 2) the decline in the fair market value of the property because of the casualty. There are numerous rules in determining the latter (decline in fair market value). Purposefully, our questions does not contain the various numbers necessary for us to properly analyze Talia's dollar amount, so we need not address the issue of measuring Talia's casualty loss. Nonetheless, we can say that Talia did incur a casualty loss and, so far, it sounds like Talia may be entitled to some tax benefit for her loss. We have much more law to cover before we can conclude if she is actually entitled to some tax benefit.

At this point, we have correctly concluded that Talia has suffered "casualty losses" from the loss of her home and belongings due to the flood. We shall move on and continue our analysis of the statute to determine how, if at all, Talia may benefit, tax-wise, from these casualty losses. Be forewarned that our analysis will follow the statutory framework of IRC § 165 casualty losses as to how we compute any allowable deduction but in proceeding in this manner, it may be a bit misleading until we hit a huge potential roadblock at the end.

Per IRC § 165, once the amount of one's *casualty loss* is determined (see our above analysis) an individual's prima facie deduction is initially limited in two ways (we'll see that the TCJA added a third hurdle). First, for **each** casualty, $100 is not deductible. [IRC 165(h)(1).] This concept is similar to that of car insurance where you may have a $100 or $500 "deductible," the amount that you have to pay before the insurance kicks in. This Code provision is basically a $100 "deductible" plan with the government – no potential benefit (tax deduction) for the first $100 of loss per casualty.

The second, and more detrimental limit is that once you take off the first $100 per casualty, the remaining aggregate amount of *casualty loss* is deductible only to the extent that it exceeds 10% of the taxpayer's adjusted gross income (AGI). [IRC § 165(h)(2)(A).] AGI is discussed elsewhere in this book, but basically it is an intermediate point in the computation of taxable income. Gross income less certain deductions (listed in IRC § 62 and known as *above the line deductions*) take you to AGI. Other deductions (known as *below the line deductions*) are then subtracted to arrive at *taxable income*. While not required for this problem, the amount calculated as a deductible *casualty loss* is included as part of a group of *below the line* deductions known collectively as *itemized deductions*. This group of deductions is taken (if larger than the taxpayer's *standard deduction*) from adjusted gross income (AGI) in computing taxable income. [See Appendix A for more information about how various items of income and deductions fit together in the computation of taxable income and AGI.] This 10% of AGI floor was introduced into tax law in the early 1980's and is a substantial hurdle for the actual deduction of casualty losses (notwithstanding an additional hurdle that came with the TCJA).

For a numeric example of how this works, please see the analysis of question 11, above. As mentioned, we do not have numbers to work with for Talia in this question 13 but the process would be the same as that for Dan in question 11, above. The one difference for Talia is that the loss of her house as well as its contents would all be from the same casualty so there would only be a single $100 "deductible" in her case (Dan had two separate casualties and calculations for him reflected two $100 "deductibles (one for each casualty).

This is where our analysis stopped for this question in prior editions of this book. In this new edition, we have to deal with a provision added to IRC § 165 by the TCJA that eliminates any prospect of a tax deduction for many individuals experiencing casualty losses but, as we shall see, may not be a hinderance for Talia. The TCJA tacked on a new subpart of IRC § 165, specifically (h)(5) and the title "Limitations for taxable years 2018 through 2025" sets up what is now another hurdle for allowing actual deductions for *casualty losses*. The pertinent part of this new subsection states that a *casualty loss* deduction will be allowed (after the above-mentioned deductible and 10% AGI floor) "*only to the extent it [the casualty loss] is attributable to a Federally declared disaster . . .*" Federally declared disasters are then defined to be a "*disaster subsequently determined by the President of the United States to warrant assistance by the Federal Government under the Robert T. Stafford Disaster Relief and Emergency Assistance Act.*" And a disaster area "*means the area so determined to warrant such assistance.*" [See IRC § 165(i)(5)]

Prior to the TCJA, there was no requirement that a *casualty loss* be coupled with a federally declared disaster. As mentioned, in prior editions of this book which predates the TCJA, Talia (and Dan in question 11, above) would have qualified for a potential deduction for both of his *casualty losses*. Unlike

Dan's situation in question 11, above, Talia's loss was the result of a flood. Therefore, any *casualty lo*ss deduction for Talia will depend on whether the flood that destroyed her house (and contents) was an event that is/was a "federally declared disaster." If yes, then then Talia's casualty loss deduction would be calculated as discussed above. If the flood is/was not a "federally declared disaster," then she is not entitled to any deduction.

Answer (a) is incorrect because it fails to recognize the new TCJA restrictions of casualty losses to federally declared disasters. This answer also appears to leave out the logistics of how one determines their actual deduction for a "correctly determined aggregate amount of the loss" (i.e., the "deductibles" and 10% of AGI floor). **Answer (b) is incorrect** because it incorrectly states that personal casualty losses no longer give rise to possible deductions. True, deductions for personal casualty losses are severely limited, but there is no blanket disallowance of deductions. **Answer (d) correctly describes the framework for calculating a personal casualty loss deduction** but fails to recognize the new TCJA restrictions of casualty losses to federally declared disasters.

14. **The correct answer is (b).** Determining Thelma's realized gain or loss in this question requires us to identify two basic components: her sales price ("amount realized" or, hereinafter, AR) and her basis in the stock ("adjusted basis or, hereinafter, AB). The difference between the two represents a <u>realized</u> gain or loss. [IRC § 1001(a).] Each of these two components, AR and AB, can present a variety of complex tax issues for exam and real-world tax purposes. The AR side is straightforward in our question and is her $6,000 sales price of the stock. Other questions in this book present more complex issues involving a taxpayer's AR. The AB component is the more challenging in this question. We will conclude, after a lengthy discussion below (mostly eliminating the possible application of some rather complex basis rules), that Thelma's AB in the stock is $5,000, resulting in a realized gain to her of $1,000.

While a taxpayer's cost is normally the starting point for determination of one's basis in property (IRC §§ 1011 and 1012), when property is received as a gift, as is the case here, there really is no "cost" to the taxpayer. The seemingly logical result of a zero basis is neither desirable nor, thankfully, appropriate. IRC § 1015 provides us with the rules for determining a donee's AB in property received as a gift. The general rule for most gifts is that the donee takes the donor's AB in the property, or what is commonly referred to as a "carryover" AB. In Thelma's case, this would be her father, Frank's original $5,000 cost. A careful reading of IRC § 1015(a), juxtaposed with our facts, requires us to examine the possible application of something called the "special loss rule." If at the time of the gift, the fair market value of the property is less than the donor's AB, then "for purposes of determining a loss" the donee takes the lower fair market value as his or her AB (and not the carryover AB from the donor). Indeed, the $4,000 value of the shares at the time of their gift to Thelma was less than Frank's AB. However, do not fall into the "let us make a quick tax rule" trap of concluding that Thelma's AB in the stock is this lower $4,000. As quoted, the statute effectively says that we apply this rule *if* the donee later sells for a *loss*. For example, if the facts were changed and Thelma later sold the stock for $1,500, the "special loss rule" would apply and her AB would properly be $4,000. However, in our facts, the stocks rebound in value and she sells them for $6,000, a gain no matter how we look at it. Therefore, the "special loss rule" is not applicable and the starting point for Thelma's AB is the general carryover basis rule for gifts: $5,000 (a carryover of Frank's AB of the same amount).

We say that $5,000 is the "starting point" for determining Thelma's AB. This is because there was a gift tax paid in connection with this gift, last year, to Thelma. A discussion of gift taxes is beyond the scope of this book, and most basic federal income tax courses. Suffice it to say that a gift tax is based on the value of the property transferred and is an obligation of the donor/transferor. It is a given, in our facts, that Frank incurred and paid a $2,000 gift tax on this gift to Thelma. While the study of gift taxes is beyond our scope, their effect on a donee/transferee's AB is not. IRC § 1015(d) provides for a "gift tax paid adjustment" to AB (an increase to AB). The method of calculating this positive, and favorable, adjustment varies depending on when the gift was made, with the critical date (of the gift) being December 31, 1976. The gift tax paid adjustment to AB for gifts made before 1977, is the subject of at least one question presented elsewhere in this book. In this question, the gift to Thelma was made "last year," and the "gift tax paid adjustment" rules for post-1976 gifts are applicable. This rule appears in IRC § 1015(d)(6), and unfortunately for students, the gift tax paid adjustment calculation for post-1976 gifts is a more difficult arithmetic affair than that for gifts made before 1977. The calculation is a prorated type of computation and is an example of what this professor's students refer to as the dreaded algebra infused "Code ratio." [Please see Appendix C for examples of "Code math."] Recognizing that any type of math formula may strike fear in the hearts of some law students, rest assured that the calculations are not really that bad.

The gift tax paid adjustment, or the amount by which Thelma can increase her $5,000 carryover AB from her father, will be represented by the variable "X" in the following formula:

$$\frac{X}{\text{Gift Tax Paid}} \quad = \quad \frac{\text{"Net Appreciation" of Property in Donor's Hands at Time of Gift}}{\text{Value of Gift at Time of Gift}}$$

The term "net appreciation" as used in the numerator on the right-hand side of this equation is simply how much the property has appreciated in value from the time the donor acquired the property until he or she made the gift. Alternatively stated, the "net appreciation" is any *positive* difference between the value of the gift at the time of the gift, and the donor's AB in the property. The above formula adjusted to reflect this definition is:

$$\frac{X}{\text{Gift Tax Paid}} \quad = \quad \frac{\text{(Value of Gift at Time of Gift – Donor's AB in Gift)}}{\text{Value of Gift at Time of Gift}}$$

Utilizing the numbers from our facts, the formula is:

$$\frac{X}{\$2,000} = \frac{(\$4,000 - \$5,000)}{\$4,000} \quad \text{or:} \quad \frac{X}{\$2,000} = \frac{\$0}{\$4,000}$$

In our facts, there was no *net appreciation* in Frank's hands. We do not calculate for a negative gift tax paid adjustment. Solving for "X" is very simple in our situation as the zero divided by a number is zero, which means **X** equals **zero**. In other words, we have no gift tax paid adjustment in our case (because there was no net appreciation of the stock in Frank's hands at the time of the gift). After all of that, (sorry, but the author hopes that going through the complete analysis will assist in understanding the material) we end up with Thelma's AB being $5,000 (the same carryover AB with no gift tax paid adjustment)

The calculation of Thelma's gain is now a simple matter. Her AR of $6,000 less her $5,000 AB results in a realized gain of $1,000. While not the subject of this question, issues of gain recognition and characterization (i.e., capital gain materials) are related testable material. For information purposes, Thelma's $1,000 gain would be recognized and characterized as a "long-term capital gain." [Please see other questions presented in this book where recognition and characterization issues are addressed.]

Answer (a) is incorrect because it incorrectly uses $4,000, the fair market value at the time of the gift, as Thelma's AB in the stock. **Answer (c) is**

incorrect because it incorrectly reflects an AB to Thelma of $7,000 (most likely from an incorrect application of the gift tax paid adjustment attempting to utilize the pre-1977 rules of adding the $2,000 gift tax paid to the $5,000 carryover AB). **Answer (d) is incorrect** because the result in this answer occurs when the donee sells property at a price between that of the donor's AB and a lower fair market value of the property at the time of the gift. This does not represent the facts in our case.

15. **The correct answer is (a).** This question may have little relevance to those students having no contact with states having "community property" laws. For those students concerned with community property, this question represents a very important "real-world" tax issue. This question centers on one's basis (or "adjusted basis" hereinafter AB) in property. A taxpayer, if given the choice between having a higher or lower AB for property with no additional costs involved, would, for income tax purposes, usually select the higher AB. The higher the AB, the lower the potentially taxable gain (or greater loss) results from a subsequent sale. There are two general rules regarding AB that come into play for this question. The first is that a taxpayer's basis in property is usually determined by its cost. [IRC §§ 1011 and 1012.] The second general rule applicable here is the determination of a taxpayer's AB in property acquired from a decedent. IRC § 1014(a)(1) provides that the basis of property acquired from a decedent shall be the property's fair market value at the date of the decedent's death (commonly referred to as a "step-up" in basis for appreciated property). Let us analyze this question and apply these rules utilizing the facts in our question, illustrated with some numbers.

> *Assume that our Wife and Husband purchased the vacant lot many years ago for $200,000. Let us further assume that the lot has appreciated in value to $800,000 and one spouse, the Wife, dies. We will analyze these facts in the alternative scenarios that the property was titled in "joint tenancy" and "community property."*

Joint Tenancy Analysis

Joint tenants each have an undivided one-half ownership interest in property while both co-tenants are alive. Joint tenancy carries with it, the right of survivorship, where, by operation of law, at the death of one co-tenant, his or her one-half interest vests in (goes to) the surviving co-tenant. At Wife's death, her one-half interest in the property would go to Husband, resulting in Husband's 100% ownership of the property. But what is Husband's AB? He already owned one-half of the property prior to his wife's death, and to this one half, we apply our "cost" AB rule; Husband's one-half of the original $200,000 purchase price is $100,000. Husband's AB in the one-half that he already owned prior to Wife's death is $100,000.

As for the one-half interest in the property owned by Wife that Husband receives by operation of law at Wife's death (as the surviving joint tenant), we apply the rules of IRC § 1014(a)(1); Husband's AB in this one-half interest received from decedent Wife is one-half of the property's $800,000 fair market date of death value, or $400,000. Husband's resulting AB is $500,000 comprised of $100,000 representing the AB for the one-half of the property that he originally owned and $400,000 representing the AB for the one-half of the property that he received from decedent Wife at her death. We see that Husband received a so-called "stepped up" basis in one-half of the property (the share coming from Wife at her death).

This result is illustrated in the following diagram:

Joint Tenancy Analysis

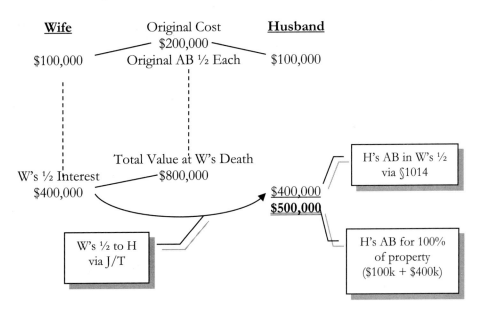

Community Property Analysis

Similar to joint tenancy, a husband and wife each has an undivided one-half interest in community property. Regular community property, as is the case here, does not have the automatic "transfer at death" mechanism of joint tenancy. A spouse is free to devise her or his one-half community property interest to anyone. Absent a devise, the deceased spouse's interest goes by state intestacy laws. To make this illustration consistent with that of joint tenancy, where the surviving spouse ends up owning 100% of the property, we will assume that Wife's will devises her one-half community property interest to Husband. In this scenario, Husband again owns 100% of the property after Wife's death, but what is his AB in this property? Applying the basic rule of IRC § 1014(a)(1) Husband's AB in the one-half interest he received from decedent Wife equals one-half of the property's $800,000 fair market date of death value, or $400,000. And the AB in the one-half interest Husband already owned? This is where a special and magical rule, at IRC § 1014(b)(6), comes into play. For AB determination purposes, this rule says that we treat the <u>Husband's</u> one-half interest in the community property (that he already owns) as if it too was received from his wife at her death. This then translates into application of the general date of death valuation as AB rule for property received from a decedent. Husband's AB in <u>his</u> one-half of the property also gets "stepped-up" to the fair market value of that one-half at Wife's death; $400,000 in our illustration. Husband's resulting AB is <u>$800,000</u> or a so-called "double step-up" in basis for community property. This result is illustrated in the following diagram:

Community Property Analysis

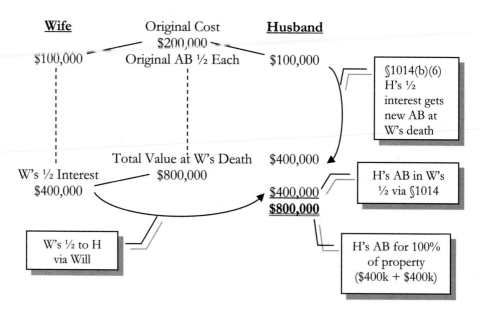

Surviving Husband has an AB of <u>$500,000</u> if they held the property as joint tenants. Alternatively, surviving Husband has an AB of <u>$800,000</u> if they held it as community property. Clearly, the latter result is better for Husband in this set of facts.

For appreciated property, this special community property provision can be a great tax savings devise that effectively makes, for income tax purposes, all unrealized appreciation and gain in the decedent's hands evaporate. While not at issue in this question (and state-specific) some community property states have developed a statutory hybrid joint-tenancy/community-property form of title: "*community property with right of survivorship.*" It has the same automatic "right of survivorship" characteristics of classic joint tenancy, and is accorded the "community property" attributes of IRC § 1014(b)(6)).

Answer (b) is incorrect because IRC § 1041 has no application with respect to the facts in this problem. **Answer (c) is incorrect** because IRC § 1014(b)(6), while not applicable to spousal joint tenancies, would produce a more favorable result to the surviving spouse vis-à-vis the surviving spouse's resulting AB in the appreciated property. **Answer (d) is incorrect** because "community property" does, indeed, produce a more favorable result to the surviving spouse in this <u>appreciating</u> property value situation vis-à-vis the surviving spouse's resulting AB in the property.

16. **The correct answer is (d).** This question is very similar to question 15, immediately preceding this question. This professor would not ask two closely related questions such as these on an exam. It is presented here, however, to reinforce understanding of the subject. The sole difference between this question and question 15, above, is that in this question, we substitute "domestic partners" in place of a married couple.

This question may have little relevance to those students having no contact with states having "community property" laws. Also, because our couple in this question are "domestic partners," the question may have limited application as domestic partners are not recognized in all states. This question is even more specific because we are dealing with California Domestic partners (the significance is explained below). For those students concerned with community property and domestic partners, this question represents a very important "real-world" tax issue. This question centers on one's basis (or "adjusted basis" hereinafter AB) in property. A taxpayer, if given the choice between having a higher or lower AB for property with no additional costs involved, would, for income tax purposes, usually select the higher AB. The higher the AB, the lower the potentially taxable gain (or greater loss) results from a subsequent sale. There are two general rules regarding AB that come into play for this question. The first is that a taxpayer's basis in property is usually determined by its cost. [IRC §§ 1011 and 1012.] The second general rule applicable here is the determination of a taxpayer's AB in property acquired from a decedent. IRC § 1014(a)(1) provides that the basis of property acquired from a decedent shall be the property's fair market value at the date of the decedent's death (commonly referred to as a "step-up" in basis for appreciated property). Let us analyze this question and apply these rules utilizing the facts in our question, illustrated with some numbers.

> *Assume that our California Domestic Partners purchased the vacant lot many years ago for $200,000. Let us further assume that the lot has appreciated in value to $800,000 when one of the domestic partners dies. We will analyze these facts in the alternative scenarios that the property was titled in "joint tenancy" and "community property."*

Joint Tenancy Analysis

Joint tenants each have an undivided one-half ownership interest in property while both co-tenants are alive. Joint tenancy carries with it, the right of survivorship, where, by operation of law, at the death of one co-tenant, his or her one-half interest vests in (goes to) the surviving co-tenant. The fact that we are substituting domestic partners for a married couple is irrelevant for this portion of our analysis. When one of the domestic partners dies, their one-half interest in the property would go to the other domestic partner, resulting in the surviving domestic partner's 100% ownership of the property. But what is the surviving domestic partner's AB? He or she already owned one-half of the property prior to their partner's death, and to this one half, we apply our "cost" AB rule; the surviving domestic partner's one-half of the original $200,000 purchase price is $100,000 Therefore, the surviving domestic partner's AB in the one-half that they already owned prior to the other domestic partner's death is $100,000.

As for the one-half interest in the property owned by deceased domestic partner that the surviving partner receives by operation of law at death (as the surviving joint tenant), we apply the rules of IRC § 1014(a)(1); the surviving domestic partner's AB in this one-half interest received from decedent domestic partner is one-half of the property's $800,000 fair market date of death value, or $400,000. The surviving domestic partner's resulting AB is $500,000 comprised of $100,000 representing the AB for the one-half of the property that he originally owned and $400,000 representing the AB for the one-half of the property that they received from decedent domestic partner at their death. We see that the surviving domestic partner received a so-called "stepped up" basis in one-half of the property (the share coming from the deceased partner at their death).

Our joint tenancy analysis is exactly as that for the married couple in question 15 (immediately preceding this question). Therefore, for property held in joint tenancy, domestic partners and married spouses are treated the same. While not at issue in questions 15 through 17, the result would be identical for any two persons holding property as joint tenants (e.g., friends, relatives, etc.).

This result is illustrated in the following diagram:

Joint Tenancy Analysis

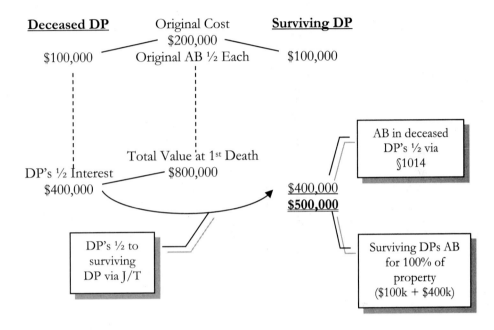

Deceased DP   Original Cost   **Surviving DP**
                              $200,000
   $100,000   Original AB ½ Each $100,000

                                                        AB in deceased
                                                        DP's ½ via
                                                        §1014

                    Total Value at 1st Death
DP's ½ Interest $800,000 $400,000
   $400,000 $500,000

         DP's ½ to   Surviving DPs AB
         surviving   for 100% of
         DP via J/T   property
                                                  ($100k + $400k)

Community Property Analysis

Again, the analysis here is almost identical to that for question 15, above. The only change is that we have California Domestic Partners in place of a married couple. California law makes the rights of a domestic partner equivalent to those of a spouse including the right to hold property between partners as **community property**. It would be logical to conclude that our analysis of community property owned by domestic partners would result in the same analysis as it was for our spouses in question 15, above. While logical, the analysis here is not the same because for federal income tax purposes, domestic partners are <u>not</u> deemed to be spouses. This means that the special "double step-up" rule for community property at the death of the first "spouse" (IRC § 1014(b)(6)) does <u>not</u> apply to our domestic partners in this question 16. Our domestic partner's property in this question is **true community property** but the statute specifically uses the phrase "the surviving *spouses* share of community property." (Emphasis added). Unfortunately, domestic partners are not spouses according to federal law and, therefore, are not able to utilize this double step in basis at the death of the first domestic partner. The end result is the same as that for our joint tenancy example above.

For appreciated property, the special community property provision in IRC § 1014 (b)(6) has no application in this question because domestic partners are not spouses and, therefore, joint tenancy and community property forms of ownership would produce the same result.

It should be noted that same-sex *married* couples <u>are</u> spouses and the special rules for community property (in IRC § 1014(b)(6)) apply the same as to any married couple.

Answer (a) is incorrect because, as discussed above, domestic partners are not considered spouses for federal tax purposes and, therefore, the stated section does not apply. **Answer (b) is incorrect** because IRC § 1041 has no application with respect to the facts in this problem. **Answer (c) is incorrect** because as discussed above, there is not tax difference for domestic partners holding property in joint tenancy or community property (so neither form of title is better than the other).

17. **The correct answer is (c).** This question is very similar to questions 15 and 16, immediately preceding this question. This professor would not ask two closely related questions such as these on an exam. It is presented here, however, to reinforce understanding of the subject.

In this question, we are faced with an asset that is continually declining in value rather than an asset, as in questions 15 and 16, which has enjoyed appreciation. The focus of this problem is also the surviving spouse's basis (or "adjusted basis" herein after AB) in the property with the higher the AB, the better for income tax purposes. The decedent spouse's one-half interest in property held in joint tenancy that passes, by operation of law, to the surviving co-tenant spouse, receives a new basis in the hands of such surviving spouse that is equal to one-half of the property's fair market value at the decedent's death. This is the general rule of IRC § 1014(a)(1). While with appreciated property, this is referred to as a "stepped-up" basis in that one-half interest, for the property that has depreciated in value, the result is a "stepped-down" basis. As for the one-half interest in joint tenancy property that the surviving spouse already owned as when his or her spouse died, the AB remains as a higher cost basis. The fact that the one-half share coming from the deceased spouse receives a "stepped-down" basis, is not favorable. However, it is only one-half of the property that gets this "stepped-down" basis treatment, the other one-half interest retaining its higher cost AB.

If the couple holds the property as community property, with the first spouse to die devising his or her one-half interest in the property to the surviving spouse, we have a different and less favorable result. The one-half interest devised to the surviving spouse, from the deceased spouse, receives a new AB equal to one-half the value of the property at the date of the decedent's death. This is pursuant to the general rule of IRC § 1014(a)(1), and is the same "stepped-down" result in this one-half interest that we saw in the preceding paragraph regarding property held in joint tenancy. Unfortunately for the surviving spouse, the one-half interest in the property that he or she already owned is also "stepped-down" pursuant to IRC § 1014(b)(6). This is the same provision that worked so well in question 15, above dealing with appreciated property, giving the surviving spouse a so-called "double step-up" in AB (both halves of community property receiving a new fair market value AB). It works the same way, and not so well, when dealing with depreciated property. This is sometimes referred to as the "double step-down" basis for depreciated property.

Answer (c), therefore is correct because at least with joint tenancy, only one-half of the property receives a "stepped down" AB for the recipient spouse. A more comprehensive analysis of this question utilizing the facts in our question illustrated with some numbers might be helpful. This illustration is very similar to that utilized in the analysis of question 15, but with the respective numbers representing the couple's original cost and fair market value at Wife's death reversed.

> *Assume that our Wife and Husband purchased the vacant lot many years ago for $800,000. Let us further assume that the lot has depreciated in value to $200,000 and one spouse, the Wife, dies. We will analyze these facts in the alternative scenarios that the property was titled in "joint tenancy" and "community property."*

Joint Tenancy Analysis

Joint tenants each have an undivided one-half ownership interest in property while both co-tenants are alive. Joint tenancy carries with it, the right of survivorship, where, by operation of law, at the death of one co-tenant, his or her one-half interest vests in (goes to) the surviving co-tenant. At Wife's death, her one-half interest in the property would go to Husband, resulting in Husband's 100% ownership of the property. But what is Husband's AB? He already owned one-half of the property prior to his wife's death, and to this one half, we apply our "cost" AB rule; Husband's one-half of the original $800,000 purchase price is $400,000. Husband's AB in the one-half that he already owned prior to Wife's death is $400,000.

As for the one-half interest in the property owned by Wife that Husband receives by operation of law at Wife's death (as the surviving joint tenant), we apply the rules of IRC § 1014(a)(1); Husband's AB in this one-half interest received from decedent Wife is one-half of the property's $200,000 fair market date of death value, or $100,000. Husband's resulting AB is $500,000 comprised of $400,000 representing the AB for the one-half of the property that he originally owned and $100,000 representing the AB for the one-half of the property that he received from decedent Wife at her death. We see that Husband received a so-called "stepped down" basis in one-half of the property (the share coming from Wife at her death). This result is illustrated in the following diagram:

Joint Tenancy Analysis

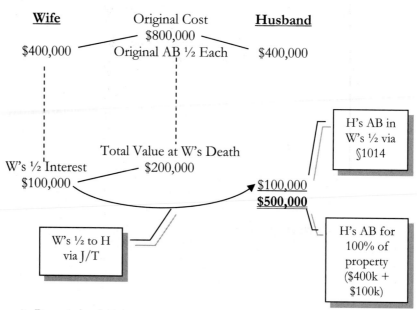

Community Property Analysis

Similar to joint tenancy, a husband and wife each has an undivided one-half interest in community property. Regular community property, as is the case here, does not have the automatic "transfer at death" mechanism of joint tenancy. A spouse is free to devise her or his one-half community property interest to anyone. Absent a devise, the deceased spouse's interest goes by state intestacy laws. To make this illustration consistent with that of joint tenancy, where the surviving spouse ends up owning 100% of the property, we will assume that Wife's will devises her one-half community property interest to Husband. In this scenario, Husband again owns 100% of the property after Wife's death, but what is his AB in this property? Applying the basic rule of IRC § 1014(a)(1) Husband's AB in the one-half interest that he received from decedent Wife equals one-half of the property's $200,000 fair market date of death value, or $100,000. And the AB in the one-half interest Husband already owned? This is where a special rule, at IRC § 1014(b)(6), comes into play. For AB determination purposes, this rule says that we treat the <u>Husband's</u> one-half interest in the community property (that he already owns) as if it too was received from his wife at her death. This then translates into application of the general date of death valuation as AB rule for property received from a decedent. Husband's AB in <u>his</u> one-half of the property also gets "stepped-down" to the fair market value of that one-half at Wife's death; $100,000 in our illustration. Husband's resulting AB is <u>$200,000</u> or a so-called "double step-down" in basis for community property that has declined in value. This result is illustrated in the following diagram:

Community Property Analysis

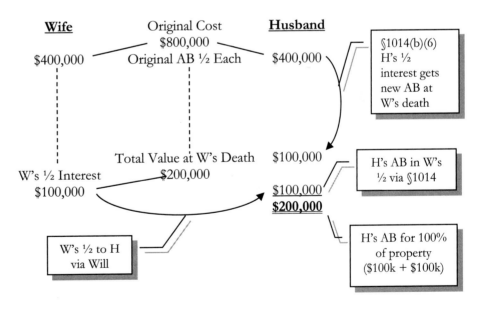

Surviving Husband has an AB of <u>$500,000</u> if they held the property as joint tenants. Alternatively, surviving Husband has an AB of <u>$200,000</u> if they held it as community property. Clearly, the latter result is worse for Husband in this set of facts.

For appreciated property, this special community property provision can be a great tax savings device that effectively makes, for income tax purposes, all unrealized appreciation and gain in the decedent's hands evaporate. However, for property that has declined in value, the special community property rule can produce unfavorable results. While not at issue in this question (and state-specific) some community property states have developed a statutory hybrid joint-tenancy/community-property form of title: "*community property with right of survivorship*." It has the same automatic "right of survivorship" characteristics of classic joint tenancy and is accorded the "community property" attributes of IRC § 1014(b)(6).

Answer (a) is incorrect because in this question, there is no step-up in basis for property that has declined in value. As discussed above, IRC §§ 1014(b)(6) and 1014(a) work in concert to produce a "double step-down" in basis for community property that has declined in value. **Answer (b) is incorrect** because IRC § 1041 has no application with respect to the facts in this problem. **Answer (d) is incorrect** because "joint tenancy" does, indeed, produce a more favorable result to the surviving spouse in this declining property value situation vis-à-vis the surviving spouse's resulting AB in the property.

18. **The correct answer is (b).** In every fact pattern in which something is sold (or otherwise disposed of), the author likes to go through the following analysis; always ask these three questions:

    1) Does the sale (or disposition) result in a <u>realized</u> gain or loss and if so, what is the <u>amount</u>? This is computing the amount of gain (or loss). It is the AR (amount realized) less one's AB (adjusted basis).

    2) If we have a <u>realized</u> gain or loss, is it <u>recognized</u> (i.e. reportable for income tax purposes)? As a taxpayer, you would like the answer to be NO for gains; I do not want to recognize, report, the gain (said another way, I'd like to be able to exclude this gain from my income).

    3) If the gain or loss is recognized, is it accorded "capital" gain or loss treatment? This is primarily the issue of "capital gains (or losses)" that are treated differently for income tax purposes.

Determining Sean's realized gain or loss in this question requires us to identify two basic components: his sales price ("amount realized" or, hereinafter, AR) and his basis in the land ("adjusted basis or, hereinafter, AB). The difference between the two represents a <u>realized</u> gain or loss. [IRC

§ 1001(a).] Each of these two components, AR and AB, can present a variety of complex tax issues for exam and real-world tax purposes. Although this question lacks numbers, conceptually both the AB and AR components are fairly straightforward in our question. Sean's AB is his original cost of the raw land. The land in question declined in value, and since Sean sold it for its then lower fair market value, he <u>realized</u> a <u>loss</u> on the sale of the land.

It should be noted that, while not at issue in this question, adjustments to a taxpayer's basis in an asset can result from many reasons including capital improvements (increasing basis), and depreciation expenses (reducing basis). [IRC § 1016.] In this question there are no indications that improvements have been made to the land. It should be noted that raw land is generally not "depreciable."

The next step in our analysis of gain/loss situations is to determine the extent to which any this <u>realized</u> loss is <u>recognized</u>. Recognition of loss basically means that it is reflected, as a deduction, in computing taxable income. IRC § 1001(c) provides that unless otherwise provided for in the Code, all realized gains and losses are recognized. Unfortunately, this is such an "otherwise provided for" non-recognition provision applicable to Sean's loss in this situation. IRC § 267 disallows deductions for losses resulting from sales between certain related individuals. In other words, a loss realized from the sale to certain related individuals will not be recognized. Sean's mother, Marta, is considered a "related" individual for purposes of this section (IRC § 267(c)(4) defines related individuals as siblings, stepsiblings, spouses, ancestors and lineal descendants). Therefore, Sean's realized loss is <u>not recognized</u>. In other words, Sean gets no income tax benefit from this loss.

Note that we need not proceed to the third step in our analysis of gain/loss situations (determining capital gain/loss treatment), because Sean's loss is not recognized. Basically, we stop at step two, as we only go to the third step in the analysis for gains/losses that are recognized (which is not the case here with Sean's loss). Students sometimes jump straight to the capital gain/loss step three without first making the critical determination of gain/loss recognition. For example, Sean's land would be considered a capital asset and would have given rise to a capital loss had his loss been recognizable. Sean does <u>not</u> have a capital loss from this sale even though the land was a capital asset in Sean's hands because the loss never gets past the "recognition" stage. Had Sean sold the land to an individual "unrelated" to him, the loss would have been recognized and we would have continued to the capital loss, step three, of our analysis.

Answer (a) is incorrect. While it is true that gifts do not result in recognized losses, sales to related parties do not necessarily result in a gift.

A sale of an asset for its full fair market value, as was Sean's sale to his mother Marta, does not result in a gift. The fact that Sean was financially strapped and that Marta felt sorry for Sean, is irrelevant in this case. **Answer (c) is incorrect** because notwithstanding other non-recognition provisions (such as our related party disallowance) realized losses from the sale of investment property are generally recognized. **Answer (d) is incorrect** because it, like answer (a), incorporates "gift" concepts that are inapplicable to the facts of this question.

19. **Answer (a) is correct.** This question is very similar to question 18 immediately above. The results, however, are very different. Although it may be tedious for the reader, a step-by-step complete analysis is appropriate for this question. As previously indicated, in every fact pattern in which something is sold (or otherwise disposed of), the author likes to go through the following analysis; always ask these three questions:

    1) Does the sale (or disposition) result in a _realized_ gain or loss and if so, what is the _amount_? This is computing the amount of gain (or loss). It is the AR (amount realized) less one's AB (adjusted basis).

    2) If we have a _realized_ gain or loss, is it _recognized_ (i.e. reportable for income tax purposes)? As a taxpayer, you would like the answer to be NO for gains; I do not want to recognize, report, the gain (said another way, I'd like to be able to exclude this gain from my income).

    3) If the gain or loss is recognized, is it accorded "capital" gain or loss treatment? This is primarily the issue of "capital gains (or losses)" that are treated differently for income tax purposes.

We will conclude that Sean's loss _is_ recognized, and it will qualify as a capital loss.

Determining Sean's realized gain or loss in this question requires us to identify two basic components: his sales price ("amount realized" or, hereinafter, AR) and his basis in the land ("adjusted basis or, hereinafter, AB). The difference between the two represents a _realized_ gain or loss. [IRC § 1001(a).] Although this question also lacks numbers, conceptually both the AB and AR components are fairly straightforward in this question. Sean's AB is his original cost of this parcel of raw land. The land in question declined substantially in value, and since Sean sold it to his brother-in-law Bob for its then lower fair market value, Sean _realized_ a _loss_ on the sale of the land.

It should be noted that, while not at issue in this question, adjustments to a taxpayer's basis in an asset can result from many reasons including capital improvements (increasing basis), and depreciation expenses (reducing basis). [IRC § 1016.] In this question there are no indications that improvements have been made to land. It should be noted that raw land is generally, not "depreciable."

The next step in our analysis of gain/loss situations is to determine the extent to which any of this <u>realized</u> loss is <u>recognized</u>. Recognition of loss basically means that it is reflected, as a deduction, in computing taxable income. IRC § 1001(c) provides that unless otherwise provided for in the Code, all realized gains and losses are recognized. In question 18, immediately preceding this question, we addressed IRC § 267, which disallows deductions for losses resulting from sales between certain related individuals. Sean's mother Marta was a "related" individual for purposes of this disallowance section. Is brother-in-law Bob considered "related" for purposes of IRC § 267? IRC § 267(c)(4) defines a "related" individual as a sibling, a stepsibling, a spouse, an ancestor (e.g., parent, grandparent, etc.), and a lineal descendant (e.g., child, grandchild, etc.). An "in-law," such as Bob, is <u>not</u>, for purposes of this section, considered related. Therefore, IRC § 267 does not, in this question, block Sean's recognition of his realized loss resulting from his sale to Bob. So far, so good.

Now to the second step of our gain/loss analysis: whether Tom's $130,000 loss is recognized. IRC § 1001(c) provides that, unless otherwise indicated in the Code, all realized gains and losses are recognized. This would cement the recognition of Tom's loss if it were not for an "otherwise indicated" Code section, namely IRC § 165. At first glance, the "general rule" in IRC § 165(a) looks to be in Tom's favor allowing a deduction for "any loss sustained during the taxable year . . ." Reading further at IRC § 165(c) we come across an ominous sounding subsection: "Limitation on losses of individuals." In class, this professor refers to this as the "section 165(c) hoop," complete with graphic depictions on the board/slides. Figuratively, the goal is to jump from the "realized" loss side, through the hoop to the land of "recognized" losses. This hoop, however, is more akin to a **semipermeable membrane** than an unobstructed open space. [Ha! Who would think we'd ever use the phrase *semipermeable membrane* in law school, let alone in a tax class?] We see, in IRC §§ 165(c)(1)-(c)(3), that business losses, investment losses and personal-use "casualty" losses, break on through to the recognized loss side. By default, however, losses from personal-use assets (other than casualty losses) do not make it through this "section 165(c) hoop" and go unrecognized. [To complete the *semipermeable membrane* analogy, their molecular size is too large to pass through to the land of *recognition*.] This explains why, for example, when you sell your personal-use car for a loss (which is almost always the case), the loss is realized but not recognized; i.e., you get no tax benefit from such a loss.

Turning to Sean in our problem, the facts indicate that he purchased and held the real estate for investment purposes and that there is no indication that he used it for personal or pleasure purposes. Even though it proved to be a poor investment for Sean, it was an investment nonetheless. Sean's realized loss, therefore, passes through this recognition hoop of IRC § 165(c) and is recognized.

Here is a copy of the slide (albeit without some cool animation and colors better depicting the semipermeable membrane) that this professor uses in class for a visual representation of IRC § 165(c).

Barring further potential nonrecognition provisions, of which there are none applicable to Sean in our facts, we proceed to the third step in our gain/loss analysis: is Sean's recognized loss on the sale of the land to Bob a "capital loss?" A capital loss analysis requires first determining that we are dealing with a "capital asset" after which the gain is characterized as having either long-term or short-term status. IRC § 1221(a) defines a capital asset in a negative fashion, but for purposes of this analysis, it includes, by process of elimination, assets held for investment and personal-use purposes. As indicated, Sean held the raw land for investment purposes. Therefore, Sean's realized, and recognized loss, is properly characterized as a <u>capital loss</u>. At this point, the analysis would normally continue to determine whether the capital loss is characterized as long-term or short-term, with long-term status reserved for those assets held for more than one year. However, we are not given the length of Sean's holding period for the land in this problem and, therefore, can go no further in our analysis.

Answer (b) is incorrect because the IRC § 267 disallowance of losses on sales between related parties does not apply in this situation, as Bob is not, for purposes of this section, considered a related party. Answer (c) is incorrect. It is correct to the extent that it reflects Sean has a recognized loss. However, this answer fails to reflect the proper characterization of the land as a capital asset. Answer (d) is incorrect because it does not properly reflect the above discussed nonrecognition rules of IRC § 165(c).

20. **The correct answer is (b).** This question, except for one critical date in the facts, is identical to another question appearing elsewhere in this book. The answer, however, is quite different with Tom realizing a $4,000 gain from the sale of the watch.

Determining Tom's realized gain or loss in this question requires us to identify two basic components: his sales price ("amount realized" or, hereinafter, AR) and his basis in the watch ("adjusted basis or, hereinafter, AB). The difference between the two represents a <u>realized</u> gain or loss. [IRC § 1001(a).] Each of these two components, AR and AB, can present a variety of complex tax issues for exam and real-world tax purposes. The AR side is straightforward in our question and is his $23,000 sales price. Other questions in this book present more complex issues involving a taxpayer's AR. The AB component is the more challenging in this question.

While a taxpayer's cost is normally the starting point for determination of one's basis in property (IRC §§ 1011 and 1012), when property is received as a gift, as is the case here, there really is no "cost" to the taxpayer. The seemingly logical result of a zero basis is neither desirable nor, thankfully, appropriate. IRC § 1015 provides us with the rules for determining a donee's AB in property received as a gift. The general rule for most gifts is that the donee takes the donor's AB in the property, or what is commonly referred to as a "carryover" AB. In Tom's case, this would be Tom's Aunt's original $18,000 cost. This is Tom's starting point in determining his AB.

We say "starting point" because there was a gift tax paid in connection with the 1990 gift to Tom. Discussion of gift taxes is beyond the scope of this book, and most basic federal income tax courses. Suffice it to say that a gift tax is based on the value of the property transferred and is an obligation of the donor/transferor. It is a given, in our facts, that Tom's Aunt incurred and paid a $7,000 gift tax on the 1990 gift to Tom. While the study of gift taxes is beyond our scope, their effect on a donee/transferee's AB is not. IRC § 1015(d) provides for a "gift tax paid adjustment" to AB (an increase to AB). The method of calculating this positive, and favorable, adjustment varies depending on when the gift was made, with the critical date (of the gift) being December 31, 1976. The gift tax paid adjustment to AB for gifts made before 1977, is the subject of at least one question presented elsewhere in this book. In this question, the gift to Tom was in <u>1990</u> and the "gift tax paid adjustment" rules for post-1976 gifts are contained in IRC § 1015(d)(6). Unfortunately for students, the gift tax paid adjustment calculation for post-1976 gifts is a more difficult arithmetic affair than that for gifts made before 1977. The calculation is a prorated type of computation and is an example of what this professor's students refer to as the dreaded algebra infused "Code ratio" [See Appendix C for explanation of "Code" math.] Recognizing that any type of math formula may strike fear in the hearts of some law students, rest assured that the calculations are not really that bad.

The gift tax paid adjustment, or the amount by which Tom can increase his $18,000 carryover AB from his aunt, will be represented by the variable "X" in the following formula:

$$\frac{X}{\text{Gift Tax Paid}} = \frac{\text{"Net Appreciation" of Property in Donor's Hands at Time of Gift}}{\text{Value of Gift at Time of Gift}}$$

The term "net appreciation" as used in the numerator on the right-hand side of this equation is simply how much the property has appreciated in value from the time the donor acquired the property until he or she made the gift. Alternatively stated, the "net appreciation" is the difference between the value of the gift at the time of the gift, and the donor's AB in the property. The above formula adjusted to reflect this definition is:

$$\frac{X}{\text{Gift Tax Paid}} = \frac{(\text{Value of Gift at Time of Gift – Donor's AB in Gift})}{\text{Value of Gift at Time of Gift}}$$

Utilizing the numbers from our facts, the formula is:

$$\frac{X}{\$7,000} = \frac{(\$21,000 - \$18,000)}{\$21,000} \qquad \text{or:} \qquad \frac{X}{\$7,000} = \frac{\$3,000}{\$21,000}$$

Our task now is to try to remember high-school algebra and solve for the variable "X." There are a variety of ways to solve for X. One such way is to first simplify the right-hand side of the equation, if possible, then isolate X on the left-hand side of the equation by multiplying both sides by the denominator on the left-hand side of the equation ; then multiply and divide the numbers on the right-hand side of the equation as necessary to find the numeric value. Another method is to "cross multiply," then isolate X and solve for its numeric value. Or, as is the case with our facts, you may be able to just "eye-ball" the answer. The value for "X" in our problem is $1,000. Tom's "gift tax paid adjustment," the amount he is entitled to add to his carryover AB is $1,000 (the solved value of "X"). Tom's resulting AB is, therefore, $19,000 (the $18,000 carryover AB plus the $1,000 gift tax paid adjustment).

The calculation of Tom's gain is now a simple matter. His AR of $23,000 less his $19,000 AB results in a realized gain of $4,000. While not the subject of this question, issues of gain recognition and characterization (i.e., capital gain materials) are related testable material. For information purposes, Tom's $4,000 gain would be recognized and characterized as a "long-term capital gain." Please see other questions presented in this book that address issues of gain and loss recognition and characterization.

Answer (a) is incorrect. This answer utilizes an incorrect interpretation of what is the pre-1977 "gift tax paid adjustment" rule that is covered in at least one question elsewhere in this book. **Answer (c) is incorrect** because it utilizes the pre-1977 "gift tax the "gift tax paid adjustment" rule, albeit in a correct manner. The gift to Tom in this question utilizes the gift tax paid adjustment for post-1976 gifts pursuant to IRC § 1015(d)(6). **Answer (d) is incorrect** because it fails to reflect any "gift tax paid adjustment," rendering Tom's AB in the watch as a straight "carryover" of $18,000. **Answer (e) is incorrect** because a correct response (b) is presented.

21. **The correct answer is (e).** Alicia falls within the so-called "wash sale" rules that prevent the recognition of the loss she sustained from her December sale of the XYZ shares. There is no question that Alicia "realized" a loss from the sale of her shares in December measured by her $10,000 cost of the shares less the $4,000 selling price (a realized loss of $6,000). IRC § 1001(c) states that unless otherwise provided for in the Code, all realized gains and losses are recognized. Unfortunately, there is such an "otherwise provided for" non-recognition provision applicable to Alicia's loss realized from the December sale of her shares.

IRC § 1091, in an attempt to prevent manipulation of losses by taxpayers, provides, in its most basic form, that if you sell shares of stock for a loss and within thirty days you purchase the same stock, you do not get to recognize the loss from the sale. This is referred to as a "wash sale." In effect, you are treated as if you never disposed of the shares in the first place. In Alicia's case, while she had no manipulative intent (trying to benefit from a loss before the end of the year and then reestablish her position in the stock a short time later), she did repurchase the same number of XYZ shares within thirty days of selling them for a loss. This law makes no motivational distinctions and, unfortunately for Alicia, prevents the recognition of her December loss.

Answer (a) is incorrect because there is no such mechanism in the statute to provide for such a result. **Answer (b) is incorrect** because Alicia's sale and repurchase precludes the recognition of the December loss. **Answer (c) is incorrect** because the wash sale rules contain no such "safe harbor" for transactions straddling different tax years. Rather, the prohibited purchase period is a straight "thirty days" (either before or, as is the more common situation as presented in our facts, after the loss sale). **Answer (d) is incorrect** because "intent" is irrelevant in application of the IRC § 1091 wash sale rules.

22. **The correct answer is (c).** This question is a companion to the immediately preceding question 21. It would be a bit unfair to ask both this and the preceding question on an exam as the answer for this question is somewhat dependent on arriving at the correct answer to question 21, above. However, it is presented to further explore the area of "wash sale" rules.

Looking at the situation logically, before going into any specific statutory rules, it would seem unfair to disallow the recognition of a loss because of the *wash sale* provisions and then not have it affect (in a positive way) the basis of the replacement shares. In our question, Alicia originally paid $10,000 for her 500 shares of XYZ stock. After selling them, she repurchased 500 shares of XYZ stock for only $3,500. In computing her gain when she sells this second block of shares (for $15,000), is it fair that she must use as her basis the $3,500 cost of these shares (resulting in a huge gain) when she was not allowed to recognize the $6,000 loss from her December sale of the shares (because of the wash sale rules)? This doesn't "smell" right and indeed, the statute provides otherwise.

Normally, a taxpayer's basis in property is its costs. [IRC §§ 1011 & 1012.] When a loss is not allowed because of the wash sale rules, the statute provides a rather cryptic definition of the basis in the new shares purchased. The statute states that "the basis of the stock . . . so sold [they are referring to the stock that was sold resulting in the wash sale] . . ., increased or decreased, as the case may be, by the difference, if any, between the price at which the property was acquired [meaning the new, replacement shares] and the price at which such substantially identical stock . . . [was] sold . . ." [IRC § 1091(d).] Okay, how about this instead? Take the basis or her first block of XYZ shares ($10,000) and decrease it by $500 (the difference between the $4,000 sales price of her old shares and the $3,500 repurchase price), resulting in a basis of $9,500. Another interpretation: Take the cost of her new shares $3,500 and add her $6,000 loss that was not allowed to be recognized because of the wash sale rules, to get her basis in the new shares of $9,500.

Confusing to say the least, but after careful thought, the result *does* make sense.

Answer (a) is incorrect because it does not reflect the special basis rules applicable to wash sales. **Answers (b) and (d) are incorrect** because they do not reflect an accurate interpretation of the basis rules applicable to wash sales. **Answer (e) is incorrect** because the correct answer (c) is presented.

23. **Answer (a) is the most accurate.** A gift of property generally does not result in realization of a gain or loss to a donor. However, under certain circumstances (i.e., if a donor receives "consideration"), a gift may in fact constitute a "part sale/part gift" with a resulting realization of gain. In a part sale/part gift situation, a gain is realized (by the donor/transferor) to the extent the consideration received (amount realized or hereinafter AR) by the donor exceeds the donor's basis (adjusted basis or hereinafter AB) in the property. [Reg. § 1.1001-1(e).] This is consistent with the general principals of IRC § 1001(a); the difference between the AR and AB represents a realized gain or loss. When Derrick made the gift of the stock to Gail, he did not receive consideration in the traditional sense. However, Derrick did receive consideration, albeit indirectly, by Gail paying the gift tax on the transfer. While an in-depth discussion of gift taxes is far beyond the scope of this book, suffice it to say that any gift tax resulting from a gift is the obligation of the *donor*. Gail's payment of Derrick's obligation *is* consideration to Derrick. Relief of Derrick's obligation (the gift tax) represents a net financial benefit or accession to wealth to him. This concept is similar to that where an employer pays an obligation owed by one of its employees. If the employer seeks no repayment by the employee, the employee is deemed to have received consideration (extra compensation). [See *Old Colony Trust Co. v. Comm'r*, 279 U.S. 716, 49 S.Ct. 499 (1929); Reg. § 1.61-14.]

Therefore, while this appears to be just a gift, it is, in reality, a part sale/part gift situation with Derrick deemed to have received consideration (AR) equal to the amount of the gift tax paid by Gail. If the gift tax paid by Gail exceeds Derrick's AB in the shares, then Derrick has a realized, and recognized, gain resulting from the transfer. [See *Diedrich v. Comm'r*, 457 U.S. 191, 102 S.Ct. 2414 (1982) (donee's payment of donor's gift tax was deemed "consideration" for purposes of determining gain to the donor).]

Answer (b) is incorrect because the gift tax paid by Gail is not income but, as discussed above, represents the AR component of a potential sales-like transfer. Derrick's income, if any, will be in the form of a gain measured by the amount of consideration that he received (AR) that is in excess of his AB. **Answer (c) is incorrect** right out of the box because the payment of gift taxes does not give rise to a deduction for federal income tax purposes. **Answer (d) is incorrect** because the fact that Gail is deemed to have paid consideration does not preclude the gift element of the transfer (the value of the shares in excess of what she is deemed to have paid for them) from exclusion under IRC § 102.

24. **The most accurate statement is (d).** Normally, recognition of a loss relating to investments requires results from some triggering event such as a sale. When a security (stock, bond, etc.) becomes *totally worthless*, it gives rise to a capital loss for most individuals. [IRC §§ 165(a) and (g)(1).] For this result to occur, the stock must be totally worthless. The regulations, at Reg. § 1.165-4(a) state: "No deduction shall be allowed under section 165(a) solely on account of a decline in the value of stock owned by the taxpayer . . . A mere shrinkage in the value of the stock owned by the taxpayer, even though extensive, does not give rise to a deduction under section 165(a) if the stock has any recognizable value . . ."

   The fact that Brenda's stock currently has <u>some</u> market value, albeit minimal, it is <u>not</u> totally worthless. Therefore **answers (a) and (b) cannot be correct.** However, if, down the road, the company does, in fact, "go under" leaving nothing for the common shareholders, then Brenda's shares *will* become *worthless*, resulting in a recognized capital loss. Because she would have held these shares for more than one year, the characterization of this capital loss would be *long-term*. [IRC § 1222.]

   Answer (c) is incorrect because recognized losses from investment assets, whether caused by sale or worthlessness, gives rise to tax benefits in the form of recognized losses (usually "capital" in nature).

   While not at issue in this problem, Brenda could force a current recognition of the loss in her shares by selling them. Please see other problems in this book addressing the realization, recognition and characterization of losses resulting from sales of assets.

25. **The correct answer is (c).** This question raises the issue of "installment sales," and the principal Code section involved is IRC § 453. The first steps of the analysis, however, is more basic: determining the amount of Michael's *realized* gain or loss, and then determining whether any such gain or loss is *recognized*. The installment sales issue addresses the *timing* of gain recognition.

Determination of Michael's *realized* gain of loss is a simple exercise in this question. Other questions in this book address more challenging aspects of gain or loss realization. Michael's *realized* gain is $150,000, the difference between the $200,000 selling price and his basis (adjusted basis or AB) or $50,000. [IRC § 1001(a).] His AB in the land is simply its cost in this situation as no improvements had been made thereto and the land is not depreciable. [See IRC §§ 1011 and 1012 (for cost basis); IRC § 1016 (for adjustments to basis).] Michael's gain from the sale of the land is also *recognized*. Pursuant to IRC § 1001(c), all gains and losses are recognized unless otherwise provided for in the Code. There are no "nonrecognition" or "exclusion" provisions applicable in Michael's situation. The key issue here is *when* Michael recognizes this gain (i.e., reports it on his income tax return as income).

With some restrictions, when a "nondealer" sells property for a gain and at least one payment is to be received after the close of the current tax year (in which the sale took place), the recognized gain is reported (for income tax purposes) as payments are received. This is commonly referred to as the installment method of reporting gain. [IRC § 453.] Michael is not a "dealer" of property (this was his only piece of investment real estate) and his sales price is to be paid to him over ten years (first payment at sale and nine additional payments at one per year).

The mechanism for calculating the amount of gain to be reported with each payment is logical, and not nearly as bad as it sounds from reading IRC § 453. In Michael's somewhat simple situation, we know that his total gain is $150,000 and that he is receiving 10% (one-tenth) of the $200,000 sales price in each of ten years (starting with the sale date). While not exactly the method prescribed in the Code, it is logical (and correct in this situation) to conclude that Michael will report 10% (one-tenth) of the $150,000 or $15,000 with each payment of $20,000 that he receives. The Code method is a bit more complex but necessary for some situations other than our simple gain situation.

The mechanism for computing installment gains that is found in the Code, establishes a "gross profit ratio" that is applied to each payment received. The *gross profit ratio* is the amount of gross profit from the sale ($150,000 for Michael) divided by the total "contract price" ($200,000 for Michael). Michael's *gross profit ratio* is 150,000/200,000 or 75%. This, then, is applied to each payment received (exclusive of any interest). 75% of the $20,000 that Michael receives as his first payment at the time of the sale, results in $15,000 of gain to be reported. Assuming Michael receives each additional $20,000 in coming years as planned, the same 75% ratio is applied to each payment (resulting in $15,000 of gain reported with each payment). While not applicable to our question, the "contract price," used in determining the *gross profit ratio*, may be different from the sales price. The "contract price" is generally the selling price, reduced by debt on the property that the buyer either assumes or takes subject to.

For "nondealers" the installment method cannot be used for sales of publicly traded stocks or other securities. There are also limitations on its use with respect to certain depreciable assets and sales between related parties. Assuming none of these situations apply (which they do not in our question), the installment method of reporting gain for "nondealers" is <u>automatic</u>, and to not use it (i.e., report all of the recognized gain at the time of sale) an individual must affirmatively "elect" to "opt-out." [IRC § 453(d).]

While not at issue in this problem, Michael will also have to report, as income, the interest received each year with respect to his installment sale of the land. Also not at issue in this problem is the characterization of Michael's *recognized* gain. Each reported installment portion of his gain will be a long-term capital gain (sale of a capital asset, the investment land, that he held for more than one year.

Answer (a) is incorrect because $20,000 represents 10% of the sales price and not the amount of Michael's recognized gain. **Answer (b) is incorrect** because the statute does not allow one to first recover one's basis before any gain is reported as income. **Answer (d) is incorrect** because, as discussed above, the installment method is the default method for Michael's reporting of gain. He would have to elect not to use the installment method.

**ANSWER KEY
EXAM VI**

FEDERAL INCOME TAX
ANSWER KEY AND EXPLANATIONS
EXAM VI

1. **Answer (d) is correct.** Situations involving the exchange, between two parties, of services and/or property, usually result in some confusion among students at first. The bottom-line answer with respect to Skip is that he rendered $4,000 worth of services, and was compensated for them, albeit not in cash form, but by receiving other "stuff" (services and property) worth $4,000. Skip has $4,000 of income as a result. Paula did two things: rendered services and disposed of XYZ Co. shares. She rendered $1,300 worth of services and was compensated for them, albeit not in cash form, but by receiving other stuff (services from Skip) worth $1,300. Paula also disposed of XYZ Co. shares worth $2,700 and received consideration for them, albeit not in the form of cash, but by receiving other stuff (services from Skip) worth $2,700. Paula's receipt of $2,700 consideration for the shares less her cost basis ("adjusted basis" hereinafter AB) of $500, results in a realized gain of $2,200.

What is bothersome for students in such exchange transactions, is the lack of cash being received for services rendered or property transferred. Somehow, the resulting income tax consequences seem to be incorrect or unfair. To more thoroughly discuss the answer to this question, the tax implications viewed from both Skip's and Paula's perspective will be discussed.

The transaction from Skip's perspective

Early on, in classroom discussion of gross income, we discover that gross income need not be in the form of cash. A lawyer, for example, who performs legal work for a client and is paid in cash, has gross income. A lawyer who performs legal work for a client and receives property as payment has gross income equal to the fair market value of the property received. A lawyer who performs legal work for a client and receives a combination of cash and property as payment has gross income equal to the cash plus the fair market value of the property received. A lawyer who performs legal work for a client and receives the client's services as payment (in exchange) has income equal to the value of the services. A lawyer who performs legal work for a client and receives cash, property and the client's services as payment has gross income equal to the cash, the fair market value of the property, and the fair market value of the services. [See Reg. § 1.61-1(d) (compensation received in forms other than in cash).] When an individual performs services and receives "something" in exchange, that "something" (or the value thereof) represents gross income. The form of that "something" is generally irrelevant. In our question, Skip rendered

$4,000 worth of services, and received $4,000 worth of stuff in return: $2,700 worth of property and $1,300 worth of Paula's services. Skip has gross income of $4,000.

In class, this professor likes to recast, or view in a different light, exchange or barter transactions in an essentially equivalent manner involving the transfer of cash back and forth between the parties. We could break down the transaction between Skip and Paula into something like this. Skip performs $4,000 worth of services for Paula and Paula pays Skip $4,000 in cash. At this point, it is clear that Skip would have income. Next, Paula performs $1,300 worth of services for Skip, and Skip pays Paula $1,300 in cash. Finally, Skip buys shares XYZ Co, stock worth $2,700 from Paula paying her $2,700 in cash. We will discuss the tax impact to Paula below, but in economic substance, viewing the transaction this way (with cash going back and forth) is the same as that given in our facts.

The transaction from Paula's perspective

Paula performed services worth $1,300 and was paid for these services, albeit not in the form of cash. We know, from our discussion above regarding Skip, that she has gross income regardless of the form of payment. So, for part of this transaction she received $1,300 worth of stuff (Skip's services) for her services, which, results in gross income of $1,300. The other part of the transaction from Paula's perspective was the disposition of the XYZ Co. shares. A sale or disposition of property results in the realization of a gain or loss to transferor measured by the difference between the "amount realized" (AR) and the transferor's AB. [IRC § 1001(a).] The AR side of this sale or disposition equation is obscured just a bit. One's AR from a sale or disposition of property is usually received in the form of cash. However, AR is broader than that and basically includes the value of any "stuff" received in exchange for property whether it be other property or services (money's worth). Here, Paula received $2,700 worth of "stuff" (Skip's services) as consideration. Paula's AB is straightforward in this question and is her $500 original cost of the shares. [See IRC §§ 1011 and 1012.] In effect, Paula sold these shares and received $2,700 consideration (in the form of Skip's services), resulting in a realized gain of $2,200 ($2,700 AR less her AB of $500). In the aggregate, therefore, Paula has $1,300 gross income resulting from her services rendered, and a $2,200 realized gain from the disposition of her XYZ Co. shares.

Let us view these tax results to Paula utilizing our "recast" cash version of this transaction. Skip performs $4,000 worth of services for Paula and Paula pays Skip $4,000 in cash. Next, Paula performs $1,300 worth of services for Skip and Skip pays Paula $1,300 in cash. Finally, Skip buys shares XYZ Co, stock worth $2,700 from Paula <u>paying</u> her $2,700 <u>in cash</u>. It is now easy to see that Paula has $1,300 of gross income for her services rendered. It is also easy to identify the stock "sale or disposition" transaction with a $2,700 sales price resulting in $2,200 of realized gain to Paula ($2,700 AR less her AB of $500).

[For more information about barter/exchange transactions, see Reg. § 1.61-1(d); Rev.Rul. 79-24, 1979-1 C.B. 60.]

Answer (a) is incorrect because "barter" transactions such as the one in our question, are not tax-free transactions. **Answer (b) is incorrect** as to Paula's income tax consequences. The exchange from Paula's perspective is actually two transactions: rendering (and being paid for) services, and the sale of her stock. This answer fails to properly identify the income tax consequences resulting from the stock sale component of the transaction. As to Skip, this answer is correct. **Answer (c) is incorrect** because it does not reflect the entire scope of the facts presented in the question. **Answer (e) is incorrect**. This answer would have been correct if Paula had paid for the extra $2,700 worth of Skip's services in cash. However, she paid for these extra services with property and, as discussed above, this represents a "sale or disposition" of the property, resulting in a gain.

2. **Answer (c) is correct.** This question, unfortunately, requires, in part, a correct analysis of the previous question. This professor would not ask such a series of interrelated multiple-choice questions on an exam. Rather, this series of questions was derived from an exam essay question.

This question presents a basic gain calculation with a slight twist. When Skip sells the XYZ Co. shares, he realizes a gain or loss measured by the difference between the sales price (or in tax terms: the amount realized or AR) and his adjusted basis (hereinafter AB) in the property. [IRC § 1001(a).] The AR portion of the equation in this problem is simply the $5,000 sales price for the XYZ Co. shares. The key component to this question is the determination of Skip's AB in the shares. We will conclude, below, that $2,700 will be his AB in the shares, thus resulting in a realized gain of $2,300 (AR of $5,000 less an AB of $2,700).

A taxpayer's cost is normally the starting point for determining one's basis in property. [IRC §§ 1011 and 1012.] Here, while it is a bit obscured, Skip paid $2,700 for the XYZ Co. shares in his exchange transaction with Paula. From the analysis of the correct answer to question 1, above, we know that Skip had, in part $2,700 of gross income, in the form of compensation, resulting from receiving the shares in the exchange (he also received an additional $1,300 of gross income, receiving Paula's services in exchange). At this point, it might be helpful to look at how we viewed the transaction in an alternate, but equivalent, form with cash going back and forth between the parties. Recall the "recast" transaction: Skip performs $4,000 worth of services for Paula and Paula <u>pays</u> Skip $4,000 <u>in cash</u>. Next, Paula performs $1,300 worth of services for Skip and Skip <u>pays</u> Paula $1,300 <u>in cash</u>. Finally, Skip buys shares XYZ Co, stock worth $2,700 from Paula <u>paying</u> her $2,700 <u>in cash</u>. Viewing the transaction from this revised vantage point, we see that Skip, in effect, paid $2,700 for the shares and that this represents his AB in the shares. This concept in determining Skip's AB in property received in payment for services rendered is sometimes referred to as "tax cost" and is described, albeit in a somewhat cryptic fashion, in the regulations at Reg. § 1.61-2(d)(2)(i).

Skip's gain calculation is now easy to accomplish. The $5,000 sales price (AR) less his $2,700 AB results in a realized gain of $2,300.

Answers (a) (b) and (d) are incorrect because none of these answers reflects a valid calculation of Skip's realized gain resulting from his sale of the XYZ Co. shares. **Answer (e) is incorrect** because a correct answer (c) is presented.

3.   **The correct answer is (b).** To answer this question, it is helpful to "recast" this exchange transaction as illustrated in the analysis of the answers to questions 1 and 2, above. Skip performs $4,000 worth of services for Paula, and Paula <u>pays</u> Skip $4,000 <u>in cash</u>. Next, Paula performs $1,300 worth of services for Skip, and Skip <u>pays</u> Paula $1,300 <u>in cash</u>. Finally, Skip buys shares XYZ Co, stock worth $2,700 from Paula <u>paying</u> her $2,700 <u>in cash</u>. We can now more easily identify "payments" that may give rise to possible deductions.

Skip effectively paid $1,300 to Paula for her expert photography assistance related to his business's website. Pursuant to IRC § 162, this expenditure qualifies for a business expense deduction.

The first sentence of IRC § 162 (which appears in subsection (a)) enumerates, for all intents and purposes, four basic requirements for a business deduction. A business deduction is allowed for all (read as one continuous phrase with four distinct requirements):
   ➢   Ordinary and necessary
   ➢   Expenses
   ➢   Paid or incurred during the taxable year
   ➢   In carrying on any trade or business.

These four requirements often represent, in federal income tax classes and in real life, separate and significant points of contention. Business deductions come in a million different flavors, but all qualifying deductions must meet those four criteria. The study, in tax classes, of business deductions can be long and comprehensive. At times, it may seem like many business deductions have their own set of rules, as if permitted by a separate Code section. There are many business deductions that almost take on a life of their own primarily because of explanations and interpretations from the Code subsections, regulations, court decisions, I.R.S. pronouncements, and the like. While some IRC § 162 business expenses require much analysis, Skip's expenditure for help with his business's website clearly meets the section's criteria and he is entitled to a $1,300 business deduction (the amount that he effectively "paid" Paula via their exchange).

While not necessary to answer our question, it should be noted that an individual can incur qualifying § 162 expenses in the context of working as an employee or in an individual's own business (someone who alternatively referred to as being self-employed, an independent contractor, or operating his or her business as an "unincorporated sole proprietorship"). Skip, in our question operating his business as an unincorporated sole proprietorship (i.e., self-employed), falls in the latter category. The requirements for deductibility pursuant to § 162 are the same for an employee or a self-employed individual. However, the effective availability of an actual business deduction, and where it is deducted, varies dramatically depending on one's "work status." The *Tax Cuts and Jobs Act* (TCJA) signed into law in December 2017 (and generally effective beginning in 2018) made significant changes, and not in a good way, for deductions of business expenses by employees. Under the TCJA (in its current state as of this writing), deductions for unreimbursed business expenses incurred by employees, have, for the most part, been "suspended" for 2018 through 2025. [IRC § 67(g)]. In other words, the TCJA has generally eliminated the actual deductibility of such business expenses if incurred as an employee. This topic, as well as one small exception, is addressed in other questions in this book.

We haven't forgotten about Paula in this question. Recall that she effectively paid Skip $4,000 for body-work on her car. Is she entitled to any deduction for this "expenditure?" Unfortunately for Paula, the answer is no. A key fact is that this was her personal-use car and from your studies in tax, you know that the general framework for tax deductions is that nothing is deductible unless there is a specific code section that allows for a deduction. There are no code sections that would give rise to a deduction for Paula and while not really necessary, IRC § 262 specifically reiterates this by denying any deduction for "personal, living, or family expenses" unless otherwise expressly provided for by a particular code section (and there are none that would so provide for Paula's costs related to her personal-use automobile.

Answer (a) is incorrect because, as explained above, the $1,300 Skip effectively paid Paula for the photography/website assistance qualifies as an IRC § 162 deductible business expense. Similar to the concept that a taxpayer in an exchange transaction can have gross income without the receipt of cash, deductible expenses do not necessarily require the payment of cash. **Answer (c) is incorrect** because although Paula effectively "paid" Skip $4,000 for the body-shop work, such an expenditure is personal in nature and does not give rise to a business expense deduction (or any deduction) for her. **Answer (d) is incorrect** although it does correctly identify the deductibility of Skip's expenditure as an IRC § 162 business expense. The $4,000 that Paula effectively "paid" Skip does not give rise to any deduction (IRC § 162 or otherwise). **Answer (e) is similarly incorrect** because no type of deductible investment-related IRC § 212 expense results from Paula's effective $4,000 payment to Skip.

4. **Answer (d) is correct.** Situations involving the exchange, between two parties, of services and/or property, usually result in some confusion among students at first. The bottom-line answer with respect to Paula in this question is that she rendered photography services to Larry, and was compensated for them, albeit not in cash form, but by receiving other "stuff" (two months use of her apartment) worth, assumingly, an equal amount. As a result, Paula has income in the amount of two months of apartment rent that she would otherwise be paying.

What is bothersome for students in such exchange transactions, is the lack of cash being received for services rendered or property transferred. Somehow, the resulting income tax consequences seem to be incorrect or unfair. A more thorough discussion of the tax implications follows immediately below.

Early on, in classroom discussion of gross income, we discover that gross income need not be in the form of cash. A lawyer, for example, who performs legal work for a client and is paid in cash, has gross income. A lawyer who performs legal work for a client and receives property as payment has gross income equal to the fair market value of the property received. A lawyer who performs legal work for a client and receives a combination of cash and property as payment has gross income equal to the cash plus the fair market value of the property received. A lawyer who performs legal work for a client and receives the client's services as payment (in exchange) has income equal to the value of the services. A lawyer who performs legal work for a client and receives cash, property and the client's services as payment has gross income equal to the cash, the fair market value of the property, and the fair market value of the services. [See Reg. § 1.61-1(d) (compensation received in forms other than in cash).] When an individual performs services and receives "something" in exchange, that "something" (or the value thereof) represents gross income. The form of that "something" is generally irrelevant. In our question, Paula rendered photography services to Larry and they agreed that she would be paid by him giving her "stuff" instead of cash. The "stuff" in this question is two months' worth of rent, rent that she would otherwise be paying for the use of her apartment. Paula has gross income equal to what she would otherwise be paying Larry in apartment rent for two months.

In class, this professor likes to recast, or view in a different light, exchange or barter transactions in an essentially equivalent manner involving the transfer of cash back and forth between the parties. While students do not always like the introduction of numbers if not necessary, using dollar amounts for this explanation may be helpful. Let's assume that Paula's monthly apartment rent is $2,500 (so two month's rent would be $5,000). Using our illustration-only facts, we could break down the transaction between Paula and Larry into something like this. Paula performs the photography services for Larry (being the photographer for his huge holiday party) and Larry pays her $5,000 in cash. At this point, it is clear that Paula would have income. Next, Paula pays Larry her apartment rent for two months equal to $5,000. Breaking down their exchange transaction into its component parts (with cash going back and forth), paints a clear picture that Paula has income and then pays her apartment rent.

While this question does not ask about the tax implications to Larry, we already know the answer from our analysis above. He would have rental income in the same amount (the two months' rent). Effectively, Paula paid that to him (in the form of "stuff"). Remember, looking at the exchange transaction broken down into its component parts we also have both Paula and Larry "paying" something to each other (again, in the form of "stuff"). We are not, in this question, addressing any possible deductions for such "payments" but if we were (or if this were an essay question where you would want to address this), Paula would not be entitled to a deduction for the two months' rent that she "paid" because this is a personal expense for which no tax deductions are provided. Potential deductions for Larry would be a more complex matter and we would need to know a lot more facts to do a proper analysis (e.g., was this a business-related party?).

As with every law school class (and in real life), students should be careful about language that is used. Often, the lay use of language does not properly align with the legal, here tax, nature of what is being said. A good example in this question that Larry "agreed to **forgive** two months' rent in exchange . . ." In the tax world, forgiveness of an amount owed (or to be owed) means that one party is letting the other party "off the hook," and is choosing to receive nothing (or not the full amount) of what is owed. This would take us to the tax topic of forgiveness of a debt where the obligor is realizing a financial benefit from the forgiveness of debt. This topic of "income from discharge of indebtedness" is the subject of other questions in this book. Here, however, Larry is not really forgiving anything owed to him by Paula. She is paying him in full, just not in the form of cash. Do not be tricked by the use of language that in a lay sense may make sense but is not an accurate depiction of what is really occurring in the transaction.

[For more information about barter/exchange transactions, see Reg. § 1.61-1(d); Rev.Rul. 79-24, 1979-1 C.B. 60.]

Answer (a) is incorrect because, as explained above, Larry did not actually forgive any amount that Paula owed (or was otherwise obligated) to him. Paula "paid" her rent to Larry, albeit in the form of services performed instead of cash. **Answer (b) is incorrect** but is accurate in some respects. Paula did furnish consideration (her services) and, therefore, did effectively furnish consideration to Larry. This answer is not correct, however, because it portrays the transaction in an incorrect light of Larry "forgiving" Paula's apartment rent, this failing to address the "income" component realized by Paula for being "paid" for her work. **Answer (c) is incorrect.** We know, from this and other questions, that barter transactions still generate taxable events notwithstanding that there is no cash being exchanged. It is true that a net accession to wealth is a core component in defining "gross income" for tax purposes. When we "recast" the exchange, it is easy to see that we really have two transactions here and as for one of them, Paula did realize a net accession to wealth when she performed services and was effectively "paid."

5. **The most accurate statement is (c).** Sam rendered services worth $4,000 and received consideration (albeit not in the form of cash) and, therefore, has $4,000 of income. The balance of the benefit that he receives is an excludable gift.

There is no doubt that Sam received economic benefit in this problem. You are also aware from your study of gross income, that the receipt of economic benefit, or a net accession to wealth, generally defines the scope of *gross income* pursuant to IRC § 61. Sam received $10,000 of economic benefit represented by the value of the life insurance policy received and, prima facie, has gross income. To completely analyze this question, it helps to identify the composition of this benefit that he received.

Early on in classroom discussion of gross income, we discover that gross income need not be in the form of cash. A lawyer, for example, who performs legal work for a client and is paid in cash, has gross income. A lawyer who performs legal work for a client and receives property as payment has gross income equal to the fair market value of the property received. A lawyer who performs legal work for a client and receives a combination of cash and property as payment has gross income equal to the cash plus the fair market value of the property received. A lawyer who performs legal work for a client and receives the client's services as payment (in exchange) has income equal to the value of the services. A lawyer who performs legal work for a client and receives cash, property, and the client's services as payment has gross income equal to the cash, the fair market value of the property, and the fair market value of the services. [See Reg. § 1.61-1(d) (compensation received in forms other than in cash).] When an individual performs services and receives "something" in exchange, that "something" (or the value thereof) represents gross income. The form of that "something" is generally irrelevant. In our question, Sam rendered $4,000 worth of services and received property, the insurance policy, in return. Granted, the $10,000 value of the insurance policy received is greater than the $4,000 worth of services Sam rendered, but there is no question that Sam was paid for his services. Therefore, he has $4,000 of gross income as compensation for his services. The extra $6,000 of value that he received is addressed in the following paragraph.

The remaining $6,000 of financial benefit Sam received also constitutes gross income (an economic benefit or net accession to wealth), unless we can identify a Code provision specifically excluding it. One specific income exclusion provision that is very relevant here is IRC § 102. This section's general rule provides for a very beneficial exclusion from income of amounts received as gifts, bequests, devises, and inheritances. [IRC § 102(a).] While not defined in statutes, a gift, for purposes of this exclusion, is a transfer made for insufficient consideration with the donor acting from "detached and disinterested generosity." [See *Comm'r v. Duberstein*, 363 U.S. 278, 80 S.Ct. 1190 (1960).] It does not take too much analysis of the facts to conclude that the extra $6,000 worth of property Sam received was a gift from Beatrice, excludable by IRC § 102. The mother/son relationship between the parties and Beatrice's statements referring to the extra amount as a "gift" are sufficient to make this conclusion. One might argue that the entire $10,000 (value of property) given to Sam should constitute an excludable gift. However, this would require that Sam's rendering of his services was gratuitous in nature and the facts do not indicate this to be the case (the familial relationship alone is not sufficient).

Answer (a) is incorrect because it does not reflect the excluded gift portion of the transaction. **Answer (b) is incorrect** because while this was a part sale/part gift transaction, it has no bearing on the amount of income that Sam is required to recognize. See question 6, below for implications of the part sale/part gift nature of this transaction. **Answer (d) is also incorrect.**

The statement about his value of services rendered equaling the consideration that he is deemed to have paid for the policy is correct (and relevant in problem 6, below). However, it does not preclude his recognition of this as income. See problem 6, below, for more information. **Answer (e) is incorrect** because the $6,000 difference represents the excluded gift portion.

6.   **The correct answer is (b).** The entire $100,000 received by Sam is excludable from his gross income pursuant to IRC §101.

This is a <u>very difficult</u> question, the answer to which will take us through many diverse income tax issues. Sam suffered a horrible loss with the death of his mother, Beatrice. Financially, however, Sam's receipt of the $100,000 life insurance proceeds represents a benefit to him that will, absent a specific exclusion provision, result in the recognition of gross income (gross income being broadly defined). IRC § 101 is a good starting place for Sam as its general rule provides that life insurance proceeds received by reason of the insured's death are excluded from gross income of the beneficiary. [IRC § 101(a).] Unfortunately, to properly analyze the income tax implications to Sam in this question, we must travel a rather bumpy road requiring careful attention to numerous statutory road signs. Needless to say, this type of multi-step analysis makes for very good testing material.

The first detour encountered is the potential that the above-mentioned general exclusion rule for life insurance proceeds (IRC § 101(a)) may not apply to those received by Sam. When there has been a transfer, for valuable consideration, of a life insurance policy during the insured's life, the aforementioned general rule of full exclusion <u>may</u> not be applicable to benefits received by reason of the insured's death. [IRC § 101(a)(2).] Sam, through his services, effectively "paid," at least in part, for the life insurance policy. In other words, Sam furnished some consideration in exchange for the policy. True, the consideration Sam furnished, $4,000, was not as much as the value of the policy that he received, $10,000, but he provided consideration nonetheless. To help clarify this, the transaction involving the transfer of the policy could be recast or viewed in an equivalent, but alternative, manner eliminating the "exchange" element, substituting it with the transfer of cash between the parties. Sam performs services for Beatrice worth $4,000. Beatrice pays Sam, in cash, the $4,000. Sam then turns around and buys, for $4,000, Beatrice's life insurance policy. Clearly, he purchased the policy for less than its $10,000 fair market value, and this bargain purchase gives rise to the gift that Sam is deemed to have received (please see the analysis for question 5, above, for more information).

As indicated, IRC § 101(a)(2) contains this "consideration" exception to the general exclusion rule of life insurance benefits. When a life insurance policy has been transferred for consideration, as it was in the facts of our question, the exclusion for benefits proceeds received at the insured's death is <u>limited</u> to the consideration paid by the transferee plus any additional premiums paid by the transferee subsequent to the transfer. In our problem, transferee Sam "paid" $4,000 in consideration for the policy plus $1,000 in policy premiums subsequent to the transfer. Applying this "consideration" limitation of IRC § 101(a)(2) to these facts, Sam's exclusion would be limited to only <u>$5,000</u> ($4,000 plus $1,000) of the $100,000 received. The $95,000 of remaining proceeds would not be excluded pursuant to this rule.

This "consideration" exception (in IRC § 101(a)(2)) to the general full exclusion rule of IRC § 101(a) has, in classic law school form, exceptions thereto. One such "exception to the exception" is at issue in this question, and it requires the application of Code sections seemingly unrelated to the insurance provisions at issue. Specifically, IRC § 101(a)(2)(a) effectively provides that you can forget the aforementioned "consideration" limitation and qualify for full exclusion of life insurance proceeds even if the policy was transferred for consideration if, the basis of the policy in the hands of the transferee is "determined in whole or in part by reference" to the basis of the policy in the hands of the transferor. In other words, even though there has been a transfer of a policy for consideration, <u>if</u> the transferee's basis is essentially a carryover basis from the transferor, the "consideration" limitation evaporates, and proceeds from the policy are fully excluded. To determine if Sam qualifies for this "exception to the exception," we must determine Sam's basis in the policy and how such basis was derived. The stakes, for Sam are dramatic: a "carryover" basis resulting in full exclusion of the $100,000 life insurance proceeds received, while a non-carryover basis results in an exclusion of only $5,000 of the $100,000 received, the balance included in his gross income.

Beatrice's transfer of the policy to Sam was, in part, a "gift" and, in part, a "sale." In such part gift/part sale situations we have two possible rules to consider in determining Sam's (the transferee's) basis (or "adjusted basis" hereinafter AB). A donee's AB in property received as a gift is generally the AB of the donor/transferor; a so-called "carryover" AB. [IRC § 1015.] The AB in property purchased, however, is generally determined by the transferee's "cost." [IRC §§ 1011 and 1012.] In part gift/part sale situations the resulting transferee's basis is the <u>greater</u> of: (1) the amount paid by the donee, or (2) the donor's basis at the time of the gift. [Reg. 1.1015-4(a), (the greater of these two is also increased for any gift tax paid adjustment – this is not present here).] Sam's AB is the greater of the $4,000 consideration he was deemed to have paid for the policy, or Beatrice's AB in the policy of $5,000 (as indicated in this question's facts). Since Beatrice's $5,000 AB exceeds the $4,000 Sam "paid," Sam's AB in the policy is $5,000, a "carryover" AB.

Now that we have determined Sam's AB in the life insurance policy to be a carryover AB, this places him squarely within the exception of IRC § 101(a)(2)(A). This, in turn, overrides the "consideration" limitation, which ultimately results in Sam's exclusion of the full $100,000 insurance proceeds received.

Had the facts to this question been altered slightly so that, for example, Beatrice's AB in the policy was only $3,000 rather than the $5,000 in our question, the results to Sam would have been quite different. In this revised hypothetical, Sam's $4,000 consideration "paid" for the policy would have been greater than Beatrice's AB, resulting in Sam having a "cost" AB in the policy rather than a "carryover" AB. In turn, he would <u>not</u> qualify under the exception in IRC § 101(a)(2)(A), which ultimately would result in his exclusion of the life insurance proceeds being limited to only $5,000 ($4,000 consideration paid for the policy plus the $1,000 he paid in premiums subsequent to the transfer).

Answer (a) is incorrect. Sam does have gross income of $4,000, but this is not as a result of receiving the policy proceeds at Beatrice's death. Rather, Sam has $4,000 of gross income when Beatrice transferred the policy to him as "payment" for his services. This answer (a) corresponds to the correct answer for question 5, above. **Answers (c) and (d) are incorrect** because both answers fail to reflect that Sam meets the requirements of IRC § 101(a)(2)(A) and is therefore entitled to fully exclude the $100,000 insurance proceeds received. Answer (d) would be the correct answer had Sam's AB in the policy transferred from Beatrice not been a "carryover" AB. For more information see the revised fact hypothetical discussed in the analysis of the correct answer (b), above. **Answer (e) is incorrect** because the correct response (b) is presented.

7. **Answer (d) best describes the income tax consequences to Maureen.** This is a complex problem (as is this entire series of questions) and involves multiple steps to arrive at the correct answer. Determining Maureen's "adjusted basis" (AB) of the property is the first important component of this question. Pursuant to IRC § 1011(a), the AB of the property is the "cost basis" of the property adjusted for certain items. The cost basis is simply the cost of the property. [IRC § 1012).] In the present case, the $125,000 Maureen paid for the property ten years ago represents her cost basis of the property.

Maureen's borrowing of the $150,000 on the equity of the property five years ago, in and of itself, is of no income tax consequence. No income is realized from borrowing of monies, as there is no net accession to wealth (a general prerequisite for income realization). [See *Comm'r v. Glenshaw Glass Co.*, 348 U.S. 426, 75 S.Ct. 473 (1955).] The act of borrowing also has no direct impact on AB. The basis of property may be affected, however, if funds are actually used to make substantial improvements to such property. [IRC § 1016(a); Reg. § 1.1016-2(a).] Here the entire proceeds of the loan were used for matters unrelated to the house, so the loan has no impact on Maureen's AB in the house (it remains at $125,000). While not pertinent to this question, your professor can easily take a problem such as this and ask about numerous other items including the deductibility of interest on this loan, the basis of the car purchased with some of the loan proceeds, etc.

A gift of property generally does not result in realization of gain or loss to a donor. However, under certain circumstances (i.e., if a donor receives "consideration"), a gift may in fact constitute a "part sale/part gift" with a resulting realization of gain. In a part sale/part gift situation, gain is realized to the extent the "amount realized" (AR) by the donor exceeds the donor's AB in the property. [Reg. § 1.1001-1(e).] This is consistent with the general principals of IRC § 1001. In the present case, while Maureen does not have any amount realized in the traditional sense (money or other property received, § 1001(b)), an amount is nonetheless realized. Pursuant to *Crane v. Commissioner* (331 U.S. 1, 67 S.Ct. 1047 (1947)), a liability associated with transferred property is considered an amount realized even when a transferee merely takes property subject to a mortgage. Therefore, Maureen's AR equals the $150,000 mortgage to which the property was taken subject to by her daughter, Denise. Again, while not part of this question, always be on the lookout for situations where the loan involved is greater than the fair market value of the property at the time of the transfer. In that case (which is not the case in our question), the fair market value is generally irrelevant, and "AR" is the full amount of the mortgage. [See *Comm'r v. Tufts* 461 U.S. 300, 103 S.Ct. 1826 (1983).]

Since the $150,000 amount realized by Maureen exceeds her AB of $125,000, a $25,000 gain is realized as a result of this "gift" to Denise. While not part of this question, pursuant to IRC § 1001(c), this gain is also recognized barring application of any nonrecognition provisions of the Code. Again, your professor could easily extend this question to encompass the IRC § 121 nonrecognition provisions for the sale of a principal residence.

Answer (a) is incorrect because no such income tax deduction exists for non-charitable gifts. There is, however, a "gift tax" provision that is often the source of confusion in this area. Gift taxes are a completely separate set of tax rules that, in general, may create a tax liability to the "donor" for the privilege of transferring wealth. The gift tax is usually not the subject of in-depth discussion in the basic federal income tax course but, rather, is often a separate law school course that also covers estate taxes and, perhaps, other subjects such as income taxation of estates and trusts, estate planning, and the like. With that said, there is a gift tax provision at IRC § 2503(b) that may exclude from taxable gifts for gift tax purposes, up to $10,000 (as indexed for inflation) per year, per donee. In other words, an individual can usually give $10,000 worth of assets (the number indexed for inflation) to a person (or any number of persons) in a year without such gift(s) counting as taxable gifts possibly subject to gift taxation. There is, however, no corresponding income tax deduction to the donor. While not part of this question, the value of gifts received by a donee ($250,000 to Denise representing the difference between the house's value and the consideration that she was deemed to have paid) is generally excludable from gross income pursuant to IRC § 102.

Answer (b) is incorrect because the $150,000 consideration deemed paid by Denise (see discussion for correct answer (d), above, is the "amount realized" component of a gain calculation, and not, income in and of itself. **Answer (c) is incorrect** because the numbers do not correspond to how a gain or loss is calculated. As indicated in the discussion for the correct response, above, a gain or loss is the difference between the amount realized by the transferor and the transferor's adjusted basis. The $400,000 in this question was the fair market value of the house at the time of the gift, but not Maureen's adjusted basis in it. **Answer (e) is incorrect** because while it is true that a portion of this transaction is a gift to Denise, and such portion most likely would be "tax-free" to Denise pursuant to IRC § 102, there still was consideration deemed paid by Denise. Because that consideration paid exceeded Maureen's adjusted basis in the property, the result is a gain realized by Maureen as discussed above.

8. **Answer (a) is correct.** This too is a difficult question involving multiple steps but caution, this easily could have been an even more difficult question. It should be noted that this series of questions was originally part of an even more "involved" essay question on one of the author's tax exams. Denise's sale does result in a realized gain and we will conclude that the entire amount of such gain will be <u>recognized</u>.

While this question does not require the actual calculation of such gain, it might be helpful to utilize the actual numbers provided and discuss the answer in this context. As with her mother, the first component of calculating Denise's gain from the house sale is to determine its adjusted basis (AB). As discussed with respect to question 7, above, the "gift" to

Denise was actually a part sale/part gift situation. In such situations, the resulting transferee's basis is the greater of: 1) the amount paid by the donee, or 2) the donor's basis at the time of the gift. [Reg. § 1.1015-4(a) (the greater of these two is also increased for any gift tax paid adjustment; this is not present here).] While in this question, Denise did not pay any monies to Maureen to acquire the house, the aforementioned *Crane* case also stands for the proposition that a mortgage loan taken "subject to" by a transferee is deemed consideration paid. Denise took the property subject to the $150,000 loan and, therefore, this is deemed the amount paid for purpose of determining Denise's AB. Since the $150,000 exceeds Maureen's basis in the house of $125,000 (see above), Denise's AB in the house is $150,000.

Denise's subsequent sale of the property results in the realization of gain. As previously discussed in the correct answer to question 7, above, the amount of this gain is the "amount realized" (AR) from its sale (the sales price) less the "adjusted basis" (AB) in the property. [IRC § 1001(a).] Here, Denise sold the property for $450,000 and this is her AR for purposes of determining her gain. [See *Crane v. Comm'r* (331 U.S. 1, 67 S.Ct. 1047 (1947) (the mortgage being taken "subject to" by the buyer is added to any cash received to determine the transferor's AR).] This results in a realized gain to Denise of $300,000 (AR of $450,000 less AB of $150,000). Again, the calculation of Denise's actual gain is not required for this particular question but might be helpful in understanding the answer to this question or similar questions that you might face on an exam.

As discussed in other questions in this book, in every fact pattern in which something is sold (or otherwise disposed of), the author likes to go through the following analysis; always ask these three questions:

1) Does the sale (or disposition) result in a realized gain or loss and if so, what is the amount? This is computing the amount of gain (or loss). It is the AR (amount realized) less one's AB (adjusted basis).

2) If we have a realized gain or loss, is it recognized (i.e. reportable for income tax purposes)? As a taxpayer, you would like the answer to be NO for gains – I do not want to recognize, report, the gain (said another way, I'd like to be able to exclude this gain from my income).

3) If the gain or loss is recognized, is it accorded "capital" gain or loss treatment? This is primarily the issue of "capital gains (or losses)" that are treated differently for income tax purposes.

We have already addressed the first issue and determined that Denise has a realized gain from the sale of her house. Again, while not required for this question, her realized gain was $300,000 (AR of $450,000 less AB of $150,000). We now move on to a key part of this question and that is item

#2 above: does Denise have to *recognize* her realized gain? Realized gains are recognized (reported as income) unless there is a particular Code provision providing for its exclusion or non-recognition. [IRC § 1001(c).] The law has, for a long time, given some relief (non-recognition) to homeowners with respect to the sale of one's principal residence. We find this in IRC § 121 and it is often referred to as an "exclusion of gain from sale of principal residence." More accurately, IRC § 121 is a non-recognition (of gain) provision. Effective for sales of a taxpayer's principal residence after May 6, 1997, IRC § 121 provides for the exclusion of up to $250,000 of gain ($500,000 in the case of certain married individuals), if certain conditions are met.

Again, it may be helpful to first present the landscape of this analysis. Immediately below is a slide that this professor uses in class to address the various components of IRC § 121. The application and analysis of these steps follows.

§121 NON-RECOGNITION

Step 1: Does non-recognition (exclusion) even apply?
      a) Ownership test **and**
      b) Use Test

         (if necessary, look to prorating provision §121(c))

Step 2: Okay, we qualify for non-recognition. Now to the new (in 2009) "overlay" for "qualified/non-qualified" use in §121(b)(5): **If required to do so**, split the **total realized gain** into two parts:

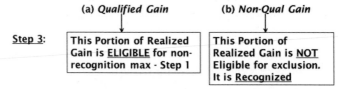

(a) *Qualified Gain*   **(b) *Non-Qual Gain***

Step 3:

This Portion of Realized Gain is **ELIGIBLE** for non-recognition max - Step 1	This Portion of Realized Gain is **NOT** Eligible for exclusion. It is **Recognized**

From 1997 through 2008 (and in prior editions of this book), IRC § 121 was much simpler. Our analysis consisted of only "Step 1," above (there were no steps 2 and 3). Fortunately for Denise, we shall see that we need not address Steps 2 & 3 in his case (please see other problems in this book that cover the entire scope of this section.)

Step 1 of our IRC § 121 analysis consists of the two basic requirements for this exclusion, commonly referred to as the "ownership" and "use" tests. The taxpayer must have owned the house for at least two years (looking back five years from the date of sale) **and** must have used it as his or her principal residence for two years (looking back five years from the date of sale). [IRC § 121(a).] This IRC § 121 exclusion provision is fertile grounds for examination questions both in multiple choice and essay forms. In this particular question, however, the determination of whether Denise can utilize this exclusion is fairly straightforward. She clearly meets the two-year "use" test having lived in this house since its purchase by her mother ten years earlier. However, she has owned the house for only one year, thus failing to meet the two-year ownership requirement. Because she has not met both of these requirements, Denise is not entitled to exclude any portion of the gain pursuant to IRC § 121.

There is a provision in the section, specifically IRC § 121(c) that provides a partial potential exclusion/non-recognition when a taxpayer fails the two-year ownership and use tests. This provision is not applicable to Denise but for information purposes, the maximum amount of the exclusion ($250,000 for single and, possibly, $500,000 for a married couple) is prorated if the taxpayer's failure to comply with the two-year provisions was for a statutorily defined "good reason." There are numerous "good reasons" identified in the code and regulations but suffice it to say that moving closer to one's existing job, as is the case for Denise in this question, is not one of them (please see the analysis, below, for incorrect answer (c) for more information). At this point we have our answer that the full amount of her realized gain will be recognized.

It is important, when analyzing an IRC § 121 question to methodically go through the aforementioned three steps in the order presented. Because Denise fails to qualify for IRC § 121 non-recognition provision, we **stop** and do not proceed to the new (as of 2008) Steps 2 & 3. These latter two steps are not at issue for Denise. Had we found that Denise was eligible for an exclusion/non-recognition of some or all of her gain from the sale of her house, we would then proceed to Steps 2 & 3. While not applicable to this question, it might be helpful to discuss the general concepts of these latter two steps to round out our discussion of the subject. These additional steps are necessary for situations where an individual has at any time during the entire period he or she owned the house, used it for something other than his or her principal residence for the entire period that they owned it (e.g., used it as a vacation home, left it vacant, rented it out, etc.). If this were the case, it can be harmful (tax-wise) and we would have much longer trek to determine the proper outcome (please see later questions in this book where these steps are implicated). Again, with respect to Denise in our question, we don't even get to Steps 2 & 3 because in Step 1, we determined that she is not even eligible for the IRC § 121 exclusion. Therefore, we need not proceed any further.

This question, as well as those earlier in this book, are meant to serve as a "soft" introduction to the IRC § 121 non-recognition provision for the gain from the sale of one's principal residence. Other questions in this book are more complex and take us down the entire tortuous road of IRC § 121.

While not at issue in this problem, it should be noted that generally, the exclusion provisions of IRC § 121 cannot be used more than once in a two-year period. [IRC § 121(b)(3).]

Back to Step 1, it should also be noted that the statute does not require that the requisite two-year "use" and "ownership" period be co-extensive. While again, this is not an issue in this question, it is a common misunderstanding (read as "good testing area") that the two "two-year" qualifying periods must be at the same time. It is also a common misunderstanding (again, read as "good testing area") that the "five-year look back period" for purposes of determining two-year ownership and use somehow requires that the taxpayer either owned or used the house for at least five years. This is not correct, and again, while this is not at issue in this question, it might be helpful for your analysis of other IRC § 121 related questions.

Answer (b) is incorrect because Denise is not entitled to the $250,000 exclusion provided in IRC § 121 as she fails the aforementioned two-year "ownership" requirement. **Answer (c) is also incorrect** but is probably the most commonly selected incorrect answer. As discussed above, there is, in IRC § 121(c), a partial or "prorated" exclusion if the taxpayer fails to meet both of the two-year tests. However, this partial exclusion is applicable only when the house sale is "by reason of a change in place of employment, health, or, to the extent provided in regulations, unforeseen circumstances." [IRC § 121(c)(2)(B).] Denise did not sell her house due to a job change or for health reasons, and there is no indication of anything that might constitute "unforeseen circumstances" in this question. Regulation § 1.121-3 contains a comprehensive discussion of the prorated exclusion including "safe harbors" for what are considered "unforeseen circumstances" as well as other factors to be considered in making this determination. However, this question contains no facts that would indicate that any of the factors enumerated in this regulation would be applicable to allow Denise to exclude a portion of the gain pursuant to IRC § 121.

Answer (d) is incorrect because there is no blanket non-recognition provision applicable to "this situation." **Answer (e) is incorrect**, but it is also the source of much confusion among students and the general public. Prior to the $250,000/$500,000 exclusion of IRC § 121, the primary provision affecting gain recognition from the sale of a principal residence was IRC § 1034. This latter section, which was repealed and replaced by current IRC § 121 in 1997, also provided for gain exclusion, but its mechanism for doing so was very different. Basically, this old section provided that if you purchased (and occupied) a new principal residence within a two-year period of selling your old principal residence (either before or, as was more common, after the sale), then gain was recognized only to the extent, if any, that the purchase price of the new house was less than the sales price of the old house. In other words, if a taxpayer always "moved-up" to a more expensive house, gain was not recognized. However, this old IRC § 1034 provision was merely a "deferral" mechanism because any gain not recognized pursuant to this provision, served to reduce the adjusted basis of the new house (to be potentially recognized upon a subsequent sale). As indicated, this old IRC § 1034 is no longer valid law (but if your professor covers this material in greater depth, be aware that prior deferrals of gain under that law may still be reflected in a taxpayer's adjusted basis for their home). Current IRC § 121 does not require that the taxpayer purchase a new house, and any gain excluded pursuant to the section is a real exclusion (not merely a deferral of recognition) with no effect on the adjusted basis of any subsequent house purchase.

Not trying to add additional confusion to the matter, there was an "old" IRC § 121 that was also repealed with enactment of current IRC § 121 in 1997. The old section was a "once in a lifetime" exclusion of a certain dollar amount of gain from the sale of a principal residence for taxpayers fifty-five years of age and older. This old IRC § 121 was in addition to old IRC § 1034 and their combination was a logistics mess (and tough area for instruction) when compared to the relatively straightforward rules of the current IRC § 121. The current IRC § 121 has no age limit, can be used over and over again to exclude gain (generally, just not more than once every two years), and has larger exclusion limitations. Again, while this old IRC § 121 is no longer valid law, it is the source of some confusion among taxpayers.

9. **Answer (a) is correct.** This question addresses an issue discussed in the analysis of the answer in question 8, immediately above. Be forewarned that there will be a lot of duplication in our analysis here. This is not to torture you with extraneous information but, rather, to properly analyze the answer independently so that you need not refer back to question 8 for important substantive material. After a somewhat lengthy analysis, we will conclude that in this question, Denise may be entitled to a partial exclusion (or non-recognition) of her gain from the sale of her home. In question 8, above, we concluded that she was not entitled to any exclusion (non-recognition) so here, she will be entitled to exclude (not recognize) **more** than zero as was the case in question 8. So, hold on as we are in for a long ride.

While this question does not require the actual calculation of such gain, it might be helpful to utilize the actual numbers provided and discuss the answer in this context. As with her mother, the first component of calculating Denise's gain from the house sale is to determine its adjusted basis (AB). As discussed with respect to question 8, above, the "gift" to Denise was actually a part sale/part gift situation. In such situations, the resulting transferee's basis is the <u>greater</u> of: 1) the amount paid by the donee, or 2) the donor's basis at the time of the gift. [Reg. § 1.1015-4(a) (the greater of these two is also increased for any gift tax paid adjustment; this is not present here).] While in this question, Denise did not pay any monies to Maureen to acquire the house, the aforementioned *Crane* case also stands for the proposition that a mortgage loan taken "subject to" by a transferee is deemed consideration paid. Denise took the property subject to the $150,000 loan and, therefore, this is deemed the amount paid for purpose of determining Denise's AB. Since the $150,000 exceeds Maureen's basis in the house of $125,000 (see above), Denise's AB in the house is $150,000.

Denise's subsequent sale of the property results in the realization of gain. As previously discussed in the correct answer to question 8, above, the amount of this gain is the "amount realized" (AR) from its sale (the sales price) less the "adjusted basis" (AB) in the property. [IRC § 1001(a).] Here, Denise sold the property for $450,000 and this is her AR for purposes of determining her gain. [See *Crane v. Comm'r* (331 U.S. 1, 67 S.Ct. 1047 (1947) (the mortgage being taken "subject to" by the buyer is added to any cash received to determine the transferor's AR).] This results in a realized gain to Denise of $300,000 (AR of $450,000 less AB of $150,000). Again, the calculation of Denise's actual gain is not required for this particular question but might be helpful in understanding the answer to this question or similar questions that you might face on an exam.

As discussed in other questions in this book, in every fact pattern in which something is sold (or otherwise disposed of), the author likes to go through the following analysis; always ask these three questions:

1) Does the sale (or disposition) result in a <u>realized</u> gain or loss and if so, what is the <u>amount</u>? This is computing the amount of gain (or loss). It is the AR (amount realized) less one's AB (adjusted basis).

2) If we have a <u>realized</u> gain or loss, is it <u>recognized</u> (i.e. reportable for income tax purposes)? As a taxpayer, you would like the answer to be NO for gains – I do not want to recognize, report, the gain (said another way, I'd like to be able to exclude this gain from my income).

3) If the gain or loss is recognized, is it accorded "capital" gain or loss treatment? This is primarily the issue of "capital gains (or losses)" that are treated differently for income tax purposes.

We have already addressed the first issue and determined that Denise has a realized gain from the sale of her house. Again, while not required for this question, her realized gain was $300,000 (AR of $450,000 less AB of $150,000). We now move on to a key part of this question and that is item #2 above: does Denise have to *recognize* her realized gain? Realized gains are recognized (reported as income) unless there is a particular Code provision providing for its exclusion or non-recognition. [IRC § 1001(c).] The law has, for a long time, given some relief (non-recognition) to homeowners with respect to the sale of one's principal residence. We find this in IRC § 121 and it is often referred to as an "exclusion of gain from sale of principal residence." More accurately, IRC § 121 is a non-recognition (of gain) provision. Effective for sales of a taxpayer's principal residence after May 6, 1997, IRC § 121 provides for the exclusion of up to $250,000 of gain ($500,000 in the case of certain married individuals), if certain conditions are met.

Again, it may be helpful to first present the landscape of this analysis. Immediately below is a slide that this professor uses in class to address the various components of IRC § 121. The application and analysis of these steps follows.

§121 NON-RECOGNITION

Step 1: Does non-recognition (exclusion) even apply?
          a) Ownership test **and**
          b) Use Test
            (if necessary, look to prorating provision §121(c))

Step 2: Okay, we qualify for non-recognition. Now to the new (in 2009) "overlay" for "qualified/non-qualified" use in §121(b)(5): **If required to do so**, split the total realized gain into two parts:

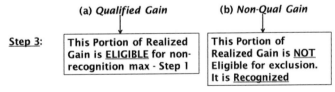

Step 3:	This Portion of Realized Gain is **ELIGIBLE** for non-recognition max - Step 1	This Portion of Realized Gain is **NOT** Eligible for exclusion. It is **Recognized**

From 1997 through 2008 (and in prior editions of this book), IRC § 121 was much simpler. Our analysis consisted of only "Step 1," above (there were no steps 2 and 3). Fortunately for Denise, we shall see that we need not address Steps 2 & 3 in his case (please see other problems in this book that cover the entire scope of this section.)

Step 1 of our IRC § 121 analysis consists of the two basic requirements for this exclusion, commonly referred to as the "ownership" and "use" tests. The taxpayer must have owned the house for at least two years (looking back five years from the date of sale) **and** must have used it as his or her principal residence for two years (looking back five years from the date of sale). [IRC § 121(a).] This IRC § 121 exclusion provision is fertile grounds for examination questions both in multiple choice and essay forms. In this particular question, however, the determination of whether Denise can utilize this exclusion is fairly straightforward. She clearly meets the two-year "use" test having lived in this house since its purchase by her mother ten years earlier. However, she has owned the house for only one year, thus failing to meet the two-year ownership requirement. On the surface, it appears that Denise is not entitled to exclude (not recognize) any of the realized gain from her house sale (this is what we concluded in question 8, above). Recall, however, that while not applicable to Denise in question 8, we did discuss a provision (IRC § 121(c)) that provides a partial potential exclusion/non-recognition when a taxpayer fails the two-year ownership and use tests. Further, as indicated in the analysis of question 8 (discussing the then incorrect answer (c)), we briefly examined IRC § 121(c) and indicated that it contains a "partial" or "prorated" exclusion for certain taxpayers failing to meet both of the two-year tests. This partial exclusion is applicable when the house sale is "by reason of a change in place of employment, health, or, to the extent provided in regulations, unforeseen circumstances." [IRC § 121(c)(2)(B).]

In this question, Denise did sell her house because of health reasons and would be entitled to a partial exclusion. Therefore, answer (a) is correct. It might be a good idea to carefully read regulation § 1.121-3 for detailed information about the prorated (partial) IRC § 121(c) exclusion including what is required for purposes of meeting the "moving for health reasons," and other, requirements.

While this question does not require that we compute Denise's maximum exclusion, it might be helpful to go through the numbers to illustrate how this partial exclusion works. To simplify the Code here, you look to see for what period of time the taxpayer actually met both the "ownership" and "use" requirements. In our case, while Denise's use easily exceeded the two-year period, her ownership was only for one year; so both requirements were met for only one year. (If you prefer, you can do this by taking whichever period, ownership or use, is less). To get the partial or prorated exclusion, you take that portion of the two-year period for which she did meet the requirements (here one of the two years or ½) and multiply that by the maximum available exclusion ($250,000 for a single person). Therefore, the actual maximum exclusion available to Denise in our problem is ½ of $250,000 or $125,000.

Even though we continue our analysis below, we have, at this point, reached the answer to our question. Denise will be entitled to exclude (not recognize) a greater amount of her gain then she could in question 8.

It is important, when analyzing an IRC § 121 question to methodically go through the aforementioned three steps in the order presented. Fortunately for Denise in this question, these latter two steps are not at issue. These additional steps are necessary for situations where an individual has at any time during the entire period he or she owned the house, used it for something other than his or her principal residence for the entire period that they owned it (e.g., used it as a vacation home, left it vacant, rented it out, etc.). If this were the case, it can be harmful (tax-wise) and we would have much longer trek to determine the proper outcome (please see later questions in this book where these steps are implicated). For Denise, the facts in this question have her using the house as her principal residence for the entire time of her ownership. Therefore, we need not proceed any further.

This question, as well as those earlier in this book, are meant to serve as a "soft" introduction to the IRC § 121 non-recognition provision for the gain from the sale of one's principal residence. Other questions in this book are more complex and take us down the entire tortuous road of IRC § 121.

While not at issue in this problem, it should be noted that generally, the exclusion provisions of IRC § 121 cannot be used more than once in a two-year period. [IRC § 121(b)(3).]

Back to Step 1, it should also be noted that the statute does not require that the requisite two-year "use" and "ownership" period be co-extensive. While again, this is not an issue in this question, it is a common misunderstanding (read as "good testing area") that the two "two-year" qualifying periods must be at the same time. It is also a common misunderstanding (again, read as "good testing area") that the "five-year look back period" for purposes of determining two-year ownership and use somehow requires that the taxpayer either owned or used the house for at least five years. This is not correct, and again, while this is not at issue in this question, it might be helpful for your analysis of other IRC § 121 related questions.

Answers (b) and (c) are incorrect because mathematically, they do not make sense. **Answer (d)** is incorrect because in the previous question there was no significance of her house location vis-à-vis her Atlanta job.

10. **The correct answer is (b).** The questions in this series are somewhat tied together and, unfortunately, if you get off track with one, it may have a ripple effect causing errors in other questions. With this question, the answer is

basically the same as in question 8 above but is, in reality, a bit more straightforward than that question. The difference in these facts is that the gift of the house from Maureen to Denise is a true gift as opposed to the part sale/part gift scenario in question 8. For purposes of this question, the only difference to Denise would be that her adjusted basis (AB) in the house is a gift "carryover" basis of $125,000. [IRC § 1015.] Again, this question does not really require that we determine Denise's AB. While Denise's AB in the house is different in this question, the balance of the analysis to question 8, above, is relevant. Looking at Denise's ownership and use for IRC § 121 gain exclusion qualification, we once again see that Denise falls short on the ownership requirement. Additionally, in this question she is not entitled to any portion or prorated exclusion, as she is not selling her house for any of the requisite reasons identified in IRC § 121(c). Therefore, she is not entitled to exclude any portion of the gain realized on the sale of her house.

Because this question is pretty much the same as question 8, above, and the author respects the value of your time, we will not replicate all of the appropriate steps to consider in answering this question. For a more complete analysis of this question, please see the analysis for question 8 (the only difference between the two being the amount of Denise's realized gain). Also, this question, as well as those earlier in this book, are meant to serve as a "soft" introduction to the IRC § 121 non-recognition provision for the gain from the sale of one's principal residence. Other questions in this book are more complex and take us down the entire tortuous road of IRC § 121.

While this question does not require that we compute the gain, for reference purposes, she would have a gain of $325,000 ($450,000 sales price (AR) less her AB of $125,000).

Answer (a) is incorrect, but it is the most commonly selected incorrect answer. Students are often confused about "tacking" (adding) on the holding period of another individual. The confusion seems to arise because there are instances, for purposes of IRC § 121 that we do tack on periods of ownership and use of another in certain instances. In addition, in some tax issues other than IRC § 121, we do "tack" (add) on the holding period of the transferor when the transferee's basis in the property is determined with reference to the basis of the transferor. Unfortunately, these two situations do not overlap here. IRC § 121(d) contains special rules for the application of that section's exclusion of gain from the sale of a principal residence. Specifically, "tacking" ownership and use periods is allowed in certain situations involving deceased and former spouses. [IRC §§ 121(d)(2) and (d)(3).] There is no general "tacking" provision for purposes of IRC §121, when property is received as a gift or other situations where there is a carryover basis. While Denise cannot tack or add on Maureen's holding period to determine her ownership for purposes of IRC § 121, she could, for example, tack on her mother's holding period for capital gain classification purposes. [IRC § 1223(2).] This latter issue, however, has no relevance for qualification under IRC § 121 exclusion of gain from the sale of a principal residence.

Answers (c) and (d) are incorrect because, as discussed in the answers to questions 8 and 9, above, current law for the potential exclusion of gain from the sale of a principal residence no longer has, a requirement, that the taxpayer purchase a replacement residence. **Answer (e) is incorrect** because there is a correct answer: (b).

11. **The best answer is (d).** As discussed in more detail below, this is a "part sale/part gift" type of transaction. Jim's transfer of the fine crystal to Tina for consideration of $5,000 exceeds his $4,000 basis in the property, resulting in a realized (and recognized) gain to him of $1,000. As to Tina, the value of the property that she received in excess of what she paid for it represents a "gift" that is excludable from gross income pursuant to IRC § 102. A more thorough explanation follows.

The sale of property usually results in the realization of a gain or loss by the transferor. A gift of property, however, generally does not result in the realization of a gain or loss to a donor. Under certain circumstances (i.e., if a donor receives "consideration"), a "part sale/part gift" type transaction results. The transfer of the fine crystal from Jim to his niece Tina represents a *part sale/part gift* transaction. The sale component exists because Jim received consideration from Tina (the $5,000 in cash). A gift component also exists because the $30,000 value of the property far exceeded the amount Tina paid for it.

Income Tax Ramifications of the *Part Sale/Part Gift* Transaction to Jim (the transferor)

In *part sale/part gift* situations, the transferor (seller/donor) realizes *gain* to the extent the consideration received ("amount realized" or hereinafter AR) by the donor exceeds the donor's basis ("adjusted basis" or hereinafter AB) in the property. [Reg. § 1.1001-1(e).] This is consistent with the general principals of IRC § 1001(a); the difference between the AR and AB represents a <u>realized</u> gain or loss. Jim received consideration of $5,000 (in the form of cash) from the transfer to Tina and this represents his AR. Jim's AB in the fine crystal is a straightforward proposition here and is his $4,000 cost. [IRC §§ 1011 and 1012.] Since Jim's $5,000 AR from the transfer exceeds his AB of $4,000, Jim realizes a gain of $1,000. Pursuant to IRC § 1001(c), this gain is also recognized barring application of any nonrecognition provisions of the Code. There are no such provisions applicable to these facts, so Jim must *recognize* this $1,000 gain.

While not part of this question, Jim's $1,000 recognized gain would be classified as a long-term capital gain (the crystal qualifying as a capital asset and Jim held the property for more than one year before "selling" it).

Also not germane to this question but it bears mentioning, is that had Jim received consideration from Tina that was less than his AB (e.g. she paid him only $3,000) the regulations provide that no loss is recognized in such a part sale/part gift scenario. [Reg. § 1.1001-1(e).] This makes sense because pure gifts (where no consideration is received) would then result in realized losses to the donor.

Income Tax Ramifications to Tina Resulting from Jim's Transfer to Her

As indicated above, despite the fact that Tina *did* furnish some consideration to Jim, she received property of a value far in excess of what she paid. Logically, this is the "gift" component of the *part sale/part gift* type of transaction. IRC § 102 provides an exclusion from income to the recipient of gifts, bequests, devises, and inheritances. While no statutory definition of a gift exists, it is generally defined as a transfer without consideration that is made out of emotions of detached and disinterested generosity. [See *Comm'r v. Duberstein*, 363 U.S. 278, 80 S.Ct. 1190 (1960).] The facts are abundant to indicate that Jim's motivations were gratuitous. Jim "was originally just going to give it to her, his *favorite* niece," but she insisted on paying him something and he "reluctantly agreed." Therefore, the gift portion of this transaction ($25,000, the difference between the property's value and what Tina paid for it) is excludable from Tina's gross income as a gift pursuant to IRC § 102.

Answer (a) is incorrect because the part sale/part gift rules preclude recognition of losses by the donor/seller. In addition, this answer is incorrect because the net $25,000 benefit that Tina received is excludable as a gift. **Answer (b) is also incorrect** but it is a commonly selected answer. Basically, most of this answer is true except for the statement that a loss results and the reason for its nonrecognition. Because this is a *part sale/part gift* transaction, the gift element effectively precludes recognition of any loss. He really does not have a loss just because of the huge gift component. Rather, he has a gain because of the *part sale/part gift* analysis. [See Reg. § 1.11001-1(e).] Students sometimes confuse gift type sales such as this with losses between certain related parties that are not recognized pursuant to IRC § 267. Actually, a careful reading of IRC 267(c)(4) defining who constitutes a "related" party, will reveal that Tina is not related to Jim for purpose of § 267. **Answer (c) is incorrect** because, as discussed above, Jim does realize (and recognize) a gain due to the amount of consideration received exceeding his AB in the property. **Answer (e) is also incorrect.** This answer properly reflects the tax ramifications to Jim but fails to reflect that there is still a gift element to the transaction and it is excludable by Tina.

12. **The correct answer is (c).** This is a somewhat complex question that takes us through many steps and, unfortunately, is based upon a substantially correct analysis of the previous question 11. This professor would not ask such a combination of interrelated multiple-choice questions on an exam. Rather, these questions were developed from an exam essay question.

In every fact pattern in which something is sold (or otherwise disposed of), the author likes to go through the following analysis; always ask these three questions:

1) Does the sale (or disposition) result in a <u>realized</u> gain or loss and if so, what is the <u>amount</u>? This is computing the amount of gain (or loss). It is the AR (amount realized) less one's AB (adjusted basis).

2) If we have a <u>realized</u> gain or loss, is it <u>recognized</u> (i.e. reportable for income tax purposes)? As a taxpayer, you would like the answer to be NO for gains – I do not want to recognize, report, the gain (said another way, I'd like to be able to exclude this gain from my income).

3) If the gain or loss is recognized, is it accorded "capital" gain or loss treatment? This is primarily the issue of "capital gains (or losses)" that are treated differently for income tax purposes.

Because this question involves a multi-step analysis and because the author recognizes the value of your time, both an **abbreviated/short** and **comprehensive/long** analyses are provided below.

The <u>abbreviated/short</u> version of the analysis for this question is that Tina's realized gain is the difference between the $28,000 sales price and her basis in the fine crystal of $5,000, or <u>$23,000</u>. Her basis in the crystal is $5,000 because it exceeds what would have been a carryover basis from Jim of $4,000. This gain is <u>recognized</u> and is characterized as a <u>short-term capital gain</u>. This is because the crystal represents a capital asset and her holding period, was only a month. Because her basis was not a carryover basis from Jim, she is unable to "tack" Jim's four-year holding period onto hers. [See IRC §§ 1221, 1222 and 1223(2).]

The following <u>comprehensive/long</u> analysis presents a step-by-step discussion of the answer to this question that can be applied to other gain/loss questions.

The first step is determining whether Tina has a <u>realized</u> a gain or loss on the sale of the fine crystal. For this, we need two basic components: her sales price ("amount realized" or, hereinafter, AR) and her basis in the crystal ("adjusted basis or, hereinafter, AB). The difference between the two represents a <u>realized</u> gain or loss. [IRC § 1001(a).] Each of these two components, AR and AB, can present a variety of complex tax issues for exam and real-world tax purposes. The AR side is straightforward in our question and is her $28,000 sales price (much to the chagrin of Jim). Other questions in this book present more complex issues involving a taxpayer's AR. In this question, the AB component is a bit more difficult to derive.

The general starting place for determining one's AB in property is one's cost. [IRC §§ 1011 and 1012.] "Adjustments" to one's basis, while not at issue in this question, can result from many reasons including capital improvements (increasing basis), and depreciation expenses (reducing basis). Applying the general cost basis rule in our question, Tina's AB would appear to be $5,000, the amount that she paid Jim for the crystal. In fact, that will be her AB, but we need to consider other issues before arriving at that answer. Recall that the initial transfer of the crystal from Jim to Tina was considered a *part sale/part gift* type of transaction. Also recall that to Jim, we had to look at the amount of consideration that he received, and if it exceeded his AB, gain resulted. In fact, that is what did happen: Jim received consideration of $5,000 from Tina and his AB in the crystal was $4,000 (his original cost). We must look to these same *part sale/part gift* rules to determine Tina's AB in such a transaction. The two possible measurements for Tina's AB are either what she paid for it (her cost basis), because this was in part a sale/purchase, or Jim's carryover AB (pursuant to the general IRC § 1015 AB rules for gifts) because this was in part a gift. The regulations provide guidance in such *part sale/part gift* situations. The transferee's basis is the <u>greater</u> of: (1) the amount paid by the donee, or (2) the donor's basis at the time of the gift. [Reg. § 1.1015-4(a) (the greater of these two is also increased for any gift tax paid adjustment; this is not present here).] Since the $5,000 Tina paid Jim exceeds Jim's AB in the crystal, Tina's AB in the crystal is $5,000.

We can now answer the question in the first step of our gain/loss analysis: the amount of Tina's <u>realized</u> gain. Tina has a <u>realized</u> gain of <u>$23,000</u>, her AR (sales price) of $28,000 less her AB (as determined above) of $5,000.

The question we ask in our analysis of gain/loss situations is to determine the extent to which any <u>realized</u> gain is <u>recognized</u>. Recognition of gain basically means that it is reported as income for income tax purposes. IRC § 1001(c) provides that unless otherwise provided for in the Code, all realized gains and losses are recognized. While not at issue in this question, always be on the lookout for various nonrecognition provisions such as with sales between spouses and certain former spouses (IRC § 1041), gain from the sale of a principal residence (IRC § 121), and other nonrecognition provisions discussed elsewhere in this book. Unfortunately for Tina, there are no exclusion or non-recognition provisions applicable in these facts and her $23,000 realized gain will be <u>recognized</u>.

The last part of the analysis is to determine whether Tina's $23,000 of recognized gain is accorded special "capital gain" treatment. Historically, gains from the sale of certain types of assets have been accorded preferential tax treatment. While it is far beyond the scope of analysis for this question, modernly, "long-term" capital gains ("net capital gains" to be more specific), while included in a taxpayer's gross and taxable incomes, may be taxed at favorable (i.e., lower) tax rates. A capital gain analysis requires first determining that we are dealing with a "capital asset" after which the gain is characterized as having either long-term or short-term status.

IRC § 1221(a) defines a capital asset in a negative fashion, but for purposes of this analysis, it includes, by process of elimination, assets held for investment and personal-use purposes. There is little question that Tina's fine crystal qualifies as a capital asset. Long-term status is reserved for those assets held for <u>more than one year</u> (short-term status for assets held one year or less). [See IRC § 1222.] Tina purchased the crystal only one month prior to selling it and, at first brush, this appears to be the end of our analysis with Tina's gain characterized as a *short-term capital gain*. This is the correct answer, but one other issue needs to be addressed. Determining the holding period, for short- and long-term gain/loss classification, is controlled by IRC § 1223. At IRC § 1223(2) we have the so-called "tacking" rule, which essentially applies to situations where the taxpayer's AB is a carryover AB. Where this is the case, the transferee can add to his or her holding period, that of the transferor. This brings us to how we determined Tina's AB above. Recall that we determined her basis to be the greater amount that she paid (the $5,000) rather than Jim's AB of $4,000. Because Tina's AB was <u>not</u> a carryover AB, Tina is <u>not</u> entitled to "tack" or add on Jim's many-year holding period to hers. Therefore, Tina's holding period is measured by her actual holding period of a month (short-term status). Note, that had the facts been different here with the consideration Tina paid being less than Jim's AB, she would have had a long-term holding period via tacking.

In summary, Tina has a *realized* <u>$23,000 gain</u> from the sale of the crystal and it is a *recognized short term-capital gain*.

The issues of recognition, capital gain/loss treatment and holding periods (including "tacking" and other special rules) are addressed in other questions in this book. Needless to say, all of this material is *super fertile* ground for exam questions.

Answer (a) is incorrect because it wrongly classifies Tina's gain as a long-term capital gain. **Answer (b) is incorrect** because it states the wrong amount of Tina's gain and incorrectly classifies it as a long-term capital gain. Note, however, that had the facts been different with Tina's consideration being *less* than Jim's AB, this answer would most likely be the correct answer. **Answer (d) is incorrect** because it states the wrong amount of Tina's gain. **Answer (e) is incorrect** because this sale by Tina is separate from the initial transfer to her by Jim. Any nonrecognition because of the § 102 gift provisions do not carry over to this subsequent sale by Tina.

13. **The most accurate statement is (c).** This question is designed to illustrate the coordination of capital gains and losses and how they are reflected in determining a taxpayer's "adjusted gross income" (hereinafter AGI). The facts present the results of four transactions that yielded capital gains and losses to Bill last year. Presentation of the gains and losses in this problem as long-term and short-term capital gains and losses presupposes that such gains and losses have been properly realized and recognized, as well as properly classified as to their long- and short-term capital gain and loss status. Questions presented elsewhere in this book address these realization, recognition, and classification issues. After a somewhat lengthy analysis below, we will conclude that Bill's AGI for last year was $57,000 representing gross income of $60,000 less $3,000 of deductible losses. In addition, he has a $2,000 long-term capital loss carryover to the current year.

Once capital gains and losses have been classified as to their long- or short-term holding status, as is the case here, IRC § 1222 effectively requires that we combine and net such gains and losses in a particular manner. Simplifying the statutory rules, we split the gains and losses up based on holding period, separating them into two groups or columns: short-term gains/losses and long-term gains/losses. Bill's capital gains and losses for last year would be grouped as follows:

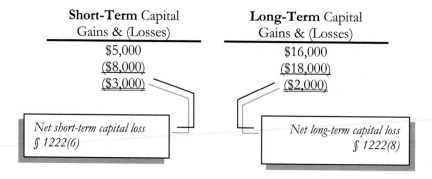

Short-Term Capital Gains & (Losses)	**Long-Term** Capital Gains & (Losses)
$5,000	$16,000
($8,000)	($18,000)
($3,000)	($2,000)

Net short-term capital loss
§ 1222(6)

Net long-term capital loss
§ 1222(8)

Note that the correct groupings of capital gains and losses presented above are different from the somewhat misleading (i.e., tricky) way in which the gains and losses are presented in the question facts. Also note from the above groupings that gains and losses are then combined and netted within their respective short-term and long-term columns.

As illustrated above, Bill has $3,000 and $2,000 of short-term and long-term capital losses, respectively, for a total of $5,000 of losses. Can Bill deduct these $5,000 of losses in computing his AGI for the year involved? IRC § 1211(b) provides the answer. An individual is allowed to first use capital losses to offset capital gains, which is what we did by netting Bill's gains and losses above. Our facts yielded losses in both the short-term and long-term columns but had there been a loss in one column and a gain in the other, we would net the two (i.e., using losses to offset gains). For an individual, once capital losses have been used to offset capital gains (accomplished by netting gains and losses), any remaining capital loss can be deducted up to a $3,000 limit. [IRC § 1211(b).] In Bill's case, he has capital losses (after netting with capital gains) totaling $5,000. Bill's deduction for capital losses last year is therefore limited to $3,000. Deductions for losses are allowed "above the line" in computing AGI. [IRC § 62.] We now have the answer to part of our question: Bill's AGI for last year was $57,000 ($60,000 of salary income less $3,000 of capital losses).

Last year, Bill had capital losses of $5,000 in the aggregate, but was allowed a deduction of only $3,000, leaving a total of $2,000 of capital losses unused (not deducted). Fortunately, individuals are entitled to carryover unused capital losses to future years (to offset future gains and/or be deducted subject to the same $3,000 per year limitation). Capital loss carryovers maintain their same status (as short or long term) for purposes of future year groupings and netting. Recall that last year, we determined Bill had net short-term capital losses of $3,000 and net long-term capital losses of $2,000. Recall that Bill was limited in his deduction of net capital losses to $3,000 resulting in $2,000 of losses to be carried over to this year. The question, at this point, is from where (short-term or long-term) does the $3,000 of losses used last year come? A corollary question is: what is the status (short-term or long-term) of the $2,000 in capital loss carried over to this year? This answer lies deeply concealed within IRC § 1212(b). The "quick and dirty" answer (that works in almost every instance) is that the "short-term" losses are the first to be used. In Bill's case, the $3,000 of capital losses allowed as a deduction last year came first, and entirely in Bill's case, from the short-term side. The status of the $2,000 capital loss carryover to this year is, by default, long-term.

This can be illustrated as follows:

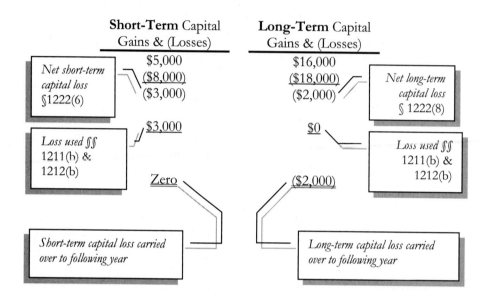

Note that our "quick and dirty" rule of IRC § 1212(b), that short-term capital losses get used first, is not something that you will find spelled out in the statute. Be aware that your professor may want to properly analyze the statutory provisions (which, in almost every case, will yield the same result as our simplified rule).

One might wonder why so much is made out of properly classifying capital gains and losses as short-term and long-term, and why there is so much attention paid, as in this question, to the proper utilization and carryover of capital losses. Historically, gains from the sale of certain types of assets (capital assets) that has been accorded preferential tax treatment. While it is far beyond the scope of the analysis for this question, modernly, "long-term" capital gains ("net capital gains" to be more specific), while included in a taxpayer's gross and taxable incomes, may be taxed at favorable (i.e., lower) tax rates. Proper classification of losses and gains (including capital loss carryovers) is critical in determining the extent of favorably taxed long-term capital gains.

Answer (a) is incorrect because it fails to recognize the $3,000 limitation for the deduction, in any one year, of excess capital losses. **Answer (b) is incorrect** because it incorrectly used long-term capital losses first to make up the $3,000 of deductible capital losses. **Answer (d) is not the best answer.** Technically, this answer could be considered a correct answer but it is not the <u>best</u> answer because it does not distinguish the status of the capital loss carryover as either short-term, long-term, or some combination thereof.

14. **Answer (e) is correct.** This is a multi-step question that combines many diverse income tax issues, requires careful attention to math (albeit only addition and subtraction), is a bit unfair because it requires, in part, a correct analysis of the previous question (13), and to top it all off, the correct answer is the hated "none of the above." While the author apologizes for such a question, and, in advance, for the lengthy analysis to follow, it is a good problem to work through a host of income tax issues.

The abbreviated analysis is that of Bill's two car sales in this year, only the first (the car inherited from Fred) results in a recognized gain or loss. He recognizes a $3,500 gain, which is considered a *long-term capital gain*. The second car sale resulted in a realized loss of $3,000 but such loss is <u>not</u> recognized (and therefore is not classified as a capital loss). Next, we take the $3,500 long-term capital gain and combine it with any capital loss carryovers from prior years (keeping short-terms and long-terms separate as is normally the case with multiple capital gains/losses). This long-term capital gain netted with the $2,000 long-term capital loss carried over from the prior year (see analysis for question 13) results in a net <u>$1,500</u> long-term capital gain for the current year. As there are no additional capital gains or losses involved Bill simply adds this $1,500 capital gain to his given $60,000 of wages resulting in an adjusted gross income (AGI) of <u>$61,500.</u> Phew! Now for the more complete analysis that is long, but hopefully, helpful for a better understanding of this and other questions.

The <u>first</u> issue to be addressed is the realization, recognition and characterization of gains or losses resulting from the sale of the two automobiles. The <u>second</u> issue is that if we determine that the car sales result in recognized capital gains or losses, how do the current year's capital gain(s) or loss(es) fit together with the long-term capital loss carryover from the prior year? And <u>third</u>, how are the capital gain(s) or loss(es) reflected in computing Bill's adjusted gross income (AGI)?

<u>Realization, Recognition, and Characterization of Gain or Loss from the Car Sales</u>

In every fact pattern in which something is sold (or otherwise disposed of), the author likes to go through the following analysis; always ask these three questions:

1) Does the sale (or disposition) result in a <u>realized</u> gain or loss and if so, what is the <u>amount</u>? This is computing the amount of gain (or loss). It is the AR (amount realized) less one's AB (adjusted basis).

2) If we have a <u>realized</u> gain or loss, is it <u>recognized</u> (i.e. reportable for income tax purposes)? As a taxpayer, you would like the answer to be NO for gains – I do not want to recognize, report, the gain (said another way, I'd like to be able to exclude this gain from my income).

3) If the gain or loss is recognized, is it accorded "capital" gain or loss treatment? This is primarily the issue of "capital gains (or losses)" that are treated differently for income tax purposes.

Determining Bill's realized gains or losses in this question requires us to identify two basic components: The sales price of the cars ("amount realized" or, hereinafter, AR) and his basis in the cars ("adjusted basis or, hereinafter, AB). The difference between the two represents a <u>realized</u> gain or loss. [IRC § 1001(a).] Let us examine the AB and AR components of each of Bill's two sales separately.

The AR for the first automobile that he sold is simple: The $7,500 sales price. As for Bill's AB in the car, a taxpayer's cost is normally the starting point for its determination. [IRC §§ 1011 and 1012.] When property is received as a bequest/devise/inheritance, as is the case here, there really is no "cost" to the taxpayer. The seemingly logical result of a zero basis is neither desirable nor, thankfully, appropriate. IRC § 1014(a)(1) provides the general rule that the basis of property acquired from a decedent shall be the property's fair market value at the date of the decedent's death. The automobile that Bill received from his uncle Fred was worth $4,000 at Fred's death and, therefore, this represents Bill's basis in the car. Note that Fred's AB (his original cost of $8,000) is irrelevant. While the fair market value basis rule of IRC § 1014(a)(1) is often referred to as the "step-up in basis" rule for receipt of appreciated property, the statutory provision also works as a "step-down" rule for depreciated property such as Fred's car. Subtracting Bill's $4,000 AB from his $7,500 AR, results in a realized <u>gain of $3,500</u>.

AR	$7,500
minus: **AB**	($4,000)
Realized gain/(loss)	$3,500

Bill's AR and AB for the second car that he sold are more straightforward. The AR is his $3,000 sales price and his AB is his original cost of $6,000. This sale results in a realized <u>loss of $3,000</u>.

AR	$3,000
minus: **AB**	($6,000)
Realized gain/(loss)	($3,000)

The next step in our analysis of gain/loss situations is to determine the extent to which these <u>realized</u> gains and losses are <u>recognized</u>. Recognition basically means that the gains and losses will be reflected or counted in the computing of taxable income. Gains or losses that are <u>not</u> recognized, are, for all intents and purposes, ignored for income tax purpose. IRC § 1001(c) provides that unless otherwise provided for in the Code, all realized gains and losses are recognized. Bill's $3,500 gain from the first car sale <u>is</u> recognized as no "non-recognition" provision of the Code applicable to these facts.

The recognition of the $3,000 loss from the second car sale presents a bit of a problem for Bill. Unfortunately, there is an "otherwise indicated" Code section, namely IRC § 165, that affects Bill's recognition of his realized loss. At first glance, the "general rule" in IRC § 165(a) looks to be in Bill's favor allowing a deduction for "any loss sustained during the taxable year . . ." Reading further at IRC § 165(c) we come across an ominous sounding subsection: "Limitation on losses of individuals." In class, this professor refers to this as the "section 165(c) hoop," complete with graphic depictions on the board/slides. Figuratively, the goal is to jump from the "realized" loss side, through the hoop to the land of "recognized" losses. This hoop, however, is more akin to a **semi-permeable membrane** than an unobstructed open space. [Ha! Who would think we'd ever use the phrase *semipermeable membrane* in law school, let alone in a tax class?] We see, in IRC §§ 165(c)(1)-(c)(3), that business losses, investment losses and personal-use "casualty" losses, break on through to the recognized loss side. By default, however, losses from personal-use assets (other than casualty losses) do not make it through this "section 165(c) hoop" and go unrecognized. [To complete the *semipermeable membrane* analogy, their molecular size is too large to pass through to the land of *recognition*.] This explains why, for example, when you sell your personal-use car for a loss (which is almost always the case), the loss is realized but not recognized – i.e., you get no tax benefit from such a loss.

Bill realized a loss on the sale of this automobile but, unfortunately, he is <u>unable</u> to *recognize* this loss – i.e., Bill gets no tax benefit from such a loss and, for the sale of this automobile, the analysis stops here.

Students are often bothered by the lack of symmetry in that gains from the sale of personal-use assets <u>are</u> recognized (must be included in income unless a specific exclusion provision is applicable) but losses from the sale of such assets are not recognized (no tax benefit for these losses). Unfortunately, income tax laws are not always fair.

Here is a copy of the slide (albeit without some cool animation and colors better depicting the semipermeable membrane) that this professor uses in class for a visual representation of IRC § 165(c).

The §165(c) Hoop

The third step in our analysis of gain/loss situations is whether Bill's gain is accorded special "capital gain" treatment. Note we are no longer concerned with his unrecognized loss on the second car sale (we go no further in the analysis once we have determined a gain or loss is <u>not</u> recognized). A capital gain analysis requires first determining that we are dealing with a "capital asset" after which the gain is characterized as being either long-term or short-term status. IRC § 1221(a) defines a capital asset in a negative fashion but for purposes of this analysis, it includes, by process of elimination, assets held for investment and personal-use purposes. Bill's car at issue at this point was used as a personal-use automobile. Therefore, Bill's $3,500 realized and recognized gain is properly characterized as a <u>capital gain</u>. Long-term status is reserved for those assets held for <u>more than one year</u> (short-term status for assets held one year or less). See § 1222. Bill sold the car that he inherited from Fred, about one month after receiving it. At first brush, Bill's capital gain from the sale of the car appears to be a short-term capital gain. Determining the holding period, for short- and long-term gain/loss classification, is controlled by IRC § 1223. While long-term status is generally reserved for assets held for more than one year, property received from a decedent effectively gets *automatic* long-term status in most situations pursuant to IRC § 1223(11). Bill's $3,500 gain is, therefore, a *long-term capital gain*.

How Capital Gains/Losses are Combined, Including Carryovers from Prior Years

As indicated in the analysis for question 13, above, capital gains and losses are separated according to their holding period, separating them into two groups or columns: short-term gains/losses and long-term gains/losses. Recall that in question 13, above, Bill had four capital gain or loss transactions and they were separated into these two groups. For reference purposes, Bill's capital gain/loss activity for the <u>prior year</u> is reproduced as follows:

Bill's Capital Gains and Losses for the <u>Prior Year</u>

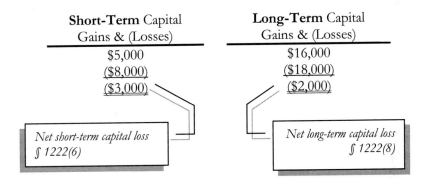

Short-Term Capital Gains & (Losses)	**Long-Term** Capital Gains & (Losses)
$5,000	$16,000
($8,000)	($18,000)
($3,000)	($2,000)
Net short-term capital loss § 1222(6)	Net long-term capital loss § 1222(8)

Without going through a complete explanation of the limits imposed on deductions of net capital losses (see analysis for question 13, above), Bill was able to use (or deduct) a total of $3,000 of these losses last year, all coming from the *short-term* side.

Again, for reference purposes, a visual depiction of how this works is reproduced as follows:

Bill's Utilization of Capital Losses in the <u>Prior Year</u>

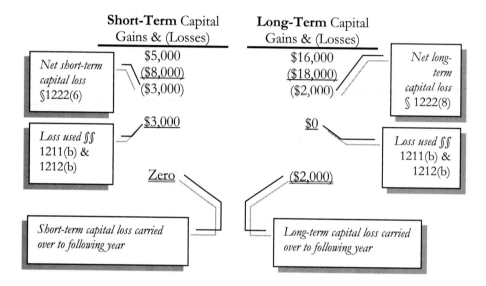

As we can see, last year, Bill was limited in the amount of capital loss he could deduct and was left with $2,000 *long-term capital loss* to be carried over to this, the current, year. From our analysis above, we know that in this year Bill has a $3,500 *long-term capital gain* from the first car sale. The mechanics of what we do now are relatively simple. We just go through the grouping and netting process again for the current year, making sure we properly reflect the carryover from the prior year.

The grouping appears as follows:

Bill's Capital Gain/Loss Analysis for the <u>Current Year</u>

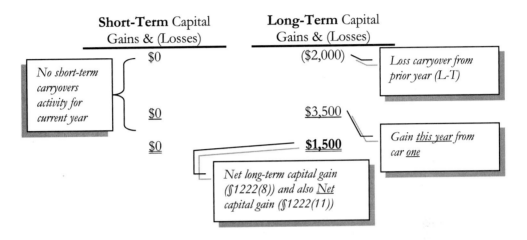

At this point, Bill has a net long-term capital gain (or net capital gain as defined in IRC § 1222(11)). The last part of this long analysis is how this gain is reflected in Bill's adjusted gross income (AGI).

<u>Bill's Adjusted Gross Income (AGI) Reflecting Capital Gain</u>

This is the easiest part. All gains (unless excluded) are reflected in a taxpayer's gross income. They may be offset by losses (as we saw in problem 13, above with Bill's capital losses offsetting his capital gains in the prior year), but the net amount of gain is included in gross income. For the current year, the facts indicate that Bill's wages are $60,000, and these, of course are part of his gross income. His $1,500 *net capital gain* is also included in gross income bringing the total to **$61,500**. Since the facts state that there are no other tax-related items for the current year, and thus no deductions to arrive at adjusted gross income (these would be IRC § 62 so-called *above the line deductions*), Bill's adjusted gross income (AGI) is **$61,500**.

At this point, students often wonder why bother with the characterization of capital gains as long-term or short-term and the accompanying netting process. All gains, whether short-term, long-term, or "ordinary" gains are, under current law, included in gross income regardless of their character. The answer is that *long-term gains* (more specifically, net-net long-term capital gains [net capital gains]) historically have been accorded special tax treatment. The details of this favorable treatment are far beyond the scope of analysis for this question, but modernly, these *long-term capital gains* (while included gross and taxable income) are treated special when it comes time to actually compute the taxpayer's tax liability. The special treatment is that these *long-term capital gains* (net capital gains) may be taxed at lower tax rates than those applied to the taxpayer's other taxable income.

Answers (a), (b), (c), and (d) are all incorrect because they represent incorrect calculations to varying degrees including incorrect analysis of the preceding question 13, incorrect determination of the long-term capital loss carryover from the prior year, incorrect recognition of the loss from the sale of car <u>two</u>, and various combinations thereof.

15. **The correct answer is (d).** IRC § 61 defines gross income as "all income from whatever source derived." From your initial study of gross income's scope, you probably found it to be broadly defined, including the taxpayer's receipt of some net economic benefit or net accession to wealth. In class, you also discover that gross income is also not limited to the receipt of cash nor, in the case of employee compensation, need it be received directly by the taxpayer. Frequent flyer miles, and "points" earned under similar travel-related programs, do represent a benefit. Theoretically, if one's employer allows an employee to use benefits that accrued while working for personal purposes, income would result. Historically, however, the I.R.S. has not pursued this issue, as the administrative and technical issues are daunting at best.

In Announcement 2002-18, the I.R.S. indicated that they "will not assert that any taxpayer has understated his federal tax liability by reason of the receipt or personal use of frequent flyer miles or other in-kind promotional benefits attributable to the taxpayer's business or official travel." [IRS Ann. 2002-10, I.R.B. 621.] However, it should be noted that this announcement goes on to say that, "[t]he relief provided by this announcement does not apply to travel or other promotional benefits that are converted to cash, to compensation that is paid in the form of travel or other promotional benefits, or in other circumstances where these benefits are used for tax avoidance purposes."

Kathleen ("Kath") will clearly have no income merely by the accrual of her frequent flyer miles. She will also have no income on redemption of the frequent flyer miles for travel, or other non-cash benefits available to her under the plan.

Answers (a) and (b) are incorrect. As discussed above, the accumulation of miles or redemption for benefits do not give rise to income. **Answer (c) is incorrect** because the Commerce Clause of the Constitution is not applicable.

16. **The most accurate answer is (b).** This is a rather difficult question and may be unanswerable depending on the depth of coverage of certain tax concepts; namely the concepts of "depreciation" and "depreciation recapture." Actually, this "most accurate" answer is a bit incomplete and, perhaps, slightly misleading (as we shall explain below). Only after eliminating the possible application of certain classic "depreciation recapture" rules that would tax some of Roberta's gain at "ordinary income rates" can we come to our conclusion that Roberta's gain from the sale of the property will be a "long-term capital gain." While this is correct, long-term capital gains are subject to differing rates and a portion of her capital gain may be taxed at a slightly higher rate that regular long-term capital gains. Yes, this is all rather confusing and again, your professor may not cover this material in great detail, if at all. Suffice it to say that the "depreciation recapture" area of tax law is extremely complex and this question (and immediately following question 17) gives us only a slight, and simplistic, peek at the subject.

We do not know the exact amount of Roberta's realized gain in this problem, but such gain will be recognized. [IRC § 1001(c).] The primary focus of this question is the character of this gain. Is some or all of it "ordinary income" which is part of the taxpayer's taxable income and taxed at applicable regular income tax rates, or is it accorded "long-term capital gain treatment (albeit at varying capital gains rates)?" *Long-term capital gains* are included in the taxpayer's taxable income, but if the taxpayer has net *long-term capital gain* (after netting with other capital gains and losses), such gain may be taxed at more favorable (lower) tax rates. [IRC § 1(h).] *Long-term capital gains* are <u>good</u> things when compared to ordinary income. A capital gain analysis requires first determining that we are dealing with a "capital asset" after which, the gain is characterized as having either long-term or short-term status.

IRC § 1221(a) defines a capital asset in a negative fashion but for purposes of this analysis, it includes, by process of elimination, assets held for investment and personal-use purposes. There is little question that Roberta's rental residence qualifies as a capital asset. Long-term status is reserved for those assets held for <u>more than one year</u> (short-term status for those assets held one year or less). [See IRC § 1222.] Roberta's purchase of the property "about four years ago" clearly confers "long-term" status to the gain. Although ultimately this is the end result, Roberta's gain is a *long-term capital gain*, we need to address a few other issues before we can conclude that this is, indeed, the most accurate answer.

Each year that Roberta owned the property, she claimed "depreciation" deductions. She benefited from these deductions in prior years as they reduced her net income from the rental activities. These depreciation deductions also reduced her basis (adjusted basis or AB) in the property (IRC § 1016) that, in turn, created a greater gain when sold (gain measured by her selling price less her AB). While this may seem like a wash; deductions in earlier years traded for a larger gain in a later year, Roberta most likely benefited from this situation. Her depreciation deductions reduced "ordinary" income (thus reducing her tax at regular tax rates) and she benefited from these deductions in earlier years. While she has a larger gain now, when the property is sold, she had the benefit of the use of the taxes saved because of the depreciation deductions. In other words, she benefited from the "time value of money" delaying income to later years. In addition, this larger gain now is favorably taxed *long-term capital gain* (albeit it at varying tax rates). Getting deductions offsetting ordinary income in earlier years in exchange for *long-term capital gain* income in later years is generally a good deal for taxpayers. There is a provision in the law, however, that can act to deny this later preferential capital-gain treatment to a portion of gain (taxing it at "ordinary income" tax rates), and it is known as "depreciation recapture."

Basically, the classic form of *depreciation recapture*, if it applies, requires that some of the gain that would otherwise be favorable *long-term capital gain*, be reclassified as *ordinary income*. Some of the depreciation taken in prior years is effectively "recaptured" as ordinary income when the property is sold. The *depreciation recapture* provision for real estate is IRC § 1250 (different provisions apply to depreciable personal property). While the rules vary based on numerous factors, the basic theme is that the amount of *depreciation recapture* (the amount of gain classified as *ordinary income*) is classically a certain percentage of "additional" depreciation that has been deducted by the taxpayer over the years. Depreciation methods are numerous and are very complex, varying by the type and use of assets. Some methods of depreciation are considered favorable or accelerated in that they produce greater depreciation deductions in the early years of the assets use. "Additional" or extra depreciation (the thing that triggers classic depreciation recapture at ordinary income tax rates) is this total amount of accelerated depreciation deductions that are in excess of what would have been the total depreciation calculated under a straight pro-rata (or "straight-line") method. How does this apply to our situation? If Roberta deducted depreciation utilizing a method that accelerated these deductions, then some of her otherwise *long-term capital* gain will be "recaptured" as ordinary income. To make this determination, we need to know what methods of depreciation were available to Roberta with respect to her rental property.

Over the years, the tax laws have changed many times regarding allowable depreciation. To act as an economic incentive, sometimes the laws have changed to allow shorter depreciation periods for assets and more accelerated methods for computing depreciation. At other times, because of fiscal restraints, depreciation periods have been lengthened and methods producing less acceleration of deductions to earlier years. Roberta's purchase of the rental property about four years ago places her firmly in the period utilizing a depreciation convention known as the "Modified Accelerated Cost Recovery System" or "MACRS." This system has basically been in place for years after 1986 (it replaced the "Accelerated Cost Recovery System" or "ACRS"). IRC § 168 spells out most of the provisions for MACRS depreciation (although oddly, the statute still uses the term Accelerated Cost Recovery System). Under MACRS, "residential rental real estate" as in Roberta's rental property, is depreciated over 27.5 years. [IRC § 168(c).] More importantly for our purpose, such property **must** use the "straight-line" method of depreciation. [IRC § 168(b)(3).] What does all this mean for our situation? Roberta had to have been using the "straight-line" method of depreciation with respect to her rental property. Straight-line depreciation is **not** an accelerated method and, therefore, no "additional" or extra depreciation is created for recapture purposes. Phew!

The bottom line is that all of Roberta's gain from the sale of her rental property is *long-term capital gain*. The IRC § 1250 *depreciation recapture* provisions requiring her to report some of her gain as ordinary income (taxed, generally, at higher regular tax rates) do not apply to her, as the depreciation deductions with respect to her property could not have been determined using any sort of accelerated method (thus creating no "additional" or extra recapturable depreciation). Again, phew!

This all sounds neat and tidy but there is one wrinkle that makes the designated "correct" answer a bit incomplete and, perhaps, a bit misleading. It is true that the classic form of depreciation recapture triggering a portion of her gain to be recaptured as ordinary income is not applicable here. A careful analysis of capital gains tax rates, however, exposes that Roberta will not benefit from the lowest beneficial capital gains rates. IRC § 1(h) lays out the various tax rates applicable to capital gains (generally, those that are long-term capital gains). Heavily dependent on a taxpayer's level of income, regular long-term capital gains rates can be zero, 15% or 20% (these comparing favorably to regular tax rates that range from 10% to 37% as of the time of this writing). IRC § 1(h) lists a potential capital gain rate of 25% on "unrecaptured section 1250 gain." We saw that Roberta did not have any "recaptured" additional depreciation that would implicate ordinary income (and tax rates commensurate thereto). "Unrecaptured section 1250 gain" is defined in IRC § 1(h)(6)(A) and while complex, it basically is the total depreciation taken (not to exceed the realized gain). So what does all of this mean for Roberta? She still is entitled to beneficial long-term capital gain rates of tax but the portion of her gain that represents the total depreciation that she took with respect to her rental property, will potentially be taxed at a slightly higher 25% capital gains rate. This is <u>not</u> depreciation recapture in the classic sense (where a portion of gain is tax as ordinary income's higher tax rates) but does impose a potentially higher capital gain tax rate for some of her gain. "Recapture light" perhaps?

Answer (a) is incorrect because, as discussed above, Roberta's rental property qualifies as a capital asset generating a *long-term capital gain* and not *ordinary* income. **Answer (c) is also incorrect.** This would be a logical answer that could not be eliminated as incorrect without a fair amount of knowledge about depreciation methods. The only available method of depreciation for Roberta's residential rental real estate was the "straight-line" method. This, in turn, does not create any amount of classic recapturable depreciation that would be treated as "ordinary income." It is true, as discussed above, that a portion of her gain (representing depreciation she took as a deduction prior to the sale) may trigger a slightly higher capital gain tax rate than that which would otherwise apply for regular long-term capital gains. **Answer (d) is incorrect** because the nonrecognition rules applying to houses only apply to a taxpayer's <u>principal residence</u> and not to rental properties.

17. **The best answer is (d).** Like problem 16, above, this question is a bit difficult and may be unanswerable depending on the depth of coverage of certain tax concepts; namely the concepts of "depreciation" and "depreciation recapture." We will conclude that because the furniture is considered "section 1245" property, Roberta must recapture, as *ordinary* income, the total amount of her depreciation deductions taken with respect to the property. As indicated in the analysis of question 16, above, the degree to which a basic income tax course covers the subject of depreciation recapture can vary dramatically (it is often not covered at all or may be mentioned as a mere side note), and questions 16 and 17 are designed to provide a very basic introduction of the concepts.

As indicated in the previous question, *depreciation recapture* provisions are designed to prevent the effective conversion of *ordinary* income (depreciation deductions reducing *ordinary* income) into favorably treated *long-term capital gain* income. The *depreciation recapture* rules vary depending on the nature of the property depreciated and, in some instances, the method of depreciation utilized. Most real property, as Roberta's rental house in the previous problem, invokes the *depreciation recapture* rules of IRC § 1250. Those rules generally require recapture of only a certain portion of the depreciation taken by the taxpayer (accelerated or "additional" amounts when compared with "straight-line" depreciation). The rules regarding most "personal" property (not personal-use property which is not subject to depreciation, but property other than "real" property) are different and are governed by

IRC § 1245. Basically, this section requires that the total amount of **all** depreciation taken with respect to such property (regardless of method) is recapturable as ordinary income. [IRC § 1245.] While there are additional issues involving IRC § 1245, the facts of this question require us to go no further in our analysis.

Roberta's business furniture is personal property to which IRC § 1245 is applicable. The gain she realized from its sale is recaptured as *ordinary* income to the extent of her depreciation deductions taken with respect to the furniture.

Answer (a) is incorrect because unlike IRC § 1250 that is applicable to most real property, IRC § 1245 recapture (applicable here) does not apply only to excess or accelerated depreciation deductions. Rather, as discussed above, it is more inclusive and generally recaptures all depreciation taken. **Answer (b) is incorrect** because IRC § 1245 *is* applicable regardless to individuals. **Answer (c) is also incorrect.** While it is well beyond the scope of this question, the sale of business assets, such as Roberta's furniture, can give rise to *capital gain* income. See IRC § 1231.

18. **Answer (d) is correct.** Generally, when a *nonbusiness* bad debt becomes *totally* worthless, the loss is treated as a "short-term capital loss" (regardless of how long the debt had been outstanding before becoming worthless). [IRC § 166(d)(1); Reg. § 1.166-5.] Greg's loan to Tony was a nonbusiness bad debt, as the loan was not made in connection with Greg's business. [IRC § 166(d)(2).] Greg, therefore, has a $5,000 short-term capital loss resulting from this bad debt. This $5,000 short-term capital loss will be combined with any of Greg's other capital gains and losses. Capital gains and losses are combined and reflected in income utilizing a particular set of rules, which is the subject of other questions in this book.

It should be noted that the rules differ for "business" bad debts. [See, generally, IRC § 166.]

Answer (a) is not the best answer because it fails to characterize the loss (and potential deduction) as a short-term capital loss. **Answer (b) is also incorrect.** While it correctly classifies the bad debt as a short-term capital loss, the loss itself is not limited to $3,000. Other questions in this book explain that the total deduction for net capital losses in any one tax year may be limited to $3,000, but this is not equivalent to what is stated in this answer (b). **Answer (c) is incorrect** because a totally worthless nonbusiness bad debt *does* give rise to the recognition of a short-term capital loss. **Answer (e) is also incorrect.** While it is true that no benefit (loss or deduction) results if the creditor has no "basis" in the bad debt, Greg did have a $5,000 basis in the debt (his basis in the promissory note). This answer does bring up a common misconception about some bad debts. For example, say you perform some services for your neighbor in return for your neighbor's promise to pay you a specified amount (the value of your services). Should your neighbor fail to pay and this debt becomes totally worthless, you are not entitled to any benefit based upon the value of your services rendered. This is because you have no basis in the debt. Had you recognized *income* upon performing the services (say under the "accrual" method of accounting), *then* you would be entitled to a benefit from the worthless debt.

19. **The correct answer is (a).** The concept of "adjusted gross income" (hereinafter AGI) is a bit amorphous, especially in one's initial study of income tax. The full comprehension of its significance sometimes does not come until very near the end of a full semester of studying tax. The long trek in the study of income, exclusions and deductions is to reach a computational goal of "taxable income" upon which tax rates are applied to get one's tax liability (before tax credits). In a nutshell, AGI is an intermediate point in this computation of taxable income.

In your study of the broad reach of gross income, you probably discuss specific statutory exclusions therefrom (such as those for gifts, bequests, etc., life insurance proceeds, and the like). In your study of *deductions*, you may cover many deductions including those for interest, business, medical, etc. expenses. As far as deductions are concerned, there are two major camps of deductions for purposes of computing taxable income. There are deductions that are subtracted from *gross income* to arrive at our intermediary AGI. These are commonly referred to as "above the line" deductions, with AGI representing "the line." The other camp of deductions is comprised of those that are subtracted from AGI to arrive at *taxable income*. These are commonly referred to as "below the line" deductions. The components making up this camp of *below the line* deductions can include something called the "standard deduction" or, in the alternative, a group of deductions called "itemized deductions." In addition, *The Tax Cuts and Jobs Act* (TCJA) signed into law in December 2017 (generally effective beginning in 2018) enacted IRC § 199A which provides for a new deduction for certain businesses (and pass-through entities). This deduction is considered a *below the line* deduction because it is deducted after the standard or itemized deduction. Historically an individual was also generally entitled to one or more personal exemption deductions that were considered *below the line* deductions, but these deductions were eliminated by the TCJA. [For more information about how this all fits together, please see IRC § 62, Appendix A, and other questions in this book.]

Why AGI is so important is the substance of this question. Some of the exclusions from gross income and deductions (both to AGI and from AGI) are based or dependent on the level of the taxpayer's AGI (in one form or another). Examples of some of these deductions and exclusions are mentioned below.

Common Examples of *Below the Line* Deductions that are Dependent or Based on AGI

> ➤ Medical care expenses deductible only to the extent that they exceed a certain percentage of AGI. [IRC § 217.]
> ➤ Qualifying casualty losses deductible (after some adjustment) only to the extent that they exceed a certain percentage of AGI. [IRC § 165(h).]
> ➤ Charitable contributions subject to a ceiling or cap in deductions based on varying percentages of AGI. [IRC § 170.]

Common Examples of *Above the Line* Deductions that are Dependent or Based on AGI

> ➤ Interest on student loans phased-out for taxpayers with AGI (modified) exceeding certain limits. [IRC § 221.]
> ➤ Certain retirement savings accounts phased-out for taxpayers with AGI (modified) exceeding certain limits. [IRC § 219.]

Common Examples of Exclusions From Income that are Dependent or Based on AGI

> ➤ Social Security benefits received not subject to exclusion from income (in varying degrees) for taxpayers with AGI (modified) exceeding certain limits. [IRC § 86.]
> ➤ Interest from U.S. Savings Bonds used for higher education not subject to exclusion from income (in varying degrees) for taxpayers with AGI (modified) exceeding certain limits. [IRC § 135.]
> ➤ Employer paid adoption assistance costs not subject to exclusion from income for taxpayers with AGI (modified) exceeding certain limits. [IRC § 137.]

As indicated by the deductions and exclusions listed above, AGI can be a very important factor, and can make a dramatic difference, in computing one's net income that is subject to tax (taxable income).

The one item presented in the question that is not dependent on AGI is the determination of a self-employed individual's "self-employment" tax. Beyond the scope of many federal income tax courses is the subject of self-employment tax. Basically, it is the *Social Security* and *Medicare* taxes that a self-employed individual has to pay on his or her net income (from such self-employed business). This tax is calculated and reported on, and payable with, an individual's regular income tax return, but it is not an income tax and the basis for its calculation is not impacted by AGI. For information purposes, the basis for calculating this tax is the individual's net income from his or her self-employed business activities (i.e., income from business as a self-employed person, independent contractor, or unincorporated sole proprietorship, less deductible business expenses associated therewith).

Answers (b), (c), and (d) are incorrect because they all contain an incorrect combination of items listed that are dependent or based on AGI. **Answer (e) is incorrect** because a correct answer (a) is present.

20. **The correct answer is (b).** While this is a year-specific question (2019) it is easily adaptable to other tax years. As computed below, for 2019 the couple's *standard deduction* is $25,700 while their *itemized deductions* total only $24,400. It is, therefore, to their advantage to take the *standard deduction* in computing their taxable income.

In very broad terms, there are two camps of deductions for purposes of computing taxable income. There are deductions that are subtracted from *gross income* to arrive at an intermediary point called *adjusted gross income* (AGI). These are commonly referred to as "above the line" deductions, with AGI representing "the line." The other camp of deductions is comprised of those that are subtracted from AGI to arrive at *taxable income*. These are commonly referred to as "below the line" deductions. The components making up this camp of *below the line* deductions can include something called the "standard deduction" or, in the alternative, a group of deductions called "itemized deductions." In addition, *The Tax Cuts and Jobs Act* (TCJA) signed into law in December 2017 (generally effective beginning in 2018) enacted IRC § 199A which provides for a new deduction for certain businesses (and pass-through entities). This deduction is considered a *below the line* deduction because it is deducted after the standard or itemized deduction. Historically an individual was also generally entitled to one or more personal exemption deductions that were considered *below the line* deductions, but these deductions were eliminated by the TCJA. [For more information about how this all fits together, please see IRC § 62, Appendix A, and other questions in this book.]

In this question, we are concerned with two components of *below the line* deductions: the *standard deduction* and *itemized deductions*. Taxpayers have a choice: deduct either 1) the *standard deduction* amount, **or** 2) the total of *itemized deductions* (after applying all necessary limits and restrictions). In calculating "taxable income," a taxpayer takes, as a deduction, the greater of these two. The two deductions will be discussed separately. We are not concerned, in this problem, with *above the line* deductions as the couple's AGI is already given: $40,000.

The Couple's *Standard Deduction*

Many years ago, the concept of the "standard deduction" was introduced into tax law as a means of reducing an individual's record-keeping needs. As indicated, the *standard deduction* may be taken in place of a group of deductions known collectively as "itemized deductions."

IRC § 63(c) is the focal point for the *standard deduction*. The amount of this *standard deduction* can vary greatly from taxpayer to taxpayer depending on various factors including marital or filing status, age, degree of visual imparity, and whether the taxpayer is a "dependent" of another. In addition, *standard deduction* amounts are subject to change each tax year (and for the most part, do change each year) based on adjustments for "inflation" (i.e., the standard deduction amounts are *indexed* for inflation). The various *standard deduction* amounts identified in the statute (throughout IRC § 63 either listed in dollars or instructions for computation) are <u>not</u> the actual amounts for the current year but, rather, are pre-inflation adjusted "base" amounts (that are well below the actual current amounts). [Appendix B contains the various *standard deduction* amounts for the year 2019 (the most current at the time of this printing).]

A highly touted component of the *Tax Cuts and Jobs Act* (TCJA) signed into law in December 2017 (generally effective beginning in 2018), was a substantial increase in the *standard deduction* amounts (beginning in 2018). For 2019, the "regular" *standard deduction* for a married couple filing a joint return is $24,400 (corresponding to the computed statutory amount of $6,000 which is 200% of the $3,000 listed for single individuals, which is unadjusted for inflation and does not reflect the TCJA's 200% of a new $12,000 listed for single individuals and also not adjusted for inflation; the latter effective for years 2018-2025). Note that this is **one** deduction for the joint return of both spouses, and <u>not</u> a deduction per spouse.

The *standard deduction* is **increased** for certain individuals based on age or visual imparity. [IRC § 63(b)(3).] For 2019, taxpayers age 65 and older (as of the end of the taxable year) are entitled to an extra $1,300 per qualifying individual when married and filing a joint return. This $1,300 for 2019 corresponds to the unadjusted for inflation amount of $600 listed in IRC § 63(f)(1). [See Appendix B for the 2019 *standard deduction* "extra amounts" for other classifications of individuals.] In our problem, Jim (but not Kathy) is the requisite age and they are entitled to "one" of these extra $1,300 standard deduction amounts. The couple's regular *standard deduction* of **$24,400** is

increased by **$1,300**, resulting in a total *standard deduction* amount of **$25,700** for 2019.

[Please see other questions in this book that address the issue of visual imparity vis-à-vis the *standard deduction* amount as well as different or limited *standard deduction* amounts in other instances.]

The Couple's *Itemized Deductions*

Jim and Kathy have four expenditures that give rise to possible *itemized deductions*: real property taxes, state income taxes, charitable contributions, and medical care expenses.

IRC § 164 is a key section for addressing deductions for both property taxes and state income taxes. This section allows a deduction for, among other taxes, state and local income and real property taxes paid. [IRC § 164(a)(1).] The $6,000 and $8,000 that Jim and Kathy paid in property taxes and state income taxes, respectively, clearly fit within this section. While the aforementioned TCJA's increase to the *standard deduction* was favorable to taxpayers, the TCJA instituted a "cap" or maximum aggregate amount deductible as state and local taxes (basically, the most common type of IRC § 164 deductions). This TCJA provision is often referred to as the "SALT" (state and local tax) deduction limit and is set at $10,000. Note that this is not a per-person cap but, an aggregate $10,000 cap for our couple. So at this point in our analysis, the couple's itemized deductions begin with **$10,000** (the SALT cap limits what would have been a $14,000 aggregate deduction prior to the TCJA). [Please see other questions in this book that address, in more detail, this new SALT limit).

The $5,300 that the Couple made in "qualified charitable donations," implicates IRC § 170. We need not go into the details of what constitutes a qualified charitable contribution or a qualified charitable organization since the facts already tell us that this is a qualified charitable donation. We need also not delve into the deduction limits imposed by this section. Suffice it to say that our couple's charitable donations do not come close to any such limits (please see other questions in this book that address IRC § 170 charitable contributions in more detail). Our couple will be allowed, as part of *itemized deductions*, **$5,300** for their charitable donations.

The $13,100 the couple spent on unreimbursed prescription drugs is the subject of IRC § 213. IRC § 213 allows for a deduction of certain qualified medical care expenses. Once one makes the determination of what constitutes "qualified" medical care expenses, the subject of this question, the deduction is allowed only to the extent that the total qualifying expenses exceeds 10% of the taxpayer's AGI. [Prior editions of this book utilized the pre-TCJA 7.5% of AGI floor.] Qualified medical care expenses include typical costs for doctors, dentists, hospital, health insurance, and the like. [See IRC § 213(d).] In addition, qualified medical care expenses include costs for prescription drugs (and insulin in those areas where its sale is allowed without a prescription). [IRC § 213(b).] All of the couple's medicine costs were for prescription drugs and therefore, the $13,100 they spent qualifies as medical care expenses. To determine their actual medical expense deduction, we need to apply the 10% of AGI nondeductible "floor." The 10% nondeductible portion equals $4,000 (10% x $40,000 AGI). Therefore, their medical expense deduction is $13,100 less $4,000, or **$9,100**.

Now it is time to add up the couple's *itemized deductions*. Their total *itemized deductions* equal the **$10,000** in property and income taxes (capped by the SALT limit of the TCJA), plus their **$5,300** in charitable donations, plus their **$9,100** medical expense deduction. The sum of these equals **$24,400.**

Comparing this *itemized deduction* total of $24,400 to their $25,700 *standard deduction*, it is obvious that it is to their benefit to use the ***standard deduction* of $25,700**.

Answer (a) is incorrect because the two deductions are <u>not</u> equal. They would have been equal (at $24,400) but for the "extra" $1,300 standard deduction because of Jim's age (being 65 or older). **Answer (c) is incorrect** because as indicated above, the *standard deduction* is the larger of the two. **Answer (d) is incorrect** because pursuant to the TCJA, personal exemption deductions have been eliminated. Even if they had not been eliminated (as was the case in prior editions of this book) the deduction for *personal exemptions* is separate and is in <u>addition</u> to the greater of the *standard deduction* or total *itemized deductions*.

21. **The best answer is (c).** This question involves determining who qualifies and someone's "dependent" for a variety of tax purposes. First and foremost, students should be aware that this question is date or year sensitive. As indicated in the preface of this book, many tax related provisions change for each tax year. Sometimes it is necessary to ask questions for a specific year as opposed to in the abstract. This is one such situation and it involves <u>who qualifies as someone's dependent.</u>

It should be noted that tax law relating to someone qualifying as a dependent and the relevance of why this is important has changed dramatically since the earlier editions of this book. It still has some significance, hence this question, but historically deductions for personal exemptions (including those for dependents) was a huge deal. The *Tax Cuts and Jobs Act* (TCJA) that was signed into law in December 2017 (generally effective beginning in 2018) eliminated deductions for personal exemptions for 2018 through

2025. While no longer a deduction, it may help to go through some explanation of what used to be the pre-TCJA law (in 2017 and earlier) and help give more meaning to the relevance of claiming another individual as one's dependent. Here is a brief explanation of prior law and then we will circle back to analyze the answer for this question 21.

> *Pre-TCJA Law; what was a personal exemption deduction and how many of them could a taxpayer deduct: Every living person has, in his or her figurative pocket, a "coupon" good for a personal exemption deduction for each tax year. There is no real "coupon" involved, but it helps to think of the personal exemption deduction as such. The amount of this exemption deduction is listed in IRC § 151 of the Code as $2,000. However, this amount has been adjusted (increased) each year since 1990 to reflect the general level of inflation. The personal exemption deduction amount in 2017, the last year for which a deduction was allowed, was $4,050 (it would have been $4,150 for 2018). The key to this problem in its prior, pre-TCJA form was determining who gets to use these personal exemption deduction "coupons" ($4,050 for 2017). Did each person get to use his or her own "coupon" and get a $4,050 deduction (for 2017), or does somebody else get to claim that person's "coupon" and take the deduction? This latter question gives rise to the issue of who qualifies as one's dependent. [This is still a relevant question after the TCJA but for tax reasons other than obtaining a now nonexistent personal exemption deduction].*
>
> *Students knowing little about income tax, probably knew something about this issue. A parent claiming his or her children as dependents and getting an extra deduction for them is precisely the issue that was in the forefront of this question in prior editions of this book. Had this problem been placed in 2017 or earlier, Tammy would have been entitled to a personal exemption deduction for herself. The issue, pre TCJA (before 2018) was whether Tammy gets to take Chuck and Ned's "coupons" and thus get more personal exemption deductions (on her income tax return for purposes of computing her taxable income). Alternatively, do Chuck and Ned get to use their own "coupons" for a personal exemption deduction (on their respective income tax returns for purposes of computing their respective taxable income)? To determine if Tammy was entitled to get Chuck and Ned's personal exemption "coupons" (claim them as dependents and get to deduct their $4,050 (for 2017) personal exemption deductions) we would have been determining if they (the kids) qualified as Tammy's dependents.*

The author hopes that this introduction of "old law" helps with what we are about to discuss with respect to our current question 21. While Tammy, in our question, no longer has any personal exemption deductions for herself or any "dependents," the determination of who qualifies as a dependent is still very relevant for other tax matters (albeit not ones generally as valuable as the pre-TCJA personal exemption deduction). The question identifies the "child tax credit" and "credit for other dependents" as two areas where determining if other individuals (here Chuck and Ned) qualify as Tammy's dependents. Questions 22 & 23 (immediately following this question 21) also address areas where it is important to determine who qualifies as a "dependent." Because the TCJA eliminated the personal exemption deduction, which was a significant tax topic and valuable deduction, many basic income tax courses no longer cover, in great detail, this accompanying topic of who qualifies as one's dependent. With that in mind, let's begin our journey (and be forewarned that it is not a particularly fun journey) into the world of "dependents."

For Chuck or Ned to be Tammy's dependent, we begin by determining whether they (the kids) are either Tammy's "*qualifying child*" or "*qualifying relative*" pursuant to IRC § 152 (it is this section that defines, through some rather complex rules, who qualifies as one's dependent). The dependent qualification process became a bit more complex with the enactment of the "*Working Families Tax Relief Act of 2004*" where the desire to have uniform definitions of certain relatives for federal tax statutes created a rather messy result for the dependency rules. What follows below may look a bit daunting, but it is not too bad once you go through each part, step by step (as applicable).

> **Requirements for <u>all</u> possible "dependents."** As indicated, a "dependent" is someone who is either a "*qualifying child*" or "*qualifying relative*" of the taxpayer. There are a bunch of requirements for each alternative (see below), but before we get to those, there are some basic requirements that must be met in order for either type of qualifying individual to be considered your "dependent." First, and logically, if you yourself (or your spouse if he or she is filing a joint return with you) can be claimed as a dependent by someone else, then you will not be entitled to claim anyone as your dependent. Next, for both a "*qualifying child*" and a "*qualifying relative*" <u>all</u> of the following requirements must be met:
> - ➤ If the potential "dependent" is married, he or she must not file a joint return with his or her spouse for the tax year (there are some exceptions to this).
> - ➤ The potential "dependent" must be a U.S. citizen, U.S. resident, U.S. national, or a resident of Canada or Mexico for some part of the tax year. [Note that non-citizen residents of Canada or Mexico may not qualify for certain dependent credits notwithstanding that they can qualify as dependents.]

If all of the above requirements are satisfied, we then move on to see if the potential individual is **<u>either</u>** a "***qualifying child***" or "***qualifying*** *relative*." If the individual meets all of the requirements of either, then this person is a "dependent" for various tax purposes (in the pre-TCJA world, this also meant that taxpayer could take as a deduction, that person's personal exemption "coupon"). Be forewarned; put aside any preconceived, non-tax, notions of who you think is considered a "child" or "relative."

Qualifying Child: An individual is considered a "***qualifying child***" of you, the taxpayer, if all of the following requirements are met:

➤ The individual is your son, daughter, stepchild, eligible foster child, brother, sister, half-brother, half-sister, stepbrother, stepsister, or a descendant of any of them (hmmmm, seems a bit odd that a sister, a nephew, and a whole lot more people are your "children").

➤ The "child" (see above) must be:

- Under age 19 at the end of the year, **or**
- Under age 24 at the end of the year and is a full-time student for some part of each of five months during the year, **or**
- Any age if permanently or totally disabled.

➤ The "child" must have, with some exceptions, lived with you for more than half of the year.

➤ The "child" must not have provided more than one half of his or her own support for the year.

Qualifying Relative: An individual is considered a "***qualifying relative***" of you, the taxpayer, if all of the following requirements are met:

➤ The individual must be either "*related*" to you or, if not "related" in the Code sense, live with you (with some exceptions) for the entire year. [See IRC §§ 152(d)(2)(A)-(d)(2)(G) for definitions of "relatives" which includes everyone from children, siblings, ancestors, aunts/uncles, etc. to a host of "in-laws," and IRC § 152(d)((2)(H) for other qualifying individuals.]

➤ The individual must have "gross income" less than the "exemption amount" for that year (for 2018, the year of our question, this amount is $4,150).

➤ The taxpayer (you – the person trying to claim the individual as a dependent) must have provided more than one-half of this person's total support for the year.

Note that there are differences and areas of overlap in the definitions of a *qualifying child* and *qualifying relative*. For example, the taxpayer's "child" may fail the requirements of a "*qualifying child*" because of their age but be considered a dependent nonetheless because such child meets the requirements of a *"qualifying relative."* Also note that because of the expansive definition of a "child" under the *qualifying child* rules, the situation could arise where an individual is a *qualifying child* of more than one taxpayer (e.g., a grandchild could be a *qualifying child* of a grandparent while, at the same time, be a *qualifying child* to the child's parent). In such cases, the *qualifying child* can be claimed as a "dependent" by only one taxpayer and generally, they can agree as to which one will be entitled to claim the dependent (with "tie-breaking" rules if they cannot so agree). Also not applicable to this question, and beyond the scope of this book, there are special rules for divorced/separated parents, multiple support arrangements, kidnapped children, and other situations.

If an individual is either a *qualifying child* or *qualifying relative* (and all of the other requirements for both are met), then that individual is your "dependent."

Finally, after all of that, we can now get back to our question. There are no problems with respect to Chuck and Ned meeting the first set of requirements applicable to both a *qualifying child* and *qualifying relative*. They are both U.S. citizens, neither is married, and, there are no facts to indicate that Tammy is a "dependent" of someone else.

Next, we look at Chuck and Ned to see if they are either a *qualifying child* or *qualifying relative*. First, we will start with Tammy's child, Chuck. Is **Chuck** a *qualifying child*? He is 1) a child, and 2) is under age 19 at the end of 2018, and 3) he lived with Tammy for more than one-half of 2018, and 4) he did not provide more than one-half of his own support (Tammy did). **Chuck**, therefore, is a *qualifying child* and, thus, a "dependent." Students are often thrown by the fact that Chuck is making $5,000 which is not less than the "exemption amount" ($4,150 in 2018, the year of this problem). However, this income limitation is part of the definition of a *qualifying relative* and not that of a *qualifying child*. So, if all of the requirements of a *qualifying child* are met, that individual's amount of gross income for the year is irrelevant. Of course, at some point, the amount of the "dependent's" income may create problems with the "one-half" support requirement.

Next, we come to **Ned**; is he a *qualifying child* of Tammy? What, you ask, why are we even discussing the possibility that Ned is Tammy's *qualifying child*? He's Tammy's nephew, not her child. Not so fast, says the Code, Ned is, indeed, a "child" as defined in IRC § 152(c)(2)(B): "a brother, sister . . . of the taxpayer or a <u>descendant</u> of any such relative. Ned meets this definition because he is the descendent (child) of Tammy's brother. Next, while Ned is not under age 19 as of the end of 2018, he is a full-time student under age 24; so far, so good. Unfortunately, Ned fails the last requirement of a *qualifying child* as he does not live with Tammy for more than one-half of the year (there are some exceptions for temporary absences, but the facts indicate that Ned lives with Tammy's sister, Susie). **Ned** therefore, is <u>not</u> Tammy's *qualifying child* and, so far, he is not Tammy's dependent.

We move on to see if, in the alternative, Ned is a *qualifying relative* entitling Tammy to claim Ned as her dependent. Unfortunately for Tammy, he (Ned) is also not a *qualifying relative*. He is "related" (a nephew is considered a relative pursuant to IRC § 152(d)(2)), and Tammy provides more than one-half of Ned's support (see below) <u>but</u>, Ned does not have gross income less than the "exemption amount." To meet this requirement, Ned would have to have, in 2018, gross income less than the exemption amount ($4,150 for 2017). Ned's $5,000 gross income is not less than $4,150. **Ned**, therefore, is also <u>not</u> Tammy's *qualifying child* and, with all alternatives for tax dependency spent, he is <u>not</u> Tammy's dependent. The bottom line; Tammy is <u>not</u> entitled to claim Ned as her dependent (and in a pre-TCJA world, Tammy would not get Ned's personal exemption deduction "coupon").

In conclusion, Chuck is Tammy's dependent (and while not the subject of this question, she may be entitled to claim a "child tax credit" or a "credit for other dependents" with respect to Chuck). Ned, however, is not Tammy's dependent for purposes of the aforementioned credits. He comes close, but does not meet the qualifications of either a *qualifying child* or *qualifying relative*.

As indicated, this question is date sensitive, applicable to the 2018 tax year but can easily be modified to accommodate subsequent years (the change would be the limit of the amount of income earned by the potential dependent; i.e., the $4,150 for 2018 is adjusted for inflation and may increase).

Answer (a) is incorrect because Ned's is not Tammy's *qualifying child.* He meets all the requirements except one; he did not live with Tammy for more than half of the year. **Answer (b) is incorrect** but is the source of much confusion. The answer is correct regarding Ned, but not Chuck. Under the definition of a *qualifying child,* there is no requirement that the possible dependent have gross income less than the exemption amount (this comes up only for the *qualifying relative* definition), and Chuck meets the definition of a *qualifying child.* As to Ned, while he comes close to being a *qualifying child*, he does not (fails the "living with the taxpayer" requirement) and, therefore, we can't ignore his gross income (which results in him failing to meet the alternative dependent definition of a *qualifying relative*). **Answer (d) is incorrect** but is also the source of some confusion. This is a bit tricky, but we saw that Ned <u>is</u> Tammy's "child" for *qualifying child* purposes (sounds strange, but the Code definition of a "child" includes Ned). Ned does not live with Tammy, so this precludes Ned from being a *qualifying child*. We then saw that Ned did not meet the alternative dependent definition of a *qualifying relative,* so this precluded Tammy from claiming Ned as her dependent. If Ned were Tammy's actual child, this would change nothing (he would still fail to be a *qualifying child* or a *qualifying relative*. **Answer (e) is incorrect** because we do have a correct response in answer (c).

22. **The best answer is (b).** It is a bit unfair to ask in conjunction with other questions in this series, as the correct answer is substantially dependent on a correct analysis of other questions in this series. This professor would not ask such a series of interrelated multiple-choice questions on an exam. Rather, this series of questions were derived from an exam essay question. We will conclude that Tammy qualifies as a "head of household" because Chuck is her *qualifying child,* and she meets the statutory requirements of this filing status.

As you have most likely discussed in class, the tax rate schedules used to compute tax liability vary depending on one's *filing status*. IRC § 1 contains these rate schedules. Be aware, that the rate schedules appearing in IRC § 1 are "indexed for inflation," so the actual rate schedules for any particular year will vary. [Please see Appendix B for inflation-adjusted information for the 2018 and 2019 tax years.] As you also have probably discussed, the rate schedules for individuals appear in order, in IRC §§ 1(a)-1(d), from the most favorable rates (the least amount of tax for any given amount of taxable income) to the least favorable rates. The primary issue for Tammy in this question is **whether she can qualify to file using the "head of household" rates** in IRC § 1(b). This rate schedule is not quite as favorable as that for "married individuals filing a joint return", but it is better than the rate schedule for "unmarried individuals" (generally known as "single").

A *head of household* is defined in IRC §2 (b), and here is where the rules get tricky (and, you might say, picky too). The statutory definition of a *head of household* is a bit more inclusive than is necessary to address the facts in this question, so it is wise to carefully read all of the provisions in IRC § 2(b) for other situations that might arise.

Generally, we start with a *head of household* being an "unmarried individual" (although there is a notable exception for certain "separated" spouses), and Tammy meets this criterion. Next, to qualify for *head of household* status, the taxpayer (Tammy) must maintain as her home, a household which is the primary home for more than ½ of the year for the taxpayer (Tammy) and at least one of the following:

> ➢ A *qualifying child* who is single (there are a few other minor items, none of which are applicable here),

> ➢ Any other "relative" (as defined in IRC §§ 152(a)(2)(A)–(2)(G)) if such person is a dependent of the taxpayer (and the taxpayer is entitled to claim the dependent's *personal exemption deduction* pursuant to IRC § 151).

Note that there are special *head of household* qualifying rules with respect to utilizing one's dependent parent who is not required to live with the taxpayer. [See IRC § 2(b)(1)(B).]

As for Tammy, she qualifies as *head of household* because her son, Chuck, lives with her for more than ½ of the year (he lives with her for the full year) and is her *qualifying child* (see Question 21, above).

As noted in the explanation to Question 21, above, the dependent qualification process became a bit more complex with the enactment of the *"Working Families Tax Relief Act of 2004"* where the desire to have uniform definitions of certain relatives for federal tax statutes created a rather messy result for the dependency rules. Surprisingly, this change to the "dependency" rules made the definition of "head of household" status a bit less complex than it had been prior to this legislative change (in the first edition of this book, the answer to this question had been one of the more "tricky" ones).

Answer (a) is incorrect because, Ned is not a qualifying dependent as required by the statute. As we saw in Question 21, Ned is not a *qualifying child* (see discussion in problem 21, above). Basically, Ned fails because he was not living with Tammy for more than one-half of the year. As noted, but not applicable here, that there are special *head of household* qualifying rules with respect to utilizing one's dependent parent who is not required to live with the taxpayer. [See IRC § 2(b)(1)(B).] **Answer (c) is incorrect** because Tammy does not meet the requirements to qualify as a *surviving spouse* pursuant to IRC § 2(a). **Answer (d) is incorrect** because, as indicated above, Tammy qualifies for the more favorable *head of household* status even though she is an unmarried individual.

23. **The best answer to this very tricky question is (b).** The author admits that this is an awful question (awful in the sense that it requires a very careful reading of detailed cross-referenced and complex statutes). However, it serves to point out how carefully one must read the sometimes seemingly undecipherable language of the Code. This question also serves as an example of miniscule Code details at, or near, their worst. It also is a bit unfair to ask in conjunction with other questions in this series, as the correct

answer is substantially dependent on a correct analysis of other questions in this series. This professor would not ask such a series of interrelated multiple-choice questions on an exam. Rather, this series of questions were derived from an exam essay question. We will conclude that all of the identified health-related costs (insurance and doctor/hospital) that Tammy paid for both Chuck and Ned will qualify as medical care expenses for purposes of a possible deduction for Tammy. To arrive at this conclusion, we must look at the deduction for medical care expenses as well as the relationships of the individuals for whom such medical costs were paid.

IRC § 213 allows for a deduction of certain qualified medical care expenses. Once one makes the determination of what constitutes "qualified" medical care expenses, the subject of this question, the deduction is allowed as an "itemized deduction" only to the extent that the total qualifying expenses exceeds 10% of adjusted gross income (AGI). Qualified medical care expenses include typical costs for doctors, dentists, hospital, health insurance, and the like. [See IRC § 213(d).] The section specifically provides, in IRC § 213(a), that qualifying medical care expenses are those paid by the taxpayer for the taxpayer, his or her spouse, or a dependent (as defined in IRC § 152, . . .).

The $1,000 of health insurance premiums Tammy paid for herself clearly qualifies as medical care expenses. The health insurance premiums and doctor/hospital costs Tammy paid for Chuck and Ned, respectively, also clearly qualify as medical care expenses under IRC § 213. The critical question now is whether Tammy, who paid for these costs, is entitled to deduct them. As for Chuck, we concluded, in Questions 21 and 22 above, that he is Tammy's dependent; a *qualifying child* to be specific. Tammy, therefore, is entitled to deduct the $1,000 in insurance premiums paid for her dependent child Chuck.

And what of the $7,000 doctor and hospital costs that Tammy paid for Ned? Is Tammy entitled to deduct them? Is Ned Tammy's "dependent (as defined in IRC § 152, . . .)? Looking back at Question 21, you may be inclined to say no because in that question, we determined that Ned was not Tammy's dependent for purposes of certain credits for dependents. Indeed, we found that Ned was neither a *qualifying child* nor *a qualifying relative*. So how, you might ask, did we come up with the answer that Tammy is entitled to deduct medical expenses that she paid for Ned. Pursuant to IRC § 213, doesn't Ned have to be her dependent for this? Well, the answer is yes and no. This professor is not fond of reading parenthetical comments, but as a student, you should not do as this professor and you should carefully read all parenthetical comments. The answer to this question lies in such a parenthetical comment. Back to IRC § 213(a) and reference to the full parenthetical text: The section specifically provides, in IRC § 213(a), that qualifying medical care expenses are those paid by the taxpayer for the taxpayer, his or her spouse, or <u>a dependent (as defined in IRC § 152, **determined without regard to subsections** (b)(1), (b)(2), and **(d)(1)(B)** thereof)</u>.

This requires some very careful reading and takes us back to the definition of a *qualifying relative* in IRC § 152(d). Recall, from other questions in this book, the requirements of a *qualifying relative*:

> **Qualifying Relative:** An individual is considered a "***qualifying relative***" of you, the taxpayer, if all of the following requirements are met:
>
> ➤ The individual must be either "*related*" to you <u>or</u>, if not "related" in the Code sense, live with you (with some exceptions) for the entire year. [See IRC §§ 152(d)(2)(A)-(d)(2)(G) for definitions of "relatives" which includes everyone from children, siblings, ancestors, aunts/uncles, etc. to a host of "in-laws," and IRC § 152(d)((2)(H) for other qualifying individuals.]
>
> ➤ ***The individual must have "gross income" less than the "exemption amount" for that year.***
>
> ➤ The taxpayer (you, the person trying to claim the individual as a dependent) must have provided more than one-half of this person's total support for the year.

Emphasis has been added to the "gross income" requirement of a *qualifying relative*. In Question 21, we determined that Ned was not a *qualifying relative* (and, therefore not Tammy's dependent) because he failed this "gross income" requirement; his $5,000 gross income was not less than the "exemption amount" ($4,150 for 2018). Also recall, however, that in Question 21, we found that Ned did meet the other two requirements (being "related" to Tammy and Tammy providing more than one-half of Ned's support). Back to IRC § 213(a) where it specifically provides that qualifying medical care expenses are those paid by the taxpayer for the taxpayer, his or her spouse, or <u>a dependent (as defined in IRC § 152, **determined without regard to subsections** (b)(1), (b)(2), and **(d)(1)(B)** thereof)</u>. Subsection (d)(1)(B) of IRC § 152 **is** the "gross income" test that Ned failed as a *qualifying relative*. And now we have our answer as to Ned's medical care expenses. Once we ignore the fact that Ned did "not have gross income less than the exemption amount" he would have been Tammy's dependent (as a *qualifying relative*). So, for purposes of IRC § 213(a) and deducting Ned's medical care costs, Ned <u>is</u> Tammy's dependent.

In summary, Tammy's expenditures for all of the items listed for her, Chuck and Ned qualify as medical care expenses for purposes of IRC § 213.

Answer (a) is incorrect but is a favorite choice. This answer incorrectly places the tougher requirement on a taxpayer deducting qualifying medical care expenses paid for another that other person qualify as a dependent of the taxpayer (for purposes of IRC § 152 and can be so claimed for sections where this tougher dependency status is required (such as for the credits mentioned in Question 21). For purposes of IRC § 213 medical deductions, we have a less restrictive definition of a dependent. Ned does not really have to be either a *qualifying child* or *qualifying relative* as defined in IRC § 152. Tammy is entitled to treat Ned as her "dependent," for IRC § 213 purposes, nonetheless. **Answer (c) is incorrect** because it fails to recognize that a taxpayer can deduct qualifying medical care expenses paid for certain other individuals. **Answer (d) is incorrect** because it fails to recognize that health insurance premiums represent qualifying medical care expenses. **Answer (e) is incorrect** because a correct response (b) is presented.

24. **The best answer is (c).** Sadly, Allison lost her spouse last year. For income tax purposes a joint return generally may be filed in the year a spouse dies. [IRC § 6013; Reg. 1.6013-3.] There are special rules regarding the allocation of income between the spouses' joint return and an income tax return for the decedent in the year of death (i.e., determining income and deductions that are included in the joint return). However, Allison, with a substantial amount of income for last year, will definitely benefit from the most favorable "married filing joint returns" income tax rates (these rates are the lowest of any filing status for any given amount of taxable income).

    Answer (a) is incorrect but is an answer that is often selected. As is more thoroughly discussed in question 25, immediately following this question, "labels" for income tax purposes do not necessarily agree with those that we use in everyday language. To everyone, except the I.R.S., Allison became a "surviving spouse" once Robert passed away. For income tax purposes, however, the term "surviving spouse" has a very particular meaning defined in IRC § 2(a). Allison is <u>not</u> a "surviving spouse" for income tax purposes, as is more thoroughly discussed in question 25, below. **Answer (b) is incorrect** because as discussed above, in the year of her husband's death, Allison may still use the married filing joint rates. The statement in this answer about one's marital status being determined as of the last day of the taxable year is, however, generally true. **Answer (d) is incorrect** because there is no rule requiring Allison to use this rate schedule.

25. **Answer (b) is correct.** Sadly, Allison lost her spouse last year and, unfortunately for tax purposes, this year she is *single* and will use the "unmarried/single" rate schedule for computing her tax liability. IRC § 1 sets out the tax computation rate schedules and as you have most likely

studied, the rate schedules vary depending on one's *filing status*. Filing status is determined as of the end of the tax year and, as indicated in the facts, Allison is single.

A word of caution about language used on exams. There are many instances where the common use of a term does not necessarily correspond to its official "tax" counterpart. Labels can be deceiving so do not be fooled by their use in lay terms on an exam. In everyday language we would refer to Allison as a "surviving spouse." Looking at IRC § 1(a) we see a favorable tax rate schedule (compared to that for unmarried individuals) for certain married individuals and *surviving spouses*. The term *surviving spouse*, however, has a very specific and much narrower definition for federal income tax purposes (and the ability to use the more favorable rate schedule). IRC § 2(a) gives the *tax label* of *surviving spouse* for only the two years after the year in which the taxpayer's spouse died <u>and</u> only if:

> ➢ Such surviving spouse maintains as his or her home a household which constitutes for the taxable year the principal place of abode (as a member of such household) of a dependent,
> ➢ Who (within the meaning of IRC § 152) is a son, stepson, daughter, or stepdaughter of the surviving spouse, and
> ➢ With respect to whom the surviving spouse is entitled to a deduction for the taxable year under IRC § 151.

Distilled, a *surviving spouse* for income tax purposes is an unmarried surviving spouse (for the two years subsequent to his or her spouse's death) who has dependent children living in his or her home. The facts state that Allison has no children. Even though to the entire non-tax world, Allison is a surviving spouse, she is not so considered for federal income tax purposes. Therefore, she is unable to use the more favorable married/surviving spouse rate schedule but, rather, must use the single/unmarried (non "heads of households") rate schedule.

Answer (a) is incorrect because, as discussed above, Allison is <u>not</u> considered a surviving spouse for federal income tax purposes. **Answer (d) is incorrect** for the same reason that she does not qualify for surviving spouse status for income tax purposes. **Answer (c) is also incorrect**. The tax rate schedule for *heads of households* is "in between" those for married/surviving spouses and unmarried/single (less favorable than the former but more favorable than the latter). Heads of households have a particular meaning for federal income tax purposes and Allison does not meet the requirements. [See IRC § 2(b) and other questions in this book addressing this issue.]

ANSWER KEY
EXAM VII

FEDERAL INCOME TAX
ANSWER KEY AND EXPLANATIONS
EXAM VII

Note: Questions 1 through 7 represent a series of questions, in this Exam VII, that concentrate on the potential nonrecognition of gain from the sale of one's principal residence. The questions in this series are in different blocks with different fact patterns and get progressively more difficult. There will be some redundancy in this answer analysis portion. These questions are, however, "doable" and will emphasize the importance of going through a fairly consistent step-by-step approach. Question 1 through 7 have all been, in some form, questions (essay or multiple choice) in this professor's actual basic income tax class. There are other questions earlier in this book that introduced us to this area of the law and beginning with this question, we begin to add real-life layers to this important area of tax law.

1. **The correct answer is (b).** This is a fairly complex question, and it requires a somewhat lengthy step-by-step analysis. This is another example of a question that, to a student studying income tax, may appear to exist purely as an academic exercise. While it does contain aspects that present an academic challenge, this question reflects a surprisingly common "real world" tax situation. We will conclude that Winnie and Herb each has a <u>realized</u> gain of $100,000 from the sale of their respective interests in the home. However, pursuant to IRC § 121, they will both be able to fully exclude their gains from recognition as income.

   As discussed in other questions in this book, in every fact pattern in which something is sold (or otherwise disposed of), the author likes to go through the following analysis; always ask these three questions:

   1) Does the sale (or disposition) result in a <u>realized</u> gain or loss and if so, what is the <u>amount</u>? This is computing the amount of gain (or loss). It is the AR (amount realized) less one's AB (adjusted basis).

   2) If we have a <u>realized</u> gain or loss, is it <u>recognized</u> (i.e. reportable for income tax purposes)? As a taxpayer, you would like the answer to be NO for gains; I do not want to recognize, report, the gain (said another way, I'd like to be able to exclude this gain from my income).

   3) If the gain or loss is recognized, is it accorded "capital" gain or loss treatment? This is primarily the issue of "capital gains (or losses)" that are treated differently for income tax purposes.

   Because this question involves a multi-step analysis and because the author recognizes the value of your time, both **abbreviated/short** and **comprehensive/long** analyses are provided below.

The abbreviated/short version of the analysis for this question begins with the understanding that at the time of the house sale, we have two separate and unmarried individuals, Winnie and Herb, each selling an undivided one-half interest in the house. Both Winnie and Herb each *realize* a $100,000 gain from the sale. This gain is the difference between the $250,000 sales price for each of their one-half shares ($500,000 combined sales price) less their respective bases of $150,000. Winnie's basis is her "cost" for the one-half interest (one-half of her original $300,000 cost for the entire house). Herb's basis in his one-half interest in the house is a "carryover" basis from Winnie's cost basis for the one-half interest because Herb received his one half interest in the house as a transfer "incident to their divorce."

Neither Winnie nor Herb will have to *recognize* their respective gains. Analyzing each of them, and their respective realized gains, *independently* (they are no longer married), they both can exclude (not recognize) their realized gain pursuant to IRC § 121, the exclusion (or nonrecognition) of gain from the sale of a personal residence.

The following comprehensive/long (very long) analysis presents a step-by-step discussion of the answer to this question that can be applied to other gain/loss questions.

As indicated above, the first question that we ask whenever there is a sale or disposition of an asset is whether there is a realized gain and if so, what is the amount? Therefore, our first step in our analysis process is determining whether Winnie and Herb have *realized* gains or losses from the sale of their respective one-half interests in the house. It is important to understand that at the time of the house sale, we have two separate and unmarried individuals, Winnie and Herb, each selling an undivided one-half interest in the house. Essentially, we have two separate sales to analyze.

To determine the *realized* gain or loss from the sale of the interests in the house, we need two basic components: the sales price ("amount realized" or, hereinafter, AR) and the basis in the property interest ("adjusted basis or, hereinafter, AB). The difference between the two represents realized gain or loss. [IRC § 1001(a).] Each of these two components, AR and AB, can present a variety of complex tax issues for exam and real-world tax purposes. The AR side for both Winnie and Herb is straightforward in our question, and is $250,000 for each of them (the combined selling price of the house was $500,000.

The general starting place for determining one's AB in property is one's cost. [IRC §§ 1011 and 1012.] "Adjustments" to one's basis, while not at issue in this question, can result from many reasons including capital improvements (increasing basis), and depreciation expenses (reducing basis). [IRC § 1016.] Applying the general cost basis rule in our question, Winnie's AB is her "cost" for the <u>one-half interest</u> (one-half of her original $300,000 cost for the entire house) or $150,000. The determination of Herb's AB is a bit more involved but not too complex. There is no indication that Herb paid anything for his one-half interest in the house. Rather, he received his one-half ownership interest pursuant to his and Winnie's divorce decree. The AB of property transferred between spouses, or former spouses that are "incident to divorce," is controlled by IRC § 1041(b). In a nutshell, it provides that when spouses transfer property to each other, or when former spouses transfer property to each other and it is "incident to their divorce," the transferee spouse (or former spouse) takes a carryover basis. This section does not distinguish as to the type of inter vivos transfer involved; it covers gifts, sales, exchanges, etc. The term "incident to divorce" means any transfer within one year of the divorce or generally within six years of the divorce such transfer is called for by the divorce instrument (e.g., divorce decree). This is not a significant issue in our case and when Herb receives the one-half interest in the house, he takes as his AB the AB that Winnie had in that one-half interest. We have already determined that Winnie's AB in the property is her cost and, therefore, Herb, like Winnie, has a $150,000 AB in his one-half interest in the house. [Technically, when Winnie transferred the one-half interest to Herb, we should also address any relevant gain. Suffice it to say, while Winnie realized some gain, it would not, pursuant to IRC § 1041(a) be recognized. So we can dispense with this and continue.]

The determination of *realized* gains or losses to Winnie and Herb is now an easy task:

Winnie		Herb
$250,000	Amount realized (AR)	$250,000
($150,000)	Adjusted basis (AB)	($150,000)
$100,000	***Realized* Gain**	**$100,000**

The next step in our analysis of gain/loss situations is to determine the extent to which any <u>realized</u> gain is <u>recognized</u>. Recognition of gain basically means that it is reported as income for income tax purposes. IRC § 1001(c) provides that unless otherwise provided for in the Code, all realized gains and losses are recognized. The law has, for a long time, given some relief (non-recognition) to homeowners with respect to the sale of one's principal residence. We find this in IRC § 121 and it is often referred to as an "exclusion of gain from sale of principal residence." More accurately, IRC § 121 is a non-recognition (of gain) provision. Effective for sales of a taxpayer's principal residence after May 6, 1997, IRC § 121 provides for the exclusion of up to $250,000 of gain ($500,000 in the case of certain married individuals), if certain conditions are met.

Again, it may be helpful to first present the landscape of this analysis. Immediately below is a slide that this professor uses in class to address the various components of IRC § 121. The application and analysis of these steps follows.

§121 NON-RECOGNITION

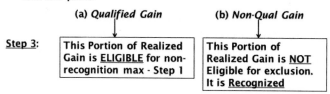

Step 1: Does non-recognition (exclusion) even apply?
    a) Ownership test **and**
    b) Use Test
       (if necessary, look to prorating provision §121(c))

Step 2: Okay, we qualify for non-recognition. Now to the new (in 2009) "overlay" for "qualified/non-qualified" use in §121(b)(5): **If required to do so**, split the **total realized gain** into two parts:

      (a) Qualified Gain   **(b) Non-Qual Gain**

Step 3:

This Portion of Realized Gain is **ELIGIBLE** for non-recognition max - Step 1	This Portion of Realized Gain is **NOT** Eligible for exclusion. It is **Recognized**

From 1997 through 2008 (and in prior editions of this book), IRC § 121 was much simpler. Our analysis consisted of only "Step 1," above (there were no steps 2 and 3). Fortunately for Winnie and Herb, we shall see that we need not address Steps 2 & 3 in his case (please see questions that follow where we must cover the entire scope of this section and address Steps 2 & 3.)

Step 1 of our IRC § 121 analysis consists of the two basic requirements for this exclusion, commonly referred to as the "ownership" and "use" tests. The taxpayer must have owned the house for at least two years (looking back five years from the date of sale) **and** must have used it as his or her principal residence for two years (looking back five years from the date of sale). [IRC § 121(a).] Because Winnie and Herb are two separate individuals, with two separate realized gains, the section requirements must be analyzed separately with respect to Winnie and Herb.

Winnie: Recognition *of Gain and Application of IRC § 121*

As to Winnie's one-half interest in the house, she easily meets the two-year "ownership" test, having owned at least a one-half interest for five years.

Winnie also easily meets the two-year "use" test as she has been using the house as her principal residence for five years. Winnie meets the requirements of IRC § 121, and she can exclude up to $250,000 of realized gain (remember, she is single at this point). Her realized gain of $100,000 does not exceed this maximum so all of her gain is excluded from gross income (or **not** *recognized*).

Herb: *Recognition* of Gain and Application of IRC § 121

It was exactly one year ago that the couple divorced, and Herb received his one-half interest in the house (pursuant to their divorce decree). In real terms, Herb has owned his one-half interest for only one year, which is less than the requisite two-year period. Herb, however, is in luck because of a "special rule" at IRC § 121(d)(3)(A) that states: "In the case of an individual holding property transferred to such individual in a transaction described in section 1041(a), the period such individual owns such property shall include the period the transferor owned the property." Herb *did* receive his one-half interest from Winnie incident to their divorce (a transaction to which IRC § 1041 applies). This special rule allows Herb to "tack," or add, Winnie's period of ownership (prior to Herb receiving his interest) onto his ownership period resulting in Herb owning his one-half interest for five years. Thus, Herb does meet the two-year ownership test.

The two-year "use" test presents a similar problem. Herb did use the house as his principal residence for one year (the year he was married to Winnie). Recall that he then moved out of the house at the couple's divorce and did not live in the house for the subsequent year. In real terms, Herb has used the house as his principal residence for only one year. Again, Herb is in luck. Another "special rule" at IRC § 121(d)(3)(B) states: "Solely for purposes of this section, an individual shall be treated as using the property as such individual's principal residence during any period of ownership which such individual's spouse or former spouse is granted use of the property under a divorce decree or separation instrument." This provision allows Herb to "tack," or add, on to his one-year use period, the one year that Winnie has used the house as her principal residence subsequent to their divorce. Fortunately for Herb, this adds up to a total of two years of use, thus meeting the two-year "use" test. Note that the tacking of use is not the same as that for ownership. Tacking of "use" is tacking the other spouse's period of use forward from the divorce. Tacking of "ownership" is tacking the other spouse's ownership back from the divorce.

With the help of these two special rules, Herb meets the requirements of IRC § 121, and he can exclude up to $250,000 of realized gain (remember, he is single at this point). His realized gain of $100,000 does not exceed this maximum, so all of his gain is excluded from gross income (or **not** *recognized*).

While not at issue in this problem, it should be noted that generally, the exclusion provisions of IRC § 121 cannot be used more than once in a two-year period. [IRC § 121(b)(3).] It is a logical assumption from the facts presented that this limitation would not apply to Herb in this question. It should also be noted that the statute does not require that the requisite two-year "use" and "ownership" period be co-extensive. While again, this is not an issue in this question, it is a common misunderstanding (read as "good testing area") that the two "two-year" qualifying periods must be at the same time. It is also a common misunderstanding (again, read as "good testing area") that the "five-year look back period" for purposes of determining two-year ownership and use somehow requires that the taxpayer either owned or used the house for at least five years. This is not correct and again, while this is not at issue in this question, it might be helpful for your analysis of other IRC § 121 related questions.

It is important, when analyzing an IRC § 121 question to methodically go through the aforementioned three steps in the order presented. The new (as of 2008) Steps 2 & 3 (see the above depiction of the author's slide used in class) are not at issue for Winnie or Herb. These additional steps are necessary for situations where an individual has at any time during the entire period he or she owned the house, used it for something other than his or her principal residence for the entire period that they owned it (e.g., used it as a vacation home, left it vacant, rented it out, etc,). If this were the case, it can be harmful (tax-wise) and we would have a much longer trek to determine the proper outcome. Fortunately for Winnie and Herb, the facts in this question have one or both of them using the house as a principal residence for the entire time of ownership. Therefore, we need not proceed any further.

Answer (a) is incorrect and would not the best answer but it does raise an interesting issue. As discussed in other questions in this book, the IRC § 121 exclusion provisions might apply on a prorated basis if one's sale of their principal residence was for reasons of health, job change, or for "unforeseen circumstances." In our problem, Herb met the two qualifying tests of IRC § 121 because of the special "tacking" rules. However, had he not met both tests for the full two-year period, would he be entitled to a prorated exclusion based on the theory that his divorce (and subsequent sale) is an "unforeseen circumstance?" The answer would be yes. Regulation § 1.121-3 contains a comprehensive discussion of the prorated exclusion including "safe harbors" for what are considered "unforeseen circumstances" as well as other factors to be considered in making this determination. The short version of the explanation here is that one would pro-rate the $250,000 exclusion (½ of $250,000 or $125,000 per person because they met the requirements for ½ the tow-year required time, or one year. The answer here too is not correct because it pro-rates the $100,000 gain for each and not the $250,000 exclusion for each. Again, however, this is not at issue in this problem. **Answer (c) is incorrect** because the nonrecognition provisions of IRC § 1041 apply only to transfers between spouses or former spouses if incident to divorce. Gains from sales to "outside" parties, such as is the case here, are not covered by IRC § 1041. **Answer (d) is incorrect** because it fails to recognize that Winnie and Herb are two separate, unmarried individuals, who have two separate *realized* gains. Please see other questions in this book that address the application of IRC § 121 to married individuals. **Answer (e) is also incorrect**. This answer does not correctly apply the "tacking" rules to the sale of Herb's one-half interest in the house nor the concept of unforeseen circumstances.

2. **The correct answer is (b).** This is a very complex question (especially as an objective, multiple choice question), and it requires a lengthy step-by-step analysis. This is another example of a question that, to a student studying income tax, may appear to exist purely as an academic exercise. While it does contain aspects that present an academic challenge, this question reflects a surprisingly common "real world" tax situation. We will conclude that Jon's $300,000 gain realized from the sale of his lakefront cabin will be eligible for some non-recognition (or exclusion) pursuant to IRC § 121. This fact pattern will require us to apportion his $300,000 gain into "qualified" and "nonqualified" portions with only the former eligible for exclusion under IRC § 121. His *qualified* portion of gain will be $160,000 and he will not have to recognize this amount. He will, however, be required to recognize the $140,000 balance of his gain (it is the *nonqualified* portion of gain that is not eligible for exclusion under IRC § 121). Now for the in-depth analysis (be forewarned that it is rather long and tedious).

As mentioned in other questions, in every fact pattern in which something is sold (or otherwise disposed of), the author likes to go through the following analysis; always ask these three questions:

1) Do we have a Realized Gain (or Loss) & how much? This is computing the amount of gain (or loss). It is the AR (amount realized) less one's AB (adjusted basis). See other problems in this book addressing this issue.

2) If yes, is the realized gain (or loss) Recognized? This simply means, is it reported in one's income for tax purposes. This is the issue that we are currently addressing. As a taxpayer, you would like the answer to be NO for gains; I do not want to recognize, report, the gain (said another way, I'd like to be able to exclude this gain from my income).

3) If gain is recognized, is it given any special character or treatment? This is primarily the issue of "capital gains (or losses)" that are treated differently for income tax purposes. This is not the issue in this question (see other problems in this book).

The facts of the question already give us the answer to our first inquiry. Jon realized a $300,000 gain from the sale of his lakefront cabin. We need not go into our usual detailed analysis of how to compute the gain as the question already supplies this. So, let's move on to the major part of this question; what amount of this $300,000 gain must Jon recognize (include in his gross income for tax reporting)? Note, that if we do find that Jon has some gain to recognize (which he will) we will not be addressing the third inquiry, above, regarding if there is any special character to Jon's gain since this is not part of this question.

On to the second question of whether or not his realized gain is **recognized** (reported in his income). As discussed in other problems in this book, all realized gains are recognized unless there is some specific "non-recognition" (or exclusion) provision in the Code. The law has, for a long time, given some relief (non-recognition) to homeowners with respect to the sale of one's principal residence. This is IRC § 121 and is the primary issue for this question.

Again, it may be helpful to first present the landscape of this analysis. Immediately below is a slide that this professor uses in class to address the various components of IRC § 121. The application and analysis of these steps follows.

§121 NON-RECOGNITION

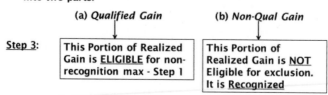

Step 1: Does non-recognition (exclusion) even apply?
a) Ownership test **and**
b) Use Test

(if necessary, look to prorating provision §121(c))

Step 2: Okay, we qualify for non-recognition. Now to the new (in 2009) "overlay" for "qualified/non-qualified" use in §121(b)(5): If required to do so, split the total realized gain into two parts:

(a) *Qualified Gain*   (b) *Non-Qual Gain*

Step 3:

| This Portion of Realized Gain is ELIGIBLE for non-recognition max - Step 1 | This Portion of Realized Gain is NOT Eligible for exclusion. It is Recognized |

From 1997 through 2008 (and in prior editions of this book), IRC § 121 was much simpler. Our analysis consisted of only "Step 1," above (there were no steps 2 and 3). The analysis for this question will, ultimately, involve Steps 2 & 3 and we shall get to those in due course. We begin with Step 1.

Step 1 of our IRC § 121 analysis consists of the two basic requirements for this exclusion, commonly referred to as the "ownership" and "use" tests. The taxpayer must have owned the house for at least two years (looking back five years from the date of sale) **and** must have used it as his or her principal residence for two years (looking back five years from the date of sale). [IRC § 121(a).]

It might be helpful to visually indicate Jon's years of ownership ('04-'18) as well as his use in each year.

   V = Vacation or Vacant (not used as his principal residence)

   H = Home; used as his principal residence   *The Sale*

'04	'05	'06	'07	'08	'09	'10	'11	'12	'13	'14	'15	'16	'17	'18
V	V	V	V	V	V	V	V	V	H	V	V	V	H	H

Beginning of 5 year window

The five-year look back period for the ownership and use tests consist of years **2014 through 2018** (the earlier years of ownership are irrelevant for this Step 1 but we will return to them, if necessary, in Steps 2 & 3)

Jon **easily meets the *ownership test*** having owned it for at least two of the five years for the look-back window (he's owned it for all five years of this look-back period for Step 1 of our IRC § 121 analysis, and even longer which will be relevant for Steps 2 & 3 of our IRC § 121 analysis). **He also meets the *use test***, having used it as his principal residence for **exactly two years** ('17 & '18) during the five-year lookback period. One may be tempted to include Jon's 2013 use of the cabin as his principal residence in determining the requisite two years of use. 2013, however, is not within the five-year statutory look-back window and we ignore it for Step 1.

At this point we are done with Step 1 of our IRC § 121 analysis and Jon is eligible to use this section to exclude (not recognize) some or all of his $300,000 gain from the sale of the lakefront cabin. Jon is single, and we know that his maximum exclusion/non-recognition amount from IRC § 121 is $250,000. In the earlier editions of this book (before Steps 2 & 3 were effective beginning in 2009) we would have been done with this problem, concluding that Jon could exclude $250,000 of his $300,000 gain and only the $50,000 balance would be recognized. This answer (which is answer (a) to this question) is no longer correct. Unfortunately for Jon, and us, we have a lot more work to do.

This question takes us to the more complex parts of IRC § 121 (enacted in 2008 and effective beginning in 2009). These are Steps 2 & 3 of our IRC § 121 analysis (see the §121 slide, above and below) and these additional steps are necessary for situations where an individual has at any time during the entire period he or she owned the house, used it for something other than their principal residence for the entire ownership period (e.g., used it as a vacation home, left vacant, rented it out, etc.). This is the case with Jon in our question.

Not to take up space and repeat material, it may be helpful to see the IRC § 121 slide, again, with all the steps:

§121 NON-RECOGNITION

Step 1: Does non-recognition (exclusion) even apply?
    a) Ownership test <u>and</u>
    b) Use Test
        (if necessary, look to prorating provision §121(c))

Step 2: Okay, we qualify for non-recognition. Now to the new (in 2009) "overlay" for "qualified/non-qualified" use in §121(b)(5): <u>If required to do so</u>, split the <u>total realized gain</u> into two parts:

      (a) *Qualified Gain*   **(b)** *Non-Qual Gain*

Step 3:

| This Portion of Realized Gain is <u>ELIGIBLE</u> for non-recognition max - Step 1 | This Portion of Realized Gain is <u>NOT</u> Eligible for exclusion. It is <u>Recognized</u> |

Here is the visual representation of Jon's 15 years of owning the cabin vis-à-vis his use:

V = Vacation or Vacant (not used as his principal residence)

H = Home; used as his principal residence   *The Sale*

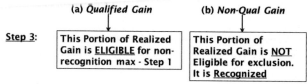

'04	'05	'06	'07	'08	'09	'10	'11	'12	'13	'14	'15	'16	'17	'18
V	V	V	V	V	V	V	V	V	H	V	V	V	H	H

We have already determined that Jon is eligible for IRC § 121 (Step 1). Note that in Step 2, we now (after the 2008 law change) must split up his gain into two parts: **qualified portion of gain** and **nonqualified portion of gain**. In class, this professor uses the term "overlay;" as we are overlaying this new (as of 2008) law requiring us to bifurcate the gain. This was not a "taxpayer friendly" change to the law and it affects many individuals, including Jon in our question. This is not a political statement but prior to this new law (enacted at the end of the George W. Bush Presidency and designed to raise revenue for the government), a gain from the sale of a personal residence was excluded (not recognized) up to the Code's $250,000 max ($500,000 for most married couples) as long as the "two year" tests were met. We generally did not care if sometime during a taxpayer's period of ownership, it was used for purposes other than their principal residence. In other words, all of their gain was generally eligible for exclusion up to the maximum amount allowed. Now, however, the gain realized must be divided up (apportioned) into *qualified* and *nonqualified* parts with only the *qualified* portion of the gain being eligible for IRC § 121 exclusion. The *nonqualified* portion of the gain is not eligible for exclusion and must be recognized.

Adding these steps means that we have more rules (often complex) and more math. As ominous as it sounds, proper application of these additional components of IRC § 121 is really not too bad. In class, this professor emphasis, over and over, how important it is to follow the Steps carefully and, in the order, presented. Do not be alarmed if this area feels difficult or even impossible. It is very common for most students to feel this way, at first, because there is so much information and rules that seem to be "all over the place." With every tax class, this professor continually encourages students, working with them using questions like these and class hypos, in class, in office hours, and sometimes by text, email and phone conversations; knowing, ultimately, that it will make sense. Every law student can make it over this hurdle with enough practice and patience.

Okay, on with our Step 2 for Jon. To apportion his gain, we need to figure out the total number of years Jon owned the cabin (total years and not just the five years ending with the sale like we did in Step 1). Per the facts, Jon owned the lakefront cabin for exactly 15 years. What portion of these total 15 years are *qualified* use years? There are some wacky rules here (we'll see them in this question and those that follow) but the general starting point is that a *qualified* use year is one in which the taxpayer used the property as their principal residence. [See IRC § 121(b)(5)] We'll show this visually in just a bit, but we know from the facts for this question, that Jon actually lived in the cabin as his principal residence for 2013, 2017 & 2018. So far, that makes 3 *qualified* years. Logically, *nonqualified* use years are, generally, those years that the taxpayer did not use the property as their principal residence. But don't do any counting for Jon just yet because we have more *qualified* years for him. Because this new bifurcating gain provision of the law did not begin until 2009, the Code, again logically, counts all years **prior to 2009** as *qualified* years. Again, we'll depict all of this visually in just a bit, but this means that the 5 years Jon owned the cabin prior to 2009 (2004 through 2008) count as *qualified* years. There is another rule that we shall see come to life in question 3 (immediately following this question 2) and cover it in that question's answer analysis.

Visually, let's see what we have as far as *qualified* and *nonqualified* years.

V = Vacation or Vacant (not used as his principal residence)

H = Home; used as his principal residence

Q = Qualified Year

NQ = Nonqualified Year   *The Sale*

'04	'05	'06	'07	'08	'09	'10	'11	'12	'13	'14	'15	'16	'17	'18
V	V	V	V	V	V	V	V	V	H	V	V	V	H	H
Q	Q	Q	Q	Q	NQ	NQ	NQ	NQ	Q	NQ	NQ	NQ	Q	Q

Okay, now what? We split-up Jon's total $300,000 gain realized from the sale of his lakefront cabin into *qualified* and *nonqualified* parts. If you prefer, we are apportioning his total gain between *qualified* and *nonqualified* components. This is Step 2 of our IRC § 121 analysis (from the slide) and we have some math!

Qualified **Portion of Gain**	*Nonqualified* **Portion of Gain**
$\dfrac{\text{[Total "Q" years]}}{\text{[Total years Owned]}} = \dfrac{8}{15}$	$\dfrac{\text{[Total "NQ" years]}}{\text{[Total years Owned]}} = \dfrac{7}{15}$
$\dfrac{8}{15} \times \$300,000 = \mathbf{\$160,000}$	$\dfrac{7}{15} \times \$300,000 = \mathbf{\$140,000}$

Almost done! Jon's *qualified* portion of his total $300,000 gain is **$160,000**. This *qualified* portion is eligible for IRC § 121 exclusion (nonrecognition) up to a maximum of $250,000 (Jon is single, and we determined this amount in Step 1 of our analysis). Because $160,000 is less than the $250,000 max, Jon can exclude (not recognize) all of this $160,000 *qualified* gain. His $140,000 *nonqualified* portion of his total gain is not eligible for IRC § 121 exclusion (nonrecognition) so, he must recognize (report in income) the entire $140,000 *nonqualified* portion of the gain.

Note that we are not, as is a common misunderstanding, apportioning the IRC § 121 $250,000 (or $500,000) maximum exclusion amount. Rather, we are apportioning the taxpayer's gain (to which we will then apply the statutory exclusion amount).

Note how this new (as of 2008) "overlay" provision of IRC § 121 hurts Jon tax-wise. Under prior longstanding tax law, he would have been able to exclude $250,000 of his $300,000 gain (recognizing only the $50,000 excess above the statutory maximum). Now, however, he is not able to avail himself of the full IRC § 121 exclusion. Only his *qualified* $160,000 portion of his $300,000 gain is excluded (and his gain recognized jumps to $140,000).

Note that this new (as of 2008) Q/NQ "overlay" does not negatively impact taxpayers who use their home as their principal residence for the entire period of ownership (i.e., there are no "NQ" years).

Phew! That was a very lengthy analysis but again, analyzing the law in a step-by-step manner will get you through it. This area of the law provides students a great opportunity to create their own hypothetical fact patterns and test themselves on applying the law. Again, at first blush, this area of law may seem daunting. When ultimately tamed and understood, however, every question becomes answerable (step-by-step analysis is the key).

Answer (a) is incorrect but, as discussed above, would have been the correct answer in prior editions of this book before concepts of *qualified* and *nonqualified* portions of gain came to life via the 2008 tax law changes to IRC § 121. **Answer (c) is not correct.** The $60,000 portion of gain indicated as qualified is the result of only including Jon's actual three years using the cabin as his principal residence. It fails to apply the statutory *qualified* label to the 5 years he owned the cabin prior to 2009 notwithstanding that the cabin was not used as his principal residence. **Answer (d) is incorrect** because Jon does qualify for some exclusion (nonrecognition) under the statute. **Answer (e) is incorrect** because it does not accurately reflect Jon's *qualified* and *nonqualified* years in apportioning his realized gain.

3.   **The correct answer is (d).** This question is very similar to question 2, immediately above. It is also a very complex question and it requires a lengthy step-by-step analysis. While somewhat redundant, much of the analysis material from the previous question 2 will be replicated here (done to alleviate the need for students to go back and forth between a previous exam answer and the analysis applicable to this question).

This is another example of a question that, to a student studying income tax, may appear to exist purely as an academic exercise. While it does contain aspects that present an academic challenge, this question reflects a surprisingly common "real world" tax situation. We will conclude that Jon's $300,000 gain realized from the sale of his lakefront cabin will be eligible for some non-recognition (or exclusion) pursuant to IRC § 121. This fact pattern will require us to apportion his $300,000 gain into "qualified" and "nonqualified" portions with only the former eligible for exclusion under IRC § 121. His *qualified* portion of gain will be $180,000 and he will not have to recognize this amount. He will, however, be required to recognize the

$120,000 balance of his gain (it is the *nonqualified* portion of gain that is not eligible for exclusion under IRC § 121). Now for the in-depth analysis (be forewarned that it is rather long and tedious).

As mentioned in other questions, in every fact pattern in which something is sold (or otherwise disposed of), the author likes to go through the following analysis; always ask these three questions:

1) Do we have a Realized Gain (or Loss) & how much? This is computing the amount of gain (or loss). It is the AR (amount realized) less one's AB (adjusted basis). See other problems in this book addressing this issue.

2) If yes, is the realized gain (or loss) Recognized? This simply means, is it reported in one's income for tax purposes. This is the issue that we are currently addressing. As a taxpayer, you would like the answer to be NO for gains; I do not want to recognize, report, the gain (said another way, I'd like to be able to exclude this gain from my income).

3) If gain is recognized, is it given any special character or treatment? This is primarily the issue of "capital gains (or losses)" that are treated differently for income tax purposes. This is not the issue in this question (see other problems in this book).

The facts of the question already give us the answer to our first inquiry. Jon realized a $300,000 gain from the sale of his lakefront cabin. We need not go into our usual detailed analysis of how to compute the gain as the question already supplies this. So, let's move on to the major part of this question; what amount of this $300,000 gain must Jon recognize (include in his gross income for tax reporting)? Note, that if we do find that Jon has some gain to recognize (which he will) we will not be addressing the third inquiry, above, regarding if there is any special character to Jon's gain since this is not an issue in this question.

On to the second question of whether or not his realized gain is ***recognized*** (reported in his income). As discussed in other problems in this book, all realized gains are recognized unless there is some specific "non-recognition" (or exclusion) provision in the Code. The law has, for a long time, given some relief (non-recognition) to homeowners with respect to the sale of one's principal residence. This is IRC § 121 and is the primary issue for this question.

Again, it may be helpful to first present the landscape of this analysis. Immediately below is a slide that this professor uses in class to address the various components of IRC § 121. The application and analysis of these steps follows.

§121 NON-RECOGNITION

Step 1: Does non-recognition (exclusion) even apply?
   a) Ownership test **and**
   b) Use Test
   (if necessary, look to prorating provision §121(c))

Step 2: Okay, we qualify for non-recognition. Now to the new (in 2009) "overlay" for "qualified/non-qualified" use in §121(b)(5): <u>If required to do so,</u> split the <u>total realized gain</u> into two parts:

(a) *Qualified Gain*   **(b)** *Non-Qual Gain*

Step 3:

This Portion of Realized Gain is <u>ELIGIBLE</u> for non-recognition max - Step 1	This Portion of Realized Gain is <u>NOT</u> Eligible for exclusion. It is <u>Recognized</u>

From 1997 through 2008 (and in prior editions of this book), IRC § 121 was much simpler. Our analysis consisted of only "Step 1," above (there were no steps 2 and 3). The analysis for this question will, ultimately, involve Steps 2 & 3 and we shall get to those in due course. We begin with Step 1.

Step 1 of our IRC § 121 analysis consists of the two basic requirements for this exclusion, commonly referred to as the "ownership" and "use" tests. The taxpayer must have owned the house for at least two years (looking back five years from the date of sale) **and** must have used it as his or her principal residence for two years (looking back five years from the date of sale). [IRC § 121(a).]

It might be helpful to visually indicate Jon's years of ownership ('04-'18) as well as his use in each year.

   V = Vacation or Vacant (not used as his principal residence)

   H = Home; used as his principal residence   *The Sale*

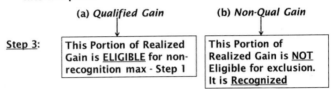

'04	'05	'06	'07	'08	'09	'10	'11	'12	'13	'14	'15	'16	'17	'18
V	V	V	V	V	V	V	V	V	H	H	V	V	H	V

Beginning of 5 year window

The five-year look back period for the ownership and use tests consist of years **2014 through 2018** (the earlier years of ownership are irrelevant for this Step 1 but we will return to them, if necessary, in Steps 2 & 3)

Jon **easily meets the *ownership test*** having owned it for at least two of the five years for the look-back window (he's owned it for all five years of this look-back period for Step 1 of our IRC § 121 analysis, and even longer which will be relevant for Steps 2 & 3 of our IRC § 121 analysis). **He also meets the *use test*,** having used it as his principal residence for **exactly two years** ('14 & '17) during the five-year lookback period. One may be tempted to include Jon's 2013 use of the cabin as his principal residence in determining the requisite two years of use. 2013, however, is not within the five-year statutory look-back window and we ignore it for Step 1.

At this point we are done with Step 1 of our IRC § 121 analysis and Jon is eligible to use this section to exclude (not recognize) some or all of his $300,000 gain from the sale of the lakefront cabin. Jon is single and we know that his maximum exclusion/non-recognition amount from IRC § 121 is $250,000. In the earlier editions of this book (before Steps 2 & 3 were effective beginning in 2009) we would have been done with this problem, concluding that Jon could exclude $250,000 of his $300,000 gain and only the $50,000 balance would be recognized. This answer (which is answer (a) to this question) is no longer correct. Unfortunately for Jon, and us, we have a lot more work to do.

This question takes us to the more complex parts of IRC § 121 (enacted in 2008 and effective beginning in 2009). These are Steps 2 & 3 of our IRC § 121 analysis (see the §121 slide, above and below) and these additional steps are necessary for situations where an individual has at any time during the entire period he or she owned the house, used it for something other than their principal residence for the entire ownership period (e.g., used it as a vacation home, left vacant, rented it out, etc.). This is the case with Jon in our question.

Not to take up space and repeat material, it may be helpful to see the IRC § 121 slide, again, with all the steps:

§121 NON-RECOGNITION

Step 1: Does non-recognition (exclusion) even apply?
   a) Ownership test <u>and</u>
   b) Use Test
      (if necessary, look to prorating provision §121(c))

Step 2: Okay, we qualify for non-recognition. Now to the new (in 2009) "overlay" for "qualified/non-qualified" use in §121(b)(5): <u>If required to do so</u>, split the <u>total realized gain</u> into two parts:

(a) *Qualified Gain*   (b) *Non-Qual Gain*

Step 3:

This Portion of Realized Gain is **ELIGIBLE** for non-recognition max - Step 1	This Portion of Realized Gain is **NOT** Eligible for exclusion. It is <u>Recognized</u>

Here is the visual representation of Jon's 15 years of owning the cabin vis-à-vis his use:

V = Vacation or Vacant (not used as his principal residence)

H = Home; used as his principal residence   *The Sale*

'04	'05	'06	'07	'08	'09	'10	'11	'12	'13	'14	'15	'16	'17	'18
V	V	V	V	V	V	V	V	V	H	H	V	V	H	V

We have already determined that Jon is eligible for IRC § 121 (Step 1). Note that in Step 2, we now (after the 2008 law change) must split up his gain into two parts: *qualified portion of gain* and *nonqualified portion of gain*. In class, this professor uses the term "overlay;" as we are overlaying this new (as of 2008) law requiring us to bifurcate the gain. This was not a "taxpayer friendly" change to the law and it affects many individuals, including Jon in our question. This is not a political comment but prior to this new law (enacted at the end of the George W. Bush Presidency and designed to raise revenue for the government), a gain from the sale of a personal residence was excluded (not recognized) up to the Code's $250,000 max ($500,000 for most married couples) as long as the "two year" tests were met. We generally did not care if sometime during a taxpayer's period of ownership, it was used for purposes other than their principal residence. In other words, all their gain was generally eligible for exclusion up to the maximum amount allowed. Now, however, the gain realized must be divided up (apportioned) *qualified* and *nonqualified* parts with <u>only the *qualified* portion of the gain being eligible for IRC § 121 exclusion</u>. The ***nonqualified*** <u>portion of the gain is not eligible for exclusion and must be recognized</u>.

Adding these steps means that we have more rules (often complex) and more math. As ominous as it sounds, proper application of these additional components of IRC § 121 is really not too bad. In class, this professor emphasis, over and over, how important it is to follow the Steps carefully and, in the order, presented. Do not be alarmed if this area feels difficult or even impossible. It is very common for most students to feel this way, at first, because there is so much information and rules that seem to be "all over the place." With every tax class, this professor continually encourages students, working with them using questions like these and class hypos, in class, in office hours, and sometimes by text, email and phone conversations, knowing, ultimately, that it will make sense. Every law student can make it over this hurdle with enough practice and patience.

Okay, on with our Step 2 for Jon. To apportion his gain, we need to figure out the total number of years Jon owned the cabin (total years and not just the five years ending with the sale like we did in Step 1). Per the facts, Jon owned the lakefront cabin for exactly 15 years. What portion of these total 15 years are *qualified* use years? There are some wacky rules here but the general starting point is that a *qualified* use year is one in which the taxpayer used the property as their principal residence. [See IRC § 121(b)(5)] We'll show this visually in just a bit, but we know from the facts for this question, that Jon actually lived in the cabin as his principal residence for 2013, 2014 & 2017. So far, that makes 3 *qualified* years. Logically, *nonqualified* use years are, generally, those years that the taxpayer did not use the property as their principal residence. But don't do any counting for Jon just yet because we have more *qualified* years for him. Because this new bifurcating gain provision of the law did not begin until 2009, the Code, again logically, counts all years **prior to 2009** as *qualified* years. Again, we'll depict all of this visually in just a bit, but this means that the 5 years Jon owned the cabin prior to 2009 (2004 through 2008) count as *qualified* years.

There is one more rule that is applicable here (we did not see this in question 2, above). Hold on tight as this rule lacks some logic. Buried in IRC § 121(b)(5)(C)(ii)(I), a *nonqualified* year does not include "any portion of the 5-year period . . . [that we used for Step 1's ownership and use tests] which is after the last date such property is used as the principal residence of the taxpayer or the taxpayer's spouse." Huh? This is always confusing to students and practitioners alike. Stated another way, you get to count as a *qualified* year, any year within our original 5-year lookback window that follows the last year, within that window, that the taxpayer actually used the property as their principal residence. Still confused? That's okay, nobody understood this when it was first enacted (the author attended a tax seminar in that year and the entire audience of hundreds of CPA's and Tax Attorneys was confused and arguing about just what this meant). We shall explain this after the visual depiction below.

Visually, let's see what we have as far as *qualified* and *nonqualified* years.

V = Vacation or Vacant (not used as his principal residence)

H = Home; used as his principal residence

Q = Qualified Year

NQ = Nonqualified Year   *The Sale*

'04	'05	'06	'07	'08	'09	'10	'11	'12	'13	'14	'15	'16	'17	'18
V	V	V	V	V	V	V	V	V	H	H	V	V	H	V
Q	Q	Q	Q	Q	NQ	NQ	NQ	NQ	Q	Q	NQ	NQ	Q	Q

We can see three *qualified* years for Jon's actual use as his principal residence in 2013, 2014 and 2017. The statutory pre-2009 years ('04-'08) represent another five *qualified* years. But how did 2018 become a *qualified* year? This is that wacky rule. Recall that 2014-2018 was our five-year window for Step 1 to determine if Jon was even eligible for some §121 exclusion (the two-year tests). The aforementioned goofy rule applies here; 2018 (a vacation year) followed a year of actual use as his principal residence (2017) so that is classified as a *qualified* year in these Steps 2 & 3). If that is the case, why don't we reclassify 2015 and 2016 as *qualified* years? They follow 2014, an actual year of use as a principal residence and 2014 is within the original 5-year lookback window? Careful reading of the code is critical; it is only years that follow the **last year** of actual use as a principal residence during this 5-year lookback period. 2014 was <u>not</u> Jon's last year of actual use as his principal residence. Rather, 2017 was his last year of actual use. So, we can't count 2015 and 2016 (they were not after his last year of use) but 2018 slots in as a *qualified* year because it follows the last year, 2017, of actual use during this 5-year lookback window. It is very important that we only use this crazy rule to determine *qualifying* years for splitting up a gain <u>after we have determined, in Step 1, that the taxpayer is eligible for exclusion under this section.</u> We will see the huge significance of this "important" point in question 4 (immediately following this question, 3).

To summarize Step 2, we ended up with Jon having **9 *qualified* years** (and 6 *nonqualified* years). *Qualified* years consist of three actual use years, five from the statutory pre-2009 period, and one more (2018) because of the goofy rule in IRC § 121(b)(5)(C)(ii)(I).

Okay, now what? We split-up Jon's total $300,000 gain realized from the sale of his lakefront cabin into *qualified* and *nonqualified* parts. If you prefer, we are apportioning his total gain between *qualified* and *nonqualified* components. This is Step 2 of our IRC § 121 analysis (from the slide) and we have some math!

Qualified **Portion of Gain**	*Nonqualified* **Portion of Gain**

$$\frac{\text{[Total “Q” years]}}{\text{[Total years Owned]}} = \frac{9}{15}$$
$$\frac{\text{[Total “NQ” years]}}{\text{[Total years Owned]}} = \frac{6}{15}$$

$$\frac{9}{15} \times \$300,000 = \mathbf{\$180,000}$$
$$\frac{6}{15} \times \$300,000 = \mathbf{\$120,000}$$

Almost done! Jon's ***qualified*** portion of his total $300,000 gain is **$180,000**. This *qualified* portion is eligible for IRC § 121 exclusion (nonrecognition) up to a maximum of $250,000 (Jon is single, and we determined this amount in Step 1 of our analysis). <u>Because $180,000 is less than the $250,000 max, Jon can exclude (not recognize) all of this $180,000 *qualified* gain.</u> His $120,000 *nonqualified* portion of his total gain is <u>not</u> eligible for IRC § 121 exclusion (nonrecognition) so, <u>he must recognize (report in income) the entire $120,000 *nonqualified* portion of the gain.</u>

Note that we are not, as is a common misunderstanding, apportioning the IRC § 121 $250,000 (or $500,000) maximum exclusion amount. Rather, we are <u>apportioning the taxpayer's gain</u> (to which we will then apply the statutory exclusion amount).

Note how this new (as of 2008) "overlay" provision of IRC § 121 hurts Jon tax-wise. Under prior longstanding tax law, he would have been able to exclude $250,000 of his $300,000 gain (recognizing only the $50,000 excess above the statutory maximum). Now, however, he is not able to avail himself of the full IRC § 121 exclusion. Only his *qualified* $180,000 portion of his $300,000 gain is excluded (and his gain recognized jumps to $120,000).

Note that this new (as of 2008) Q/NQ "overlay" does not negatively impact taxpayers who use their home as their principal residence for the entire period of ownership (i.e., there are no "NQ" years).

Phew! That was a very lengthy analysis but again, analyzing the law in a step-by-step manner will get you through it. This area of the law provides students a great opportunity to create their own hypothetical fact patterns and test themselves on applying the law. Again, at first blush, this area of law may seem daunting. When ultimately tamed and understood, however, every question becomes answerable (step-by-step analysis is the key).

Answer (a) is incorrect but, as discussed above, would have been the correct answer in prior editions of this book before concepts of *qualified* and *nonqualified* portions of gain came to life via the 2008 tax law changes to IRC § 121. **Answer (b) is not correct.** The $220,000 portion of gain indicated as qualified is the result of including an additional two years of *qualified* use by improperly applying the wacky rule of IRC § 121(b)(5)(C)(ii)(I). As discussed, 2015 and 2016 follow an actual use year (2014) within the 5-year window, they do not follow the **last** year of actual use in that window (only 2018 gets reclassified as *qualified* according to this rule. **Answer (c) is incorrect** it fails to utilize the rule in IRC § 121(b)(5)(C)(ii)(I) to pick up one extra *qualified* year. The prorated gain numbers incorrect reflect only 8 total *qualified* years. **Answer (e) is incorrect** because a correct response in reflected in answer (d).

4. **The correct answer is (d).** This question is very similar to questions 2 and 3, immediately above, but the answer is **very** different. This question is, when all is said and done, less complex that the two immediately preceding questions. It is vitally important to approach this question, like the others, utilizing a careful step-by-step analysis. Much of the analysis material from the previous questions 2 and 3 will be replicated here (done to alleviate the need for students to go back and forth between a previous exam answer and the analysis applicable to this question).

    This is another example of a question that, to a student studying income tax, may appear to exist purely as an academic exercise. While it does contain aspects that present an academic challenge, this question reflects a surprisingly common "real world" tax situation. We will conclude that **none** of Jon's $300,000 gain realized from the sale of his lakefront cabin will be eligible for non-recognition (or exclusion) pursuant to IRC § 121. Unlike questions 2 and 3, immediately above, our fact pattern in this question 4 will not require us to apportion any of Jon's gain into *qualified* or *nonqualified* components. He will not be eligible for any exclusion (or nonrecognition) because he will fail the initial core requirements of IRC § 121. Now for the in-depth analysis (albeit not as long as those for questions 2 and 3, above).

    As mentioned in other questions, in every fact pattern in which something is sold (or otherwise disposed of), the author likes to go through the following analysis; always ask these three questions:

    1) Do we have a Realized Gain (or Loss) & how much? This is computing the amount of gain (or loss). It is the AR (amount realized) less one's AB (adjusted basis). See other problems in this book addressing this issue.

    2) If yes, is the realized gain (or loss) Recognized? This simply means, is it reported in one's income for tax purposes. This is the issue that we are currently addressing. As a taxpayer, you would like the answer to be NO for gains – I do not want to recognize, report, the

gain (said another way, I'd like to be able to exclude this gain from my income).

3) If gain is recognized, is it given any special character or treatment? This is primarily the issue of "capital gains (or losses)" that are treated differently for income tax purposes. This is not the issue in this question (see other problems in this book).

The facts of the question already give us the answer to our first inquiry. Jon realized a $300,000 gain from the sale of his lakefront cabin. We need not go into our usual detailed analysis of how to compute the gain as the question already supplies this. So, let's move on to the major part of this question; what amount of this $300,000 gain must Jon recognize (include in his gross income for tax reporting)? Note, that if we do find that Jon has some gain to recognize (which he will) we will not be addressing the third inquiry, above, regarding if there is any special character to Jon's gain since this is not an issue in this question.

On to the second question of whether or not his realized gain is *recognized* (reported in his income). As discussed in other problems in this book, all realized gains are recognized unless there is some specific "non-recognition" (or exclusion) provision in the Code. The law has, for a long time, given some relief (non-recognition) to homeowners with respect to the sale of one's principal residence. This is IRC § 121 and is the primary issue for this question.

Again, it may be helpful to first present the landscape of this analysis. Immediately below is a slide that this professor uses in class to address the various components of IRC § 121. The application and analysis of these steps follows.

§121 NON-RECOGNITION

Step 1: Does non-recognition (exclusion) even apply?
    a) Ownership test **and**
    b) Use Test
    (if necessary, look to prorating provision §121(c))

Step 2: Okay, we qualify for non-recognition. Now to the new (in 2009) "overlay" for "qualified/non-qualified" use in §121(b)(5): <u>If required to do so</u>, split the <u>total realized gain</u> into two parts:

(a) *Qualified Gain*   **(b)** *Non-Qual Gain*

Step 3:

This Portion of Realized Gain is <u>ELIGIBLE</u> for non-recognition max - Step 1	This Portion of Realized Gain is <u>NOT</u> Eligible for exclusion. It is <u>Recognized</u>

From 1997 through 2008 (and in prior editions of this book), IRC § 121 was much simpler. Our analysis consisted of only "Step 1," above (there were no steps 2 and 3). The analysis for this question will **not**, ultimately, involve Steps 2 & 3. We begin, and end, with Step 1.

Step 1 of our IRC § 121 analysis consists of the two basic requirements for this exclusion, commonly referred to as the "ownership" and "use" tests. The taxpayer must have owned the house for at least two years (looking back five years from the date of sale) **and** must have used it as his or her principal residence for two years (looking back five years from the date of sale). [IRC § 121(a).]

It might be helpful to visually indicate Jon's years of ownership ('04-'18) as well as his use in each year.

    V = Vacation or Vacant (not used as his principal residence)

    H = Home; used as his principal residence   *The Sale*

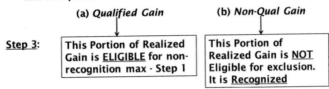

'04	'05	'06	'07	'08	'09	'10	'11	'12	'13	'14	'15	'16	'17	'18
V	V	V	V	V	V	V	V	V	H	H	V	V	V	V

Beginning of 5 year window

The five-year look back period for the ownership and use tests consist of years **2014 through 2018** (the earlier years of ownership are irrelevant for this Step 1 but we will return to them, if necessary, in Steps 2 & 3)

Jon **easily meets the *ownership test*** having owned it for at least two of the five years for the look-back window (he's owned it for all five years of this look-back period for Step 1 of our IRC § 121 analysis, and even longer which will be relevant for Steps 2 & 3 of our IRC § 121 analysis).

Unfortunately**, Jon fails to meet the *use test*.** Recall that for this first Step, we are examining only the five-year lookback period and in doing so, we see that during this period (2014 through 2018), he used the lakefront cabin as his principal residence in only **one** of these years (2014). Having failed to meet both tests, Jon is not eligible for any exclusion (nonrecognition) pursuant to IRC § 121. We **stop** at this point and do not go on to Steps 2 & 3. Going through our analysis on a step-by-step basis is absolutely critical in this question (see the discussion, below, explaining how one can get caught up in this section and sometimes it is difficult to accept what ends up being a rather straightforward, and not a very involved or deep, result. Jon's entire $300,000 will be recognized (IRC § 121 does not provide him with any exclusion (nonrecognition) for his gain).

It should be noted that other questions in this book address situations where a taxpayer fails to meet the two-year use and ownership tests but, nonetheless, is entitled to a partial exclusion (nonrecognition) in certain situations. This is IRC § 121(c). As discussed in other questions, this partial exclusion is applicable <u>only</u> when the house sale is "by reason of a change in place of employment, health, or, to the extent provided in regulations, unforeseen circumstances." [IRC § 121(c)(2)(B).] There are no facts here to indicate Jon sold his lakefront cabin for any such reasons. Regulation § 1.121-3 contains a comprehensive discussion of the prorated exclusion including "safe harbors" for what are considered "unforeseen circumstances" as well as other factors to be considered in making this determination. However, this question contains no facts that would indicate that any of the factors enumerated in this regulation would be applicable to allow Jon to exclude a portion of his gain pursuant to IRC § 121.

So that's it? Don't we move on to determine which of Jon's years of ownership are *qualified* and *nonqualified*? The simple answer is **NO** but doing so is common and can be a recipe for disaster. Again, conquering IRC § 121 questions require a step-by-step discipline. We would move on to Steps 2 & 3 only if we first find that Jon is eligible for some exclusion (which he is not in this question). The following is a common example of a student essay answer using our facts and we will see how easy it is to get into trouble (and make this a much more difficult question than it is). Can you spot where this sample student answer goes off course?

For §121 purposes, Jon does meet the "ownership" test (he has owned it for at least two years looking back five years from the sale). He does not, however, appear to meet the "use" test as he used the cabin for only one year, and not two, during the five-year lookback period from the date of sale. The facts do not indicate any reason that would be considered a "valid" reason for a prorated exclusion (§121(c)).

Jon's only year of "use" during the qualifying lookback period was in 2014 where he lived there for principal residence purposes. Other provisions in §121 provide that he can count, as qualifying years, any year(s) following the last year of actual use in the five-year lookback period. Since 2014 was the last year back in the five-year period and he used it that year as his principal residence, the Code lets him count, as qualifying years, the next four years (2015, 2016, 2017, & 2018). Therefore, looking at it in light of this rule, Jon is now considered to meet the two-year "use" test and can, therefore, utilize the §121 exclusion. [This sample answer then goes on to explain the maximum exclusion amount and goes down the rabbit hole in a lengthy, drawn-out discussion of apportioning his $300,000 gain into qualifying and nonqualifying parts, etc.]

Unfortunately, this professor has seen many similar answers over the years. Sadly, in addition to being incorrect, the extra time spent doing a "deep dive" is also costly as this is valuable time lost that could have been used on other questions (or parts of an essay). So where did this answer go awry? This sample answer had it correct to begin with that Jon fails the "use" test and that should have been the end of the story (no exclusion via IRC § 121, nor an IRC §121(c) prorated exclusion with these facts). It should have ended there with a conclusion that Jon's entire $300,000 gain would be recognized.

Unfortunately, this sample student answer did not go through a step-by-step analysis and jumped to the issue of *qualified* years (and this professor's heart sinks because seeing the words *qualified years* triggers an "oh no, don't go there" response). Once there we determine that Jon is ineligible for an IRC § 121 exclusion by not meeting the "use" test, then we **stop**. Conflating the next step's determination of *qualified* years (about which we should not even inquire) and using the quirky rules to conclude that we have five *qualified* years within the five-year lookback period, this sample student answer essentially "bootstrapped" Jon into meeting the "use" test (which he does not). With time constraints on exams, such an error is understandable. So too is a possible student disbelief that with all of the facts, there surely has to be more to the answer than Jon not meeting initial, Step 1 requirements.

Answers (a), (b), and (c) are incorrect because each, to some degree, incorrect concludes that Jon's gain from the sale of his cabin is eligible for exclusion (or nonrecognition) pursuant to IRC § 121. As discussed above,

he fails the two-year "use" test that is the gateway Step 1 in a proper IRC §
121 analysis. **Answer (e) is incorrect** because a correct response in reflected
in answer (d).

5. **The correct answer is (c).** This is a very complex question (especially as
    an objective multiple choice question). In this series of questions (5 through
    7) we are examining some of the most examples of the application of IRC §
    121's exclusion (nonrecognition) of gain from the sale of a principal
    residence. These are very difficult questions, and each requires a somewhat
    lengthy step-by-step analysis. This is another example of a question that, to
    a student studying income tax, may appear to exist purely as an academic
    exercise. While it does contain aspects that present an academic challenge,
    this question reflects a surprisingly common "real world" tax situation (this
    set of questions is actually based on a real-life facts). For this question, we
    will conclude that Jamie and Manuel each has a _realized_ gain of $200,000
    from the sale of their respective interests in the home. We shall also
    conclude, in this question, that both are eligible for some exclusion
    (nonrecognition) pursuant to IRC § 121. Ultimately, after a very long
    analysis, each will be entitled to exclude (not recognize) only $120.000 or
    their $200,000 gain via IRC § 121 (leaving $80,000 for each to recognize).

    Be forewarned, this will be a very long and multi-step analysis and it is easy
    to get lost with so many steps and parties. However, this is about as difficult
    as it gets and while it may take multiple times going through all of this mess,
    as long as you proceed step-by-step, you can master any fact pattern. So,
    let's get started.

    As discussed in other questions in this book, in every fact pattern in which
    something is sold (or otherwise disposed of), the author likes to go through
    the following analysis; always ask these three questions:

    1) Does the sale (or disposition) result in a _realized_ gain or loss and if
        so, what is the _amount_? This is computing the amount of gain (or
        loss). It is the AR (amount realized) less one's AB (adjusted basis).

    2) If we have a _realized_ gain or loss, is it _recognized_ (i.e. reportable for
        income tax purposes)? As a taxpayer, you would like the answer to
        be NO for gains; I do not want to recognize, report, the gain (said
        another way, I'd like to be able to exclude this gain from my
        income).

    3) If the gain or loss is recognized, is it accorded "capital" gain or loss
        treatment? This is primarily the issue of "capital gains (or losses)"
        that are treated differently for income tax purposes.

Because this question involves a multi-step analysis and because the author recognizes the value of your time, both **abbreviated/short** and **comprehensive/long** analyses are provided below.

The abbreviated/short version of the analysis for this question begins with the understanding that at the time of the condo sale, we have two separate and unmarried individuals, Jamie and Manuel, each selling an undivided one-half interest in the condo. Both Jamie and Manuel each *realize* a $200,000 gain from the sale. This gain is the difference between the $250,000 sales price for each of their one-half shares ($500,000 combined sales price) less their respective bases of $50,000. Jamie's basis is her "cost" for the one-half interest (one-half of her original $100,000 cost for the entire condo). Manuel's basis in his one-half interest in the condo is a "carryover" basis from Jamie's cost basis for the one-half interest because Manuel received his one-half interest in the condo as a transfer "incident to their divorce."

Each of their respective $200,000 gain will be apportioned between "qualified" and "nonqualified" portions with only the former being excluded (not recognized) pursuant to IRC § 121. Using numbers, both Jamie and Manuel will each have $120,000 of *qualified* gain (excluded/not recognized under IRC § 121. Each will also have $80,000 of *nonqualified* gain that must be recognized (reported as income).

The following comprehensive/long (excruciatingly long) analysis presents a step-by-step discussion of the answer to this question that can be applied to other gain/loss questions.

As indicated above, the first question that we ask whenever there is a sale or disposition of an asset is whether there is a realized gain and if so, what is the amount? Therefore, our first step in our analysis process is determining whether Jamie and Manuel have *realized* gains or losses from the sale of their respective one-half interests in the condo. It is important to understand that at the time of the condo sale, we have two separate and unmarried individuals, Jamie and Manuel, each selling an undivided one-half interest in the condo. Essentially, we have two separate sales to analyze.

To determine the *realized* gain or loss from the sale of the interests in the condo, we need two basic components: the sales price ("amount realized" or, hereinafter, AR) and the basis in the property interest ("adjusted basis or, hereinafter, AB). The difference between the two represents realized gain or loss. [IRC § 1001(a).] Each of these two components, AR and AB, can present a variety of complex tax issues for exam and real-world tax purposes. The AR side for both Jamie and Manuel is straightforward in our question and is $250,000 for each of them (the combined selling price of the condo was $500,000.

The general starting place for determining one's AB in property is one's cost. [IRC §§ 1011 and 1012.] "Adjustments" to one's basis, while not at issue in this question, can result from many reasons including capital improvements (increasing basis), and depreciation expenses (reducing basis). [IRC § 1016.] Applying the general cost basis rule in our question, Jamie's AB is her "cost" for the <u>one-half interest</u> (one-half of her original $100,000 cost for the entire condo) or $50,000. The determination of Manuel's AB is a bit more involved but not too complex. There is no indication that Manuel paid anything for his one-half interest in the condo. Rather, he received his one-half ownership interest pursuant to his and Jamie's divorce decree. The AB of property transferred between spouses, or former spouses that are "incident to divorce," is controlled by IRC § 1041(b). In a nutshell, it provides that when spouses transfer property to each other, or when former spouses transfer property to each other and it is "incident to their divorce," the transferee spouse (or former spouse) takes a carryover basis. This section does not distinguish as to the type of inter vivos transfer involved; it covers gifts, sales, exchanges, etc. The term "incident to divorce" means any transfer within one year of the divorce or generally within six years of the divorce such transfer is called for by the divorce instrument (e.g., divorce decree). This is not a significant issue in our case and when Manuel receives the one-half interest in the condo, he takes as his AB the AB that Jamie had in that one-half interest. We have already determined that Jamie's AB in the property is her cost and, therefore, Manuel, like Jamie, has a $50,000 AB in his one half interest in the condo. [Technically, when Jamie transferred the one-half interest to Manuel, we should also address any relevant gain. Suffice it to say, while Jamie realized some gain, it would not, pursuant to IRC § 1041(a) be recognized. So we can dispense with this and continue.]

The determination of *realized* gains or losses to Jamie and Manuel is now an easy task:

	Jamie		Manuel
	<u>Jamie</u>		<u>Manuel</u>
Amount realized (AR)	$250,000		$250,000
Adjusted basis (AB)	($ 50,000)		($ 50,000)
***Realized* Gain**	**$200,000**		**$200,000**

The next step in our analysis of gain/loss situations is to determine the extent to which any <u>realized</u> gain is <u>recognized</u>. Recognition of gain basically means that it is reported as income for income tax purposes. IRC § 1001(c) provides that unless otherwise provided for in the Code, all realized gains and losses are recognized. The law has, for a long time, given some relief (non-recognition) to homeowners with respect to the sale of one's principal residence. We find this in IRC § 121 and it is often referred to as an "exclusion of gain from sale of principal residence." More accurately, IRC § 121 is a non-recognition (of gain) provision. Effective for sales of a taxpayer's principal residence after May 6, 1997, IRC § 121 provides for the exclusion of up to $250,000 of gain ($500,000 in the case of certain married individuals), if certain conditions are met.

Again, it may be helpful to first present the landscape of this analysis. Immediately below is a slide that this professor uses in class to address the various components of IRC § 121. The application and analysis of these steps follows.

§121 NON-RECOGNITION

Step 1: Does non-recognition (exclusion) even apply?
　　　a) Ownership test **and**
　　　b) Use Test
　　　　(if necessary, look to prorating provision §121(c))

Step 2: Okay, we qualify for non-recognition. Now to the new (in 2009) "overlay" for "qualified/non-qualified" use in §121(b)(5): **If required to do so**, split the **total realized gain** into two parts:

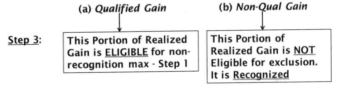

(a) *Qualified Gain*	(b) *Non-Qual Gain*
Step 3: This Portion of Realized Gain is **ELIGIBLE** for non-recognition max - Step 1	This Portion of Realized Gain is **NOT** Eligible for exclusion. It is **Recognized**

From 1997 through 2008 (and in prior editions of this book), IRC § 121 was much simpler. Our analysis consisted of only "Step 1," above (there were no steps 2 and 3). For Jamie and Manuel in this question, we shall also have to cover the additional Steps 2 & 3 (for each, individually).

Step 1 of our IRC § 121 analysis consists of the two basic requirements for this exclusion, commonly referred to as the "**ownership**" and "**use**" tests. The taxpayer must have owned the house for at least two years (looking back five years from the date of sale) **and** must have used it as his or her principal residence for two years (looking back five years from the date of sale). [IRC § 121(a).]

It might be helpful to visually indicate Jamie's and Manuel's years of ownership as well as their use in each year. For reasons explained later, we'll be consistent and use the same ten-year period (Jamie's ownership) for both of them.

Jamie:

V = Vacation or Vacant (not used as her principal residence)

H = Home; used as her principal residence

Beginning of 5 year window

The five-year look back period for the ownership and use tests consist of years **2014 through 2018** (the earlier years of ownership are irrelevant for this Step 1 but we will return to them when covering Steps 2 & 3)

Jamie **easily meets the *ownership test*** having owned it for at least two of the five years for the look-back window (she's owned it for all five years of this look-back period for Step 1 of our IRC § 121 analysis, and even longer which will be relevant for Steps 2 & 3 of our IRC § 121 analysis). **She also meets the *use test***, having used it as his principal residence for **exactly two years** ('16 & '17) during the five-year lookback period. One may be tempted to include Jamie's 2013 use of the condo as her principal residence in determining the requisite two years of use. 2013, however, is not within the five-year statutory look-back window and we ignore it for Step 1.

Manuel:

V = Vacation or Vacant (not used as his principal residence)

H = Home; used as his principal residence

Beginning of 5 year window

The five-year look back period for the ownership and use tests consist of years **2014 through 2018** (the earlier years of ownership are irrelevant for this Step 1 but we will return to them when covering Steps 2 & 3)

The couple divorce on 1/1/16 and that is when Manuel received his one-half interest in the condo (pursuant to the divorce decree). In real terms, Manuel has owned his one-half interest for three years ('16, '17 & '18). **Manuel, therefore, meets the *ownership test*.** While he meets the *ownership test* all by himself, there is a "special rule" at IRC § 121(d)(3)(A) that states: "In the case of an individual holding property transferred to such individual in a transaction described in section 1041(a), the period such individual owns such property shall include the period the transferor owned the property." Manuel *did* receive his one-half interest from Jamie incident to their divorce (a transaction to which IRC § 1041 applies). This special rule allows Manuel to "tack," or add, Jamie's period of ownership (prior to Manuel receiving his interest) onto his ownership period resulting in Manuel owning his one-half interest for the same ten-year period as Jamie.

The two-year "use" test appears to present a problem for Manuel as in real terms, he did not use the condo as his principal residence for any of the years in the five-year lookback period. Manuel, however, is in luck. Another "special rule" at IRC § 121(d)(3)(B) states: "Solely for purposes of this section, an individual shall be treated as using the property as such individual's principal residence during any period of ownership which such individual's spouse or former spouse is granted use of the property under a divorce decree or separation instrument." This provision allows Manuel to "tack," or add the **two** years that Jamie has used the condo as her principal residence subsequent to their divorce. He cannot, however, tack on or count as "use" years the post-divorce that Jamie was granted use of the condo but did not actually use it for her principal residence. [See Reg. § 121-4(b)(2).] **This means that Manuel also meets the *use* test.** Note that the tacking of use is not the same as that for ownership. Tacking of "use" is tacking the other spouse's period of use forward from the divorce. Tacking of "ownership" is tacking the other spouse's ownership back from the divorce.

At this point we are done with Step 1 of our IRC § 121 analysis and both Jamie and Manuel are eligible to use this section to exclude (not recognize) some or all of their respective $200,000 gain from the sale of the condo. Jamie and Manuel are both single (in the year the condo sold) and we know that their maximum exclusion/non-recognition amount from IRC § 121 is $250,000, each. In the earlier editions of this book (before Steps 2 & 3 were effective beginning in 2009) we would have been done with this problem, concluding that both Jamie and Manuel could each exclude their respective $200,000 gain since it is less than the $250,000 maximum amount. This answer (which is answer (a) to this question) is no longer correct. Unfortunately for Jamie and Manuel, and us, we have a lot more work to do.

This question takes us to the more complex parts of IRC § 121 (enacted in 2008 and effective beginning in 2009). These are Steps 2 & 3 of our IRC § 121 analysis (see the §121 slide, above and below) and these additional steps are necessary for situations where an individual has at any time during the entire period he or she owned the condo, used it for something other than their principal residence for the entire ownership period (e.g., used it as a vacation home, left vacant, rented it out, etc.). This is the case with Jamie and Manuel in our question.

Not to take up space and repeat material, it may be helpful to see the IRC § 121 slide, again, with all the steps:

§121 NON-RECOGNITION

Step 1: Does non-recognition (exclusion) even apply?
　　　a) Ownership test <u>and</u>
　　　b) Use Test
　　　　　(if necessary, look to prorating provision §121(c))

Step 2: Okay, we qualify for non-recognition. Now to the new (in 2009) "overlay" for "qualified/non-qualified" use in §121(b)(5): <u>If required to do so</u>, split the <u>total realized gain</u> into two parts:

　　　　　(a) *Qualified Gain*　　　　**(b) *Non-Qual Gain***

Step 3:

This Portion of Realized Gain is <u>ELIGIBLE</u> for non-recognition max - Step 1	This Portion of Realized Gain is <u>NOT</u> Eligible for exclusion. It is <u>Recognized</u>

It might be helpful to again depict Jamie's and Manuel's years of ownership as well as their use in each year for the full ten year period of ownership.

Jamie:

V = Vacation or Vacant (not used as her principal residence)

H = Home; used as her principal residence

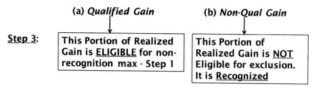

Marriage　　　*Divorce*　　　*The Sale*

'09	'10	'11	'12	'13	'14	'15	'16	'17	'18
V	V	H	H	H	V	V	H	H	V

Beginning of 5 year window

Manuel (including "tacked on" ownership and use; see above discussion):

V = Vacation or Vacant (not used as his principal residence)

H = Home; used as his principal residence

Marriage　　　*Divorce*　　　*The Sale*

'09	'10	'11	'12	'13	'14	'15	'16	'17	'18
V	V	H	H	H	V	V	H	H	V

Beginning of 5 year window

We have already determined that both Jamie and Manuel are eligible for IRC § 121 (Step 1). Note that in Step 2, we now (after the 2008 law change) must split up his gain into two parts: *qualified portion of gain* and *nonqualified portion of gain*. In class, this professor uses the term "overlay;" as we are overlaying this new (as of 2008) law requiring us to bifurcate the gain. This was not a "taxpayer friendly" change to the law and it affects many individuals, including Jamie and Manuel in our question. This is not a political statement but prior to this new law (enacted at the end of the George W. Bush Presidency and designed to raise revenue for the government), a gain from the sale of a personal residence was excluded (not recognized) up to the Code's $250,000 max ($500,000 for most married couples) as long as the "two year" tests were met. We generally did not care if sometime during a taxpayer's period of ownership, it was used for purposes other than their principal residence. In other words, all of their gain was generally eligible for exclusion up to the maximum amount allowed. Now, however, the gain realized must be divided up (apportioned) into *qualified* and *nonqualified* parts with <u>only the *qualified* portion of the gain being eligible for IRC § 121 exclusion. The *nonqualified* portion of the gain is not eligible for exclusion and must be recognized.</u>

Adding these steps means that we have more rules (often complex) and more math. As ominous as it sounds, proper application of these additional components of IRC § 121 is really not too bad. In class, this professor emphasis, over and over, how important it is to follow the Steps carefully and, in the order, presented. Do not be alarmed if this area feels difficult or even impossible. It is very common for most students to feel this way, at first, because there is so much information and rules that seem to be "all over the place." With every tax class, this professor continually encourages students, working with them using questions like these and class hypos, in class, in office hours, and sometimes by text, email and phone conversations; knowing, ultimately, that it will make sense. Every law student can make it over this hurdle with enough practice and patience.

Okay, on with our Step 2 for Jamie and Manuel. To apportion their respective gains, we need to figure out the total number of years they owned the condo (total years and not just the five years ending with the sale like we did in Step 1). Ownership for both Jamie and Manuel will be the same after application of our special tacking rule in Step 1, above. Per the facts, Jamie (and, effectively, Manuel) owned the condo for exactly 10 years. What portion of these total 10 years are *qualified* use years? There are some wacky rules here (we may see them in this question and those that follow) but the general starting point is that a *qualified* use year is one in which the taxpayer used the property as their principal residence. [See IRC § 121(b)(5)] We'll show this visually in just a bit but we will first analyze these years using Jamie. Per statute, Manuel's "years" will be the same (*qualified* years include those of a spouse or former spouse). We know from the facts for this question that Jamie actually lived in the condo as her principal residence for 2011, 2012, 2013, 2016 & 2017. So far, that makes 5 *qualified* years. Logically, *nonqualified* use years are, generally, those years that the taxpayer did not use the property as their principal residence. But don't do any counting for Jamie (and Manuel) just yet because we have more *qualified* years. Because this new bifurcating gain provision of the law did not begin until 2009, the Code, again logically, counts all years **prior to 2009** as **qualified** years. Since the condo was purchased in 2009, this is not applicable in our question.

There is one more rule that is applicable here. Hold on tight as this rule lacks some logic. Buried in IRC § 121(b)(5)(C)(ii)(I), a *nonqualified* year does not include "any portion of the 5-year period . . . [that we used for Step 1's ownership and use tests] which is after the last date such property is used as the principal residence of the taxpayer or the taxpayer's spouse." Huh? This is always confusing to students and practitioners alike. Stated another way, you get to count as a *qualified* year, any year within our original 5-year lookback window that follows the last year, within that window, that the taxpayer actually used the property as their principal residence. Still confused? That's okay, nobody understood this when it was first enacted (the author attended a tax seminar in that year and the entire audience of hundreds of CPA's and Tax Attorneys was confused and arguing about just what this meant). We shall explain this after the visual depiction below.

Visually, let's see what we have as far as *qualified* and *nonqualified* years. Remember, this will be the same for both Jamie and Manuel (a qualified year for one spouse is the same for the other spouse or former spouse).

V = Vacation or Vacant (not used as his principal residence)

H = Home; used as his principal residence

Q = Qualified Year

NQ = Nonqualified Year   *The Sale*

'09	'10	'11	'12	'13	'14	'15	'16	'17	'18
V	V	H	H	H	V	V	H	H	V
NQ	NQ	Q	Q	Q	NQ	NQ	Q	Q	Q

We can see five *qualified* years for Jamie's (and, by statute, Manuel's) actual use as a principal residence in 2011, 2012, 2013, 2016 and 2017. But how did 2018 become a *qualified* year? This is that wacky rule. Recall that 2014-2018 was our five-year window for Step 1 to determine if Jamie and Manuel were even eligible for some §121 exclusion (the two-year tests). The aforementioned goofy rule applies here; 2018 (a vacant year) followed the last year of actual use as a principal residence (2017) so that is classified as a *qualified* year in these Steps 2 & 3). It is very important that we only use this crazy rule to determine *qualifying* years for splitting up a gain <u>after we have determined, in Step 1, that the taxpayer is eligible for exclusion under this section.</u> We will see the huge significance of this "important" point in the question 6 (immediately following this question 5).

To summarize Step 2, we ended up with Jamie and Manuel each having **6 qualified years** (and 4 *nonqualified* years). *Qualified* years consist of five actual use years and one more (2018) because of the goofy rule in IRC § 121(b)(5)(C)(ii)(I).

Okay, now what? We split-up each of Jamie's and Manuel's $200,000 respective gain realized from the sale of the condo into *qualified* and *nonqualified* parts. If you prefer, we are apportioning each of their total gain between *qualified* and *nonqualified* components. This is Step 2 of our IRC § 121 analysis (from the slide) and we have some math! This is the same calculation for Jamie's $200,000 realized gain as well as Manuel's $200,000 realized gain.

Qualified **Portion of Gain**	*Nonqualified* **Portion of Gain**
$\dfrac{\text{[Total "Q" years]}}{\text{[Total years Owned]}} = \dfrac{6}{10}$	$\dfrac{\text{[Total "NQ" years]}}{\text{[Total years Owned]}} = \dfrac{4}{10}$
$\dfrac{6}{10} \times \$200{,}000 = \mathbf{\$120{,}000}$	$\dfrac{4}{10} \times \$200{,}000 = \mathbf{\$80{,}000}$

Almost done! Jamie and Manuel each have, as a **qualified** portion of each of their total $200,000 gain, an amount equal to **$120,000**. This *qualified* portion is eligible for IRC § 121 exclusion (nonrecognition) up to a maximum of $250,000 for each of them (Both Jamie and Manuel are single, and we determined this amount in Step 1 of our analysis). <u>Because $120,000 is less than the $250,000 max, both Jamie and Manuel can exclude (not recognize) all of their respective $120,000 *qualified* gain.</u> Their $80,000 *nonqualified* portion of total gain (each) is <u>not</u> eligible for IRC § 121 exclusion (nonrecognition) so, <u>both of them must recognize (report in their respective incomes) the entire $80,000 (each) *nonqualified* portion of the gain.</u>

Note that we are not, as is a common misunderstanding, apportioning the IRC § 121 $250,000 (or $500,000) maximum exclusion amount. Rather, we are <u>apportioning the taxpayer's gain</u> (to which we will then apply the statutory exclusion amount).

Note how this new (as of 2008) "overlay" provision of IRC § 121 hurts Jamie and Manuel tax-wise. Under prior longstanding tax law, each of them would have been able to exclude the entire amount of their respective $200,000 gain. Now, however, they are not able to avail themselves of the full IRC § 121 exclusion. Only their *qualified* $120,000 portion of each of their respective $200,000 gain is excluded (and each of their gain recognized jumps to $80,000).

Note that this new (as of 2008) Q/NQ "overlay" does not negatively impact taxpayers who use their home as their principal residence for the entire period of ownership (i.e., there are no "NQ" years).

Phew! That was a very lengthy analysis but again, analyzing the law in a step-by-step manner will get you through it. This area of the law provides students a great opportunity to create their own hypothetical fact patterns and test themselves on applying the law. Again, at first blush, this area of law may seem daunting. When ultimately tamed and understood, however, every question becomes answerable (step-by-step analysis is the key).

Answer (a) is incorrect. Jamie's gain is not fully excludable, as discussed above, and Manuel is eligible to use IRC § 121 to exclude a portion of his gain. **Answer (b) is incorrect** but, as discussed above, would have been the correct answer in prior editions of this book before concepts of *qualified* and *nonqualified* portions of gain came to life via the 2008 tax law changes to IRC § 121. **Answer (d) is not correct.** The first part of this answer is correct with respect to Jamie. However, it is incorrect that Manuel's amount of gain excluded will be less than that for Jamie; they are both entitled to the same degree of gain exclusion. **Answer (e) is incorrect** because it fails to recognize that Jamie and Manuel are two separate, unmarried individuals, who have two separate *realized* gains. Please see other questions in this book that address the application of IRC § 121 to married individuals.

6. **The correct answer is (d).** This question is very similar to questions 5, immediately above, but the answer is **very** different. This question is, when all is said and done, less complex that the immediately preceding question. It is vitally important to approach this question, like the others, utilizing a careful step-by-step analysis. Much of the analysis material from the previous questions 5 will be replicated here (done to alleviate the need for students to go back and forth between a previous exam answer and the analysis applicable to this question).

This is another example of a question that, to a student studying income tax, may appear to exist purely as an academic exercise. While it does contain aspects that present an academic challenge, this question reflects a surprisingly common "real world" tax situation. We will conclude that **none** of either Jamie's or Manuel's $200,000 respective gain realized from the sale of their condo will be eligible for non-recognition (or exclusion) pursuant to IRC § 121. Unlike question 5, immediately above, our fact pattern in this question 6 will not require us to apportion any of Jamie' or Manuel's gain into *qualified* or *nonqualified* components. We do not get that far. <u>Neither of them will be eligible for any exclusion (or nonrecognition)</u> because they both fail the initial core requirements of IRC § 121. Now for the in-depth analysis (albeit not as long as that for question 5, above).

As mentioned in other questions, in every fact pattern in which something is sold (or otherwise disposed of), the author likes to go through the following analysis; always ask these three questions:

1) Do we have a Realized Gain (or Loss) & how much? This is computing the amount of gain (or loss). It is the AR (amount realized) less one's AB (adjusted basis). See other problems in this book addressing this issue.

2) If yes, is the realized gain (or loss) Recognized? This simply means, is it reported in one's income for tax purposes. This is the issue that we are currently addressing. As a taxpayer, you would like the answer to be NO for gains – I do not want to recognize, report, the gain (said another way, I'd like to be able to exclude this gain from my income).

3) If gain is recognized, is it given any special character or treatment? This is primarily the issue of "capital gains (or losses)" that are treated differently for income tax purposes. This is not the issue in this question (see other problems in this book).

As indicated above, the first question that we ask whenever there is a sale or disposition of an asset is whether there is a realized gain and if so, what is the amount? Therefore, our first step in our analysis process is determining whether Jamie and Manuel have *realized* gains or losses from the sale of their respective one-half interests in the condo. It is important to understand that at the time of the condo sale, we have two separate and unmarried individuals, Jamie and Manuel, each selling an undivided one-half interest in the condo. <u>Essentially, we have two separate sales to analyze.</u>

To determine the *realized* gain or loss from the sale of the interests in the condo, we need two basic components: the sales price ("amount realized" or, hereinafter, AR) and the basis in the property interest ("adjusted basis or, hereinafter, AB). The difference between the two represents <u>realized</u> gain or loss. [IRC § 1001(a).] Each of these two components, AR and AB, can present a variety of complex tax issues for exam and real-world tax purposes. The AR side for both Jamie and Manuel is straightforward in our question and is $250,000 for each of them (the combined selling price of the condo was $500,000.

The general starting place for determining one's AB in property is one's cost. [IRC §§ 1011 and 1012.] "Adjustments" to one's basis, while not at issue in this question, can result from many reasons including capital improvements (increasing basis), and depreciation expenses (reducing basis). [IRC § 1016.] Applying the general cost basis rule in our question, Jamie's AB is her "cost" for the one-half interest (one-half of her original $100,000 cost for the entire condo) or $50,000. The determination of Manuel's AB is a bit more involved but not too complex. There is no indication that Manuel paid anything for his one-half interest in the condo. Rather, he received his one-half ownership interest pursuant to his and Jamie's divorce decree. The AB of property transferred between spouses, or former spouses that are "incident to divorce," is controlled by IRC § 1041(b). In a nutshell, it provides that when spouses transfer property to each other, or when former spouses transfer property to each other and it is "incident to their divorce," the transferee spouse (or former spouse) takes a carryover basis. This section does not distinguish as to the type of inter vivos transfer involved; it covers gifts, sales, exchanges, etc. The term "incident to divorce" means any transfer within one year of the divorce or generally within six years of the divorce such transfer is called for by the divorce instrument (e.g., divorce decree). This is not a significant issue in our case and when Manuel receives the one-half interest in the condo, he takes as his AB the AB that Jamie had in that one-half interest. We have already determined that Jamie's AB in the property is her cost and, therefore, Manuel, like Jamie, has a $50,000 AB in his one-half interest in the condo. [Technically, when Jamie transferred the one-half interest to Manuel, we should also address any relevant gain. Suffice it to say, while Jamie realized some gain, it would not, pursuant to IRC § 1041(a) be recognized. So we can dispense with this and continue.]

The determination of *realized* gains or losses to Jamie and Manuel is now an easy task:

Jamie		Manuel
$250,000	Amount realized (AR)	$250,000
($ 50,000)	Adjusted basis (AB)	($ 50,000)
$200,000	***Realized* Gain**	**$200,000**

The next step in our analysis of gain/loss situations is to determine the extent to which any realized gain is recognized. Recognition of gain basically means that it is reported as income for income tax purposes. IRC § 1001(c) provides that unless otherwise provided for in the Code, all realized gains and losses are recognized. The law has, for a long time, given some relief (non-recognition) to homeowners with respect to the sale of one's principal residence. We find this in IRC § 121 and it is often referred to as an "exclusion of gain from sale of principal residence." More accurately, IRC § 121 is a non-recognition (of gain) provision. Effective for sales of a taxpayer's principal residence after May 6, 1997, IRC § 121 provides for the exclusion of up to $250,000 of gain ($500,000 in the case of certain married individuals), if certain conditions are met.

Again, it may be helpful to first present the landscape of this analysis. Immediately below is a slide that this professor uses in class to address the various components of IRC § 121. The application and analysis of these steps follows.

§121 NON-RECOGNITION

<u>Step 1</u>: Does non-recognition (exclusion) even apply?
   a) Ownership test <u>and</u>
   b) Use Test

   (if necessary, look to prorating provision §121(c))

<u>Step 2</u>: Okay, we qualify for non-recognition. Now to the new (in 2009) "overlay" for "qualified/non-qualified" use in §121(b)(5): <u>If required to do so</u>, split the <u>total realized gain</u> into two parts:

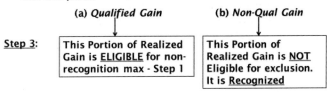

(a) *Qualified Gain*	(b) *Non-Qual Gain*
This Portion of Realized Gain is <u>ELIGIBLE</u> for non-recognition max - Step 1	**This Portion of Realized Gain is <u>NOT</u> Eligible for exclusion. It is <u>Recognized</u>**

Step 3:

From 1997 through 2008 (and in prior editions of this book), IRC § 121 was much simpler. Our analysis consisted of only "Step 1," above (there were no steps 2 and 3). For Jamie and Manuel in this question, we shall also have to cover the additional Steps 2 & 3 (for each, individually).

<u>**Step 1 of our IRC § 121 analysis**</u> consists of the two basic requirements for this exclusion, commonly referred to as the **"ownership"** and **"use"** tests. The taxpayer must have owned the condo for at least two years (looking back five years from the date of sale) **and** must have used it as his or her principal residence for two years (looking back five years from the date of sale). [IRC § 121(a).]

It might be helpful to visually indicate Jamie's and Manuel's years of ownership as well as their use in each year. For reasons explain later, we'll be consistent and use the same ten-year period (Jamie's ownership) for both of them.

Jamie:

V = Vacation or Vacant (not used as her principal residence)

H = Home; used as her principal residence

	'09	'10	'11	'12	'13	'14	'15	'16	'17	'18
	V	V	H	H	H	V	V	H	V	V

Beginning of 5 year window

The five-year look back period for the ownership and use tests consist of years **2014 through 2018** (the earlier years of ownership are irrelevant for this Step 1 but we will return to them when covering Steps 2 & 3)

Jamie **easily meets the *ownership test*** having owned it for at least two of the five years for the look-back window (she's owned it for all five years of this look-back period for Step 1 of our IRC § 121 analysis, and even longer which will be relevant for Steps 2 & 3 of our IRC § 121 analysis).

Unfortunately**, Jamie fails to meet the *use test*.** Recall that for this first Step, we are examining only the five-year lookback period and in doing so, we see that during this period (2014 through 2018), she used the condo as her principal residence in only **one** of these years (2016). Having failed to meet both tests, Jamie is not eligible for any exclusion (nonrecognition) pursuant to IRC § 121.

Before proceeding any further, let's look at Manuel's situation vis-à-vis the ownership and use tests.

Manuel:

V = Vacation or Vacant (not used as his principal residence)

H = Home; used as his principal residence

	'09	'10	'11	'12	'13	'14	'15	'16	'17	'18
			H	H	H	V	V	V	V	V

Beginning of 5 year window

The five-year look back period for the ownership and use tests consist of years **2014 through 2018** (the earlier years of ownership are irrelevant for this Step 1 but we will return to them when covering Steps 2 & 3)

The couple divorce on 1/1/16 and that is when Manuel received his one-half interest in the condo (pursuant to the divorce decree). In real terms,

Manuel has owned his one-half interest for three years ('16, '17 & '18). **Manuel, therefore, meets the *ownership test.*** While he meets the *ownership test* all by himself, there is a "special rule" at IRC § 121(d)(3)(A) that states: "In the case of an individual holding property transferred to such individual in a transaction described in section 1041(a), the period such individual owns such property shall include the period the transferor owned the property." Manuel *did* receive his one-half interest from Jamie incident to their divorce (a transaction to which IRC § 1041 applies). This special rule allows Manuel to "tack," or add, Jamie's period of ownership (prior to Manuel receiving his interest) onto his ownership period resulting in Manuel owning his one-half interest for the same ten-year period as Jamie.

The two-year "use" test, however, presents an insurmountable problem for Manuel. In real terms, he did not use the condo as his principal residence in any of the years in the five-year window. You may recall, from question 5, immediately above, that we used a special rule for tacking Jamie's post-divorce "use." This "special rule" at IRC § 121(d)(3)(B) states: "Solely for purposes of this section, an individual shall be treated as using the property as such individual's principal residence during any period of ownership which such individual's spouse or former spouse is granted use of the property under a divorce decree or separation instrument." This provision allows Manuel to "tack," or add Jamie's 2016 year of use. He cannot, however, tack on or count as "use" years the post-divorce that Jamie was granted use of the condo but did not actually use it for her principal residence. [See Reg. § 121-4(b)(2).] **Therefore, Manuel also fails to meet the *use test.*** Recall that for this first Step, we are examining only the five-year lookback period and in doing so, we see that during this period (2014 through 2018), even after using the special "tacking" rule, he is deemed to have used the condo as his principal residence (through Jamie's use) in only **one** of these years (2016). Having failed to meet both tests, Manuel is not eligible for any exclusion (nonrecognition) pursuant to IRC § 121.

We **stop** at this point and do not go on to Steps 2 & 3. Going through our analysis on a step-by-step basis is absolutely critical in this question (see the discussion, below, explaining how one can get caught up in this section and sometimes it is difficult to accept what ends up being a rather straightforward, and not a very involved or deep, result. Both Jamie's and Manuel's entire $200,000 (each) will be recognized (IRC § 121 does not provide them with any exclusion (nonrecognition) for his gain).

It should be noted that other questions in this book address situations where a taxpayer fails to meet the two-year use and ownership tests but, nonetheless, is entitled to a partial exclusion (nonrecognition) in certain situations. This is IRC § 121(c). As discussed in other questions, this partial exclusion is applicable only when the condo sale is "by reason of a change in place of employment, health, or, to the extent provided in regulations, unforeseen circumstances." [IRC § 121(c)(2)(B).] While the regulations indicate that "divorce" can be a precipitating unforeseen circumstance for a sale before each of the two-year tests are met, there are no facts in our question that indicate that their sale of the condo was a result of their divorce (i.e., their divorce does not appear to have prevented them from meeting the two-year "use" test). Rather, the facts indicate that they remained on good terms after their divorce and neither of them envisioned selling the condo. While worthy of some discussion (say on an essay exam), there is really no compelling argument here that they should be entitled to a partial exclusion of their gain pursuant to IRC § 121(c).

So that's it? Don't we move on to determine which of Jamie's and Manuel's years of ownership are *qualified* and *nonqualified*? The simple answer is **NO** but doing so is common and can be a recipe for disaster. Again, conquering IRC § 121 questions require a step-by-step discipline. We would move on to Steps 2 & 3 only if we first find that Jamie or Manuel is eligible for some exclusion (which they are not in this question). The following is a common example of a student essay answer using our facts and we will see how easy it is to get into trouble (and make this a much more difficult question than it is). Can you spot where this sample student answer goes off course?

> *For §121 purposes, both Jamie nor Manuel meet the "ownership" test (they have each owned their respective one-half interests in the condo for at least two years looking back five years from the sale). Neither of them, however, appear to meet the "use" test as Jamie used the condo for only one year, and not two, during the five-year lookback period from the date of sale. Similarly, even through the "tacking" provisions in the statute, Manuel would also have only one year of use. The facts do not indicate any reason that would be considered a "valid" reason for a prorated exclusion (§121(c)).*

> *Jamie's (and by statute, Manuel's) only year of "use" during the qualifying lookback period was in 2016 when Jamie lived there as a principal residence purposes. Other provisions in §121 provide that we can count, as qualifying years, any year(s) following the last year of actual use in the five-year lookback period. Since 2016 was in the five-year lookback period and Jamie (and Manuel via statute) used it that year as her principal residence, the Code lets her count, as qualifying years, the next two years (2017, & 2018). These are also considered qualifying years for Manuel via the statute. Therefore, looking at it in light of this rule, both Jamie and Manuel are now considered to meet the two-year "use" test and can, therefore, utilize the §121 exclusion. [This sample answer then goes on to explain the maximum exclusion amount and goes down the rabbit hole in a lengthy, drawn-out discussion of apportioning their respective $200,000 gain into qualifying and nonqualifying parts, etc.]*

Unfortunately, this professor has seen many similar answers over the years. Sadly, in addition to being incorrect, the extra time spent doing a "deep dive" is also costly as this is valuable time lost that could have been used on other questions (or parts of an essay). So where did this answer go awry? This sample answer had it correct to begin with that both Jamie and Manuel fail the "use" test and that should have been the end of the story (no exclusion via IRC § 121, nor an IRC §121(c) prorated exclusion with these facts). It should have ended there with a conclusion that Jamie and Manuel will each have to recognize their entire respective $200,000 gain.

Unfortunately, this sample student answer did not go through a step-by-step analysis and jumped to the issue of *qualified* years (and this professor's heart sinks because seeing the words *qualified years* triggers an "oh no, don't go there" response). Once we determine that both Jamie and Manuel are ineligible for an IRC § 121 exclusion by not meeting the "use" test, then we **stop**. Conflating the next step's determination of *qualified* years (about which we should not even inquire) and using the quirky rules to conclude that we have three *qualified* years within the five-year lookback period, this sample student answer essentially "bootstrapped" both Jamie and Manuel into meeting the "use" test (which they do not). With time constraints on exams, such an error is understandable. So too is a possible student disbelief that with all of the facts, there surely has to be more to the answer than Jamie and Manuel not meeting initial, Step 1 requirements.

Answers (a), (b), and (c) are incorrect because each, to some degree, incorrect concludes that either Jamie's or Manuel's (or both) respective gain from the sale of the condo is eligible for exclusion (or nonrecognition) pursuant to IRC § 121. As discussed above, they both fail the two-year "use" test that is the gateway Step 1 in a proper IRC § 121 analysis. **Answer (e) is incorrect** because a correct response in reflected in answer (d).

7. **The correct answer is (c).** Wow, talk about an incredibly difficult question (especially as an objective multiple choice question). Heck, even for an essay question, this would be an "I hate my professor" question. Nonetheless, it is a good question for helping understand the often-complex nature of IRC § 121's exclusion/nonrecognition of gain from the sale of a principal residence. This question 7 may be the most difficult question in this book on this subject. Interestingly, this question is very similar to one that was asked of this author (the names and dates were changed, but the underlying facts are very close to what happened to real-life former spouses selling a jointly owned condo).

    For this question, we will conclude that Jamie and Manuel each has a <u>realized</u> gain of $200,000 from the sale of their respective interests in the condo. We shall also conclude, in this question, that **Manuel is eligible for some exclusion (nonrecognition) pursuant to IRC § 121 of his gain**, but in a bizarre twist of law, **Jamie** is <u>**not**</u> eligible to exclude (not recognize) any portion of her gain. **After a very long analysis, Manuel** will be entitled to exclude (not recognize) $120.000 or his $200,000 gain via IRC § 121 (leaving $80,000 for each to recognize), and unfortunately, **Jamie** will have to recognize her entire $200,000 gain.

Be forewarned, this will be a very long and multi-step analysis and it is easy to get lost with so many steps and parties. However, this is about as difficult as it gets and while it may take multiple times going through all of this mess, as long as you proceed step-by-step, you can master any fact pattern. So, let's get started.

As mentioned in other questions, in every fact pattern in which something is sold (or otherwise disposed of), the author likes to go through the following analysis; always ask these three questions:

1) Do we have a Realized Gain (or Loss) & how much? This is computing the amount of gain (or loss). It is the AR (amount realized) less one's AB (adjusted basis). See other problems in this book addressing this issue.

2) If yes, is the realized gain (or loss) Recognized? This simply means, is it reported in one's income for tax purposes. This is the issue that we are currently addressing. As a taxpayer, you would like the answer to be NO for gains – I do not want to recognize, report, the gain (said another way, I'd like to be able to exclude this gain from my income).

3) If gain is recognized, is it given any special character or treatment? This is primarily the issue of "capital gains (or losses)" that are treated differently for income tax purposes. This is not the issue in this question (see other problems in this book).

As indicated above, the first question that we ask whenever there is a sale or disposition of an asset is whether there is a realized gain and if so, what is the amount? Therefore, our first step in our analysis process is determining whether Jamie and Manuel have *realized* gains or losses from the sale of their respective one-half interests in the condo. It is important to understand that at the time of the condo sale, we have two separate and unmarried individuals, Jamie and Manuel, each selling an undivided one-half interest in the condo. <u>Essentially, we have two separate sales to analyze.</u>

To determine the *realized* gain or loss from the sale of the interests in the condo, we need two basic components: the sales price ("amount realized" or, hereinafter, AR) and the basis in the property interest ("adjusted basis or, hereinafter, AB). The difference between the two represents <u>realized</u> gain or loss. [IRC § 1001(a).] Each of these two components, AR and AB, can present a variety of complex tax issues for exam and real-world tax purposes. The AR side for both Jamie and Manuel is straightforward in our question and is $250,000 for each of them (the combined selling price of the condo was $500,000.

The general starting place for determining one's AB in property is one's cost. [IRC §§ 1011 and 1012.] "Adjustments" to one's basis, while not at issue in this question, can result from many reasons including capital improvements (increasing basis), and depreciation expenses (reducing basis). [IRC § 1016.] Applying the general cost basis rule in our question, Jamie's AB is her "cost" for the <u>one-half interest</u> (one-half of her original $100,000 cost for the entire condo) or $50,000. The determination of Manuel's AB is a bit more involved but not too complex. There is no indication that Manuel paid anything for his one-half interest in the condo. Rather, he received his one-half ownership interest pursuant to his and Jamie's divorce decree. The AB of property transferred between spouses, or former spouses that are "incident to divorce," is controlled by IRC § 1041(b). In a nutshell, it provides that when spouses transfer property to each other, or when former spouses transfer property to each other and it is "incident to their divorce," the transferee spouse (or former spouse) takes a carryover basis. This section does not distinguish as to the type of inter vivos transfer involved; it covers gifts, sales, exchanges, etc. The term "incident to divorce" means any transfer within one year of the divorce or generally within six years of the divorce such transfer is called for by the divorce instrument (e.g., divorce decree). This is not a significant issue in our case and when Manuel receives the one-half interest in the condo, he takes as his AB the AB that Jamie had in that one-half interest. We have already determined that Jamie's AB in the property is her cost and, therefore, Manuel, like Jamie, has a $50,000 AB in his one-half interest in the condo. [Technically, when Jamie transferred the one-half interest to Manuel, we should also address any relevant gain. Suffice it to say, while Jamie realized some gain, it would not, pursuant to IRC § 1041(a) be recognized. So we can dispense with this and continue.]

The determination of *realized* gains or losses to Jamie and Manuel is now an easy task:

<u>Jamie</u>		<u>Manuel</u>
$250,000	Amount realized (AR)	$250,000
($ 50,000)	Adjusted basis (AB)	($ 50,000)
$200,000	***Realized* Gain**	**$200,000**

The next step in our analysis of gain/loss situations is to determine the extent to which any <u>realized</u> gain is <u>recognized</u>. Recognition of gain basically means that it is reported as income for income tax purposes. IRC § 1001(c) provides that unless otherwise provided for in the Code, all realized gains and losses are recognized. The law has, for a long time, given some relief (non-recognition) to homeowners with respect to the sale of one's principal residence. We find this in IRC § 121 and it is often referred to as an "exclusion of gain from sale of principal residence." More accurately, IRC § 121 is a non-recognition (of gain) provision. Effective for sales of a taxpayer's principal residence after May 6, 1997, IRC § 121 provides for the exclusion of up to $250,000 of gain ($500,000 in the case of certain married individuals), if certain conditions are met.

Again, it may be helpful to first present the landscape of this analysis. Immediately below is a slide that this professor uses in class to address the various components of IRC § 121. The application and analysis of these steps follows.

§121 NON-RECOGNITION

Step 1: Does non-recognition (exclusion) even apply?
      a) Ownership test <u>and</u>
      b) Use Test
         (if necessary, look to prorating provision §121(c))

Step 2: Okay, we qualify for non-recognition. Now to the new (in 2009) "overlay" for "qualified/non-qualified" use in §121(b)(5): <u>If required to do so</u>, split the <u>total realized gain</u> into two parts:

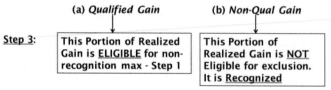

(a) *Qualified Gain*	(b) *Non-Qual Gain*
Step 3: **This Portion of Realized Gain is <u>ELIGIBLE</u> for non-recognition max - Step 1**	**This Portion of Realized Gain is <u>NOT</u> Eligible for exclusion. It is <u>Recognized</u>**

From 1997 through 2008 (and in prior editions of this book), IRC § 121 was much simpler. Our analysis consisted of only "Step 1," above (there were no steps 2 and 3). In this question 7, we shall see that for Manuel, but not Jamie, it will be necessary to cover the additional Steps 2 & 3.

<u>**Step 1 of our IRC § 121 analysis**</u> consists of the two basic requirements for this exclusion, commonly referred to as the "**ownership**" and "**use**" tests. The taxpayer must have owned the house for at least two years (looking back five years from the date of sale) **and** must have used it as his

or her principal residence for two years (looking back five years from the date of sale). [IRC § 121(a).]

It might be helpful to visually indicate Jamie's and Manuel's years of ownership as well as their use in each year. For reasons explain later, we'll be consistent and use the same ten-year period (Jamie's ownership) for both of them.

Quick visual depiction of Jamie's and Manuel's years at issue:

V = Vacation or Vacant (not used as her principal residence)

H = Home; used as her principal residence

Jamie; Step 1 Analysis:

The five-year look back period for the ownership and use tests consist of years **2014 through 2018** (the earlier years of ownership are irrelevant for this Step 1 but we will return to them when discussing Steps 2 & 3 that will be applicable to Manuel).

Jamie **easily meets the *ownership test*** having owned it for at least two of the five years for the look-back window (she's owned it for all five years of this look-back period for Step 1 of our IRC § 121 analysis, and even longer which will be relevant for Steps 2 & 3 of our IRC § 121 analysis).

Unfortunately, **Jamie fails to meet the *use test***. Recall that for this first Step, we are examining only the five-year lookback period and in doing so, we see that during this period (2014 through 2018), she did not use the condo as her principal residence in any of these years. Having failed to meet both tests, Jamie is not eligible for any exclusion (nonrecognition) pursuant to IRC § 121.

Before moving on to examine Manuel's situation, we should explore a "special rule" that we utilized in the preceding question 5 and 6 involving Manuel's ability to "tack" on and count as his "use" the years of a former spouse. This "special rule" at IRC § 121(d)(3)(B) states: "Solely for purposes of this section, an individual shall be treated as using the property as such individual's principal residence during any period of ownership which such individual's spouse or former spouse is granted use of the property under a divorce decree or separation instrument." Recall from the introductory facts, the couple's divorce decree gave **Jamie** (not Manuel) exclusive rights to possession of the condo. If Jamie had used the condo as her principal residence for 2016 through 2018), this special rule would have allowed Manuel to also count these years as if he were also using the condo (we saw this in questions 5 and 6 for Manuel). Casually, without careful reading of the statute, this rule is often incorrectly viewed as "actual use by a former spouse also counts as use by the other former spouse." If this was the law, then Jamie could count Manuel's use of the condo for these three years as "use" years for her in determining whether she meets the two-year "use" test. Unfortunately, that is **not** the law and this "special rule" will have no impact on Jamie (i.e., she will **not** be able to count as her use, those three years that Manuel used the condo). Jamie, the former spouse who was granted exclusive rights to use the condo can allow her former spouse, Manuel, to use the condo. However, for determining Jamie's use, she was the former spouse who was granted these rights pursuant to their decree and she cannot count as her "use" years the years Manuel live there. The statute's special rule is designed to work in the opposite direction; the former spouse who does not have such rights to use the property can count, as "use" years, those post-divorce years used by the spouse who has such rights. Jamie was kind to let Manuel live in the condo for those three years but the statute does not allow her to "tack" on those years for determining her use for meeting the two-year test. Confusing? Yes. Is it fair to Jamie that this special rule works only in one direction does not apply to her? No, but, unfortunately, that is the law.

As for Jamie, we **stop** at this point and do not go on to Steps 2 & 3 for her. Jamie fails the "use" test and she goes no further. She does not met the core requirements of IRC § 121 (our Step 1) and, <u>therefore, she is ineligible to exclude (not recognize) any portion of her $200,000 gain from the sale of her one-half of the condo. She must recognize (report as income) the entire amount of her gain.</u>

At this point, we have part of our answer; the tax ramifications to Jamie. The balance of this answer analysis will only be applicable to Manuel.

Manuel; Step 1 Analysis:

V = Vacation or Vacant (not used as his principal residence)

H = Home; used as his principal residence

Beginning of 5 year window

The five-year look back period for the ownership and use tests consist of years **2014 through 2018** (the earlier years of ownership are irrelevant for this Step 1, but we will return to them when covering Steps 2 & 3)

The couple divorce on 1/1/16 and that is when Manuel received his one-half interest in the condo (pursuant to the divorce decree). In real terms, Manuel has owned his one-half interest for three years ('16, '17 & '18). **Manuel, therefore, meets the *ownership test*.** While he meets the *ownership test* all by himself, there is a "special rule" at IRC § 121(d)(3)(A) that states: "In the case of an individual holding property transferred to such individual in a transaction described in section 1041(a), the period such individual owns such property shall include the period the transferor owned the property." Manuel *did* receive his one-half interest from Jamie incident to their divorce (a transaction to which IRC § 1041 applies). This special rule allows Manuel to "tack," or add, Jamie's period of ownership (prior to Manuel receiving his interest) onto his ownership period resulting in Manuel owning his one-half interest for the same ten-year period as Jamie.

Manuel also meets the *use test*. During our five-year look back window (2014 through 2018) Manuel used the condo as his principal residence for three years (2016, 2017 and 2018). There are no special "tacking" rules at work here as Manuel's three years of use are solely by reason of him using the condo as his principal residence. Had Jamie instead of Manuel been living there for those three years, we would discuss the aforementioned "special rule" allowing Manuel to count or tack on Jamie's use as his use (again, because Jamie was the former spouse who, pursuant to their divorce decree, was granted the exclusive right to use it). As indicated above, that rule does not work to help Jamie in our situation.

At this point we are done with Step 1 of our IRC § 121 analysis. In a somewhat bizarre combination of the facts and the law, we have a mixed result. **Jamie** is ineligible to utilize IRC § 121 to exclude (not recognize) any portion of her $200,000 gain (i.e., she must recognize all of it). **Manuel**, on the other hand, is eligible to use this section to exclude (not recognize) some or all of his $200,000 gain from the sale of his one-half interest in the condo.

Manuel is single (in the year the condo sold) and we know that his maximum exclusion/non-recognition amount from IRC § 121 is $250,000. In the earlier editions of this book (before Steps 2 & 3 were effective beginning in 2009) we would have been done with this problem, concluding that Manuel (but not Jamie) could exclude all his $200,000 gain since it is less than the $250,000 maximum amount. Unfortunately for Manuel, and us, we have more work to do.

This question takes us to the more complex parts of IRC § 121 (enacted in 2008 and effective beginning in 2009). These are Steps 2 & 3 of our IRC § 121 analysis (see the §121 slide, above and below) and these additional steps are necessary for situations where an individual has at any time during the entire period he or she owned the condo, used it for something other than their principal residence for the entire ownership period (e.g., used it as a vacation home, left vacant, rented it out, etc.). This is the case with Manuel in this question. Recall that we are done, tax-wise, with Jamie and since she did not meet the core (our Step 1) ownership and use tests, we do not proceed to Steps 2 & 3 for her.

Not to take up space and repeat material, it may be helpful to see the IRC § 121 slide, again, with all the steps:

§121 NON-RECOGNITION

Step 1: Does non-recognition (exclusion) even apply?
   a) Ownership test <u>and</u>
   b) Use Test
   (if necessary, look to prorating provision §121(c))

Step 2: Okay, we qualify for non-recognition. Now to the new (in 2009) "overlay" for "qualified/non-qualified" use in §121(b)(5): <u>If required to do so</u>, split the <u>total realized gain</u> into two parts:

	(a) *Qualified Gain*	**(b)** *Non-Qual Gain*
Step 3:	This Portion of Realized Gain is <u>ELIGIBLE</u> for non-recognition max - Step 1	This Portion of Realized Gain is <u>NOT</u> Eligible for exclusion. It is <u>Recognized</u>

It might be helpful to again depict and Manuel's years of ownership as well as their use in each year for the full ten-year period of ownership. Again, we are doing this analysis only for Manuel (Jamie failed the Step 1 tests and none of her gain is eligible for exclusion/nonrecognition under IRC § 121).

Manuel (including "tacked on" ownership; see above discussion):

V = Vacation or Vacant (not used as his principal residence)

H = Home; used as his principal residence

Marriage   *Divorce*   *The Sale*

'09	'10	'11	'12	'13	'14	'15	'16	'17	'18
V	V	H	H	H	V	V	H	H	H

Beginning of 5 year window

We have already determined that Manuel (but not Jamie) is eligible for IRC § 121 (Step 1). Note that in Step 2, we now (after the 2008 law change) must split up his gain into two parts: ***qualified portion of gain*** and ***nonqualified portion of gain***. In class, this professor uses the term "overlay;" as we are overlaying this new (as of 2008) law requiring us to bifurcate the gain. This was not a "taxpayer friendly" change to the law and it affects many individuals, including Manuel in our question. This is not a political statement but prior to this new law (enacted at the end of the George W. Bush Presidency and designed to raise revenue for the government), a gain from the sale of a personal residence was excluded (not recognized) up to the Code's $250,000 max ($500,000 for most married couples) as long as the "two year" tests were met. We generally did not care if sometime during a taxpayer's period of ownership, it was used for purposes other than their principal residence. In other words, all of their gain was generally eligible for exclusion up to the maximum amount allowed. Now, however, the gain realized must be divided up (apportioned) into ***qualified*** and ***nonqualified*** parts with <u>only the ***qualified*** portion of the gain being eligible for IRC § 121 exclusion. The ***nonqualified*** portion of the gain is not eligible for exclusion and must be recognized.</u>

Adding these steps means that we have more rules (often complex) and more math. As ominous as it sounds, proper application of these additional components of IRC § 121 is really not too bad. In class, this professor emphasis, over and over, how important it is to follow the Steps carefully and, in the order, presented. Do not be alarmed if this area feels difficult or even impossible. It is very common for most students to feel this way, at first, because there is so much information and rules that seem to be "all over the place." With every tax class, this professor continually encourages students, working with them using questions like these and class hypos, in class, in office hours, and sometimes by text, email and phone conversations; knowing, ultimately, that it will make sense. Every law student can make it over this hurdle with enough practice and patience.

Okay, on with our Step 2 for Manuel. To apportion his gain, we need to figure out the total number of years he owned the condo (total years and not just the five years ending with the sale like we did in Step 1). Per the facts, Jamie owned the condo for exactly 10 years. While this portion of our answer analysis concerns only Manuel, his ownership years include his actual post-divorce years and, via the previously discussed ownership tacking rules, the pre-divorce years that Jamie owned it. What portion of these total 10 years are *qualified* use years? There are some wacky rules that we have seen in other question, but for this question 7, it will be fairly straightforward. The general starting point is that a *qualified* use year is one in which the taxpayer used the property as their principal residence. [See IRC § 121(b)(5)] We'll show this visually in just a bit, but we will first analyze these years. We know from the facts for this question that Manuel actually lived in the condo as his principal residence for 2011, 2012, 2013, 2016, 2017 & 2018. So far, that translates to 6 *qualified* years. It should be noted that it is irrelevant that Manuel's first three years were ones where he and Jamie were not yet married. Use is use. *Nonqualified* use years are, logically and generally, those years that the taxpayer did not use the property as their principal residence. Normally we would warn about rushing to conclusions about *qualified years,* but with our facts, we do not have a situation that would implicate other rules that might result in additional *qualified* years (e.g., pre-2009 years being qualified because of the effective date of this part of the statute, and other somewhat wacky rules that are discussed in other questions in this book).

Visually, let's see what we have as far as *qualified* and *nonqualified* years. Remember, this analysis is only for Manuel (Jamie, unfortunately, did not make it out of our Step 1 and none of her gain is eligible for IRC § 121 nonrecognition treatment).

V = Vacation or Vacant (not used as his principal residence)

H = Home; used as his principal residence

Q = Qualified Year

NQ = Nonqualified Year   *The Sale*

'09	'10	'11	'12	'13	'14	'15	'16	'17	'18
V	V	H	H	H	V	V	H	H	H
NQ	NQ	Q	Q	Q	NQ	NQ	Q	Q	Q

We can see six *qualified* years for Manuel's actual use as a principal residence in 2011, 2012, 2013, 2016, 2017 and 2018. And for this question, we have identified all of the *qualified* years (see other questions in this book where various statutory special rules can produce additional *qualified* years).

To summarize Step 2, we ended up with Manuel having **6 *qualified* years** (and 4 *nonqualified* years).

Okay, now what? We split-up Manuel's $200,000 realized gain from the sale of the condo into *qualified* and *nonqualified* parts. If you prefer, we are apportioning his total gain between *qualified* and *nonqualified* components. This is Step 2 of our IRC § 121 analysis (from the slide) and we have some math! Recall that this calculation is only for Manuel's $200,000 realized gain.

***Qualified* Portion of Gain**	***Nonqualified* Portion of Gain**
$\dfrac{\text{[Total "Q" years]}}{\text{[Total years Owned]}} = \dfrac{6}{10}$	$\dfrac{\text{[Total "NQ" years]}}{\text{[Total years Owned]}} = \dfrac{4}{10}$
$\dfrac{6}{10} \times \$200{,}000 = \mathbf{\$120{,}000}$	$\dfrac{4}{10} \times \$200{,}000 = \mathbf{\$80{,}000}$

Almost done! Manuel's ***qualified*** portion his total $200,000 gain is equal to **$120,000**. This *qualified* portion is eligible for IRC § 121 exclusion (nonrecognition) up to a maximum of $250,000 (Manuel is single, and we determined this amount in Step 1 of our analysis). <u>Because $120,000 is less than the $250,000 max, Manuel can exclude (not recognize) all of his $120,000 *qualified* gain.</u> His $80,000 *nonqualified* portion of total gain is <u>not</u> eligible for IRC § 121 exclusion (nonrecognition) so, Manuel <u>must recognize (report in their respective incomes) the entire $80,000 *nonqualified* portion of the gain.</u>

Note that we are not, as is a common misunderstanding, apportioning the IRC § 121 $250,000 (or $500,000) maximum exclusion amount. Rather, we are <u>apportioning the taxpayer's gain</u> (to which we will then apply the statutory exclusion amount).

Note how this new (as of 2008) "overlay" provision of IRC § 121 hurts Manuel tax-wise. Under prior longstanding tax law, he would have been able to exclude the entire amount of his $200,000 realized gain. Now, however, he is not able to avail himself of the full IRC § 121 exclusion. Only his *qualified* $120,000 portion of his $200,000 gain is excluded (and his gain recognized jumps to $80,000).

Note that this new (as of 2008) Q/NQ "overlay" does not negatively impact taxpayers who use their home as their principal residence for the entire period of ownership (i.e., there are no "NQ" years).

Phew! That was a very lengthy analysis but again, analyzing the law in a step-by-step manner will get you through it. This area of the law provides students a great opportunity to create their own hypothetical fact patterns and test themselves on applying the law. Again, at first blush, this area of law may seem daunting. When ultimately tamed and understood, however, every question becomes answerable (step-by-step analysis is the key).

Answer (a) is incorrect. Jamie cannot exclude any portion of her realized gain pursuant to IRC § 121 and Manuel is eligible to use the section to exclude a portion of his gain. **Answer (b) is also incorrect** because again, Jamie is not eligible for any exclusion and while Manuel is eligible to utilize IRC § 121, it will not serve to exclude his entire $200,000 gain. **Answer (d) is incorrect.** This answer is correct regarding Manuel, but not for Jamie (she is not eligible for any exclusion). **Answer (e) is also incorrect.** While Jamie is ineligible for any IRC § 121 exclusion, Manuel, as discussed above, is entitled to exclude a portion of his $200,000 gain.

8. **Answer (a) is correct.** This question involves determining who qualifies and someone's "dependent" for a variety of tax purposes. First and foremost, students should be aware that this question is date or year sensitive. As indicated in the preface of this book, many tax related provisions change for each tax year. Sometimes it is necessary to ask questions for a specific year as opposed to in the abstract. This is one such situation and it involves <u>who qualifies as someone's dependent.</u> **We will conclude that Daniel is Mom's dependent.**

It should be noted that tax law relating to someone qualifying as a dependent and the relevance of why this is important has changed dramatically since the earlier editions of this book. It still has some significance, hence this question, but historically deductions for personal exemptions (including those for dependents) was a huge deal. The *Tax Cuts and Jobs Act* (TCJA) that was signed into law in December 2017 (generally effective beginning in 2018) eliminated deductions for personal exemptions for 2018 through 2025. While no longer a deduction, it may help to go through some explanation of what used to be the pre-TCJA law (in 2017 and earlier) and help give more meaning to the relevance of claiming another individual as one's dependent. Here is a brief explanation of prior law and then we will circle back to analyze the answer for this question 8.

> *Pre-TCJA Law; what was a personal exemption deduction and how many of them could a taxpayer deduct:* Every living person has, in his or her figurative pocket, a "coupon" good for a personal exemption deduction for each tax year. There is no real "coupon" involved, but it helps to think of the personal exemption deduction as such. The amount of this exemption deduction is listed in IRC § 151 of the Code as $2,000. However, this amount has been adjusted (increased) each year since 1990 to reflect the general level of inflation. The personal exemption deduction amount

in 2017, the last year for which a deduction was allowed, was $4,050 (it would have been $4,150 for 2018 and slightly more for 2019). The key to this problem in its prior, pre-TCJA form was determining who gets to use these personal exemption deduction "coupons" ($4,050 for 2017). Did each person get to use his or her own "coupon" and get a $4,050 deduction (for 2017), or does somebody else get to claim that person's "coupon" and take the deduction? This latter question gives rise to the issue of who qualifies as one's dependent. [This is still a relevant question after the TCJA but for tax reasons other than obtaining a now nonexistent personal exemption deduction].

Students knowing little about income tax, probably knew something about this issue. A parent claiming his or her children as dependents and getting an extra deduction for them is precisely the issue that was in the forefront of this question in prior editions of this book. Had this problem been placed in 2017 or earlier, Mom would have been entitled to a personal exemption deduction for herself. The issue, pre TCJA (before 2018) was whether Mom gets to take Daniel's "coupon" and thus get an additional personal exemption deductions (on her income tax return for purposes of computing her taxable income). Alternatively, does Daniel get to use his own "coupon" for a personal exemption deduction (on his income tax returns for purposes of computing his taxable income)? To determine if Mom was entitled to get Daniel's personal exemption "coupon" (claim him as dependents and get to deduct his $4,050 (for 2017) personal exemption deductions) we would have been determining if he (Daniel) qualified as Mom's dependent.

The author hopes that this introduction of "old law" helps with what we are about to discuss with respect to our current question 8. While Mom, in our question, no longer has any personal exemption deductions for herself or any "dependents," the determination of who qualifies as a dependent is still very relevant for other tax matters (albeit not generally for items as valuable as the pre-TCJA personal exemption deduction). We shall see that in the questions that follow, determining Daniel's dependency status will, nonetheless, be very important. Because the TCJA eliminated the personal exemption deduction, which was a significant tax topic and valuable deduction, many basic income tax courses no longer cover, in great detail, this accompanying topic of who qualifies as one's dependent. With that in mind, let's begin our journey (and be forewarned that it is not a particularly fun journey) into the world of "dependents."

For Daniel to be Mom's dependent, we begin by determining whether he is either Mom's *"qualifying child"* or *"qualifying relative"* pursuant to IRC § 152 (it is this section that defines, through some rather complex rules, who qualifies as one's dependent). The dependent qualification process became a bit more complex with the enactment of the *"Working Families Tax Relief Act of 2004"* where the desire to have uniform definitions of certain relatives for federal tax statutes created a rather messy result for the dependency rules. What follows below may look a bit daunting, but it is not that bad once you go through each part, step by step (as applicable).

Requirements for <u>all</u> possible "dependents." As indicated, a "dependent" is someone who is either a "*qualifying child*" or "*qualifying relative*" of the taxpayer. There are a bunch of requirements for each alternative (see below), but before we get to those, there are some basic requirements that must be met in order for either type of qualifying individual to be considered your "dependent." First, and logically, if you yourself (or your spouse if he or she is filing a joint return with you) can be claimed as a dependent by someone else, then you will not be entitled to claim anyone as your dependent. Next, for both a "*qualifying child*" and a "*qualifying relative*" **all** the following requirements must be met:

> ➢ If the potential "dependent" is married, he or she must not file a joint return with his or her spouse for the tax year (there are some exceptions to this).
> ➢ The potential "dependent" must be a U.S. citizen, U.S. resident, U.S. national, or a resident of Canada or Mexico for some part of the tax year. [Note that non-citizen residents of Canada or Mexico may not qualify for certain dependent credits notwithstanding that they can qualify as dependents.]

If all of the above requirements are satisfied, we then move on to see if the potential individual is **either** a "*qualifying child*" or "*qualifying relative*.*" If the individual meets all the requirements of <u>either</u>, then this person is a "dependent" for various tax purposes (in the pre-TCJA world, this also meant that the taxpayer could take as a deduction, that person's personal exemption "coupon"). Be forewarned; put aside any preconceived, non-tax, notions of who you think is considered a "child" or "relative."

Qualifying Child: An individual is considered a "*qualifying child*" of you, the taxpayer, if all of the following requirements are met:

> ➢ The individual is your son, daughter, stepchild, eligible foster child, brother, sister, half-brother, half-sister, stepbrother, stepsister, or a descendant of any of them (hmmmm, seems a bit odd that a sister, a nephew, and a whole lot more people are your "children").
> ➢ The "child" (see above) must be:
>> ▪ Under age 19 at the end of the year, **or**
>> ▪ Under age 24 at the end of the year and is a full-time student for some part of each of five months during the year, **or**

- Any age if permanently or totally disabled.

➢ The "child" must have, with some exceptions, lived with you for more than half of the year.

➢ The "child" must not have provided more than one-half of his or her own support for the year.

Qualifying Relative: An individual is considered a *"qualifying relative"* of you, the taxpayer, if all of the following requirements are met:

➢ The individual must be either *"related"* to you <u>or</u>, if not "related" in the Code sense, live with you (with some exceptions) for the entire year. [See IRC §§ 152(d)(2)(A)-(d)(2)(G) for definitions of "relatives" which includes everyone from children, siblings, ancestors, aunts/uncles, etc. to a host of "in-laws," and IRC § 152(d)((2)(H) for other qualifying individuals.]

➢ The individual must have "gross income" less than the "exemption amount" for that year (for 2018, the year of our question, this amount is $4,150).

➢ The taxpayer (you – the person trying to claim the individual as a dependent) must have provided more than one-half of this person's total support for the year.

Note that there are differences and areas of overlap in the definitions of a *qualifying child* and *qualifying relative*. For example, the taxpayer's "child" may fail the requirements of a *"qualifying child"* because of their age but be considered a dependent nonetheless because such child meets the requirements of a *"qualifying relative."* Also note that because of the expansive definition of a "child" under the *qualifying child* rules, the situation could arise where an individual is a *qualifying child* of more than one taxpayer (e.g., a grandchild could be a *qualifying child* of a grandparent while, at the same time, be a *qualifying child* to the child's parent). In such cases, the *qualifying child* can be claimed as a "dependent" by only one taxpayer and generally, they can agree as to which one will be entitled to claim the dependent (with "tie-breaking" rules if they cannot so agree). Also not applicable to this question, and beyond the scope of this book, there are special rules for divorced/separated parents, multiple support arrangements, kidnapped children, and other situations.

If an individual is either a *qualifying child* or *qualifying relative* (and all of the other requirements for both are met), then that individual is your "dependent."

Finally, after all of that, we can now get back to our question. There are no problems with respect to Daniel meeting the first set of requirements applicable to both a *qualifying child* and *qualifying relative*. Daniel is both a U.S. citizen, he is not married, and, there are no facts to indicate that Mom is a "dependent" of someone else.

Next, we look to see if Daniel is either a *qualifying child* or *qualifying relative*. Is **Daniel** a *qualifying child?* He is 1) a child, and 2) is <u>not under</u> age 19 (he is 22) at the end of 2019, but he is under age 24 and a full-time student, and 3) he lived with Mom for more than one-half of 2019, and 4) he did not provide more than one-half of his own support (Mom did). **Daniel**, therefore, is a *qualifying child* and, thus, is Mom's "dependent." Students are often thrown by the fact that Daniel is making $13,000 which is not less than the "exemption amount" ($4,150 in 2018 and while not available at the time of this writing, probably slightly higher, perhaps $4,200 for 2019). However, this income limitation is part of the definition of a *qualifying relative* and not that of a *qualifying child*. So if all of the requirements of a *qualifying child* are met, that individual's amount of gross income for the year is irrelevant. Of course, at some point, the amount of the "dependent's" income may create problems with the "one-half" support requirement.

Because Daniel is a *qualifying child*, he is Mom's "dependent." We do not need to address the issue of whether or not Daniel is a *qualifying relative* because to be a dependent, one need only be either a *qualifying child* or a *qualifying relative.*

In conclusion, Daniel is Mom's dependent (and while not the subject of this question, she may be entitled to claim a "child tax credit" or a "credit for other dependents" with respect to Daniel). This will also be of importance to Daniel in the questions that follow.

As indicated, this question is date sensitive, applicable to the 2019 tax year but can easily be modified to accommodate subsequent years (the change would be the limit of the amount of income earned by the potential dependent; i.e., the $4,150 for 2018 is adjusted for inflation and may increase; we assumed it to be, perhaps, $4,200 in 2019).

Answer (b) is incorrect because, as discussed above, Daniel's gross income can exceed the statutory amount if the other requirements of a *qualifying child* are met, which they are (his income can exceed the statutory amount as long as he is either under 19 or a full-time student less than 24 years of age). **Answer (c) is incorrect** because providing more than one-half of the support of one's child are not the only requirements of determining dependency. **Answer (d) is not correct.** While it is true that Daniel's level of gross income would disqualify him from being a Mom's *qualifying relative*, he is not too old to be considered Mom's *qualifying child*. With respect to the latter, while he is not under the age of 19, he is a full-time student under the age of 24.

9. **Answer (c) is correct.** Many years ago, the concept of the "standard deduction" was introduced into tax law as a means of reducing an individual's record-keeping needs. The *standard deduction* may be taken in place of a group of deductions known collectively as "itemized deductions." Probably the most commonly known components of this latter group of *itemized deductions* include charitable contributions, deductible interest and taxes and qualifying medical deductions. Taxpayers have a choice: deduct either 1) the total of itemized deductions (after applying all necessary limits and restrictions as discussed elsewhere in this book), **or** 2) the *standard deduction* amount. In calculating "taxable income," a taxpayer takes as a deduction the <u>greater</u> of these two. [Please see Appendix A for more information about *where* these deductions fit within the framework of calculating taxable income.]

IRC § 63(c) is the focal point for the *standard deduction*. The amount of this *standard deduction* can vary greatly from taxpayer to taxpayer depending on various factors including marital or filing status, age, degree of visual imparity, and whether the taxpayer is a "dependent" of another. In addition, *standard deduction* amounts are subject to change each tax year (and for the most part, do change each year) based on adjustments for "inflation" (i.e., the standard deduction amounts are *indexed* for inflation). The various *standard deduction* amounts listed in the statute (throughout IRC § 63) are <u>not</u> the actual amounts for the current year but, rather, are pre-inflation adjusted "base" amounts (that are well below the actual current amounts). [Appendix B contains the various *standard deduction* amounts for the year 2019 (the most current at the time of this printing).]

A highly touted component of the *Tax Cuts and Jobs Act* (TCJA) signed into law in December 2017 (generally effective beginning in 2018), was a substantial increase in the *standard deduction* amounts (beginning in 2018). For 2019, the "regular" *standard deduction* for a single individual is $12,200 (corresponding to the special TCJA 2018-2025 statutory amount of $12,000 which is unadjusted for inflation). For couples filing a joint return, the 2019 standard deduction is $24,400 (corresponding to the computed 200% of the single special TCJA 2018-2025 statutory amount of $12,000 which is unadjusted for inflation). There are other standard deductions for other filing status' not applicable for this question).

It sounds simple for Daniel; he's single so his standard deduction for 2019 is $12,200, right? For 2019, that is the "regular" *standard deduction* amount for a single individual (it is the TCJA's base adjusted for inflation). Unfortunately for Daniel, he will not be entitled to this amount because of a special limitation provision in IRC § 63(c)(5). As indicated in our facts, and as discussed in problem 8, above, Daniel is Mom's dependent. This dependency status implicates IRC § 63(c)(5) which may limit the standard deduction for an individual in Daniel's situation; someone who can be claimed as a dependent by another. [Note the language in this subsection is a bit confusing at it references an IRC § 151 personal exemption deduction. Read that as "one who qualifies as a dependent." The section for a personal exemption deduction, IRC § 151, still exists post TCJA, but the actual exemption deduction allowed is zero for 2018-2025.] For **2019**, the limit imposed by this provision for Daniel's *standard deduction* is:

> **The greater of:**
> 1) $1,100, or
> 2) Daniel's "earned" income + $350.

> Please note that the $1,100 and $350 amounts above are for 2019, and correspond to the statutory amounts of $500 and $250, respectively (that are unadjusted for inflation).

"Earned income" for this special limitation, basically means wages, salaries and other compensation-like income. It does not include more passive income such as interest and dividends. In *this* question, Daniel has no *earned income,* so applying this special provision to Daniel, his *standard deduction* is <u>$1,100</u>.

Note, that the above special limitation calculation <u>cannot</u> yield a *standard deduction* that is greater than that which would otherwise apply to the individual (without applying this special provision). [IRC § 63(c)(5).] This is not the case for Daniel in this question.

Answer (a) is incorrect because while $12,200 represents the basic 2019 *standard deduction* for single individuals, it does not apply to Daniel. Rather, as discussed above, the special limitation provision of IRC § 63(c)(5) is applicable to him. **Answer (b) is incorrect.** $3,000 represents the basic *standard deduction* for single individuals as listed in the statute. This statutory amount is unadjusted for the changes made by the TCJA and is also not adjust for inflation. However, as indicated above, Daniel is not entitled to this amount because of IRC § 63(c)(5). **Answer (d) is incorrect** because at a minimum, Daniel is entitled to some amount of *standard deduction* ($1,100 in his case). **Answer (e) is incorrect** because the correct answer (c) is presented.

10. **The correct answer is (e).** This is another one of those awful "none of the above" answers, but for this question, we will conclude that Daniel's

"standard deduction" for 2019 is $2,350 (and this is not presented as an answer choice).

Many years ago, the concept of the "standard deduction" was introduced into tax law as a means of reducing an individual's record-keeping needs. The *standard deduction* may be taken in place of a group of deductions known collectively as "itemized deductions." Probably the most commonly known components of this latter group of *itemized deductions* include charitable contributions, deductible interest and taxes, and qualifying medical deductions. Taxpayers have a choice: deduct either 1) the total of itemized deductions (after applying all necessary limits and restrictions as discussed elsewhere in this book), **or** 2) the *standard deduction* amount. In calculating "taxable income," a taxpayer takes as a deduction the <u>greater</u> of these two. [Please see Appendix A for more information about *where* these deductions fit within the framework of calculating taxable income.]

IRC § 63(c) is the focal point for the *standard deduction*. The amount of this *standard deduction* can vary greatly from taxpayer to taxpayer depending on various factors including marital or filing status, age, degree of visual imparity, and whether the taxpayer is a "dependent" of another. In addition, *standard deduction* amounts are subject to change each tax year (and for the most part, do change each year) based on adjustments for "inflation" (i.e., the standard deduction amounts are *indexed* for inflation). The various *standard deduction* amounts listed in the statute (throughout IRC § 63) are <u>not</u> the actual amounts for the current year but, rather, are pre-inflation adjusted "base" amounts (that are well below the actual current amounts). [Appendix B contains the various *standard deduction* amounts for the year 2019 (the most current at the time of this printing).]

A highly touted component of the *Tax Cuts and Jobs Act* (TCJA) signed into law in December 2017 (generally effective beginning in 2018), was a substantial increase in the *standard deduction* amounts (beginning in 2018). For 2019, the "regular" *standard deduction* for a single individual is $12,200 (corresponding to the special TCJA 2018-2025 statutory amount of $12,000 which is unadjusted for inflation). For couples filing a joint return, the 2019 standard deduction is $24,400 (corresponding to the computed 200% of the single special TCJA 2018-2025 statutory amount of $12,000 which is unadjusted for inflation). There are other standard deductions for other filing status'.)

It sounds simple for Daniel; he's single so his standard deduction for 2019 is $12,200, right? For 2019, that is the "regular" *standard deduction* amount for a single individual (it is the TCJA's base adjusted for inflation). Unfortunately for Daniel, he will not be entitled to this amount because of a special limitation provision in IRC § 63(c)(5). As indicated in our facts, and as discussed in problem 8, above, Daniel is Mom's dependent. This dependency status implicates IRC § 63(c)(5) which may limit the standard deduction for an individual in Daniel's situation; someone who can be claimed as a dependent by another. [Note the language in this subsection is a bit confusing at it references an IRC § 151 personal exemption deduction. Read that as "one who qualifies as a dependent." The section for a personal exemption deduction, IRC § 151, still exists post TCJA, but the actual exemption deduction allowed is zero for 2018-2025.] For **2019**, the limit imposed by this provision for Daniel's *standard deduction* is:

>**The greater of:**
>   1) $1,100, or
>   2) Daniel's "earned" income + $350.

>Please note that the $1,100 and $350 amounts above are for 2019 and correspond to the statutory amounts of $500 and $250, respectively (that are unadjusted for inflation).

"Earned income" for this special limitation, basically means wages, salaries and other compensation-like income. It does not include more passive income such as interest and dividends. In *this* question, Daniel has *earned income* of $2,000. Applying the above special provision, Daniel's *standard deduction*, for 2019, is the greater of $1,100, or $2,350 ($2,000 + $350). Daniel's *standard deduction*, in *this* question is, therefore $2,350.

Note, that the above special limitation calculation <u>cannot</u> yield a *standard deduction* that is greater than that which would otherwise apply to the individual (without such applying this special provision). [IRC § 63(c)(5).] This is not the case for Daniel in this question.

Answer (a) is incorrect because Daniel, as discussed above, is entitled to some amount of *standard deduction*. **Answer (b) is incorrect** because Daniel had a sufficient amount of "earned income" that, when applying the special limitation provision, yields an amount greater than $1,100. **Answer (c) is incorrect** because it fails to add the $350 to his "earned income" of $2,000 in arriving at the correct *standard deduction* amount. **Answer (d) is incorrect** because in Daniel's situation, he is not entitled to the full *standard deduction* of $12,200 (for 2019) for single individuals.

11. **The correct answer is (c).** For this question, we will conclude that Daniel is entitled to the full "standard deduction" amount for single individuals: $12,200 for 2019.

Many years ago, the concept of the "standard deduction" was introduced into tax law as a means of reducing an individual's record-keeping needs. The *standard deduction* may be taken in place of a group of deductions known collectively as "itemized deductions." Probably the most commonly known components of this latter group of *itemized deductions* include charitable contributions, deductible interest and taxes and qualifying medical deductions. Taxpayers have a choice: deduct either 1) the total of itemized deductions (after applying all necessary limits and restrictions as discussed elsewhere in this book), **or** 2) the *standard deduction* amount. In calculating "taxable income," a taxpayer takes as a deduction the <u>greater</u> of these two. [Please see Appendix A for more information about *where* these deductions fit within the framework of calculating taxable income.]

IRC § 63(c) is the focal point for the *standard deduction*. The amount of this *standard deduction* can vary greatly from taxpayer to taxpayer depending on various factors including marital or filing status, age, degree of visual imparity, and whether the taxpayer is a "dependent" of another. In addition, *standard deduction* amounts are subject to change each tax year (and for the most part, do change each year) based on adjustments for "inflation" (i.e., the standard deduction amounts are *indexed* for inflation). The various *standard deduction* amounts listed in the statute (throughout IRC § 63) are <u>not</u> the actual amounts for the current year but, rather, are pre-inflation adjusted "base" amounts (that are well below the actual current amounts). [Appendix B contains the various *standard deduction* amounts for the year 2019 (the most current at the time of this printing).]

A highly touted component of the *Tax Cuts and Jobs Act* (TCJA) signed into law in December 2017 (generally effective beginning in 2018), was a substantial increase in the *standard deduction* amounts (beginning in 2018). For 2019, the "regular" *standard deduction* for a single individual is $12,200 (corresponding to the special TCJA 2018-2025 statutory amount of $12,000 which is unadjusted for inflation). For couples filing a joint return, the 2019 standard deduction is $24,400 (corresponding to the computed 200% of the single special TCJA 2018-2025 statutory amount of $12,000 which is unadjusted for inflation). There are other standard deductions for other filing status' not applicable for this question).

It sounds simple for Daniel; he's single so his standard deduction for 2019 is $12,200, right? For 2019, that is the "regular" *standard deduction* amount for a single individual (it is the TCJA's base adjusted for inflation). Maybe, but he may not be entitled to this amount because of a special limitation provision in IRC § 63(c)(5). As indicated in our facts, and as discussed in problem 8, above, Daniel is Mom's dependent. This dependency status implicates IRC § 63(c)(5) which may limit the standard deduction for an individual in Daniel's situation; someone who can be claimed as a dependent by another. [Note the language in this subsection is a bit confusing at it references an IRC § 151 personal exemption deduction. Read that as "one who qualifies as a dependent." The section for a personal exemption deduction, IRC § 151, still exists post TCJA, but the actual exemption deduction allowed is zero for 2018-2025.] For **2019**, the limit imposed by this provision for Daniel's *standard deduction* is:

> **The greater of:**
> 1) $1,100, or
> 2) Daniel's "earned" income + $350.

> Please note that the $1,100 and $350 amounts above are for 2019 and correspond to the statutory amounts of $500 and $250, respectively (that are unadjusted for inflation).

"Earned income" for this special limitation, basically means wages, salaries, and other compensation-like income. It does not include more passive income such as interest and dividends. In *this* question, Daniel has *earned income* of $13,000. Applying the above special provision, Daniel's *standard deduction* is the greater of $1,100, or $13,350 ($9,000 + $300). It would <u>appear</u>, therefore, that Daniel's *standard deduction*, in *this* question is $13,350. This special limitation calculation <u>cannot</u> yield a *standard deduction* that is greater than that which would otherwise apply to the individual (without applying this special provision). [IRC § 63(c)(5).] The regular *standard deduction* for a single individual (for 2019) is <u>$12,200</u> and this, therefore, is the proper amount that can be claimed by Daniel.

Answer (a) is incorrect because it fails to recognize that the standard deduction computed under the special "limitation" provision cannot exceed the regular *standard deduction* for such individual (without application of the special limitation provision). **Answer (b) is also incorrect.** This answer fails to add the $350 to Daniel's earned income for purposes of the special limitation provision in IRC § 63(c)(5). In any event, the amount still cannot exceed what would be his regular *standard deduction* of $12,200 (for 2019). **Answer (d) is incorrect** because it is the wrong number (it represents the unadjusted for inflation regular, post TCJA, *standard deduction* amount). **Answer (e) is incorrect** because the correct answer (c) is presented.

12. **The correct answer is (c).** This question is designed to illustrate how the various components of income and deductions fit together to compute taxable income. This computation requires information about Daniel's income and deductions. A visual computational framework for taxable income is as follows:

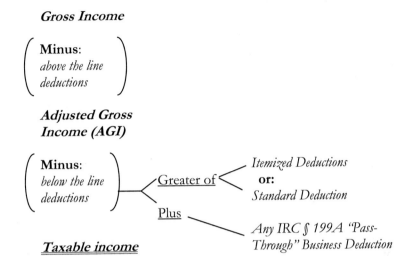

It should be noted that the calculation of *taxable income* has changed since the prior editions of this book. *The Tax Cuts and Jobs Act* (TCJA) signed into law in December 2017 (generally effective beginning in 2018) removed one "category" of deductions (personal exemption(s)) and added, for some business-related activities, another category of deductions (the so-called "pass-through" deduction). In class, this professor also explains the computation of *taxable income* in a **six-step** approach as follows:

Step 1:   Determine what is included in the taxpayer's *Gross Income*
(This reflects all income and exclusions therefrom.)

Step 2:   Determine the taxpayer's *Adjusted Gross Income (AGI)*
(This requires subtracting from *Gross income* any deductions that are allowed *above the line* pursuant to IRC § 62; Appendix A for more information.)

Step 3:   Determine the total amount of the taxpayer's *Itemized Deductions*
(This requires applying any applicable limitations, floors, or restrictions for certain types of these deductions; see Appendix A for more information.)

Step 4:   Determine the amount of the taxpayer's *Standard Deduction*
(This is year-specific and varies by filing status, age, degree of visual impairment, and limitations for certain dependents.)

Step 5:   Determine the amount of any available TCJA *IRC § 199A Pass-Through business-related deduction*.

(In prior editions of this book, and pre-TCJA law, this step used to be determining the amount of the taxpayer's *Personal Exemption Deduction(s)*. Under the TCJA, these deductions have been eliminated for 2018-2025)

Step 6: Compute *Taxable Income* by subtracting from AGI (amount in Step 2):

     1) Either *itemized deductions* (amount in **Step 3**), or the *standard deduction* (amount in **Step 4**), whichever is the **greater** of the two, **and**

     2) Any IRC § 199A *Pass-Through business-related deduction* (amount in **Step 5**).

Daniel's gross income for 2019 consists solely of the $13,000 in interest that he receives (facts from question 9, above). The general facts of this series of questions indicate that Daniel has no *above the line* deductions for 2019. In addition, the general facts indicate that he has no qualifying "itemized deductions" for 2019. From question 10, above, we saw that Daniel's *standard deduction* for 2019 was limited to only $1,100. Finally, Daniel will not have any IRC § 199A *Pass-Through business-related deduction*. [Other questions in this book address this deduction which may be available to some self-employed type businesses; this has no application to Daniel.]

Applying this **six-step** computation approach to Daniel, we have the following:

     Step 1: *Gross income* = $13,000
     Step 2: *Adjusted gross income (AGI)* = $13,000
     Step 3: *Itemized deductions* = $0
     Step 4: *Standard deduction* = $1,100
     Step 5: IRC § 199A *Pass-Through business-related deduction* = $0
     Step 6: *Taxable income* = $13,000
                     ($ 1,100) [the greater of $0 or $1,100]
                     ($ 0)
                     $11,900

A visual depiction of Daniel's *taxable income* computation for 2019 is as follows:

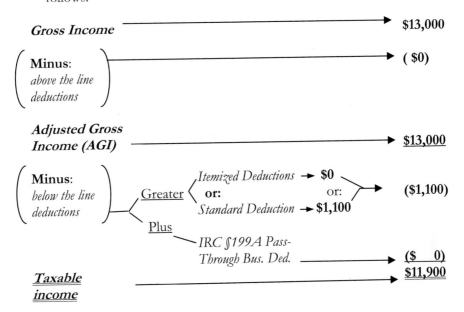

Gross Income ⟶ **$13,000**

Minus:
above the line deductions ⟶ ($0)

Adjusted Gross Income (AGI) ⟶ **$13,000**

Minus:
below the line deductions

Greater ⟨ *Itemized Deductions* ⟶ **$0**
 or: or: ⟶ **($1,100)**
Standard Deduction ⟶ **$1,100**

Plus

IRC §199A Pass-Through Bus. Ded. ⟶ **($ 0)**

Taxable income ⟶ **$11,900**

Answer (a) is incorrect because Daniel does, as indicated above, have taxable income. **Answer (b) is incorrect** because this answer reflects a regular $12,200 *standard deduction* that is not available to Daniel is this question. **Answer (d) is incorrect** because it does not reflect the $1,100 *standard deduction* to which Daniel is entitled.

13. **The correct answer is (b).** In this question, the facts indicate that Daniel provides all of his own support for 2019. Because of this change, Daniel is no longer Mom's *dependent*, as he had been in the other questions in this series. This fact has an impact on one deduction that is important in computing his *taxable income*: the *standard deduction*.

As for the *standard deduction*, because Daniel is not Mom's dependent he is not restricted to the special limitation calculation discussed in questions 9 through 11, above. Rather, he is entitled to the regular *standard deduction* for single individuals of $12,200 (for 2019).

Applying this **six-step** computation approach, Daniel's *taxable income* for 2019 is $800, computed as follows:

 Step 1: *Gross income* = $13,000
 Step 2: *Adjusted gross income (AGI)* = $13,000
 Step 3: *Itemized deductions* = $0

Step 4: *Standard deduction* = $12,200
Step 5: *IRC § 199A Pass-Through business-related deduction* = $0
Step 6: *Taxable income* = $13,000
                                ($12,200) [the greater of $0 or $12,200]
                                (\$ 0)
                                \$ 800

A visual depiction of the *taxable income* calculation is as follows:

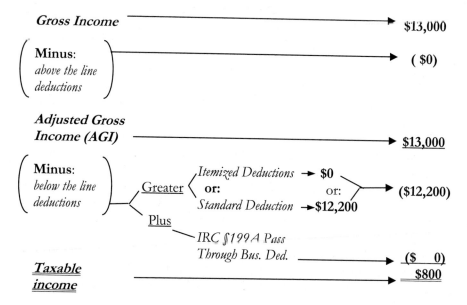

Gross Income ————————————————————▶ **$13,000**

(**Minus:** *above the line deductions*) ————————————▶ **($0)**

Adjusted Gross Income (AGI) ————————————▶ **$13,000**

(**Minus:** *below the line deductions*) — Greater ⟨ *Itemized Deductions* ▶ **$0** or: *Standard Deduction* ▶**$12,200** ⟩ or: ————▶ **($12,200)**

Plus — *IRC §199A Pass Through Bus. Ded.* ————————▶ **(\$ 0)**

__Taxable income__ ————————————————————▶ **$800**

Answer (a) is incorrect based on the calculations above. **Answer (c) is incorrect** because this answer does not properly reflect the full *standard deduction* to which Daniel is entitled. **Answer (d) is incorrect** because Daniel will not be entitled to any *IRC § 199A Pass-Through business-related deduction*. [Other questions in this book address this deduction which may be available to some self-employed type businesses; this has no application to Daniel.] **Answer (e) is incorrect** because a correct answer (b) is presented.

14. **Answer (e) is correct.** This first question in this long "taxable income" series of questions is fairly straightforward and not too difficult. Early in your class discussion of "gross income" for income tax purposes, you learned that its scope is very broad. Not only does IRC § 61 proclaim that gross income includes "all income from whatever source derived," its definition encompasses net economic benefits or net accessions to wealth experienced by an individual. Generally, to exclude from gross income any such benefit received, a specific statutory provision must apply.

Thian clearly must include in his gross income for 2019, the $27,000 in wages that he received. There is no statutory provision excluding such wages from gross income. The other cognizable economic benefit Thian receives is the $30,000 scholarship. Ostensibly, this would also be included in his gross income. However, IRC § 117 provides that "qualified scholarships" (or fellowships) are excluded from gross income.

Generally, a *qualified scholarship* is one that is used to pay for a student's tuition and fees required for enrollment, fees, books, supplies, and equipment required for courses. [IRC §§ 117(a) and 117(b).] While not at issue in this question, any scholarship monies for room and board are not excludable *qualified scholarships*. In addition, this general scholarship exclusion rule applies only to students who are candidates for a degree, and who are students attending a qualified educational organization, the latter defined as a school that normally maintains a regular faculty, curriculum and regularly enrolled student body in attendance. [IRC §§ 117(b)(2)(A) and 170(b)(1)(A)(ii).] While not pertinent to our facts, the growing trend of "distance learning" raises interesting questions as to what constitutes a "school" for scholarship exclusion purposes. Thian's $30,000 scholarship is solely for his tuition and his enrollment at an accredited law school satisfies the other requirements for exclusion. IRC § 117 makes no distinction between graduate and undergraduate levels of education for exclusion purposes.

Thian's *gross income* for 2019 is $27,000, representing his wages for the year. The $30,000 law school scholarship is fully excludable from gross income pursuant to IRC § 117.

Answer (a) is incorrect because there is no such restriction for exclusion of qualified scholarships under IRC § 117. While not pertinent to our facts, the exclusion of certain tuition reduction programs for employees of educational institutions is usually <u>not</u> applicable to graduate study. **Answer (b) is also incorrect.** Thian is entitled to a full exclusion of his scholarship pursuant to IRC § 117. Another Code provision, IRC § 127, provides for a different, and more limited, exclusion for "employer-provided" educational assistance. Thian's scholarship is not an employer-provided educational benefit. Even if Thian's employer was providing educational assistance for his law school study, this answer is incorrect because the 2001 Tax Act extended the application of the IRC § 127 exclusion for employer-provided educational assistance to graduate level study starting in 2002. **Answer (c) is also incorrect.** This answer correctly outlines the exclusion provided in IRC § 127 for employer-provided educational assistance. However, Thian's scholarship is not an employer-provided educational benefit. Rather, Thian's scholarship is a fully excludable qualified scholarship pursuant IRC

§ 117. **Answer (d) is incorrect** because the scholarship exclusion provisions of IRC § 117 are not so limited in its application.

15. **The best answer is (a).** In earlier editions of this book, this was a very complex question requiring numerous calculations and a very long discussion of various component parts. Now, however, this question is relatively easy. Neither of these two expenditures (tuition or room & board) will give rise to any deductions for Thian. We shall see, in later questions, that he may be entitled to some "tax credits," but no deductions. [Later, we discuss the difference between a deduction and a credit. Both are good things for taxpayers but work differently; a deduction reduces taxable income upon which a tax is computed whereas a credit comes in after the tax has been computed and it reduces the tax itself.]

This question used to implicate IRC § 222. This was a good section for students as it provided a deduction, up to a certain amount (generally $4,000 per year) for "qualified tuition and expenses." The section was rather complex (as was the explanation to this answer in prior editions) and required numerous calculations that affected the amount of the deduction depending on the taxpayer's level of income. The deduction allowed by IRC § 222 was a valuable "above the line" deduction (used to compute one's Adjusted Gross Income; please see other questions in this book that address the importance of "above" versus "below" the line deductions.

The IRC § 222 deduction expired at the end of 2017 and while there has been some congressional discussion of reinstating it, as of this writing, there is little hope of this happening. The actual section still appears in the Code in all of its past glory, but it is all for naught as stated in IRC § 222(e) "Termination. – This section shall not apply to taxable years beginning after December 31, 2017."

Had we gone through a complete analysis of IRC § 222 (say, had Thian's first year of law school been 2017 or earlier) we would have found that he would have been entitled to deduct a portion of the $10,000 paid for tuition (specifically, it would have entitled him to a $4,000, above the line deduction). We also would have determined that his room and board costs would not have given rise to a deduction because they are not "qualified tuition and related expenses" as required by the statute. **This is, in effect, our correct answer (a) to this question.**

Answer (b) is not correct but would have been the correct answer if IRC § 222 was still in effect. **Answer (c) is incorrect** for a variety of reasons. IRC § 222 is no longer applicable but if it were, his payment of the spring 2020 tuition in 2019 would still count in computing the deduction. The statement about room and board and IRC § 117 does not make sense; the tax concept of an exclusion from income is inconsistent with a deduction for something paid. **Answer (d) is incorrect.** Like answer (c), the concept of an exclusion for something paid does not make sense tax-wise. As addressed in question 14, above, the scholarship he received is properly excludable under IRC § 117, that section has nothing to do with a possible deduction for education-related expenses. The part of the answer concerning any deduction for his room and board costs is, however, correct. **Answer (e) is not the best answer.** It is correct that Thian is not entitled to any deductions for this question, but the stated reason is incorrect. Under the no longer relevant IRC § 222, which would, in earlier years, entitled him to some deduction for his tuition, there was no distinction for qualifying costs incurred in undergraduate or graduate settings.

16. **The best answer is (d).** An income tax credit is a very valuable tax benefit as it represents a dollar-for-dollar reduction of a taxpayer's computed tax liability. There are two major tax credits with respect to "higher" education: the "American Opportunity Credit" and the "Lifetime Learning Credit." IRC § 25A is the primary Code section dealing with both of these credits. We will conclude, below, that the $10,000 Thian paid in law school tuition (in 2019) will be qualified expenses for purposes of determining the *Lifetime Learning Credit*.

As indicated, IRC § 25A contains provisions for both the *American Opportunity* and the *Lifetime Learning* credits. The former (*American Opportunity Credit*) is not applicable in our case, as that credit is generally available for certain qualifying higher education costs associated with only the first four years of undergraduate (post-secondary) education. [IRC § 25A(b)(2)(C).] Since Thian already completed four years of *post-secondary* education in obtaining his bachelor's degree, this alone would make him ineligible for the *American Opportunity Credit*. Additionally, IRC § 25A(b)(2)(D) denies the credit to anyone convicted of a "Federal or State felony offense consisting of the possession or distribution of a controlled substance . . . " Thian's felony drug possession conviction would make him ineligible for the *American Opportunity Credit* even if he had not already completed four years of *post-secondary* education. Not intended as a political statement, but the author, as well as many in the tax field, finds in a bit odd that a conviction for any other felony (e.g., murder, rape, arson, burglary, kidnapping, etc.) does not result in denial of this credit.

Because the *American Opportunity Credit* will not be available to Thian, our focus turns to the *Lifetime Learning Credit* and the statutory provisions in IRC § 25A(c).

Basically, the *Lifetime Learning Credit* equals 20% of up to $10,000 of "qualified tuition and related expenses." Tuition, fees and books (but not room or board) to attend most post-secondary institutions (colleges, universities, vocational schools, etc.) are considered "qualified tuition and related expenses." This credit, unlike the *American Opportunity Credit*, is available for undergraduate and graduate studies. Mathematically, the maximum credit available for 2019 is $2,000 (20% of $10,000).

For Thian, the $10,000 paid for law school tuition represents his "qualified tuition and related expenses" for the purposes of the *Lifetime Learning Credit*. While $5,000 of this amount represents tuition for the spring 2019 semester, such prepayments are allowed (for credit purposes) as long as the semester, for which the tuition is paid, begins within three months of the following year. This does not present a problem in the present case. While the answer to this problem does not require the computation of Thian's *Lifetime Learning Credit*, his "potential" credit would be $2,000 (20% of the $10,000 paid, which is also the maximum amount of qualified expenditures eligible in computing the credit). This is his "potential" credit because this credit, like many other credits, deductions and exclusions, is "phased-out" for taxpayer's with income levels above a certain amount. For illustration purposes, for 2019 the phase-out of this credit begins and ends at $58,000 and $68,000 of adjusted gross income (AGI as modified), respectively (for married individuals filing a joint return, the 2019 "phase-out" range is $116,000 through $136,000). We do not know, at this point, whether Thian's potential *Lifetime Learning Credit* will be reduced because we have yet to compute his AGI.

At this point in this series of questions, we also do not know if Thian will qualify as Marlo's "dependent." This will determine who is entitled to potentially benefit from the *Lifetime Learning Credit*. We shall make this determination is later problems in this set. If Thian is Marlo's dependent, then she will be entitled to any credit (utilizing her tax information for the aforementioned income-related limitations). If Thian is not Marlo's dependent, then this credit will be his to utilize (using his tax information for the income-related limitations).

[For more information about the *American Opportunity Credit* and the *Lifetime Learning Credit*, see I.R.S. Pub. 970, "Tax Benefits for Higher Education."]

Answers (a) and (b) are incorrect because Thian's expenses associated with Thian's graduate studies do not qualify for the *American Opportunity Credit*. As discussed above, that credit is generally available only for the first four years of *post-secondary* education. Also, Thian is ineligible for the *American Opportunity Credit* because of his felony drug possession conviction.

In addition, costs for room/board are not qualifying expenses for the *American Opportunity Credit* (as indicated in answer (a)). **Answer (c) is incorrect** because, as discussed above, the entire $10,000 tuition that Thian paid in 2019 qualifies notwithstanding that $5,000 of this amount represents tuition for the <u>spring 2020</u> semester. **Answer (e) is incorrect** because a correct response (d) is presented.

17. **The best answer is (c).** This is also a difficult question. While in this question we need not determine Thian's actual deduction for his student loan interest, we will be doing so in other questions in this series, where it will be necessary to compute *adjusted gross income (AGI)* and *taxable income*. As discussed below, Thian might be entitled to deduct, some or all, of the $1,000 interest paid pursuant to IRC § 221.

The analysis starts with IRC § 163. This is the primary section at issue for deductions related to interest paid. For casual readers of the Code, IRC § 163(a) provides a simple and broad sounding deduction for interest stating, in part: "There shall be allowed as a deduction all interest paid . . . within the taxable year on indebtedness." Under this general definition, the interest that Thian pays on his law school loans would give rise to a deduction. However, the Tax Reform Act of 1986 added subsection (h) to § 163, located quite some written distance from the general allowance for interest deductions of subsection (a). IRC § 163(h) starts out deceptively, and unfavorably, simple by stating, in part: "In the case of a taxpayer other than a corporation, no deduction shall be allowed . . . for personal interest paid . . . during the taxable year."

The definition of *personal interest*, which is not deductible, is found in IRC § 163(h)(2) and takes the form of a negative definition; *personal interest* is interest "other than" those listed in subparagraphs (A) through (F). The key, therefore, to finding interest that <u>is</u> deductible, is to fit within one of these specified categories of what does <u>not</u> constitute nondeductible personal interest. Among the categories of interest that are <u>not</u> personal interest is what might be the familiar category of "qualified residence interest" (typical interest paid on a home mortgage). [IRC § 163(h)(2)(D).] Somewhat less familiar, but logically not included as personal interest, is "interest properly allocable to a trade or business." [IRC § 163(h)(2)(A).] Also listed among the categories of interest that is <u>not</u> considered personal interest is, "any interest allowable as a deduction under IRC § 221 (relating to interest on educational loans)." [IRC § 163(h)(2)(F).] We will, below, conclude that the interest Thian pays on his student loans in 2019, *may* qualify as deductible education loan interest pursuant to IRC § 221.

So far, Thian's loan qualifies. Qualified educational loans do <u>not</u> include money borrowed from certain "related parties." [IRC § 221(d)(1).] Thian's loans were from traditional law school loan sources (not from "related" individuals) and her loans are considered *qualified education loans* used for *qualified higher education expenses*. It should be noted that your professor may dive deeper into the complex waters of what constitutes *qualified educational loans* and *qualified higher education expenses*. Our question does not require us to do so.

IRC § 221 (which came to life in 1998) allows for a limited deduction for certain interest paid on certain educational loans. This deduction, if allowed, is a valuable "above the line" deduction; a deduction from gross income in computing adjusted gross income (AGI). To qualify as an educational loan for this section, the loan proceeds generally must be used for tuition, fees, books, room/board or related expenses while attending a college, university or vocational school. This includes graduate, post graduate studies, professional degree programs, etc. So far, Thian's loan qualifies. Qualified educational loans do <u>not</u> include money borrowed from certain "related parties." [IRC § 221(d)(1).] Thian's loans were from federally sponsored loan sources (not from "related" individuals), and his loans are considered qualified educational loans used for qualified higher education expenses. Recall from the introductory fact pattern, Thian obtained these loans for his undergraduate education which was prior to his felony drug possession conviction. While it is not at issue and has no bearing for our question, the unfortunate real-life ramifications of such a conviction would make it very difficult for Thian to obtain any new federally sponsored student loans.

The interest Thian pays on this qualified higher education loan is subject to two important limitations. First, the amount of interest deductible under IRC § 221 is limited, by statute, to $2,500 per year (in the aggregate for all such loans). Thian's $1,000 of interest does not exceed this limit. If allowed, as discussed below, this deduction is taken "above the line" in computing Thian's *adjusted gross income (AGI)* (i.e., it is an amount that is subtracted from *gross income* to compute AGI). [Please see Appendix A for more information about how income and deductions fit together to compute AGI and taxable income.]

The second important limitation kicks in if the taxpayer's *adjusted gross income (AGI)*, as modified by IRC § 221(b)(2)(C), exceeds certain levels. If it does, the otherwise allowed IRC § 221 interest deduction is reduced or "phased-out" utilizing a formula contained in the statute. Pursuant to IRC § 221(b)(2)(B), the level of "modified adjusted gross income" at which this deduction starts to "phase-out" (be reduced) is $50,000 for single individuals or $100,00 for married individuals filing a joint return. The deduction for student loan interest is completely eliminated for single individuals with "modified adjusted gross income" of $65,000 or more, and at $130,000 or more for married individuals filing a joint return. The statute uses the term "modified adjusted gross income" because true adjusted gross income will reflect any deduction allowed by this IRC § 221 (see above). Modified adjusted gross income is basically *adjusted gross income* computed before you compute any possible deduction under this IRC § 221 (and other sections not applicable to this problem). [IRC § 221(b)(2)(C).] It is **very important to note** that these "phase-out" thresholds appearing here and in the statute are "adjusted for inflation: (i.e., these threshold amounts are *indexed* for inflation) and are <u>not</u> the actual amounts for the current year (2019 in our question) but, rather, are the pre-inflation "phase-out" amounts.

For 2019, the year in question in our problem, the level of "modified adjusted gross income" at which this deduction starts to "phase-out" is $70,000 for single individuals or $140,000 for married individuals filing a joint return. For 2019, the deduction for student loan interest is completely eliminated for single individuals with "modified adjusted gross income" of $85,000 or more, and at $170,000 or more for married individuals filing a joint return. [Appendix B contains the "phase-out" threshold amounts for the year 2019 (the most current at the time of this printing)].

The exact amount of Thian's deduction pursuant to IRC § 221, if any, will be determined in later questions that involve computation of his *AGI* and *taxable income*. But at this point, we can say that Thian will be entitled to deduct some or all his $1,000 interest paid depending on the amount of his *AGI* (as modified). **This, essentially, is our answer (c).**

Answer (a) is incorrect because *personal interest* is not deductible at all pursuant to IRC § 163(h). **Answer (b) is incorrect** because the interest Thian pays on his student loans might (and will as is discussed in later questions) be deductible student loan interest pursuant to IRC § 221. **Answer (d) is also incorrect.** Before 2002, the deductibility of student loan interest under IRC § 221 was generally limited to interest paid only during the first 60 months of loan payments. This provision was repealed, effective for 2002, by then current legislation. **Answer (e) is incorrect** because, as discussed above, deductions allowed for student loan interest pursuant to IRC § 221 are deductible *above the line* in computing *adjusted gross income (AGI)*.

18. **Answer (d) is correct.** For most individuals, IRC § 164 is the delimiting section for deducting taxes paid. State income taxes are among those listed as deductible (IRC § 164(a)(3)), so Thian's $1,000 of state income taxes qualify as a deductible expense. The statute also allows deductions for state and local personal property taxes. [IRC § 164(a)(2).] Thian's $800 of state intangibles tax fits into this category. An intangibles tax, in its most common form (which is not that common as very few states, or subdivisions thereof,

assess such a tax), is an annual tax based on the value (ad-valorem) of securities (stocks, bonds, etc.) owned by the taxpayer. Securities are considered "intangible" personal property, and the annual ad-valorem tax thereon, as well as ad-valorem taxes on other personal property are very similar to state and local real property taxes (also deductible under IRC § 164). The difference between "personal" property taxes and "real" property taxes is the character of the underlying property subject to tax: personal (including intangible) property and real property, respectively. Another common example in some states is a portion of a taxpayer's car registration fee. Many states, but not all, assess, as a component of "DMV" fees based on the value of the vehicle. This would also be a qualifying "tax" on personal property for IRC § 164 purposes.

Prior to the enactment of the *1986 Tax Reform Act*, taxpayers were also entitled to deduct federal and state gasoline taxes under IRC § 164. Now, however, federal and state gasoline are not listed as a deductible tax in IRC § 164 and, therefore, are generally not deductible. This is not to be confused with a possible deduction of "state and local sales taxes" in lieu of "state and local income taxes" (see questions elsewhere in this book that address this).

While not necessary to answer this question, it should be noted that deductible taxes, pursuant to IRC § 164, are part of the large group of "itemized deductions" that might come into play in computing taxable income. See problem 24, below, for the composition of Thian's itemized deductions in this series of questions, and their relevance in computing Thian's taxable income.

Again, not part of this question, but the *Tax Cuts and Jobs Act* (TCJA) signed into law in December 2017 (generally effective beginning in 2018) instituted a "cap" on the aggregate amount of state and local taxes deductible per year. The so-called SALT (state and local tax) limit; beginning in 2018, the deduction for all such taxes is capped at $10,000 (this is the same for single, married filing jointly, etc. and not a per-person cap). Other questions in this book address, in much more detail, this SALT limit and its ramifications for tax and real-life economic purposes. At this point in this block of questions, we are not determining Thian's actual IRC § 164 total deduction for such taxes. Rather, we are analyzing which taxes paid are part of the deductible pool.

Answers (a), (b), (c), and (e) are incorrect because they do not reflect the correct combination of deductible taxes.

19. **The correct answer is (b).** IRC § 213 allows for a deduction of certain qualified medical care expenses. Once one makes the determination of what

constitutes "qualified" medical care expenses, the subject of this question, the deduction is allowed as an "itemized deduction" only to the extent that the total qualifying expenses exceeds 10% of Adjusted Gross Income (AGI). Qualified medical care expenses include typical costs for doctors, dentists, hospital, health insurance, and the like. [See IRC § 213(d).]

Addressing first the easier issue of Thian's over-the-counter allergy medicines that were recommended by his doctor. While logically it would appear that such costs would qualify, the Code specifically allows deductions only for prescription drugs (and insulin in those areas where its sale is allowed without a prescription). [IRC § 213(b).] Therefore, none of the $400 that Thian paid for the allergy medicine will qualify as medical care expenses even though his physician recommended the medicine.

The $4,000 in veterinary fees that Thian paid with respect to his Seeing Eye dog presents other issues. IRC § 213 allows a deduction for medical care expenditures made for the taxpayer, his or her spouse, or *dependents*. Non-humans, however, do not qualify as dependents and Thian's vet bills for his Seeing Eye dog are not deductible by *this* means. However, the vet bills are deductible by Thian for other reasons. While not really necessary for the answer to this question, it is helpful to address the tax ramifications (deductibility) of the cost, if any, that Thian had to pay to acquire the Seeing Eye dog. For the sake of discussion, let us say that Thian had to purchase the Seeing Eye dog. This purchase would not really constitute an "expense," but, rather, would be considered a "capital expenditure." *Capital expenditures* and *expenses* are usually mutually exclusive items, with IRC § 213 medical deductions limited to qualified medical care *expense*. However, if the capital expenditure primarily health-related, which would be the case in our as-sumed hypothetical of Thian purchasing the Seeing Eye dog, it is not precluded from qualifying as a medical care expense. The regulations, at Reg. § 1.213-1(e)(iii), indicate that costs for such medically related *capital expenditures* as Seeing Eye dogs, artificial teeth and limbs, wheelchairs, and the like represent *qualifying medical care expenses*. [Reg. § 1.213-1(e)(iii).] The regulations go on to provide that 100% of the operating and maintenance costs associated with such capital expenditures are deductible regardless of the amount, if any, of the original expenditure for the medically related expenditure that qualified as a medical related expense. Therefore, notwithstanding how much, if anything, Thian paid for the Seeing Eye dog, the entire $4,000 in veterinary fees (considered maintenance expenses for the dog) qualifies as a medically related expense.

As indicated above, the aggregate of Thian's qualifying medical expenses, $4,000 in this case, is deductible, as an itemized ("below the line") deduction to the extent that they exceed 10% of his adjusted gross income (AGI). See later questions in this set for this computation in conjunction with computing his taxable income for the year.

Answer (a) is incorrect. While this answer correctly states the non-deductibility of his over-the-counter allergy medicines, it is not correct regarding the vet fees. As indicated above, the deduction of the maintenance costs for the Seeing Eye dog is not predicated upon either Thian paying for the dog or whether or not, if he did pay for it, the cost was deductible. **Answer (c) is also incorrect.** Again, this answer correctly states the non-deductibility of his over-the-counter allergy medicines. However, it is incorrect regarding the vet fees. True, Thian is not entitled to deduct them because the dog is not his dependent but, rather, as explained above they represent qualifying medical care expenses for *Thian*. **Answer (d) is incorrect** on both counts: the non-deductibility of the vet fees and the deductibility of the over-the-counter allergy medicines. **Answer (e) is incorrect** because it incorrectly includes, as qualifying medical care expenses, the costs for his over-the-counter allergy medicines.

20. **The correct answer is (c).** Each year, Americans give billions of dollars to charities. Fostering charitable giving has long been an important component of government policy. A deduction, for income tax purposes, for contributions made to charitable organizations has had a long-time presence in our country's tax structure. IRC § 170(a) facilitates deductions for contributions of cash and property to qualified charities. One need not be a student in income tax to surmise that the American Heart Association qualifies as a charitable organization. Indeed, the American Heart Association is a qualified charitable organization as generally defined in IRC § 170(c), and Thian's cash gifts thereto will be tax deductible (subject to limits discussed below).

The total amount of an individual's charitable deductions in any one year is limited or capped at a ceiling that varies depending on the nature of the contribution (cash or property) and the charitable recipients. This deduction ceiling or limit for cash gifts made to most charitable organizations (commonly referred to as "public charities") is 60% of the taxpayer's "contribution base." [IRC § 170(b)(1)(A) & (b)(1)(G)] Thian's cash contributions to the American Red Cross (representing all of his qualified charitable contributions in the year for this question) are deductible up to 60% of his contribution base. This, we will see in later questions, does not pose a limitation to Thian's charitable deductions. While not necessary to answer this question, an individual's "contribution base" is basically the individuals adjusted gross income (AGI) calculated before deducting any "net operating loss" (NOL) carryback (most individuals do not have a NOL carryback so their AGI is their "contribution base"). [See IRC § 170(b)(1)(H).]

In prior editions of this book, the above-described "cap" for charitable contributions was 50% (and had been so for decades). The *Tax Cuts and Job's Act* (TCJA) signed into law in December 2017 (generally effective beginning in 2018) raised this cap to 60%.

While also not a part of this question, it should be noted that charitable contributions made in any year that, in the aggregate, exceed the deduction ceiling, are carried forward for up to the next five tax years (and deductible subject to the applicable year's limits).

What <u>is</u> pertinent for this question, is where, in computing taxable income, charitable contributions are deductible. In very broad terms, and very important for this series of questions, there are two camps of deductions for purposes of computing taxable income. There are deductions that are subtracted from *gross income* to arrive at an intermediary point called *adjusted gross income* (AGI). These are commonly referred to as "above the line" deductions, with AGI representing "the line." The other camp of deductions is comprised of those that are subtracted from AGI to arrive at *taxable income*. These are commonly referred to as "below the line" deductions. The components making up this camp of *below the line* deductions can include something called the "standard deduction" or, in the alternative, a group of deductions called "itemized deductions." In addition, some taxpayers with business-related expenses may be entitled to a TCJA-enacted "pass-through" deduction via IRC § 199A. [Please see other questions in this book and Appendix A for more information about how income and deductions fit together in computing taxable income and AGI.]

Deductions for charitable contributions fit into the *itemized deduction* camp which are, as a group, part of the *below the line* deductions; possible deductions subtracted from adjusted gross income (AGI) in computing taxable income. [Please see Appendix A, and later questions in this series (especially questions 23 and 24).]

Answer (a) is incorrect. While this answer correctly recognized that Thian's $3,000 cash contribution to the American Heart Association gives rise to a charitable contribution deduction, it is incorrect regarding "where" the deduction is taken. **Answer (b) is incorrect** because charitable deductions (and other *itemized deductions*) are not predicated upon one's status as a dependent of another. **Answer (d) is incorrect** because, as indicated above, the charitable deduction limit is essentially 60% of the taxpayer's AGI. The $3,000 contributed is not close to approaching this limit. Please see questions 23 and 24 for a more complete picture of Thian's AGI and taxable income).

21. **Answer (d) is the most accurate.** It is virtually a given that Thian's "legitimate, unreimbursed business expenses" qualify as deductible IRC § 162 trade or business expenses. The first sentence of IRC § 162 (contained in subsection (a)) enumerates, for all intents and purposes, the basic requirements for a business deduction. A deduction is allowed for all "ordinary and necessary" "expenses" "paid or incurred during the taxable year" "in carrying on any trade or business." The compartmentalized quotation marks signify what are commonly considered the four basic requirements for a business deduction. These four requirements often represent, in tax classes and in real life, separate and significant points of contention. Business deductions come in a million different flavors, but all qualifying deductions meet those four criteria. The study, in tax classes, of business deductions can be long and comprehensive. Presumptively, Thian's $600 expenditures relating to his paralegal job meet all of the IRC § 162 requirements.

The key issues in this question are where and how, in computing Thian's taxable income, this $600 is deductible. The requirements for deductibility pursuant to § 162 are the same for an employee or a self-employed individual. However, the effective availability of an actual business deduction, and where it is deducted, varies dramatically depending on one's "work status." The *Tax Cuts and Jobs Act* (TCJA) signed into law in December 2017 (and generally effective beginning in 2018) made significant changes, and not in a good way, for deductions of business expenses by employees. While individuals who are self-employed are entitled to deduct IRC § 162 business expenses *above the line* (to compute adjusted gross income) under the TCJA, it is a very different story for the exact same business expenses incurred by employees. In prior editions of this book, the law still allowed for business deductions for employees (albeit *below the line* as part of the *itemized deduction* group of deduction and subject to various statutory deduction floors). Now, pursuant to the TCJA, deductions for unreimbursed business expenses incurred by employees, have, for the most part, been "suspended" for 2018 through 2025. [IRC § 67(g)].

In prior editions of this book, answer (c) was correct and reflects the pre-TCJA tax results for this question. Now, however, answer (d) correctly reflect the TCJA's elimination of actual deductions by employees for otherwise qualifying IRC § 162 business expenses. We shall see, in question 24, below, this reflected in computing Thian's taxable income for 2019.

Answer (a) is incorrect because for most individuals, *above the line* deductions of IRC § 162 business expenses are reserved for the self-employed (a.k.a., independent contractor, unincorporated sole proprietor). **Answer (b) is incorrect** because the business expenses in question relate to Thian's trade/business while employed as a paralegal. They have nothing to do with his law school education. **Answer (c) is also incorrect.** In prior editions of this book, this was the correct answer. Now, however, even though Thian's expenditures are qualifying IRC § 162 business expenses, employees are no longer entitled to an actual deduction under the TCJA. **Answer (e) is incorrect** because while Thian is Marlo's dependent (see a later question in this set), this does not preclude Thian from utilizing itemized deductions.

22. **The correct answer is (e).** Many years ago, the concept of the "standard deduction" was introduced into tax law as a means of reducing an individual's record-keeping needs. The *standard deduction* may be taken in place of a group of deductions known collectively as "itemized deductions." Probably the most commonly known components of this latter group of *itemized deductions* include charitable contributions, deductible interest and taxes and qualifying medical deductions. Taxpayers have a choice: deduct either 1) the total of itemized deductions (after applying all necessary limits and restrictions as discussed elsewhere in this book), **or** 2) the *standard deduction* amount. In calculating "taxable income," a taxpayer takes as a deduction the <u>greater</u> of these two. [Please see Appendix A for more information about *where* these deductions fit within the framework of calculating taxable income.]

IRC § 63(c) is the focal point for the *standard deduction*. The amount of this *standard deduction* can vary greatly from taxpayer to taxpayer depending on various factors including marital or filing status, age, degree of visual imparity, and whether the taxpayer is a "dependent" of another. In addition, *standard deduction* amounts are subject to change each tax year (and for the most part, do change each year) based on adjustments for "inflation" (i.e., the standard deduction amounts are *indexed* for inflation). The various *standard deduction* amounts listed in the statute (throughout IRC § 63) are <u>not</u> the actual amounts for the current year but, rather, are pre-inflation adjusted "base" amounts (that are well below the actual current amounts). [Appendix B contains the various *standard deduction* amounts for the year 2019 (the most current at the time of this printing).]

A highly touted component of the *Tax Cuts and Jobs Act* (TCJA) signed into law in December 2017 (generally effective beginning in 2018), was a substantial increase in the *standard deduction* amounts (beginning in 2018). For 2019, the "regular" *standard deduction* for a single individual is $12,200 (corresponding to the special TCJA 2018-2025 statutory amount of $12,000 which is unadjusted for inflation). For couples filing a joint return, the 2019 standard deduction is $24,400 (corresponding to the computed 200% of the single special TCJA 2018-2025 statutory amount of $12,000 which is unadjusted for inflation). The regular *standard deduction* is **increased** for certain individuals based on age or visual imparity. [IRC § 63(b)(3).] For 2019, single individuals (and heads of households) with severe visual impairment, as defined below, are entitled to an extra $1,650 of *standard deduction*. This $1,650 for 2019 corresponds to the unadjusted for inflation amount of $750 listed in IRC § 63(f)(3). [See Appendix B for the 2019 *standard deduction* "extra amounts" for other classifications of individuals.] The degree of visual impairment that generates this extra amount is defined in the Code as an individual whose "central visual acuity does not exceed 20/200 in the better eye with correcting lenses, or if his visual acuity is greater than 20/200 but is accompanied by a limitation in the fields of vision such that the widest diameter of the visual field subtends an angle no greater than 20 degrees." [IRC § 63(f)(4).] The facts indicate that Thian's eyesight would meet this definition thereby entitling him to an extra $1,650 of *standard deduction*. Barring any other factors, Thian's *standard deduction* for 2019 is **$13,850** ($12,200 + $1,650).

Before concluding that Thian's *standard deduction* for 2019 is $13,850, we need to address one additional item. IRC § 63(c)(5) contains a provision possibly reducing the amount of certain individual's *standard deduction*. For a taxpayer who can be claimed as a "dependent" by another individual, this provision dictates the use of a formula for determining the dependent taxpayer's *standard deduction*. For **2019**, the limit imposed by this provision for the *standard deduction* is:

The greater of:
1) $1,100, or
2) The dependent taxpayer's "earned" income + $350.

If a taxpayer is required to use this "dependent" formula for the *standard deduction*, the amount would always be limited by the non-dependent *standard deduction* for the taxpayer.

We will conclude that Thian is <u>not</u> Marlo's dependent and, therefore, his *standard deduction* will be $13,850 (and not be determined by the above formula for dependent taxpayers). To reach this conclusion, and confirm that Thian is entitled to his full single (plus visually impaired extra) *standard deduction*, we must go through a rather complex analysis to determine whether or not Thian is Marlo's dependent. Here goes:

As with the other questions in this set, they are year-specific (but can easily be adapted to years other than 2019 as in our set of questions.

Recall that we are going through this "dependent" exercise to determine if Thian must use a different set of rules for calculating his *standard deduction* than is normally the case (the usual result is that dependents do not benefit from the full *standard deduction* for non-dependents). While this is important for us at this point in this set of questions, it should be noted that tax law relating to someone qualifying as a dependent and the relevance of why this is important has changed dramatically since the earlier editions of this book. It still has some significance, hence this question, but historically deductions for personal exemptions (including those for dependents) was a huge deal. The *Tax Cuts and Jobs Act* (TCJA) that was signed into law in December 2017 (generally effective beginning in 2018) eliminated deductions for personal exemptions for 2018 through 2025. While no longer a deduction, it may help to go through some explanation of what used to be the pre-TCJA law (in 2017 and earlier) and help give more meaning to the relevance of claiming another individual as one's dependent. Here is a brief explanation of prior law and then we will circle back to analyze whether or not Thian is Marlo's dependent.

> ### Pre-TCJA Law; what was a personal exemption deduction and how many of them could a taxpayer deduct:
> *Every living person has, in his or her figurative pocket, a "coupon" good for a personal exemption deduction for each tax year. There is no real "coupon" involved, but it helps to think of the personal exemption deduction as such. The amount of this exemption deduction is listed in IRC § 151 of the Code as $2,000. However, this amount has been adjusted (increased) each year since 1990 to reflect the general level of inflation. The personal exemption deduction amount in 2017, the last year for which a deduction was allowed, was $4,050 (it would have been $4,150 for 2018 and slightly more for 2019). The key to this problem in its prior, pre-TCJA form was determining who gets to use these personal exemption deduction "coupons" ($4,050 for 2017). Did each person get to use his or her own "coupon" and get a $4,050 deduction (for 2017), or does somebody else get to claim that person's "coupon" and take the deduction? This latter question gives rise to the issue of who qualifies as one's dependent. [This is still a relevant question after the TCJA but for tax reasons other than obtaining a now nonexistent personal exemption deduction].*
>
> *Students knowing little about income tax, probably knew something about this issue. A parent claiming his or her children as dependents and getting an extra deduction for them is precisely the issue that was in the forefront of this question in prior editions of this book. Had this problem been placed in 2017 or earlier, Marlo would have been entitled to a personal exemption deduction for herself. The issue, pre TCJA (before 2018) was whether Marlo gets to take Thian's "coupon" and thus get an additional personal exemption deductions (on her income tax return for purposes of computing her taxable income). Alternatively,*

does Thian get to use his own "coupon" for a personal exemption deduction (on his income tax returns for purposes of computing his taxable income)? To determine if Marlo was entitled to get Thian's personal exemption "coupon" (claim him as dependents and get to deduct his $4,050 (for 2017) personal exemption deductions) we would have been determining if he (Thian) qualified as Marlo's dependent.

The author hopes that this introduction of "old law" helps with what we are about to discuss with respect to our current question. While Marlo, in our question, no longer has any personal exemption deductions for herself or any "dependents," the determination of whether Thian qualifies as her dependent will control the previously discussed *standard deduction* issue. Because the TCJA eliminated the personal exemption deduction, which was a significant tax topic and valuable deduction, many basic income tax courses no longer cover, in great detail, this accompanying topic of who qualifies as one's dependent. With that in mind, let's begin our journey (and be forewarned that it is not a particularly fun journey) into the world of "dependents."

For Thian to be Marlo's dependent, we begin by determining whether he is either Marlo's *"qualifying child"* or *"qualifying relative"* pursuant to IRC § 152 (it is this section that defines, through some rather complex rules, who qualifies as one's dependent). The dependent qualification process became a bit more complex with the enactment of the *"Working Families Tax Relief Act of 2004"* where the desire to have uniform definitions of certain relatives for federal tax statutes created a rather messy result for the dependency rules. What follows below may look a bit daunting, but it is not too bad once you go through each part, step by step (as applicable).

Requirements for all possible "dependents." As indicated, a "dependent" is someone who is either a *"qualifying child"* or *"qualifying relative"* of the taxpayer. There are a bunch of requirements for each alternative (see below), but before we get to those, there are some basic requirements that must be met in order for either type of qualifying individual to be considered your "dependent." First, and logically, if you yourself (or your spouse if he or she is filing a joint return with you) can be claimed as a dependent by someone else, then you will not be entitled to claim anyone as your dependent. Next, for both a *"qualifying child"* and a *"qualifying relative"* **all** the following requirements must be met:

➢ If the potential "dependent" is married, he or she must not file a joint return with his or her spouse for the tax year (there are some exceptions to this).

➢ The potential "dependent" must be a U.S. citizen, U.S. resident, U.S. national, or a resident of Canada or Mexico for some part of the tax year. [Note that non-citizen residents of Canada or Mexico may not qualify for certain dependent credits notwithstanding that they can qualify as dependents.]

If all of the above requirements are satisfied, we then move on to see if the potential individual is **either** a "***qualifying child***" or "***qualifying relative***." If the individual meets all the requirements of <u>either</u>, then this person is a "dependent" for various tax purposes (in the pre-TCJA world, this also meant that taxpayer could take as a deduction, that person's personal exemption "coupon"). Be forewarned; put aside any preconceived, non-tax, notions of who you think is considered a "child" or "relative."

Qualifying Child: An individual is considered a "***qualifying child***" of you, the taxpayer, if all of the following requirements are met:

> The individual is your son, daughter, stepchild, eligible foster child, brother, sister, half-brother, half-sister, stepbrother, stepsister, or a descendant of any of them (hmmmm, seems a bit odd that a sister, a nephew, and a whole lot more people are your "children").

> The "child" (see above) must be:
>   - Under age 19 at the end of the year, **or**
>   - Under age 24 at the end of the year and is a full-time student for some part of each of five months during the year, **or**
>   - Any age if permanently or totally disabled.

> The "child" must have, with some exceptions, lived with you for more than half of the year.

> The "child" must not have provided more than one-half of his or her own support for the year.

Qualifying Relative: An individual is considered a "***qualifying relative***" of you, the taxpayer, if all of the following requirements are met:

> The individual must be either "*related*" to you <u>or</u>, if not "related" in the Code sense, live with you (with some exceptions) for the entire year. [See IRC §§ 152(d)(2)(A)-(d)(2)(G) for definitions of "relatives" which includes everyone from children, siblings, ancestors, aunts/uncles, etc. to a host of "in-laws," and IRC § 152(d)((2)(H) for other qualifying individuals.]

> The individual must have "gross income" less than the "exemption amount" for that year (for 2018, the year of our question, this amount is $4,150).

> ➤ The taxpayer (you – the person trying to claim the individual as a dependent) must have provided more than one-half of this person's total support for the year.

Note that there are differences and areas of overlap in the definitions of a *qualifying child* and *qualifying relative*. For example, the taxpayer's "child" may fail the requirements of a "*qualifying child*" because of their age but be considered a dependent nonetheless because such child meets the requirements of a "*qualifying relative*." Also note that because of the expansive definition of a "child" under the *qualifying child* rules, the situation could arise where an individual is a *qualifying child* of more than one taxpayer (e.g., a grandchild could be a *qualifying child* of a grandparent while, at the same time, be a *qualifying child* to the child's parent). In such cases, the *qualifying child* can be claimed as a "dependent" by only one taxpayer and generally, they can agree as to which one will be entitled to claim the dependent (with "tie-breaking" rules if they cannot so agree). Also, not applicable to this question, and beyond the scope of this book, there are special rules for divorced/separated parents, multiple support arrangements, kidnapped children, and other situations.

If an individual is either a *qualifying child* or *qualifying relative* (and all of the other requirements for both are met), then that individual is your "dependent."

Finally, after all of that, we can now get back to our question. There are no problems with respect to Thian meeting the first set of requirements applicable to both a *qualifying child* and *qualifying relative*. Thian is a U.S. citizen, he is not married, and, we have no facts to indicate that "Marlo" is a dependent of someone else.

Next, we look to see if Thian is either a *qualifying child* or *qualifying relative*. Is **Thian** a *qualifying child*? The short answer is <u>no</u>. While he is a "child," lived with Marlo for more than half of the year, and he did not provide more than one-half of his own support (see below for discussion of support), he fails the "age" component: he is 27 (he is not permanently or totally disabled). It doesn't matter that he is a student because that "exception" will only carry you up to age 24. **Thian**, therefore, is <u>not</u> Marlo's *qualifying child* and, so far, he is not Marlo's dependent.

We move on to see if, in the alternative, Thian is a *qualifying relative* entitling Marlo to claim Thian as her dependent. Unfortunately for Marlo, but fortunately for Thian, he (Thian) is also not a *qualifying relative*. He is "related" (a child is considered a relative pursuant to IRC § 152(d)(2)), and Marlo provides more than one-half of Thian's support (see below) <u>but</u>, Thian does not have gross income less than the "exemption amount." To meet this requirement, Thian would have to have, in 2019, gross income less than the "exemption amount." This is all rather confusing after the TCJA, there are no personal exemptions; but there is an exemption amount. For 2018, the exemption amount was $4,150. As of this writing, the exemption amount for 2019 is not available but it is anticipated to be slightly more, perhaps $4,200. We know from Question 14, above, that Thian's gross income for 2019 is $27,000, far from being less than the estimated $4,200 for 2019. **Thian**, therefore, is also <u>not</u> Marlo's qualifying child and, with all alternatives for tax dependency spent, he is <u>not</u> Marlo's dependent.

While not really an issue in this problem, we should address the "support" requirements of both a *qualifying child* and a *qualifying relative*. It does not change our conclusion, but as we indicated, above, that Marlo does, in 2019, provide more than one-half of Thian's support. The facts indicate that "[n]otwithstanding the scholarship awarded to Thian, Marlo provided more than one-half of his support for 2019." Thian's scholarship does not count in determining the amount of support provided to him and the relative share that Marlo provides (i.e., she, as the facts indicate, furnishes more than one-half of his support – not counting the scholarship). The reason why Thian's scholarship is not factored into the support equation is because of a special provision (good testing nuance) at IRC § 152(f)(5). In general, it provides that scholarships are not counted as support if received by a son, stepson, daughter or stepdaughter of the taxpayer. If Marlo were Thian's aunt instead of his mother, then the scholarship *would* figure into the support test. Another testing nuance upon a nuance; the *scholarship*, for purposes of this support issue, need not be a "qualified scholarship" excludable by the recipient under IRC § 117 (Thian's scholarship happens to be excludable from his gross income as we saw in question 14, above).

So, after our long adventure into the world of dependents, we can now say, for certain, that Thian is not Marlo's dependent. This, in turn, takes us back to the conclusion that Thian is entitled to his $13,850 *standard deduction* for 2019. He is not relegated to the limited *standard deduction* for individuals who are dependents of another. [Please see other questions in this book that address the issue of age vis-à-vis the *standard deduction* amount as well as different or limited *standard deduction* amounts in other instances.]

Answer (a) is incorrect. This answer incorrectly reflects what is the non-applicable special *standard deduction* limiting provision of IRC § 63(c)(5). This provision is not applicable to Thian because he is not Marlo's dependent. **Answer (b) is also incorrect.** While this answer provides a better rendition of the special *standard deduction* limiting provision of IRC § 63(c)(5), this provision is not applicable in Thian's case. In addition, this answer fails to reflect the "extra" amount of standard deduction to which Thian is entitled because of his visual impairment. **Answer (c) is incorrect** because it fails to reflect the "extra" amount of standard deduction to which Thian is entitled due to his visual impairment. **Answer (d) is incorrect** because it utilizes an incorrect number for the "extra" standard deduction. While not at issue in this problem, the "extra" standard deduction amount for a married individual in 2019 is $1,300. This answer uses this improper amount as Thian's "extra" standard deduction.

23. **The correct answer is (c).** This question, and question 24 below, are the culminating questions for this series and are presented to illustrate how the many components of income and deductions fit together to calculate adjusted gross income (AGI) in this problem (and continuing to "taxable income" in problem 24). Ultimately, we will determine that Thian's AGI for 2019 is <u>$26,000</u>. It may be somewhat comforting to know that the analysis of Thian's AGI (and *taxable income* in question 24) is less complex compared to a similar question in prior editions of this book. We shall explain as we move through our analysis.

The answer to this question (and *taxable income* computation in question 24) draws upon our answers to questions 14, 15, and 17 through 22. While we are computing Thian's AGI in this question, we will consider the entire *taxable income* framework.

The computation framework for taxable income is as follows:

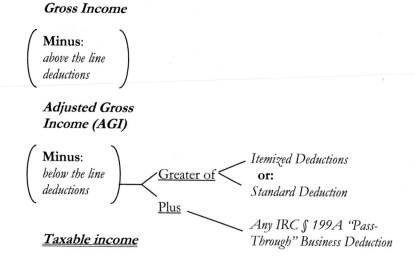

It should be noted that the calculation of *taxable income* has changed since the prior editions of this book. *The Tax Cuts and Jobs Act* (TCJA) signed into law in December 2017 (generally effective beginning in 2018) removed one "category" of deductions (personal exemption(s)) and added, for some business-related activities, another category of deductions (the so-called "pass-through" deduction). In class, this professor also explains the computation of *taxable income* in a **six-step** approach as follows:

Step 1:   Determine what is included in the taxpayer's *Gross Income* (This reflects all income and exclusions therefrom.)

Step 2:   Determine the taxpayer's *Adjusted Gross Income (AGI)* (This requires subtracting from *Gross income* any deductions that are allowed *above the line* pursuant to IRC § 62; Appendix A for more information.)

Step 3:   Determine the total amount of the taxpayer's *Itemized Deductions* (This requires applying any applicable limitations, floors, or restrictions for certain types of these deductions; see Appendix A for more information.)

Step 4:   Determine the amount of the taxpayer's *Standard Deduction* (This is year-specific and varies by filing status, age, degree of visual impairment, and limitations for certain dependents.)

Step 5:   Determine the amount of any available TCJA *IRC § 199A Pass-Through business-related deduction.*

(In prior editions of this book, and pre-TCJA law, this step used to be determining the amount of the taxpayer's *Personal Exemption Deduction(s)*. Under the TCJA, these deductions have been eliminated for 2018-2025)

Step 6:   Compute *Taxable Income* by subtracting from AGI (amount in Step 2):
  1) Either *itemized deductions* (amount in **Step 3**), or the *standard deduction* (amount in **Step 4**), whichever is the **greater** of the two, **and**
  2) Any *IRC § 199A Pass-Through business-related deduction* (amount in **Step 5**).

As indicated, we are concerned with AGI in this question and we begin with step one, determining Thian's "gross income." Thian's *gross income* was calculated in problem 14, above, as $27,000. Recall that this was derived from Thian's $27,000 in wages for 2019. He was not required to include, in gross income, the $30,000 law school scholarship pursuant to IRC § 117.

We now turn to the issue of deductions. In previous questions in this series, we identified the following possible deductions for Thian:

Question 15: Possible deduction for *qualified tuition and related expenses* for amount Thian paid for law school tuition paid and room/board. IRC §222.

Question 17: Possible IRC § 221 deduction for *interest on education loans.*

Question 18: Possible IRC § 164 deduction for *taxes paid* (his state income tax of $1,000 and intangibles tax of $800).

Question 19: Possible IRC § 213 deduction for *qualified medical care expenses* (the veterinary fees for his Seeing Eye dog).

Question 20: Possible IRC § 170 deduction for *charitable contributions.*

Question 21: Possible IRC § 162 deduction for *business expenses* (associated with his paralegal job).

Question 22: Possible IRC § 63 *standard deduction.*

Determination of Thian's *AGI* (step two in our taxable income calculation) requires that we first identify which of the above possible deductions are allowed in its computation. Recall that deductions are basically divided into two camps: the so-called *above the line* deductions (for computing *AGI*) and the *below the line* deductions (subtracted from *AGI* to arrive at *taxable income*). IRC § 62 is the "signpost" section that lists those deductions that are available for computing *AGI*. This is the origin of the terms *above the line* deductions and those that are allowed *below the line*. The **line** is AGI (it is, literally, a line on an individual's tax return).

For Thian, he one or two possible *above the line* deductions: IRC § 222 (*qualified tuition and related expenses*) and IRC § 221, (*interest on education loans*). Calculating Thian's "actual" deductions for these three items can be a challenging task, and each of the two possible deductions will be analyzed separately; beginning with IRC § 222 which corresponds to question 15 in this set.

IRC § 222 Qualified Tuition and Related Expenses

This comes from earlier question 15 and, as mentioned in the answer analysis for that question, in earlier editions of this book, this was a very complex issue. Recall, however, that now we do not have much to do here as neither of his two education-related expenditures (tuition or room & board) give rise to any deductions for Thian. **Therefore, we have no** deduction, either *above* or *below* the line, to consider in computing Thian's AGI (or, later, his *taxable income*).

IRC § 222 **was** a good section for students as it provided a deduction, up to a certain amount (generally $4,000 per year) for "qualified tuition and expenses." The section was rather complex (as was the explanation to this answer in prior editions) and required numerous calculations that affected the amount of the deduction depending on the taxpayer's level of income. The deduction allowed by IRC § 222 was an *above the line* deduction and if the section was still in force, we would have computed Thian's deduction and taken it here in computing his AGI. The IRC § 222 deduction expired at the end of 2017 and while there has been some congressional discussion of reinstating it, as of this writing, there is little hope of this happening. The actual section still appears in the Code in all of its past glory, but it is all for naught as stated in IRC § 222(e) "Termination. – This section shall not apply to taxable years beginning after December 31, 2017."

If the section was still applicable, we would have found that the $10,000 Thian paid in tuition would have entitled him to a $4,000 deduction. Again, this would have been an *above the line* deduction that would come into play here in computing his AGI.

We did see, in question 16, that the tuition paid may give rise to a credit; the *lifetime learning credit*. While a credit is very valuable in actually reducing an individual's tax liability, it does not factor in to calculating an individual's AGI or *taxable income*. Deductions are reflected in computing, ultimately, *taxable income*, upon which a preliminary tax is based (and credits reduce the actual tax). Thian gets no deduction for these costs so we have nothing to consider in this question or question 24 where we are computing his AGI and *taxable income*, respectively. His expenditure for tuition does, however, help him out tax-wise but that is in the form of a tax-reducing credit (which is not part of this question or question 24).

IRC § 221 Interest on Education Loans

In 2019, Thian paid $1,000 in interest on his undergraduate student loans (used for tuition). IRC § 221 is a complex section with many requirements and was discussed at some length in question 17, above. Recall that once we determined that the loans involved were "qualified educational loans" the statute imposes two important limitations regarding the deduction of this interest: a $2,500 maximum interest deduction, and a "phase-out" of the deduction for taxpayers making over a certain threshold amount of income. Thian's $1,000 in interest paid does not exceed the statutory maximum. At this point, however, we need to determine if Thian's deduction is affected by the "phase-out" mechanism.

Referring to question 17, above, this "phase-out" starts for single individuals with *AGI* (as modified) of $70,000 (for 2019). Recall that the statute uses the term "modified adjusted gross income" because true *AGI* will ultimately reflect any deduction allowed for education interest under IRC § 221. "Modified adjusted gross income" (or MAGI) is defined in IRC § 221(b)(2)(c) as sort of a "pretend" *AGI* amount. *MAGI* is *AGI* before considering this possible IRC § 221 interest deduction <u>and</u> the possible IRC § 222 education expense deduction (which is now zero beginning in 2018 but had been based on a different *MAGI* permutation). [Not relevant now, but in prior editions of this book we would have first discussed Thian's possible IRC § 221 deduction <u>before</u> we would have discussed his possible deduction under IRC § 222. When an individual had both of these possible deductions, as did Thian in prior editions of this book, the code requires a certain order of computation – different *MAGI's* if you prefer – and the IRC § 221 deduction is computed before that in IRC § 222.]

Now back to Thian's situation and *MAGI*. Without regard to IRC § 221 (or the now defunct IRC § 222, his AGI would be $27,000. This is his $27,000 of gross income less, so far, no pertinent *above the line* deductions. This $27,000 is Thian's *MAGI* for purposes of determining his possible student loan interest deduction under IRC § 221. Again, the phase-out for single individuals (for 2019) starts at $70,000 of *MAGI* (and is fully eliminated when *MAGI* reaches $85,000). Thian's *MAGI* is well below the start of the phase-out range. Therefore, Thian is entitled to an *above the line* deduction for the full $1,000 of student loan interest he paid in 2019.

Thian's Real *AGI*

We now have all of the necessary component parts to compute Thian's actual *AGI*. Thian's *AGI*, for 2019, is $26,000 computed as follows:

$ 27,000	Gross Income
($ 1,000)	Student loan interest deduction (IRC § 221)
($ 0)	Higher education expense deduction (IRC § 222)
$ 26,000	**Adjusted Gross Income (*AGI*)**

Answers (a), (b), and (d) are all incorrect because none of these answers reflects the proper computation of Thian's *AGI*. **Answer (e) is incorrect** because a correct answer (a) is presented.

24. **The correct answer to is this comprehensive question is (a).** This question represents the culmination for this series of questions: computation of taxable income. Understandably, this is a difficult question to present in a multiple-choice format, as it draws upon the answers to many

of the previous questions. It is presented, nonetheless, to illustrate how the many components of income and deductions fit together to calculate *taxable income*. Ultimately, we will determine that Thian's *taxable income* for 2019 is **$12,150.**

It may be somewhat comforting to know that the analysis of Thian's *taxable income* is less complex compared to a similar question in prior editions of this book. We shall explain as we move through our analysis.

The answer to this question (and *taxable income* computation in question 24) draws upon our answers to questions 14, 15, and 17 through 23. Reproduced again, is the computational framework for *taxable income*.

The answer to this question draws upon our answers to questions 11 through 13, and 15 through 23.

Gross Income

$\left(\begin{array}{l} \textbf{Minus:} \\ \textit{above the line} \\ \textit{deductions} \end{array} \right)$

Adjusted Gross Income (AGI)

$\left(\begin{array}{l} \textbf{Minus:} \\ \textit{below the line} \\ \textit{deductions} \end{array} \right)$ — Greater of — *Itemized Deductions*
or:
Standard Deduction

Plus — *Any IRC § 199A "Pass-Through" Business Deduction*

Taxable income

It should be noted that the calculation of *taxable income* has changed since the prior editions of this book. *The Tax Cuts and Jobs Act* (TCJA) signed into law in December 2017 (generally effective beginning in 2018) removed one "category" of deductions (personal exemption(s)) and added, for some business-related activities, another category of deductions (the so-called "pass-through" deduction). In class, this professor also explains the computation of *taxable income* in a **six-step** approach as follows:

Step 1:   Determine what is included in the taxpayer's *Gross Income* (This reflects all income and exclusions therefrom.)

Step 2:   Determine the taxpayer's *Adjusted Gross Income (AGI)*

(This requires subtracting from *Gross income* any deductions that are allowed *above the line* pursuant to IRC § 62; Appendix A for more information.)

Step 3:   Determine the total amount of the taxpayer's *Itemized Deductions* (This requires applying any applicable limitations, floors, or restrictions for certain types of these deductions; see Appendix A for more information.)

Step 4:   Determine the amount of the taxpayer's *Standard Deduction* (This is year-specific and varies by filing status, age, degree of visual impairment, and limitations for certain dependents.)

Step 5:   Determine the amount of any available TCJA *IRC § 199A Pass-Through business-related deduction*.

    (In prior editions of this book, and pre-TCJA law, this step used to be determining the amount of the taxpayer's *Personal Exemption Deduction(s)*. Under the TCJA, these deductions have been eliminated for 2018-2025)

Step 6:   Compute *Taxable Income* by subtracting from AGI (amount in Step 2):
    1)   Either *itemized deductions* (amount in **Step 3**), or the *standard deduction* (amount in **Step 4**), whichever is the **greater** of the two, **and**
    2)   Any *IRC § 199A Pass-Through business-related deduction* (amount in **Step 5**).

Question 23, above, addressed the complicated calculation of Thian's 2019 *AGI*, "Step Two" in our *taxable income* computation. We determined Thian's *AGI* for 2019 to be <u>$26.000</u> computed as follows:

```
$ 27,000   Gross Income
($ 1,000)  Student loan interest deduction (IRC § 221)
($      0) Higher education expense deduction (IRC § 222)
 $ 26,000  Adjusted Gross Income (AGI)
```

We will now proceed through the remaining steps (3 through 6) to calculate Thian's *taxable income*.

Step 3 – *Itemized Deductions*

Referring to the computational framework of computing *taxable income*, above, itemized deductions, as a group, are to be compared with the *standard deduction*. The taxpayer, in computing *taxable income* will take the greater of these two, plus any IRC § 199A *Pass-Through business-related deduction).* All of these deductions are known as *below the line* deductions. Looking back to the analysis of question 23 (and questions 12, 13, 15-22), we identified Thian's possible deductions as follows:

Question 15:   Possible deduction for *qualified tuition and related expenses* for amount Thian paid for law school tuition paid and room/board. IRC §222.

Question 17:   Possible IRC § 221 deduction for *interest on education loans.*

Question 18:   Possible IRC § 164 deduction for *taxes paid* (his state income tax of $1,000 and intangibles tax of $800).

Question 19:   Possible IRC § 213 deduction for *qualified medical care expenses* (the veterinary fees for his Seeing Eye dog).

Question 20:   Possible IRC § 170 deduction for *charitable contributions.*

Question 21:   Possible IRC § 162 deduction for *business expenses* (associated with his paralegal job).

Question 22:   Possible IRC § 63 *standard deduction.*

In determining Thian's *AGI,* we dispensed with two possible deductions: IRC § 221 student loan interest (from question 17) and IRC § 222 higher education expenses (from question 15). Thian's *standard deduction* (from question 22) and any available TCJA *IRC § 199A Pass-Through business-related deduction* are addressed below in Steps 4 and 5, respectively. By process of elimination, the deductions that may be part of Thian's *itemized deductions* are the following:

- The $1,000 state income tax paid (IRC § 164 – from question 18).
- The $800 in state intangibles tax paid (IRC § 164 – from question 18).
- The $4,000 in qualified medical care expenses (IRC § 213 – from question 19).
- The $3,000 in charitable contributions (IRC § 170 – from question 20).
- The $600 in business expenses paid (IRC § 162 – from question 21).

Some of the deductions that comprise *itemized deductions* are subject to various limitations as discussed in each of the questions dealing with a particular deduction. A summary and calculation of each component of Thian's *itemized deductions* follows.

State Income and Intangibles Taxes

Pursuant to the *Tax Cuts and Jobs Act* (TCJA) signed into law in December 2017 (generally effective beginning in 2018), these IRC § 164 deductions (often referred to as "SALT;" state and local taxes) are subject to a $10,000 aggregate cap. Thian's $1,000 and $800 expenditures for state income and intangibles tax, respectively ($1,800 total), is well below the TCJA's SALT cap, so his $1,800 total will be part of Thian's *itemized deductions*. [Please see other questions in this book where the SALT cap is implicated.]

Qualified Medical Care Expenses

Pursuant to IRC § 213, these expenses are deductible only to the extent that they exceed 10% of the taxpayer's *AGI* (see question 19 above). This is known as the 10% of AGI "floor" and for Thian, his IRC § 213 actual medical deduction is:

$4,000   Qualifying medical care expenses
($2,600) 10% of Thian's *AGI* (.10 x $26,000)
$1,400   **Thian's Actual Medical Deduction**

Charitable Contributions

As discussed in question 20, above, the deduction for most cash charitable contributions is limited (a ceiling) to 60% of a taxpayer's *AGI*. 60% of Thian's $26,000 AGI is $15,600. Because Thian's $3,000 in charitable contributions do not exceed this ceiling, the full $3,000 will be part of Thian's *itemized deductions*.

Business Expenses

As discussed in question 21, above, the qualifying requirements for legitimate IRC § 162 business expenses are the same for individuals engaged in business on a self-employed basis (independent contractor, unincorporated sole proprietorship, etc.) or engaged in business as an employee. For self-employed individuals, IRC § 162 business expenses are allowed as an *above the line* deduction. For employees, such business expenses were allowed *below the line*, subject to a certain % of AGI floor (similar to medical expenses, above). In prior editions of this book, we would go through these calculations. Now, however, this is no longer necessary. As indicated in the analysis of question 21 (and other questions in this book), the TCJA **eliminated** (for 2018-2025) deductions of otherwise valid IRC § 162 business expenses when incurred by **employees**. Thian, in our question, incurred these qualifying IRC § 162 business expenses as an employee and, therefore, is not entitled to any deduction. His $600 in business expenses for 2019 will **not** be part of his itemized deductions.

Thian's Total *Itemized Deductions* for 2019
His total itemized deductions, after applying any applicable limits and restrictions, is $5,500 computed as follows:

$1,800	State income and intangibles taxes
$1,400	Medical care expense deduction
$3,000	Charitable contributions
$ 0	IRC § 162 Business expense deduction
$6,200	**Thian's Itemized deductions Total**

Step 4 – Thian's *Standard Deduction*
Thian's *standard deduction* was computed in question 22, above. Recall that his *standard deduction* for 2019 is **$13,850**. The regular *standard deduction* amount for a single individual (for 2019) is $12,200. However, recall that because of Thian's visual imparity, he is entitled to increase the regular *standard deduction* by $1,650 (for 2019).

Step 5 – Thian's available TCJA *IRC § 199A Pass-Through business-related deduction.*
As indicated above, in prior editions of this book, and pre-TCJA law, this step used to be determining the amount of the taxpayer's *Personal Exemption Deduction(s)*. Under the TCJA, the *personal exemption deduction(s)* have been eliminated for 2018-2025).

Other questions in this book discuss, in some detail, the new TCJA IRC §199A so called *Pass-Through* deduction for certain business-related entities. This is a separate *below the line* deduction (independent from regular IRC § 162 business deductions) for certain business operating as partnerships, LLC's, S Corporations, and come unincorporated sole proprietorships. Thian's job an employee is not one to which this *pass-through* deduction is applicable. If Thian was operating his own business, then we would go through the extremely complex rules to determine the availability of any such IRC § 199A deduction (the law is so complex that it took over a year from enactment for the Treasury to give guidance as to how to apply the new rules; with some items remaining to be completely fleshed out). Thian has no deduction in this area for 2019.

Step 6 – Putting it All Together – Thian's *Taxable Income* for 2019

Applying this **six-step** computation approach to Thian, we have the following:

Step 1: *Gross income* = $27,000
Step 2: *Adjusted gross income (AGI)* = $26,000
Step 3: *Itemized deductions* = $6,200
Step 4: *Standard deduction* = $13,850
Step 5: *§ 199A pass-through deduction* = $0
Step 6: **Taxable income** = $26,000 (AGI)

§199A pass-through ded.	($ 13,850)	The **greater of:** $6,200
	($ 0)	*Itemized,* **or**
	$ 12,150	$13,850 *Standard Deduction*

A visual depiction of Thian's *taxable income* computation for 2019 is as follows:

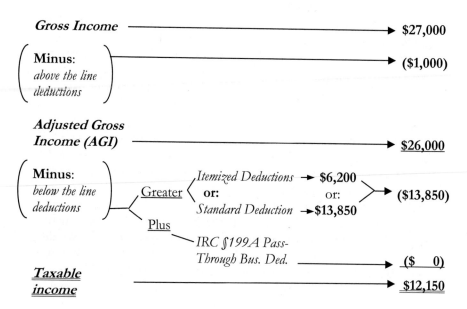

Gross Income ──────────────▶ **$27,000**

Minus:
above the line deductions ──────────────▶ **($1,000)**

Adjusted Gross Income (AGI) ──────────────▶ **$26,000**

Minus:
below the line deductions

Greater {
Itemized Deductions ▶ **$6,200**
or:
Standard Deduction ▶**$13,850**
} or: ──▶ **($13,850)**

Plus

IRC *§199A Pass-Through Bus. Ded.* ──────────────▶ **($ 0)**

Taxable income ──────────────▶ **$12,150**

Answers (b) through (d) are all incorrect because none of these answers reflects the proper computation of Thian's *taxable income*. **Answer (e) is incorrect** because a correct answer (a) is presented.

25. The best answer to this somewhat tricky question is (a). IRC § 213 allows for a deduction of certain qualified medical care expenses. Once one makes the determination of what constitutes "qualified" medical care expenses, the subject of this question, the deduction is allowed as an "itemized deduction" only to the extent that the total qualifying expenses exceeds 10% of adjusted gross income (AGI). Qualified medical care expenses include typical costs for doctors, dentists, hospital, health insurance, and the like. [See IRC § 213(d).] The section specifically provides, in IRC § 213(a), that qualifying medical care expenses are those paid by the taxpayer for the taxpayer, his or her spouse, or <u>a dependent (as defined in IRC § 152, . . .)</u>.

The costs for Thian's doctor visits clearly qualify as medical care expenses. However, is Marlo entitled to deduct them? Is Thian Marlo's "dependent (as defined in IRC § 152, . . .)? Looking back at Question 22 of this series, you may be inclined to say <u>no</u> because in that question, we determined that Thian was not Marlo's dependent (we were determining Thian's *standard deduction* and dependency status would have impacted our analysis). Indeed, we found that Thian was <u>neither</u> a *qualifying child* nor *a qualifying relative*.

So how, you might ask, did we come up with the answer that Marlo is entitled to deduct Thian's medical expenses that she paid. Pursuant to IRC § 213 doesn't Thian have to be her dependent for this? Well, the answer is yes and no. This professor is not fond of reading parenthetical comments, but as a student, you should not do as this professor and you should carefully read all parenthetical comments. The answer to this question lies in such a parenthetical comment. Back to IRC § 213(a) and reference to the <u>full</u> parenthetical text: The section specifically provides, in IRC § 213(a), that qualifying medical care expenses are those paid by the taxpayer for the taxpayer, his or her spouse, or <u>a dependent (as defined in IRC § 152, **determined without regard to subsections** (b)(1), (b)(2), and **(d)(1)(B)** thereof)</u>.

This requires some very careful reading and takes us back to the definition of a *qualifying relative* in IRC § 152(d). Recall, from other questions in this book, the requirements of a *qualifying relative*:

> **Qualifying Relative:** An individual is considered a "***qualifying relative***" of you, the taxpayer, if all of the following requirements are met:
> > ➤ The individual must be either "*related*" to you <u>or</u>, if not "related" in the Code sense, live with you (with some exceptions) for the entire year. [See IRC §§ 152(d)(2)(A)-(d)(2)(G) for definitions of "relatives" which includes everyone from children, siblings,

> ancestors, aunts/uncles, etc. to a host of "in-laws," and IRC § 152(d)((2)(H) for other qualifying individuals.]

> ➤ *The individual must have "gross income" less than the "exemption amount" for that year.*

> ➤ The taxpayer (you, the person trying to claim the individual as a dependent) must have provided more than one-half of this person's total support for the year.

Emphasis has been added to the "gross income" requirement of a *qualifying relative*. In Question 22 of this series, we determined that Thian was not a *qualifying relative* (and, therefore not Marlo's dependent) because he failed this "gross income" requirement; his $27,000 gross income was not close to being less than the "exemption amount" (estimated to be $4,200 for 2019). Also recall, however, that in Question 22 of this series, we found that Thian did meet the other two requirements (being "related" to Marlo and Marlo providing more than one-half of Thian's support). Back to IRC § 213(a) where it specifically provides that qualifying medical care expenses are those paid by the taxpayer for the taxpayer, his or her spouse, or <u>a dependent (as defined in IRC § 152, **determined without regard to subsections** (b)(1), (b)(2), and **(d)(1)(B)** thereof)</u>. Subsection (d)(1)(B) of IRC § 152 **is** the "gross income" test that Thian failed as a *qualifying relative*. And now we have our answer. Once we ignore the fact that Thian did "not have gross income less than the exemption amount" he would have been Marlo's dependent (as a *qualifying relative*). So, for purposes of IRC § 213(a) and deducting Thian's medical care costs, Thian <u>is</u> Marlo's dependent.

In summary, Marlo's payments for Thian's doctor bills qualify as medical care expenses for purposes of determining Marlo's medical deduction under IRC § 213.

Answer (b) is not correct because for purposes of IRC § 213 medical deductions, Thian does not really have to be either a *qualifying child* or *qualifying relative*. Marlo is entitled to treat Thian as her dependent, for IRC § 213 purposes, nonetheless. **Answer (c) is not correct** because you cannot just get a medical deduction for paying anyone's medical bills. Here Thian must qualify as Marlo's dependent under the special rules for IRC § 213 (the special version of the IRC § 152 dependency rules) in order for Marlo to deduct the medical care expenses she paid for Thian. **Answer (d) is not correct** because Marlo need not be entitled to claim Thian's as her dependent on her tax return. For IRC § 213, we have a special, more lenient definition of who qualifies as a dependent for medical care expenses paid for another.

1. **The correct response is (d).** Many years ago, the concept of the "standard deduction" was introduced into tax law as a means of reducing an individual's record-keeping needs. The *standard deduction* may be taken in place of a group of deductions known collectively as "itemized deductions." Probably the most commonly known components of this latter group of *itemized deductions* include charitable contributions, deductible interest and taxes, and qualifying medical deductions. Taxpayers have a choice: deduct either 1) the total of itemized deductions (after applying all necessary limits and restrictions as discussed elsewhere in this book), **or** 2) the *standard deduction* amount. In calculating "taxable income," a taxpayer takes as a deduction the <u>greater</u> of these two. [Please see Appendix A for more information about *where* these deductions fit within the framework of calculating taxable income.]

    IRC § 63(c) is the focal point for the *standard deduction.* The amount of this *standard deduction* can vary greatly from taxpayer to taxpayer depending on various factors including marital or filing status, age, degree of visual imparity, and whether the taxpayer is a "dependent" of another. In addition, *standard deduction* amounts are subject to change each tax year (and for the most part, do change each year) based on adjustments for "inflation" (i.e., the standard deduction amounts are *indexed* for inflation). The various *standard deduction* amounts identified in the statute (throughout IRC § 63 either listed in dollars or instructions for computation) are <u>not</u> the actual amounts for the current year but, rather, are pre-inflation adjusted "base" amounts (that are well below the actual current amounts). [Appendix B contains the various *standard deduction* amounts for the year 2019 (the most current at the time of this printing).]

    A highly touted component of the *Tax Cuts and Jobs Act* (TCJA) signed into law in December 2017 (generally effective beginning in 2018), was a substantial increase in the *standard deduction* amounts (beginning in 2018). For 2019, the "regular" *standard deduction* for a single individual is $12,200 (corresponding to the special TCJA 2018-2025 statutory amount of $12,000 which is unadjusted for inflation). For couples filing a joint return, the 2019 standard deduction is $24,400 (corresponding to the computed 200% of the single special TCJA 2018-2025 statutory amount of $12,000 which is unadjusted for inflation). There are other standard deductions for other filing status' not applicable for this question).

    The *standard deduction* is **increased** for certain individuals based on age or visual imparity. [IRC § 63(b)(3).] For 2019, taxpayers age 65 and older (as of the end of the taxable year) are entitled to an extra $1,300 per qualifying individual when married and filing a joint return. This $1,300 for 2019 corresponds to the unadjusted for inflation amount of $600 listed in IRC § 63(f)(1). [See Appendix B for the 2019 *standard deduction* "extra amounts" for other classifications of individuals.] Both Susan and Wally are the requisite age and they are **each** entitled and extra $1,300 *standard deduction* amount ($2,600 extra in total). Therefore, *standard deduction* for 2019 is **$27,000** ($24,400 + $1,300 + $1,300).

[Please see other questions in this book that address the issue of visual imparity vis-à-vis the *standard deduction* amount as well as different or limited *standard deduction* amounts in other instances.]

Answer (a) is incorrect because is the pre-TCJA, unadjusted for inflation amount listed in IRC § 63 for a married couple. **Answer (b) is incorrect** because while it has the correct base, statutory TCJA *standard deduction* amount for a married couple, it fails to reflect the adjustment for inflation, Also it fails to reflect the extra *standard deduction* to which both of our taxpayers are entitled base on their respective ages. **Answer (c) is incorrect** because while it is the proper inflation-adjusted 2019 *standard deduction* for a married couple, it fails to reflect that our couple is entitled to <u>two</u> of the extra $1,300 amounts (for 2019) because they are both ages 65 or older. **Answer (e) is incorrect** because a correct answer (d) is presented.

2. **The correct answer (a).** The *Tax Cuts and Jobs Act* (TCJA), signed into law in December 2017 (generally effective beginning in 2018) brought many tax law changes to both individuals and corporations. Our focus, of course, are the changes affecting individuals. A flagship component of the TCJA was a so called "Pass-Through" deduction for certain businesses. IRC § 199A was newly added by the TCJA and is the source of this new deduction. This is an exceptionally complex piece of legislation and this subject may be covered in varying degrees in your basic federal income tax course (from mentioning it in passing to a comprehensive study of the provisions). This question is designed to give you some idea of this new *pass-through* deduction works and where it all fits in the grand scheme of calculating an individual's *taxable income*. <u>After much introduction, we will conclude that Susan's law practice will generate a $14,000 IRC § 199A *pass-through* deduction</u>.

It is important to understand what this deduction is and where it fits in determining *taxable income*. This *pass-through* deduction is not a regular IRC § 162 business expense deduction. Regular business deductions are covered in many other questions in this book and the core section for them, IRC § 162, has not changed much over the years. For a self-employed individual, these traditional business deductions are often referred to as *above the line* deductions and are utilized in computing one's net profit from one's business. In our question, we are already given this net profit for her law practice ($70,000), this being her gross income from her business less traditional IRC § 162 business expenses. This TCJA *pass-through* deduction is something new and is **not** an actual business deduction in determining Susan's net profit from her law practice. Rather, it is an extra, add-on *below the line* deduction taken after (and in addition to) the deduction for the greater of *itemized deductions* or the *standard deduction*.

A visual depiction of *taxable income* may be helpful (we have seen this in numerous questions in this book):

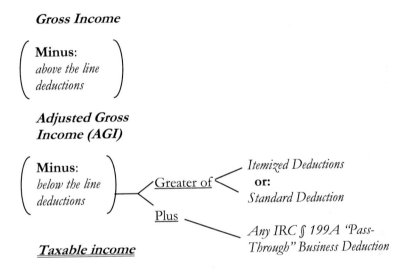

Note the placement of the IRC § 199A *pass-through* deduction. As indicated, the computation of this deduction can be extraordinarily complex. It took the Treasury over one year to issue guidance for this section (with some intricate questions left unanswered).

To qualify for a *pass-through* deduction, one must be operating their business in a proper form. These include:

- A self-employed business (also known as an unincorporated sole proprietorship or someone who is working as an independent contractor).
- A partnership
- A limited liability partnership (LLP)
- An S-Corporation
- A limited liability corporation (LLC)

Susan's unincorporated sole proprietorship meets this first test. There was some confusion surrounding the "naming" of the IRC § 199A as a *pass-through* deduction because the word "pass-through" is normally associated only with the latter four types of entities listed above.

The basic *pass-through* deduction is a flat 20% of such business's "qualified business income" (QBI). The definition of QBI can be very complex and an in-depth discussion is well beyond the scope of this question. It can become especially difficult when an individual has more than one business. Fortunately for Susan, and us, she has only one business (her law practice) and the definition of QBI for her purposes is simple; the net profit from her business. We already know this for Susan's law practice; her net profit (and her QBI for the *pass-through* calculation) is given at $70,000. Remember, this **net** $70,000 figure already reflects her regular IRC § 162 business deductions.

The **tentative** *pass-through* deduction for Susan's law practice is 20% of her $70,000 (QBI), or **$14,000**. We will ultimately determine that this will be her actual IRC § 199A *pass-through* deduction (and we will reflect this in question 4 where we compute the couple's *taxable income*). Before we can label this the correct answer, we must consider some important limitations and special rules for the IRC § 199A deduction.

There is a *taxable income* limitation in IRC § 199A(a) that the *pass-through deduction* cannot exceed 20% of an individual's (or couple's) *taxable income* (i.e., there is a 20% of *taxable income* cap for this deduction). Right away you will notice we are in somewhat of a conundrum. If the *pass-through* deduction is one that will ultimately determine *taxable income*, how can we compute this 20% *taxable income* cap for the deduction? Subsection (e) comes to the rescue and defines *taxable income* for purposes of determining the *pass-through* deduction as a "pretend" *taxable income* without regard to any *pass-through* deduction. We now have to effectively compute Susan and Wally's *taxable income* as if IRC § 199A did not exist. Fortunately for us, the calculation, while taking up some space in our analysis, is not too bad. We'll call it their ***"pretend taxable income."***

We shall borrow an abbreviated visual depiction of their *taxable income* from other questions in this book and explain the items below.

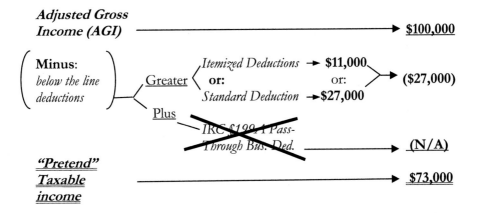

The couple's AGI is comprised of Wally's $10,000 in wages, plus, their $20,000 in regular bank interest, plus Susan's **net** profit of $70,000 from her law practice for a total of $100,000. We don't have the detailed figures comprising Susan's $70,000 net profit but if we were being technical, her business's gross revenues would be included in gross income and her regular IRC § 162 business expenses would be *above the line* deductions. Therefore, this abbreviated "pretend" *taxable income* appears in truncated form (missing gross income and *above the line* deductions); but, we get to the same place for AGI.

We know, from question 1, in this set, that the couple's *standard deduction* is $27,000 for 2019 (the regular *standard deduction* for a married couple plus two extra amounts because of their age – see question 1 for a more thorough analysis. We have not addressed the couple's itemized deductions for 2019, but the only possible one indicated is their $11,000 charitable contribution. We will discuss this more thoroughly in question 4 of this set but suffice it to say, this represents their total itemized deductions for 2019. For *taxable income* computations (real or "pretend"), we would select the greater of their $27,000 *standard deduction* or *itemized deductions* of $11,000 in their case. Clearly, their *standard deduction* is the greater of the two.

At this point, we can finalize our computation of their "pretend" *taxable income*. Recall that we are doing this to make sure that their tentative $14,000 *pass-through* deduction does not exceed the 20% of *taxable income* cap. So let's check the limitation. The 20% of "pretend *taxable income*" of $73,000 equals $14,600. Recall that we calculated the couple's tentative *pass-through* deduction to be $14,000. This means that their tentative $14,000 *pass-through* deduction is not limited by this provision. Alas, we still have more to discuss.

If a taxpayer has income above certain thresholds, then the *pass-through* deduction is reduced and, potentially eliminated. Fortunately, these thresholds are well beyond Susan and Wally's level of income, so we need not delve into the morass of this area. For information, the 2019 beginning threshold of *taxable income* that would cause concern is $321,400 for a married couple ($160,700 for a single individual). Above these levels, the *pass-through deduction* is phased-out or limited.

There is another component to determining the *pass-through* deduction that has been the source of much confusion and misunderstanding. The IRC § 199A *pass-through* deduction distinguishes between different types of business activities. Individuals engaged in a "specified service trade or business" (SSTB) are not favored business activities for the deduction. Generally, if one's business consists primarily providing services, it is an SSTB. Not an exhaustive list, but they include: attorneys, accountants, doctors, dentists, other health-related fields, performing arts, consulting, athletics, financial services, and the like. When the TCJA enacted IRC § 199A, many thought that net income from these service businesses would not qualify for the new *pass-through* deduction. This may have come from a quick reading of the statute where *qualified business income* (QBI, upon which the deduction is based) does not include income from SSTB's (see IRC § 199(d)(1)). Reading deeper into the statute, one finds that this is not really the case unless a taxpayer has income above certain threshold amount (amounts a certain amount above those previously discussed). Non SSTB's may still be entitled to an IRC § 199A *pass-through* deduction even when net income exceeds the various thresholds (whereas, it is phased-out and eventually eliminated for SSTB's who hit the threshold income levels). Super clear, yes?

Susan's business is clearly a "specified service trade or business" (SSTB) but because their income does not come close to beginning of the phase-out amount ($321,400 for their 2019 joint return), her law practice's net income counts at QBI and the couple is entitled to a *pass-through* deduction.

Now we come to our conclusion. Susan's $70,000 of net income from her law practice is qualified business income (they're income is not high enough to be affected by the SSTB thresholds). Also the 20% general deduction (20% of $70,000, or $14,000) does not run afoul of the 20% of "pretend taxable income" cap (see above), so this brings us to our answer that she is entitled to a **$14,000** IRC § 199A *pass-through* deduction in computing taxable income.

Please see question 4 where we see how this is reflected when we compute the couple's "real" *taxable income*.

Answers (b) and (c) are incorrect because, as discussed above, neither of these accurately reflect the law. **Answer (d) is incorrect** because it is the wrong amount (the amount indicated in this answer is 20% of their *pretend taxable income* and not 20% of her net business income. **Answer (e) is incorrect** because a correct answer is presented in (a).

3. **The correct answer (c).** This question is almost identical to question 2, above, but with one slight twist. It would be unfair, in an actual objective exam, to ask to such closely related questions when they would both involve an in-depth analysis, plus this professor does not like to ask questions where the answer to one is dependent on determining the correct answer in another question. In this book, however, this question is designed to assist in understanding the law. This answer analysis will be, in many parts, repetitive from that for question 2, above. We will ultimately determine that Susan's business will generate a $13,600 IRC § 199A *pass-through* deduction for 2019

The *Tax Cuts and Jobs Act* (TCJA), signed into law in December 2017 (generally effective in 2018) brought many tax law changes to both individuals and corporations. Our focus, of course, are the changes affecting individuals. A flagship component of the TCJA was a so called "Pass-Through" deduction for certain businesses. IRC § 199A was newly added by the TCJA and is the source of this new deduction. This is an exceptionally complex piece of legislation and this subject may be covered in varying degrees in your basic federal income tax course (from mentioning it in passing to a comprehensive study of the provisions). This question is designed to give you some idea of this new *pass-through* deduction works and where it all fits in the grand scheme of calculating an individual's *taxable income*. After much introduction, we will conclude that Susan's law practice will generate a $13,600 IRC § 199A *pass-through* deduction. This is, in comparison to the deduction in question 2, above, $400 less than the $14,000 for that question.

It is important to understand what this deduction is and where it fits in determining *taxable income*. This *pass-through* deduction is not a regular IRC § 162 business expense deduction. Regular business deductions are covered in many other questions in this book and the core section for them, IRC § 162, has not changed much over the years. For a self-employed individual, these traditional business deductions are often referred to as *above the line* deductions and are utilized in computing one's net profit from one's business. In our question, we are already given this net profit for her law practice ($70,000), this being her gross income from her business less traditional IRC § 162 business expenses. This TCJA *pass-through* deduction is something new and is **not** an actual business deduction in determining Susan's net profit from her law practice. Rather, it is an extra, add-on *below the line* deduction taken after (and in addition to) the deduction for the greater of *itemized deductions* or the *standard deduction*.

A visual depiction of *taxable income* may be helpful (we have seen this in numerous questions in this book):

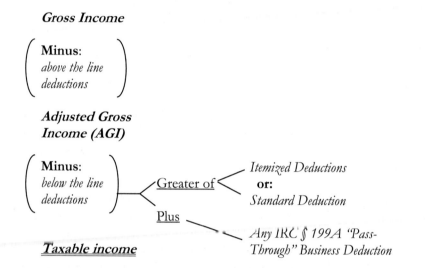

Note the placement of the IRC § 199A *pass-through* deduction. As indicated, the computation of this deduction can be extraordinarily complex. It took the Treasury over one year to issue guidance for this section (with some intricate questions left unanswered).

To qualify for a *pass-through* deduction, one must be operating their business in a proper form. These include:

- A self-employed business (also known as an unincorporated sole proprietorship or someone who is working as an independent contractor).
- A partnership
- A limited liability partnership (LLP)
- An S-Corporation
- A limited liability corporation (LLC)

Susan's unincorporated sole proprietorship meets this first test. There was some confusion surrounding the "naming" of the IRC § 199A as a *pass-*

through deduction because the word "pass-through" is normally associated only with the latter four types of entities listed above.

The basic *pass-through* deduction is a flat 20% of such business's "qualified business income" (QBI). The definition of QBI can be very complex and an in-depth discussion is well beyond the scope of this question. It can become especially difficult when an individual has more than one business. Fortunately for Susan, and us, she has only one business (her law practice) and the definition of QBI for her purposes is simple; the net profit from her business. We already know this for Susan's law practice; her net profit (and her QBI for the *pass-through* calculation) is given at $70,000. Remember, this **net** $70,000 figure already reflects her regular IRC § 162 business deductions.

The **tentative** *pass-through* deduction for Susan's law practice is 20% of her $70,000 (QBI), or $14,000. We will ultimately determine that her actual IRC § 199A *pass-through* deduction for this one-off question 3, will be $400 less, or **$13,600**. In order to determine why her actual *pass-through* deduction is less, we must examine some important limitations and special rules for the IRC § 199A deduction.

There is a *taxable income* limitation in IRC § 199A(a) that the *pass-through deduction* cannot exceed 20% of an individual's (or couple's) *taxable income* (i.e., there is a 20% of *taxable income* cap for this deduction). Right away you will notice we are in somewhat of a conundrum. If the *pass-through* deduction is one that will ultimately determine *taxable income*, how can we compute this 20% *taxable income* cap for the deduction? Subsection (e) comes to the rescue and defines *taxable income* for purposes of determining the *pass-through* deduction as a "pretend" *taxable income* without regard to any *pass-through* deduction. We now have to effectively compute Susan and Wally's *taxable income* as if IRC § 199A did not exist. Fortunately for us, the calculation, while taking up some space in our analysis, is not too bad. We'll call it their **"*pretend taxable income.*"**

We shall borrow an abbreviated visual depiction of their *taxable income* from other questions in this book and explain the items below.

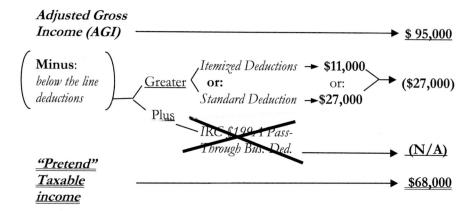

The couple's AGI is comprised of Wally's $10,000 in wages, plus, in this question, their $15,000 in regular bank interest (this is the one number that has changed from those in question 2). Plus, Susan's **net** profit of $70,000 from her law practice for a total of $95,000 ($5,000 less than in the previous question 2 representing the lower bank interest in this question 3). We don't have the detailed figures comprising Susan's $70,000 net profit but if we were being technical, her business's gross revenues would be included in gross income and her regular IRC § 162 business expenses would be *above the line* deductions. Therefore, this abbreviated "pretend" *taxable income* appears in truncated form (missing gross income and *above the line* deductions); but, we get to the same place for AGI.

We know, from question 1, in this set, that the couple's *standard deduction* is $27,000 for 2019 (the regular *standard deduction* for a married couple plus two extra amounts because of their age (see question 1 for a more thorough analysis). We have not addressed the couple's itemized deductions for 2019, but the only possible one indicated is their $11,000 charitable contribution. We will discuss this more thoroughly in question 4 of this set but suffice it to say, this represents their total itemized deductions for 2019. For *taxable income* computations (real or "pretend"), we would select the greater of their $27,000 *standard deduction* or *itemized deductions* of $11,000 in their case. Clearly, their *standard deduction* is the greater of the two.

At this point, we can finalize our computation of their "pretend" *taxable income*. Recall that we are doing this to make sure that their tentative $14,000 *pass-through* deduction does not exceed the 20% of *taxable income* cap. So let's check the limitation. **The 20% of "pretend *taxable income*" of $68,000**

equals $13,600. Recall that we calculated the couple's tentative *pass-through* deduction to be $14,000. This means that their tentative $14,000 *pass-through* deduction is limited by this provision and their tentative *pass-through* deduction is now **$13,600** (compared to $14,000 in question 2 that was not limited by this *pretend taxable income* cap. Alas, we still have more to discuss.

If a taxpayer has income above certain thresholds, then the *pass-through* deduction is reduced and, potentially eliminated. Fortunately, these thresholds are well beyond Susan and Wally's level of income, so we need not delve into the morass of this area. For information, the 2019 beginning threshold of *taxable income* that would cause concern is $321,400 for a married couple ($160,700 for a single individual). Above these levels, the *pass-through deduction* is phased-out or limited.

There is another component to determining the *pass-through* deduction that has been the source of much confusion and misunderstanding. The IRC § 199A *pass-through* deduction distinguishes between different types of business activities. Individuals engaged in a "specified service trade or business" (SSTB) are not favored business activities for the deduction. Generally, if one's business consists primarily providing services, it is an SSTB. Not an exhaustive list, but they include: attorneys, accountants, doctors, dentists, other health-related fields, performing arts, consulting, athletics, financial services, and the like. When the TCJA enacted IRC § 199A, many thought that net income from these service businesses would not qualify for the new *pass-through* deduction. This may have come from a quick reading of the statute where *qualified business income* (QBI, upon which the deduction is based) does not include income from SSTB's (see IRC § 199(d)(1)). Reading deeper into the statute, one finds that this is not really the case unless a taxpayer has income above certain threshold amount (amounts a certain amount above those previously discussed). Non SSTB's may still be entitled to an IRC § 199A *pass-through* deduction even when net income exceeds the various thresholds (whereas, it is phased-out and eventually eliminated for SSTB's who hit the threshold income levels). Super clear, yes?

Susan's business is clearly a "specified service trade or business" (SSTB) but because their income does not come close to beginning of the phase-out amount ($321,400 for their 2019 joint return), her law practice's net income counts at QBI and the couple is entitled to a *pass-through* deduction.

Now we come to our conclusion. Susan's $70,000 of net income from her law practice is qualified business income (they're income is not high enough to be affected by the SSTB thresholds). What would generally be a 20% general deduction (20% of $70,000, or $14,000) will, unfortunately, run afoul of the 20% of "pretend taxable income" cap (see above). Recall that in this one-off problem 3, their interest income was less. This, in turn, reduced the couple's *pretend taxable* income down to $68,000 which resulted in a lower limit for the possible *pass-through* deduction (20% of $68,000 = $13,600). This brings us to our answer that their IRC § 199A *pass-through* deduction for 2019 is $13,600 or $400 lower than it was in question 2 (where it was not limited).

Answer (a) is incorrect because while the *pass-through* deduction is based on her net business income, their other income items are reflected in their "taxable income" is necessary to compute any limiting caps (as was the case in this question). **Answer (b) is incorrect** because she was, in both questions 2 and 3, entitled to an IRC §199A *pass-through* deduction. **Answer (d) is incorrect** because it is the wrong amount and represents an incorrect calculation of how the reduction in their interest income affects their *pass-through* deduction (the $1,000 is 20% of the $500 amount by which their interest income was reduced in this question). Answer (e) is incorrect because the correct reduction of their *pass-through* deduction is reflected in answer (c).

4. **Answer (a) is correct.** This question is designed to illustrate how the various components of income and deductions fit together to compute taxable income. This computation requires information about Susan and Wally's income and deductions. The computational framework for taxable income is as follows:

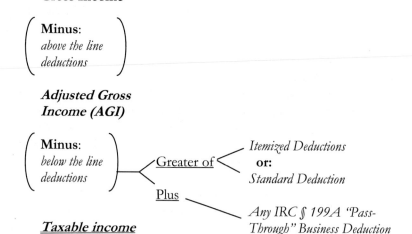

It should be noted that the calculation of *taxable income* has changed since the prior editions of this book. *The Tax Cuts and Jobs Act* (TCJA) signed into law in December 2017 (generally effective beginning in 2018) removed one "category" of deductions (personal exemption(s)) and added, for some business-related activities, another category of deductions (the so-called "pass-through" deduction). In class, this professor also explains the computation of *taxable income* in a **six-step** approach as follows:

Step 1:   Determine what is included in the taxpayer's *Gross Income* (This reflects all income and exclusions therefrom.)

Step 2:   Determine the taxpayer's *Adjusted Gross Income (AGI)* (This requires subtracting from *Gross income* any deductions that are allowed *above the line* pursuant to IRC § 62; Appendix A for more information.)

Step 3:   Determine the total amount of the taxpayer's *Itemized Deductions* (This requires applying any applicable limitations, floors, or restrictions for certain types of these deductions; see Appendix A for more information.)

Step 4:   Determine the amount of the taxpayer's *Standard Deduction* (This is year-specific and varies by filing status, age, degree of visual impairment, and limitations for certain dependents.)

Step 5:   Determine the amount of any available TCJA *IRC § 199A Pass-Through business-related deduction*.

                (In prior editions of this book, and pre-TCJA law, this step used to be determining the amount of the taxpayer's *Personal Exemption Deduction(s)*. Under the TCJA, these deductions have been eliminated for 2018-2025)

Step 6:   Compute *Taxable Income* by subtracting from AGI (amount in Step 2):
                1)   Either *itemized deductions* (amount in **Step 3**), or the *standard deduction* (amount in **Step 4**), whichever is the **greater** of the two, **and**
                2)   Any *IRC § 199A Pass-Through business-related deduction* (amount in **Step 5**).

The couple's AGI is comprised of Wally's $10,000 in wages, plus, in this question, their $15,000 in regular bank interest (this is the one number that has changed from those in question 2). Plus, Susan's **net** profit of $70,000 from her law practice for a total of $95,000. We don't have the detailed figures comprising Susan's $70,000 net profit but if we were being technical, her business's gross revenues would be included in gross income and her regular IRC § 162 business expenses would be *above the line* deductions. The facts indicate that they had no other *above the line* deductions. Therefore, we effectively completed steps 1 and 2 to arrive at their AGI (which, as indicate below), is $100,000.

As far as other deductions are concerned, the general facts of this series of questions indicate that for 2019 the couple had $11,000 of cash contributions to qualified charities. Pursuant to IRC § 173, this gives rise to a deduction. Charitable deductions are part of a group of *below the line* deductions known collectively as "itemized deductions." This group of deductions also includes such items as qualifying medical care expenses, and certain interest and taxes paid, among others. Some of these itemized deductions are subject to certain restrictions and limitations. The total amount of charitable contributions deductible in any one year is subject to certain limits or caps depending on the type of contribution and the charitable recipient. For most cash contributions, the deduction cannot exceed 60% of the taxpayer's AGI. Our couple's $11,000 of charitable contributions does not exceed 60% of their $100,000 AGI (see AGI calculation below).

There are two other deductions that need to be addressed before we have all the components necessary to compute Susan and Wally's taxable income: their *standard deduction* and their IRC § 199A *pass-through* deduction, if any. As discussed in question 1, above, our couple is entitled to a $27,000 *standard deduction* for 2019. Recall that because they both are 65 years of age or older, their basic married *standard deduction* of $24,400 (for 2019) was increased by $2,600 (an extra $1,300 for each of them).

We move to their last possible deduction; the IRC § 199A *pass-through* business-related item. Reverting to our original facts, we went through the long analysis of this *pass-through* deduction in question 2 and determined that they are entitled to a $14,000 deduction.

Applying this **six-step** computation approach (beginning with AGI in step 3), our couple's *taxable income* for 2019 is $59,000, computed as follows:

Step 1: *Gross income* = Unknown
Step 2: *Adjusted gross income (AGI)* = $100,000
Step 3: *Itemized deductions* = $11,000
Step 4: *Standard deduction* = $27,000
Step 5: IRC § 199A *pass-through deduction* = $14,000
Step 6: *Taxable income* = $100,000
                            ($27,000) [greater of $11,000 or $27,000]
                            ($14,000)
                            $59,000

A visual depiction of the *taxable income* calculation is as follows:

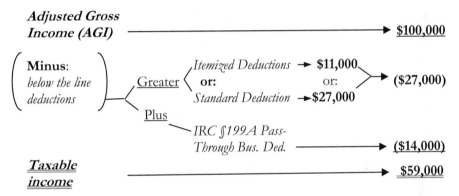

Adjusted Gross Income (AGI) → $100,000

Minus: *below the line deductions* — Greater — Itemized Deductions → $11,000 or: Standard Deduction → $27,000 or: → ($27,000)

Plus — IRC §199A Pass-Through Bus. Ded. → ($14,000)

Taxable income → $59,000

Answer (b) is incorrect because this answer reflects the incorrect *standard deduction*. It utilizes only the basic 2019 $24,400 amount but fails to add the additional amounts because they are both 65 or older. **Answer (c) is also incorrect.** This answer reflects the correct *standard deduction* amount but fails to reflect their IRC § 199A *pass-through* deduction. **Answer (d) is incorrect** because it also fails to reflect the available *pass-through* deduction plus incorporates an incorrect *standard deduction amount* (not including the extra amounts because of their respective ages). **Answer (e) is incorrect** because a correct answer (a) is presented.

5.   **Answer (e) is correct.** *As with the other questions in this set, this question 5 is year-specific (2019) and is intended to illustrate a basic calculation of federal income tax liability. [Appendix B, contains relevant, year-specific information applicable to 2019.] This question, like all questions in this set, is easily adaptable to years other than 2019. Also, this professor would have such a question in an objective portion of an exam because it requires that you have the correct answer for the previous question. For our purposes,*

however, it provides a logical conclusion to this set of questions and one can always look at the "correct" answer to question 4, above, before tackling this tax computation question.

Computation of the actual tax is a rather anticlimactic event in the study of tax. When one hears the word "tax," most people tend to think of what we are doing here; computing the actual tax. From your study of federal income tax, you know that most of the "action" in tax is not the actual tax calculation. Rather, it is what constitutes *taxable income*. What is include or excluded from gross income? What is allowed or not allowed as a deduction? How do we put the various components together to compute *taxable income*? Understanding the component parts is what studying tax is all about and comprises the vast majority of questions in this book. Students quickly learn that when tax is "in the political news," the usual focus is on "tax rates," often with a promise that, "[I]f elected, I'll push for lower tax rates." Students, in tax class, also quickly learn that "tax rates" are simple and only a small part of the government tax revenue picture. Students know that the real question should be, "What is going to happen to the tax base?" The tax base contains the big issues of what will be included or excluded from income and which deductions will be increased/added and which deductions will be decreased/disappear? Tax legislative history is replete of reductions in tax rates only to have a corresponding increase in the tax base (increases in *taxable incomes* with fewer exclusions from income and reductions in tax deductions). Enough with tax policy and politics. We do, at some point, need to compute the tax. Let's get to it.

Computing Susan and Wally's "regular" tax liability (ignoring any possible additional taxes and before any tax credits) is a rather straightforward mathematical exercise. IRC § 1 sets out the tax computation rate schedules and as you have most likely studied, the rate schedules vary depending on one's *filing status*. Filing status is determined as of the end of the tax year and for our couple, they will "married filing a joint return." A married couple (but not domestic partners) usually file "jointly" as this the most favorable set of tax rates (i.e., will produce the lowest amount of tax for any given amount of taxable income). Married individuals cannot file as "single" and another set of rates, "married filing separately," is the least favorable for taxpayers. A full discussion of the various filing statuses is beyond the scope of this book, and the initial set of facts indicate that our couple are filing a joint return for 2019. Their regular tax, using the 2019 tax rate schedules is **$6,692.** Now a bit more on how we arrive at this amount.

Once the proper filing status is determined, the actual calculation of the regular income tax is a simple matter. The rate schedules for individuals are found in IRC § 1(a), but the schedules that appear in the Code should <u>not</u> be used for actual tax calculations. One reason is that the rate schedules are "indexed" for inflation and change every year. In addition, the *Tax Cuts and Jobs Act* (TCJA) signed into law in December 2017 (generally effective beginning in 2018) added an entirely new set of rates. The TCJA left the "old" rates in IRC § 1(a) alone and added subsection (j): "Modifications for taxable years 2018 through 2025." The rates the various sub-parts of this TCJA subjection (j) are those for computing taxes for the year 2018. These too are indexed for inflation and every year and the Treasury announces the actual rates as adjusted for inflation (these are published in an official-type notice, but the aforementioned code sections are not amended every year to reflect the actual rates). [Please see Appendix B for the various rate schedules applicable to 2019.] In general, the tax rate schedules reflect a "graduated" nature of the income tax; lower rates for lower levels of taxable income with progressively higher incremental tax rates on higher levels of income. One can see this just by looking at the unadjusted for inflation tax rates in IRC § 1(a) and 1(j) (the latter as part of the TCJA).

The tax rate schedules are based on *taxable income* (this is why a correct computation of *taxable income* is so important). Recall, from question 4, above, that our couple's taxable income for 2019 is $59,000. Utilizing the "married filing jointly" rate schedule for 2019, $59,000 of taxable income places Susan and Wally in the 12% "marginal" tax bracket. The progressive nature of the rate schedules insures that only a portion of their $59,000 of taxable income will be taxed at this rate. Other portions of her $59,000 taxable income are taxed, in 2019, at a lower rate 10% (see other questions later in this book with greater amounts of *taxable income* where multiple rate brackets are used in computing the tax). Applying the 2019 married filing jointly tax rate schedule to their $59,000, the tax is: $1,940 plus 12% of the difference between their $59,000 taxable income and $19,400. This translates to $1,940 + (12% x ($59,000 - $19,400)), or $1,940 + (12% x $39,600), or $1,940 + $4,752, or **$6,692**. Note that the rate schedules automatically compute the tax on amounts of income at the lower marginal rates. For example, in our couple's case, the $1,940 in the rate schedule represents the tax on the first $19,400 of taxable income (applying here, the lower 10% marginal tax rate on the first $19,400).

Answers (a) and (b) are not correct because both are based on incorrect *taxable income* amounts. Answer (a) is the tax on $100,000 which is the couple's *gross income* (and not their *taxable income*). Answer (b) is the tax on a *taxable income* that does not reflect their IRC § 199A *pass-through* deduction. **Answer (c) is incorrect.** This answer does not correctly use the rate schedule. It wrongly calculates their tax based on 12% of their total *taxable income* thus failing to reflect the graduated nature of income tax rates. **Answer (d) is incorrect** but reflects a common error. This amount is the tax using the proper rate schedules and the couple's correct *taxable income*, but it is using the tax rate schedules in the code (IRC § 1(j)) which do not reflect the 2019 adjustment for inflation. This answer would have been correct if we were applying the tax rates for 2018 [See Appendix B for the various actual tax rates for 2019.]

6. **Answer (c) is correct.** *This question is year-specific (2019) and is intended to illustrate a basic calculation of federal income tax liability. [Appendix B, contains relevant, year-specific information applicable to 2019.] This question is easily adaptable to years other than 2019.*

Computation of the actual tax is a rather anticlimactic event in the study of tax. When one hears the word "tax," most people tend to think of what we are doing here; computing the actual tax. From your study of federal income tax, you know that most of the "action" in tax is not the actual tax calculation. Rather, it is what constitutes *taxable income*. What is include or excluded from gross income? What is allowed or not allowed as a deduction? How do we put the various components together to compute *taxable income*? Understanding the component parts is what studying tax is all about and comprises the vast majority of questions in this book. Students quickly learn that when tax is "in the political news," the usual focus is on "tax rates," often with a promise that, "[I]f elected, I'll push for lower tax rates." Students, in tax class, also quickly learn that "tax rates" are simple and only a small part of the government tax revenue picture. Students know that the real question should be, "What is going to happen to the tax base?" The tax base contains the big issues of what will be included or excluded from income and which deductions will be increased/added and which deductions will be decreased/disappear? Tax legislative history is replete of reductions in tax rates only to have a corresponding increase in the tax base (increases in *taxable incomes* with fewer exclusions from income and reductions in tax deductions). Enough with tax policy and politics. We do, at some point, need to compute the tax. Let's get to it.

Sadly, Carol lost her spouse at a young age. Computing her "regular" tax liability (ignoring any possible additional taxes and before any tax credits) is a rather straightforward mathematical exercise. IRC § 1 sets out the tax computation rate schedules and as you have most likely studied, the rate schedules vary depending on one's *filing status*. Filing status is determined as of the end of the tax year and Carol's status is that of an "unmarried individual (other than a surviving spouse or head of household)." The resulting tax using the 2019 tax rate schedules is **$18,174** (rounded down to the nearest dollar).

A word of caution about language used on exams. There are many instances where the common use of a term does not necessarily correspond to its official "tax" counterpart. Labels can be deceiving and do not be fooled by their use in lay terms on an exam. In everyday language we would refer to Carol as a "surviving spouse." Looking at IRC § 1(a) (and § 1(j), see below) we see a favorable tax rate schedule (compared to that for unmarried individuals) for certain married individuals and *surviving spouses*. The term *surviving spouse*, however, has a very specific and much narrower definition for federal income tax purposes (and the ability to use the more favorable rate schedule). IRC § 2(a) attaches the *tax label* of *surviving spouse* for the year in which the taxpayer's spouse died. It also extends this *surviving spouse* label for the two years after the year in which the taxpayer's spouse died, **but** only if:

> ➤ Such surviving spouse maintains as his or her home a household which constitutes for the taxable year the principal place of abode (as a member of such household) of a dependent
> ➤ Who (within the meaning of IRC § 152) is a son, stepson, daughter, or stepdaughter of the surviving spouse, and
> ➤ With respect to whom the surviving spouse is entitled to a deduction for the taxable year under IRC § 151.

Distilled, a *surviving spouse* for income tax purposes is generally an unmarried surviving spouse for the year in which the taxpayer's spouse dies and also for the two years subsequent to his or her spouse's death but for the latter, only if the surviving spouse has a dependent child living in his or her home. Carol is not, for tax purposes, a *surviving spouse* because Robert died too long ago (five years earlier). We need not even consider if Carol had any dependent children (which she did not) because the extra two-year *surviving spouse* label, for taxes, would have already expired. Even though to the entire non-tax world, Carol is a surviving spouse, she is not so considered for federal income tax purposes. Therefore, she is unable to use the more favorable married/surviving spouse rate schedule but, rather, must use the single/unmarried (non "heads of households") rate schedule.

Once the proper filing status is determined, the actual calculation of the regular income tax is a simple matter. The rate schedules for individuals are found in IRC § 1(a), but the schedules that appear in the Code should not be used for actual tax calculations. One reason is that the rate schedules are "indexed" for inflation and change every year. In addition, the *Tax Cuts and Jobs Act* (TCJA) signed into law in December 2017 (generally effective beginning in 2018) added an entirely new set of rates. The TCJA left the "old" rates in IRC § 1(a) alone and added subsection (j): "Modifications for taxable years 2018 through 2025." The rates the various sub-parts of this TCJA subjection (j) are those for computing taxes for the year 2018. These too are indexed for inflation and every year and the Treasury announces the actual rates as adjusted for inflation (these are published in an official-type notice, but the aforementioned code sections are not amended every year to reflect the actual rates). [Please see Appendix B for the various rate schedules applicable to 2019.] In general, the tax rate schedules reflect a "graduated" nature of the income tax; lower rates for lower levels of taxable income with progressively higher incremental tax rates on higher levels of income. One can see this just by looking at the unadjusted for inflation tax rates in IRC § 1(a) and 1(j) (the latter as part of the TCJA).

Utilizing the unmarried (single) rate schedule for 2019, $100,000 of taxable income places Carol in the 24% "marginal" tax bracket. The progressive nature of the rate schedules insures that only a portion of her $100,000 of taxable income will be taxed at this rate. Other portions of her $100,000 taxable income are taxed, in 2019, at rates of 10%, 12%, and 22%. Applying the 2019 single tax rate schedule to her $100,000, the tax is: $14,382.50 plus 24% of the difference between her $100,000 taxable income and $84,200. This translates to $14,385.50 + (24% x ($100,000 - $84,200)), or $14,385.50 + (24% x $15,800), or $14,382.50 + $3,792, or **$18,174** (rounded down to the nearest dollar). Note that the rate schedules automatically compute the tax on amounts of income at the lower marginal rates. For example, in Carol's case, the $14,382.50 in the rate schedule represents the tax on the first $84,200 of taxable income (applying all of the lower marginal rates to lower levels of income).

Answer (a) is incorrect because this number represents the "regular" income tax using the tax rate schedule for married individuals filing joint returns and *surviving spouse*. Notice that the computed tax using this rate schedule is more favorable than that for single individuals. **Answer (b) is incorrect** because this number represents the "regular" income tax using the tax rate schedule for "heads of households." Carol does not qualify for this favorable (compared to single) rate schedule. Qualification as a "head of household" is determined by IRC § 2(b). **Answer (d) is also incorrect**. This answer was computed applying a static 24% tax rate. This is Carol's "marginal" rate bracket, but only a portion of her income is taxed at this rate. **Answer (e) is incorrect** because a correct answer (c) is presented.

7. **Answer (b) is correct.** *This question is year-specific (2019) and is intended to illustrate a basic calculation of federal income tax liability. [Appendix B, contains relevant, year-specific information applicable to 2019.] This question is very similar to question 6, above, but for the sake of providing a complete analysis, much of the answer analysis to the previous question will be repeated here. This question is easily adaptable to years other than 2019.*

Computation of the actual tax is a rather anticlimactic event in the study of tax. When one hears the word "tax," most people tend to think of what we are doing here; computing the actual tax. From your study of federal income tax, you know that most of the "action" in tax is not the actual tax calculation. Rather, it is what constitutes *taxable income*. What is include or excluded from gross income? What is allowed or not allowed as a deduction? How do we put the various components together to compute *taxable income*? Understanding the component parts is what studying tax is all about and comprises the vast majority of questions in this book. Students quickly learn that when tax is "in the political news," the usual focus is on "tax rates," often with a promise that, "[I]f elected, I'll push for lower tax rates." Students, in tax class, also quickly learn that "tax rates" are simple and only a small part of the government tax revenue picture. Students know that the real question should be, "What is going to happen to the tax base?" The tax base contains the big issues of what will be included or excluded from income and which deductions will be increased/added and which deductions will be decreased/disappear? Tax legislative history is replete of reductions in tax rates only to have a corresponding increase in the tax base (increases in *taxable incomes* with fewer exclusions from income and reductions in tax deductions). Enough with tax policy and politics. We do, at some point, need to compute the tax. Let's get to it.

Sadly, Carol lost her spouse at a young age. Computing her "regular" tax liability (ignoring any possible additional taxes and before any tax credits) is a rather straightforward mathematical exercise. IRC § 1 sets out the tax computation rate schedules and as you have most likely studied, the rate schedules vary depending on one's *filing status*. Filing status is determined as of the end of the tax year and Carol's status is that of a "head of household." The resulting tax using the 2019 tax rate schedules is **$16,754**.

A word of caution about language used on exams. There are many instances where the common use of a term does not necessarily correspond to its official "tax" counterpart. Labels can be deceiving and do not be fooled by their use in lay terms on an exam. In everyday language we would refer to Carol as a "surviving spouse." Looking at IRC § 1(a) (and § 1(j), see below) we see a favorable tax rate schedule (compared to that for unmarried individuals) for certain married individuals and *surviving spouses*. The term *surviving spouse*, however, has a very specific and much narrower definition for federal income tax purposes (and the ability to use the more favorable rate schedule). IRC § 2(a) attaches the *tax label* of *surviving spouse* for the year in which the taxpayer's spouse died. It also extends this *surviving spouse* label for the two years after the year in which the taxpayer's spouse died, **but** only if:

> ➤ Such surviving spouse maintains as his or her home a household which constitutes for the taxable year the principal place of abode (as a member of such household) of a dependent

> ➢ Who (within the meaning of IRC § 152) is a son, stepson, daughter, or stepdaughter of the surviving spouse, and
> ➢ With respect to whom the surviving spouse is entitled to a deduction for the taxable year under IRC § 151.

Distilled, a *surviving spouse* for income tax purposes is generally an unmarried surviving spouse for the year in which the taxpayer's spouse dies and also for the two years subsequent to his or her spouse's death but for the latter, only if the surviving spouse has a dependent child living in his or her home. Carol is not, for tax purposes, a *surviving spouse* because Robert died too long ago (five years earlier). Even though, in this question, Carol has a dependent child (Samantha), she still does not qualify as a *surviving spouse* because that status lasts for only two years following the death of her husband. Robert died five years ago, so that two-year period has expired. Even though to the entire non-tax world, Carol is a surviving spouse, she is not so considered for federal income tax purposes. Therefore, she is unable to use the more favorable married/surviving spouse rate schedule.

Might Carol be entitled to use the "heads of households" filing status for 2019? The tax rates are not as favorable as for married filing joint taxpayers (and tax-defined surviving spouses), but they are better than the tax rates for single/unmarried (non "heads of households") individuals. A *head of household* is defined in IRC §2 (b), and here is where the rules get tricky (and, you might say, picky too). The statutory definition of a *head of household* is a bit more inclusive than is necessary to address the facts in this question, so it is wise to carefully read all the provisions in IRC § 2(b) for other situations that might arise.

Generally, we start with a *head of household* being an "unmarried individual" (although there is a notable exception for certain "separated" spouses), and Carol meets this criterion. Next, to qualify for *head of household* status, the taxpayer (Carol) must maintain as her home, a household which is the primary home for more than ½ of the year for the taxpayer (Carol) and at least one of the following:

> ➢ A *qualifying child* who is single (there are a few other minor items, none of which are applicable here),
> ➢ Any other "relative" (as defined in IRC §§ 152(a)(2)(A)–(2)(G)) if such person is a dependent of the taxpayer (and the taxpayer is entitled to claim the dependent's *personal exemption deduction* pursuant to IRC § 151).

Note that there are special *head of household* qualifying rules with respect to utilizing one's dependent parent who is not required to live with the taxpayer. [See IRC § 2(b)(1)(B).]

As for Carol, she qualifies as *head of household* because her daughter, Samantha, lives with her for more than ½ of the year (she lives with her for the full year) and is her *qualifying child*. Please see other questions in this book for a more thorough discussion of who constitutes a *qualifying child*. For our purposes, Samantha is a *qualifying child* because she is Carol's child, is under a certain age (19), lives with Carol, and is supported by her.

Once the proper filing status is determined, the actual calculation of the regular income tax is a simple matter. The rate schedules for individuals are found in IRC § 1(a), but the schedules that appear in the Code should <u>not</u> be used for actual tax calculations. One reason is that the rate schedules are "indexed" for inflation and change every year. In addition, the *Tax Cuts and Jobs Act* (TCJA) signed into law in December 2017 (generally effective beginning in 2018) added an entirely new set of rates. The TCJA left the "old" rates in IRC § 1(a) alone and added subsection (j): "Modifications for taxable years 2018 through 2025." The rates the various sub-parts of this TCJA subjection (j) are those for computing taxes for the year 2018. These too are indexed for inflation and every year and the Treasury announces the actual rates as adjusted for inflation (these are published in an official-type notice, but the aforementioned code sections are not amended every year to reflect the actual rates). [Please see Appendix B for the various rate schedules applicable to 2019.] In general, the tax rate schedules reflect a "graduated" nature of the income tax; lower rates for lower levels of taxable income with progressively higher incremental tax rates on higher levels of income. One can see this just by looking at the unadjusted for inflation tax rates in IRC § 1(a) and 1(j) (the latter as part of the TCJA).

Utilizing the heads of household rate schedule for 2019, $100,000 of taxable income places Carol in the 24% "marginal" tax bracket. The progressive nature of the rate schedules insures that only a portion of her $100,000 of taxable income will be taxed at this rate. Other portions of her $100,000 taxable income are taxed, in 2019, at rates of 10%, 12%, and 22%. Applying the 2019 heads of household tax rate schedule to her $100,000, the tax is: $12,962 plus 24% of the difference between her $100,000 taxable income and $84,200. This translates to $12,962 + (24% x ($100,000 - $84,200)), or $12,962 + (24% x $15,800), or $12,962 + $3,792, or **$16,754**. Note that the rate schedules automatically compute the tax on amounts of income at the lower marginal rates. For example, in Carol's case, the $12,962 in the rate schedule represents the tax on the first $84,200 of taxable income (applying all of the lower marginal rates to lower levels of income).

Answer (a) is incorrect because this number represents the "regular" income tax using the tax rate schedule for married individuals filing joint returns and *surviving spouse*. Notice that the computed tax using this rate schedule is more favorable than that for taxpayers using a different filing status. **Answer (c) is incorrect** because this number represents the "regular" income tax using the tax rate schedule for unmarried individuals (single) other than those who qualify as a head of household. While Carol is single, she does qualify for the more favorable (compared to single) head of household tax rate schedule. **Answer (d) is also incorrect**. This answer was computed applying a static 24% tax rate. This is Carol's "marginal" rate bracket, but only a portion of her income is taxed at this rate. **Answer (e) is incorrect** because a correct answer (b) is presented.

8. **The best answer, albeit not complete, is (b).** IRC § 61 defines gross income as "all income from whatever source derived." From your initial study of gross income's scope, you probably found it to be broadly defined, including the taxpayer's receipt of some net economic benefit or net accession to wealth. We really need go no further than IRC § 61 itself to find that "dividends" are specifically identified as an item of "gross income." [IRC § 61(a)(7).] We ultimately will conclude that Marilee and Bill must include, in income, the dividends received and that "answer (b)" is the most accurate of those provided. As discussed below, it may not be a complete answer, but it is the most accurate answer.

    Traditionally, dividends have been included in gross income and have not been accorded any special tax treatment; they were just part of income, which was part of "adjusted gross income" (AGI), which ultimately became part of an individual's "taxable income" (which was then subject to tax at "regular" tax rates varying with the individual's level of taxable income). A big change in the tax law with respect to dividends, occurred with the enactment of the "*Jobs and Growth Tax Relieve and Reconciliation Act of 2003*." Starting in 2003, certain dividends, called "qualified dividends" would receive preferential tax treatment. Here is where the answer gets a bit tricky, and why you may be fooled into selecting an alternative, albeit incorrect, answer. Starting with this 2003 law, dividends, while still included in income (and ultimately part of taxable income) are, when it comes time to actually compute the income tax, taxed at favorable (lower) marginal tax rates than those in the regular income tax rate schedules (regular income tax marginal rates range from 10% to 37% (for 2019) depending on one's taxable income. The more favorable capital gains tax rates have a maximum rate of 20% (this is for high-income individuals with *taxable income* in excess of almost $500,000). The marginal capital gains tax rate for most individuals is 15% and this rates drops to zero for individuals with lower taxable income (for 2019, these are individuals with *taxable income* less than around $40,000 for single filers and around $80,000 for married filing jointly. [IRC § 1(h)(11).] Again, these "qualified dividends" are still included in income (in full) but do receive preferential tax treatment when it comes to actually applying the tax rates to compute the individual's federal income tax.

While somewhat beyond the scope of this question, but helpful in understanding the material, "qualified dividends" are generally those dividends received from domestic (U.S.) corporations and certain qualified foreign corporations. [See IRC § 1(h)(11)(B) & (C) for more information.] It should also be noted that the statute contains rules requiring ownership of the dividend paying stocks for a certain period of time before the "ex-dividend" date (the date the corporation sets for shareholders of record/ownership to receive upcoming dividends). In our question, the dividends that Marilee and Bill receive would, with all likelihood, be considered "qualified dividends." A complete answer, and the source of confusion as to why (b) is the most accurate, is that the dividends that Marilee and Bill receive in 2019 would be included in their gross income, but when calculating their actual income tax, would be taxed at favorable capital gains rates (which would be lower than their regular income tax rates).

Answer (a) is incorrect because while their dividends are probably "qualified dividends," they are <u>not</u>, as such, excluded from income. **Answer (c) is on the right track, but incorrect nonetheless.** This is the most commonly selected answer because it does contain some correct information about the preferential tax treatment of "qualified dividends," and the taxpayer's dividends, in this question, are probably "qualified dividends." However, the beginning of this answer, that the dividends are excluded from income, is not correct. As discussed above, they are still part of the taxpayer's gross income (and AGI and Taxable Income, playing an important role in all sorts of things relating thereto). **Answer (d) is incorrect** because dividends do constitute gross income. While not implicated in this question, and well beyond the scope of this book, dividends may represent a tax-free return in certain rare instances. **Answer (e) is incorrect** because even though the taxpayer's dividends are "qualified dividends," this is not how such dividends are treated for tax purposes.

9. **The best answer is (a).** Hey, sometimes it is very difficult to come up with at least four good answers. The author apologizes for answer (d) although it sounds quite nice.

The *Tax cuts and jobs act* (TCJA) was signed into law in December 2017 and was generally effective beginning in 2018. The TCJA made numerous tax law changes for both corporations and individuals. Concentrating on individuals, the TCJA, among other things, increased the standard deduction, added the new IRC § 199A pass-through deduction, reduced income tax rates, eliminated "personal exemption" deductions, eliminated most business deductions for employees, placed a $10,000 cap on deductions for state and local taxes (SALT), reduced the deductibility of home loan interest, (and we could go on). Almost all the tax changes affecting individuals are effective for years 2018 through 2025. This, in the tax world, is commonly referred to as a "sunset provision"

The TCJA's *sunset provisions* are there in order to comply with certain congressional budget constraints. Historically, many tax laws (and other laws) have been enacted with *sunset clauses* and most such situations were not driven, primarily, by budget matters. For example, a certain provision of the law may change for a limited period of time to act as a short-term adjustment or stimulus and then that provision goes away after a certain period of time.

As enacted, the portions of the TCJA that have this *sunset provision* limited shelf life of years 2018 through 2025 (see above for examples of a few of these) will disappear after December 31, 2025 unless affirmatively changed by Congress and enacted into law. If this is not done, then all such affected provisions of the TCJA will revert to their status immediately prior to the enactment of the TCJA (i.e., the tax laws for these affected areas will be as they were prior to the TCJA).

Will some of the "time limited" provisions of the TCJA be made permanent? Will subsequent legislation reverse, before 2025, some of its changes to tax law? Only time will tell but if history is any guide, it is highly unlikely that everything will now remain unchanged. As of this writing, for example, congress is already debating the elimination of the TCJA's $10,000 cap for the state and local tax (SALT) deduction. Motivated by a combination of the TCJA's SALT cap and a larger standard deduction, there is, as of this writing, talk of changing tax law to make charitable contributions deductible irrespective of whether a taxpayer chooses to take the *standard deduction* or "itemizes" deductions.

Perhaps by the next edition of this book, the author can remove this question and the tax laws will be in less of a state of flux? We can only hope!!!

Answer (b) is incorrect because there is no "triggering" mechanism with respect to the Act's *sunset clause*. **Answer (c) is incorrect** because the TCJA contains no such provision for an automatic extension of the provision ending after 2025. **No comment about answer (d).**

10. **The best answer is (b).** A deduction serves to reduce *taxable income*. Tax rates are then applied to *taxable income* to compute the amount of tax. Tax "credits" then serve to reduce the actual tax liability. In other words, tax credits are a "dollar for dollar" reduction in the amount of tax owed while a

deduction only serves to reduce the amount of net income used to compute the tax. Because net income is not taxed at rates anywhere close to 100%, a credit is more valuable.

An illustration might be helpful. Suppose an individual has net or taxable income of $10,000 and, unrealistically, the tax rate is a flat 25%. Let us compare a $2,000 *deduction* with a $2,000 *credit*.

The Deduction
A $2,000 *deduction* would reduce net or taxable income to $8,000 ($10,000 less $2,000). Their tax, at 25%, would be **$2,000**.

The Credit
Net or taxable income of $10,000 taxed, at 25%, is $2,500. A $2,000 *credit* would reduce this $2,500 tax by $2,000, resulting in a tax of only **$500**.

It should be noted that in some instances, an individual might have a choice of taking either a deduction or a credit for a particular item. Although very rare, in such instances a *deduction* may provide for greater overall tax savings when compared to a *credit*.

Answers (a) and (c) are incorrect as discussed above. **Answer (d) is not the best answer** because a credit does not necessarily represent previously paid taxes. Rather, many credits are for current year's expenditures for which a benefit, in the form of a credit, has been granted by the Code.

11. **The correct answer is (a).** Tax credits are usually quite beneficial to a taxpayer as they serve to reduce the taxpayer's actual tax liability (computed by applying the appropriate tax rates to a taxpayer's *taxable income*). Some tax credits are allowed only to the extent that they reduce tax liability to zero and are referred to as "nonrefundable credits." In other words, these types of credits do not result in a refund to the taxpayer once tax liability has been reduced to zero. Other tax credits are not so limited and can generate a refund to the taxpayer notwithstanding a "zero" tax liability. This latter group of tax credits is referred to as "refundable" credits.

Most statutory provisions for "nonrefundable" credits for individuals are contained in Subpart A (of Subtitle A, Chapter 1, Subchapter A, Part IV), beginning IRC § 21 (Expenses for household and dependent care services necessary for gainful employment). Most statutory provisions for "refundable" credits for individuals are contained in Subpart C (of Subtitle A, Chapter 1, Subchapter A, Part IV), beginning IRC § 31 (Tax withheld on wages). IRC § 32 provides for the *earned income credit*, and this credit is "refundable." IRC § 25A contains provisions for the *lifetime learning credit* (and "American Opportunity" credit) and this credit is "nonrefundable."

Answers (b), (c), and (d) are all incorrect because they all incorrectly reflect, to some degree the "refundable" or "nonrefundable" nature of the two credits.

12. **The best answer is (c).** This question (and question 13, below) implicates the "child and dependent care" tax credit in IRC § 21. The scope of possible federal income tax issues to address in a semester's income tax course is huge and it is impossible to cover all issues in great depth. Coverage, in class, of the childcare credit ranges from no mention of it to a full, in-depth analysis. Most likely, Baxter will be entitled to some amount of childcare credit for the amount he pays for someone to come to his house to look after his daughter Celia.

Basically, IRC § 21 allows a <u>tax credit</u> (reduction of computed tax liability) for amounts paid for the care of certain qualifying individuals that enables the taxpayer to be "gainfully employed" (to work). While the determination of who constitutes a "qualifying individual" can be somewhat involved in certain situations, the most common qualifying individual is: "a dependent of the taxpayer (as defined in section 152(a)(1)) who has not attained the age of 13." [IRC § 21(b)(1)(A).] Celia qualifies, as she is five years old and is Baxter's dependent. Determining what qualifies as childcare expenses can also be much more complex than presented in our facts. Generally, however, they are costs to care for a child that enable the taxpayer to work. [IRC § 21(b)(2).] Baxter's payments for childcare would easily meet this requirement.

While exact numbers are not necessary to answer this question, the maximum amount of childcare expenses that qualify for this credit is $3,000 for one qualifying individual, or $6,000 for two or more qualifying individuals. [IRC § 21(c).] The actual credit, before limitations mentioned below, is equal to 35% of the childcare expenses (limited to the $3,000/$6,000 maximum). This 35% credit percentage is reduced for taxpayer's with adjusted gross income (AGI) in excess of $15,000. [IRC § 21(a)(2).] The actual reduction mechanism is a bit awkward, but the reduction in the credit percentage is gradual for individuals with AGI to $43,000. At that upper level of AGI, the credit percentage remains static at 20%. Therefore, individuals with AGI in excess of $43,000 are still entitled to a credit of 20% of their qualifying childcare expenses.

Based on the limited information that we have in this question, Baxter is entitled to some amount of childcare credit pursuant to IRC § 21.

While we do not have numbers in this question, an example might be helpful. Let's assume that Baxter paid $4,500 in qualifying childcare expenses for his daughter, Celia. Assume, for this illustration, that Baxter's AGI is $80,000. The maximum amount of childcare expenses for purposes of this credit is $3,000 (it is $6,000 for two or more qualifying individuals), so although Baxter paid $4,500 in childcare expenses, only $3,000 will be eligible for calculating the credit. As indicated above, the actual credit will be this $3,000 multiplied by a percentage. The statutory percentage of 35% is for individuals with AGI not more than $15,000. As mentioned, this percentage decreases, gradually, down to 20% for individuals with an AGI of $43,000 or greater. Baxter's $80,000 AGI means that he will use 20% for the calculation. In our illustration, Baxter's childcare credit will be 20% of $3,000 or **$600**. Had Baxter's AGI been $15,000 or less, his credit would be 35% of $3,000 or $1,050.

It should be mentioned that the IRC § 21 childcare credit is a nonrefundable credit (it cannot reduce tax liability below zero resulting in an excess that is refunded to the taxpayer).

Answer (a) is incorrect. While the amount of the credit percentage declines as one's AGI increases, the credit percentage is not reduced below 20%. **Answer (b) is also incorrect.** A medical care component of childcare is not required for this tax credit. Had the costs actually been for Celia's health care needs, they might give rise to a deduction as a medical care expense under IRC § 213. **Answer (d) is also incorrect.** IRC § 262 provides that "unless expressly provided" in the Code, no deductions are allowed for personal, living and family expenses. While the childcare tax credit is not a deduction, the credit is expressly provided for in IRC § 21.

13. **Answer (d) is correct.** This question (and question 12, above) implicates the "child and dependent care" tax credit in IRC § 21. The scope of possible federal income tax issues to address in a semester's income tax course is huge, and it is impossible to cover all of the issues in great depth. Coverage, in class, of the childcare credit ranges from no mention of it to a full, in-depth analysis.

Basically, IRC § 21 allows a <u>tax credit</u> (reduction of computed tax liability) for amounts paid for the care of certain qualifying individuals that enables the taxpayer to be "gainfully employed" (to work). While the determination of who constitutes a "qualifying individual" can be somewhat involved in certain situations, the most common qualifying individual is: "a dependent of the taxpayer (as defined in section 152(a)(1)) who has not attained the age of 13." [IRC § 21(b)(1)(A).] Each of Pamela's three children qualify because they are all less than 13 years old and all three are Pamela's dependents.

Determining what qualifies as childcare expenses can also be much more complex than presented in our facts. Generally, however, they are costs to care for a child that enable the taxpayer to work. [IRC § 21(b)(2).] For "qualifying individuals" of the type described in this question (dependents under 13), costs for day care facilities can qualify as childcare expenses. To qualify, such a facility must "comply with all applicable laws and regulations of a State or unit of local government," and the facility "(i) provides care for more than six individuals (other than the individuals who reside at the facility), and (ii) receives a fee, payment . . . for providing services for any of the individuals (regardless of whether such facility is operated for profit)." [IRC §§ 21(b)(2)(C) and 21(b)(2)(D).] It is clear, from our facts, that Pamela's costs for day care will qualify for the credit.

The maximum amount of childcare expenses that qualify for this credit is $3,000 for one qualifying individual, or $6,000 for two or more qualifying individuals. [IRC § 21(c).] Pamela's expected day care costs of $4,000 per each of her three children will, pursuant to this provision, be limited to a maximum of $6,000 (the limit for two *or more* children). The actual credit, before limitations mentioned below, is equal to 35% of the childcare expenses (limited to the $3,000/$6,000 maximum). This 35% credit percentage is reduced for taxpayer's with adjusted gross income (AGI) in excess of $15,000. [IRC § 21(a)(2).] The actual reduction mechanism is a bit awkward, but the reduction in the credit percentage is gradual for individuals with AGI up to $43,000. (The reduction in the credit percentage is 1% for each $2,000, or fraction thereof, that the taxpayer's AGI exceeds $15,000.) At that upper level of AGI, the credit percentage remains static at 20%. Therefore, individuals with AGI in excess of $43,000 are still entitled to a credit of 20% of their qualifying childcare expenses. Pamela's expected AGI of $45,000 would result in a credit percentage of 20%.

Based on Pamela's estimated numbers, her childcare tax credit, pursuant to IRC § 21, will be **$1,200** ($6,000 x 20%).

It should be mentioned that the IRC § 21 childcare credit is a nonrefundable credit (it cannot reduce tax liability below zero resulting in an excess that is refunded to the taxpayer).

Answer (a) is incorrect. This incorrect number is derived as follows: $4,000 costs (which should be limited) x 3 people (credit limit is same for 2 or more) x 20% (the correct credit percentage). **Answer (b) is also incorrect**. This incorrect number is derived as follows: $3,000 costs (correctly limited) x 2 people (correctly limited) x 35% (the incorrect full credit percentage not allowed for Pamela because of her AGI). **Answer (c) is also incorrect**. This incorrect number is derived as follows: $3,000 costs (correctly limited) x 3 (not correct because the credit limit is same for 2 or more) x 20% (the correct credit percentage). **Answer (e) is incorrect** because a correct answer (d) is presented.

14. **The correct answer is (a).** This question involves the "adoption expense" tax credit in IRC § 23. The scope of possible federal income tax issues to address in a semester's income tax course is huge, and it is impossible to cover all other issues in great depth. Coverage, in class, of the adoption tax credit ranges from no mention of it to a more comprehensive analysis. It also should be noted that this question is somewhat year-specific (for 2019 as for dollar amounts).

Basically, IRC § 23 allows a <u>tax credit</u> (reduction of computed tax liability) for amounts paid for certain costs associated with adopting an eligible individual. Qualified costs include reasonable and necessary adoption fees, court costs, attorney fees and other expenses that are directly related to the legal adoption of an eligible individual. [IRC § 23(d).] An eligible individual is generally a child under 18 or who is physically or mentally incapable of caring for himself or herself. There is another category of eligible individuals identified as "special needs" children. Most likely, all of Sonia's adoption related costs listed above would be considered qualified costs. In addition, her new son Adam is an eligible individual.

The basic adoption tax credit is the amount of qualifying costs paid with respect to the adoption up to a maximum of $10,000 per child. [IRC § 23(a)(1).] This statutory $10,000 maximum is indexed for inflation for years after 2002. [IRC § 23(h).] The 2019 maximum is $14,080 per child. While not applicable in our case, there are slightly different rules relating to adoptions of "special needs" individuals that apply starting in 2003. Like many other tax benefits, this adoption credit "phases-out" or is reduced if the taxpayer has too much income. While not necessary to answer this question, the Code states that this phase-out begins $150,000 of adjusted gross income (AGI) as modified (by items not pertinent to our facts). [IRC § 23(b)(2).] This $150,000 threshold is also indexed for inflation for years after 2002 and for 2019, this threshold is $211,160. The mechanism for computing this "phase-out" is rather complex and need not be discussed with specificity for our problem. Pursuant to the numbers stated in the Code, any possible adoption credit is fully "phased-out" (i.e., eliminated) for individuals with "inflation adjusted" (after 2002) AGI (as modified) of $190,000 or more (translating to $251,160 for 2019). Sonia should be entitled to some amount of adoption credit for her adoption related costs assuming her income is not at levels that preclude the tax credit.

It should be noted that there are many issues relating to the adoption credit in IRC § 23 that are not pertinent to our somewhat basic problem on the subject. It should also be mentioned that the IRC § 23 adoption credit is a nonrefundable credit (it cannot reduce tax liability below zero resulting in an excess that is refunded to the taxpayer). Also, this credit, along with some other nonrefundable credits, may be otherwise limited for certain individuals. [IRC § 26(a)(1).] It also should be noted that legislation in 2001 amended this credit in ways that are generally favorable to taxpayers (qualifying amounts and threshold) and the above discussion reflects these changes.

Answer (b) is incorrect. This credit was set to expire at the end of 2001, except as it applied to adoptions of "special needs" individuals. However, legislation in 2001 reinstated this credit (and made it more favorable to taxpayers) effective for years beginning in 2002. For adoption of "special needs" individuals, starting in 2003, different (and more beneficial rules) might be applicable for certain taxpayers. **Answer (c) is incorrect** because the answer reflects the stated Code amount that, after 2002, adjusts for inflation. As indicated in the discussion above, the 2019 "inflation-adjusted" maximum is $14,080. **Answer (d) is also incorrect.** As discussed above, IRC § 23 *does* provide a potential credit for adoption related costs. It should be noted that the latter part of this answer, regarding exclusion from income of employer provided adoption costs, is correct under certain conditions. IRC § 137 enumerates the tax rules for such employer adoption assistant programs.

15. **The best answer is (b).** The area of retirement and pension accounts is vast and an in-depth discussion is well beyond the scope of this book. This question is designed to address some of the basic points relating to one form of retirement accounts: the Individual Retirement Account or IRA. Also, this question is somewhat year-specific regarding the impact of Justin's alimony payments (see below).

There are many varieties of individual retirement accounts (IRA's) including traditional IRA's, Roth IRA's, SEP IRA's, and Coverdell Education Savings Accounts. The traditional IRA (the oldest in the IRA family) is the subject of this question. An IRA is an individual's own personal retirement plan. IRA's have been around for some time, and while the rules and restrictions associated with them have changed many times, the basic concept of them has remained the same. Put money into an IRA now while working and get a tax deduction for the contribution. The money in the IRA is invested and its earnings are not currently subject to tax (so called "tax free compounding"). Funds are withdrawn from the IRA years later (at retirement). While these later withdrawals are fully taxable, the taxpayer has received the benefit of the "time value of money" along with the advantage of the "tax-free" accumulations in the account. In addition, at the time of withdrawals, the taxpayer may be in a lower income tax bracket (or tax rates have declined). All in all, it makes for a nice deal. However, there are various restrictions and limitations regarding their use and availability. IRC § 219 is the principal section with respect to "traditional" IRA's.

First there is a specific dollar limitation for contributions to an IRA. The amounts vary depending on the year and one's age. The statutory contribution limit is set at $5,000 per year, but this amount is indexed for inflation (the maximum contribution for 2019, the latest available at the time of this writing, is $6,000. For individuals 50 and older, there are additional "catch-up" contribution amounts.

The above contribution limits also serve as the maximum deduction amounts for such contributions. The deduction for contributions is fairly simple for an individual (or his or her spouse) who is <u>not</u> a participant in some other qualified employer-sponsored retirement/pension plan. For such individuals, the maximum deduction, in any particular year, is the applicable maximum amount listed above, or the individual's compensation for the year, whichever is less. Unfortunately, these simple deduction rules will not apply to Justin, as he *is* a participant in his company's pension/retirement plan.

If the individual (or his or her spouse) *is* an active participant in a qualified employer-sponsored retirement/pension plan, then the amount of the contribution to an IRA that is deductible may be reduced or eliminated depending on the amount of the taxpayer's adjusted gross income (AGI). As with many other tax benefits, the maximum deductible contribution is "phased-out" (reduced or eliminated) as the level of an individual's income increases. The mechanism of the phase-out for deductible IRA contributions is somewhat complex and the threshold amounts where the "phase-outs" begin and end vary considerably depending on the year, the taxpayer's filing status, and other factors. To give an example, for a single individual in 2019, the phase-out of the deduction for contributions to an IRA begin at AGI levels of $64,000 and the deduction is completely phased-out (i.e., eliminated) for individuals with AGI of $74,000 or more. Justin, in our problem, is a participant in his company's pension/retirement plan, so depending on his AGI, his deductions for contributions to an IRA may be reduced or eliminated.

The tax laws regarding alimony are discussed in other questions in this book. The *Tax Cuts and Jobs Act* (TCJA) signed into law in December 2017 (effective generally in 2018 but 2019 in the case of divorces and the tax treatment of alimony). Long story short, the TCJA upended some 77 years of fairly consistent tax law regarding alimony. Historically, alimony was income to the recipient ex-spouse and a corresponding deduction to the payor ex-spouse. The TCJA has stricken the tax controlling sections for alimony and effective for divorces after 2018, alimony is not income to the recipient ex-spouse nor is it a deduction for the payor ex-spouse (a complete reversal of what had been settled law for 77 years). <u>Because Justin's divorce was prior to 2019, the historical rules continue to apply vis-à-vis his alimony payments and they constitute deductions for Justin. In addition, Justin's deductions for alimony payment are *above the line* and, therefore, are reflected in the determination of his AGI. Moving on to the next logical step, for Justin's IRA contribution deduction purposes, the alimony payments to his ex-wife, Ellen are beneficial (they serve to reduce his AGI and thereby increasing the possibility of some deduction for IRA contributions).</u> [Note that had their divorce been after 2018, alimony payments would not have an impact on his AGI (as they are no longer deductible under the TCJA) and, therefore, would not be relevant for IRA contribution limitation purposes.]

It should be noted that for participants in qualified employer-sponsored pension/retirement plans whose deduction for IRA contributions are reduced or eliminated, contributions can still be made to a "traditional" IRA (subject to the contribution limits previously discussed). There is no immediate tax benefit in such cases and upon withdrawal from the IRA, different tax treatment results.

It should be noted that in addition to the limits and restrictions mentioned above, the timing of withdrawals from an IRA is restricted and severe penalties can apply for noncompliance.

It should also be noted that not all IRA's have the same basic theme as the "traditional" IRA. For example, the Roth IRA is, to some degree, a reversal of the traditional rules; no deduction for current contributions, but the later withdrawals are tax-free.

Answer (a) is incorrect because participation in such a company plan does not necessarily preclude deductible contributions to an IRA. Rather, as discussed above, the deduction may be allowed to some degree depending on the individual's AGI. **Answer (c) is incorrect** because Justin's alimony payments are relevant. His divorce was prior to the TCJA changes affecting alimony deductions for the payor ex-spouse and in his case, his alimony payments serve to reduce his AGI (which is the determining factor for deductible contributions in his case). **Answer (d) is incorrect** because while there has been discussion about eliminating the restriction of participation in other plans for purposes of deductible IRA contributions, this has not happened as of this writing. It is interesting to note that for a period of time some years ago, this was not a restricting factor for deductible IRA contributions (i.e., at one time, an individual could be a participant in an employer's pension/retirement plan and still make deductible IRA contributions without regard to the amount of one's AGI).

16. **The correct answer is (a).** As indicated in the analysis of question 15, above, the area of retirement plans, including the numerous varieties of individual retirement accounts (IRA's) can be very complex. This question is designed to illustrate a few basic rules applicable to "traditional" IRA's. IRC § 219 is the primary section applicable to "traditional" IRA's.

As indicated in the analysis of question 15, above, there are various restrictions and limitations relating to contributions and deductions for IRA's. First there is a specific dollar limitation for contributions to an IRA. The amounts vary depending on the year and one's age. The statutory contribution limit is set at $5,000 per year, but this amount is indexed for inflation (the maximum contribution for 2019, the latest available at the time of this writing, is $6,000. For individuals 50 and older, there are additional "catch-up" contribution amounts.

The above contribution limits also serve as the maximum deduction amounts for such contributions. The deduction for contributions is fairly simple for an individual (or his or her spouse) who is <u>not</u> a participant in some other qualified employer-sponsored retirement/pension plan. For such individuals, the maximum deduction in any particular year is the applicable maximum amount listed above, <u>or the individual's compensation for the year, whichever is less</u>. These are the rules that are applicable to Ellen because she is not a participant in any other pension or retirement plan. At first glance, one may think that while the maximum deduction in 2019 is $6,000, Ellen's compensation of only $1,500 would limit her deduction to that amount. Fortunately, for Ellen, alimony received (and includible in income as is the case here) is considered "compensation" for purposes of determining deductible IRA contributions. [Formerly identified in IRC 219(f)(1), but with the TCJA change in alimony rules effective in 2019, this section no longer specifically identifies alimony; as compensation. The Treasury, however, still considers alimony from pre-2019 divorces that is included in the recipient's gross income, to be "earned for purposes of computing the IRA limit.] Therefore, Ellen could be entitled to a full $6,000 deduction (in 2019) for her contribution of that amount to a "traditional" IRA.

As indicated in question 15, above, and other questions in this book, the *Tax Cuts and Jobs Act* (TCJA) signed into law in December 2017 (generally effective in 2018 but 2019 in the case of divorces and the tax treatment of alimony). Long story short, the TCJA upended some 77 years of fairly consistent tax law regarding alimony. Historically, alimony was income to the recipient ex-spouse and a corresponding deduction to the payor ex-spouse. The TCJA has stricken the tax controlling sections for alimony and effective for divorces after 2018, alimony is not income to the recipient ex-spouse nor is it a deduction for the payor ex-spouse (a complete reversal of what had been settled law for 77 years). Because Justin's divorce was prior to 2019, the historical rules continue to apply vis-à-vis his alimony payments and they constitute deductions for Justin and Income to Ellen. As discussed above, the alimony Ellen receives is also considered "compensation" for purposes of computing her IRA contribution (here in 2019). Note that had their divorce been after 2018, alimony payments would not, pursuant to the TCJA, be included in Ellen's gross income and, accordingly, would not be considered "compensation" and for purposes of determining her maximum IRA contribution.

Because Ellen is not a participant in a company-sponsored retirement/pension plan, we need not be concerned with possible reductions or elimination of the IRA contribution deduction based on the amount of her AGI as discussed in the answer to Question 15, above.

It should be noted that in addition to the limits and restrictions mentioned above, the timing of withdrawals from an IRA is restricted and severe penalties can apply for noncompliance.

It should also be noted that not all IRA's have the same basic theme as the "traditional" IRA. For example, the Roth IRA is, to some degree, a reversal of the traditional rules – no deduction for current contributions, but the later withdrawals are tax-free.

Answer (b) is not correct for our fact pattern. Because the couple's divorce was before 2019, the alimony received by Ellen is included in her income and is also considered "compensation" for determining deductible contribution limits. Note that this would be the correct answer had their divorce been after 2018 when the new TCJA rules would be in effect. **Answer (c) is incorrect** because the amount of her AGI is irrelevant as she is not a participant in another qualified pension/retirement plan. **Answer (d) is incorrect** because full-time employment is not a requirement for deductible IRA contributions.

17. **Answer (b) is correct.** This question raises the very complex issue of the "alternative minimum tax" or AMT. Both in concept and real-world application, the many complex aspects of the AMT can be intimidating and extremely difficult to compute. The study of the AMT varies considerably among law school tax courses: from no mention at all, to a full-blown, in-depth analysis of its provisions and method of computation. For this book, the author has chosen to merely introduce the subject and forego analysis

of the many in-depth, analytical rules. This choice was made primarily to leave room for the host of other tax issues that require discussion. The author acknowledges that this level of coverage may be disappointing for those students whose professor more fully covers the AMT in class.

The AMT is a separate calculation of an individual's income tax (using special rates) that is based not on regular *taxable income* but, rather, "alternative minimum taxable income." If the individual's resulting tax utilizing the AMT computations is **greater** than the individual's income tax computed by traditional means, the taxpayer will pay (as a forced alternative) the higher amount. [IRC § 55] Technically, the amount by which the AMT exceeds the taxpayer's regularly computed tax is an addition to the taxpayer's regular tax. The word "minimum," in "alternative minimum tax" does not have a favorable meaning to the taxpayer and the AMT is not a good thing for taxpayers.

The impetus for the AMT was to prevent taxpayers with "high" levels of income from paying too little income tax, because they took advantage of too many favorable benefits accorded them under the law. The "alternative" tax that such individuals are required to pay at a "minimum" is based on a modification of the taxpayer's *taxable income*. Basically, there are certain items (usually deductions) that are considered "tax preference" items, and if the taxpayer, in computing *taxable income,* has benefited from them, then they will be reflected (in an unfavorable manner) in determining the basis for computing the AMT. In addition, there are certain AMT adjustments that substitute an AMT treatment of a particular item for that item reflected using regular income tax rules. Tax preference items and AMT adjustments encompass such things as depreciation and depletion, certain tax exempt interest, intangible drilling costs, various *itemized deductions*, "passive losses," and many others.

Because of changing taxpayer dynamics and the scope of "tax preference" items, more and more individuals (even those who are considered "middle-class" vis-à-vis income levels), were becoming subject to the AMT; something which, many argue, was not the purpose of the AMT when enacted. To this issue, the *Tax Cuts and Jobs Act* (TCJA) signed into law in December 2017 (generally effective beginning in 2018) made significant changes to the AMT. Through a combination of relaxed laws in IRC § 55 (increased amounts of income exempted in computing AMT) and changes to individual's itemized deductions (capped state and local income tax deductions, reduced deductions for certain interest, etc.), the TCJA has impacted, positively, who is now subject to the AMT (i.e., the number of individual's snagged by this tax has been greatly reduced).

Answers (a), (c) and (d) are all incorrect because they do not reflect the nature of the alternative minimum tax.

18. **The best answer is (c).** This question addresses an income tax doctrine known as the "tax benefit rule." Basically stated, when a taxpayer recovers an amount that was deducted (or credited) in an earlier year, the recovery is included in the taxpayer's gross income in the current year <u>unless, and to the extent</u> the deduction (or credit) did <u>not</u> benefit the taxpayer (reducing his or her tax) in the earlier year. [IRC § 111.] In our facts, if the medical costs Victor incurred and paid last year *benefited him* (reduced his *taxable income*, which, in turn, reduced his income tax) the recovery (to the extent it served to reduce his *taxable income*) will be income in this year. However, if these costs did not benefit him last year tax-wise, the recovery will not be included in income this year.

There is little doubt that Victor's hospital costs were "qualified medical care expenses" pursuant to IRC § 213. Whether his costs qualify as medical care expenses is not really at issue in the question. Rather, "how" and "where" these medical care expenses were deductible *is the primary issue*. Figuring out *how* and *where* these expenses were deductible will determine if Victor *benefited* by their deduction (which in turn, determines whether he has to include their refund in gross income in the current year).

The first stop is IRC § 213 itself. A "deduction" for qualified *medical care expenses* is allowed only to the extent that total qualifying expenses for the year exceed 10% of adjusted gross income (AGI). Therefore, if Victor's total qualifying medical care expenses last year did not exceed 10% of his AGI, he would not have benefited from these expenditures and, therefore, the refund would not be included in his income for this year. However, to the extent that his qualifying medical care expenses last year *did* exceed 10% of his AGI, we have to continue to the next step of our analysis to see if he benefited from the deduction.

Deducted medical care expenses (those in excess of 10% of a taxpayer's AGI) are part of a larger group of deductions known collectively as "itemized deductions." This group of *itemized deductions* also includes such items as deductible taxes (IRC § 164), deductible interest (IRC § 163), charitable deductions (IRC § 170), and casualty losses (IRC § 165(h)). Some of these items that make up *itemized deductions* contain their own "percentage of AGI" floor or ceiling to determine deductibility. When computing an individual's *taxable income* this group of *itemized deductions* is compared to another major deduction known as the "standard deduction." While other questions in this book explore the *standard deduction* in greater detail, every individual is entitled to a *standard deduction* of some amount (it varies depending on numerous factors). An individual **takes the greater of: the standard deduction** or *total allowed itemized deductions* in computing taxable income.

Looking at Victor's situation for last year, in order for him to have benefited from his medical care costs they first would have had to exceed 10% of his AGI to make it into the group of *itemized deductions* (and then only the amount exceeding this 10% of AGI floor). And then, this entire group of *itemized deductions* (as adjusted if necessary) would have had to exceed Victor's standard deduction. Only to the extent that his medical care expenses made it over both of these hurdles, must Victor include their refund in his income for this year.

[Please see Appendix A for more information on how income and deductions fit together in computing taxable income and AGI. There are also series of questions in this book that explore the comprehensive nature of taxable income.]

Answer (a) is incorrect because the answer fails to recognize the second "hurdle" that Victor's total *itemized deductions* exceeded his *standard deduction*. **Answer (b) is incorrect** because it fails to recognize the first "hurdle" that Victor could have benefited from his medical care costs only to the extent that they exceeded 10% of his AGI. **Answer (d) is incorrect** because that is not how the statute deals with this issue. **Answer (e) is incorrect** because the statute does not allow for this choice in handling this issue.

19. **The best answer is (e).** The general statute of limitations for an individual amending a prior return to claim a refund or credit is the <u>later</u> of:
    ➤ Three years from the date the return was filed (or the due date of the return if the return was filed before the due date), or
    ➤ Two years from the date the tax was paid.

The facts indicate that Kim has consistently filed her income tax returns on a timely basis. In fact, she consistently files them at least one month prior to the regular April 15th due date for income tax returns. Applying the rule that is applicable to Kim (the first of the two listed above), she can file amended returns for any years' returns where the due date for filing such returns was in the last three years. The distinction between "filing dates" and "due dates" can be critical. Note that Kim's "open" period is actually longer than three years from the actual filing dates of her returns.

After a careful reading of the applicable section (IRC § 6511(a)), students logically come away with a different answer, namely (d). IRC § 6511(a) states, in part, that the taxpayer has the later of "3 years from the *time the return was filed*, or 2 years from the time the tax was paid" in which to file a claim for refund or credit (an amended return). With not so much as a clue in IRC §6511, another Code section, IRC § 6513, indicates that for purposes of IRC § 6511, a return that is actually filed before its due date (as is the case for Kim's prior returns) is considered filed on the due date. This is the reason for the parenthetical comment appearing above in the first of the two rules listed.

Although not required for this question, the appropriate form for most individuals for filing an amended income tax return is *Form 1040X*.

Answer (a) is not the best answer. While it is true that unclaimed benefits in a prior year cannot be claimed in the current year, this answer does not provide the possibility of amending prior income tax returns to claim the missed benefit. **Answer (b) is also not the best answer.** This answer is partially correct but it does not contain necessary information about the periods for which amended returns can be filed. **Answer (c) is incorrect** because claiming the benefits in the current year is not a valid option. **Answer (d) is also incorrect.** This is the most commonly selected answer because it appears to reflect the rules of IRC § 6513. However, IRC § 6511 indicates that if the returns are filed prior to their due dates, the due dates are considered the time of filing for purposes of the three-year general rule for filing amended returns.

20. The correct answer is (a). This is a tax procedure question that may or may not be covered in depth in your federal income tax class. However, basic knowledge of the court system, as it relates to federal tax issues, is important if not for anything more than making jurisdictional sense of the cases that you may read. This professor seems to recall learning in the first-year law school civil procedure course that individuals are generally precluded from "forum shopping." This, generally, is not the case with respect to federal tax matters. Most court actions, regarding an individual federal income tax matter, can be brought by the taxpayer in either: 1) the U.S. Tax Court, 2) the U.S. District Court (in the jurisdiction in which the taxpayer resides), or 3) the U.S. Court of Federal Claims (located in Washington D.C.). All three of these "trial" courts generally have "subject matter jurisdiction" with respect to federal income tax issues for individuals.

While not required for this question, the requirements, procedural matters, and adjudication options differ between these three courts. See question 21, below, for a discussion of one such difference.

Answers (b), (c) and (d) are incorrect because all, to varying degrees, identify or fail to identify valid courts in which Terrance can resolve his income tax issue. **Answer (e) is incorrect** because a correct response (a) is presented.

21. **The best answer is (d).** As indicated in the analysis of question 20, above, an individual contesting a proposed federal income tax deficiency generally has three court options: U.S. Tax Court, U.S. District Court in which the taxpayer resides, and the U.S. Court of Federal Claims. The U.S. Tax Court is unique, among the options, in that the taxpayer need not pay the proposed assessment before litigating the matter. [See IRC § 6213 (regarding petitions to Tax Court).] If Terrance wishes to have his tax matter heard by either the U.S. District or the U.S. Court of Federal Claims, he must first pay the proposed assessment and sue for a refund.

While not required for this question, there are other requirements, procedural matters, and adjudication options that differ depending on the trial court chosen by the taxpayer in which to adjudicate the tax issue in question.

Answer (a) is incorrect because, as discussed above, petitioning to the U.S. Tax Court does not require that the taxpayer first pay the proposed assessment. **Answer (b) is incorrect** because, as discussed above, bringing issue to either the U.S. District Court or U.S. Court of Federal Claims requires that the taxpayer first pay the proposed assessment and then sue for a refund. **Answer (c) is incorrect** and represents an answer that is opposite that of the correct answer.

22. **The correct answer is (d).** The Revenue Act of 1913 was the first piece of legislation to levy a Constitutionally-valid income tax upon individuals.

Answer (a) is incorrect because the 16th Amendment permitted Congress to "lay and collect taxes on incomes, from whatever source derived." It did not actually impose a tax upon individuals but only allowed such a tax to be imposed. **Answer (b) is incorrect** because Article 1, § 8 of the Constitution merely authorizes Congress "to lay and collect taxes, duties, imposts and excises." It did not actually impose any tax, but only gave Congress this power. **Answer (c) is incorrect** because Article 1, § 9 of the Constitution requires that "direct taxes" be allocated to the states based upon their respective populations. A direct tax is one that is required to be paid by the specific members of the targeted tax group and cannot be shifted to others outside of the group.

23. **Answer (a) is the most accurate.** Betty could claim that by imposing a tax based upon her income from previous years, Congress violated her Due Process rights under the 5th Amendment. However, the Court held in *Brushaber* (a landmark case) that the Due Process clause does not pose such

a restriction upon Congress. [*Brushaber v. Union Pac. R. Co.*, 240 U.S. 1, 36 S. Ct. 236 (1916).] Therefore, Congress is able to tax in a retrospective manner despite the taxpayer's lack of foresight that their income will be subjected to a tax in future years. So, Betty will not be successful in making such an argument.

Answer (b) is incorrect because the Court in *Brushaber* specifically eliminated this argument in such situations. **Answer (c) is incorrect** because the 16th Amendment does not constrain Congress to tax only income earned during the current tax year. **Answer (d) is incorrect** because Congress is permitted to modify the tax structure and there are no restrictions placed upon this power.

24. **The best answer is (b).** Although the 5th Amendment provides that "no person shall be compelled in any criminal case to be a witness against himself," self-incrimination does not apply with respect to the requirement that each taxpayer file a tax return (and properly report income). Therefore, even though Dave would incriminate himself if he were to file a proper tax return, which would disclose income received from illegal sources, he cannot claim that the 5th Amendment provides any protection in such a situation.

Answer (a) is incorrect because Dave would not prevail if he were to make such an argument since the privilege against self-incrimination does not apply to such a situation. **Answer (c) is incorrect** because the 16th Amendment requires that all income "from whatever source derived" be disclosed upon a tax return even if it is derived from illegal sources. **Answer (d) is incorrect** because state law is not a consideration in such a situation, but federal law governs in order to advance consistency in the application of tax laws from state to state.

25. **Answer (b) is correct.** Sales taxes and "value added taxes" are common examples of consumption-based taxes (taxes paid based on consumption of products and, sometimes, services). Higher income individuals would save more under such a regressive structure. Since the consumption tax would simply impose a tax whenever goods are purchased, it would create a heavier burden on lower and middle class taxpayers, who would effectively be forced to pay a greater portion or percentage of their income in the form of a tax. Proportionally, individuals with a higher level of income would pay a smaller share of their income in the form of a tax. Therefore, such a tax has been criticized as unfair.

Answer (a) is incorrect because a consumption tax would actually simplify the administration of taxes by eliminating the various regulations that govern the current tax system. **Answer (c) is incorrect** because increased litigation has not been argued as a major concern. **Answer (d) is incorrect** because such a scheme would inhibit tax evasion since taxpayers would be forced to pay a tax upon purchase rather than being forced to determine the tax based on past events (filing tax returns and paying tax based, primarily, on a self-assessed basis).

Appendix

Appendix A

Framework for Taxable Income

How Income and Deductions Fit Together in Computing Taxable Income

The computation of *taxable income* as well as *adjusted gross income (AGI)* requires knowledge of what is includible and excludable from a taxpayer's gross income, as well as what constitutes deductible and nondeductible expenses. In addition, a key point in determining a taxpayer's *taxable income* or *AGI* is knowing **where** various deductions are taken. The following is a visual depiction of the *taxable income* and *AGI* calculations showing many of the most common elements of income, exclusion, and deductions. This is **not** an all-inclusive list of such items.

Please be aware that many of the elements listed below are subject to various limitations and restrictions that are discussed throughout the questions in this book.

Please see the following page for Flowchart

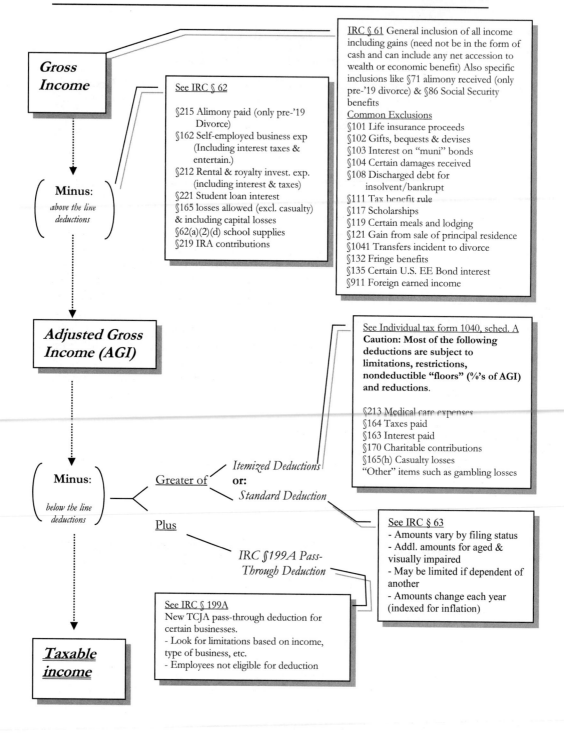

Gross Income

IRC § 61 General inclusion of all income including gains (need not be in the form of cash and can include any net accession to wealth or economic benefit) Also specific inclusions like §71 alimony received (only pre-'19 divorce) & §86 Social Security benefits

Common Exclusions
§101 Life insurance proceeds
§102 Gifts, bequests & devises
§103 Interest on "muni" bonds
§104 Certain damages received
§108 Discharged debt for insolvent/bankrupt
§111 Tax benefit rule
§117 Scholarships
§119 Certain meals and lodging
§121 Gain from sale of principal residence
§1041 Transfers incident to divorce
§132 Fringe benefits
§135 Certain U.S. EE Bond interest
§911 Foreign earned income

(**Minus:**
above the line deductions)

See IRC § 62

§215 Alimony paid (only pre-'19 Divorce)
§162 Self-employed business exp (Including interest taxes & entertain.)
§212 Rental & royalty invest. exp. (including interest & taxes)
§221 Student loan interest
§165 losses allowed (excl. casualty) & including capital losses
§62(a)(2)(d) school supplies
§219 IRA contributions

Adjusted Gross Income (AGI)

See Individual tax form 1040, sched. A
Caution: Most of the following deductions are subject to limitations, restrictions, nondeductible "floors" (%'s of AGI) and reductions.

§213 Medical care expenses
§164 Taxes paid
§163 Interest paid
§170 Charitable contributions
§165(h) Casualty losses
"Other" items such as gambling losses

(**Minus:**
below the line deductions)

Greater of   *Itemized Deductions*
or:
Standard Deduction

Plus

IRC §199A Pass-Through Deduction

See IRC § 63
- Amounts vary by filing status
- Addl. amounts for aged & visually impaired
- May be limited if dependent of another
- Amounts change each year (indexed for inflation)

See IRC § 199A
New TCJA pass-through deduction for certain businesses.
- Look for limitations based on income, type of business, etc.
- Employees not eligible for deduction

Taxable income

Appendix B

Tax Year 2019 – Year-Specific Information

Many Code items, that are pertinent to questions appearing in this book, vary from year to year. Some items, such as the *standard deduction* are "indexed for inflation" while others are changed statutorily as a result of new legislation. Some items, such as tax rates, will be changing each year due to both inflation-indexing and statutory changes.

Some of the questions appearing in this book are year-specific. Of these, many are based upon the 2019 tax year, the most current year available at the time of this publication. These questions were included not, necessarily, for the purpose of covering specifically the 2019 tax year but, rather, to provide a computational or "real-world" foundation to explore certain income tax topics. These questions are easily adaptable to years subsequent to 2019. The new, as of this writing, *Tax Cuts and Jobs Act* (TCJA) signed into law in December 2017 (generally effective beginning in 2018), made significant changes to numerous aspects of tax law affecting individuals. While too numerous to mention here, many of the questions presented were designed to give you an idea of the "tax world" both before the TCJA and after it became law. Keep in mind that tax law is always in a state of flux and there is no guarantee that any question in this book will remain pertinent, or continue to have the proper answer analysis, in the future.

Provided below, are most of the 2019 year-specific items that have been discussed with respect to questions presented in this book. Please see individual questions for more information about any particular item (and for those not listed).

The *Personal Exemption Deduction* for 2019

Sort of a misleading heading as the IRC § 151(d)(1) actual deduction for personal exemptions is zero ($0). The TCJA effectively eliminated this deduction for tax years 2018 through 2025. There continues to be, technically, an "exemption amount" but this is not for deduction purposes. For example, in questions involving who qualifies as one's *dependent,* the income of an individual may be relevant and its amount relative to the "exemption amount" can have far-reaching consequences. So while the deduction for personal exemptions has been eliminated by the TCJA, there still is an "exemption amount." As of this writing, the exact amount for 2019 is not known but is estimated to be $4,200 (the exemption amount for 2018, the first year for which the TCJA eliminated the personal exemption deduction, was $4,150 and indexing for inflation should result in a slightly higher 2019 amount).

The *Standard Deduction(s)* for 2019

Regular *standard deduction* amounts:

      $24,400 Married filing joint returns (& surviving spouses)
      $18,350 Heads of Household
      $12,200 Single individuals
      $12,200 Married individuals filing separately

"Extra" *standard deduction* amounts (additions to above) for individuals 65 years of age and older, or severely visually impaired. [See IRC § 63(c)(3),]:

      $1,300 Married individuals (& surviving spouses)
      $1,650 Single individuals and Heads of Household

Restricted *standard deduction* for individuals who can be claimed as a dependent of another. [See IRC § 63(c)(5).]:

      The greater of (but not to exceed *std deduction* without regard to this provision):
            1) $1,100, or
            2) The individual's "earned income" plus $350.

The IRC § 132(f) "Qualified Parking" Fringe Tax-Free Limit for 2019

The maximum allowed exclusion for 2019 is $265 per month of parking value.

IRC §221 Qualified Student Loan Interest Deduction for 2019.

The maximum deduction allowed for 2019 and later years is $2,500.

The "phase-out" ranges of "modified adjusted gross income" (MAGI) for 2019 are:

      $70,000 – $85,000
      ($140,000 – $170,000 for joint filers)

"Phase-Out" of IRC § 135 U.S. Savings Bond Interest Used for Education for 2019

The 2019 "phase-out" range for the IRC § 135 exclusion for U.S. Savings Bonds used for higher education expenses is "modified adjusted gross income" (MAGI) between $81,100 and $96,100 (between $121,600 and $151,600 for joint filers).

2019 Income Tax Rates are on the Following Page

TAX RATES FOR 2019

IRC § 1(a)(2)/(j)(2)(A) (Married filing joint returns and surviving spouses)

If taxable income is	The tax is
- Not over $19,400	10% of taxable income
- Over $19,400 but not over $78,950	$1,940 plus 12% of excess over $19,400
- Over $78,950 but not over $168,400	$9,086 plus 22% of excess over $78,950
- Over $168,400 but not over $321,450	$28,762 plus 24% of excess over $168,400
- Over $321,450 but not over $408,200	$65,497 plus 32% of excess over $321,450
- Over $408,200 but not over $612,350	$93,257 plus 35% of excess over $408,200
- Over $612,350	$164,709.50 plus 37% of excess over $612,350

IRC § 1(b)/(j)(2)(B) (Head of household)

If taxable income is	The tax is
- Not over $13,850	10% of taxable income
- Over $13,850 but not over $52,850	$1,385 plus 12% of excess over $13,850
- Over $52,850 but not over $84,200	$6,065 plus 22% of excess over $52,850
- Over $84,200 but not over $160,700	$12,962 plus 24% of excess over $84,200
- Over $160,700 but not over $204,100	$31,322 plus 32% of excess over $160,700
- Over $204,100 but not over $510,300	$45,210 plus 35% of excess over $204,100
- Over $510,300	$152,380 plus 37% of excess over $510,300

IRC § 1(c)/(j)(2)(C) (Unmarried individuals other than surviving spouse & head of households (i.e., this usually means **Single** individuals)

If taxable income is	The tax is
- Not over $9,700	10% of taxable income
- Over $9,700 but not over $39,475	$970 plus 12% of the excess over $9,700
- Over $39,475 but not over $84,200	$4,543 plus 22% of excess over $39,475
- Over $84,200 but not over $160,725	$14,382.50 plus 24% of excess over $84,200
- Over $160,725 but not over $204,100	$32,748.50 plus 32% of excess over $160,725
- Over $204,100 but not over $510,300	$46,628.50 plus 35% of excess over $204,100
- Over $510,300	$153,798.50 plus 37% of excess over $510,300

IRC § 1(d)/(j)(2)(D) (Married filing separate returns)

If <u>taxable</u> income is	The tax is
- Not over $9,700	10% of taxable income
- Over $9,700 but not over $39,475	$970 plus 12% of the excess over $9,700
- Over $39,475 but not over $84,200	$4,543 plus 22% of excess over $39,475
- Over $84,200 but not over $160,725	$14,382.50 plus 24% of excess over $84,200
- Over $160,725 but not over $204,100	$32,748.50 plus 32% of excess over $160,725
- Over $204,100 but not over $306,175	$46,628.50 plus 35% of excess over $204,100
- Over $306,175	$82,354.75 plus 37% of excess over $306,175

Appendix C

Code Math – Almost Everything You Need to Know About Tax Math

Introduction

The study of federal income taxation involves some math. However, the math utilized is <u>very basic</u> and should not be a source of concern for those of you who do not get excited at the sight of numbers. Actually, the only math skills necessary are those from the four basic "arithmetic" food groups: addition, subtraction, multiplication, and division.

If any difficulty should arise, it will probably not be with the math itself. Rather, it will be interpreting how and when the sections of the Internal Revenue Code ("Code") tell you to add, subtract, multiply and divide. The following is a summary of the necessary math concepts and some samples of how the language of the Code may signal you to use a particular math function.

<u>Addition</u>

Code language: "The sum of [X] plus [Y]."

This means: X + Y

For example, see IRC § 1001(b) discussing computation of "amount realized." It equals "the sum of any money received plus the fair market value of property (other than money) received."

<u>Subtraction</u>

Code language: "The excess of [X] over [Y]." It really should say: "The excess of [X], <u>if any</u>, over [Y]."

This means: X - Y. However, by definition, the result will not be a less than zero.

For example, see IRC § 1001(a) discussing gain realized from the sale of property as "the excess of the amount realized therefrom over the adjusted basis." This means the "amount realized" minus the "adjusted basis." A source of common confusion; the word "over" in this context does **not** mean the fraction X divided by Y.

Multiplication

Code language: "[X] multiplied by [Y]" or, "the product of [X] and [Y]."

Both of these means: X multiplied by Y.

For example, see IRC § 68(b)(2) discussing certain inflation adjustments re deductions ". . . shall be increased by an amount equal to -- (A) such dollar amount, multiplied by (B) the cost-of-living adjustment determined . . ."

Sometimes when the Code wants you to multiply something by a percentage, the language will read [X] percent of [Y]. This means [Y] multiplied by [X] percent.

The Code Ratios

This is probably the most dreaded math language of the Internal Revenue Code.

Code language (from IRC §1015(d)(6)(A)): "[The adjustment to basis] shall be an amount which bears the same ratio to the amount of tax so paid as -- (i) the net appreciation in value of the gift, bears to (ii) the amount of the gift."

We have "bears" in the code? What are bears doing in tax law?

Here you are solving for an unknown amount [adjustment to basis] which we will call **X**. Expressed in equation form, the above language means:

X / *Amount of tax paid* = *The net appreciation in value of the gift* / *Amount of gift*

Recalling high-school algebra may be uncomfortable, but with only one variable to solve for, the math is usually not too bad. There are various ways to solve for the unknown such as "simplifying the equation and then isolating **X** on one side, "cross-multiplying" (always a neat trick), and the like.

Other Combinations of Math Functions

It is very common that the Code will use a combination of the above math functions in one code provision. The key with these encounters is to make sure you perform each math function separately and in the correct order. These may sound tough at first, but once you see the pattern, it becomes easy.

For an example, see IRC § 68 which says ". . . the amount of the itemized deductions otherwise allowable for the taxable year shall be reduced by the lesser of: (1) 3 percent of the excess of adjusted gross income over the applicable amount, or (2) 80 percent of the amount of the itemized deductions otherwise allowable for such taxable year." This is telling you to first subtract the "applicable amount" from "adjusted gross income" and then (if the result is positive) multiply the result by three percent (.03). Once you have done that, you then must take the amount of "itemized deductions otherwise allowable" and multiply that by 80% (.80). You then take the lesser of those two calculations and subtract it from the amount of the "itemized deductions otherwise allowable."

WOW! Don't worry, it sounds much worse than it is.